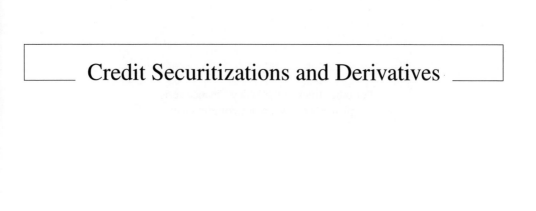

Credit Securitizations and Derivatives

Credit Securitizations and Derivatives

Challenges for the Global Markets

Edited by

Daniel Rösch
Harald Scheule

A John Wiley & Sons, Ltd., Publication

This edition first published 2013
Copyright © 2013 John Wiley & Sons Ltd

Registered Office
John Wiley & Sons Ltd, The Atrium, Southern Gate, Chichester, West Sussex, PO19 8SQ, United Kingdom

For details of our global editorial offices, for customer services and for information about how to apply for
permission to reuse the copyright material in this book please see our website at www.wiley.com.

Wiley publishes in a variety of print and electronic formats and by print-on-demand. Some material included with
standard print versions of this book may not be included in e-books or in print-on-demand. If this book refers to
media such as a CD or DVD that is not included in the version you purchased, you may download this material at
http://booksupport.wiley.com. For more information about Wiley products, visit www.wiley.com.

Library of Congress Cataloging-in-Publication Data (CIP) To follow

A catalogue record for this book is available from the British Library.

ISBN 978-1-119-96396-7 (hardback) ISBN 978-1-119-96604-3 (ebk)
ISBN 978-1-119-96605-0 (ebk) ISBN 978-1-119-96606-7 (ebk)

Set in 10/12pt Times by Aptara, Inc., New Delhi, India
Printed in Great Britain by CPI Group (UK) Ltd, Croydon, CR0 4YY

Contents

Foreword

Thilo Liebig

Deutsche Bundesbank[1]

Credit risk is at the core of commercial banking. In recent years, we have seen the rampant emergence of new techniques for credit risk management, especially securitization and credit derivatives such as credit default swaps (CDS). Both instruments have in common that they allow banks to separate credit origination from credit risk. From an economic point of view, this separation is reasonable: banks can extend their lending and are no longer constrained by their risk-taking capacity. By securitizing the loans and buying or selling credit protection, banks make the credit risk tradable and shift the credit risk out of their balance sheets to other market participants who are better able to bear this risk or wish to diversify their portfolio.

From the standpoint of financial stability, however, during the financial crisis, securitization and credit derivatives sometimes failed to meet the high expectations placed on them. Separating credit origination from the credit risk occasionally gave the wrong incentives. Since they were able to dispense with the risk, banks no longer had a strong incentive to carefully select and monitor the borrowers. As a result, credit standards began to deteriorate; loans to the sub-prime sector grew to a high level. Moreover, the banks' additional lending capacity increased the mortgage supply in the US, thereby amplifying a bubble in the US housing market. Incentive problems of a different kind are said to have mattered for rating agencies as well. In fact, rating agencies earned a large amount in fees by providing ratings for securitizations and were blamed for having rated them too positively.

Another issue was the lack of transparency: by securitization, credit risk was believed to have been shifted out of the banks' balance sheets. However, it turned out that it had never really left the banking sector but instead had been repackaged into complex and opaque financial products and placed in off-balance-sheet entities known as "special purpose vehicles". It is also true that securitization makes credit risk tradable so that loans become as liquid as securities. Nevertheless, during the crisis when liquidity was needed most, the markets dried up, leaving the banks with "toxic" assets that could be sold only at a large discount. In the case of credit derivatives, the problem was that it became unclear which financial institutions – and to what extent – were ultimately exposed to the underlying default risk.

---

[1] The views expressed in this paper are those of the author and do not necessarily reflect the opinions of the Deutsche Bundesbank.

This book is designed to help gain an understanding of the principles underlying credit risk and its management. It is only if these principles are well understood that we can hope to make securitizations and credit derivatives into sustainable risk management techniques that foster financial stability. This book also covers financial stability issues, for instance, liquidity, regulation and counterparty risk.

Credit derivatives and securitizations are a cornerstone of modern finance, especially for banks that are active internationally. For a large number of people, a sound grasp of these risk management techniques is crucial. I am thinking of practitioners in banks who manage the risk of large credit and security portfolios. It seems self-evident that such people really understood what they were doing. The crisis, however, showed that some banks were engaged in securitization and credit derivatives without having the necessary expertise. Having learned the lessons of the crisis, regulators are making considerable progress in addressing the main problems associated with securitization and credit derivatives. I am referring here to the tighter regulation of risk weights for securitization and the central counterparties for clearing such credit derivatives that have been traded over the counter.

In addition, CDS premia are a valuable tool for financial stability analysis, where CDS prices can be used as an additional indicator to assess the credit quality of a bank, especially if the bank is not listed and does not have many outstanding bonds that are traded. In this context, it is necessary to understand such credit derivatives properly in order to know what the prices can tell us – and what they cannot.

Securitization and credit derivatives provide a wide range of research fields. Apart from the financial stability aspects (which, I believe, merit a book of their own), there are still some open questions concerning the limitations of the theoretical models. At the time I was writing this foreword, the yield on five-year German government bonds was about 0.6% p.a., yet the corresponding yearly CDS premium was 1%. Thus, in principle, it would be possible to offer credit protection and sell the underlying five-year German government bond, thereby earning the CDS premium, which is higher than the coupon of the underlying bond. As far as I understand it, CDS pricing is based on arbitrage arguments. The question is: can the current models explain such discrepancies or do they need to be expanded? We should keep in mind that credit risk models are, in the end, a simplification of the real world and subject to a process of permanent revision. Academics and other researchers, therefore, need to acknowledge the limitations of their models and, more importantly, to advise caution to those people who apply them in practice. To my mind, credit risk models should not be used to create a false sense of confidence, but rather to improve our understanding. Therefore, the clear message of this book to the reader is that, before applying any model, it is necessary to obtain a more detailed insight into the complexities of credit risk, the regulatory environment, and incentives for market players in order to form an opinion on it.

Securitizations and credit derivatives are still relatively new financial instruments. Applied properly, they have the potential to become a standard tool in risk management, comparable to derivatives for classical market risk, which – when they were introduced in the 1970s and 1980s – we also learned the hard way how to employ and regulate.

Part I
Introduction

1
Credit Securitizations and Derivatives

Daniel Roesch[1] and Harald Scheule[2]
[1] University of Hannover
[2] University of Technology, Sydney

The Global Financial Crisis (GFC) led to an unprecedented and, by most of us, unexpected increase of impairment and loss rates for securitizations and derivatives. The disappointment of investors manifested in the criticism of models applied for measuring credit portfolio risk in relation to credit securities and derivatives.

Credit portfolio securitizations and derivatives are primarily OTC market instruments with exposures totaling approximately \$40 trillion. Securitizations involve the sale of assets into bankruptcy-remote special purpose vehicles, which are funded by investors of different seniorities (tranches). Based on the nature of the securitized asset portfolios, important transaction types include asset-backed securities, collateralized debt obligations, home equity loan-backed securities and mortgage-backed securities. On the other side, credit derivatives are generally unfunded contracts and share similar structures and appraisal challenges with securitizations.

This exciting and timely book provides regulators with an overview of the risk inherent in credit securitizations and derivatives. The book aims to help quantitative analysts improve risk models and managers of financial institutions evaluate the performance of existing risk models and future model needs. The book addresses challenges in relation to the evaluation of credit portfolio securitizations and derivatives and covers the following areas:

- credit portfolio risk measurement,
- credit portfolio risk tranching,
- credit ratings,
- credit default swaps, indices and tranches,
- counterparty credit risk and clearing of derivatives contracts,
- liquidity risk,
- regulation.

The following provides a first introduction to some of these areas.

1.1 ECONOMIC CYCLES AND CREDIT PORTFOLIO RISK

The Global Financial Crisis (GFC) had its origin in the US mortgage market. During the GFC various changes in key macroeconomic variables were observed: (i) declining house prices, where changes in house prices often exceeded their equity finance, (ii) higher mortgage reset rates despite declining risk-free interest rates, (iii) decreases in GDP coinciding with higher unemployment rates and lower per capita earnings. This economic downturn spread to other

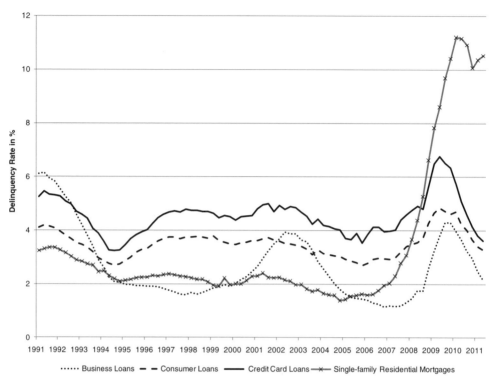

Figure 1.1   Delinquency rates, all commercial US banks, seasonally adjusted.
Note: This chart shows the delinquency rates for business loans, consumer loans, credit card loans and single-family residential mortgages. Delinquency rates are the ratios of the dollar amount of a bank's delinquent loans to the dollar amount of total loans outstanding in that category.
Source: Board of Governors of the US Federal Reserve System.

asset classes, financial products and eventually financial markets in many other countries through various mechanisms.

Figure 1.1 shows the delinquency rates for business loans, consumer loans, credit card loans and single-family residential mortgages. Traditionally, credit risk moves in parallel for the various loan classes. This trend was reversed in 2007 when delinquency rates for single-family residential mortgages dramatically increased to historically unprecedented levels (gray line with black markers).

Demyanyk et al. (2011) and others confirm that house prices are a major driver of mortgage credit risk. Figure 1.2 compares the delinquency rates for single-family residential mortgages with the growth rate of the Case–Shiller house price index for 10 major Metropolitan Statistical Areas in the United States (Greater Boston, Chicago metropolitan area, Denver-Aurora Metropolitan Area, Las Vegas metropolitan area, Greater Los Angeles, South Florida metropolitan area, New York metropolitan area, San Diego County, California, San Francisco–Oakland–Fremont, CA and Washington Metropolitan Area). The negative correlation between the two variables is apparent. More interestingly, the decrease in growth rates in 2006/07 anticipates the subsequent increase in mortgage delinquency rates.

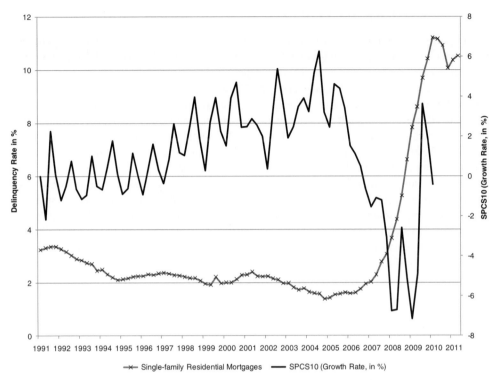

Figure 1.2   Delinquency rates for single-family residential mortgages with the Case–Shiller house price index.
Note: This chart shows the negative relationship between delinquency rates for single-family residential mortgages and the Case–Shiller house price index.

The cyclical movement of credit risk poses a challenge to practitioners, prudential regulators and academics as cyclical patterns may be included to various degrees in risk measures. Rösch and Scheule (2005) highlight the two extremes. The first extreme is the through-the-cycle (TTC) approach, which averages over the business cycle and is often promoted by banks in order to avoid cyclical regulatory capital requirements. The problem with cyclical regulatory capital requirements is that banks may be exposed to raise capital during economic downturns (when risk is high) when share prices are low and when capital supply is limited.

The second extreme is the point-in-time approach (PIT), which makes a prediction for future periods. PIT models are more accurate as they are generally based on forecast models, which explain the credit risk for a future point in time by information which is available at the time when the forecast is made.

Similar model approaches are common for other risk dimensions such as loss rates given default, and exposures given default (compare Bade, Rösch and Scheule, 2011 and Rösch and Scheule, 2010). Many recent current contributions in literature aim to improve the measurement of mortgage risk by building PIT risk models which include dynamic risk drivers such as real estate prices.

1.2 CREDIT PORTFOLIO RISK MEASUREMENT

Credit portfolio risk models measure the risk for loan portfolios. Such models are generally based on a set of parameters such as probabilities of default, loss rates given default, exposures at default and default correlations. Mortgage portfolios are retail portfolios and are characterized by a large number of mortgages. The US delinquency rates, which are presented in Figure 1.1, may be used as proxies for the portfolio default rate as they average over many individual exposures. Default rates are low in economic booms and high in economic downturns. Financial institutions generate default rate distributions around the current default rate and derive key portfolio measures, such as expected loss or value at risk. In addition, economic and regulatory capital may be derived from such distributions.

Figure 1.3 shows the default rate distribution for delinquency rates for single-family residential mortgages in the first quarter of 2006, which represents the economic boom state and 2011, which represents the economic downturn state. The application of TTC models will lead to time-invariant measures of portfolio risk while the application of PIT models will lead to time-varying measures of portfolio risk. Real-world models have mixed properties and the PIT-character of risk models accelerated the need for financial institutions to recapitalize during the GFC. The current discussion in literature focuses on the trade-off between (i) achieving

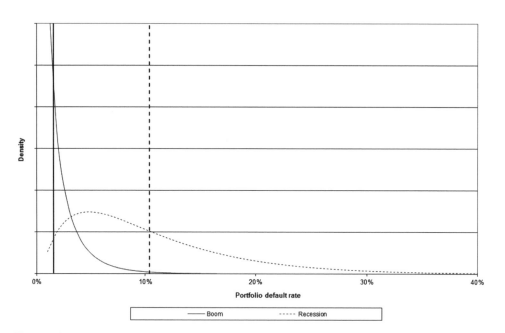

Figure 1.3 Credit portfolio loss distributions.
Note: The application of TTC models will lead to time-invariant measures of portfolio risk while the application of PIT models will lead to time-varying measures of portfolio risk.
Source: Own calculations based on delinquency rates for single-family residential mortgages in the first quarter of 2006 (expected default rate: 1.59%), which represents the economic book state, and 2011 (expected default rate: 10.37%), which represents the economic downturn state. A Basel II asset correlation for residential mortgage loans of 15% and the Vasicek density was assumed in deriving the numbers underlying the figure.

model accuracy and therefore capital adequacy, and (ii) a reduction of capital cyclicality. A Basel II asset correlation for residential mortgage loans of 15% and the Vasicek density was assumed in deriving the numbers underlying the figure. The vertical lines indicate the expected default rates of 1.59% and 10.37% for the two states.

1.3 CREDIT PORTFOLIO RISK TRANCHING

Credit derivatives and securitizations are often subject to tranching, which is highly sensitive to the systematic exposure. The interaction between states of the economy and the risk exposure for tranches is forcefully shown in Figure 1.3. The attachment risk increases for senior tranches more so than for junior tranches from economic booms to economic downturns. For example, if a structure has an equity, mezzanine and junior tranche with attachment levels 0%, 5% and 20%, then the attachment probability for the mezzanine tranche is 5.18% in a boom and 74.55% in a recession. The attachment probability for the senior tranche is 0.02% in a boom and 10.53% in a recession. The attachment probability for the equity tranche is converging to one for large portfolios in both economic scenarios. Rösch and Scheule (2012) analyze the risk, capital adequacy and policy implications in relation to securitizations.

1.4 CREDIT RATINGS

The disappointment of investors also manifested in the criticism of models applied by credit rating agencies (CRAs). First contributions analyze the ratings of securitizations in more general terms or in relation to different asset classes such as collateralized debt obligations. Benmelech and Dlugosz (2009) analyze collateralized loan obligations (CLOs) rated by Standard & Poor's and find a mismatch between credit ratings and the quality of the underlying loan portfolios. Bolton et al. (2011) analyze CRA securitization rating performance with regard to the business cycle. Griffin and Tang (2012) compare CRA model methodologies with CRA ratings for collateralized debt obligations. Coval et al. (2009) argue that model risk and the exposure to systemic risk of securitization may explain the increase of impairment rates during the GFC.

1.5 ACTUARIAL VS. MARKET CREDIT RISK PRICING

So far, we have focused on actuarial, so-called real-world risk measures. Credit risks are priced in many markets such as lending markets, deposit markets, corporate bond markets, securitization markets or credit derivatives markets. Many risk models rely on market prices to measure the inherent level of risk. However, Figure 1.4 shows that a gap between actuarial and market priced losses exists and that this gap widens during an economic downturn. In addition, the volatility of market-based risk measures is larger than the volatility of real-world risk measures.

Market participants as well as researchers are currently scrutinizing the accuracy of market-based risk models and implications on financial institutions' risk measurement, management and reporting.

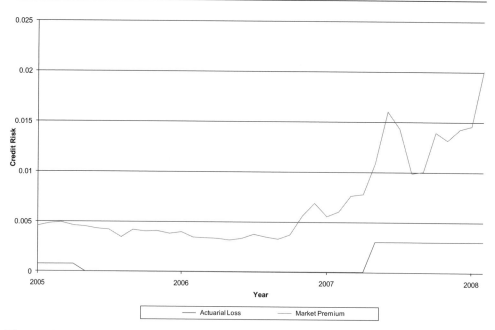

Figure 1.4 Actuarial losses and market premiums.
Note: Actuarial loss rates are calculated as default rates multiplied by average loss rates given default for on BAA-rated bonds. Market premium is calculated as the average credit spread of credit default swaps of BAA-rated bonds.
Source: Bloomberg and Moody's rating agency.

1.6 REGULATION

Prudential regulators of financial institutions aim to ensure that, under all reasonable circumstances, financial promises made by the institutions are met within a stable, efficient and competitive financial system. The enhancement of prudential regulations is an important element in ensuring the stability of financial institutions, markets and instruments.

In response to the GFC, the G-20 countries have proposed a new set of regulatory requirements with regard to (a) capital, (b) accounting and (c) liquidity of financial institutions, also known as Basel III. These revised requirements are based on national feedback such as the Turner Review (FSA 2009). For example, the Turner Review outlined various changes for prudential regulation: (i) increasing the quantity and quality of bank capital, (ii) increasing the trading book capital, (iii) avoiding pro-cyclicality in relation to bank capital regulations, (iv) creating counter-cyclical capital buffers, (v) offsetting pro-cyclicality in published accounts, (vi) implementing a gross leverage ratio backstop and (vii) containing liquidity risks in individual banks and at the systemic level.

These new rules have been expressed under Basel III, which aims to increase capital and liquidity of banks as well as in national regulations such as the Dodd–Frank Wall Street Reform and Consumer Protection Act of 2010 in the US.

Surprisingly, few measures relate to minimum standards for financial risk models. It is this area where research may make a major contribution. New policies require the understanding of the characteristics of financial risks with regard to level, idiosyncratic and systematic risk, as well as the impact on the capital adequacy of banks and risk transfer mechanisms such as securitizations.

1.7 THANK YOU

It is apparent from these examples that many global challenges for credit securitizations and derivatives persist and that more knowledge on these issues is required. This book is a first step into this direction. Leading academics and practitioners from many institutions and places have come together over the past two years to share their insights and recent research findings on credit securitizations and derivatives. This book aims to transfer this knowledge to the wider community. This research was supported by the Centre for International Finance and Regulation (project number E001) which is funded by the Commonwealth and NSW Governments and supported by other Consortium members (see www.cifr.edu.au). We would like to thank the Centre for International Finance and Regulation and the Hong Kong Institute for Monetary Research for their support. We hope you have a great reading time and that the book will provide further stimulus for research and impact in the practice of credit securitizations and derivatives.

REFERENCES

Bade, B., Rösch, D., Scheule, H., 2011. Default and recovery risk dependencies in a simple credit risk model. European Financial Management, 17 (1), 120–144.
Benmelech, E., Dlugosz, J., 2009. The alchemy of CDO credit ratings. Journal of Monetary Economics, 56, 617–634.
Bolton, P., Freixas, X., Shapiro, J., 2011. The Credit Ratings Game. Journal of Finance, 67(1), 85–112.
Coval, J., Jurek, J., Stafford, E., 2009. The economics of structured finance. Journal of Economic Perspectives, 23, 3–25.
Demyanyk, Y., Koijen, R., Hemert, O. V., 2011. Understanding the subprime mortgage crisis, 24(6), 1848–1880.
Fitch Ratings. 2006. Exposure Draft: Introducing the Fitch VECTOR Default Model Version 3.0.
FSA. 2009. The Turner review: A regulatory response to the global banking crisis. Financial Services Authority, UK, March.
Griffin, J. M., Tang, D., 2012. Did subjectivity play a role in CDO credit ratings? Forthcoming Journal of Finance.
International Swaps and Derivative Association 2009. ISDA Market Survey Historical Data. www.isda.org.
Moody's 2006. CDOROM v2.3 User Guide.
Rösch, D., Scheule, H., 2005. A multi-factor approach for systematic default and recovery risk. Journal of Fixed Income, 15(2), 63–75.
Rösch, D., Scheule, H., 2010. Downturn credit portfolio risk, regulatory capital and prudential incentives. International Review of Finance, 10(2), 185–207.
Rösch, D., Scheule, H., 2012. Capital Incentives and Adequacy for Securitizations, 2012. Journal of Banking and Finance, 36, 733–748.
Standard & Poor's 2005. CDO Evaluator Version 3.0: Technical Document.

2

Developments in Structured Finance Markets

Sebastian Löhr

University of Hannover

2.1 IMPAIRMENTS OF ASSET-BACKED SECURITIES AND OUTSTANDING RATINGS

In 2010 the number of impaired Asset-backed Securities (ABS) fell for the first time in five years to 8,071 from 14,242 in 2009 (Moody's, 2011). By contrast, there were only 106 ABS impairments reported for 2006 which was several months before the Global Financial Crisis (GFC) began in June 2007.[1]

Before analyzing the impairments by year, as well as further market developments, the major ABS structures and their functionality are briefly discussed: the US Securities and Exchange Commission (SEC, 2004) defines ABS as financial securities "that are backed by a discrete pool of self-liquidating financial assets." The SEC (2004) further defines asset-backed securitization in its regulation rules as

> "a financing technique in which financial assets [...] are pooled and converted into instruments that may be offered and sold in the capital markets. In a basic securitization structure, an entity, often a financial institution and commonly known as a 'sponsor' originates or otherwise acquires a pool of financial assets, such as mortgage loans [...]. It then sells the financial assets [...] to a specially created investment vehicle that issues [...] asset-backed securities. Payment on the asset-backed securities depends primarily on the cash flows generated by the assets in the underlying pool and other rights designed to assure timely payment, such as liquidity facilities, guarantees or other features generally known as credit enhancements."[2]

Based on this definition Figure 2.1 summarizes the functionality of a simple asset securitization focusing on the loss flow in such a structure. Corresponding to the SEC's definition of ABS, the underlying asset pool, which is also called the collateral, typically consists of debt assets that are unable to be traded individually. These debt assets are represented by single-name *Loan 1* to *10* on the left hand side of Figure 2.1. Furthermore, *Loan 1* to *Loan 8* (in any order) constitute the specified pool of loans (collateral), which is tranched afterwards.

Through pooling and tranching – as main characteristics of securitizations – the original debt claims are converted to tradeable financial instruments (tranches) that may be sold to external investors in accordance to their individual risk-return profile.[3] The investor's risk-return profile is determined by his internal willingness to face risk related to the respective security. Depending on the instrument's inherent risk, an investor may expect a premium that compensates him for bearing this risk.[4] The Capital Asset Pricing Model (CAPM), for example, is the most popular factor model for pricing the risk of assets (compare Sharpe, 1964).

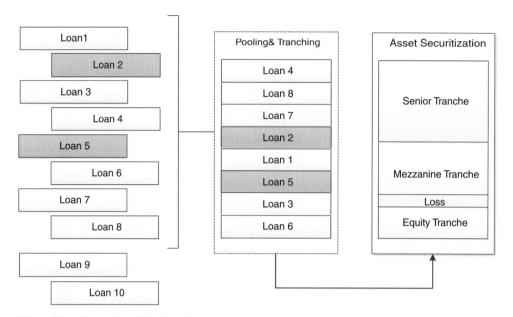

Figure 2.1   Illustration of the loss-flow in a simple asset securitization.
Note: This figure shows the loss flow in a simple asset securitization. Other elements such as premium flows, issuance and rating structures and involved participants are omitted for simplicity.

Löhr et al. (2010) show how to calculate credit risk premiums of tranches which compensate for the default risk in securitizations.

The asset securitization in Figure 2.1 consists of three tranches representing generic tranche types: the equity, mezzanine and senior tranche. Often, the originator (sponsor) partly retains the issued securitization to signal the credit quality of underlying debt claims.[5] The retained part of the securitization is mostly the equity tranche, which is also called first loss piece, since it covers first losses in the collateral (see Renault, 2007).

If losses in the collateral exceed the size of the equity tranche, measured in its nominal or in percentage of the total portfolio loss, then the next tranche of higher seniority suffers from defaults in the collateral and so on. Referring to Figure 2.1, the cumulated losses of *Loan 2* and *Loan 5* exceed the thickness of the equity tranche and thus also hit the mezzanine tranche. Eventually, both tranches are impaired, the equity tranche completely and the mezzanine tranche in parts. Thus investors of both tranches suffer from losses in the collateral: while the nominal of the equity tranche investor has been entirely eliminated, the exceeding losses are covered by the investor who holds the mezzanine tranche. Consequently, the nominal of senior tranche holders remains unaffected. Hence, according to this subordination principle, subordinated tranches provide loss buffers for more senior tranches. In this way, tranche losses are generally restricted to the nominal or principal of the respective tranche (thickness). Thus the risk profiles of securitized tranches may clearly differ from each other in terms of default risk and related losses strongly depending on i) the risk characteristics of the collateral and ii) the seniority of the tranche.

Finally, each security funds a fraction of the underlying pool and transfers the related risk to the investors, such as banks, insurance companies, hedge funds and investment banks. In turn, tranche investors receive a premium payment which is periodically paid out, e.g. quarterly, and which is a compensation for the default risk. Thus related cash flows can be distinguished by their payment directions into the premium leg (pass-through structure) and the protection leg.[6] The premium leg contains the investors' risk premium paid by the issuer. The risk premium is mostly raised from cash flows generated by the collateral through interest and/or liquidation payments. Premium payments also follow the subordination principle: hence, the premium claims of senior tranche investors are firstly served stepwise followed by claims of investors who purchased subordinated tranches (waterfall principle). Since premium payments strongly depend on the risk profile of securitized tranches, the premiums for the equity tranches are generally much higher than the respective ones of more senior tranches. The protection leg (contingent payments) has to be paid from investors to its counterparts in terms of a default event within the collateral to compensate for occurred losses. In general, the definition of a default event may vary. However, in standard securitizations such default events are triggered by delayed or failed interest payments and liquidation.[7]

To achieve an appropriate risk profile of the entire credit exposure, both the originator as well as the contract counterparties may engage in asset securitizations. Required customization as well as optimization of the counterparts' credit portfolio risk can easily be executed with credit derivatives involving so-called bespoke, or customized, CDO tranches (Rajan et al., 2007). Bespoke securitizations are often generated in cooperation with rating agencies such as Moody;s, S&P and Fitch. For example, a single investor announces his individual risk-return preference, e.g. expressed by a desired tranche rating in line with a risk-adjusted premium claim, to the issuer and the cooperating rating agency.[8] In the following, the issuer defines both the collateral and the tranche sizes as well as subordination in order to meet the rating agency's requirements to achieve the target rating.[9] Afterwards, the individually securitized tranche is purchased by the investor who adds diversity to his portfolio. Besides bespoke asset securitization the ABS market offers a variety of business opportunities for global rating agencies, which is also indicated by a rapidly increasing number of tranche ratings, as is shown later on.

To alleviate the following market analysis of structured securities Figure 2.2 provides an overview of the major ABS structures.

In general ABS may be seen as hypernym for all asset-backed securities (wide sense), but more specifically ABS are themselves seen as financial securities backed by, e.g. home equity loans (HEL), auto loans, leases, credit card receivables, student loans, aircraft leases

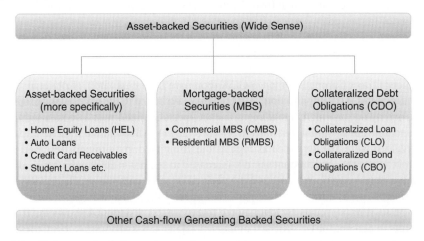

Figure 2.2   Major asset-backed security structures.
Note: This figure summarizes the three major classes of asset-backed securities and their sub-classes.

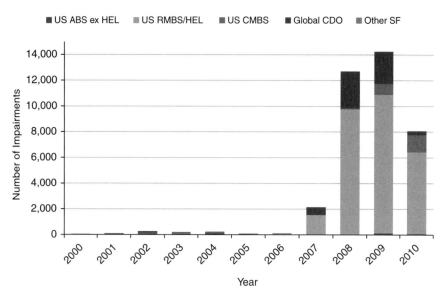

Figure 2.3   Impairments of structured securities.
Note: This figure shows the the amount of impairments for major US asset-backed security classes. *Other SF* contains structured finance securities that are not categorized in the four major sectors (ABS, CDO, CMBS and RMBS).
Data Source: Moody's (2011).

etc. Other sub-classes of ABS are Mortgage Backed Securities (MBS) and Collateralized Debt Obligations (CDO). MBS can further be separated into Commercial MBS and Residential MBS.[10] Collateralized Loan Obligations (CLO) as well as Collateralized Bond Obligations (CBO) represent sub-categories of CDOs. Hence, depending on the underlying collateral and its characteristics, ABS structures may be further sub-classified.

Figure 2.3 underlines the development of annual impairments of structured finance securities (x-axis) from 2000 to 2010 (y-axis) for major asset-backed security (ABS) structures (Moody's, 2011).[11]

In contrast to the period from 2000 to 2006, where 1,064 cumulated impairments occurred, the number of impairments dramatically increased in the years 2007 to 2009 triggered by the Global Financial Crisis (GFC).[12] The events of the GFC come along with strongly increasing credit spreads[13] particularly on the credit derivative markets around the world, e.g. the markets for Credit Default Swaps (CDS) or other structured finance securities such as the popular credit indices iTraxx Europe and the US CDX (compare Löhr et al., 2010; Löhr et al., 2012).[14]

The sharp rise of ABS impairments in 2007 can be attributed to the US housing crisis, which was spawned by nationwide US housing price declines combined with a sudden tightening of credit standards and rising interest rates (Moody's, 2011). Although the tranche impairments in 2007 (2,153) were already twice as high as the cumulated impairments observed over the previous six years, the total amount rapidly increased to 12,719 in 2008, which was almost six times higher than in 2007. With 14,242 the peak of impairments was reached in 2009 due to 13,618 principal write-downs (95.61%) and 624 interest shortfalls (4.39%).[15]

Based on total impairments by year shown in Figure 2.3, Figure 2.4 shows the fraction of impairments in percent for US ABS excluding (ex) HEL, US RMBS/HEL, US CMBS, global CDO and other Structured Finance (SF) securities.

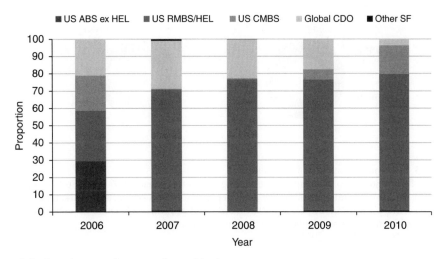

Figure 2.4   Impairments of structured securities by sector.
Note: This figure shows the percentages of material impairments related to the four major asset-backed security classes (or sectors): *US ABS ex Home Equity Loans* (HEL), *US RMBS/HEL, US CMBS, Global CDO* and *Other SF*. *Other SF* contains structured finance securities that are not categorized in the four major sectors. Proportions are reported for 2006 to 2010.
Data Source: Moody's (2011).

While the US ABS ex HEL market exhibited the highest default frequency until 2007 with on average 36.6% over the years 2000 up to 2006, impairments are clearly dominated by US RMBS/HEL since 2007. In contrast to 2006, where we observed almost balanced impairments across all major ABS classes (except other SF), especially the market for US Residential Mortgage Backed Securities (RMBS), Home Equity Loans (HEL) and global Collateralized Debt Obligations (CDO) suffered from default events related to its borrowers in later years.

In 2007, 1,505 tranche defaults in the US RMBS/HEL market account for more than 69.9%, followed by impairments of global CDO tranches with a proportion of 27.7%. Thus both securitization classes accounted for more than 97.6% of reported tranche defaults in the first year of the GFC.

In the following years, there was again a slight shift in the proportion of sectoral impairments: up to the impairment peak in 2009 the US RMBS/HEL proportion of tranche defaults increased to 75.6% (10,774), while the respective proportion of global CDOs clearly decreased to 17.5%. But despite this decrease the absolute number of 2,496 impairments was relatively high and still higher than the overall impairments in 2007.

In 2010, US RMBS/HEL accounted for 78.7%, US Commercial MBS for 16.6% and global CDOs for 3.8% of the 8,071 reported tranche defaults. Thereby, the new impairments of US CMBS increased by 59% from 839 to 1,337. However, we observe a decrease of almost 47% in new impairments in comparison to the previous year in total across the reported ABS classes. The decrease of impairments from absolute 2,496 to 304 (about 88%) is even higher in the global CDO market.

Figure 2.5 shows the proportion of outstanding ratings across the reported ABS classes for January 2007 and 2010 (compare Moody's, 2008, 2011).

Moody's (2011) reports that the number of new ratings by closing year exponentially increased from 1993 to 2006 and reached its peak in 2006 with over 27,000 ratings. During the

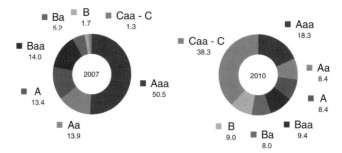

Figure 2.5   Comparison of outstanding ratings.
Note: This figure shows the percentage of outstanding ratings for January 2007 (total: 86,671) and January 2010 (total: 94,326). The ratings refer to the entire reported asset-backed security market, particularly to *US ABS ex HEL, US RMBS/HEL, US CMBS, Global CDO* and *Other SF*. Other SF contains structured finance securities that are not categorized in the four major sectors.
Data Source: Moody's (2008, 2011).

turmoil in the global financial markets, the number of new ratings decreased strongly and fell below 2,500 in 2010 which is the second lowest level since 1993 (compare Moody's, 2011). Consequently, the number of outstanding ratings moderately declines for the second year in a row across all ABS classes.

In 2010 – analogously to 2007 (reported in parentheses) – the US RMBS/HEL were leading the outstanding ratings, approximately accounting for 61.4% (60.1%), followed by US CMBS approximately accounting for 9.3% (9.8%) and global CDOs approximately accounting for 13.4% (13.4%).

While the distribution of outstanding ratings was heavily skewed in the beginning of 2007 towards Investment Grade (IG) ratings, the respective distribution for 2010 was not: with over 50% "Aaa"-rated tranches the IG ratings making up 91.8% of all asset-backed security ratings in 2007. In contrast, approximately 55.3% of all structured ratings were below the IG rating in the beginning of 2010. The proportion of tranches in the "Aaa" category experienced a decline of over 36%, while the amount of non-IG rated tranches was about 6.7 times higher than in 2007, despite the numerous impairments in the previous years.

Figure 2.6 shows the distribution of material impairments by original rating of structured securities in 2010.

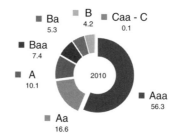

Figure 2.6   Impairments of asset-backed securities by original rating in percent.
Note: This figure shows the distribution of material impairments, defined as interest shortfalls or principal write-downs, by the original rating of asset-backed securities for the year 2010 in percent.
Data Source: Moody's (2011).

As already indicated, in 2010 most tranche impairments occurred in rating category "Aaa" which is expected to contain the most secure tranches in terms of default risk. Interestingly, tranches of category "Caa" to "C" exhibiting the lowest creditworthiness represent the smallest group of defaulted securities. Overall, 90.4% of impaired tranches were labeled with an IG rating, which underlines the shortcomings of current rating metrics.

These rating-based descriptives lead to two major results: firstly, the distress on the global financial markets arrived, with strongly increasing material impairments across all securitized asset classes. From an economic perspective a dramatic increase of physical defaults was observed across various financial instruments, e.g. bonds, loans, leases, structured products, even during the economic downturn, either caused by principal write-downs or continuing interest shortfalls. However, structured financial instruments seem to have been particularly affected by the financial turmoil, since its investors were faced with unexpected high default frequencies/rates, even though they invested in "Aaa"-rated securities.

Under the assumption that global economic movements are caused by unobservable systematic risk which affects all economic sectors simultaneously, one may conclude that particularly structured finance instruments are exposed to systematic risk due to pooling and tranching. The impacts of systematic risk are especially observable in economic downturns since this economic distress becomes manifest in an increase of impairments (downside risk). On the other hand, the systematic upside risk is rather negligible since default events are rarely triggered by economic upturns.

Eventually, these market developments indicate not only that structured finance products exhibit a higher sensitivity to systematic risk than other financial instruments such as classical bonds, but also that the systematic risk sensitivity is monotonically increasing with the tranches' seniority.[16]

Despite the absence of exact knowledge about the established rating methodologies, one may secondly conclude that ratings are not appropriately measuring default risk of structured securities at all. Rather, they seem to underestimate risk characteristics of structured financial products, especially in times of market crisis, as could be deduced by market participants from the recent GFC. From this point of view, it is assumed that agency ratings do not reflect appropriately the risk characteristics of structured financial products – neither in terms of default risk nor in terms of losses caused by such impairments. For that reason, particularly investors in structured products bore unexpectedly high default rates and also suffered from related severe losses due to the numerous tranche impairments.

In conclusion, it is suggested that current rating metrics do not account appropriately for systematic risks inherent in asset-backed securities, since they obviously underestimate cyclical influences which affect impairments.

2.2 ISSUANCE OF ASSET-BACKED SECURITIES AND OUTSTANDING VOLUME

One way to examine the economic relevance and popularity of asset securitizations in global financial markets is to analyze recorded issuance activities and outstanding volumes of these securities.

Starting with a description of the developments on current structured finance markets, Figure 2.7 compares the market issuance from 1996 to 2010 concerning both major ABS classes, namely asset- and mortgage-backed securities. Referring to ABS, the upper graph of Figure 2.7 compares the issuance volume related to the US and Europe.[17] In the lower graph

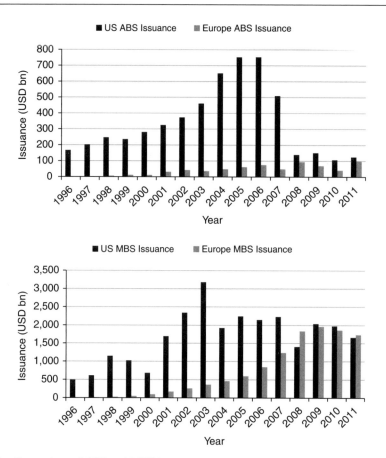

Figure 2.7   Comparison of ABS and MBS issuance.
Note: This figure compares the ABS issuance (upper graph) and MBS issuance (lower graph) with respect to the US and Europe from 1996 to 2011 in USD billions (bn).
Data Source: SIFMA (2012a,c).

the security issuance is analogously compared with respect to MBS. The issuance volume is denoted in USD billions (bn) on the y-axes from 1996 to 2010 (x-axes).

Similarly to the developments of tranche impairments shown in Figure 2.3, the US ABS issuance increased more than 19 years in row and reached its all-time high in 2006 with over 753 USD bn (upper graph). In the following years it dramatically fell (107 USD bn in 2010).[18] From 2010 to 2011 we saw the first issuance increase of almost 16% to more than 124 USD bn after four weak years. This increase in volume comes along with the decrease in new material impairments which was described earlier.

Even though first European securitizations were already recorded in 1987, the total market for ABS was comparably less developed in Europe until 1997. While the US ABS issuance was at 202 USD bn, its European pendant solely denoted at 1.08 USD bn. However, from 1997 to 2011 the developments in terms of absolute growth were still dominated by the US markets, but the relative growth rates indicate the increasing importance of the European market segment: despite a moderate break down in 2007 due to the turmoil in global financial markets, the European security issuance increased to more than 98 USD bn, which is more than 90 times higher than the volume in 1997. Due to the increasing demand for European ABS structures both ABS markets (US and Europe) exhibit a comparable level in issuance, which also underlines the emergence of Europe as one of the major global security markets.

Similar developments may be observed with regard to MBS markets (lower graph). Until 2010 the US MBS issuance was dominating the respective European one in absolute pattern. Interestingly, after the US issuance peak in 2003 (over 3,179 USD bn) the volume declined to 1,924 USD bn in 2004, but varies around 2,000 USD bn, with the exception of 2008, where the issuance fell to 1,403 USD bn, which was about 37% less volume than in the previous year. Thus, in contrast to the ABS markets, one may conclude that the US MBS markets experienced a relatively strong issuance of structured securities despite the turmoil on the global financial markets.

Similar to European ABS, European MBS have increased since 1987. During the next decade the issuance increased moderately from 1.0 USD bn to about 9.76 USD bn in 1996. In the following years the demand for European MBS increased, with an all-time high in 2009 with over 1,961 USD bn, which is more than 200 times higher than the issuance in 1996. Nevertheless, the absolute volume is slightly lower than the respective one on US markets. This has changed in the years 2009 to 2011: while the US market issuance has decreased about 18.7% the European issuance has declined only about 11.5%. Thus, in 2011, the absolute US issuance volume was 1,660 USD bn while the European was 1,736 US bn, which was historically the first time that the US MBS issuance was below the European one.

2.3 GLOBAL CDO ISSUANCE AND OUTSTANDING VOLUME

Since many practitioners and researchers widely view CDOs as one of the most important financial innovations of the past decade and identify CDOs as a major source for credit losses in the recent credit crisis (compare Longstaff, 2010), the remainder of this chapter focuses on CDOs as a heavily – and most critically – discussed ABS class. To underline their special role on global financial markets, both the global CDO issuance and CDO outstandings are addressed from several perspectives.

Initially, North America and Europe were the main markets for credit derivatives such as credit default swaps and CDOs. Recently, trading activities have begun in Asia, Japan and a number of emerging markets (Rajan et al., 2007). Although the list of participants has grown, banks are major market participants next to others such as hedge funds, monoline insurers, reinsurers, pensions funds, mutual funds and corporations. Nowadays, most market participants are buyers as well as sellers of default protection (Rajan et al., 2007).

Figure 2.8 compares the global CDO issuance (black line) with the US bond issuance (dashed line). The primary y-axis denotes the US bond issuance in USD billions (bn) and the secondary y-axis shows the global CDO issuance from 2000 to 2011 (x-axis).

After four years of moderate CDO issuance growth from 67.99 USD bn in 2000 to 86.63 USD bn in 2003, the issuance growth rate strongly increased over the next three years. This led to a peak in 2006 that is marked by an issuance of more than 520 USD bn. Therefore, during these three years the market demand for global CDOs rapidly increased and was six times higher than in 2003. In line with the distress on financial markets the global issuance fell for three years in a row and reached its recorded all-time low at 4.3 USD bn in 2009. Since 2010 the volume is again rising and was recorded at almost 13 USD bn in 2011.[19]

While varying around approximately 800 USD bn between 2000 and 2005, the issuance on US bond markets increased moderately in 2006 to 1,058 USD bn from 752 USD bn in 2005.

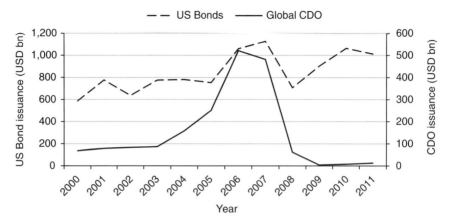

Figure 2.8   The global CDO and bond issuance from 2000 to 2011.
Note: This figure shows the the global CDO issuance (secondary y-axis) from 2000 to 2011. Respective developments in the US bond market are also denoted (primary y-axis).
Data Source: SIFMA (2012a).

In contrast to the CDO markets the bond issuance grew also in 2007 up to 1,127 USD bn (almost 6.5%). Further, the volume was just declining in 2008 to 707 USD bn due to the crisis. Thus the issuance fell approximately back to the level established between 2000 and 2005. Additionally, the US bond issuance rebounded fast to over 1,000 USD bn in 2010, which is close to the former peak in 2007.

By contrast, the global CDO issuance broke down heavily during the GFC and only started recovering in 2011, while the US bond market was seemingly much less affected by the recent turmoil. Additionally, the default rates were much lower in this period on corporate bond markets than for comparably rated asset securitizations (compare Moody's, 2010a,b).

These market developments suggest that corporate bonds and structured finance securities vary in their risk characteristics, and they also indicate differences in the instruments' sensitivities to systematic risk, which are explicitly addressed by Löhr et al. (2011).

Before current market developments for global CDO issuance and outstandings are analyzed in detail, the most common types of CDOs are briefly contrasted. As a sub-class of asset-backed securities in general, CDOs may further be categorized, among others, by its type, purpose, collateral or domination. Regarding the type of CDOs, one may distinguish between *Cash Flow, Synthetic, Hybrid* and *Market Value CDOs*. Generally, *Cash Flow, Synthetic, Hybrid* and *Market Value CDOs* refer to the source of funds related to the securitization. In a *Cash Flow CDO* a portfolio of individual debt assets, such as loans, bonds (high yield or IG bonds), other ABS or MBS etc., is physically acquired at the launch of the deal and securitized afterwards. Although there is only little change on the asset side during the securitization's term, the focus lies on the management of the collateral to maintain a pre-specified credit quality of the underlying assets, particularly when credit impairments occur so that a single-name asset must be replaced (compare Batchvarov, 2007).[20]

Typically, a special purpose entity (SPE) is involved – in Europe often called a special purpose vehicle – that is especially designed to acquire the collateral of the securitization and issues bonds to investors for cash used to purchase the underlying *Cash Pool* (compare SEC, 2005).[21] In this way the originator legally conveys the ownership of the debt assets to the SPE (true sale transaction) and is thus isolated from the financial risks, e.g. credit risk and market risk of the entire securitization. Thus, a SPE can be characterized by its narrow as well as its temporary objectives. This mechanism of course may create a number of moral hazard risks since the originator is aware that he may not suffer any credit losses on the loans he makes because they will be sold as repackaged CDOs (compare Longstaff, 2010).

Eventually, the issuer engaged in such off-balance sheet transactions looks less leveraged and may be permitted to borrow money on capital markets at cheaper interest rates. Further, the originator raises liquidity, increasing his financial flexibility through the sale of receivables (off-balance sheet financing).

By isolating inherent credit risks and transferring them to external investors, the financial institution may also optimize its credit portfolio risk. For example, through the sale of sectoral concentrated debt assets such as ship financing and auto loans, concentration risk may be reduced (diversification effects). In consequence, the issuing bank may achieve a release of required regulatory capital. The reduction of regulatory requirements is among others, a frequent reason for issuing *Balance Sheet CDOs*. By contrast, if the sale of receivables is recognized on the (consolidated) balance sheet of the originator then this securitization is called an on-balance sheet transaction (on-balance sheet financing).

As already indicated, structured finance securities fulfill numerous useful functions. In addition to enhancing liquidity and facilitating lower-cost funding there are further reasons for the originator to engage in these securitized transactions such as managing risk, e.g. by diversifying credit portfolio risk, trading various components of credit risk and separating legal from beneficial ownership.[22] On the other hand, investors are also able to customize the exposures they want to hold in their portfolios (FCIC, 2011).[23] Once credit risk or specified elements of credit risk have been separated – such as default risk and related losses, spread volatility, counterparty risk and correlation risk – market participants can choose which ones they want to hold or to hedge.[24] Derivative contracts are thus naturally two-sided and allow long and short positions to be taken on each element of credit risk (Rajan et al., 2007).

For example, investors can use structured securities to get access to products whose spread would otherwise be either too high or too low for their needs (Rajan et al., 2007). An investor looking for "A"-rated risk can either purchase a junior tranche (note) backed by "AAA"-collateral or, instead, invest in a senior tranche that is backed by "B"-rated assets in the structured credit market.

In contrast to *Cash Flow CDOs*, *Synthetic CDOs* do not involve cash assets, but take on credit exposures through embedding credit default swaps (CDS) or baskets of CDS (compare Longstaff and Rajan, 2008).

A CDS is a credit derivative that is linked to a specified credit risky asset or basket of assets (reference asset or underlying). In a CDS contract the protection seller, e.g. an external investor, offers protection against the default risk of the underlying, and compensates the protection buyer for losses related to the reference asset in terms of an default event such as an interest shortfall or principal impairment (similar to an insurance contract). In turn, the protection buyer, e.g. a bank owning the underlying, periodically pays a risk premium (spread) to the investor – usually on the outstanding nominal – for taking the default risk.[25]

Most popular examples for standardized *Synthetic CDOs* are credit indices, namely the iTraxx Europe and the CDX index families. As already mentioned, each index represents a basket containing 125 of such CDS contracts on corporate names.[26] Thus, *Synthetic CDOs* use, for example, CDS contracts to synthetically replicate *Cash Flow CDOs*.

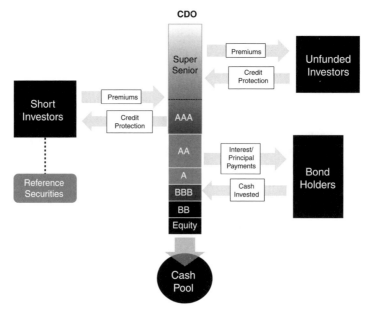

Figure 2.9   Complexity of hybrid CDO: an example.
Note: This figure shows an example for a complex hybrid CDO structure, similarly to FCIC (2011).

Since many CDOs actually take on credit risk through both cash assets and CDS, the boundary between *Cash Flow CDOs* and *Synthetic CDOs* is often blurred. To avoid mis-specifications these structures can be summarized below *Hybrid CDOs* (intermediate securities).[27]

Apart from other involved parties, e.g. underwriter, special purpose entity, credit rating agency (CRA), trustee, Figure 2.9 points out that *Hybrid CDOs* involving CDS contracts may lead to complex securitization structures.

The invested capital is typically provided by *Bond Holders* acquiring securitized tranches of the CDO. Due to the credit quality of tranches which is indicated through its CRA rating, e.g. "BB", "BBB", "A", *Bond Holders* obtain interest payments throughout the tranches' maturity – periodically on the remaining nominal – and the residual principal at maturity. Eventually, the size of principal re-payment depends on the losses of the respective tranche until maturity. If the principal covering for tranche losses expires, the investor of this tranche neither receives, any principal payback nor any interest payments.

In contrast to funded investors, here the *Bond Holders*, unfunded investors typically buy the most senior tranche and are effectively engaged in a CDS with the "CDO." Such investors therefore offer credit protection to losses occurring in the super senior tranche and receive in turn premiums (also periodically) for facing the default risk of that tranche.

Additional funds are generated by *Short Investors*, who enter into CDS with the "CDO." They demand credit protection related to own *Reference Securities* such as other ABS, which are independent of the major CDO (compare Figure 2.9). Offering credit protection for losses in these *Reference Securities* the "CDO" receives CDS premiums (funds). But if losses occur within the external collateral (*Reference Securities*), the "CDO" has to provide protection payments to the *Short Investors*.[28] Through embedding CDS contracts in securitizations a possibility was created for market participants to bet for or against the performance of these securities. Generally, through offering *Synthetic CDOs* the demand for this kind of betting heavily increased and added liquidity to the market, which is sometimes referred to as social utility (FCIC, 2011).

Funds generated through premiums by the *Short Investors* can be retained on cash reserve accounts and used to cover losses within the most senior tranches.[29] If funds are not enough to cover losses, e.g. in the super senior tranche, then *Unfunded Investors* in this tranche have to cover the remaining losses according to signed swap contracts.

Underwriters of securitizations, such as investment banks, profit from underwriting fees of between 0.5% to 1.50% of the total deal (see FCIC, 2011). In this way underwriters raise investment capital from investors on behalf of the securitization's issuer, e.g. the originating bank. In collaboration with a hired asset manager of the CDO, or asset management firm, that selects the collateral, the underwriter structures the securitization related to a tranche's thickness, subordination and credit quality in order to meet the desired requirements of involved parties, such as the originator himself, investors or credit rating agencies.[30] Thus, the underwriter acts as an intermediary between the issuer and potential investors in the financial markets.

For i) bearing the market risk while holding issued securities on its own books until all securitized tranches are completely sold to market participants, ii) shorting many of these deals and iii) providing sale channels facilitating transactions between buyer and seller of credit default swap protection, the underwriter is rewarded with a compensating fee. Further proceeds often result from an exclusive sale agreement on the securities. Indeed, the originator is insulated from the market risk related to the entire issuance of the securitization on capital markets at a sufficient price.

Generally, CDO tranches may find their way into several asset securitizations, which boosts the complexity of the overall mosaic capturing all cross-links and other dependencies related to structured finance products (compare FCIC, 2011). Often single mortgage-backed securities are referenced multiple times in *Synthetic CDOs*. As long as the reference securities perform well, investors betting that the tranche will fail (short investors) would make regular payments to the protection sellers. If the reference securities default, then the long investors would make large payments to the protection buyer (short investor). For example, if the reference securities, e.g. bonds, are worth 10 USD million and there are bets placed through CDS contracts on that securities worth 50 USD million, then on the basis of the performance of 10 USD million in bonds, more than 60 USD million could potentially change hands.

Due to the structure of such synthetic CDOs, losses from the bursting of the housing bubble were multiplied exponentially during the GFC through *Synthetic CDOs* by magnifying the overall risk (compare FCIC, 2011).

However, investors often relied on the rating agencies' opinions rather than conducting their own credit analysis. It was thus a great business for rating agencies such as Moody's, S&P and Fitch since they were paid according to the size of each deal.[31]

In providing credit ratings the agencies were faced with two key challenges: first, estimating the probability of default for the MBS purchased by the CDO or its synthetic equivalent and second, gauging the correlation between defaults measuring the dependency between security defaults at the same time.

To estimate the default probability, Moody's relied almost exclusively on its own ratings of the mortgage-backed securities purchased by the CDO (FCIC, 2011). The rating agencies rarely "looked through" the securities to the underlying, e.g. sub-prime mortgages, which led to problems for Moody's and investors (FCIC, 2011).

Necessary assessments may be even more difficult in complex CDO structures. On the other hand, the increased complexity of structured products also allowed rating agencies to increase their proceeds since it was even harder for investors to provide their own due diligence. This led to situations in which investors relied more heavily on ratings than for other types of rated financial instruments such as corporate bonds (FCIC, 2011).

Market Value CDOs represent another type of CDOs. *Market Value CDOs* can be characterized by frequent trading activities in order to maintain a specified ratio of the collateral's market value to the structure's obligations.[32] Typically, the collateral must be liquidated, either in part or in whole, if the specified ratio falls below a specified threshold (compare Moody's, 1998). Revenues from liquidated collateral are used to reduce the liabilities to tranche investors until the specified ratio is again fulfilled (re-balancing). Overall, *Market Value CDOs* tend to offer a variety of useful applications, even in structures of unpredictable cash flows, such as distressed debt (compare Moody's, 1998).

Referring to the purpose of a CDO, another couple of sub-categories is represented by *Arbitrage CDOs* and *Balance Sheet CDOs*. In an *Arbitrage CDO*, whether cash, synthetic or hybrid, the respective arranger undertakes transactions that are mainly targeted at spread differences between relatively high yielding pool assets (spread on loans or CDS) and lower yielding CDO liabilities (spread on CDO note) (compare Renault, 2007). Thus assets of an *Arbitrage CDO* are particularly purchased for arbitrage transactions rather than holding these assets on the originator's book. Note that all sub-categories do not obviate each other. So *Arbitrage CDOs* may refer to *Cash Flow*, *Synthetic*, *Hybrid* and *Market Value CDOs*.

Based on the global CDO issuance by year shown in Figure 2.8, Figure 2.10 shows the distribution of the global CDO issuance (y-axes) by type and purpose for the period 2005 to 2011 (x-axes) denoted in USD billions (bn). Thus the upper graph refers to several securitization types and the lower graph to its purposes.[33]

The percentage of *Cash Flow/Hybrid CDOs* dominated the issuance volume in each year from 2005 to 2011 (upper graph). Despite a decline from 82% in 2005 to 59% in 2009, in 2010 almost each issuance was of this type (99.5%). Further, its proportion remained relatively stable at 70% in 2007 and 2008.

While in 2005 and 2006 *Synthetic CDOs* represented the second major issuance type with 17.7% and 12.8%, respectively, the proportion shifted in 2007 as *Market Value CDOs* accounted for 19.3% and *Synthetic CDOs* only for 10.1%. Until 2009 this gap widened to 35.1% (*Market Value*) versus 5.9% (*Synthetic*), so that the global issuance of *Market Value CDOs* accounted for more than one third of the total volume. However, in 2010 only 11% was attributed to *Market Value CDOs*.

Until 2009, the global CDO issuance by purpose was clearly dominated by *Arbitrage CDOs*. From 2005 to 2009 this kind of CDO issuance accounted for at least 77%. In 2010 and 2011 the demand for *Balance Sheet CDOs* strongly increased from 20.6% in 2009 to 57.9% and 58.8%, respectively. Thus, in these years the issuance market was slightly dominated by *Balance Sheet CDOs*, which underlines the rising attractiveness of these securitizations.

Next, Figure 2.11 shows the global CDO issuance with respect to the collateral (upper graph), and the denomination (lower graph) for 2005 to 2011 (x-axes) in USD billions (bn). Categorized outstandings are denoted on the y-axes. The total issuance by year corresponds to those plotted in the previous Figures 2.8 and 2.10. The issuance by collateral shown in the upper graph is distinguished in *High Yield* and *Investment Grade Bonds*, *High Yield Loans*, *Mixed Collateral*, *Structured Finance* and *Other*.

Investment Grade Bonds are defined as bonds that are rated by authorized credit rating agencies with an investment grade rating being equal or above "Baa3" ("BBB") in terms of

Global CDO Issuance by Type

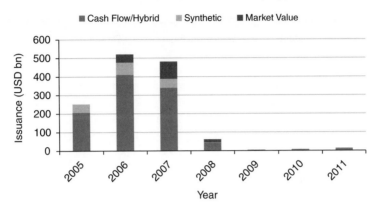

Global CDO Issuance by Purpose

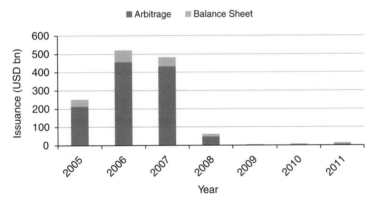

Figure 2.10   Comparison of global CDO issuance by type and purpose.
Note: This figure shows the global CDO issuance by type divided into *Cash Flow CDO/Hybrid*, *Synthetic* and *Market Value CDO* (upper graph), and also by purpose (lower graph) distinguished between *Arbitrage* and *Balance Sheet CDO*.
Data Source: SIFMA (2012b).

the Moody's (S&P) rating scale. On the other hand, bonds that are rated below the investment grade are defined as *High Yield Bonds*. With respect to the data, *High Yield Loans* are defined as debt assets of borrowers with senior unsecured debt ratings that are at financial close below Moody's "Baa3" or S&P's "BBB" (SIFMA, 2012b).

Structured Finance collateral includes underlying assets such as RMBS, CMBS, ABS, CMO, CDO, CDS, and other securitized or structured products (SIFMA, 2012b). In category *Other* SIFMA (2012a) summarizes collateral such as funds, insurance receivables, cash and assets that are not captured by the other categories noted above. Further, a CDO that has 51% or more of a single collateral type, is included in this bucket, otherwise in *Mixed Collateral*.

With an absolute issuance of 746.94 USD bn from 2005 to 2011 (relative 55.72%) structured finance (SF) securities represent the major collateral related to the total global CDO issuance

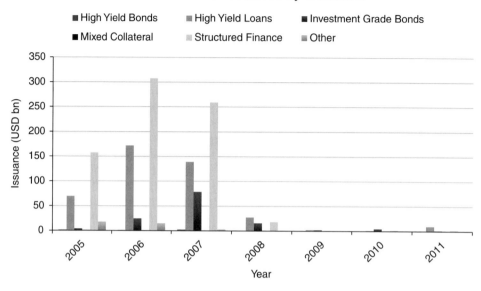

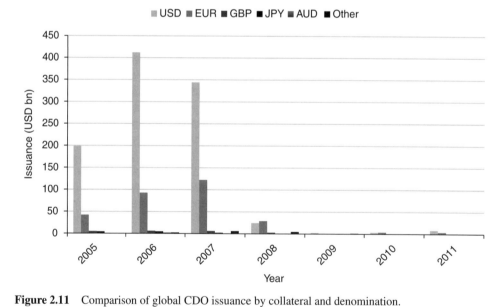

Figure 2.11   Comparison of global CDO issuance by collateral and denomination.
Note: This figure shows the global CDO issuance by its collateral in the upper graph and by its denomination in the lower one. The collateral is distinguished in *High Yield* and *Investment Grade Bonds*, *High Yield Loans*, *Mixed Collateral*, *Structured Finance* and *Other*. The category *Other* refers to collateral assets such as funds, insurance receivables, cash, and assets that are not captured by the other categories noted above. With respect to the lower chart, *Other* refers to currencies other than USD, EUR, GBP, JPY and AUD.
Data Source: SIFMA (2012a).

of 1,340 USD bn. This collateral type was followed by high yield loans with 420.85 USD bn (relative 31.4%) and IG bonds with 131.08 USD bn (relative 9.8%).

In 2006 the percentage of SF was 59.1% with absolute 307 USD bn, which was more than 12.3 times higher than the IG collateral and 1.79 times higher than the high yield loan issuance (24.86 USD bn, and 171.9 USD bn compared to 520.64 USD bn in total). Up to 2009 the SF as well as the HYL issuance was rapidly decreasing: while the SF accounted for 7.64% (absolute 0.33 USD bn), HYL accounted for 46.9% (absolute 2 USD bn) of the annual issuance of 4.33 USD bn. Interestingly, that was less than 1% of the total issuance in 2006.

After four years in a row, the issuance slightly increased in 2010 for the first time in both collateral groups. Finally, the demand for HYL recovered faster since the percentage was 76.9% with 10.01 USD bn in 2011, and thus 8.74 times higher than in 2010. By contrast, the SF issuance increased by 14.1% compared to 2010 to 1.98 USD bn in 2011.

Interestingly, the percentage of IG bonds (IGB) strongly increased from 2005 to 2010 from 1.5% to 62.6%. Additionally, the demand for IGB (78.51 USD bn) was more than 3 times higher than in the year before (24.86 USD bn). In 2010 the IGB collateral was more than 4 times higher than the HYL and 2.8 times higher than the SF collateral. These market developments indicate that the confidence in structured markets massively declined, but they also show that the investors' confidence has slightly returned since 2010. Thus the market demand for more secured products like IG bonds seems to increase again and HYL are preferred over the structured collateral.

Additionally, most of the global CDO securities are either denoted in US dollars or in Euros and account together for at least 96% of the global issuance in 2005 to 2007. Thus, the USD issuance is around 75% throughout. With 29.2 USD bn (relative 47.12f%) the EUR issuance was in 2008 the first time above the USD notations since 2000. In 2011 around two thirds (65.1%) of the issuance was denoted in USD and about one third in EUR (30.1%).

Intuitively, another important indicator for current market developments is the outstanding of global CDOs. For this reason, Figure 2.12 reports the global CDO outstanding in USD bn (y-axis) by type and purpose from 2005 to 2011 (x-axis).

From 1995 to 2007 the outstandings of global CDOs rapidly grew from 1.39 UDS bn to more than 1,363 USD bn. After its peak in 2007 these outstandings declined for four years in a row to approximately 951 USD bn.[34]

From 2005 to 2007 *Cash Flow and Hybrid CDOs* dominated the global outstandings. All CDO outstandings that could not be captured by other categories are summarized below *Unknown* (see SIFMA, 2012b). From 2008 to 2011 around 50% of the entire outstandings were attributed to that category.

In 2011 *Cash Flow and Hybrid CDOs* accounted with 434.8 USD bn for approximately 45.7%, while solely 2.3% could be attributed to *Synthetic Funded CDOs* (absolute 21.9 USD bn). In contrast to 2006, where the attributed volume was at an all-time high of 56.2 USD bn, accounting for 5.2% of the total outstanding, the *Synthetic Funded CDO* outstandings denoted at an all-time low in 2011 due to a decline for 7 years in a row.

In 2005, the volume of 6 USD bn accounted for only 0.8% of the global outstanding. The proportions of *Market Value CDO* have also decreased since 2005. Related outstandings decreased absolutely and relatively, reaching an all-time low in 2011 of 1.1 USD bn (0.1%).

Overall, neither *Synthetic Funded CDOs* nor *Market Value CDOs* seem to play a major role on global CDO markets. Instead, at least *Cash Flow and Hybrid CDOs* are identified as one of the most important securities on current markets accounting for almost 50% of the securitized market volume.[35]

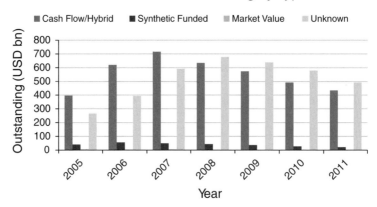

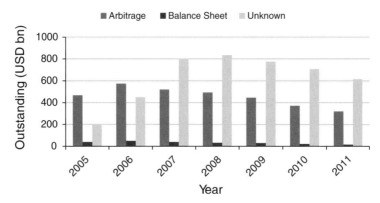

Figure 2.12 Comparison of global CDO outstanding by type and purpose.
Note: This figure shows the outstanding of global CDOs by type (*Cash Flow/Hybrid, Synthetic* and *Market Value CDOs*) in the upper graph and by purpose (*Arbitrage* and *Balance Sheet CDOs*) in the lower graph. All CDO structures that may not be allocated in any of the other categories are included in category *Unknown*.
Data Source: SIFMA (2012b).

Related to the purpose of global CDOs, *Arbitrage CDOs* were dominating *Balance Sheet CDOs* in terms of global outstandings from 1999 to 2005. In 2006, *Arbitrage CDOs* reached its all-time high with over 574 USD bn or 53.4% of total outstandings. In line with the turmoil in financial markets the volume declined to 320 USD bn in 2011 which denoted 33.7% of the annual outstandings. Simultaneously, proportion of *Balance Sheet CDO* also continuously declined from 5.63% in 2005 (absolute about 40 USD bn) to 1.64% in 2011 with an absolute volume of about 15.61 USD bn.

However, *Unknown CDOs* which are not attributable to one of both standard categories play a major role and account for 28.45% of the outstandings (201.8 USD bn) in 2005. Their proportion continuously increased to 64.66% of the total outstandings with an absolute volume of 615 USD bn in 2011.

CONCLUDING REMARKS

- Structured finance securities such as Collateralized Debt Obligations facilitate the isolation of credit risk and its transfer to external investors.
- Numerous useful applications of structured products made these financial instruments the most popular tools in the last decade.
- During the GFC the default rates of structured securities increased dramatically, even those of "Aaa"-rated tranches.
- More than 90% of the reported impairments referred to IG-rated securities indicating the shortcomings of the current rating metrics.
- Seemingly, securitizations exhibit specific risk characteristics not sufficiently reflected by credit ratings due to their high sensitivity to systematic risk.
- Within the financial turbulences, impairments were concentrated in the market for RMBS, HELs and CDOs.
- The demand for US ABS and global CDOs was dramatically affected, but less strongly the demand on US MBS markets.
- Indeed, the European ABS issuance tended to move sideways on a relatively low level, while the MBS issuance clearly increased, even in the GFC.
- In 2011 the European ABS issuance reached the US level with almost 98 USD bn, while the MBS issuance was above the US one for the first time.
- Related to the global CDO issuance an all-time low was reached in 2009 with less than 1% of the volume in 2006.
- After four years in a row the global CDO issuance increased for the first time in 2010, with changed major collateral types.
- Interestingly, since 2010 more secured collateral, such as IG bonds and high-yield loans, are preferred over structured collateral.
- Due to the numerous tranche impairments as well as the decreased issuance, the global CDO outstanding was also slightly decreasing from 2008 to 2011.
- Since 2010 when the number of tranche impairments fell for the first time in five years, the confidence in structured securities has begun to return slightly.

NOTES

1. For a chronology of the GFC see BIS (2009).
2. In § 364 of the Standard Financial Accounting Standards No. 140 securitizations are similarly defined as "the process by which financial assets are transformed into securities." (FASB, 2000).
3. Risk is defined here as uncertainty measured in terms of standard deviation of expectations, e.g. referring to expected returns and expected losses (compare Modigliani and Pogue, 1974). Of course, other definitions of risk are available.
4. Under the assumption that risk-averse investors attempt to maximize their expected returns according to their individually acceptable levels of risk – which is one of the most important capital market theories – there should exist a relationship between expected return and risk (compare Modigliani and Pogue, 1974).
5. Examples for such originators are banks, monoline insurers, reinsurers, pensions funds and others (compare Rajan et al., 2007).
6. Both payment legs play a crucial role for further valuation purposes referring to structured securities, compare Löhr et al. (2010).

7. Moody's, one of the leading rating agencies worldwide, for example, defines an interest impairment, which is also an default event, as an interest shortfall continuing for 12 months or more (see Moody's, 2011).
8. A rating expresses an opinion about the creditworthiness of the obligor related to his ability to fulfill future interest and liquidation payments (liabilities).
9. The Moody's long-term ordinal rating scale for bonds and structured finance, for example, reaches from "Aaa" (highest creditworthiness) to "C" (lowest creditworthiness), embedding 21 categories (grades) (see Moody's, 2009).
10. Agency MBS are securities issued or guaranteed by government-sponsored enterprises such as Fannie Mae or Freddie Mac, representing a major category of MBS in the U.S. (see SEC, 2011).
11. Note that Moody's definition of material impairments includes a downgrade to "Ca" or "C," which often occurs far in advance of any interest shortfall or principal write-down.
12. For more detailed information on the chronology of the GFC compare BIS (2010).
13. A credit spread may simply be seen as premium compensating, e.g. investors, for the related default risk.
14. These credit indices are baskets containing 125 liquid CDS contracts (equally-weighted) either from U.S. entities having investment grade (IG) ratings (CDX) or from European entities (iTraxx). For further information on CDOs and credit indices see Longstaff and Rajan (2008).
15. In the previous five years the proportion of principal write-downs on the total impairments was above 99% throughout. The number of interest shortfalls is generally small because most either can be cured (repaid) or become principal impairments.
16. Löhr et al. (2011) demonstrate that pooling and tranching in asset securitizations lead to concentration effects of systematic risk exposures, which are higher in tranches of high seniority.
17. According to the Securities Industry and Financial Markets Association, "European securities are defined as securitizations with collateral predominantly from the European continent, including Turkey, Kazakhstan, the Russian Federation, and Iceland" (SIFMA, 2012a).
18. The collateral assets of U.S. ABS refer to auto loans and leases, credit card receivables, equipment, home equity loans, manufactured housing, student loans and other asset categories that do not fit any other categories. The European ABS refer to auto loans, consumer loans, credit card receivables, leases and others in the sense of above. For more details compare SIFMA (2012a,c).
19. Note that unfunded synthetic CDO tranches are not included in this data set (compare SIFMA, 2012a).
20. This is often handled by an employed CDO manager, who also selects the initial asset pool (collateral).
21. SPE are often located in countries with lax taxation, e.g. the Cayman Islands. However, issues concerning the taxation or accounting standards of SPE, among others, are not the central topic of this exercise and are therefore omitted. For further information see, e.g. SEC (2005).
22. For example, investors may use default swaps to to add names to their portfolios in order to diversify their exposures away from large and concentrated holdings in, e.g. plain-vanilla credit, interest-rate product classes (Rajan et al., 2007).
23. An useful illustration of the practical importance of structured products can be found in Rajan et al. (2007).
24. For example, various correlation risks of single-tranche CDO swap (STCDO) spreads are explicitly addressed in Löhr et al. (2010).
25. For more information, also for CDS markets compare Gandhi et al. (2011).
26. See note 14 or compare www.markit.com for further information.
27. Other illustrated examples for *Hybrid CDOs* as well as more detailed information are either given in Rajan et al. (2007) or in Jobst (2007).
28. Other instruments that are used to protect investors against losses are, among others, credit enhancements such as over-collateralization of the assets sold, cash reserve accounts and guarantees (compare SEC, 2005).

29. Generally, a cash reserve account is a form of credit protection funded from a portion of proceeds from the securitization transaction. Principal losses and/or interest shortfalls are first covered by that reserve up to the amount funded in such account. Thus a cash reserve provides a form of credit enhancement to the third-party investors of the securitization, e.g. *Unfunded investors*.

30. Note that an experienced CDO manager is crucial for both the construction and maintenance of the collateral.

31. Moody's set for a "standard" CDO 500,000 USD and as much as 850,000 USD for a "complex" CDO in 2006 and 2007, see FCIC (2011).

32. The obligation of a CDO is the sum of amortized principal and accrued interest, that has to be paid to investors of tranches until maturity.

33. With respect to the data source, in this analysis only funded *Synthetic CDOs* are considered. Funded tranches require the deposit of cash to an SPV account at the inception of the deal to collateralize the SPE's potential swap obligations in the transaction (compare SIFMA, 2012a).

34. Note that source data for outstanding global CDOs are not the same for global CDO issuance. Due to differences in underlying data, contents are not directly comparable. For more details compare SIFMA (2012b).

35. Note that the results of this exercise strongly depend on the quality of the data.

REFERENCES

Batchvarov, A., 2007. Overview of Structured Credit Markets. The Handbook of Structured Finance, 1–27.

BIS, 2009. BIS 79th Annual Report, June 2009. Bank for International Settlements.

BIS, 2010. BIS Quarterly Review: International Banking and Financial Market Developments, June 2010. Bank for International Settlements.

FASB, 2000. Statement of Financial Accounting Standards No. 140. Financial Accounting Standards Board of the Financial Accounting Foundation, www.fasb.org.

FCIC, 2011. The Financial Crisis Inquiry Report. The Financial Crisis Inquiry Commission, www.fcic.com.

Gandhi, P., Longstaff, F. A., Arora, N., 2011. Counterparty Credit Risk and the Credit Default Swap Market. Working Paper.

Jobst, N., 2007. Recent and Not So Recent Developments in Synthetic Collateral Debt Obligations. The Handbook of Structured Finance, (Arnaud de Servigny and Norbert Jobst (Eds)), 465–542.

Löhr, S., Claußen, A., Rösch, D., 2011. An Analytical Approach for Systematic Risk Sensitivity of Structured Financial Products. Working Paper.

Löhr, S., Claußen, A., Rösch, D., 2012. Valuation of Systematic Risk in Credit Default Swap Spreads. Working Paper.

Löhr, S., Mursajew, O., Rösch, D., Scheule, H., 2010. Dynamic Implied Correlation Modeling and Forecasting in Structured Finance. Working Paper.

Longstaff, F. A., 2010. The Subprime Credit Crisis and Contagion in Financial Markets. Journal of financial economics 97(3), 436–450.

Longstaff, F. A., Rajan, A., 2008. An Empirical Analysis of the Pricing of Collateralized Debt Obligations. The journal of finance 63(2), 529–563.

Modigliani, F., Pogue, G. A., 1974. An Introduction to Risk and Return: Concepts and Evidence. Financial analysts journal 30(3), 69–86.

Moody's, 1998. Moody's Approach to Rating Market-Value CDOs. Moody's Investors Service, www.moodys.com.

Moody's, 2008. Default & Loss Rates of Structured Finance Securities: 1993–2007. Moody's Investors Service, www.moodys.com.

Moody's, 2009. Moody's Rating Symbols & Definitons. Moody's Investors Service, www.moodys.com.

Moody's, 2010a. Corporate Default and Recovery Rates 1920–2009. Moody's Investors Service, www.moodys.com.

Moody's, 2010b. Default & Loss Rates of Structured Finance Securities: 1993–2009. Moody's Investors Service, www.moodys.com.

Moody's, 2011. Default & Loss Rates of Structured Finance Securities: 1993–2010. Moody's Investors Service, www.moodys.com.

Rajan, A., Glen, M., Ratul, R., 2007. The Structured Credit Handbook. John Wiley & Sons, Hoboken, NJ.

Renault, O., 2007. Cash and Synthetic Collateral Debt Obligations: Motivations and Investments Strategies. In: de Servigny, A., Jobst, N. (Eds), The Handbook of Structured Finance. McGraw-Hill Professional, pp. 373–396.

SEC, 2004. Regulation AB: Asset-Backed Securities. U.S. Securities and Exchange Commission, Release Nos. 33-8518.

SEC, 2005. Report and Recommendations Pursuant to Section 401(c) of the Sarbanes-Oxley Act of 2002 On Arrangements with Off-Balance Sheet Implications, Special Purpose Entities, and Transparency of Filings by Issuers. U.S. Securities and Exchange Commission, www.sec.gov.

SEC, 2011. Disclosure for Asset-Backed Securities Required by Section 943 of the Dodd-Frank Wall Street Reform and Consumer Protection Act. U.S. Securities and Exchange Commission, Release Nos. 33-9175.

Sharpe, W. F., 1964. Capital Asset Prices: A Theory of Market Equilibrium under Conditions of Risk. The journal of finance 19(3), 425–442.

SIFMA, 2012a. European Securitization. The Securities Industry and Financial Markets Association, www.sifma.org.

SIFMA, 2012b. Global CDO. The Securities Industry and Financial Markets Association, www.sifma.org.

SIFMA, 2012c. U.S. Asset-backed Securities. The Securities Industry and Financial Markets Association, www.sifma.org.

Part II

Credit Portfolio Risk Measurement

3

Mortgage Credit Risk

Min Qi[1]
Office of the Comptroller of the Currency

A crisis is a terrible thing to waste.

—Paul Romer

3.1 INTRODUCTION

Mortgages used to have low credit risk compared to other consumer credit products, such as credit cards, and have been the dominating asset category in the securitization market. The non-agency asset-backed securities (ABS) and mortgage-backed securities (MBS) market experienced explosive growth in the years leading to the mortgage crisis. The LoanPerformance ABS database shows that non-prime mortgage originations increased nearly 13-fold from $65 billion in 1998 to a peak of $932 billion in 2005 whereas the LoanPerformance MBS database shows that jumbo mortgage originations increased nearly 4-fold from $45 billion in 2000 to a peak of $222 billion in 2003 (Figure 3.1). The US sub-prime mortgage crisis started in 2007 and quickly evolved into a global financial crisis that brought down some of the major mortgage lenders and caused sky rocketing losses to investors of mortgage-backed securities and asset-backed securities. As a result, the ABS and MBS market dropped significantly in 2007 and dried up in 2008 and 2009.

There might be many factors contributing to the recent mortgage and financial crisis. These include historically low interest rates that helped create a house price bubble and a liquidity bubble; the "originate to sell" business model that disconnects mortgage loan originator from the performance of the loans underwritten; the push to increase home ownership that contributed to the loosening of underwriting standards; the deregulation of the banks in the late 1990s; the "shadow banking system" that allows excessive leverage and maturity mismatch and increases the fragility of the entire financial system; the capital framework (Basel I) that is not risk-sensitive, leaving ample room for regulatory capital arbitrage; financial "over engineering" that created arcane artificial securities (e.g. synthetic CDOs) from doubtful mortgages of which no one understood the true risk underneath; the credit rating agencies, which produced over-optimistic ratings due to misaligned incentives and used over-simplistic models that do not adequately account for all the risks in the securities rated; and the system of Wall Street compensation that rewarded short-term risk taking.

In this chapter, we focus on mortgage credit risk measurement and modeling, the weakness of which also contributed to the recent mortgage and financial crisis. Had the credit risk been accurately measured and predicted, lenders could have properly priced the loans at origination

---

[1] The author wishes to thank Jiguang (George) Fang and Roderick (Keith) Friend for research assistance, and Dennis Glennon for helpful comments. The views expressed in this chapter are those of the author and do not necessarily represent the views of the Office of the Comptroller of the Currency, or the US Treasury Department. The author is responsible for all remaining errors.

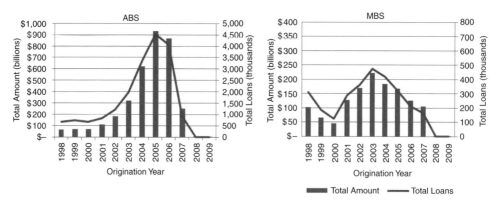

Figure 3.1 ABS and MBS origination volume.
Data Source: LoanPerformance ABS/MBS.

to cover their expected and unexpected losses, set aside an appropriate amount of reserve to cover expected losses, held adequate capital to absorb any unexpected losses, and rating agencies could have produced ratings that reflected the true level of risk in the securities rated.

Several stylized facts can be observed from the historical mortgage foreclosure rates shown in Figure 3.2. First, sub-prime mortgages experienced much higher foreclosure rates than prime mortgages for both fixed rate mortgage (FRM) and adjustable rate mortgage (ARM) in any given year from 1998 to 2011, and the differences were larger in economic downturns than during the benign years. Second, while there was no dramatic difference in foreclosure rates between adjustable and fixed rate mortgages before 2006, adjustable rate mortgages have experienced much higher foreclosure rates than fixed rate mortgages since 2007. Third, foreclosure rates had been low and stable through 2007 for prime mortgages, but are high and cyclical for sub-prime mortgages. Fourth, the rises in foreclosure rates in the early 2000s and

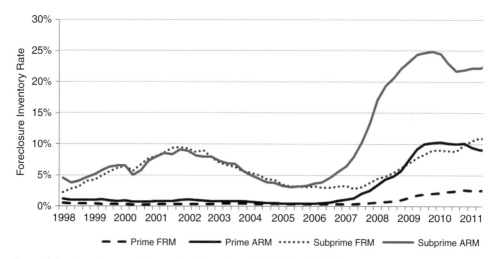

Figure 3.2 Foreclosure rate by product type from 1998Q1 to 2011Q3.
Data Source: Mortgage Bankers Association/Haver. Percent of mortgages in foreclosure, not seasonally adjusted.

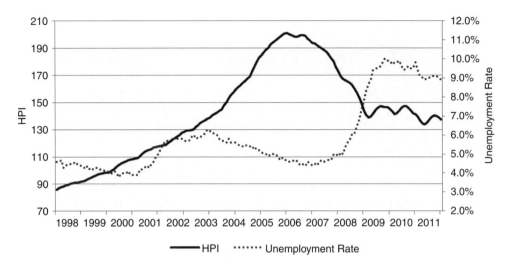

Figure 3.3   House price index and unemployment rate.
Data Source: CoreLogic national HPI including distressed sales (Jan 2000 = 100); BLS unemploymen-
trate, 16 years +, seasonally adjusted.

in the recent mortgage crisis coincided with the rises in unemployment rate and the drop in
house price index shown in Figure 3.3.

Additional observations can be made from the 90 or more days past due (or 90+DPD)
and foreclosure rates shown in Figure 3.4. First, among the loans originated in 2003–2007
in both ABS and MBS markets, more recent vintages show higher delinquency rates and
foreclosure rates than earlier vintages at any month since origination except after 3–4 years
since origination for the 2007 vintage. Second, the delinquency rates peaked faster for the
recent vintages than the earlier vintages. For example, in the ABS market the delinquency rate
peaked around three years from origination for the 2007 vintage, whereas it peaked around six
years from origination for the 2004 vintage. All ABS vintages shown in Figure 3.4 seem to
have experienced the highest delinquency rate in 2010, a year with peak unemployment rate
and bottom house price index as shown in Figure 3.3. This suggests that there is cyclicality
in mortgage defaults in addition to seasoning and vintage effects. Third, for the same vintage
and at the same month since origination, delinquency rate and foreclosure rate in the ABS
market are much higher and peaked quicker than in the MBS market. Finally, foreclosure rates
show a similar vintage pattern except that none of the vintages have truly peaked yet, despite
a small dip in 2010–2011 for all five vintages, caused by the temporary foreclosure freeze as
the robo-signing scandal went public.

In summary, we show in this section that mortgage credit risk can have significant variation
with borrower and loan characteristics (prime vs. subprime, fixed rate vs. adjustable rate), over
the life of the loan (seasoning effect) and with the economic and market conditions (credit
cycle effect). To help capture these variations, in Section 3.2 we provide a brief discussion
on the five "C"s of credit traditionally applied to assess mortgage credit risk. We then further
discuss the determinants of the key parameters of mortgage portfolio risk models, namely,
the probability of default (PD), loss given default (LGD) and exposure at default (EAD) in
Section 3.3. Section 3.4 presents modeling methods that are relevant for modeling PD, LGD
and EAD. Importance and supervisory expectations of model risk management, especially

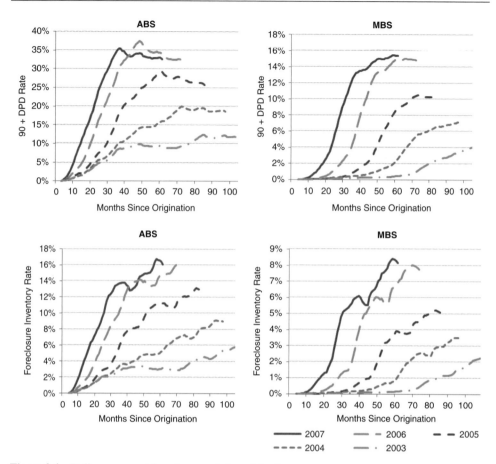

Figure 3.4   Delinquency and foreclosure rate by origination year.
Data Source: LoanPerformance ABS/MBS.
Delinquency is defined according to the MBA methods.

model validation and back-testing, are discussed in Section 3.5. Some concluding remarks are provided in Section 3.6.

3.2   FIVE "C"S OF CREDIT AND MORTGAGE CREDIT RISK

In practice the five "C"s of credit (Figure 3.5) are traditionally used to gauge a borrower's ability and willingness to repay, the lack of which can lead to default and credit loss.

- Capacity: What is the borrower's capacity or ability to repay the loan? How much is their income? Income to debt (DTI) ratio? Is the borrower financially constrained? How much is their credit card and other line of credit utilization rate?
- Character: Does the borrower pay rent, debts, child support and other financial obligations on time? Has the borrower ever been delinquent on any of his or her financial obligations? What is the borrower's credit score?

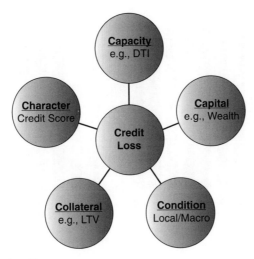

Figure 3.5 Five "C"s of credit.

- Capital: How much wealth has the borrower in case the borrower has financial trouble down the road (e.g. loss of income due to unemployment)? How much is the down payment or home equity (home value minus loan amount) at origination? How much is the updated home equity, especially after the borrower gets a second or third mortgage secured by the same home?
- Collateral: What is the condition and value of the collateral, an important driver of home equity?
- Condition: What is the local, regional and national housing market and economic conditions, such as changes in home price index, unemployment rate and interest rate? Any change in policy or regulation (for example, change in personal bankruptcy law in the US in 2005, or implementation of the Home Affordable Modification Program)?

The relative importance of each "C" could vary from time to time. For example, subprime borrowers showed lower foreclosure rates when house prices were rising and the unemployment was low (e.g. 2005 and 2006) than prime borrowers when house prices were low and the unemployment was high (e.g. 2009 and 2010). As such, lenders and investors should evaluate the five "C"s of credit not only at the time of loan origination, but also regularly during the remaining life of the loan, as the borrower and loan characteristics as well as the housing and economic conditions can change and sometimes dramatically so.

The relative importance of each "C" can also vary across each dimension of mortgage credit risk, namely, probability of default (or PD) which measures the likelihood of a loan becoming default; loss given default (LGD) which measures the loss severity (or the loss per dollar of exposure) in case a default event occurs; and exposure at default (or EAD) which measures the exposure size at the time of default. Detailed discussion on the determinants of each risk dimensions are discussed in Section 3.3 and the modeling methods for each risk dimensions are discussed in Section 3.4.

Although the escalating mortgage credit losses in recent years shown in Section 3.1 seemed to have surprised most mortgage lenders and investors, there had been signs of deterioration in the five "C"s in the years of excess credit growth preceding the mortgage crisis. For example,

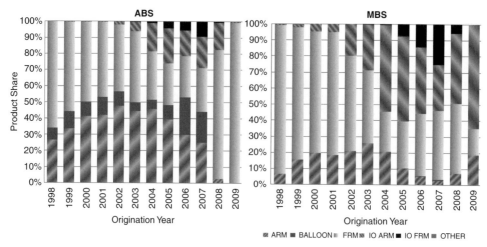

Figure 3.6 Product type at origination.
Data Source: LoanPerformance.

the share of fixed rate mortgage and adjustable rate mortgage originations had been declining, whereas there had been substantial increase in originations of interest only (IO) mortgages in both the ABS and MBS markets, and balloon mortgages in the ABS market (Figure 3.6). Since IO and balloon mortgages have lower monthly payments, the increasing originations of these mortgage products signaled an increasing number of home buyers who had bought a home that they could not really afford. This is consistent with the rising debt-to-income ratio (DTI) from 1998 to 2009 (Figure 3.7).

The share of fully documented loans had been steadily declining from 2000 to 2007 in the ABS market and from 2001 to 2007 in the MBS market (Figure 3.8). In contrast, the share of low or no doc loans had been steadily increasing, indicating the loosening of the underwriting standards during this period of time.

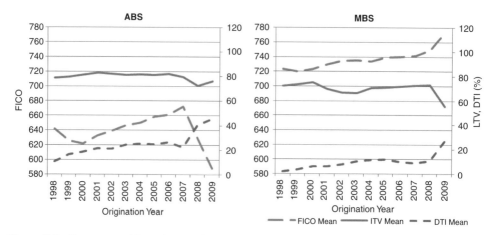

Figure 3.7 Borrower and loan characteristics at loan origination.
Source: LoanPerformance ABS/MBS.

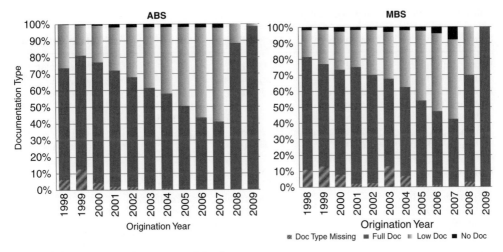

Figure 3.8   Documentation type at origination.
Source: LoanPerformance ABS/MBS.

Had the five "C"s of credit been accurately measured at the time of mortgage origination and updated in a timely fashion during the remaining life of the loan, mortgage default and loss severity models could have been developed and updated from historical and recent mortgage performance experiences. Although they may not have captured the full extent of the mortgage default and losses during the recent mortgage crisis, such models coupled with pessimistic house price forecasts could have helped predict much of the subprime mortgage defaults for loans originated in 2006 and 2007 (Amromin and Paulson, 2009).

3.3   DETERMINANTS OF MORTGAGE DEFAULT, LOSS GIVEN DEFAULT AND EXPOSURE AT DEFAULT

Credit loss can be decomposed into three components: probability of default (or PD) which measures the likelihood of a loan becomes default; loss given default (LGD) which measures the loss severity (or the loss per dollar of exposure) in case a default event occurs; and exposure at default (or EAD) which measures the exposure size at the time of default. EAD is usually no more than the outstanding amount for close-ended loans, such as mortgages and home equity loans, but can be much larger than the outstanding amount for open-ended loans, such as home equity lines of credit.

PD, LGD, EAD and asset value correlations are the key parameters in mortgage portfolio risk models. Studies documenting the determinants of mortgage PD, LGD and EAD are summarized in this section (and see Chapter 4 for asset value correlation).

3.3.1   Determinants of Mortgage Default

Mortgage default can be caused by the borrower's lack of ability or willingness or both to repay the loan. Mortgage default due to the borrower's lack of ability to repay the loan (for example, due to interest rate reset, divorce, loss of income, new medical expense) is often referred to as hardship default or trigger event default. Strategic or ruthless default refers to the situation

Table 3.1 Examples of empirical mortgage default studies.

Study	Sample Size	Sample Period	Source	Default Definition
Bajari, Chu and Park (BCP 2008)	134,952	2000–2007 origination	LPC	Foreclosure or REO
Foote, Gerardi and Willen (FGW 2009)	100,000 under water mortgages	1987–2007	Massachusetts Registry of Deeds	Foreclosure
Amromin and Paulson (AP 2009)	68,000 prime 62,000 sub-prime	2004–2007 origination	LPS	60+DPD, foreclosure, REO
Elul, Souleles, Chomsisengphet, Glennon and Hunt (ESCGH 2010)	364,000	2005–2006 Vintage, performance thr 04/2009	LPS: OO SF FRM, Equifax	60+ DPD
Goodman, Ashworth, Landy and Yin (GALY 2010)	—	2006–2009	LPC, BLS, Amherst Securities	60+ DPD
Demyanyk, Koijen and van Hemert (DKH 2011)	20,000	2004–2009	LPC, TransUnion, BLS	Borrower's largest mortgage moves to worse state
Herkenhoff (H 2012)	2,915	2009	PSID Survey	Missed 2–6 payments as of interview date
Li, Qi and Zhao (LQZ 2012)	26,800 ARM2 15,850 ARM3	2008–2009	OCC/OTS Mortgage Metrics	60+DPD

where a borrower stops paying mortgages when the borrower has the ability but not the incentive to repay (for example, when the house is worth substantially less than the mortgage). There is a large and still rapidly growing literature on mortgage default. In this section we highlight only a few representative studies that cover various modeling methods and use various data sources (Table 3.1). Interested readers are referred to Herkenhoff (2012) for a more comprehensive review of the literature both before and after the 2007–2009 mortgage crisis.

Foote, Gerardi and Willen (2009) use the Massachusetts Registry of Deeds to investigate the effect of negative equity on mortgage default and find that the majority of people with negative equity do not default. However, as the authors acknowledge, their equity proxy is fairly crude and does not take into consideration amortization or refinancing activity due to the lack of current mortgage balances, mortgage type (fixed or adjustable rate), initial interest rate and cash out amount in refinance in the data they used. It is thus unclear how sensitive the results would be had the home equity been more accurately estimated for each homeowner covered in this study.

Goodman, Ashworth, Landy and Yin (2010) show that mortgage default rates rose long before the unemployment rate picked up. CLTV always plays a critical role in determining default rates, whereas unemployment rate does not matter at all for mortgages with low CLTVs. However, at CLTV > 1.2, unemployment amplifies the likelihood a borrower will default. The authors thus conclude that CLTV, the key measure of equity, is a far more important predictor of default than unemployment, but the interactions between the two cannot be neglected. Since this study does not contain any model or regression analysis, it is not clear whether the conclusions of this study would hold had more risk factors and the causality between house price change and unemployment been controlled for.

Elul, Souleles, Chomsisengphet, Glennon and Hunt (2010) combine loan-level mortgage data with credit bureau information about the borrower's other debts to assess the relative importance of two key drivers of mortgage default: negative equity and illiquidity measured by high credit card utilization rates. They find that both variables are significant with comparable marginal effects. Moreover, the effect of illiquidity on default generally increases with high combined loan to value ratios and is significant even for low CLTV. County-level unemployment shocks are also associated with higher default risk (though less so than high utilization) and strongly interact with CLTV. In addition, having a second mortgage implies significantly higher default risk, particularly for borrowers who have a first-mortgage LTV approaching 100%. It is not clear why the effect of illiquidity on default is significant even for low CLTV as homeowners can get a home equity loan or line, or sell their house, to improve their liquidity, especially given that the interest rate of the latter is usually a lot lower than carrying over credit card balances.

Herkenhoff (2012) use household survey data to simultaneously test the impact of job loss, negative equity, illiquidity, their interactions and prior mortgage modification on mortgage default. The paper finds that the best absolute predictors of default are prior mortgage modification (14% more likely to default), severe negative equity, i.e. CLTV > 1.2 (11.2% more likely to default), and job loss (8.2% more likely to default). People with both moderate negative equity (CLTV between 1 and 1.2) and job loss are 37% more likely to default than those with just negative equity. However, job loss and the interaction between job loss and severe negative equity are insignificant, indicating that once someone is severely underwater (CLTV > 1.2), job loss is irrelevant and the borrower is likely to default regardless of whether or not they are out of work. This study supports policy initiatives to stabilize the housing market through indirect economic channels that generate long run job growth rather than temporarily modifying mortgages.

To be eligible for mortgage modification programs, such as Home Affordable Mortgage Program (HAMP), some borrowers might intentionally skip mortgage payments that they can afford. Li, Qi and Zhao (2012) use the mortgage modification program established as part of the October 2008 Countrywide legal settlement as a natural experiment to study this type of strategic default that is induced by loan modification. They find the extent of Countrywide settlement-induced strategic default is roughly 4–5 percentage points within the first three months after the settlement, representing a 25–80% increase in default rates depending on loan type and vintage. This finding is important for proper assessment of the economic impact of any loan modification programs.

Overall the existing studies have found the relevance of various loan and borrower characteristics, local/ national economic and housing market conditions, and the interactions between certain risk drivers in the determination of mortgage default. These determinants, their effect on default, as well as examples of empirical studies that document these findings are summarized in Table 3.2.

3.3.2 Determinants of Mortgage LGD

There is great uncertainty in loss severity of defaulted mortgages, ranging from 0% to 100% of the exposure amount. One cannot accurately model mortgage credit loss without an accurate model of mortgage LGD. While there has been a large and still rapidly growing literature on mortgage default, there are only a handful of studies on mortgage LGD despite its importance,

Table 3.2 Determinants of mortgage default.

Determinant	Effect on Default	Empirical Evidence
Loan characteristics		
loan to value (LTV) (origination, updated, combined)	Loans with higher LTV (or less house equity) are more likely to default	AP 2009, ESCGH 2010, GALY 2010, DKH 2011, H 2012, LQZ 2012
Loan size	Positive or nonlinear	AP 2009, ESCGH 2010, LQZ 2012
Loan age	Nonlinear	BCP 2008
Delinquency (present and past)	Loans delinquent before or now are more likely to default	LQZ 2012
Origination channel (bank vs. broker or correspondent)	Loans originated by broker or correspondent are more likely to default	ESCGH 2010
Modified	Modified loans are more likely to default	H 2012
Documentation level (no, low, full)	Low/no doc loans are more likely to default	ESCGH 2010, LQZ 2012
Loan type (traditional vs. pay option, interest only and balloon)	Non-traditional loans are more likely to default	ESCGH 2010, LQZ 2012
Prime vs. sub-prime	Sub-prime loans are more likely to default	FGW 2009, GALY 2010
Property type (single family, condo, co-op)	Mixed findings	FGW 2009, ESCGH 2010
Owner occupancy	Insignificant	AP 2009
Loan purpose (purchase or refinance)	Loans for purchase are more likely to default	AP 2009
Interest rate at origination	Loans with higher initial interest rate are more likely to default	FGW 2009, AP 2009, ESCGH 2010
Margin rate	ARMs with higher margin rate are more likely to default	AP 2009
Borrower characteristics		
Credit score (origination, updated)	Borrowers with higher credit scores are less likely to default	BCP 2008, ESCGH 2010, DKH 2011
Change in credit score	Borrowers with improving credit scores are less likely to default	DKH 2011
Liquid asset to income ratio	Borrowers with low liquid assets (savings, checking and money market accounts) are more likely to default	H 2012
Unsecured debt to income ratio	Borrowers with high levels of unsecured debt to income are more likely to default, especially for those with negative house equity	H 2012
Debt to income (DTI) or debt payment to income (PTI)	Borrowers with higher DTI or PTI are more likely to default	BCP 2008, AP 2009, DKH 2011
Credit card utilization rate	Borrowers facing liquidity constraints and having higher credit card utilization rate are more likely to default	BCP 2008, ESCGH 2010, DKH 2011
Job loss	Borrowers who just lost jobs are more likely to default	H 2012

Table 3.2   (*Continued*)

Determinant	Effect on Default	Empirical Evidence
Economic and market conditions		
House price index growth	Loans are less likely to default with higher HPI growth	AP 2009
Unemployment rate	Loans are more likely to default with higher or rising unemployment rate	BCP 2008, FGW 2009, AP 2009, ESCGH 2010, DKH 2011
Interest rate	Higher current interest rate is associated with higher likelihood of default	DKH 2011
Zip-level median income	Loans are less likely to default in zip code with higher median income	AP 2009, FGW 2009
Zip-level default rate	Loans are more likely to default in zip code with higher default rate	LQZ 2012

partly due to the lack of publicly available data that can adequately capture the economic loss from mortgage defaults. We review several representative studies of mortgage LGD in this section (Table 3.3).

Clauretie and Herzog (1990) study the effect of state foreclosure laws (judicial procedure, statutory right of redemption and deficiency judgment) on loan losses for mortgages insured by private mortgage insurance (PMI) and by government, such as Federal Housing Administration (FHA). They find that judicial procedure and statutory right of redemption extend the foreclosure and liquidation processes and thus are associated with larger loan losses. They also show that deficiency judgment reduces loss severity for PMI that has no incentive conflict due to its coinsurance feature, while deficiency judgment has no significant impact on the recovery rate for FHA insurance, with which incentive conflict arises due to the lack of a coinsurance arrangement.

Lekkas, Quigley and van Order (1993) empirically test the frictionless form of the options-based mortgage default theory. They find that higher initial loan-to-value (LTV) ratios, regions with higher default rates (Texas) and younger loans are associated with significantly higher loss severities whereas the difference between contract and current interest rates has no impact on loss severities; consequently, they reject the propositions about loss severity implied by the frictionless form of the options-based mortgage default theory. Crawford and Rosenblatt (1995) extend options-based mortgage default theory to include transaction costs and show theoretically and empirically the effect of frictions on the individual strike price that affects loss severity.

The regression analysis in the above three studies can explain only a small portion of the total variations in loan-level mortgage LGD (R^2 ranges from 0.02 to 0.14). Pennington-Cross (2003) and Calem and LaCour-Little (2004) study determinants of mortgage loss severity based on government-sponsored enterprise (GSE) data, and their regression analysis shows improved explanatory power. The R^2 reported in Calem and LaCour-Little is 0.25, whereas it is 0.95 to 0.96 in Pennington-Cross (2003). Although the latter study reports very high R^2, it uses a much smaller sample and covers a shorter sample period (1995–1999) that contains no serious housing market depreciation. Coupled with the problems in LGD definition and the timing of the current loan-to-value calculation, the findings of Pennington-Cross (2003) should be interpreted with caution.

Table 3.3   Examples of empirical mortgage LGD studies.

Study	Sample Size	Sample Period	Source	LGD Definition	$\bar{R}^2$
Clauretie and Herzog (CH 1990)	408 85,000	1980–1987 1972–1988 (claims paid)	PMI via Moody's FHA	Direct loss paid/previous year end risk (UPB-house value)/original loan amount	0.56–0.57 0.04–0.05
Lekkas, Quigley and van Order (LQO 1993)	9,457	1975–1990 (originated)	Freddie Mac	(UPB-Appraised value)/ UPB (UPB-Sale price)/UPB	0.06–0.07*
Crawford and Rosenblatt (CR 1995)	1,191	1988–1992 (foreclosed)	A large northeastern thrift	(UPB-REO sale price)/UPB (UPB-min(original appraised value, original purchase price))/UPB	0.02–0.03* 0.09–0.14*
Pennington-Cross (PC 2003)	16,272	1995–1999 (foreclosed)	GSEs	(UPB-sale price)/UPB	0.95–0.96
Calem and LaCour-Little (CL 2004)	120,289	1989–1997 (originated)	GSEs	(UPB-Gross sale proceeds)/UPB	0.25*
Qi and Yang (QY 2009)	106,857	1990–2003	MICA PMI	(UPB+ACRINT+ FCLEXP+PROEXP-NETREC)/UPB	0.61
Zhang, Ji and Liu (ZJL 2010)	833,319	1998–2009	LPC ABS	—	0.20
Leow and Mues (LM 2012)	140,000	1983–2001	A major UK bank	—	0.27

Note: *indicates R^2.

Qi and Yang (2009) study LGD using a large set of historical loan-level default and recovery data of high loan-to-value residential mortgages from several private mortgage insurance companies. They show that LGD can largely be explained by various characteristics associated with the loan, the underlying property, and the default, foreclosure and settlement process, among which the current LTV is the single most important determinant. More importantly, mortgage loss severity in distressed housing markets is significantly higher than under normal housing market conditions. These findings have important policy implications for several key issues in Basel II implementation.

Zhang, Ji and Liu (2010) test the relationship between LGD and the housing market cycle measure by the house price movements up to the point of the mortgage origination. They find that housing price history has a significant and long-lasting impact on LGD with explanatory power that far exceeds the original LTV and other loan and property characteristics.

Overall the existing studies have found the relevance of various loan and property characteristics, and economic and market conditions on mortgage loss given default. In addition, LGD can also vary with state foreclosure laws and workout methods. These determinants, their effect on LGD, as well as examples of empirical studies that document these findings are summarized in Table 3.4.

Table 3.4 Determinants of mortgage LGD.

Determinant	Effect on LGD	Empirical Evidence
Loan characteristics		
loan-to-value (LTV): (origination, updated, combined)	Loans with higher LTV (or less house equity) tend to have higher LGD	CH 1990, LQO 1993, P 2003, CL 2004, QY 2009, ZJL 2010, LM 2012
Loan age	LGD tends to decrease with loan age	LQO 1993, P 2003, QY 2009
Loan size	LGD tends to decrease with loan size	P 2003, QY 2009, ZJL 2010
Documentation	Low doc loans tend to have higher LGD	ZJL 2010
Junior liens	Junior liens tend to have higher LGDs	ZJL 2010
Loan purpose	Cash out refinance is associated with higher LGD although refinance is associated with lower LGD than purchase	QY 2009, ZJL 2010
Sub-prime	Sub-prime mortgages tend to have higher LGD	P 2003
Foreclosure time line	The longer it takes from last mortgage payment to foreclosure, the higher the LGD	CR 1995, ZJL 2010
Interest rate	LGD tends to increase with interest rate	ZJL 2010
Loan type	40-year fixed rate, interest-only ARM, balloon and ARM tend to have higher LGD than 30-year fix rate mortgage	ZJL 2010
Property characteristics		
Owner occupied	LGD tends to be lower if the home is owner occupied	QY 2009, ZJL 2010
Single family	LGD tends to be lower for single family home	QY 2009
Condo	LGD tends to be lower for condo	QY 2009
Manufactured house	Manufactured house tends to have higher LGD	ZJL 2010
State foreclosure laws		
Judicial process	States that follow judicial foreclosure process tend to have higher LGD	CH 1990, CR 1995, P 2003, QY 2009
Statutory right of redemption	States with statutory right of redemption tend to have higher LGD	CH 1990, CR 1995, QY 2009
Deficiency judgment	States prohibiting deficiency judgment tend to have higher LGD	CH 1990, CR 1995
Economic and market conditions		
House price appreciation (HPA)	Rising house price is associated with lower LGD	CH 1990, ZJL 2010
Lagged HPA	The lagged HPAs tend to have mostly positive effects on LGD	ZJL 2010
HPA volatility	LGD tends to be higher with higher house price volatility	ZJL 2010
Change in unemployment rate	Rise in unemployment rate is associated with higher LGD	CH 1990
Median income in the property zip code to the property MSA	LGD tends to be lower if borrower has relatively higher income	CL 2004
Stress	LGD tends to be higher in stressed housing market	QY 2009
Workout strategy		
Deed in lieu	Deed in lieu of foreclosure is associated with lower LGD	CR 1995
Pre-foreclosure sale	Pre-foreclosure sale is associated with lower LGD	QY 2009

3.3.3 Determinants of Mortgage EAD

Retail mortgage credit exposures can be divided into term loans (e.g. mortgages and home equity loans, or HELOAN) or revolving loans (e.g. home equity lines of credit, or HELOC). Mortgages and HELOANs are closed-ended loans extended for a specific period of time, and EAD for term loans is simply the amount outstanding (including accrued but unpaid interest and fees). HELOCs, by contrast, are open-ended, variable-rate revolving facilities that allow a borrower to draw up to a specific line amount at the borrower's discretion. Meanwhile, a bank may reduce credit limit or prohibit future draws to reduce loss. The eventual exposure will be a result of a "race to default," with the borrower drawing additional funds and the bank restricting access to these funds. Accurate modeling of HELOC loss thus requires accurate modeling of the net addition to the amount outstanding as the borrower approaches default.

A good introduction and comparison of alternative EAD measures and approaches are provided by Moral (2006) and Valvonis (2008). While there are several studies of consumer credit card EAD (for example, Valvonis (2008) and Qi (2009)), the literature on HELOC EAD is very limited. In their analysis of home equity capital requirements under Basel II, Agarwal, Ambrose, Chomsisengphet and Liu (2006) simply use an average LEQ of 40% for HELOC without considering any possible variations due to differences in account or borrower characteristics and macroeconomic conditions. Despite the lack of academic studies on HELOC EAD, industry practices have evolved. In the US, banks that are subject to Basel II capital requirements have developed HELOC EAD models using risk drivers that are similar to those used in mortgage default models, although the relative importance of these risk drivers can differ in default and EAD models.

3.4 MODELING METHODS FOR DEFAULT, LGD AND EAD

Default, LGD and EAD have statistically distinct properties that require appropriate statistical modeling methods. Default is a random dichotomous event, while LGD is a continuous variable usually bounded between 0% and 100% and sometimes showing a bi-modal distribution. Commonly used EAD approaches, such as LEQ, CCF and EADF, are continuous random variables that may or may not be bounded depending on borrower and lender behavior. Compared to LGD and EAD, modeling methods for default have been fairly well established. We briefly summarize the relevant modeling methods in Table 3.5. Interested readers are referred to Feldman and Gross (2005) and Demyanyk and Hasan (2009) for a comprehensive coverage of various default modeling methods, and Qi and Zhao (2011) for a comparison of alternative LGD modeling methods. The modeling methods for EAD are still evolving; several examples are provided in Table 3.5.

3.5 MODEL RISK MANAGEMENT

Models are extensively used in all aspects of credit risk management, especially in mortgage origination, pricing, account management, capital and reserve determination, stress testing, as well as in loan sales, portfolio securitization and hedging. Models can certainly improve business decisions, but if inadequate or misused, they can cause adverse consequences including severe financial losses for lenders and investors, such as those experienced in the 2007–2009

Mortgage Credit Risk   49

Table 3.5 Modeling methods relevant for mortgage default, LGD and EAD.

Modeling Methods	Example
Default	
Decision tree	FG 2005
Maximum Entropy	SG 2007
Probit model with partial observability	BCP 2008
Competing hazards with unobserved borrower heterogeneity	BCP 2008
Competing risk proportional hazard	FGW 2009
Dynamic logit	ESCGH 2010
Multiple probit	DKH 2011
Linear probability model	H 2012
Nonparametric local average treatment effect	LQZ 2012
LGD	
Quantile regression	SW 2007
OLS regression	QY 2009, QZ 2011
Fractional response regression	QZ 2011
Inverse Gaussian regression	QZ 2011
Inverse Gaussian regression with beta transformation	QZ 2011
Regression tree	QZ 2011
Neural network	QZ 2011
2-stage combining a repossession probability model and a haircut model	LM 2012
EAD[a]	
Generalized linear model with beta link function	Jacobs 2010
OLS, censored OLS	Qi 2009
Tobit with random effects and double censure	JLS 2009
OLS with random effects	JLS 2009
Within-group estimation	JLS 2009

[a]The author is not aware of any empirical mortgage EAD studies. The EAD studies listed here are on a range of non-mortgage revolving exposures or commitments. Many of the modeling methods listed under LGD can potentially be adopted for EAD modeling.

mortgage and financial crisis. Those consequences should be addressed by active management of model risk.

The Office of the Comptroller of the Currency (OCC) has adopted the Supervisory Guidance on Model Risk Management (or OCC Bulletin 2011–12) since April 2011. This guidance was jointly developed by the OCC and the Board of Governors of the Federal Reserve System. It articulates the elements of a sound program for effective management of risks that arise when using quantitative models in bank decision making, and provides guidance to OCC examining personnel and national banks on prudent model risk management policies, procedures, practices and standards.

Model risk management begins with robust model development, implementation and use. Another essential element is a sound model validation process. A third element is governance, which sets an effective framework with defined roles and responsibilities for clear communication of model limitations and assumptions, as well as the authority to restrict model usage. In this chapter, we highlight the various aspects of the sound model validation process. Interested readers are referred to the bulletin, which is public and can be downloaded from http://www.occ.treas.gov/news-issuances/bulletins/2011/bulletin-2011-12.html for more details on model validation and other parts of this supervisory guidance.

Model validation is the set of processes and activities intended to verify that models are performing as expected, in line with their design objectives and business uses. Effective validation helps ensure that models are sound. It also identifies potential limitations and assumptions and assesses their possible impact. Sound model validation process should include evaluation of conceptual soundness, ongoing monitoring and outcomes analysis.

Evaluation of conceptual soundness: This element involves assessing the quality of the model design and construction based on developmental evidence supporting all model choices, including the overall theoretical construction, key assumptions, variable selection, data and specific mathematical calculations, as well as model limitations. Sensitivity analysis should be employed to check the impact of small changes in inputs and parameter values on model outputs. Stress testing should be conducted to check model performance over a wide range of inputs and parameter values, including extreme values, to verify that the model is robust. Validation should ensure that judgment exercised in model design and construction is well informed, carefully considered and consistent with published research and with sound industry practice. Developmental evidence should be reviewed before a model goes into use and also as part of the ongoing validation process, in particular whenever there is a material change in the model.

Ongoing monitoring: Through process verification and benchmarking, ongoing monitoring confirms that the model is appropriately implemented and is being used and is performing as intended. Ongoing monitoring is essential to evaluate whether changes in products, exposures, activities, clients or market conditions necessitate adjustment, redevelopment or replacement of the model and to verify that any extension of the model beyond its original scope is valid. Any model limitations identified in the development stage should be regularly assessed over time, as part of ongoing monitoring. Many of the tests and model performance measures employed as part of model development should be included in ongoing monitoring and be conducted and tracked on a regular basis to incorporate additional information as it becomes available.

Outcomes analysis: Outcomes analysis compares model outputs to corresponding actual outcomes. The precise nature of the comparison depends on the objectives of a model, and might include an assessment of the accuracy of estimates or forecasts, an evaluation of rank-ordering ability or other appropriate tests. Back-testing is an important form of outcomes analysis; it involves the comparison of actual outcomes with model forecasts during a sample time period not used in model development. Models with long forecast horizons should be back-tested, but given the amount of time it would take to accumulate the necessary data, "early warning" metrics can be developed to measure performance beginning very shortly after model introduction and analyze performance trend over time.

The widespread use of vendor and other third-party products—including data, parameter values and complete models—poses unique challenges for validation and other model risk management activities because the modeling expertise is external to the user and because some components are considered proprietary. Many investors blindly relying on agency ratings or third-party models suffered huge losses during the 2007–2009 mortgage and financial crisis. As such, it is especially important to manage model risk of vendor and third-party products.

A central principle for managing model risk is the need for "effective challenge" of models: critical analysis by objective, informed parties who can identify model limitations and assumptions and produce appropriate change. Effective challenge depends on a combination of incentives, competence and influence, the lack of which could result in ineffective model risk management and open the door to credit losses from model failures.

3.6 CONCLUSIONS

Paul Romer, an influential American economist, once said "a crisis is a terrible thing to waste." Mortgages, once a strong driving force behind economic growth for many countries and wealth creation for homeowners, lenders and investors worldwide, turned into the driving force behind the 2007–2009 mortgage and financial crisis. While many lessons can be learned and reforms can be implemented, future crises cannot be avoided if the weaknesses in mortgage credit risk measurement, models and model risk management practices persist.

The stylized facts from mortgage delinquency and foreclosure show that mortgage risk can vary with many factors that can be broadly categorized into the well-known five "C"s of credit: Capacity, Character, Capital, Collateral and Condition. There had been signs of deterioration in these factors in the years of excess credit growth preceding the mortgage crisis. The crisis has since created a surge in interest in and attention to measuring and modeling mortgage credit losses, including default, loss given default and exposure at default.

Representative academic studies are reviewed in this chapter. A comprehensive list of significant risk drivers of mortgage default and loss given default that have been documented in the literature are summarized in this chapter for reference purposes. Modeling methods relevant for mortgage default, loss given default and exposure at default modeling are briefly summarized as well. While there is a large and still rapidly growing literature on mortgage default and a handful of studies on mortgage loss given default, exposure at default remains an under-studied area.

The extensive use of models in all aspects of mortgage credit portfolio risk analysis and the failure of these models to predict the losses experienced in the 2007–2009 mortgage crisis call for improvements in not only risk measurement and modeling, but also model risk management. Effective model risk management begins with robust model development, implementation and use. It also requires a sound model validation process, and strong governance, policies and controls.

REFERENCES

Agarwal, S., Ambrose, B. W., Chomsisengphet, S., Liu, C., 2006. An empirical analysis of home equity loan and line performance. Journal of Financial Intermediation 15, 444–469.

Amromin, G., Paulson, A. L., 2009. Comparing patterns of default among prime and subprime mortgages. Federal Reserve Bank of Chicago Economic Perspectives, 2Q, 18–37

Bajari, P., Chu, C. S., Park, M., 2008. An Empirical Model of Subprime Mortgage Default from 2000 to 2007. NBER Working Paper #14625.

Calem, P. S., LaCour-Little, M., 2004. Risk-based capital requirements for mortgage loans. Journal of Banking and Finance 28, 647–672.

Clauretie, T. M., Herzog, T., 1990. The effect of state foreclosure laws on loan losses: Evidence from the mortgage insurance industry. Journal of Money, Credit, and Banking 22(2), 221–233.

Crawford, G. W., Rosenblatt, E., 1995. Efficient mortgage default option exercise: Evidence from loss severity. The Journal of Real Estate Research 10(5), 543–555.

Demyanyk, Y., Hasan, I., 2009. Financial crises and bank failures: A review of prediction methods. Omega 38(5), 315–324.

Demyanyk, Y., Koijen, R. S. J., Van Hemert, O. A. C., 2011. Determinants and Consequences of Mortgage Default. Federal Reserve Bank of Cleveland Working Paper.

Elul, R., Souleles, N. S., Chomsisengphet, S., Glennon, D., Hunt, R., 2010. What "triggers" mortgage default. American Economic Review 100(2), 490–494.

Feldman, D., Gross, S., 2005. Mortgage default: Classification tree analysis. The Journal of Real Estate Finance and Economics 30(4), 369–396.

Foote, C. L., Gerardi, K., Willen, P. S., 2008. Negative equity and foreclosure: Theory and evidence. Journal of Urban Economics 64(2), 234–245.

Goodman, L. S., Ashworth, R., Landy, B., Yin, K., 2010. Negative equity trumps unemployment in predicting defaults. The Journal of Fixed Income 19(4), 67–72.

Herkenhoff, K., 2012. Job Loss, Defaults, and Policy Implications. UCLA Working Paper.

Jacobs, M. Jr., 2010. An empirical study of exposure at default. Journal of Advanced Studies in Finance 1(1), 31–59.

Jimenez, G., Lopez, J. A., Saurina, J., 2009. Empirical analysis of corporate credit lines. The Review of Financial Studies 22(12), 5069–5098.

Lekkas, V., Quigley, J. M., Van Order, R., 1993. Loan loss severity and optimal mortgage default. Journal of the American Real Estate and Urban Economics Association 21(4), 353–371.

Leow, M., Mues, C., 2012. Predicting loss given default (LGD) for residential mortgage loans: a two-stage model and empirical evidence for UK bank data. International Journal of Forecasting 28(1), 183–195.

Li, X., Qi, M., Zhao, X., 2012. The Extent of Strategic Defaults Induced by Mortgage Modification Programs. OCC and York University Working Paper.

Moral, G., 2006. EAD estimates for facilities with explicit limits. In The Basel II Risk Parameters: Estimation, Validation and Stress Testing, Englemann, B., Rauhmeier, R. (Eds). Springer: Berlin.

OCC Bulletin 2011–16, 2011. Supervisory guidance on model risk management, http://www.occ.treas.gov/news-issuances/bulletins/2011/bulletin-2011-12.html.

Pennington-Cross, A., 2003. Subprime and Prime Mortgages: Loss Distributions. Office of Federal Housing Enterprise Oversight Working Paper

Qi, M., 2009. Exposure at Default of Unsecured Credit Cards. OCC Working Paper.

Qi, M., Yang, X., 2009. Loss given default of high loan-to-value residential mortgages. Journal of Banking & Finance 33, 788–799.

Qi, M., Zhao, X., 2011. Comparison of modeling methods for Loss Given Default. Journal of Banking & Finance 35, 2842–2855.

Somers, M., Whittaker, J., 2007. Quantile regression for modelling distributions of profit and loss. European Journal of Operational Research 183(3), 1477–1487.

Stokes, J. R., Gloy, B. A., 2007. Mortgage delinquency migration: An application of maximum entropy econometrics. Journal of Real Estate Portfolio Management 13(2), 153–160.

Valvonis, V., 2008. Estimating EAD for retail exposures for Basel II purposes. Journal of Credit Risk 4(1), 79–109.

Zhang, Y., Ji, L., Liu, F., 2010. Local Housing Market Cycle and Loss Given Default: Evidence from Sub-prime Residential Mortgages. International Monetary Fund Working Paper.

4

Credit Portfolio Correlations and Uncertainty

Steffi Höse and Stefan Huschens
Technische Universität Dresden

4.1 INTRODUCTION

In light of the current financial crisis, financial institutions are under pressure to implement a meaningful sensitivity analysis and a sound stress-testing practice for the parameters of the credit portfolio models used. Although these models differ in their assumptions and complexity, default probabilities and asset (return) correlations are typical input parameters. The literature focuses mainly on the point estimation of these parameters, see Gordy (2000, p. 146), Frey and McNeil (2003), de Servigny and Renault (2004, pp. 185f.), McNeil and Wendin (2007), and on the interval estimation of default probabilities, see Höse and Huschens (2003), Christensen et al. (2004), Trück and Rachev (2005), Pluto and Tasche (2005), Hanson and Schuermann (2006), Pluto and Tasche (2006). In contrast, this chapter concentrates on the statistical interval estimation of asset correlations. There are at least six methods for the estimation of asset correlations depending on the type of available data: (a) the estimation of default correlations from default data and the derivation of implicit asset correlations by using a factor model; (b) the estimation of asset correlations from time series of transformed default rates, e.g. probits of default rates, see Höse and Huschens (2011a); (c) the estimation of asset correlations from time series of asset returns, sometimes approximated by correlations from time series of equity returns, see Bluhm et al. (2010, pp. 167ff.); (d) the estimation of asset correlations from time series of individual rating migrations; (e) the estimation of asset and default correlations from time series of credit spreads; (f) the estimation of asset correlations from historical loss data, see FitchRatings (2008, pp. 4–7).

In this chapter, the second approach is used to estimate asset correlations in a generalized asymptotic single risk factor (ASRF) model allowing non-Gaussian idiosyncratic risk factors. Within this model, point estimators for asset correlations are derived and confidence intervals for a single asset correlation as well as simultaneous confidence intervals for two or more asset correlations are developed. In the standard Gaussian ASRF model, which builds the basis for the calculation of the regulatory capital requirements according to Basel II and has also become a standard credit portfolio model in the banking industry, alternative parameterizations of the dependence structure are given by default correlations and survival time correlations. For these two types of correlation parameters, point and interval estimators are derived as well.

The resulting confidence intervals quantify the parameter uncertainty and can be understood as a statistical approach to sensitivity analysis. They can also be used to identify meaningful stress scenarios for the three different correlation parameters.[1] In order to illustrate this idea and the calculation of the confidence intervals presented here, an example with three correlation scenarios is considered.

A short extract of this chapter containing only the confidence intervals for asset correlations given in (4.14) and in the third statement of Theorem 2 has already been published in conference proceedings, see Höse and Huschens (2011a). In this chapter, a more general model allowing non-Gaussian idiosyncratic risk factors is considered and additional upper and lower bounds for asset correlations and confidence statements for default and survival time correlations are given.

4.2   GAUSSIAN AND SEMI-GAUSSIAN SINGLE RISK FACTOR MODEL

A credit portfolio classified in R different risk categories (such as rating classes, segments, industry sectors, risk buckets) is considered for T subsequent periods. Assuming an ASRF model with infinite granularity in each risk category, as suggested by the Basel Committee on Banking Supervision (2006, p. 64), the distribution of the credit portfolio loss in period $t \in \{1, \ldots, T\}$ is approximated by the distribution of $\sum_{r=1}^{R} w_{tr} \tilde{\pi}_{tr}$, which describes the systematic part of the portfolio loss. The loss contributions $w_{tr} \geq 0$ of all loans assigned to risk category r in period t are thus assumed to be known. If a Gaussian ASRF model[2] is assumed, then the stochastic default probabilities

$$\tilde{\pi}_{tr} \overset{\text{def}}{=} \Phi \left(\frac{\Phi^{-1}(\pi_r) - \sqrt{\varrho_r} Z_t}{\sqrt{1 - \varrho_r}} \right), \qquad Z_t \sim N(0, 1) \tag{4.1}$$

of all obligors in risk category r and period t are functions of the model parameters $0 < \pi_r < 1$ and $0 < \varrho_r < 1$. In this context, Φ denotes the distribution function of the standardized Gaussian distribution and Φ^{-1} its inverse. Equation (4.1) results from a linear single risk factor model, in which the stochastic default probability $\tilde{\pi}_{tr}$ is the conditional default probability of all obligors in risk category r given Z_t. The Gaussian distributed random variable Z_t represents the systematic or common risk factor of period t that simultaneously affects the creditworthiness of the obligors in all risk categories of that period. It can be shown that the stochastic default probability $\tilde{\pi}_{tr}$ follows a Vasicek distribution with parameters π_r and ϱ_r, see Vasicek (2002). The parameter $\pi_r = \mathbb{E}[\tilde{\pi}_{tr}]$ is the *mean* or *unconditional default probability* of all obligors in risk category r, see Bluhm et al. (2010, p. 90). The parameter ϱ_r is the correlation of the risk drivers $\sqrt{\varrho_r} Z_t + \sqrt{1 - \varrho_r} U_{tri}$ and $\sqrt{\varrho_r} Z_t + \sqrt{1 - \varrho_r} U_{trj}$, where the systematic risk factor Z_t and the idiosyncratic risk factors U_{tri} and U_{trj} of two different obligors i and j in risk category r and period t are stochastically independent with distribution function Φ. Since these risk drivers can be interpreted as asset returns, the parameter ϱ_r can be interpreted as the *asset (return) correlation* of two different obligors in risk category r.

A generalized version of the ASRF model – called semi-Gaussian ASRF model – results, if a Gaussian systematic risk factor is assumed, but non-Gaussian individual risk factors are allowed. More precisely, identically distributed individual risk factors following a standardized distribution with invertible (continuous and strictly increasing) distribution function Ψ_r are assumed for each risk category $r = 1, \ldots, R$. In this case, Equation (4.1) generalizes to

$$\tilde{\pi}_{tr} \overset{\text{def}}{=} \Psi_r \left(\frac{G_r^{-1}(\pi_r) - \sqrt{\varrho_r} Z_t}{\sqrt{1 - \varrho_r}} \right), \qquad Z_t \sim N(0, 1) \tag{4.2}$$

with model parameters $0 < \pi_r < 1$ and $0 < \varrho_r < 1$. Here, G_r denotes the distribution function of the risk driver $\sqrt{\varrho_r} Z_t + \sqrt{1 - \varrho_r} U_{tri}$, where the systematic risk factor Z_t has distribution function Φ and the idiosyncratic risk factor U_{tri} of obligor i in risk category r and period t has distribution function Ψ_r with $\mathbb{E}[U_{tri}] = 0$ and $\mathbb{V}[U_{tri}] = 1$. In addition, all risk factors are assumed to be stochastically independent. In this generalized model, the stochastic default probability $\tilde{\pi}_{tr}$ is still the conditional default probability of all obligors in risk category r given the systematic risk factor Z_t of period t. The random variable $\tilde{\pi}_{tr}$ in (4.2) follows a generalized Vasicek distribution with parameters π_r and ϱ_r and generating distribution functions Φ for the systematic risk factor and Ψ_r for the idiosyncratic risk factors in risk category r, see Definition 3.14 in Höse and Huschens (2010). In the semi-Gaussian ASRF model, parameter ϱ_r is still the correlation of two different risk drivers in risk category r and can therefore be interpreted as the asset (return) correlation of two different obligors in this risk category. As a result, the asset returns of all obligors in the same risk category r are equicorrelated and the equicorrelation parameter ϱ_r cannot be negative. Since $\varrho_r = 0$ implies $G_r = \Psi_r$, a constant default probability $\tilde{\pi}_{tr} = \pi_r$ and stochastically independent default events result. This case is not economically relevant and therefore not considered here. Thus the semi-Gaussian ASRF model is parameterized by the vector $\pi = (\pi_1, \ldots, \pi_R)$ of default probabilities and the vector $\varrho = (\varrho_1, \ldots, \varrho_R)$ of asset correlations with (π, ϱ) in the parameter space $]0, 1[^R \times]0, 1[^R$.

Within the semi-Gaussian ASRF model, the stochastic default probabilities $\tilde{\pi}_{tr}$ can be identified with observed default rates assuming *infinite granularity* for each risk category and ignoring sampling errors caused by the finite number of obligors in each risk category. Using this idea, the observable random variables

$$X_{tr} \stackrel{\text{def}}{=} \Psi_r^{-1}(\tilde{\pi}_{tr}) = \frac{G_r^{-1}(\pi_r) - \sqrt{\varrho_r} Z_t}{\sqrt{1 - \varrho_r}} \tag{4.3}$$

are linear transformations of the standardized Gaussian distributed systematic risk factors Z_t.[3] Therefore they are Gaussian distributed with expected values

$$\mu_r \stackrel{\text{def}}{=} \mathbb{E}[X_{tr}] = \frac{G_r^{-1}(\pi_r)}{\sqrt{1 - \varrho_r}}, \tag{4.4}$$

variances

$$\sigma_r^2 \stackrel{\text{def}}{=} \mathbb{V}[X_{tr}] = \frac{\varrho_r}{1 - \varrho_r} \tag{4.5}$$

and covariances

$$\mathbb{C}ov[X_{tr}, X_{ts}] = \sigma_r \sigma_s, \qquad r \neq s$$

for $r, s = 1, \ldots, R$ and $t = 1, \ldots, T$.

In the following sections, it is assumed that the random variables $Z_1, \ldots, Z_T$ are stochastically independent.[4] This assumption implies via (4.2) and (4.3) that the random vectors $(X_{t1}, \ldots, X_{tR})$ for $t = 1, \ldots, T$ are stochastically independent.

4.3 INDIVIDUAL AND SIMULTANEOUS CONFIDENCE BOUNDS AND INTERVALS

In this section, the terminology for confidence statements is clarified, before in two further sections confidence intervals for asset and for default and survival time correlations are derived.

Definition 1   *Let θ be a parameter with parameter space $\Theta \subseteq \mathrm{R}$ and let $0 < \alpha < 1$ be a given probability.*

1. *A statistic[5] L is called* $(1 - \alpha)$*-lower confidence bound (LCB) for* θ*, if*

$$P_\theta(L \leq \theta) = 1 - \alpha \quad \text{for all} \quad \theta \in \Theta. \tag{4.6}$$

2. *A statistic U is called* $(1 - \alpha)$*-upper confidence bound (UCB) for* θ*, if*

$$P_\theta(\theta \leq U) = 1 - \alpha \quad \text{for all} \quad \theta \in \Theta. \tag{4.7}$$

3. *For two statistics A and B the stochastic interval* $I = [A, B]$ *is called* $(1 - \alpha)$*-confidence interval (CI) for* θ*, if*

$$P_\theta(A \leq \theta \leq B) = 1 - \alpha \quad \text{for all} \quad \theta \in \Theta. \tag{4.8}$$

4. *For the confidence bounds and the confidence interval defined by* (4.6), (4.7) *and* (4.8), $1 - \alpha$ *is called the* confidence level.

It should be noted that the weaker concept with

$$P_\theta(L \leq \theta) \geq 1 - \alpha \quad \text{for all} \quad \theta \in \Theta$$

is also called the lower confidence bound for θ with confidence level $1 - \alpha$, where the number $\inf_{\theta \in \Theta} P_\theta(L \leq \theta)$ is called the *confidence coefficient*.[6] In the stronger concept used here, the coverage probability $P_\theta(L \leq \theta)$ is equal to $1 - \alpha$ for all $\theta \in \Theta$, which implies that $1 - \alpha$ is the confidence coefficient and α is the constant error probability. Confidence intervals following this concept are also called exact confidence intervals with level $1 - \alpha$.

How confidence intervals can be constructed from confidence bounds is stated in the following lemma.

Lemma 1   *Let* $\alpha_1 > 0$, $\alpha_2 > 0$ *and* $\alpha_1 + \alpha_2 < 1$. *If the statistic L is a* $(1 - \alpha_1)$*-LCB for* θ, *the statistic U is a* $(1 - \alpha_2)$*-UCB for* θ *and*

$$P_\theta(L \leq U) = 1 \quad \text{for all} \quad \theta \in \Theta,$$

then the stochastic interval $[L, U]$ *is a* $(1 - \alpha_1 - \alpha_2)$*-CI for* θ.

The proof of this lemma and of all other theorems stated here can be found in the appendix. The next definition clarifies the statistical terminology for simultaneous confidence statements, see Bickel and Doksum (1977, p. 162).

Definition 2   *Let* $0 < \alpha < 1$ *and* $\theta = (\theta_1, \ldots, \theta_R)$ *be a parameter vector with parameter space* $\Theta \subseteq \mathbb{R}^R$.

1. *The R-dimensional statistic* $(L_1, \ldots, L_R)$ *is called* simultaneous $(1 - \alpha)$*-LCB for* θ*, if*

$$P_\theta(L_1 \leq \theta_1, \ldots, L_R \leq \theta_R) = 1 - \alpha \quad \text{for all} \quad \theta \in \Theta.$$

2. *The R-dimensional statistic* $(U_1, \ldots, U_R)$ *is called* simultaneous $(1 - \alpha)$*-UCB for* θ*, if*

$$P_\theta(\theta_1 \leq U_1, \ldots, \theta_R \leq U_R) = 1 - \alpha \quad \text{for all} \quad \theta \in \Theta.$$

3. *An R-dimensional stochastic interval* $I_1 \times \ldots \times I_R$, *where* $I_r = [A_r, B_r]$ *with statistics* A_r *and* B_r, *is called* simultaneous $(1 - \alpha)$*-CI for* θ*, if*

$$P_\theta(\theta_1 \in I_1, \ldots, \theta_R \in I_R) = 1 - \alpha \quad \text{for all} \quad \theta \in \Theta.$$

4.4 CONFIDENCE INTERVALS FOR ASSET CORRELATIONS

For the observable random variables X_{tr} a parametric model is given by (4.2), (4.3) and the assumption of the stochastic independence of the systematic risk factors $Z_1, \ldots, Z_T$. In this model, point and interval estimators for asset correlations can be developed as follows.

Equations (4.4) and (4.5) define bijections between $(\mu_r, \sigma_r^2) \in \mathbb{R} \times]0, \infty[$ and $(\pi_r, \varrho_r) \in]0, 1[^2$ for all $r = 1, \ldots, R$. Therefore two alternative parameterizations of the semi-Gaussian ASRF model are given by $(\mu_1, \ldots, \mu_R, \sigma_1^2, \ldots, \sigma_R^2)$ and (π, ϱ).

For $T > 1$, the variance σ_r^2 in (4.5) may be estimated by the sample variance

$$\hat{\sigma}_r^2 \overset{\text{def}}{=} \frac{1}{T} \sum_{t=1}^{T} (X_{tr} - \bar{X}_r)^2, \qquad \bar{X}_r \overset{\text{def}}{=} \frac{1}{T} \sum_{t=1}^{T} X_{tr}. \tag{4.9}$$

Using

$$\varrho_r = \frac{\sigma_r^2}{1 + \sigma_r^2}, \tag{4.10}$$

which is equivalent to (4.5), the point estimator $\hat{\sigma}_r^2$ for the variance σ_r^2 can be transformed into the point estimator

$$\hat{\varrho}_r = \frac{\hat{\sigma}_r^2}{1 + \hat{\sigma}_r^2} \tag{4.11}$$

for the asset correlation ϱ_r. The estimator $(\bar{X}_1, \ldots, \bar{X}_R, \hat{\sigma}_1^2, \ldots, \hat{\sigma}_R^2)$ is the maximum likelihood estimator for $(\mu_1, \ldots, \mu_R, \sigma_1^2, \ldots, \sigma_R^2)$. From (4.10) and the fact that $x \mapsto \frac{x}{1+x}$ defines a bijection between $]0, \infty[$ and $]0, 1[$, it follows that $(\bar{X}_1, \ldots, \bar{X}_R, \hat{\varrho}_1, \ldots, \hat{\varrho}_R)$ is the maximum likelihood estimator for the parameter vector $(\mu_1, \ldots, \mu_R, \varrho_1, \ldots, \varrho_R)$. For a direct derivation of the maximum likelihood estimator $\hat{\varrho}_r$ in the special case of the Gaussian ASRF model see Düllmann and Trapp (2004, pp. 8–9). For $T = 1$, the trivial point estimators $\hat{\sigma}_r^2 = \hat{\varrho}_r = 0$ result, which are useless for the construction of confidence intervals.

Since the observations $X_{1r}, \ldots, X_{Tr}$ are independent and identically Gaussian distributed, $(1 - \alpha)$-confidence bounds and intervals for parameter σ_r^2 can be constructed with standard textbook methods based on the point estimator $\hat{\sigma}_r^2$ for σ_r^2 and on the chi-squared distribution. Using relation (4.11), the resulting confidence bounds and intervals for σ_r^2 can be transformed into confidence bounds and intervals for ϱ_r.

Theorem 1 *Let the semi-Gaussian ASRF model given by (4.2) hold for $T > 1$ periods with stochastically independent random variables $Z_1, \ldots, Z_T$. Let $0 < \alpha < 1$ and $\alpha_1 > 0, \alpha_2 > 0$ with $\alpha_1 + \alpha_2 = \alpha$.*
  Then for $r = 1, \ldots, R$

1. the statistic

$$L_{\varrho_r}^\alpha \overset{\text{def}}{=} \frac{T \hat{\varrho}_r}{T \hat{\varrho}_r + \chi_{T-1,1-\alpha}^2 (1 - \hat{\varrho}_r)} \tag{4.12}$$

  is a $(1 - \alpha)$-LCB for the asset correlation ϱ_r,
2. the statistic

$$U_{\varrho_r}^\alpha \overset{\text{def}}{=} \frac{T \hat{\varrho}_r}{T \hat{\varrho}_r + \chi_{T-1,\alpha}^2 (1 - \hat{\varrho}_r)} \tag{4.13}$$

  is a $(1 - \alpha)$-UCB for the asset correlation ϱ_r, and

3. each stochastic interval

$$I_{\varrho_r}^\alpha = \left[L_{\varrho_r}^{\alpha_1}, U_{\varrho_r}^{\alpha_2} \right] \tag{4.14}$$

is a $(1 - \alpha)$-CI for the asset correlation ϱ_r,

where the estimators $\hat{\varrho}_r$ are defined by (4.11) and $\chi_{T-1,\alpha}^2$ denotes the α-quantile of a chi-squared distribution with $T - 1$ degrees of freedom.

The statements in Theorem 1 imply individual probability statements for each risk category $r \in \{1, \ldots, R\}$. For example, it follows from the third statement of Theorem 1 that

$$P_{\pi,\varrho}(\varrho_r \in I_{\varrho_r}^\alpha) = 1 - \alpha \quad \text{for all} \quad \pi \in]0, 1[^R, \varrho \in]0, 1[^R.$$

In practice, a usual choice for α_1 and α_2 is $\alpha_1 = \alpha_2 = \alpha/2$ with $\alpha \in \{0.1\%, 1\%, 5\%, 10\%\}$. Since the quantile $\chi_{T-1,1-\alpha}^2$ is strictly decreasing in α, the resulting lower confidence bound in (4.12) is strictly increasing in α. Since $\chi_{T-1,\alpha}^2$ is strictly increasing in α, the resulting upper confidence bound in (4.13) is strictly decreasing in α. This monotonicity is a desirable property of confidence bounds, see Cox and Hinkley (1974, p. 208), and facilitates the use of confidence bounds and intervals for the purpose of sensitivity analysis. Decreasing α towards zero leads to increasing sets of stress scenarios for the asset correlation parameter. However, it should be noted that a very small $\alpha = \alpha_1 + \alpha_2$ leads to a useless confidence interval $I_{\varrho_r}^\alpha$, since

$$\lim_{\alpha_1 \to 0} L_{\varrho_r}^{\alpha_1} = 0 \quad \text{and} \quad \lim_{\alpha_2 \to 0} U_{\varrho_r}^{\alpha_2} = 1.$$

For inference statements about the economic capital, simultaneous inference statements for the R risk categories are needed. This means e.g. the quantification of the simultaneous probability

$$P_{\pi,\varrho}(\varrho_1 \in I_1, \ldots, \varrho_R \in I_R) = P_{\pi,\varrho}(\varrho \in I_1 \times \ldots \times I_R)$$

with suitable constructed intervals $I_1, \ldots, I_R$ which depend on the observations. In general, the construction of simultaneous confidence intervals is a challenging task, where approximations and inequalities such as the Bonferroni inequality are required. In the case of the semi-Gaussian ASRF model, however, the special structure with only one source of randomness, which influences all stochastic default probabilities in the same direction,[7] makes it possible to derive simultaneous confidence intervals directly from the univariate intervals.[8] The structure of the semi-Gaussian ASRF model induces a degenerate simultaneous distribution of the R different variance estimators.

Lemma 2 *Let the semi-Gaussian ASRF model given by (4.2) hold for $T \geq 1$ periods. Then the equations*

$$\frac{\hat{\sigma}_1^2}{\sigma_1^2} = \frac{\hat{\sigma}_2^2}{\sigma_2^2} = \ldots - \frac{\hat{\sigma}_R^2}{\sigma_R^2} \tag{4.15}$$

hold for the parameters σ_r^2 in (4.5) and their estimators $\hat{\sigma}_r^2$ in (4.9).

It should be noted that the point estimators $\hat{\varrho}_1, \ldots, \hat{\varrho}_R$ lie in a one-dimensional manifold given by

$$\frac{\frac{1}{\hat{\varrho}_1} - 1}{\frac{1}{\varrho_1} - 1} = \frac{\frac{1}{\hat{\varrho}_2} - 1}{\frac{1}{\varrho_2} - 1} = \cdots = \frac{\frac{1}{\hat{\varrho}_R} - 1}{\frac{1}{\varrho_R} - 1},$$

which is implied by (4.10), (4.11) and (4.15). This manifold is a subset of the hypercube $]0, 1[^R$ built by the parameter space for the parameter vector $\varrho = (\varrho_1, \ldots, \varrho_R)$. On the contrary, the parameter vector ϱ is not restricted by the model to lie in a subspace of this hypercube.

Using Lemma 2, simultaneous confidence bounds and intervals for the parameter vector ϱ can be derived, which are given in the following theorem.

Theorem 2   *Let the assumptions of Theorem 1 hold, then*

1. *the statistic $(L^\alpha_{\varrho_1}, \ldots, L^\alpha_{\varrho_R})$ with $L^\alpha_{\varrho_r}$ from (4.12) is a simultaneous $(1 - \alpha)$-LCB for ϱ,*
2. *the statistic $(U^\alpha_{\varrho_1}, \ldots, U^\alpha_{\varrho_R})$ with $U^\alpha_{\varrho_r}$ from (4.13) is a simultaneous $(1 - \alpha)$-UCB for ϱ, and*
3. *each R-dimensional stochastic interval $I^\alpha_{\varrho_1} \times \cdots \times I^\alpha_{\varrho_R}$ with $I^\alpha_{\varrho_r}$ from (4.14) is a simultaneous $(1 - \alpha)$-CI for ϱ.*

If instead of the estimator $\hat{\sigma}_r^2$ given in Equation (4.9) the alternative estimator

$$\tilde{\sigma}_r^2 \stackrel{\text{def}}{=} \frac{1}{T-1} \sum_{t=1}^{T} (X_{tr} - \bar{X}_r)^2$$

is used, then analogously to (4.11) the alternative estimator

$$\tilde{\varrho}_r = \frac{\tilde{\sigma}_r^2}{1 + \tilde{\sigma}_r^2}$$

for the asset correlation ϱ_r results. For these alternative estimators, Theorems 1 and 2 hold, if $T\hat{\varrho}_r$ is replaced by $(T-1)\tilde{\varrho}_r$ and $(1 - \hat{\varrho}_r)$ is replaced by $(1 - \tilde{\varrho}_r)$ in equations (4.12) and (4.13).

4.5 CONFIDENCE INTERVALS FOR DEFAULT AND SURVIVAL TIME CORRELATIONS

The confidence statements for asset correlations from Section 4.4 can be used to derive corresponding confidence statements for default and survival time correlations if these correlations can be written as monotone functions of the asset correlations. The link between the three correlation concepts is the simultaneous default probability of two different obligors, which depends on the asset correlation and determines together with other parameters the default and survival time correlations. In a semi-Gaussian ASRF model, the simultaneous default probability in risk category r is in general a non-tractable function

$$\pi_{rr} = G_{rr}\big(G_r^{-1}(\pi_r), G_r^{-1}(\pi_r)\big)$$

of the asset correlation ϱ_r. Here, G_r denotes the distribution function of the risk driver $\sqrt{\varrho_r}Z_t + \sqrt{1 - \varrho_r}U_{tri}$ and G_{rr} denotes the joint distribution function of two different risk drivers in risk category r. Both distribution functions G_r and G_{rr} depend in a non-trivial manner on ϱ_r. Only in the special case of the Gaussian ASRF model, the simultaneous default probability π_{rr} of two different obligors in risk category r can be calculated as the quadrant probability of the bivariate standard normal distribution,

$$\pi_{rr} = \Phi_2(\Phi^{-1}(\pi_r), \Phi^{-1}(\pi_r); \varrho_r), \qquad (4.16)$$

see Bluhm et al. (2010, p. 81). Here $\Phi_2(\cdot, \cdot; \varrho_r)$ denotes the distribution function of the bivariate standard normal distribution with correlation parameter ϱ_r. Therefore in this section the special case of the Gaussian ASRF model is assumed.

4.5.1   Confidence Intervals for Default Correlations

The *default correlation* of two different obligors in risk category r with asset correlation ϱ_r is in the Gaussian ASRF model given by

$$\delta_r = h(\varrho_r; \pi_r) \overset{\text{def}}{=} \frac{\Phi_2(\Phi^{-1}(\pi_r), \Phi^{-1}(\pi_r); \varrho_r) - \pi_r^2}{\pi_r(1 - \pi_r)}, \qquad (4.17)$$

see McNeil et al. (2005, p. 345). Function $h(\cdot; \pi_r) :]0, 1[\to]0, 1[$ is a continuous and strictly increasing bijection, see Höse and Huschens (2008, Lemma 1). Therefore the R-dimensional function with r-th component $h(\cdot; \pi_r)$ is a one-to-one mapping from $]0, 1[^R$ to $]0, 1[^R$. This justifies another parametrization of the Gaussian ASRF model by the vector π of default probabilities and the vector

$$\delta \overset{\text{def}}{=} (\delta_1, \ldots, \delta_R) \in]0, 1[^R$$

of default correlations. For each vector $\varrho \in]0, 1[^R$ there exists one and only one vector $\delta \in]0, 1[^R$ and vice versa.

From $\hat{\varrho}_r$ and (4.17) the point estimator

$$\hat{\delta}_r = h(\hat{\varrho}_r; \pi_r) \qquad (4.18)$$

for the default correlation $\delta_r = h(\varrho_r; \pi_r)$ results.

Theorem 3   *Let the Gaussian ASRF model given by (4.1) hold for $T > 1$ periods with stochastically independent random variables $Z_1, \ldots, Z_T$. Let $0 < \alpha < 1$ and $\alpha_1 > 0, \alpha_2 > 0$ with $\alpha_1 + \alpha_2 = \alpha$. Let function h be defined by (4.17).*
    Then for $r = 1, \ldots, R$ holds:

1. The statistic

$$L_{\delta_r}^\alpha \overset{\text{def}}{=} h(L_{\varrho_r}^\alpha; \pi_r) \qquad (4.19)$$

   is a $(1 - \alpha)$-LCB for the default correlation δ_r, where the estimator $L_{\varrho_r}^\alpha$ is defined by (4.12).
2. The statistic

$$U_{\delta_r}^\alpha \overset{\text{def}}{=} h(U_{\varrho_r}^\alpha; \pi_r) \qquad (4.20)$$

   is a $(1 - \alpha)$-UCB for the default correlation δ_r, where the estimator $U_{\varrho_r}^\alpha$ is defined by (4.13).
3. Each stochastic interval

$$I_{\delta_r}^\alpha = \left[L_{\delta_r}^{\alpha_1}, U_{\delta_r}^{\alpha_2} \right] \qquad (4.21)$$

   is a $(1 - \alpha)$-CI for the default correlation δ_r.

Simultaneous confidence intervals for the parameter vector δ of default correlations are given in the following theorem.

Theorem 4   *Let the assumptions of Theorem 3 hold, then*

1. *the statistic $(L_{\delta_1}^\alpha, \ldots, L_{\delta_R}^\alpha)$ with $L_{\delta_r}^\alpha$ from (4.19) is a simultaneous $(1 - \alpha)$-LCB for δ,*
2. *the statistic $(U_{\delta_1}^\alpha, \ldots, U_{\delta_R}^\alpha)$ with $U_{\delta_r}^\alpha$ from (4.20) is a simultaneous $(1 - \alpha)$-UCB for δ, and*
3. *each R-dimensional stochastic interval $I_{\delta_1}^\alpha \times \cdots \times I_{\delta_R}^\alpha$ with $I_{\delta_r}^\alpha$ from (4.21) is a simultaneous $(1 - \alpha)$-CI for δ.*

4.5.2   Confidence Intervals for Survival Time Correlations

The Gaussian ASRF model can be imbedded in a time-continuous framework based on the intensity approach, see Höse and Huschens (2008, p. 37), where the creditworthiness of the obligors is measured by correlated stochastic survival times. In this framework, a positive stochastic survival time with continuous distribution function F_r and one-period default probability $\pi_r = F_r(1)$ is assigned to each obligor in risk category r. Additionally, the simultaneous distribution function F_{rr} of the survival times of two different obligors in risk category r with asset correlation ϱ_r is given by the bivariate normal copula, i.e. by the function

$$F_{rr}(s, t; \varrho_r, F_r) \overset{\text{def}}{=} \Phi_2(\Phi^{-1}(F_r(s)), \Phi^{-1}(F_r(t)); \varrho_r). \tag{4.22}$$

In this framework, the simultaneous one-period default probability of two different obligors in risk category r is $\pi_{rr} = F_{rr}(1, 1; \varrho_r, F_r)$ with π_{rr} given in (4.16). For two positive survival times with finite and positive variances and with the same distribution function F_r, the *survival time correlation* in risk category r is given by

$$\theta_r = H(\varrho_r; F_r), \tag{4.23}$$

where function $H(\cdot; F_r) : \,]0, 1[\rightarrow \,]0, 1[$ is a continuous and strictly increasing bijection defined by

$$H(\varrho_r; F_r) \overset{\text{def}}{=} \frac{\int_0^\infty \int_0^\infty [F_{rr}(s, t; \varrho_r, F_r) - F_r(s)F_r(t)]\,\mathrm{d}s\,\mathrm{d}t}{\int_0^\infty t^2 \mathrm{d}F_r(t) - \left(\int_0^\infty t\,\mathrm{d}F_r(t)\right)^2}, \tag{4.24}$$

see Höse and Huschens (2008, Lemma 2). Consequently, for given distribution functions $F_1, \ldots, F_R$, the R-dimensional function with r-th component $H(\cdot; F_r)$ is a one-to-one mapping from $]0, 1[^R$ to $]0, 1[^R$. This justifies a further parametrization of the Gaussian ASRF model by the vector π of default probabilities and the vector

$$\theta \overset{\text{def}}{=} (\theta_1, \ldots, \theta_R) \in \,]0, 1[^R$$

of survival time correlations.

From $\hat{\varrho}_r$ and (4.23) the point estimator

$$\hat{\theta}_r = H(\hat{\varrho}_r; F_r) \tag{4.25}$$

for the survival time correlation $\theta_r = H(\varrho_r; F_r)$ results.

Theorem 5   *Let the Gaussian ASRF model given by (4.1) hold for $T > 1$ periods with stochastically independent random variables $Z_1, \ldots, Z_T$. Let $0 < \alpha < 1$ and $\alpha_1 > 0$, $\alpha_2 > 0$ with $\alpha_1 + \alpha_2 = \alpha$. Let $F_1, \ldots, F_R$ be continuous distribution functions with $F_1(0) = \cdots = F_R(0) = 0$ and $F_1(1) = \pi_1, \ldots, F_R(1) = \pi_R$. Let any survival time with distribution function F_r have finite and positive variance so that function H in (4.24) is defined. Further, let* *simultaneous distribution functions $F_{11}, \ldots, F_{RR}$ be defined by (4.22). Then for $r = 1, \ldots, R$ holds:*

1. The statistic

$$L_{\theta_r}^{\alpha} \overset{\text{def}}{=} H(L_{\varrho_r}^{\alpha} ; F_r) \tag{4.26}$$

is a $(1 - \alpha)$-LCB for the survival time correlation θ_r, where the estimator $L_{\varrho_r}^{\alpha}$ is defined by (4.12).

2. The statistic

$$U_{\theta_r}^{\alpha} \overset{\text{def}}{=} H(U_{\varrho_r}^{\alpha} ; F_r) \tag{4.27}$$

is a $(1 - \alpha)$-UCB for the survival time correlation θ_r, where the estimator $U_{\varrho_r}^{\alpha}$ is defined by (4.13).

3. Each stochastic interval

$$I_{\theta_r}^{\alpha} = \left[L_{\theta_r}^{\alpha_1}, U_{\theta_r}^{\alpha_2}\right] \tag{4.28}$$

is a $(1 - \alpha)$-CI for the survival time correlation θ_r.

Simultaneous confidence intervals for the parameter vector θ of survival time correlations are given in the following theorem.

Theorem 6 *Let the assumptions of Theorem 5 hold. Then*

1. the statistic $(L_{\theta_1}^{\alpha}, \ldots, L_{\theta_R}^{\alpha})$ with $L_{\theta_r}^{\alpha}$ from (4.26) is a simultaneous $(1 - \alpha)$-LCB for θ,
2. the statistic $(U_{\theta_1}^{\alpha}, \ldots, U_{\theta_R}^{\alpha})$ with $U_{\theta_r}^{\alpha}$ from (4.27) is a simultaneous $(1 - \alpha)$-UCB for θ, and
3. each R-dimensional stochastic interval $I_{\theta_1}^{\alpha} \times \ldots \times I_{\theta_R}^{\alpha}$ with $I_{\theta_r}^{\alpha}$ from (4.28) is a simultaneous $(1 - \alpha)$-CI for θ.

The most important model for stochastic survival times is given by the distribution function

$$F_r(t) = \begin{cases} 1 - e^{-\lambda_r t}, & t \geq 0, \\ 0, & \text{otherwise} \end{cases}$$

with constant intensity rate (hazard rate) $\lambda_r > 0$. In this special case, the default probability is determined by the intensity rate via

$$\pi_r = F_r(1) = 1 - e^{-\lambda_r}$$

and function (4.24) simplifies to

$$H(\varrho_r; F_r) = \int_{-\infty}^{\infty} \int_{-\infty}^{\infty} \ln \Phi(x) \ln \Phi(y) \varphi_2(x, y; \varrho_r) dx dy - 1, \tag{4.29}$$

see Höse and Huschens (2008, Theorem 6), where $\varphi_2(\cdot, \cdot; \varrho_r)$ denotes the density function of the bivariate standard normal distribution with correlation parameter ϱ_r. It should be noted that the survival time correlation given in (4.29) does not depend on the parameter λ_r. As a result, for each risk category the same functional relationship between the asset correlation and the survival time correlation holds.

Table 4.1 Point estimates for asset, default and survival time correlations, calculated for five default probabilities and three correlation scenarios (correlations and probabilities in percent).

r	π_r	Scenario A			Scenario B			Scenario C		
		$\hat{\varrho}_r$	$\hat{\delta}_r$	$\hat{\theta}_r$	$\hat{\varrho}_r$	$\hat{\delta}_r$	$\hat{\theta}_r$	$\hat{\varrho}_r$	$\hat{\delta}_r$	$\hat{\theta}_r$
1	0.1	5	0.07	4.12	23.41	0.81	20.08	25.89	1	22.32
2	0.5	.	0.25	.	21.35	1.78	18.23	14.73	.	12.40
3	1.0	:	0.41	:	19.28	2.28	16.39	10.54	:	8.79
4	5.0		1.20		12.99	3.44	10.89	4.22		3.47
5	10.0	5	1.78	4.12	12.08	4.55	10.12	2.86	1	2.34

4.6 EXAMPLE

The concepts of the previous sections are now illustrated in an example with five rating categories, where the corresponding unconditional default probabilities π_r are shown in the second column of Table 4.1.

In order to calculate confidence intervals in a Gaussian ASRF model, three different scenarios for the point estimates of the correlation parameters are considered. In scenario A, the point estimates $\hat{\varrho}_r$ for the asset correlations ϱ_r are chosen as 5% for each rating category,[9]

$$\hat{\varrho}_1 = \cdots = \hat{\varrho}_R = 0.05.$$

In scenario B, point estimates

$$\hat{\varrho}_r = 0.24 - 0.12\frac{1 - e^{-50\pi_r}}{1 - e^{-50}}$$

according to the Basel Committee on Banking Supervision (2006, p. 64) are assumed. For scenarios A and B, the point estimates $\hat{\delta}_r$ for the default correlations δ_r result from (4.18) and the point estimates $\hat{\theta}_r$ for the survival time correlations θ_r result from (4.25) with function H from (4.29). In scenario C, all point estimates $\hat{\delta}_r$ for the default correlations δ_r are assumed to be equal,

$$\hat{\delta}_1 = \cdots = \hat{\delta}_R = 0.01.$$

In this scenario, the point estimates $\hat{\varrho}_r$ for the asset correlations ϱ_r are determined by $0.01 = h(\hat{\varrho}_r; \pi_r)$. The corresponding point estimates $\hat{\theta}_r$ for the survival time correlations θ_r result from (4.25) with function H from (4.29).

Using the point estimates from the three correlation scenarios A, B and C, which are summarized in Table 4.1, the corresponding interval estimates are derived from the theorems given above. For this purpose, a sample size $T = 20$ is assumed, which, for example, results from default rates observed quarterly over the last five years. Furthermore, error probabilities $\alpha_1 = \alpha_2 = 2.5\%$ are assumed, which lead to the coverage probability of 95% for the confidence intervals.

Table 4.2 shows the values of the 95%-confidence intervals $I_{\varrho_r}^{5\%} = [L_{\varrho_r}^{2.5\%}, U_{\varrho_r}^{2.5\%}]$ for the asset correlations ϱ_r. These values have been calculated using Theorem 1. In scenario A, the assumed point estimates for the asset correlations are 5% for all rating categories so that

Table 4.2   95%-confidence intervals for the asset correlations, calculated for five default probabilities, three correlation scenarios and sample size $T = 20$.

r	Scenario A	Scenario B	Scenario C
1	[0.0310, 0.1057]	[0.1569, 0.4071]	[0.1754, 0.4397]
2		[0.1418, 0.3787]	[0.0952, 0.2795]
3	$\vdots$	[0.1269, 0.3491]	[0.0669, 0.2092]
4		[0.0833, 0.2510]	[0.0261, 0.0900]
5	[0.0310, 0.1057]	[0.0772, 0.2358]	[0.0176, 0.0619]

the resulting five interval estimates for the asset correlations are identical. In scenarios B and C, the estimated asset correlation decreases with increasing default probability. Therefore the length of the corresponding confidence intervals also decreases.

According to Theorem 2, the Cartesian products of the interval estimates given in the columns of Table 4.2 form simultaneous interval estimates for the parameter vector $(\varrho_1, \ldots, \varrho_5)$. The values of the simultaneous 95%-confidence intervals for the vector of asset correlations are

$$[0.0310, 0.1057] \times \cdots \times [0.0310, 0.1057],$$

$$[0.1569, 0.4071] \times \cdots \times [0.0772, 0.2358]$$

and

$$[0.1754, 0.4397] \times \cdots \times [0.0176, 0.0619],$$

in scenarios A, B and C, respectively.

The 95%-confidence intervals $I_{\delta_r}^{5\%} = [L_{\delta_r}^{2.5\%}, U_{\delta_r}^{2.5\%}]$ for the default correlations δ_r are calculated according to Theorem 3 and given in Table 4.3. Although the point estimates for the asset correlations are 5% for all rating categories in scenario A, the resulting interval estimates for the default correlations differ due to the fact that the default probabilities of the five rating categories differ. Using Theorem 4, the Cartesian products of the interval estimates given in the columns of Table 4.3 form simultaneous interval estimates for the parameter vector $(\delta_1, \ldots, \delta_5)$. In scenario B,

$$[0.0038, 0.0298] \times \cdots \times [0.0281, 0.0968]$$

is a simultaneous 95%-confidence interval for the vector of default correlations.

Table 4.3   95%-confidence intervals for the default correlations, calculated for five default probabilities, three correlation scenarios and sample size $T = 20$.

r	Scenario A	Scenario B	Scenario C
1	[0.0004, 0.0020]	[0.0038, 0.0298]	[0.0046, 0.0368]
2	[0.0014, 0.0063]	[0.0095, 0.0514]	[0.0055, 0.0285]
3	[0.0024, 0.0100]	[0.0127, 0.0601]	[0.0057, 0.0258]
4	[0.0072, 0.0272]	[0.0208, 0.0771]	[0.0061, 0.0227]
5	[0.0109, 0.0393]	[0.0281, 0.0968]	[0.0061, 0.0223]

Table 4.4 95%-confidence intervals for the survival time correlations, calculated for five default probabilities, three correlation scenarios, sample size $T = 20$ and constant intensity rate.

r	Scenario A	Scenario B	Scenario C
1	[0.0255, 0.0882]	[0.1324, 0.3619]	[0.1486, 0.3935]
2		[0.1193, 0.3347]	[0.0792, 0.2420]
3	⋮	[0.1064, 0.3067]	[0.0554, 0.1784]
4		[0.0692, 0.2160]	[0.0214, 0.0749]
5	[0.0255, 0.0882]	[0.0640, 0.2023]	[0.0144, 0.0512]

The 95%-confidence intervals $I_{\theta_r}^{5\%} = [L_{\theta_r}^{2.5\%}, U_{\theta_r}^{2.5\%}]$ for the survival time correlations θ_r are given in Table 4.4. They are calculated using Theorem 5 and function H from (4.29). In scenario A, all point estimates for the survival time correlations are equal so that the resulting five interval estimates are identical. Using Theorem 6, the Cartesian products of the interval estimates given in the columns of Table 4.4 form simultaneous interval estimates for the parameter vector $(\theta_1, \ldots, \theta_5)$. In scenario B,

$$[0.1324, 0.3619] \times \cdots \times [0.0640, 0.2023]$$

is a simultaneous 95%-confidence interval for the vector of survival time correlations.

4.7 CONCLUSION

In factor models, asset correlations determine the dependence structure of default events and have, together with the portfolio weights, great impact on the economic capital. Thus the implementation of a meaningful sensitivity analysis for correlation parameters is important.

This chapter focuses on a statistical sensitivity analysis of asset, default and survival time correlations based on the statistical interval estimation of these correlation parameters. To this end, a semi-Gaussian ASRF model with a Gaussian distributed systematic risk factor but arbitrarily distributed idiosyncratic risk factors is considered. Using this model, point and interval estimators for asset correlations are derived from time series of transformed default rates assuming that the systematic risk factors for the different periods are stochastically independent. Using the special structure of the ASRF model with only one systematic risk factor in each period, the individual confidence intervals for single asset correlations given in Theorem 1 provide the basis for simultaneous confidence intervals for all asset correlations given in Theorem 2. In the same way, individual confidence intervals for default correlations given in Theorem 3 and for survival time correlations given in Theorem 5 lead to simultaneous confidence intervals for all default correlations given in Theorem 4 and for all survival time correlations given in Theorem 6. The advantage of these confidence statements is that they are given as a closed-form expression, are not the result of time-consuming Monte Carlo simulations and are exact in the sense that they have the desired coverage probability even for short time series of default rates.

The application of this methodology to an example with five rating categories shows the inferential uncertainty about the asset, default and survival time correlations. This parameter uncertainty is mirrored by the length of the confidence intervals and is, for a fixed confidence level, only caused by the statistical variability inherent in the observed data. In that sense, these confidence intervals can be understood as a statistical approach to sensitivity analysis in order to identify meaningful stress scenarios for correlations. The stress level involved may be systematically altered by the variation of the confidence level used, where higher confidence levels lead to wider confidence intervals. In contrast, stress tests based on historical simulation are limited by the range of the observed data so that inference beyond the observations is not possible, e.g. stress scenarios in the extreme tails of distributions cannot be considered. It should be noted that in the ASRF model, the upper bounds of the estimated confidence intervals do not necessarily lead to the highest stress level if the value at risk is used as a risk measure. Höse and Huschens (2008) have shown that the conditional default probabilities for a given realization of the systematic risk factor, i.e. the contributions of the risk categories to the value at risk of the portfolio, do not necessarily increase with increasing asset, default or survival time correlations. If, in contrast, the tail value at risk, which is also known as the average value at risk, is used as a risk measure, then the contributions of the risk categories to the tail value at risk increase with increasing correlations, see Höse and Huschens (2011b). This gives a further criterion, in addition to the usual argument of subadditivity, to favor the risk measure tail value at risk over the value at risk.

APPENDIX

Proof of Lemma 1

$$
\begin{aligned}
P_\theta(L \le \theta \le U) &= 1 - P_\theta(L > \theta) - P_\theta(U < \theta) + P_\theta(L > \theta, U < \theta) \\
&= 1 - P_\theta(L > \theta) - P_\theta(U < \theta) \\
&= P_\theta(L \le \theta) - (1 - P_\theta(U \ge \theta)) \\
&= P_\theta(L \le \theta) + P_\theta(U \ge \theta) - 1 \\
&= (1 - \alpha_1) + (1 - \alpha_2) - 1 \\
&= 1 - \alpha_1 - \alpha_2.
\end{aligned}
$$

The second equality follows from $P_\theta(L \le U) = 1$.   □

Remark   In the following proofs all probabilities $P(\cdot)$ depend on the parameter vectors π and ϱ. To simplify the notation, $P(\cdot)$ instead of $P_{\pi,\varrho}(\cdot)$ is used. The probability equalities and inequalities in the proofs hold for all $\pi \in]0, 1[^R$ and all $\varrho \in]0, 1[^R$.

Proof of Theorem 1

1. From the stochastic independence of $Z_1, \ldots, Z_T$, it follows that the random variables $X_{1r}, \ldots, X_{Tr}$ from (4.3) are stochastically independent and $\dfrac{T\hat{\sigma}_r^2}{\sigma_r^2} \sim \chi^2_{T-1}$. This implies

$$
1 - \alpha = P\left(\frac{T\hat{\sigma}_r^2}{\sigma_r^2} \le \chi^2_{T-1,1-\alpha}\right) = P\left(\sigma_r^2 \ge \frac{T\hat{\sigma}_r^2}{\chi^2_{T-1,1-\alpha}}\right),
$$

i.e. $\dfrac{T\hat{\sigma}_r^2}{\chi_{T-1,1-\alpha}^2}$ is a lower $(1-\alpha)$-confidence bound for σ_r^2. Using (4.5) and (4.11), then

$$
1 - \alpha = P\left(\sigma_r^2 \geq \frac{T\hat{\sigma}_r^2}{\chi_{T-1,1-\alpha}^2}\right)
$$

$$
= P\left(\frac{\varrho_r}{1-\varrho_r} \geq \frac{\hat{\varrho}_r}{1-\hat{\varrho}_r} \frac{T}{\chi_{T-1,1-\alpha}^2}\right)
$$

$$
= P\left(\varrho_r \geq \frac{T\hat{\varrho}_r}{T\hat{\varrho}_r + \chi_{T-1,1-\alpha}^2(1-\hat{\varrho}_r)}\right)
$$

$$
= P\left(\varrho_r \geq L_{\varrho_r}^{\alpha}\right).
$$

2. Analogous to the previous part of the proof, it follows

$$
P(U_{\varrho_r}^{\alpha} \geq \varrho_r) = 1 - \alpha
$$

from

$$
P\left(\frac{T\hat{\sigma}_r^2}{\sigma_r^2} \geq \chi_{T-1,\alpha}^2\right) = 1 - \alpha.
$$

3. From $\chi_{T-1,\alpha_2}^2 < \chi_{T-1,1-\alpha_1}^2$ and $P(\hat{\sigma}_r = 0) = P(\hat{\varrho}_r = 0) = 0$, it follows that $P(L_{\varrho_r}^{\alpha_1} < U_{\varrho_r}^{\alpha_2}) = 1$. Lemma 1 implies $P(\varrho_r \in I_{\varrho_r}^{\alpha}) = 1 - \alpha$. $\qquad \square$

Proof of Lemma 2 From (4.3), (4.4) and (4.5), it follows that

$$
\frac{X_{t1} - \mu_1}{\sigma_1} = \ldots = \frac{X_{tR} - \mu_R}{\sigma_R} = -Z_t, \quad t = 1, \ldots, T,
$$

which implies

$$
\frac{\bar{X}_1 - \mu_1}{\sigma_1} = \ldots = \frac{\bar{X}_R - \mu_R}{\sigma_R}
$$

with $\bar{X}_r$ from (4.9). Forming the differences

$$
\frac{X_{tr} - \bar{X}_r}{\sigma_r} = \frac{X_{tr} - \mu_r}{\sigma_r} - \frac{\bar{X}_r - \mu_r}{\sigma_r},
$$

squaring and summation yields

$$
\frac{\sum_{t=1}^{T}(X_{t1} - \bar{X}_1)^2}{\sigma_1^2} = \ldots = \frac{\sum_{t=1}^{T}(X_{tR} - \bar{X}_R)^2}{\sigma_R^2}
$$

and therefore (4.15). $\qquad \square$

Proof of Theorem 2   The first statement of the theorem follows from

$$P(\varrho_1 \geq L_{\varrho_1}^{\alpha}, \ldots, \varrho_R \geq L_{\varrho_R}^{\alpha}) = P\left(\bigcap_{r=1}^{R} \left\{\frac{T\hat{\sigma}_r^2}{\sigma_r^2} \leq \chi_{T-1,1-\alpha}^2\right\}\right)$$

$$= P\left(\frac{T\hat{\sigma}_1^2}{\sigma_1^2} \leq \chi_{T-1,1-\alpha}^2\right)$$

$$= 1 - \alpha,$$

where the first equality follows from the proof of the first statement of Theorem 1 and the second equality is implied by Lemma 2. The second statement of the theorem follows analogously to the derivation of the first statement. Combining these two statements, the third statement follows.   □

Proof of Theorem 3   From the first and second statement of Theorem 1 and the strictly increasing monotonicity of the continuous bijection $h(\cdot; \pi_r)$, it follows

$$1 - \alpha = P\left(L_{\varrho_r}^{\alpha} \leq \varrho_r\right) = P\left(h\left(L_{\varrho_r}^{\alpha}; \pi_r\right) \leq h(\varrho_r; \pi_r)\right) = P\left(L_{\delta_r}^{\alpha} \leq \delta_r\right)$$

and

$$1 - \alpha = P\left(U_{\varrho_r}^{\alpha} \geq \varrho_r\right) = P\left(h\left(U_{\varrho_r}^{\alpha}; \pi_r\right) \geq h(\varrho_r; \pi_r)\right) = P\left(U_{\delta_r}^{\alpha} \geq \delta_r\right).$$

Further, equation

$$P\left(L_{\varrho_r}^{\alpha_1} \leq \varrho_r \leq U_{\varrho_r}^{\alpha_2}\right) = 1 - \alpha$$

from the third statement of Theorem 1 implies

$$1 - \alpha = P\left(h\left(L_{\varrho_r}^{\alpha_1}; \pi_r\right) \leq h(\varrho_r; \pi_r) \leq h\left(U_{\varrho_r}^{\alpha_2}; \pi_r\right)\right) = P\left(L_{\delta_r}^{\alpha_1} \leq \delta_r \leq U_{\delta_r}^{\alpha_2}\right).$$

                                                                                                                        □

Proof of Theorem 4   The first statement of the theorem follows from

$$1 - \alpha = P\left(\varrho_1 \geq L_{\varrho_1}^{\alpha}, \ldots, \varrho_R \geq L_{\varrho_R}^{\alpha}\right)$$

$$= P\left(h(\varrho_1; \pi_1) \geq h\left(L_{\varrho_1}^{\alpha}; \pi_1\right), \ldots, h(\varrho_R; \pi_R) \geq h\left(L_{\varrho_R}^{\alpha}; \pi_R\right)\right)$$

$$= P(\delta_1 \geq L_{\delta_1}^{\alpha}, \ldots, \delta_R \geq L_{\delta_R}^{\alpha}),$$

where the first equality is implied by the first statement of Theorem 2 and the second equality follows from the bijection property of functions $h(\cdot; \pi_r), \ldots, h(\cdot; \pi_R)$, which is stated in Höse and Huschens (2008, Lemma 1). Analogous to this derivation, the second and third statements of this theorem follow from the second and third statements of Theorem 2, respectively.   □

Proofs of Theorems 5 and 6   The proofs are analogous to that of Theorems 3 and 4, replacing function $h(\cdot; \pi_r)$ by the monotone and strictly increasing function $H(\cdot; F_r)$.   □

NOTES

1. For stress-testing practice in financial institutions, see Rösch and Scheule (2008).
2. For this ASRF model with Gaussian distributed individual and systematic risk factors see Vasicek (1991), Vasicek (2002), Schönbucher (2003, pp. 309–312) and Gordy (2003).
3. In case of a Gaussian ASRF model with $\Psi_r = G_r = \Phi$ for all $r = 1, \ldots, R$, the observable random variables $X_{tr} = \Phi^{-1}(\tilde{\pi}_{tr})$ are called probits, since Φ^{-1} is also known as the probit function. Höse (2007, pp. 194ff.) derives simultaneous confidence sets for default probabilities and asset correlations based on probits of default rates and calls this approach the transformation method. Alternative approaches to estimate such simultaneous confidence sets can be found in Rösch and Scheule (2007) and Höse (2007, chapters 4.3.2 and 6.2).
4. This assumption may be relaxed using a dynamic model, e.g. an autoregressive stochastic process as discussed in Höse and Vogl (2006). In this case, the construction of confidence intervals for asset correlations is much more complicated, as the correlation structure induced by the dynamic model has to be taken into account.
5. A statistic is a random variable, which is a function of the observations. The distribution of these observations and therefore the distribution of the statistic itself depends on the parameter $\theta \in \Theta$. More technically, the family of probability measures $\{P_\theta \mid \theta \in \Theta\}$ has to be considered.
6. For the definition of the weaker concept of lower and upper confidence bounds see Dudewicz and Mishra (1988, p. 572). Confidence bounds are also called confidence limits, see Zacks (1971, p. 499).
7. More technically, this property is called comonotonicity, see McNeil et al. (2005, p. 199).
8. This idea has been already used for the derivation of simultaneous confidence intervals for default probabilities, if asset correlations are fixed and given, see Höse and Huschens (2003).
9. For example in the empirical study of FitchRatings (2008, pp. 10, 12) an asset correlation of 5.2% was estimated for US corporate loans.

REFERENCES

Basel Committee on Banking Supervision, June 2006. International convergence of capital measurement and capital standards – A revised framework, comprehensive version. http://www.bis.org/publ/bcbs128.htm, Accessed March 1, 2012.

Bickel, P. J., Doksum, K. A., 1977. Mathematical Statistics: Basic Ideas and Selected Topics. Prentice Hall, Englewood Cliffs.

Bluhm, C., Overbeck, L., Wagner, C., 2010. Introduction to Credit Risk Modeling, 2nd Edition. Chapman & Hall/CRC, Boca Raton.

Christensen, J. H. E., Hansen, E., Lando, D., 2004. Confidence sets for continuous-time rating transition probabilities. Journal of Banking & Finance 28(11), 2575–2602.

Cox, D. R., Hinkley, D. V., 1974. Theoretical Statistics. Chapman & Hall, London.

de Servigny, A., Renault, O., 2004. Measuring and Managing Credit Risk. McGraw-Hill, New York.

Dudewicz, E. J., Mishra, S. N., 1988. Modern Mathematical Statistics. Wiley, New York.

Düllmann, K., Trapp, M., June 2004. Systematic risk in recovery rates – an empirical analysis of U.S. corporate credit exposures. Deutsche Bundesbank, Discussion Paper Series 2: Banking and Financial Supervision, No 02.

FitchRatings, May 2008. Basel II correlation values: an empirical analysis of EL, UL and the IRB model. http://www.securitization.net/pdf/Fitch/BaselII_19May08.pdf, Accessed March 1, 2012.

Frey, R., McNeil, A. J., 2003. Dependent defaults in models of portfolio credit risk. The Journal of Risk 6(1), 59–92.

Gordy, M. B., 2000. A comparative anatomy of credit risk models. Journal of Banking & Finance 24(1–2), 119–149.

Gordy, M. B., 2003. A risk-factor model foundation for ratings-based bank capital rules. The Journal of Financial Intermediation 12(3), 199–232.

Hanson, S., Schuermann, T., 2006. Confidence intervals for probabilities of default. Journal of Banking & Finance 30(8), 2281–2301.

Höse, S., 2007. Statistische Genauigkeit bei der simultanen Schätzung von Abhängigkeitsstrukturen und Ausfallwahrscheinlichkeiten in Kreditportfolios. Shaker Verlag, Aachen.

Höse, S., Huschens, S., 2003. Simultaneous confidence intervals for default probabilities. In: Schader, M., Gaul, W., Vichi, M. (Eds), Between Data Science and Applied Data Analysis. Springer, Berlin, pp. 555–560.

Höse, S., Huschens, S., 2008. Worst-case asset, default and survival time correlations. The Journal of Risk Model Validation 2(4), 27–50.

Höse, S., Huschens, S., 2010. Model risk and non-Gaussian latent risk factors. In: Rösch, D., Scheule, H. (Eds), Model Risk – Identification, Measurement and Management. Risk Books, London, pp. 45–73.

Höse, S., Huschens, S., 2011a. Confidence intervals for asset correlations in the asymptotic single risk factor model. In: Hu, B., Morasch, K., Pickl, S., Siegle, M. (Eds), Operations Research Proceedings 2010. Springer Verlag, Berlin, pp. 111–116.

Höse, S., Huschens, S., 2011b. Stochastic orders and non-Gaussian risk factor models. Review of Managerial Science,Online: DOI 10.1007/s11846-011-0071-8.

Höse, S., Vogl, K., 2006. Modeling and estimating the credit cycle by a probit-AR(1)-process. In: Spiliopoulou, M., Kruse, R., Borgelt, C., Nürnberger, A., Gaul, W. (Eds), From Data and Information Analysis to Knowledge Engineering. Springer, Berlin, pp. 534–541.

McNeil, A. J., Frey, R., Embrechts, P., 2005. Quantitative Risk Management: Concepts, Techniques and Tools. Princeton University Press, Princeton.

McNeil, A. J., Wendin, J. P., 2007. Bayesian inference for generalized linear mixed models of portfolio credit risk. Journal of Empirical Finance 14(2), 131–149.

Pluto, K., Tasche, D., August 2005. Thinking positively. Risk 18(8), 72–78.

Pluto, K., Tasche, D., 2006. Estimating probabilities of default for low default portfolios. In: Engelmann, B., Rauhmeier, R. (Eds), The Basel II Risk Parameters: Estimation, Validation, and Stress Testing. Springer, Berlin, pp. 79–103.

Rösch, D., Scheule, H., Spring 2007. Stress-testing credit risk parameters: an application to retail loan portfolios. The Journal of Risk Model Validation 1(1), 55–75.

Rösch, D., Scheule, H. (Eds), 2008. Stress Testing for Financial Institutions: Applications, Regulations and Techniques. Risk Books, London.

Schönbucher, P. J., 2003. Credit Derivatives Pricing Models: Models, Pricing and Implementation. John Wiley & Sons, Chichester.

Trück, S., Rachev, S. T., 2005. Credit portfolio risk and probability of default confidence sets through the business cycle. The Journal of Credit Risk 1(4), 61–88.

Vasicek, O., December 2002. Loan portfolio value. Risk 15(12), 160–162.

Vasicek, O. A., 1991. Limiting loan loss probability distribution. http://www.moodysanalytics.com/~/media/Insight/Quantitative-Research/Portfolio-Modeling/91-08-09-Limiting-Loan-Loss-Probability-Distribution.ashx, Accessed March 1, 2012.

Zacks, S., 1971. The Theory of Statistical Inference. Wiley, New York.

5

Credit Portfolio Correlations with Dynamic Leverage Ratios

Carl Chiarella[†], Ming Xi Huang[*] and Chi-Fai Lo[‡]

*†*University of Technology, Sydney
‡*The Chinese University of Hong Kong*

5.1 INTRODUCTION

Default correlations have been an important research area in credit risk analysis. There are a number of approaches to credit risk modeling, for example, the Gaussian copula method, the reduced-form approach and the structural approach. In the structural approach, default happens when the firm value falls below a default threshold. For example the fundamental model of Merton (1974) assumed that default could only happen at the maturity date of the bond. This was later modified by Black and Cox (1976) to allow default before the maturity date. Longstaff and Schwartz (1995) combine the early default mechanism in Black and Cox (1976) and the stochastic interest rate model of Vasicek (1977). Their model also accommodates the complicated liability structures and payoffs by deriving the solution as a function of a ratio of the firm value to the bond payoff value. Instead of using a constant default threshold, Briys and de Varenne (1997) consider a time-dependent default threshold and assume that it depends on the risk-free interest rate.

Later developments by Collin-Dufresne and Goldstein (2001) and Hui et al. (2006) consider the stationary leverage ratio for modeling credit risk. Collin-Dufresne and Goldstein (2001) assume that the default threshold changes dynamically over time, in particular that the dynamics of the log-default threshold is mean-reverting. This setting captures the fact that firms tend to issue debt when their leverage ratios fall below some target, and replace maturing debt when their leverage ratios are above this target. Hui et al. (2006) generalize the Collin-Dufresne and Goldstein (2001) model to consider the situation in which the default threshold is stochastic and follows a mean-reverting lognormal diffusion process with time-dependent parameters. The bond pricing functions in Collin-Dufresne and Goldstein (2001) and Hui et al. (2006) are in terms of the ratio of the default threshold to the firm value. The default threshold is assumed to be the total liabilities of the firm. For such a combined measure of the default risk of the firm, Hui et al. (2007) proposed a dynamic leverage ratio model, where default is driven by the firm's leverage ratio when it is above a certain level.

The aim of this chapter is to extend the dynamic leverage ratio model of Hui et al. (2007) to the two-firm case so as to study the implications for default correlations. The two-firm model has been proposed by Zhou (2001), who extends the one-firm model of Black and Cox (1976) to the two-firm situation. In Zhou (2001) the arrival of the default is driven by firms' asset

A long version of this chapter is published in *Quantitative Finance Research Centre Working Paper Series* University of Technology, Sydney, "Modelling default correlations in a two-firm model with dynamic leverage ratios", No. 304

values and the short-term risk-free interest rate is deterministic. In contrast to Zhou (2001), the arrival of default in the two-firm model in this chapter is driven by firms' leverage ratios, and the risk-free interest rate is stochastic. We also extend the methods and techniques applied in Hui et al. (2007) for solving the first passage time problem to a two-dimensional situation. The third aim of this chapter is to develop numerical schemes which apply more generally.

The remainder of this chapter is organized as follows. Section 5.2 reviews the dynamic leverage ratio model of Hui et al. (2007), and the techniques used by these authors to solve the first-passage-time problem: the method of images and the time varying barrier technique for dealing with time-dependent parameters. Section 5.3 extends the dynamic leverage ratio model to the two-firm situation for the valuation of default correlations. Section 5.4 shows the numerical results for the impact on joint survival probabilities and default correlations across a range of different scenarios, for example, different correlation levels, drift rates, volatilities and initial leverage ratios. Section 5.5 concludes.

5.2   THE HUI ET AL. (2007) MODEL

The Hui et al. (2007) model assumes that corporate bond prices depend on a firm's leverage ratio and the risk-free interest rate. The leverage ratio L is assumed to be the ratio of the firm's total liability to the firm's value. The leverage ratio is assumed to follow the geometric Brownian motion

$$dL = \mu_L(t)Ldt + \sigma_L(t)LdZ_L, \tag{5.1}$$

where $\mu_L(t)$ and $\sigma_L(t)$ are the time-dependent drift rate and the volatility of the proportional change in the leverage ratio, respectively and Z_L is a Wiener process under the historical measure $\mathbb{P}$. The dynamics of the risk-free interest rate is assumed to be given by the Hull and White (1990) model, so that

$$dr = \kappa_r(t)\left[\theta_r(t) - r\right]dt + \sigma_r(t)dZ_r, \tag{5.2}$$

where the risk-free interest r is mean-reverting to the long-run mean $\theta_r(t)$ at speed $\kappa_r(t)$, $\sigma_r(t)$ is the instantaneous volatility of interest rate changes and Z_r is a Wiener process under the historical measure $\mathbb{P}$.

The Wiener increments dZ_L and dZ_r are assumed to be correlated with[1]

$$\mathbb{E}[dZ_L dZ_r] = \rho_{Lr}(t)dt. \tag{5.3}$$

In Hui et al. (2007), default occurs when the firm's leverage ratio rises above a predefined level $\widehat{L}$ anytime during the life of the bond, and bondholders receive nothing upon default. Otherwise, bondholders receive the par value of the bond at the maturity T. Applying the arbitrage pricing argument, the corporate bond price $P(L, r, t)$ (which is a function of the leverage ratio L, the short term interest rate r and time t) is given by

$$-\frac{\partial P}{\partial t} = \frac{1}{2}\sigma_L^2(t)L^2\frac{\partial^2 P}{\partial L^2} + \widetilde{\mu}_L(t)L\frac{\partial P}{\partial L} + \rho_{Lr}(t)\sigma_L(t)\sigma_r(t)L\frac{\partial^2 P}{\partial L\partial r}$$

$$+\frac{1}{2}\sigma_r^2(t)\frac{\partial^2 P}{\partial r^2} + \kappa_r(t)[\widetilde{\theta}_r(t) - r]\frac{\partial P}{\partial r} - rP, \tag{5.4}$$

for $t \in (0, T)$, $L \in (0, \widehat{L})$ and subject to the boundary conditions

$$P(L, r, T) = 1, \quad P(\widehat{L}, r, t) = 0. \tag{5.5}$$

Here

$$\tilde{\mu}_L(t) = \mu_L(t) - \lambda_L \sigma_L(t), \tilde{\theta}_r(t) = \theta_r(t) - \frac{\lambda_r \sigma_r(t)}{\kappa_r(t)}, \tag{5.6}$$

where λ_L and λ_r are the market prices of risk[2] of the leverage ratio and interest rate processes, respectively.

Hui et al. (2007) employed the separation of variables method to simplify the problem (5.4) by setting

$$P(L, r, t) = B(r, t)\widehat{P}(L, t), \tag{5.7}$$

where $B(r, t)$ is the risk-free bond price and $\widehat{P}(L, t)$ which is a function defined on $L < \widehat{L}$ in the period $(0, T)$ satisfies the partial differential equation[3]

$$-\frac{\partial \widehat{P}}{\partial t} = \frac{1}{2}\sigma_L^2(t)L^2\frac{\partial^2 \widehat{P}}{\partial L^2} + [\tilde{\mu}_L(t) + \rho_{Lr}(t)\sigma_L(t)\sigma_r(t)b(t)]L\frac{\partial \widehat{P}}{\partial L}, \tag{5.8}$$

subject to the boundary conditions

$$\widehat{P}(L, T) = 1, \widehat{P}(\widehat{L}, t) = 0. \tag{5.9}$$

Equation (5.8) can be transformed further to a simpler form by using the normalized log-leverage ratio $x = \ln(L/\widehat{L})$, and $\tau = T - t$ the time-to-maturity. Then $\bar{P}(x, \tau) \equiv \widehat{P}(\widehat{L}e^x, \tau)$ can be shown to satisfy the partial differential equation

$$\frac{\partial \bar{P}}{\partial \tau} = \frac{1}{2}\sigma_L^2(\tau)\frac{\partial^2 \bar{P}}{\partial x^2} + \gamma(\tau)\frac{\partial \bar{P}}{\partial x}, \tag{5.10}$$

for $\tau \in (0, T)$ and $x \in (\infty, 0)$, subject to the boundary conditions

$$\bar{P}(x, 0) = 1, \tag{5.11}$$
$$\bar{P}(0, \tau) = 0, \tag{5.12}$$

and it turns out that $\gamma(\tau) = \tilde{\mu}_L(\tau) + \rho_{Lr}(\tau)\sigma_L(\tau)\sigma_r(\tau)b(\tau) - \frac{1}{2}\sigma_L^2(\tau)$.

The solution to (5.10) can be written as

$$\bar{P}(x, \tau) = \int_{-\infty}^{0} f(x, y; \tau)\bar{P}(y)dy, \tag{5.13}$$

where $\bar{P}(x, 0) \equiv \bar{P}(y)$ is the initial condition given in (5.11), $f(x, y; \tau)$ is the transition probability density function for x starting at the value $x(0) = y$ at $\tau = 0$ and ending at the value x at τ, and it is subject to the zero boundary condition in (5.12).

5.2.1 The Method of Images for Constant Coefficients

It is the boundary condition (5.12) that gives the defaultable bond pricing problem its particular structure and difficulty. This is essentially a barrier type condition and in one form or another requires the solution of the first passage time[4] problem associated with the partial differential equation (5.10). To solve this type of problem, Hui et al. (2007) apply the method of images. When the model parameters are first assumed to be constant, is $\sigma_L(\tau) = \sigma_L$, $\gamma(\tau) = \gamma$ and

$\rho_{Lr} = 0$, the exact solution of the transition probability density function is[5]

$$f(x, y; \tau) = \exp\left\{ -\frac{\gamma}{\sigma_L^2}(x - y) - \frac{\gamma^2}{2\sigma_L^2}\tau \right\}\left[g\left(x, y; \sigma_L^2\tau\right) - g\left(x, -y; \sigma_L^2\tau\right)\right], \quad (5.14)$$

where

$$g(x, y; v) = \frac{e^{-(x-y)^2/2v}}{\sqrt{2\pi v}}. \quad (5.15)$$

Albanese and Campolieti (2006) use an alternative approach, namely the reflection principle, to obtain the transition probability density function, and show that it is indeed the same transition probability density function for the survival probability for the absorption not yet having occurred during a period of time $\xi = t - t_0$, that is

$$F(x, \xi) = \int_{-\infty}^{0} f(x, y; \sigma_L^2\xi)dy. \quad (5.16)$$

5.2.2 The Method of Images for Time-Varying Coefficients

If the coefficients in the partial differential equation (5.10) are time-dependent, the application of the method of images will not be as straightforward as in the case of constant coefficients. Indeed, the exact solution $\bar{P}(x, \tau)$ cannot be solved by applying the method of images and only, an approximate solution can be obtained instead. Hui et al. (2007) apply a simple approach that was developed by Lo et al. (2003) to construct an approximate solution, namely $\bar{P}_\beta(x, \tau)$, which satisfies the partial differential equation (5.10) is subject to the initial condition (5.11). The approach of Lo et al. (2003) is to set the zero boundary condition of $\bar{P}_\beta(x, \tau)$ at a time-varying barrier, namely $x^*(\tau)$, which is normalized along the log-leverage ratio x-axis, that is

$$\bar{P}_\beta(x^*(\tau), \tau) = 0. \quad (5.17)$$

The dynamic form of $x^*(\tau)$ is assumed to be

$$x^*(\tau) = -\int_0^\tau \gamma(v)dv - \beta \int_0^\tau \sigma_L^2(v)dv, \quad (5.18)$$

where β is a real parameter, which may be chosen in some optimal way so as to minimize the deviation between the time-varying barrier $x^*(\tau)$ and the exact barrier at $x = 0$.

By applying the method of images, the approximate solution is given by

$$\bar{P}_\beta(x, \tau) = \int_{-\infty}^{0} f_\beta(x, y; \tau)\bar{P}_\beta(y)dy, \quad (5.19)$$

where $\bar{P}_\beta(y) = 1$ at $\tau = 0$ is the initial condition, and $f_\beta(x, y; \tau)$ is the transition probability density function for the process restricted to the region $x \in (-\infty, x^*(\tau))$ and has the form[6]

$$f_\beta(x, y, \tau) = \exp\left\{ \beta[x - y - x^*(\tau)] - \frac{1}{2}\beta^2 \int_0^\tau \sigma_L^2(v)dv \right\}$$

$$\times\left[g\left(x - x^*(\tau), y; \int_0^\tau \sigma_L^2(v)dv\right) - g\left(x - x^*(\tau), -y; \int_0^\tau \sigma_L^2(v)dv\right)\right]. \quad (5.20)$$

The survival probability for the absorption not yet having occurred during a period of time $\xi = t - t_0$ is thus

$$F_\beta(x, \xi) = \int_{-\infty}^{0} f_\beta(x, y; \xi) dy. \tag{5.21}$$

Note that the accuracy of the approximate solution depends on the choice of the values of β. Lo et al. (2003) illustrate certain forms of β that provide accurate results, for example by setting $x^*(0) = x^*(T) = 0$. A particular form of β can be obtained by using Equation (5.18), so that

$$\beta = -\frac{\int_0^T \gamma(v) dv}{\int_0^T \sigma_L^2(v) dv}. \tag{5.22}$$

Other methodologies of choosing the optimal values of β are discussed in Lo et al. (2003).

5.3 MODELLING DEFAULT CORRELATIONS IN A TWO-FIRM MODEL

5.3.1 Default Correlations

Default correlation measures the likelihood of firms defaulting together. The mathematical expression of default correlation given by Zhou (2001) is

$$\rho_D = \frac{\text{JPD} - \text{PD}_1\text{PD}_2}{\sqrt{\text{PD}_1(1 - \text{PD}_1)}\sqrt{\text{PD}_2(1 - \text{PD}_2)}}, \tag{5.23}$$

where JPD is the joint default probability of the two firms $i = 1, 2$ and PD_i are individual default probabilities of the two firms.

Default correlation in (5.23) can be explained as the normalized difference between both firms defaulting at the time when they are correlated and both firms defaulting at the time when they are uncorrelated.

To use (5.23), individual default probabilities need to be obtained by solving Equation (5.16) or (5.21). The JPD can be expressed in terms of joint survival probability JSP according to

$$\text{JPD} = \text{JSP} - 1 + \text{PD}_1 + \text{PD}_2, \tag{5.24}$$

where JSP will be determined in the following subsections.

5.3.2 A Two-Firm Model with Dynamic Leverage Ratios

To evaluate the joint survival probability of two firms, we consider a financial instrument – namely a credit-linked note (CLN) that is exposed to the default risk of the note issuer and the reference asset. A credit-linked note allows the issuer to transfer the credit risk of holding a bond to the investors. If the bond issuer (or the"reference obligor") is solvent, the note issuer is obligated to pay to the note-holders the note face value at maturity. If the reference obligor goes bankrupt, the note-holders receive a recovery rate or in the worst case they receive nothing. The note-holders are also exposed to the default risk of the note issuer. Therefore, the price of the note is linked to the performance of the reference asset and the default risk of the note issuer. To model the CLN, we extend the Hui et al. (2007) dynamic leverage ratio model to the two firm situation and incorporate the stochastic risk-free interest rate.

Let L_1 and L_2 denote respectively the leverage ratios of the note issuer and the reference obligor, and assume that they follow the dynamics

$$dL_i = \mu_i L_i dt + \sigma_i L_i dZ_i, \, (i = 1, 2), \tag{5.25}$$

where μ_i and σ_i denote the constant drift rate and volatility of the proportional change in leverage ratios respectively, and Z_1 and Z_2 are Wiener processes under the historical measure $\mathbb{P}$. The Wiener increments dZ_1 and dZ_2 are assumed to be correlated with

$$\mathbb{E}[dZ_1 dZ_2] = \rho_{12} dt, \tag{5.26}$$

where ρ_{12} denotes the correlation coefficient of the proportional leverage ratio level of the two firms.

Let the dynamics of the instantaneous spot rate of interest follow the Vasicek (1977) process

$$dr = \kappa_r (\theta_r - r) dt + \sigma_r dZ_r, \tag{5.27}$$

where the instantaneous spot rate of interest r is mean-reverting to the constant long-term mean θ_r at constant speed κ and Z_r is a Wiener process under the historical measure $\mathbb{P}$. The Wiener processes Z_i and Z_r are correlated with

$$\mathbb{E}[dZ_i dZ_r] = \rho_{ir} dt, \, (i = 1, 2), \tag{5.28}$$

where ρ_{ir} denotes the correlation coefficient between the proportional changes of the leverage ratio level of firm i and the instantaneous spot rate of interest.

Assume default(s) occur anytime during the life of the credit linked note when either firm's leverage ratio rises above a predefined default threshold $\widehat{L}_i$, that is $L_i \geq \widehat{L}_i$. If both firms' leverage ratios never reach $\widehat{L}_i$, the note holder receives the face value, which is assumed to be equal to unity. If default occurs, the firm defaults on all of its obligations immediately, and the note holder receives nothing (that is there is no recovery) upon default of either firm.[7]

Let $P(L_1, L_2, r, t)$ be the price of a credit-linked note. Applying the arbitrage pricing argument, the partial differential equation for the price is given by

$$-\frac{\partial P(L_1, L_2, r, t)}{\partial t} = \frac{1}{2}\sigma_1^2 L_1^2 \frac{\partial^2 P}{\partial L_1^2} + \frac{1}{2}\sigma_2^2 L_2^2 \frac{\partial^2 P}{\partial L_2^2} + \frac{1}{2}\sigma_r^2 \frac{\partial^2 P}{\partial r^2} + \rho_{12}\sigma_1\sigma_2 L_1 L_2 \frac{\partial^2 P}{\partial L_1 \partial L_2}$$
$$+ \rho_{1r}\sigma_1\sigma_r L_1 \frac{\partial^2 P}{\partial L_1 \partial r} + \rho_{2r}\sigma_2\sigma_r L_2 \frac{\partial^2 P}{\partial L_2 \partial r}$$
$$+ \widetilde{\mu}_1 L_1 \frac{\partial P}{\partial L_1} + \widetilde{\mu}_2 L_2 \frac{\partial P}{\partial L_2} + \kappa_r [\widetilde{\theta}_r - r]\frac{\partial P}{\partial r} - rP. \tag{5.29}$$

on the interval $L_i \in (0, \widehat{L}_i)$ $(i = 1, 2)$, $t \in (0, T)$ and subject to the boundary conditions

$$P(L_1, L_2, r, T) = 1, \tag{5.30}$$
$$P(\widehat{L}_1, L_2, r, t) = 0, \, P(L_1, \widehat{L}_2, r, t) = 0. \tag{5.31}$$

The parameters $\tilde{\mu}_i$ and $\tilde{\theta}_r$ incorporate the market prices of risk, λ_i, λ_r (assumed to be constant), associated with the leverage ratios and interest rate processes respectively and are defined as

$$\tilde{\mu}_i = \mu_i - \lambda_i \sigma_i, \, (i = 1, 2), \text{ and } \tilde{\theta}_r = \theta_r - \frac{\lambda_r \sigma_r}{\kappa_r}. \tag{5.32}$$

Extending the method of separation of variables used in Hui et al. (2007) to the two-firm case, we seek to express the credit linked note price in the separable form

$$P(L_1, L_2, r, t) = B(r, t)\widehat{P}(L_1, L_2, t), \tag{5.33}$$

where $B(r, t)$ is the risk-free bond price, and $\widehat{P}(L_1, L_2, t)$ satisfies

$$-\frac{\partial \widehat{P}}{\partial t} = \frac{1}{2}\sigma_1^2 L_1^2 \frac{\partial^2 \widehat{P}}{\partial L_1^2} + \rho_{12}\sigma_1\sigma_2 L_1 L_2 \frac{\partial^2 \widehat{P}}{\partial L_1 \partial L_2} + \frac{1}{2}\sigma_2^2 L_2^2 \frac{\partial^2 \widehat{P}}{\partial L_2^2}$$
$$+ [\tilde{\mu}_1 + \rho_{1r}\sigma_1\sigma_r b(t)] L_1 \frac{\partial \widehat{P}}{\partial L_1} + [\tilde{\mu}_2 + \rho_{2r}\sigma_2\sigma_r b(t)] L_2 \frac{\partial \widehat{P}}{\partial L_2}, \tag{5.34}$$

subject to the boundary conditions

$$\widehat{P}(L_1, L_2, T) = 1, \, \widehat{P}(\widehat{L}_1, L_2, t) = 0, \, \widehat{P}(L_1, \widehat{L}_2, t) = 0. \tag{5.35}$$

In (5.34) $b(t)$ is a time-dependent parameter depending on the speed of mean reversion of the spot rate of interest and is given by

$$b(t) = \frac{e^{-\kappa_r(T-t)} - 1}{\kappa_r}. \tag{5.36}$$

Define the volatility adjusted log-leverage ratios $X_i = \ln(L_i/\widehat{L}_i)/\sigma_i$, and denote $\widehat{P}(\widehat{L}_1 e^{\sigma_1 X_1}, \widehat{L}_2 e^{\sigma_2 X_2}, t)$ by $\bar{P}(X_1, X_2, \tau)$, so that in terms of the time-to-maturity variable $\tau = T - t$, the partial differential equation (5.34) becomes

$$\frac{\partial \bar{P}}{\partial \tau} = \frac{1}{2}\frac{\partial^2 \bar{P}}{\partial X_1^2} + \rho_{12}\frac{\partial^2 \bar{P}}{\partial X_1 \partial X_2} + \frac{1}{2}\frac{\partial^2 \bar{P}}{\partial X_2^2} + \gamma_1(\tau)\frac{\partial \bar{P}}{\partial X_1} + \gamma_2(\tau)\frac{\partial \bar{P}}{\partial X_2}, \tag{5.37}$$

on the interval of $X_i \in (-\infty, 0)$ $(i = 1, 2)$, $\tau \in (0, T)$ and subject to the boundary conditions with a new notation that $X_i(0) = Y_i$ $(i = 1, 2)$ at time-to-maturity $\tau = 0$. Thus we write

$$\bar{P}(Y_1, Y_2) \equiv \bar{P}(X_1, X_2, 0) = 1, \tag{5.38}$$
$$\bar{P}(0, X_2, \tau) = 0, \tag{5.39}$$
$$\bar{P}(X_1, 0, \tau) = 0. \tag{5.40}$$

The drift coefficients $\gamma_i(\tau)$ in (5.37) are defined as

$$\gamma_i(\tau) = [\tilde{\mu}_i + \rho_{ir}\sigma_i\sigma_r b(\tau) - \sigma_i^2/2]/\sigma_i, \, (i = 1, 2). \qquad (5.41)$$

The solution to the partial differential equation (5.37) is given by the integral

$$\bar{P}(X_1, X_2, \tau) = \int\limits_{-\infty}^{0} \int\limits_{-\infty}^{0} f(X_1, X_2, Y_1, Y_2; \tau)\bar{P}(Y_1, Y_2)dY_1 dY_2, \qquad (5.42)$$

where $f(X_1, X_2, Y_1, Y_2; \tau)$ is the transition probability density function for transition from the values $X_1(0) = Y_1$ and $X_1(0) = Y_2$ at time-to-maturity $\tau = 0$ below the barriers to the values X_1 and X_2 at time-to-maturity τ within the region $X_1 \in (-\infty, 0)$ and $X_2 \in (-\infty, 0)$.

5.3.3 Method of Images for Constant Coefficients at Certain Values of ρ_{12}

The zero boundary conditions in (5.39)–(5.40) require the solution of the first passage time problem[8] associated with the partial differential equation (5.37). To solve this problem, Chiarella et al. (2012)[9] extend the method of images to the two-dimensional heat equation when it is subject to zero boundary conditions. In order to apply the solution developed in Chiarella et al. (2012), we assume that the partial differential equation (5.37) has constant coefficients. This can be achieved by setting $\rho_{ir} = 0$, so that the drift terms are no longer time-dependent, that is $\gamma_i = [\tilde{\mu}_i - \sigma_i^2/2]/\sigma_i, \, (i = 1, 2)$. Next, we transform the partial differential equation (5.37) with constant coefficients to the two-dimensional heat equation as illustrated in Chiarella et al. (2012) Appendix D. The exact solution for the transition probability density function f is thus given by

$$f(X_1, X_2, Y_1, Y_2; \tau) = \exp\left\{\eta_1(X_1 - Y_1) + \eta_2(X_2 - Y_2) + \xi\tau\right\}$$

$$\times\left[g(X_1, X_2, Y_1, Y_2; \tau) + \sum_{k=1}^{m}(-1)^k g(X_1, X_2, Y_1^k, Y_2^k; \tau)\right], \qquad (5.43)$$

where g is the bivariate transition probability density function for transition from y_1, y_2 to x_1, x_2 in time period τ, and has the form

$$g(x_1, x_2, y_1, y_2; \tau)$$
$$= \frac{1}{2\pi\tau\sqrt{1 - \rho_{12}^2}} \exp\left\{-\frac{(x_1 - y_1)^2 - 2\rho_{12}(x_1 - y_1)(x_2 - y_2) + (x_2 - y_2)^2}{2\tau(1 - \rho_{12}^2)}\right\}, \qquad (5.44)$$

with

$$\eta_1 = \frac{\gamma_2\rho_{12} - \gamma_1}{1 - \rho_{12}^2}, \, \eta_2 = \frac{\gamma_1\rho_{12} - \gamma_2}{1 - \rho_{12}^2}, \qquad (5.45)$$

$$\xi = -\frac{\left(\frac{1}{2}\gamma_1^2 - \rho_{12}\gamma_1\gamma_2 + \frac{1}{2}\gamma_2^2\right)}{1 - \rho_{12}^2}. \qquad (5.46)$$

Here m is the total number of images used to form a closed-loop in such a way that the desired boundary conditions at $X_1 = 0$ and $X_2 = 0$ are preserved, as explained in Chiarella et al. (2012) Appendix D. The Y_1^k and Y_2^k are obtained recursively from the relations between successive images

$$Y_1^k = \begin{cases} -Y_1^{k-1} & \text{for odd } k, \\ Y_1^{k-1} - 2\rho_{12}Y_2^{k-1} & \text{for even } k, \end{cases} \tag{5.47}$$

$$Y_2^k = \begin{cases} Y_2^{k-1} - 2\rho_{12}Y_1^{k-1} & \text{for odd } k, \\ -Y_2^{k-1} & \text{for even } k, \end{cases} \tag{5.48}$$

where $Y_1^1 = -Y_1, Y_2^1 = Y_2 - 2\rho_{12}Y_1$.

Denote by $F(X_1, X_2, \xi)$ the joint survival probability for absorption not yet having occurred during a period of time $\xi = t - t_0$, that is

$$F(X_1, X_2, \xi) = \int_{-\infty}^{0} \int_{-\infty}^{0} f(X_1, X_2, Y_1, Y_2; \xi)dY_1 dY_2, \tag{5.49}$$

where $f(X_1, X_2, Y_1, Y_2; \xi)$ satisfies the same partial differential equation as $\bar{P}$ as in (5.37). Note that the solution (5.43) is obtained by applying the method of images and is valid for the values of ρ_{12} given in Table 5.1, see Chiarella et al. (2012) Appendix E for the proof.

5.3.4 Method of Images for Time-Varying Coefficients at Certain Values of ρ_{12}

If the coefficients in the partial differential equation (5.37) are time-dependent, we extend the approach of Lo et al. (2003) discussed in Subsection 5.2.2 to the two-firm case. Denote by $\bar{P}_\beta$ as an approximation to the exact solution $\bar{P}$ of the partial differential equation (5.37). It satisfies the same partial differential equation

$$\frac{\partial \bar{P}_\beta}{\partial \tau} = \frac{1}{2}\frac{\partial^2 \bar{P}_\beta}{\partial X_1^2} + \rho_{12}\frac{\partial^2 \bar{P}_\beta}{\partial X_1 \partial X_2} + \frac{1}{2}\frac{\partial^2 \bar{P}_\beta}{\partial X_2^2} + \gamma_1(\tau)\frac{\partial \bar{P}_\beta}{\partial X_1} + \gamma_2(\tau)\frac{\partial \bar{P}_\beta}{\partial X_2}. \tag{5.50}$$

With the zero boundary conditions:

$$\bar{P}_\beta(X_1^*(\tau), X_2, \tau) = 0, \ \bar{P}_\beta(X_1, X_2^*(\tau), \tau) = 0, \tag{5.51}$$

where $X_1^*(\tau)$ and $X_2^*(\tau)$ are time-varying barriers along the X_1-axis and X_2-axis respectively. Now X_1 and X_2 are restricted to the region $X_1 \in (-\infty, X_1^*(\tau))$ and $X_2 \in (-\infty, X_2^*(\tau))$.

Table 5.1 The relation between the number of images m required to form the "closed-loop" and the corresponding value of ρ_{12}.

Total No. of Images m	ρ_{12}	Values of ρ_{12}
3	$-\cos\frac{\pi}{2}$	0
5	$-\cos\frac{\pi}{3}$	-0.5
7	$-\cos\frac{\pi}{4}$	-0.707
9	$-\cos\frac{\pi}{5}$	-0.809
:	:	:
13	$-\cos\frac{\pi}{7}$	-0.901
:	:	:
m	$-\cos\frac{2\pi}{(m+1)}$	:

Applying a similar approach as in Subsection 5.2.2, the time-varying barriers are given by

$$X_i^*(\tau) = -\int_0^\tau \gamma_i(v)dv - \beta_i\tau, \, (i = 1, 2). \tag{5.52}$$

The two real adjustable constants β_1 and β_2 control the shape of the time-varying barriers $X_1^*(\tau)$ and $X_2^*(\tau)$ and are chosen so that they remain as close as possible to the exact barriers $X_1 = 0$ and $X_2 = 0$ respectively.

The solution $\bar{P}_\beta$ can be written as

$$\bar{P}_\beta(X_1, X_1, \tau) = \int_{-\infty}^0 \int_{-\infty}^0 f_\beta(X_1, X_2, Y_1, Y_2; \tau)\bar{P}_\beta(Y_1, Y_2)dY_1dY_2, \tag{5.53}$$

where $\bar{P}_\beta(Y_1, Y_2) = 1$ is the initial condition, and $f_\beta(X_1, X_2, Y_1, Y_2; \tau)$ is the joint transition probability density function for the processes restricted to the region $X_i \in (-\infty, X_i^*(\tau))$ ($i = 1, 2$) and has the form

$$f_\beta(X_1, X_2, Y_1, Y_2; \tau)$$
$$= e^{\bar{\eta}_1[X_1-X_1^*(\tau)-Y_1]+\bar{\eta}_2[X_2-X_2^*(\tau)-Y_2]+\bar{\xi}\tau}\Big[g(X_1 - X_1^*(\tau), X_2 - X_2^*(\tau), Y_1, Y_2; \tau)$$
$$+ \sum_{k=1}^m (-1)^k g(X_1 - X_1^*(\tau), X_2 - X_2^*(\tau), Y_1^k, Y_2^k; \tau)\Big]. \tag{5.54}$$

Here $\bar{\eta}_1, \bar{\eta}_2$ and $\bar{\xi}$ are constants given by (see Chiarella et al. (2012) Appendix F for the proof)

$$\bar{\eta}_1 = \frac{-\beta_2\rho_{12} + \beta_1}{1 - \rho_{12}^2}, \, \bar{\eta}_2 = \frac{-\beta_1\rho_{12} + \beta_2}{1 - \rho_{12}^2}, \, \bar{\xi} = -\frac{\frac{1}{2}\beta_1^2 - \rho_{12}\beta_1\beta_2 + \frac{1}{2}\beta_1^2}{1 - \rho_{12}^2}. \tag{5.55}$$

Then the corresponding joint survival probability $F_\beta(X_1, X_2, \xi)$ for absorption not yet having occurred during the period of time $\xi = t - t_0$, is given by

$$F_\beta(X_1, X_2, \xi) = \int_{-\infty}^0 \int_{-\infty}^0 f_\beta(X_1, X_2, Y_1, Y_2; \xi)dY_1dY_2. \tag{5.56}$$

We note that the solutions (5.49) and (5.56) can be expressed in terms of the cumulative bivariate normal distribution function $N_2(\cdot)$. Chiarella et al. (2012)[10] illustrate the implementation of (5.49) and (5.56) in terms of $N_2(\cdot)$, where the computation of the joint survival probabilities is done in an efficient and accurate way. A range of different analytical approximate methods have been proposed for the evaluation of $N_2(\cdot)$. In this chapter, we apply the widely cited Drezner (1978) method, which is based on direct computation of the double integral by the Gauss quadrature method.[11]

We emphasize that the solutions (5.43) and (5.54) obtained by applying the method of images are only valid for the particular values of the correlation coefficient ρ_{12} shown in Table 5.1. In the next subsection we will develop numerical methods to solve the problem for all values of ρ_{12}.

5.3.5 Alternative Methodologies for General Values of ρ_{12}

We apply the alternating direction implicit (ADI) method to develop an efficient numerical solution to the partial differential equation (5.37), which has a cross-derivative term and time-dependent drift terms. A recent study conducted by in't Hout and Welfert (2007) has shown that the ADI finite difference schemes introduced by Douglas and Rachford (1956) are unconditionally stable in applications to two-dimensional partial differential equations with a cross-derivative term and drift terms that is they are stable without any restriction on the time step. Therefore, we apply this scheme to solve the partial differential equation (5.37). An outline of the scheme can be found in Chiarella et al. (2012) Appendix I.

We also develop a Monte Carlo (MC) scheme as a benchmark. By the Feynman–Kac formula, the stochastic differential equations associated with the partial differential equation (5.37) are

$$dL_1 = [\tilde{\mu}_1 + \rho_{1r}\sigma_1\sigma_r b(t)] L_1 dt + \sigma_1 L_1 d\tilde{Z}_1, \tag{5.57}$$

$$dL_2 = [\tilde{\mu}_2 + \rho_{2r}\sigma_2\sigma_r b(t)] L_2 dt + \sigma_2 L_2 d\tilde{Z}_2, \tag{5.58}$$

where $\tilde{Z}_1$ and $\tilde{Z}_2$ are Wiener processes under the risk-neutral measure $\tilde{\mathbb{P}}$, and the Wiener increments $d\tilde{Z}_1$ and $d\tilde{Z}_2$ are correlated with $\mathbb{E}[d\tilde{Z}_1 d\tilde{Z}_2] = \rho_{12}dt$.

We rewrite (5.57) and (5.58) in terms of uncorrelated Wiener processes W_1, W_2, and change variables to the normalized log-leverage ratios $x_i = ln(L_i/\hat{L}_i)$. Then (5.57) and (5.58) become

$$dx_1 = \left[\tilde{\mu}_1 + \rho_{1r}\sigma_1\sigma_r b(t) - \frac{1}{2}\sigma_1^2\right] dt + \sigma_1 dW_1, \tag{5.59}$$

$$dx_2 = \left[\tilde{\mu}_2 + \rho_{2r}\sigma_2\sigma_r b(t) - \frac{1}{2}\sigma_2^2\right] dt + \sigma_2\left(\rho_{12}dW_1 + \sqrt{1 - \rho_{12}^2}dW_2\right). \tag{5.60}$$

Default occurs anytime in the time interval $t \in (0, T)$ if either firm's leverage ratio L_i is on or above the default threshold $\hat{L}_i$ (that is $x_1 \geq 0$ or $x_2 \geq 0$). Therefore, to ensure that default events are captured, the simulation time step Δt should be as small as possible. For example, Figure 5.1 shows that, if $\Delta t = t_2 - t_1$, and the barrier is breached at $t^*(t_1 < t^* < t_2)$ the default event will not be captured, and, a smaller $\Delta t = t^* - t_1$ would be required. The details of the Monte Carlo scheme for evaluating of the joint survival probability are discussed in Chiarella et al. (2012) Appendix J.

5.4 NUMERICAL RESULTS

This section will show some numerical results on joint survival probabilities, default correlations and the price of the credit-linked note. We choose the set of parameters to be consistent with Hui et al. (2007), thus allowing us to compare the effect of going from a one-firm model to a two-firm model. It is quite natural to set the default threshold at $\hat{L}_1 = \hat{L}_2 = 1$, to reflect the fact that the firm's debt level is equal to its asset level. This is equivalent to what is done by Collin-Dufresne and Goldstein (2001) where default occurs when the log-leverage ratio hits the barrier at zero. A firm can also be forced to default when its debt level is close to its asset level, for example 90% $(\hat{L}_i = 0.9)$, or higher than its asset level at 110% $(\hat{L}_i = 1.1)$. However, the framework of the two-firm model can easily be adjusted to handle these more

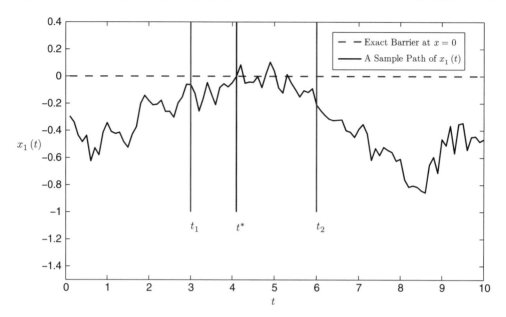

Figure 5.1   A typical path of $x_1(t)$ from a simulation of (5.59), (5.60) with $\Delta_t = t_2 - t_1$.

general situations, because the model is formulated in terms of the normalized log-leverage ratios, $\ln(L_i/\widehat{L}_i)(i = 1, 2)$.

The leverage ratios used for different individual ratings are the typical values of industry medians given by Standard and Poor's (2001). Following the same setting in Hui et al. (2007), the values of the volatility of leverage ratios are assumed to be similar to asset volatilities[12], the values of which are close to the estimates of Delianedis and Geske (2003), who observed that the volatility value is 0.17 for AA and A-rated firms and 0.27 for B-rated firms. Taking these values as reference points, volatilities for other rating categories can be determined. The values of leverage ratios and volatilities used for different individual ratings are shown in Table 5.2, which is adapted from Table 1 of Hui et al. (2007).

The time horizon is fifteen years which is the same as in Hui et al. (2007), who compared the individual default probabilities to S&P historical cumulative default rates for which the available data is up to fifteen years.

We evaluate the joint survival probabilities based on the alternating direction implicit scheme outlined in Appendix I of Chiarella et al. (2012). The spatial steps used are $\Delta x = 8.47E\text{-}03$ and $\Delta y = 6.03E\text{-}03$ and the time step used is $\Delta t = 0.01$. The accuracy of this setting will be discussed in the following subsection and it is found to result in a reasonable level of accuracy (error starts at less than 0.2% and by fifteen years has risen to around 1.3%).

Table 5.2   Parameters used for individual ratings.

Credit Rating	AAA	AA	A	BBB	BB	B	CCC
Leverage ratios L_i (%)	3.1	9.5	17.2	31.5	49.5	53.8	73.2
Volatilities σ_i	0.127	0.156	0.184	0.213	0.241	0.270	0.299

The default correlations are evaluated based on the equation given in (5.23). The individual default probabilities are computed by using Equation (5.16) for the case of constant coefficients and Equation (5.21) for the case of time-varying coefficients. Note that all quantities here are evaluated under the risk-neutral measure.

In the following subsections, we first investigate the accuracy of using different numerical methods; we then study the impact on joint survival probabilities and default correlations of a range of different scenarios, for example, paired firms having different credit quality, different values for correlation coefficients, drift levels, volatilities and initial leverage ratios, and the price of the credit-linked note in Subsection 5.4.8 below.

5.4.1   Accuracy

When the coefficients are constant, the solution obtained by the method of images approach (in Subsection 5.3.3) is exact. Therefore, we use the method of images (MOI) results as a benchmark for comparing the accuracy of the alternating direction implicit (ADI) and Monte Carlo methods.

First, we compare alternating direction implicit results to the exact solution. We consider a CCC–BBB rated pair of firms. The exact analytical solution by the method of images is only valid for specific values of the correlation coefficient ρ_{12} (see Table 5.1), and we use $\rho_{12} = -0.9$ (corresponding to $\rho_{12} = -\cos\frac{\pi}{7}$ in Table 5.1). Note that x and y are volatility normalized log-leverage ratios (i.e. $x = \ln(L_1/\widehat{L}_1)/\sigma_1$, $y = \ln(L_2/\widehat{L}_2)/\sigma_2$), it turns out that in order to increase accuracy, spatial steps may be chosen in a way that the given values of L_1 and L_2 are very close to grid points.

Table 5.3 shows that the relative percentage error of the overall results are smaller than 0.2% for the time step 0.01 and spatial steps less than 0.04. The results are further improved (error $< 0.02\%$) when the time step is 0.001 and spatial steps < 0.01. We have found that other choices of ρ_{12} (for example $\rho_{12} = 0$ and $\rho_{12} = -0.5$) give similar convergence results.

Next, we compare the Monte Carlo results to the exact solution in order to gauge their accuracy. Table 5.4 shows that the relative percentage errors with 3,650 time steps per year (i.e. 10 time steps in a day) is around 1% where the number of paths is $M = 500,000$ or $M = 1,000,000$. The relative percentage errors are reduced further to $< 0.4\%$ when the number of time steps is increased to 36,500 (i.e. 100 time steps in a day).

Table 5.3   Comparison of the joint survival probability based on the ADI method and the exact solution using the MOI. The time period is one year and other parameters used are $L_1 = 73.2\%$, $L_2 = 31.5\%$, $\sigma_1 = 0.299$, $\sigma_2 = 0.213$, $\tilde{\mu}_1 = \tilde{\mu}_2 = 0$, $\rho_{1r} = \rho_{2r} = 0$, $\rho_{12} = -0.9$. These data are for a CCC–BBB rated pair of firms.

Douglas–Rachford ADI Results Compared to Exact Solutions				
Δt	Δx	Δy	$\rho_{12} = -0.9$	Relative % error
0.01	3.19E-02	2.27E-02	0.74884	0.15970%
0.01	8.47E-03	6.03E-03	0.74867	0.13714%
0.001	8.47E-03	6.03E-03	0.74779	0.01886%
0.001	4.21E-03	3.00E-03	0.74774	0.01321%
	MOI exact results		0.74764	–

Table 5.4 Comparison of the joint survival probabilities based on the Monte Carlo method and the exact solution using the MOI. The time period is fifteen years and other parameters used are $L_1 = 73.2\%$, $L_2 = 31.5\%$, $\sigma_1 = 0.299$, $\sigma_2 = 0.213$, $\tilde{\mu}_1 = \tilde{\mu}_2 = 0$, $\rho_{1r} = \rho_{2r} = 0$, $\rho_{12} = -0.9$. These data are for a CCC–BBB rated pair of firms.

	Monte Carlo Results Compared to Exact Solutions		
n	M	$\rho_{12} = -0.9$	Relative % error
3,650	500,000	0.2835	1.1670%
3,650	1,000,000	0.2830	0.9590%
36,500	500,000	0.2812	0.3243%
36,500	1,000,000	0.2804	0.0549%
MOI exact results		0.2803	–

We note that when the coefficients are time-dependent, the solution obtained by the method of images approach is not exact (see Subsection 5.3.4). Therefore, we use the Monte Carlo results as a benchmark for comparing the accuracy of the the approximate solution of MOI results and the ADI results. Table 5.5 shows that the relative percentage error of the approximate results of the MOI over time is $< 1\%$. The relative percentage error of the ADI results overall are less than 1% except at fifteen years (around 1.3%).

5.4.2 The Impact of Correlation between Two Firms

We use the CCC and BBB paired firms to demonstrate the effect of the correlation coefficient. We consider the correlation levels of $\rho_{12} = -0.9, -0.5, -0.1, 0.5$ and 0.9. In order to isolate

Table 5.5 The accuracy of MOI for time-dependent coefficients that was developed in Subsection 5.3.4, and the accuracy of the ADI method. This table was calculated by comparing the results of joint survival probability to the MC results. The time period is fifteen years and other parameters used are $L_1 = 73.2\%$, $L_2 = 31.5\%$, $\sigma_1 = 0.299$, $\sigma_2 = 0.213$, $\tilde{\mu}_1 = \tilde{\mu}_2 = 0$, $\rho_{12} = -0.9$ and $\rho_{1r} = \rho_{2r} = -0.75$. For the MC method we use: $N_t = 36,500$ and $M = 1$ million. For the ADI method we use: $\Delta\tau = 0.01$, $\Delta x = 8.47\text{E-}03$ and $\Delta y = 6.03\text{E-}03$.

Year	MC	MOI	Relative % Error of MOI to MC	ADI	Relative % Error of ADI to MC
1	0.7421	0.7409	-0.1587	0.7419	-0.0230
2	0.5997	0.5988	-0.1562	0.5994	-0.0567
3	0.5249	0.5240	-0.1612	0.5244	-0.0907
4	0.4766	0.4757	-0.1861	0.4760	-0.1330
5	0.4408	0.4405	-0.0652	0.4407	-0.0224
6	0.4134	0.4131	-0.0762	0.4132	-0.0399
7	0.3912	0.3907	-0.1167	0.3908	-0.0846
8	0.3725	0.3719	-0.1555	0.3721	-0.1260
9	0.3563	0.3559	-0.1318	0.3560	-0.1034
10	0.3424	0.3419	-0.1319	0.3420	-0.1016
11	0.3301	0.3297	-0.1411	0.3299	-0.1017
12	0.3193	0.3188	-0.1376	0.3191	-0.0696
13	0.3096	0.3092	-0.1103	0.3097	0.0403
14	0.3009	0.3008	-0.0101	0.3020	0.3698
15	0.2930	0.2939	0.3063	0.2969	1.3387

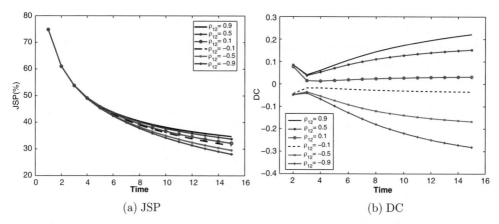

(a) JSP   (b) DC

Figure 5.2 (a) The impact of the correlation coefficient ρ_{12} on joint survival probability; (b) The impact of the correlation coefficient ρ_{12} on default correlation. Here CCC–BBB paired firms are used and the parameters used are $L_1 = 73.2\%$, $L_2 = 31.5\%$, $\sigma_1 = 0.299$, $\sigma_2 = 0.213$, $\widetilde{\mu}_1 = \widetilde{\mu}_2 = 0$, $\rho_{1r} = \rho_{2r} = 0$, $\rho_{12} = -0.9, -0.5, -0.1, 0.5$ and 0.9.

the effects of the drift terms of the leverage ratio processes and correlation of the interest rate process, we set $\widetilde{\mu}_i = 0$ and $\rho_{ir} = 0$ $(i = 1, 2)$. We will study later in this section the impact of these two factors on joint survival probabilities and default correlations.

Figure 5.2(a) plots the joint survival probability of firm i $(i = 1, 2)$ from the beginning to the end of the investment period of fifteen years. It shows the impact on joint survival probabilities of the correlation coefficient ρ_{12} between CCC–BBB paired firms over the time horizon. First, we observe that the joint survival probability declines over time. Second, the joint survival probability decreases with the level of correlation coefficient ρ_{12}. It reflects the fact that when firms' leverage ratios move in opposite directions there is a lower joint survival probability than when the move is in same direction. When firms' leverage ratios move in opposite directions, as the leverage ratio of firm 1 moves closer to the default barrier (and so is more unlikely to survive), firm 2 moves away from the default barrier (and is more likely to survive), so the chance of both firms surviving is small, because the two firms are always in opposite situations. In contrast when firms' leverage ratios move in the same direction, for example, both firms' leverage ratios move away from the default barrier (and both firms are more likely to survive at the same time). In the case of firms' leverage ratios moving closer to the default barrier at the same time, the defaulting probability of both firms defaulting at the same time increases, while the chance of default separately decreases. Recalling (5.24), we see that as a result the joint survival probability increases.

We also observe that the variation of ρ_{12} makes little difference to the value of the joint survival probabilities with there being no discernable difference up to six years and a difference of 6.71% at fifteen years for $\rho_{12} = 0.9$ and -0.9.

Figure 5.2(b) plots the default correlation of firm 1 and firm 2 from the beginning to the end of the investment period of 15 years. The figure shows the impact on default correlations of the correlation coefficient ρ_{12} between a CCC–BBB rated pair of firms. First, we note that the sign of default correlations are the same as the correlation coefficient between two firms' leverage ratios ρ_{12}, which agrees with what was found by Zhou (2001) and Cathcart and El-Jahel (2002). Second, we observe that the magnitude of default correlation values (i.e.

the absolute values) increases as the absolute values of correlation coefficient ρ_{12}. Here, the magnitude of default correlation measures the strength of default of firm 1 relative to firm 2, and the sign of default correlation indicates how this default signal works on firm 2.

In the case of a positive correlation coefficient, firm 2 will be disadvantaged by the default of firm 1. An example is when firm 1 is the creditor of firm 2, as firm 1 defaults, firm 2 becomes distressed and is more likely to default at the same time. If the firms' leverage ratios are positively correlated, as firm 1 defaults, the default signal will cause a rise of firm 2's leverage ratio and it will move closer to the default barrier, thus increasing the probability of firm 2 defaulting at the same time.

In the case of a negative correlation coefficient, firm 2 will benefit from the default of firm 1. For example, if the two firms are competitors, then if firm 1 defaults, firm 2 might profit by obtaining its customers and receiving a discount from its suppliers, as such, firm 2 will be less likely to default at the same time. From the modeling point of view, if the firm's leverage ratios are negatively correlated, the default signal from firm 1 will cause firm 2's leverage ratio to move in the opposite direction and away from the default barrier, thus firm 2 is less likely to default the same time.

We also note that the default correlation values at the very beginning of the time horizon are rising. This is an artificial effect due to division by the very small values of individual default probability for BBB-rated firm (for example, $PD_{BBB} = 6.97838 \times 10^{-5}$). In order to avoid division by the extreme small values, in the remaining figures (part (b) only), the plot of default correlations will start from time equal to three years.

5.4.3 The Impact of Dfferent Credit Quality Paired Firms

This subsection shows the impact of the difference of the credit pairing of firms on joint survival probabilities and default correlations by using CCC–CCC, CCC–BBB and BBB–BBB pairing of firms. To illustrate the effect of positive and negative correlation between two firms, the two non-extreme values of correlation coefficient $\rho_{12} = -0.5, 0.5$ are used here and in the rest of the section.

Figure 5.3(a) shows the impact on joint survival probabilities for CCC–CCC, CCC–BBB and BBB–BBB pairing of firms. First, we observe that the JSP of good credit quality firms is higher than that of low credit quality firms. Second, we find that JSP curves decrease slowly over time for BBB–BBB paired firms, while for CCC–CCC paired firms, JSP curves more rapidly flatten out towards the long run value. We also notice that the effect of leverage ratio correlation on CCC–CCC paired firms is more significant than BBB–BBB paired firm, where lower credit quality firms are more sensitive to the change of correlation levels than are good credit quality firms.

For good credit quality firms, their initial leverage ratios are lower and distant from the default barrier, therefore, the joint survival probability is higher than for lower credit quality firms. If firm 1 has defaulted, firm 2 will experience a rise (decline) in its leverage ratio because of the positive (negative) correlation, however, because of the low initial leverage ratio of firm 2, this rise (decline) in the leverage ratio of firm 2 does not effect significantly its default probability. However, if firm 2 is of low credit quality, its initial leverage ratio is high and closer to the default barrier, this rise (decline) in leverage ratios will increase (decrease) the probability of bringing firm 2 into default.

Figure 5.3(b) illustrates the impact on default correlations. It shows that at a given maturity the absolute values of DC increases as the firm's credit quality decreases. It shows the fact

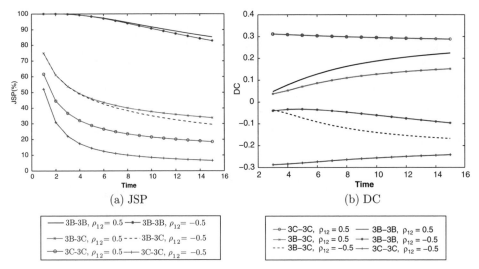

(a) JSP   (b) DC

3B-3B, $\rho_{12}=0.5$	3B-3B, $\rho_{12}=-0.5$
3B-3C, $\rho_{12}=0.5$	3B-3C, $\rho_{12}=-0.5$
3C-3C, $\rho_{12}=0.5$	3C-3C, $\rho_{12}=-0.5$

3C-3C, $\rho_{12}=0.5$	3B-3B, $\rho_{12}=0.5$
3B-3C, $\rho_{12}=0.5$	3B-3B, $\rho_{12}=-0.5$
3B-3C, $\rho_{12}=-0.5$	3C-3C, $\rho_{12}=-0.5$

Figure 5.3 (a) The impact of different credit rated pairing of firms on joint survival probability; (b) The impact of different credit rated pairing of firms on default correlation. Here CCC–CCC, CCC–BBB and BBB–BBB paired firms are used and the parameters used are $L_{CCC} = 73.2\%$, $L_{BBB} = 31.5\%$, $\sigma_{CCC} = 0.299$, $\sigma_{BBB} = 0.213$, $\tilde{\mu}_1 = \tilde{\mu}_2 = 0$, $\rho_{1r} = \rho_{2r} = 0$, $\rho_{12} = -0.5$ and 0.5.

that the lower is the credit quality of paired firms, the higher the strength of default of firm 1 relative to firm 2. However, an interesting result is that for a good quality (BBB–BBB) pair of firms, if they are positively correlated, the default correlation is higher than that of a good quality and low quality pairing of firms. But this situation is reversed (as far as the comparison of the absolute values of default correlation is concerned) if they are negatively correlated. It is difficult to relate this finding to any empirical evidence, though clearly it points to the need for more empirical research in this area. We also observed that DC curves of CCC–CCC increase quickly at the short term and flatten at the long-term, however DC curves of BBB–BBB and CCC–BBB paired firms increase slowly over time. These effects make sense in that the impact of firm 1 defaulting on firm 2 occurs quickly for low credit quality firms, but for good credit quality firms, such an impact increases gradually over time.

5.4.4 The Impact of Volatilities

We consider the volatility levels ranging between $\sigma_i = 0.25$ and 0.5. Figure 5.4(a) shows that the higher the volatility level the lower the joint survival probability. This result seems to reflect the fact that when the proportional change in leverage ratios is more volatile, the chance of the leverage ratio hitting the default point is higher, so the joint survival probability is lower.

Figure 5.4(b) shows that the values of default correlation increase with volatility levels. In terms of the two-firm model, the higher the volatility level, the larger the range in which the leverage ratio can move. For example, when firm 1 defaults, the impact on firm 2's leverage ratio can move with a larger amplitude towards the default barrier (if the firms are positively correlated) than the smaller amplitude when using a smaller volatility level, therefore the

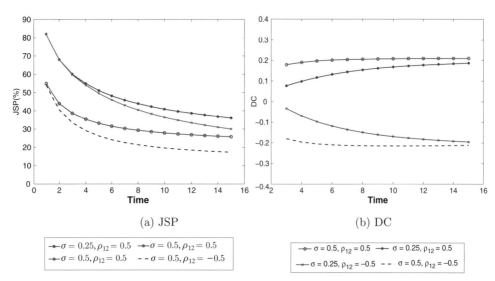

Figure 5.4   (a) The impact of volatility levels on joint survival probability; (b) The impact of volatility levels on default correlation. Here CCC–BBB paired firms are used and the parameters used are $L_1 = 73.2\%$, $L_2 = 31.5\%$, $\sigma_1 = \sigma_2 = \sigma = 0.25$ and 0.5, $\tilde{\mu}_1 = \tilde{\mu}_2 = 0$, $\rho_{1r} = \rho_{2r} = 0$, $\rho_{12} = -0.5$ and 0.5.

probability of firm 2 defaulting at the same time increases. We also note that the effect of changing volatility level on DC is more significant at the short term.

5.4.5   The Impact of Drift Levels

We consider the drift levels $\tilde{\mu}_1 = \tilde{\mu}_2 = -0.1, 0, 0.1$. Note that $\tilde{\mu}_i$ is measured under the risk-neutral measure. Figure 5.5(a) shows that the joint survival probability increases as the drift level decreases. Recall that $\tilde{\mu}_1$ and $\tilde{\mu}_2$ are the growth rates of proportional changes in the leverage ratio, which means the higher the drift level, the higher the leverage ratio over time, and thus the probability of the leverage ratio hitting the default barrier is high, therefore the joint survival probability declines with the rise of the drift level. We note that the joint survival probability is very sensitive to changes of the drift levels. We also observe that the effect of the correlation coefficient ρ_{12} is more pronounced for larger values of drift levels. There is no significant impact of ρ_{12} on joint survival probabilities in the case of negative drift, but a noticeable impact when the value of the drift is positive. For example, if the drift is negative, then this would mean a negative growth rate of the proportional change in leverage ratio on average, where a firm's leverage ratio decreases and moves away from the default barrier over time. If firm 1 defaults, firm 2 will be less impacted because its leverage ratio is heading away from the default barrier even though the correlation coefficient is positive (note that the impact of ρ_{12} is not significant for negative drift), and so is less likely to default at the same time. The situation will reverse itself for a positive drift.

Figure 5.5(b) shows that the default correlation is sensitive to the change in the drift levels. It also shows that the higher the drift level, the higher values of default correlation. If a firm's leverage ratio grows to a higher value on average, the credit quality of the firm decreases dramatically, and the impact on default correlation is similar to the previous discussion (see

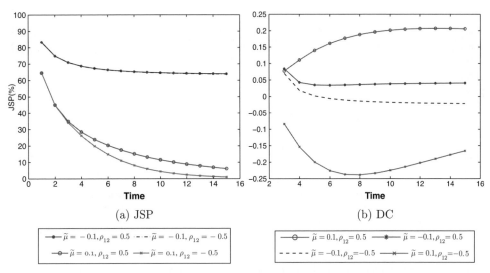

Figure 5.5 (a) The impact of mean levels on joint survival probability; (b) The impact of mean levels on default correlation. Here CCC–BBB paired firms are used and the parameters used are $L_1 = 73.2\%$, $L_2 = 31.5\%$, $\sigma_1 = 0.299$, $\sigma_2 = 0.213$, $\tilde{\mu}_1 = \tilde{\mu}_2 = \tilde{\mu} = -0.1$ and 0.1, $\rho_{1r} = \rho_{2r} = 0$, $\rho_{12} = -0.5$ and 0.5.

Subsection 5.4.3) on the impact of different credit quality firms, that is the lower the credit quality of firms, the higher the strength of default of firm 1 relative to firm 2.

5.4.6   The Impact of Initial Value of Leverage Ratio Levels

We consider the initial value of leverage ratio levels $L_1 = L_2 = 31.5\%$ (corresponding to BBB-rated firms) and $L_1 = L_2 = 80\%$ (corresponding to CCC-rated firms). Figure 5.6(a) shows that joint survival probability generally decreases over time. It shows that the lower the initial value of leverage ratio levels, the higher the joint survival probability. The joint survival probability is more sensitive to the change in the correlation coefficient ρ_{12} when the initial value of leverage ratio is high. This result is similar to the results observed in Figure 5.3(a). Figure 5.6(b) shows that the higher the leverage ratio levels, the higher the default correlations (in absolute values). That is the lower quality of these two firms, the greater is the default probability between them.

5.4.7   Impact of Correlation between Firms and Interest Rates

This subsection presents the impact of interest rate risk on joint survival probabilities and default correlations. Note that when the correlation with the interest ratio process ρ_{ir} is non-zero, the joint survival probability and the probability of individual defaults are related to the parameter κ_r that controls the speed of the mean reversion of the interest rate process via the time-dependent coefficient $b(t)$, which is given in (5.36). We consider $\kappa_r = 1.0$, $\sigma_r = 0.03162$ which is consistent with the values used by Hui et al. (2007). The values of the correlation coefficients between firms' leverage ratios and interest rates are taken at the mid values $\rho_{1r} = \rho_{2r} = -0.5, 0.5$.

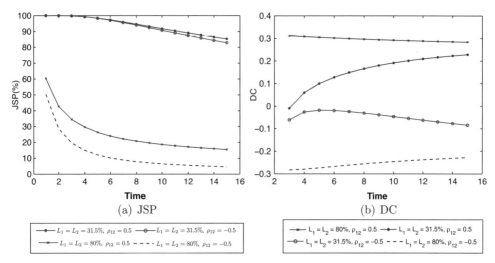

Figure 5.6 (a) The impact of initial leverage ratio levels on joint survival probability; (b) The impact of initial leverage ratio levels on default correlation. Here initial leverage ratios used are in case (i) $L_1 = L_2 = 31.5\%$ and in case (ii) $L_1 = L_2 = 80\%$. Other parameters used are $\sigma_1 = \sigma_2 = 0.213$, $\tilde{\mu}_1 = \tilde{\mu}_2 = 0$, $\rho_{1r} = \rho_{2r} = 0$, $\rho_{12} = -0.5$ and 0.5.

Figure 5.7-(a) shows that the joint survival probability increases as the correlation coefficient ρ_{ir} increases. Recall the definition of $b(t)$ in (5.36), which is a negative time-dependent function, thus the drift of the leverage ratio is actually negatively proportional to the correlation level. Therefore, the higher the correlation coefficient ρ_{ir}, the smaller the drift level, and so the leverage ratio moves to a smaller value on average. At a lower level of leverage ratio, the

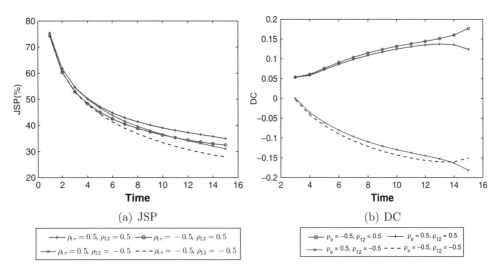

Figure 5.7 (a) The impact of the correlation coefficient ρ_{ir} on joint survival probability; (b) The impact of the correlation coefficient ρ_{ir} on default correlation. Here CCC–BBB paired firms are used and the parameters used are $L_1 = 73.2\%$, $L_2 = 31.5\%$, $\sigma_1 = 0.299$, $\sigma_2 = 0.213$, $\tilde{\mu}_1 = \tilde{\mu}_2 = 0$, $\rho_{12} = -0.5, 0.5$, $\rho_{1r} = \rho_{2r} = -0.5, 0.5$, the maturity of risk-free bond price is $T = 15$, $\kappa_r = 1.0$ and $\sigma_r = 0.03162$.

chance of hitting the default barrier is smaller, and thus the higher the chance of surviving over time. But we note that the effect of the interest rate becomes weaker at about year 13 where the the solid line with crosses and solid line with circles cross. This effect comes from the time-dependent function $b(t)$, and thus the fact that the interest rate impact on the drift rate is time-varying. We also observe that the joint survival probability is not very sensitive to the change of the correlation level to interest rate risk.

Figure 5.7(b) shows that the level of DC increases as the correlation coefficient ρ_{ir} declines, but the impact is not significant. We also observe the time-varying function of interest rate parameters impact on the DC at about year 13, which is similar to the result observed in Figure 5.7(a).

5.4.8 The Price of Credit-Linked Notes

The focus of this chapter has mostly been on default correlations and joint survival probabilities, but the other application of the two-firm model is to price the credit-linked note. In this subsection, we illustrate the impact on the prices of credit-linked notes with respect to variation in the values of correlation coefficients between two firms and with respect to different credit quality paired firms.

Recall from (5.33) that the price of a credit-linked note is the product of the function $\widehat{P}(L_1, L_2, t)$ and the risk-free bond price $B(r, t)$ of the Vasicek (1977) model.[13] For the numerical calculations we use parameters similar to Hui et al. (2007), where $r = 5\%$, $\kappa_r = 1$, $\widetilde{\theta}_r = 5\%$ and $\sigma_r^2 = 0.001$.

Figure 5.8(a) shows the impact on credit-linked note prices of different values of the correlation coefficient ρ_{12} of BBB–CCC paired firms. The parameters used to calculate $\widehat{P}(L_1, L_2, t)$

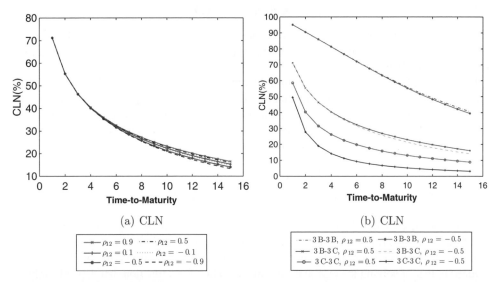

(a) CLN   (b) CLN

Figure 5.8 (a) The impact of the correlation coefficient ρ_{12} on credit-linked note prices, where CCC–BBB paired firms are used; (b) The impact of different credit rated pairings of firms' credit-linked note prices, where CCC–CCC, CCC–BBB and BBB–BBB paired firms are used. Here parameters used are $L_{CCC} = 73.2\%$, $L_{BBB} = 31.5\%$, $\sigma_{CCC} = 0.299$, $\sigma_{BBB} = 0.213$, $r = 5\%$, $\kappa_r = 1$, $\widetilde{\theta}_r = 5\%$, $\sigma_r^2 = 0.001$, $\widetilde{\mu}_1 = \widetilde{\mu}_2 = 0$, $\rho_{1r} = \rho_{2r} = 0$ and the payoff is 1. The correlation coefficient ρ_{12} used in (a) is $\rho_{12} = -0.9, -0.5, -0.1, 0.5$ and 0.9; in (b) is $\rho_{12} = -0.5$ and 0.5.

are the same as in Figure 5.2(a). We observe that the credit-linked note prices decrease with respect to time-to-maturity as the correlation coefficient ρ_{12} decreases. This may be due to the fact that when firms' leverage ratios move in the same direction the price of a credit-linked note is higher than that for moves in the opposite direction. If firms' leverage ratios move in opposite directions, as firm 1's leverage ratio moves closer to the default barrier (and is less likely to survive), firm 2 moves away from the default barrier (and is more likely to survive), so the chance of both firms surviving is small because they are always moving in opposite directions, therefore, the price of credit-linked note is lower.

Figure 5.8(b) shows the impact on credit-linked note prices for BBB–BBB, BBB–CCC and CCC–CCC paired firms over the time-to-maturity. The parameters used to evaluate $\widehat{P}(L_1, L_2, t)$ are the same as in Figure 5.3(a). We observe that the price of a credit linked note of BBB–BBB paired firms is the highest, while the price of CCC–CCC paired firms is the lowest. This result seems sensible since the price of credit-linked note issued by good credit quality firms is higher than that issued by lower credit quality firms.

We also observe that the impact of the correlation coefficient ρ_{12} or the credit quality of firms on the price of credit linked note is the same as the impact on joint survival probabilities (see Figure 5.2(a) and Figure 5.3(a)). This is because the function (5.42) and the joint survival probability function (5.49) both depend principally on the same transition probability density function, as the payoff of the credit-linked note is the par value (see (5.30)). Therefore, if we use the same risk-free bond price function, the impact of other parameters on credit-linked note prices will be similar to the impact on joint survival probabilities as illustrated in the previous subsections.

5.5 CONCLUSION

The aim of this chapter has been to extend the dynamic leverage ratio model of Hui et al. (2007) to the two-firm case so as to study its implications for default correlations and joint survival probabilities.

In Section 5.2, we reviewed the one-firm dynamic leverage ratio model of Hui et al. (2007) for corporate bond pricing. In their model, by using the method of separation of variables, the corporate bond price can be interpreted as the product of a riskless bond price and a function depending only on the firm's leverage ratio. The risk-free bond price has a known closed-form solution, therefore the main focus is on solving for the partial differential equation that depends only on the firm's leverage ratio. We reviewed the method of images for obtaining a closed-form solution in terms of cumulative normal distribution functions and then the time-varying barrier method proposed by Lo et al. (2003) to deal with the case in which parameters are time-varying.

In Section 5.3, we developed the framework for the dynamic leverage ratio model in the two-firm situation for pricing financial derivatives involving default risks among two firms using the credit-linked note as the motivating example. We showed that the problem can be reduced to that of solving the partial differential equation for a function that depends only on the two firms' leverage ratios. We also extended the method of images to the two-dimensional heat equation case and obtained the analytical solution subject to zero boundary conditions. This result was then applied to solve the partial differential equation with constant coefficients. For time-dependent coefficients, we extended the time varying barrier approach to obtain an approximate solution. However, we saw that the limitation of the method of images applied in the two-dimensional situation is that it works only for certain values of the correlation coefficient between the dynamic leverage ratios of firms.

In order to obtain solutions for general values of the correlation coefficient, we considered the alternating direction implicit numerical method in Subsection 5.3.5, in particular the alternating direction implicit numerical scheme based on Douglas and Rachford (1956). We also developed a Monte Carlo scheme to serve as a benchmark. A discussion on the accuracy for different methods is shown in Subsection 5.4.1.

In Section 5.4, we investigated the impact on joint survival probabilities and default correlations of different values of the model parameters. The main findings is that the joint survival probabilities rise if there is (i) a decrease in the leverage ratio volatility, the average mean levels, the initial leverage ratios, or (ii) an increase in the correlation coefficient between leverage ratios processes, or in the correlation coefficient between the leverage ratio and the interest rate processes. We also found that the default correlation (in absolute values) rises if there is (i) an increase in the firms' leverage ratios correlation, or their volatilities, or average mean levels, or initial leverage ratios, or (ii) a decrease in the correlation between firm's leverage ratio and the interest rate.

We note that these findings are based on a study of the impact of the model parameters chosen. Whilst there is a rationale for these values as we have explained, it remains a task for future research to calibrate the types of model discussed here to market data.

NOTES

1. Explicit expressions of the parameters $\mu_L(t)$, $\sigma_L(t)$ and the correlation coefficient $\rho_{Lr}(t)$ related to the firm's value, the firm's total liabilities and interest rate processes can be found in Hui et al. (2006).
2. There are no explicit expressions of the market prices of risk in Hui et al. (2007), and here we simply assume that they are constant.
3. Note that the fact that the drift of the dynamic leverage ratio does not depend on the risk-free interest rate allows the separation of variables technique to work in this situation. A derivation of (5.8) can be found in the Appendix of Hui et al. (2007). Under the risk-neutral measure, the growth rates of the firm's asset value and the firm's total liabilities equal the risk-free interest rate, and as a result $\tilde{\mu}_L(t)$ is independent of the risk-free interest rate.
4. In statistics, the first passage time is the time when a stochastic process first enters a threshold state. Here the first passage time is the first time x crosses the barrier at $x = 0$.
5. See Chiarella et al. (2012) Appendix A for the proof.
6. See Chiarella et al. (2012) Appendix B for the proof.
7. There could be a recovery payment if the default event happens. However, the assumption of zero recovery captures the worst situation in which investors lose all their investment on credit-linked notes. The framework can easily be adjusted to handle the case of some residual recovery rate.
8. Here the first passage time is the first time X_i ($i = 1,2$) crosses the barrier at $X_i = 0$.
9. See Chiarella et al. (2012) Appendix C.
10. See Appendix G of Chiarella et al. (2012).
11. For more details of this method and a comparison of speed and accuracy to other approximate methods, see Agca and Chance (2003).
12. This follows from the assumption that the volatilities of firms' liabilities are not significant, as can be seen from the mathematical relationship between volatilities of leverage ratio, firm's asset values and liabilities in Appendix A of Hui et al. (2006). Under this assumption the volatility of the leverage ratio is then close to the volatility of the firm asset value.
13. The solution of the Vasicek model can be found for example in Wilmott et al. (1995) or Hull (2000).

REFERENCES

Agca, S., Chance, D. M. 2003. Speed and accuracy comparison of bivariate normal distribution approximations for option pricing. Journal of Computational Finance 6(4), 61–96.

Albanese, C., Campolieti, G. 2006. Advanced Derivatives Pricing and Risk Management: Theory, Tools and Hands-on Programming Applications. Elsevier Academic Press.

Black, F., Cox, J. 1976. Valuing corporate securities: Some effects of bond indenture provisions. Journal of Finance 35, 351–367.

Briys, E., de Varenne, F. 1997. Valuing risky fixed rate debt: An extension. Journal of Financial and Quantitative Analysis 32(2), 239–248.

Cathcart, L., El-Jahel, L. 2002. Defaultable bonds and default correlation. Working Paper, Imperial College, London.

Chiarella, C., Huang, M. X., Lo, C. F. 2012. Modelling default correlations in a two-firm model with dynamic leverage ratios. Working Paper, Quantitative Finance Research Centre Working Paper Series, University of Technology, Sydney, No. 304.

Collin-Dufresne, P., Goldstein, R. S. 2001. Do credit spreads reflect stationary leverage ratios? Journal of Finance 56, 1929–1957.

Delianedis, G., Geske, R. 2003. Credit risk and risk neutral default probabilities: information about rating migrations and defaults, EFA 2003 Annual Conference Paper No. 962. Available at SSRN: http://ssrn.com/abstract=424301 or http://dx.doi.org/10.2139/ssrn.424301.

Douglas, J., Rachford, H. H. 1956. On the numerical solution of heat conduction problems in two and three space variables. Transactions of the American Mathematical Society 82, 421–439.

Drezner, Z., 1978. Computation of the bivariate normal integral. Mathematics of Computation 32(141), 277–279.

Hui, C. H., Lo, C. F., Huang, M. X. 2006. Are corporates' target leverage ratios time-dependent? International Review of Financial Analysis 15, 220–236.

Hui, C. H., Lo, C. F., Huang, M. X., Lee, H. C. 2007. Predictions of default probabilities by models with dynamic leverage ratios. Working Paper, Available at SSRN: http://ssrn.com/abstract=1113726.

Hull, J., White, A. 1990. Pricing interest-rate-derivative securities. Review of Financial Studies 3(4), 573–592.

Hull, J. C., 2000. Options, Futures, & Other Derivatives. 4th Ed. Prentice-Hall, Inc.

in't Hout, K. J., Welfert, B. D. 2007. Stability of ADI schemes applied to convection-diffusion equations with mixed derivative terms. Applied Numerical Mathematics 57(1), 19–35.

Lo, C. F., Lee, H. C., Hui, C. H. 2003. A simple approach for pricing Black-Scholes barrier options with time-dependent parameters. Quantitative Finance 3, 98–107.

Longstaff, F. A., Schwartz, E. S. 1995. A simple approach to valuing risky fixed and floating rate debt. Journal of Finance 50(3), 789–819.

Merton, R. 1974. On the pricing of corporate debt: The risk structure of interest rates. Journal of Finance 29, 449–470.

Standard, Poor's, August, 2001. Adjusted key U.S. industrial financial ratios. Corporate Ratings 10.

Vasicek, O. A. 1977. An equilibrium characterisation of term structure. Journal of Financial Economics 5, 177–188.

Wilmott, P., Howison, S., Dewynne, J. 1995. The Mathematics of Financial Derivatives: A Student Introduction. Cambridge University Press.

Zhou, C. 2001. An analysis of default correlations and multiple defaults. The Review of Financial Studies 14, 555–576.

6

A Hierarchical Model of Tail-Dependent Asset Returns

Natalia Puzanova*†

6.1 INTRODUCTION

This chapter introduces a multivariate stochastic model for logarithmic asset returns which accounts for such stylized facts as skewness and excess kurtosis of the marginal probability distributions of asset returns and tail dependence of their joint distributions. The model is derived by evaluating initially independent Brownian motions, grouped by sectors, at the sector-specific stochastic chronometers. This stochastic time represents the irregular information flow relevant for doing business in the respective sector. As the companies in different sectors may also not be entirely independent of one another, the sector-specific stochastic chronometers are themselves evaluated at an independent common stochastic chronometer that represents the flow of general information relevant for all firms in the market, such as changes in the overall macroeconomic conditions.

The specific time-change procedure described is a novelty of my approach. To the best of my knowledge, the first example of utilization of a two-stage stochastic time change in order to generate multidimensional Lévy processes with a *hierarchical* dependence structure. The model's hierarchical structure has the advantage of allowing for a *stronger dependence within* given economic or geographic sectors or certain sub-portfolios as compared to a *weaker dependence between* the sectors/sub-portfolios. Moreover, the magnitude of sector-specific parameters governing tail dependence may vary from one sector to another.

Both distinguishing properties of the specific multivariate model introduced here – (i) the hierarchical dependence structure and (ii) the tail dependence – are highly relevant from the perspective of credit portfolio modeling. The first property is desirable because companies in the same sector usually exhibit stronger dependence. The degree of dependence between the companies operating in different sectors, however, is lower but still different from zero because of the influence of a common macroeconomic environment. The second property is crucial because it allows for mutually dependent extremely negative asset returns. And since the structural approach for credit risk modeling explains the failure of a company as its asset value drops below the value of its outstanding debt, the lower-tail dependence of asset returns makes the clustering of default events possible. In turn, joint default events are the main source of tail risk in a portfolio, as measured by Value at Risk or Expected Shortfall.

---

*Deutsche Bundesbank.

†This chapter presents the author's personal opinions and does not necessarily reflect the views of the Deutsche Bundesbank or its staff.

In summary, this chapter contributes to the existing literature on the (multivariate) stochastic credit risk modeling in the following way:

- It introduces an iterative stochastic time change resulting in a Lévy process with different dependence properties of its multivariate parts. This process might prove advantageous for the dynamic modeling of asset returns, especially if individual returns are skewed and/or leptokurtic and returns from certain predefined sectors exhibit (an asymmetric) tail dependence.
- It investigates the dependence properties of the underlying static marginal copulas. At the lower level of hierarchy, the marginal copulas firstly join single asset returns within given sectors or sub-portfolios, allowing for tail dependence. At the higher level of hierarchy, asset returns from different sectors/sub-portfolios are linked together such that inter-sector dependence is weaker than intra-sector dependence.
- This chapter also provides a practical link between the concept of nested Archimedean copulas for joint characteristic functions and the multivariate distributions arising from an iterative stochastic time change, a link which merits further investigation.
- Considering an application to portfolio credit risk modeling in a static setup, this chapter illustrates the extent of model risk for the portfolio tail risk measures primarily compared to a Gaussian framework with the same asset correlation.
- For the purposes of credit portfolio modeling, this chapter provides an Importance Sampling algorithm for the proposed framework, which may considerably improve simulation efficiency.

Regarding the related literature, I refer to the seminal paper by Madan et al. (1998), in which the authors introduce the Variance Gamma process into the option price literature. I also refer to the papers on using Gamma-time-changed Brownian motion in the *portfolio* context by Luciano and Schoutens (2006) and Moosbrucker (2006), among others. It is worth stressing, however, that those papers which focus on the portfolio settings impose strict restrictions on the choice of dependence parameters. That is, even if certain sub-portfolios can be defined within the portfolio under consideration, the parameters associated with the underlying stochastic time have to be identical across the sub-portfolios. I use a specific model construction to avoid any such parameter restrictions, allowing the sub-portfolio-specific parameters to be set individually.

In general, Lévy processes provide a convenient framework for modelling the empirical phenomena from finance: since the sample paths can have jumps, the generating distributions can be fat-tailed and skewed. I refer to Schoutens (2005) and Cont and Tankov (2003) for more useful information on the application of Lévy processes in finance. The particular interest in time-changed Lévy processes for multivariate modeling arises from the hypothesis of common jump arrivals across different assets, which can induce a strong dependence in the tail. This hypothesis was investigated by Bollerslev et al. (2011), who found strong evidence for asymptotic tail dependence in stock returns, with most of it directly attributable to the systematic jump tails and strong dependencies between the sizes of the simultaneously occurring jumps. Although my model does not account for dependencies between the jumps' sizes, this feature can be incorporated by using (positively) correlated Brownian motions at the first modeling stage. I leave this model extension, however, for future research.

The remainder of this chapter is structured as follows. Section 6.2 provides details on the derivation of the dynamic hierarchical model for tail-dependent asset returns, its static copula and on a Monte Carlo sampling algorithm. Section 6.3 gives an application example and illustrates the model risk in terms of the portfolio tail losses for dependence structures with and without tail dependence. In order to increase the efficiency of portfolio tail risk simulation, Section 6.4 elaborates an Importance Sampling algorithm. Section 6.5 concludes and summarizes the main results.

6.2   THE VARIANCE COMPOUND GAMMA MODEL

I begin this section by deriving a novel multivariate model for logarithmic asset returns which I term Variance Compound Gamma (VCG). The underlying stochastic process is a four-parameter Lévy process designed as a time-changed multivariate uncorrelated Brownian motion with drift. The random time at which the Brownian motion is evaluated is given by an increasing Lévy process (subordinator) termed Compound Gamma (CG). The CG process itself is a time-changed Gamma process evaluated at a random time given by another Gamma process. This specific two-stage time change procedure has a major advantage in that it creates hierarchical dependence between asset return processes.

This section is structured as follows. I introduce the VCG process for dependent asset returns in Subsection 6.2.1. I consider its implications for the static dependence structure in Subsection 6.2.2 and provide a sampling algorithm for the VCG random variables in Subsection 6.2.3. In Subsection 6.2.4 I further investigate the properties of the implicit marginal copulas.

6.2.1   Multivariate Process for Logarithmic Asset Returns

The departing point in the construction of the VCG model are Brownian logarithmic asset returns $\{R_i\}_{t\geq0}$ for n companies under consideration:

$$R_i(t) = \mu_i\, t + \sigma_i\, W_i(t), \quad i = 1, \ldots, n. \tag{6.1}$$

In this equation $\mu \neq 0$ and $\sigma > 0$ are the drift and volatility parameters of the Brownian motion respectively, and $\{W(t)\}_{t\geq0}$ denotes a Wiener process.

Using Brownian definition (6.1) would have several disadvantages, which have been pointed out by Luciano and Schoutens (2006), among others: a symmetric and mesokurtic distribution of the asset return $R_i(t)$ for all $t > 0$; the almost surely continuous sample paths of the return process $\{R_i(t)\}$ and, hence, anticipated default times; a dependence structure which only allows for linear correlation. To overcome those drawbacks, the authors suggest applying a stochastic time change, i.e. evaluating the Brownian process at a random time. The random time is a stochastic process introduced instead of the deterministic variable t. It can be interpreted as business time, i.e, an information arrival process. When the random time used is a subordinator, its main distinguishing properties are non-decreasing sample paths and stationary and independent increments (see Sato, 1999, p. 137). Therefore, as Luciano and Schoutens put it, three following properties of information flow arise:

- the amount of available information cannot decrease,
- the amount of information released within one period of time only depends on the length of that period,
- the amount of new information is not affected by the information already released.

The authors work out the details for a Gamma-time change, which results in a (pure jump) Variance Gamma process of asset returns. They evaluate all n individual Brownian motions on a common Gamma process introducing a stochastic business time in which the general market operates. That way, dependence properties are identical for all firms under consideration, irrespective of the different sectors in which they may operate.

I extend the approach described above by constructing stochastic business times which are specific to certain groups of firms and are subordinated with respect to the common business time of the general macroeconomic environment. Let $\{Y_j(t)\}_{t\geq 0}$, $j = 1, \ldots, m$, where m denotes the number of sectors in the market, be a set of independent subordinators. A process $\{Y_j(t)\}$ represents the information flow only relevant for the firms operating in the sector j. I time-change each of those processes by evaluating them on a common stochastic time denoted by $\{Z^{mrkt}(t)\}_{t\geq 0}$. This common subordinator $\{Z^{mrkt}(t)\}$ represents the general information flow relevant for every firm in the market, irrespective of the sector it belongs to. It may be regarded as information about changes in the overall macroeconomic conditions. According to Sato (1999, p. 201), the resulting interdependent Lévy processes $\{Z_j(t)\}_{t\geq 0}$ with

$$Z_j(t) := Y_j(Z^{mrkt}(t)), \quad j = 1, \ldots, m, \tag{6.2}$$

are again subordinators and thus can act as business times. A business time $\{Z_j(t)\}$ incorporates both the information specific to sector j and the general macroeconomic information.

Now, let $\{R_{ji}\}_{t\geq 0}$ denote the asset return process of the ith firm in sector j. Then, the model for asset returns can be written as follows:

$$R_{ji}(t) = \mu_{ji} Z_j(t) + \sigma_{ji} W_{ji}(Z_j(t)), \tag{6.3}$$
$$Z_j(t) = Y_j(Z^{mrkt}(t)),$$
$$i = 1, \ldots, n_j, \quad j = 1, \ldots, m, \quad \sum_{j=1}^{m} n_j = n,$$

the processes $\{W_{ji}(t)\}$, $\{Y_j(t)\}$ and $\{Z^{mrkt}(t)\}$ being mutually independent. The representation (6.3) can be generalized by adding a drift term $\alpha_{ji} t$ with $\alpha_{ji} \neq 0$.

Thus far, the model specification has been kept very general. It holds for all subordinator settings $\{Z^{mrkt}(t)\}$ and $\{Y_j(t)\}$. In the following sections, however, I provide details on a specific hierarchical model which results from using Gamma subordinators for the business times $\{Z^{mrkt}(t)\}$ and $\{Y_j(t)\}$. The business time $\{Z_j(t)\}$ then arises as a Gamma subordinator evaluated at a Gamma random time and is therefore termed Compound Gamma (CG).

In order to complete the model specification, I need to define parameters of the Gamma processes involved. A Gamma process has independently Gamma-distributed increments characterized by two parameters: the shape parameter $\beta > 0$ and the rate or inverse scale parameter $\lambda > 0$. Thus, for each $t > 0$,

$$Z^{mrkt}(t) \sim \Gamma(t \, \beta_{Z^{mkrt}}, \lambda_{Z^{mkrt}}), \tag{6.4}$$

$$Y_j(t) \sim \Gamma(t \, \beta_{Y_j}, \lambda_{Y_j}). \tag{6.5}$$

Taking into account the scaling property of a Gamma process $\{X(t)\}$:

$$b \, X(t; \beta, \lambda) \overset{d}{=} X(t; \beta, \lambda/b), \quad b > 0 \quad \forall \, t > 0,$$

a scaling constant b may always be chosen such that $\lambda_{Z^{mkrt}}/b = \beta_{Z^{mkrt}}$ holds in (6.4). Furthermore, because any scaling constant of the subordinator $\{Z^{mrkt}(t)\}$ can be absorbed by the shape parameter of the subordinand $\{Y_j(t)\}$ (to see it, put $bZ^{mkrt}(t)$ instead of t into (6.5)), I define $\beta_{Z^{mkrt}} = \lambda_{Z^{mkrt}}$ without loss of generality. Because of

$$\beta_{Z^{mkrt}} = \frac{1}{t} \frac{E[Z^{mrkt}(t)]^2}{\mathrm{var}(Z^{mrkt}(t))} \quad \text{and} \quad \lambda_{Z^{mkrt}} = \frac{E[Z^{mrkt}(t)]}{\mathrm{var}(Z^{mrkt}(t))},$$

$\beta_{Z^{mkrt}} = \lambda_{Z^{mkrt}}$ implies $E[Z^{mrkt}(t)] = t$. Thus, the only free parameter we can decide on for the process parametrization is the variance of the Gamma process $\{Z^{mkrt}(t)\}$ at $t = 1$, which I denote $\kappa_{Z^{mkrt}}$:

$$Z^{mrkt}(t) \sim \Gamma(t/\kappa_{Z^{mrkt}}, 1/\kappa_{Z^{mrkt}}) \quad \forall t > 0. \tag{6.6}$$

Based on a similar scaling property of the CG process, and due to the fact that each scaling constant of the CG subordinator can be absorbed by the parameters of the Brownian motion because of

$$b\, W(t) \overset{d}{=} W(b^2\, t), \quad b > 0 \quad \forall t > 0,$$

I choose $\beta_{Y_j} = \lambda_{Y_j} = 1/\kappa_{Y_j}$ with $\kappa_{Y_j} := \mathrm{var}(Y_j(1))$, i.e.

$$Y_j(t) \sim \Gamma(t/\kappa_{Y_j}, 1/\kappa_{Y_j}) \quad \forall t > 0. \tag{6.7}$$

The CG process $\{Z_j(t)\}$ will thus be characterized by two distribution parameters: $\kappa_{Z^{mrkt}}$ and κ_{Y_j}. One implication of (6.7) is $E[Z_j(t)] = t$, $j = 1, \ldots, m$, i.e. the stochastic business time equals the physical time in expectation.

For a fixed t the random variable $Z_j(t)$ follows the CG distribution. The CG distribution, denoted here by $f(\cdot)$, can be specified as a mixture of a Gamma density function, denoted by $g(\cdot)$, with a stochastic, Gamma-distributed shape parameter:

$$f\left(x; \kappa_{Z^{mrkt}}, \kappa_{Y_j}\right) = \int_0^\infty g\left(x; \frac{\tau}{\kappa_{Y_j}}, \frac{1}{\kappa_{Y_j}}\right) g\left(\tau; \frac{t}{\kappa_{Z^{mrkt}}}, \frac{1}{\kappa_{Z^{mrkt}}}\right) d\tau. \tag{6.8}$$

Thus, I use the term "Compound Gamma" in the sense of Giese (2004) and not in the sense of a mixture over the stochastic *scale* parameter as introduced by Dubey (1970).

Even though the CG distribution does not possess a closed-form expression, it is sufficient to know the Laplace transform (LT) of the CG variable $Z_j(t)$. This LT can be derived using the identity for the subordinated Lévy processes given in Sato (1999, p. 201):

$$\varphi_{Z_j(t)}(v) = \varphi_{Z^{mrkt}(t)}[-t^{-1} \ln\{\varphi_{Y_j(t)}(v)\}]. \tag{6.9}$$

$\varphi_X(\cdot)$ denotes the LT of the positive random variable X with $\varphi_X(v) = E[\exp\{vX\}]$. Since the LT of the Gamma variable $Z^{mrkt}(t)$ is defined as

$$\varphi_{Z^{mrkt}(t)}(v) = (1 + v\kappa_{Z^{mrkt}})^{-t/\kappa_{Z^{mrkt}}}, \tag{6.10}$$

I can write for (6.9):

$$\varphi_{Z_j(t)}(v) = \left[1 + \frac{\kappa_{Z^{mrkt}}}{\kappa_{Y_j}} \ln(1 + v\,\kappa_{Y_j})\right]^{-t/\kappa_{Z^{mrkt}}}. \tag{6.11}$$

Based on (6.11), the characteristic function (cf) of the asset return process defined in (6.3) can be derived according to the formula in Sato (1999, S. 197 f.) for the general case of a Lévy subordination. Because $\{R_{ji}(t)\}_{t \geq 0}$ arises from the Brownian subordination with a CG process, I term this process Variance Compound Gamma (VCG), similarly to the Variance Gamma

process introduced into the option pricing literature by Madan et al. (1998). The VCG process
is a pure-jump Lévy process whose cf is given by:

$$\phi_{R_{ji}(t)}(\theta) = \varphi_{Z_j(t)}[-\psi_{X_{ji}}(\theta)] \tag{6.12}$$

$$= \left[1 + \frac{\kappa_{Z^{mrkt}}}{\kappa_{Y_j}} \ln \left\{ 1 - \kappa_{Y_j} \left(i\theta\mu_{ji} - \frac{1}{2}\theta^2\sigma_{ji}^2 \right) \right\} \right]^{-t/\kappa_{Z^{mrkt}}}, \tag{6.13}$$

where $i\mu_{ji}\theta - \frac{1}{2}\theta^2\sigma_{ji}^2 =: \psi_{X_{ji}}(\theta)$ is the characteristic exponent of the normal distribution.
I denote $\phi_X(\cdot)$ and $\psi_X(\cdot)$ the cf and characteristic exponent of the random variable X, with
$\phi_X(\theta) = E[\exp\{i\theta X\}] = \exp\{\psi_X(\theta)\}$.

The increments of the asset return process $\{R_{ji}(t)\}$ are independently VCG distributed. The
VCG distribution arises from a normal mean-variance mixture with a CG mixing probability
density (see also Equation (6.15) below) and is not known in closed form. Therefore, I only
derive an integral expression for the VCG probability distribution function (pdf) in Appendix
A. Due to its four parameters $\mu_{ji} \in \mathbb{R}$, σ_{ji}, κ_{Y_j}, $\kappa_{Z^{mrkt}} \in \mathbb{R}_+$, the VCG distribution possesses a
flexible functional form, which is illustrated in Figure 6.1 for $t = 1$. The plots were obtained
by means of inverting the cf (6.13) using a fast Fourier transform algorithm.

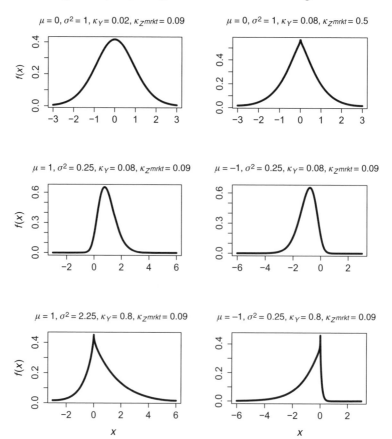

Figure 6.1   The shape of the Variance Compound Gamma probability distribution function for selected
parameters.

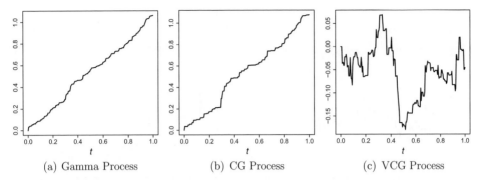

(a) Gamma Process   (b) CG Process   (c) VCG Process

Figure 6.2 Simulated sample paths of Gamma, Compound Gamma (CG) and Variance Compound Gamma (VCG) processes with parameters $\mu = -0.02$, $\sigma = 0.2$, $\kappa_Y = 0.01$ and $\kappa_{Z^{mrkt}} = 0.01$. The sample path of the Gamma process was used as a realization of the stochastic time for the simulation of the CG process. Subsequently, the sample path of the CG process was used for the simulation of the VCG process.

The moments of a VCG process can be calculated as polynomials in cumulants. Because the cf is given by a simple closed formula (6.13), cumulants of a VCG process can be obtained as derivatives of the cumulant-generating function defined as the logarithm of the cf. But for the cumulants of higher orders it is easier to use the mixture representation of the random variable $R_{ji}(t)$ and to apply the law of total cumulance introduced by Brillinger (1969). I give the first four moments – the mean, variance, skewness and excess kurtosis – in Appendix A. Referring to these moments, I describe μ_{ji} as a skewness parameter, σ_{ji} as a variance parameter and κ_{Y_j} and $\kappa_{Z^{mrkt}}$ as kurtosis parameters.

Figure 6.2 shows a simulated sample path of a Gamma process (a), a realization of the CG process based thereupon (b) and a realization of the corresponding VCG process (c). Additionally, I plot in Figure 6.3 some simulated sample paths of two correlated VCG processes. Since the processes arise as the uncorrelated Brownian motions evaluated on the same CG random time, the jumps occur at identical times, but the direction and the size of the jumps are conditionally independent.

In the next subsection I take a closer look at the static multivariate dependence structure implied by the VCG model.

6.2.2 Dependence Structure

In this subsection, I investigate in detail the dependence structure resulting from the two-stage time change described previously. For this purpose, I focus on the static case of the model (6.3) with $t = 1$ and, thus, drop the time index t:

$$R_{ji} = \mu_{ji} Z_j + \sigma_{ji}\sqrt{Z_j} W_{ji}. \tag{6.14}$$

This stochastic model has the following mixture representation:

$$F_{R_{ji}}(x) = \int_0^\infty \Phi\left(\frac{x - \mu_{ji} z_j}{\sigma_{ji}\sqrt{z_j}}\right) dH_{Z_j}(z_j) \tag{6.15}$$

$$= \int_0^\infty \int_0^\infty \Phi\left(\frac{x - \mu_{ji} z_j}{\sigma_{ji}\sqrt{z_j}}\right) dM_{Z_j|Z^{mrkt}}(z_j \mid z^{mrkt}) \, dM_{Z^{mrkt}}(z^{mrkt}).$$

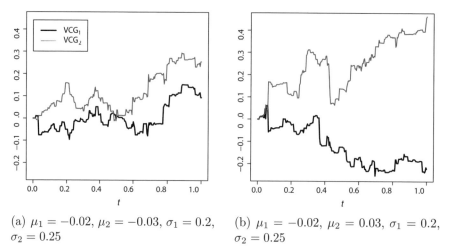

(a) $\mu_1 = -0.02$, $\mu_2 = -0.03$, $\sigma_1 = 0.2$,   (b) $\mu_1 = -0.02$, $\mu_2 = 0.03$, $\sigma_1 = 0.2$,
$\sigma_2 = 0.25$ $\sigma_2 = 0.25$

Figure 6.3 Simulated sample paths of two correlated Variance Compound Gamma (VCG) processes. Each pair of processes was evaluated based on a realization of the Compound Gamma stochastic time with parameters $\kappa_Y = 0.01$ and $\kappa_{Z^{mrkt}} = 0.01$.

This is the mixture representation of the univariate VCG cumulative distribution function (cdf) $F(\cdot)$ of an asset-return variable. Here I denote a Gamma cdf $M(\cdot)$, a CG cdf $H(\cdot)$ and the standard Gaussian cdf $\Phi(\cdot)$. Notation in form $Y \mid X$ refers to the distribution of a random variable Y conditional on X.

The hierarchical framework introduced in Subsection 6.2.1 implies that, firstly, conditional on a realization of the market business time, the asset returns of the companies in one sector are independent from those in other sectors. Additionally, when realizations of the sector-specific business times are also known, the asset returns of all companies become mutually independent. Keeping this in mind and taking (6.15) into account, I can write the mixture representation of the multivariate asset return distribution as follows:

$$F_{\mathbf{R}}(\mathbf{x}) = \int_0^\infty \int_0^\infty \prod_{i=1}^{n_1} \Phi\left(\frac{x_{1i} - \mu_{1i}z_1}{\sigma_{1i}\sqrt{z_1}}\right) dM_{Z_1 \mid Z^{mrkt}}(z_1 \mid z^{mrkt}) \times \cdots \tag{6.16}$$

$$\times \int_0^\infty \prod_{i=1}^{n_m} \Phi\left(\frac{x_{mi} - \mu_{mi}z_m}{\sigma_{mi}\sqrt{z_m}}\right) dM_{Z_m \mid Z^{mrkt}}(z_m \mid z^{mrkt})\, dM_{Z^{mrkt}}(z^{mrkt}).$$

Although the corresponding pdf can only be given in its integral representation (see Appendix A), the joint cf of asset returns has a relatively simple form (cf. (6.9) to (6.13)):

$$\phi_{R_{11},\ldots,R_{mn_m}}(\theta_{11},\ldots,\theta_{mn_m}) = E_{Z^{mrkt}}\left[\prod_{j=1}^m E_{Z_j \mid Z^{mrkt}}\left[\prod_{i=1}^{n_j} \phi_{R_{ji} \mid Z_j}(\theta_{ji})\right]\right] \tag{6.17}$$

$$= \varphi_{Z^{mrkt}}\left[-\sum_{j=1}^m \ln\left\{\varphi_{Y_j}\left(-\sum_{i=1}^{n_j} \psi_{X_{ji}}(\theta_{ji})\right)\right\}\right]$$

$$= \left[1 + \kappa_{Z^{mrkt}} \sum_{j=1}^m \frac{1}{\kappa_{Y_j}} \ln\left\{1 - \kappa_{Y_j} \sum_{i=1}^{n_j}\left(i\theta_{ji}\mu_{ji} - \frac{1}{2}\theta_{ji}^2\sigma_{ji}^2\right)\right\}\right]^{-1/\kappa_{Z^{mrkt}}} \tag{6.18}$$

The linear dependence between VCG-distributed asset returns can be described using the Pearson's correlation coefficient. Correlation between the asset returns of any two firms arises from the common business time they are evaluated at. Within a sector j both the general market and the sector-specific stochastic times take part in the covariation of asset returns. The corresponding correlation coefficient is given by:

$$\text{corr}(R_{ji}, R_{jk}) = \frac{\mu_{ji}\,\mu_{jk}\,(\kappa_{Z^{mrkt}} + \kappa_{Y_j})}{\sqrt{\sigma_{ji}^2 + \mu_{ji}^2(\kappa_{Z^{mrkt}} + \kappa_{Y_j})}\sqrt{\sigma_{jk}^2 + \mu_{jk}^2(\kappa_{Z^{mrkt}} + \kappa_{Y_j})}}. \tag{6.19}$$

For any two firms which belong to the distinct sectors j and l, the covariation is only due to the market business time, and the correlation coefficient is given by:

$$\text{corr}(R_{ji}, R_{lk}) = \frac{\mu_{ji}\,\mu_{lk}\,\kappa_{Z^{mrkt}}}{\sqrt{\sigma_{ji}^2 + \mu_{ji}^2(\kappa_{Z^{mrkt}} + \kappa_{Y_j})}\sqrt{\sigma_{lk}^2 + \mu_{lk}^2(\kappa_{Z^{mrkt}} + \kappa_{Y_l})}}. \tag{6.20}$$

When both skewness parameters have the same sign, the asset returns are positively correlated. Otherwise they are negatively correlated. If at least one of the firms in a pair under consideration has a zero skewness parameter, the asset returns are uncorrelated. Nevertheless, they are still associated, since they are driven by a common factor. Apart from the skewness parameters, the magnitude of the linear correlation coefficient also depends on the variance parameters of the Gamma variables: the smaller a parameter $\kappa_{(\cdot)}$, i.e. the closer the corresponding business time is to the physical time, the smaller the correlation between two asset returns.

As for the non-linear dependence structure, the overall, intra-sector and inter-sector copulas implied by the VCG model of asset returns can only be specified implicitly. The overall implicit copula, which joins n marginal VCG distributions to the multivariate distribution given in (6.16), has the general form:

$$C(u_{11}, \ldots, u_{mn_m}) = F_{\mathbf{R}}\big(F_{R_{11}}^{-1}(u_{11}), \ldots, F_{R_{mn_m}}^{-1}(u_{mn_m})\big). \tag{6.21}$$

The arguments u_{ji} are probability-integral transforms of R_{ji}: $u_{ji} = F_{R_{ji}}(R_{ji} = x_{ji})$. I term the function in (6.21) the hierarchical VCG copula.

Two special cases of marginal copulas of (6.21) are of interest. Firstly, the n_j-dimensional marginal copula of the asset returns $\mathbf{R}_j$, all of which belong to the same sector j:

$$C(u_{j1}, \ldots, u_{jn_j}) = F_{\mathbf{R}_j}\big(F_{R_{j1}}^{-1}(u_{j1}), \ldots, F_{R_{jn_j}}^{-1}(u_{jn_j})\big). \tag{6.22}$$

This copula links marginal VCG distributions which share the same sector-specific business time Z_j to the multivariate VCG distribution of vector $\mathbf{R}_j$, with a joint cdf given by

$$F_{\mathbf{R}_j}(\mathbf{x}_j) = \int_0^\infty \prod_{i=1}^{n_j} F_{R_{ji}|Z_j}(x_{ji})\,dH_{Z_j}(z_j)$$

$$= \int_0^\infty \prod_{i=1}^{n_j} \Phi\left(\frac{x_{ji} - \mu_{ji}z_j}{\sigma_{ji}\sqrt{z_j}}\right) dH_{Z_j}(z_j). \tag{6.23}$$

I term the implicit *intra-sector* copula (6.22) the VCG copula.

The second special case is the marginal copula of asset returns $\mathbf{R}_i$, each of which belongs to a different sector:

$$C(u_{1i}, \ldots, u_{mi}) = F_{\mathbf{R}_i}\left(F_{R_{1i}}^{-1}(u_{1i}), \ldots, F_{R_{mi}}^{-1}(u_{mi})\right). \tag{6.24}$$

This copula joins marginal VCG distributions associated with *different* sector-specific business times Z_j to a multivariate grouped VCG distribution given by[1]

$$F_{\mathbf{R}_i}(\mathbf{x}_i) = \int_0^\infty \prod_{j=1}^m F_{R_{ji}|Z^{mrkt}}(x_{ji}) \, dM_{Z^{mrkt}}(z^{mrkt}) \tag{6.25}$$

$$= \int_0^\infty \prod_{j=1}^m \int_0^\infty \Phi\left(\frac{x_{ji} - \mu_{ji}z_j}{\sigma_{ji}\sqrt{z_j}}\right) g\left(z_j; \frac{z^{mrkt}}{\kappa_{Y_j}}, \frac{1}{\kappa_{Y_j}}\right) dz_j \cdot g\left(z^{mrkt}; \frac{1}{\kappa_{Z^{mrkt}}}, \frac{1}{\kappa_{Z^{mrkt}}}\right) dz^{mrkt}.$$

I term the implicit *inter-sector* copula (6.24) the grouped VCG copula.

Whereas there is no closed solution for the copulas implied by the multivariate VCG setting, it is easy to define explicit copulas for the corresponding joint cfs. In fact, they can be specified in terms of the Hierarchical Archimedean Copulas (HAC), as shown in Appendix B. Interestingly, Wang (1999) has already pointed out that copula formulas can be applied to marginal cfs in order to obtain some new multivariate distributions. This would also allow application of efficient numerical fast Fourier transform techniques for calculating the aggregate loss distribution of correlated risks.

I adapt the copula concept to the marginal cfs of asset returns. Defining the arguments of the copulas as $v_{ji} := \phi_{R_{ji}}(\theta_{ji})$ (see (6.13)) instead of u_{ji}, I obtain the following HAC representation of the overall cf (6.18):

$$C^{Z^{mrkt}}\left(C^{Z_1}\left(v_{11}, \ldots, v_{1n_1}\right), \ldots, C^{Z_m}\left(v_{m1}, \ldots, v_{mn_m}\right)\right)$$

$$= \varphi_{Z^{mrkt}}\left[\sum_{j=1}^m \varphi_{Z^{mrkt}}^{-1} \circ \varphi_{Z_j}\left(\sum_{i=1}^{n_j} \varphi_{Z_j}^{-1}(v_{ji})\right)\right]. \tag{6.26}$$

The corresponding n_j-dimensional marginal Archimedean copula for the companies belonging to the same sector j is then given by:

$$C^{Z_j}\left(v_{j1}, \ldots, v_{jn_j}\right) = \varphi_{Z_j}\left[\sum_{i=1}^{n_j} \varphi_{Z_j}^{-1}(v_{ji})\right] \tag{6.27}$$

and the copula for the companies belonging to different sectors is given by:

$$C^{Z^{mrkt}}\left(v_{1i}, \ldots, v_{mi}\right) = \varphi_{Z^{mrkt}}\left[\sum_{j=1}^m \varphi_{Z^{mrkt}}^{-1}(v_{ji})\right]. \tag{6.28}$$

The functions (6.26) to (6.28) turn out to be exactly the same as the conventional (nested) Archimedean copulas which arise from a Gamma-mixture of powers introduced by Puzanova (2011).

Before I proceed to the properties of the copulas introduced, I first provide a sampling algorithm for the hierarchial VCG model, which I will use for simulation purposes.

6.2.3   Sampling

In order to generate realizations from the hierarchical VCG model with the joint distribution function defined in (6.16), only algorithms for the simulation of Gamma and normal random variables are needed. Such algorithms belong to the standard configuration of statistical and mathematical software.

Sampling algorithm 1: Monte Carlo for VCG asset returns

- Sample $Z^{mrkt} \sim \Gamma(1/\kappa_{Z^{mrkt}}, 1/\kappa_{Z^{mrkt}})$.
- Sample $Z_j \mid Z^{mrkt}$, $j = 1, \dots, m$ from the independent Gamma distributions with parameters $\left(Z^{mrkt}/\kappa_{Y_j}, 1/\kappa_{Y_j}\right)$.
- Sample $W_{ji} \overset{iid}{\sim} N(0, 1)$, $j = 1, \dots, m$, $i = 1, \dots, n_j$.
- The VCG realizations are given by $R_{ji} = \mu_{ji} \cdot (Z_j \mid Z^{mrkt}) + \sigma_{ji}\sqrt{Z_j \mid Z^{mrkt}}\, W_{ji}$.

6.2.4   Copula Properties

To investigate the dependence properties of the copulas implied by the VCG model and to acquire some feeling for their sensitivity with respect to the parameters, I first use the information provided by contour and scatter plots for the two-dimensional marginal copulas.

Since a copula function is invariant under any strictly increasing transformation of the marginal distributions, I begin with the standardization of asset returns. Using the expectation and variance given in (A.1) and (A.2) respectively, I can write the following stochastic representation for standardized asset returns $\tilde{R}_{ji}$:

$$\tilde{R}_{ji} = -\mu_{ji} + \mu_{ji}Z_j + \sqrt{Z_j\left[1 - \mu_{ji}^2(\kappa_{Z^{mrkt}} + \kappa_{Y_j})\right]}\, W_{ji}. \tag{6.29}$$

Now the location parameter is different from zero: it equals $-\mu_{ji}$. The scale parameter of the Gaussian part σ_{ji} has no effect on the dependence structure: it disappears in the course of the standardization procedure.

To produce a contour plot of a two-dimensional VCG copula according to representation (6.22), I make use of the cf of VCG returns, which can be inverted numerically using a fast Fourier transform. The results for various parameter settings are plotted in Figure 6.4. For the usual case of negatively skewed asset returns, the plotted level curves lie between those of the maximum copula and independence copula (i.e. the copula of comonotone random variables): cf. Figure 6.5. Moreover, the positive dependence is stronger for larger values of the shape parameters.

In addition to this information, the scatter plots in Figure 6.6, generated by simulation, provide some insight into how strongly the underlying random variables are associated. On the one hand, we observe more points on the increasing diagonal for the larger parameter values, which is evidence of a stronger positive association. On the other hand, the pairwise realizations cluster in the lower left-hand corner of a unit square, indicating lower-tail dependence which is stronger for larger values of the skewness parameters μ.

It is worth noting that the (tail) dependence properties of the jointly VCG distributed variables change depending on the sign of the skewness parameters. If both skewness parameters are positive, the underlying random variables are still positively dependent and the contour plots do not change, but the points in the scatter plots cluster in the upper right-hand corner of a unit square (a 180° rotation), indicating upper tail dependence. If only one of the skewness

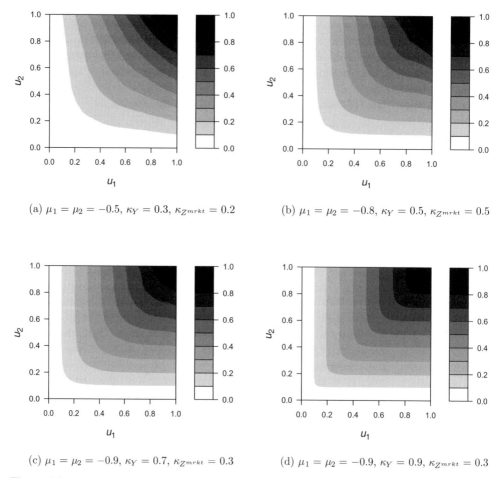

(a) $\mu_1 = \mu_2 = -0.5$, $\kappa_Y = 0.3$, $\kappa_{Zmrkt} = 0.2$

(b) $\mu_1 = \mu_2 = -0.8$, $\kappa_Y = 0.5$, $\kappa_{Zmrkt} = 0.5$

(c) $\mu_1 = \mu_2 = -0.9$, $\kappa_Y = 0.7$, $\kappa_{Zmrkt} = 0.3$

(d) $\mu_1 = \mu_2 = -0.9$, $\kappa_Y = 0.9$, $\kappa_{Zmrkt} = 0.3$

Figure 6.4 Contour plots of a Variance Compound Gamma copula for different parameter values. Obtained using numerical techniques.

parameters is positive, the contour lines lie between those of the independence and minimum copula (i.e. the copula of countermonotone random variables; see Figure 6.5), since the underlying random variables are negatively dependent. As for the scatter plots, they undergo a reflection across either the horizontal (if $\mu_1 < 0$ and $\mu_2 > 0$) or the vertical (if $\mu_1 > 0$ and $\mu_2 < 0$) line which passes through the point 0.5.

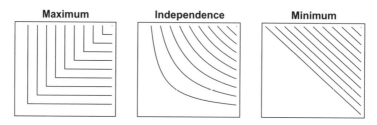

Figure 6.5 Contour plots of the maximum, independence and minimum copulas.

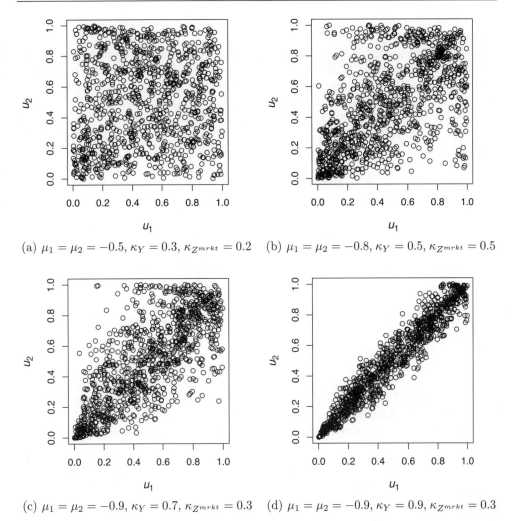

(a) $\mu_1 = \mu_2 = -0.5$, $\kappa_Y = 0.3$, $\kappa_{Z^{mrkt}} = 0.2$ (b) $\mu_1 = \mu_2 = -0.8$, $\kappa_Y = 0.5$, $\kappa_{Z^{mrkt}} = 0.5$

(c) $\mu_1 = \mu_2 = -0.9$, $\kappa_Y = 0.7$, $\kappa_{Z^{mrkt}} = 0.3$ (d) $\mu_1 = \mu_2 = -0.9$, $\kappa_Y = 0.9$, $\kappa_{Z^{mrkt}} = 0.3$

Figure 6.6 Scatter plots of 1,000 realizations from the Variance Compound Gamma copula for different parameter values.

The lower-tail dependence property of the VCG asset return model can be interpreted as the tendency of extreme, negative asset returns to occur simultaneously, e.g. during market crashes and economic downturns. In statistical terms, the coefficient of lower-tail dependence, λ_L (upper-tail dependence, λ_U) expresses the limiting conditional probability of the joint exceedance of a lower (upper) quantile. For continuous cdfs, those coefficients are given as

$$\lambda_L = \lim_{u \downarrow 0} \frac{C(u, u)}{u}, \tag{6.30}$$

$$\lambda_U = \lim_{u \uparrow 1} \frac{1 - 2u + C(u, u)}{1 - u}, \tag{6.31}$$

provided the limits exist. If the corresponding limit lies in the interval (0, 1] then the copula exhibits tail dependence.

Since the tail dependence coefficients for the VCG copula cannot be computed analytically, I use the sample versions of λ_L and λ_U in order to gauge the magnitude of the tail dependence. The sample estimates based on formulae (6.30) and (6.31) are discussed, for example, in Schmidt and Stadtmüller (2006). Let $\{(x_1, y_1), (x_2, y_2), \ldots, (x_s, y_s)\}$ denote a random sample of s observations from a vector (X, Y). Let $k \in (0, 1)$ be the threshold parameter to be chosen by the statistician. Then the sample version of the tail dependence parameters can be represented as:

$$\widehat{\lambda}_L = \frac{1}{k \cdot s} \sum_{i=1}^{s} \mathbf{1}\big(Rank(x_i) \leq k \cdot s \quad \text{and} \quad Rank(y_i) \leq k \cdot s\big), \tag{6.32}$$

$$\widehat{\lambda}_U = \frac{1}{k \cdot s} \sum_{i=1}^{s} \mathbf{1}\big(Rank(x_i) > s - k \cdot s \quad \text{and} \quad Rank(y_i) > s - k \cdot s\big).$$

$\mathbf{1}(A)$ is an indicator function which equals one if condition A is true and zero otherwise. In Figure 6.7 I illustrate the sample tail dependence coefficients for two parameter settings. In both cases the estimate of λ_L shown for $u < 0.5$ converges to a value greater than zero, indicating positive lower-tail dependence. For $u > 0.5$ the estimate of λ_U converges to zero, indicating no upper-tail dependence.

In addition to the graphical illustrations, I report in Table 6.1 the sample version of the concordance measure known as Kendall's tau and the estimates of the lower-tail dependence coefficient for the two-dimensional VCG copula for a wider range of parameters. Both estimates are calculated on the basis of a simulated sample of jointly VCG distributed returns.

Let us first consider the concordance. Again, let $\{(x_1, y_1), (x_2, y_2), \ldots, (x_s, y_s)\}$ denote a random sample of s observations from a vector (X, Y). Then pairs (x_i, y_i) and (x_j, y_j) are

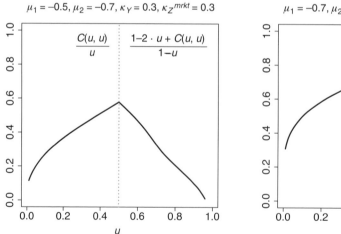
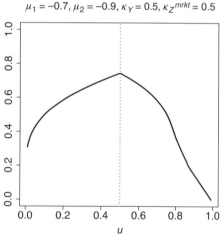

Figure 6.7 A graphical representation of the tail dependence parameters for a two-dimensional Variance Compound Gamma (VCG) copula for two different parameter sets. Lower and upper tail dependence coefficients are given for $u < 0.5$ and $u > 0.5$ respectively, based on 10^6 simulated realizations from the VCG copula.

Table 6.1 Kendall's tau and lower-tail dependence for the VCG copula.

κ_{Zmrkt}	μ	$\widehat{\tau}$			$\widehat{\lambda}_L$		
		$\kappa_Y = 0.2$	$\kappa_Y = 0.5$	$\kappa_Y = 0.9$	$\kappa_Y = 0.2$	$\kappa_Y = 0.5$	$\kappa_Y = 0.9$
0.1	−0.5	0.0450	0.0793	0.1210	0.0624	0.0970	0.1457
	−0.7	0.0841	0.1610	0.2687	0.0766	0.1521	0.2491
	−0.9	0.1420	0.2926	0.5581	0.1076	0.2327	0.4994
0.2	−0.5	0.0543	0.0887	0.1328	0.0706	0.1098	0.1610
	−0.7	0.1151	0.1892	0.3017	0.1010	0.1710	0.2743
	−0.9	0.1935	0.3502	0.6690	0.1465	0.2700	0.6013
0.3	−0.5	0.0671	0.1001	0.1445	0.0797	0.1170	0.1703
	−0.7	0.1408	0.2181	0.3324	0.1191	0.1913	0.3004
	−0.9	0.2420	0.4160	0.8351	0.1809	0.3209	0.7896

Note: The sample versions of Kendall's tau (τ) and of the lower-tail dependence coefficient (λ_L) are given for the two-dimensional Variance Compound Gamma (VCG) copula for various parameter settings. Parameter μ is always identical for a pair of random variables. Each estimate is computed based on 10^6 realizations of the jointly VCG distributed standardized variables specified in (6.29). I use 1% of the smallest realizations in order to estimate λ_L.

concordant if either $x_i < x_j$ and $y_i < y_j$, or $x_i > x_j$ and $y_i > y_j$. They are discordant if either $x_i < x_j$ and $y_i > y_j$, or $x_i > x_j$ and $y_i < y_j$. Nelsen (1999, pp. 125–126) explains that a pair of random variables is concordant if "large" values of one tend to be associated with "large" values of the other and gives the sample version of Kendall's tau as

$$\widehat{\tau} = \frac{c - d}{c + d},$$

where c denotes the number of concordant pairs in the random sample, and d denotes the number of discordant pairs. The consistent monotonically increasing pattern in the estimates of τ listed in the left-hand panel of Table 6.1 indicates that the VCG copula family is ordered with respect to each of the parameters μ, κ_Y and κ_{Zmrkt} in the sense of concordance ordering.

Now we turn to the lower-tail dependence property. I use expression (6.32) for the estimation of the lower-tail dependence coefficient and set the threshold value k to 1%. That is, for the estimation I only use 1% of the smallest realizations. The right-hand panel of Table 6.1 shows that the magnitude of lower-tail dependence for the two-dimensional VCG copula increases in the copula parameters.

Overall, I conclude that the degree of positive dependence and the dependence of extremely negative realizations of jointly VCG distributed random variables both increase along with increasing values of skewness and kurtosis parameters. An evident increase in positive dependence which goes along with rising variance of the common CG mixing variable given by $\text{var}(Z_j) = \kappa_{Zmrkt} + \kappa_{Y_j}$ is due to the growing impact of the stochastic business time on the otherwise independent random variables. An increase in the absolute values of the negative skewness parameters is accompanied by a pronounced rise in lower-tail dependence since negative realizations of both associated random variables are more likely to occur together.

As for the two-dimensional grouped VCG copula, which is the copula of the asset returns of companies operating in two different sectors, I abstain from providing a graphical representation of its dependence properties. The copula's properties do not depend on the sector-specific parameter κ_Y. Moreover, in simulation studies for this copula I could not identify any evidence of lower-tail dependence. Apart from that, the inter-sector, grouped VCG copula is smaller (in the sense of concordance ordering) than the intra-sector VCG copula for two VCG random

Table 6.2   Kendall's tau for the grouped VCG copula.

$\kappa_{Z^{mrkt}}$	$\widehat{\tau}$		
	$\mu = -0.5$	$\mu = -0.7$	$\mu = -0.9$
0.1	0.0132	0.0291	0.0524
0.2	0.0291	0.0556	0.1056
0.3	0.0413	0.0851	0.1606

Note: The sample version of Kendall's tau (τ) is given for the two-dimensional grouped Variance Compound Gamma (VCG) copula. Each estimate is computed based on 10^6 realizations of the jointly grouped VCG distributed standardized variables specified in (6.29). The estimates reported here are those for $\kappa_Y = 0.5$ and various values of parameters $\kappa_{Z^{mrkt}}$ and μ. Parameters κ_Y and μ are always identical for a pair of random variables.

variables, as can be seen by comparing the results in Table 6.2 with those in Table 6.1. Because of the consistent monotonically increasing pattern in the estimates of τ listed in Table 6.2, I conclude that the grouped VCG copula family is ordered with respect to each of the parameters μ and $\kappa_{Z^{mrkt}}$.

Finally, addressing the issue of model risk, I show by means of a graphical representation in Figure 6.8 that the tail behavior of two models with exactly the same correlation of asset returns may be quite different. I compare realizations of two jointly normally distributed random variables with those of the VCG-distributed variables. I calibrate the parameters of the bivariate VCG distribution so as to achieve the level of linear correlation specified for the Gaussian model. In the two upper scatter plots of uncorrelated asset returns we observe that, under the VCG distribution assumptions, large negative and positive realizations are more likely due to positive excess kurtosis driven by variance parameters of Gamma random times. For the positive correlation (the two lower scatter plots), negative skewness of VCG random variables leads to lower-tail dependence not observed in the Gaussian case. Applied for the purposes of credit risk modeling, this implies more joint default events and larger credit portfolio losses, as discussed in the following section.

6.3   AN APPLICATION EXAMPLE

In this section I carry out a simulation study for two credit portfolios in order to show the extent of model risk in terms of significant differences in the tail risk measures obtained for different models of asset returns with an identical linear correlation structure but different tail dependence properties.

The section is organized as follows. In Subsection 6.3.1 the variables of interest are defined: portfolio loss rate, Value at Risk (VaR) and Expected Shortfall (ES). Then the test portfolios and the model parameters used for the simulation exercise are specified in Subsections 6.3.2 and 6.3.3 respectively. Finally, the simulation results for different model settings are discussed in Subsection 6.3.4.

6.3.1   Portfolio Setup

In the tradition of default-only credit risk models, I look at the probability distribution of the portfolio losses at the one-year risk horizon, whereas the losses can only materialize if one or more borrowers default on their obligations. Let n denote the number of borrowers in the

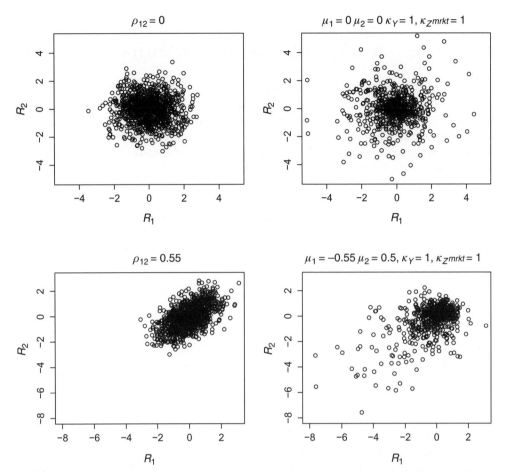

Figure 6.8 Comparison of scatter plots of 1,000 realizations of standardized, normally (left-hand column) and Variance Compound Gamma, VCG (right-hand column) distributed random variables R_1 and R_2 for different parameter values. The VCG parameters are calibrated so as to ensure the same linear correlation in a respective row.

portfolio. For each borrower i there is one, and only one, (aggregate) credit exposure. The borrower's loss given default in monetary units equals its potential exposure at default less the expected recovery. This loss given default of the borrower i divided by the loss given default of the all borrowers in portfolio results in the loss given default rate denoted by LGD_i. The portfolio loss rate, denoted PL, is a random variable defined as the sum over the individual loss rates L_i, with L_i being equal to zero when the ith borrower survives beyond the risk horizon and equal to LGD_i when the borrower defaults on its obligations.

The event of borrower i's default is determined in the tradition of structural credit risk models by the standardized returns on the borrower's market value of assets $\tilde{R}_i$ falling below the default threshold. The default threshold is defined by the borrower's one-year probability of default PD_i and equals $F_{\tilde{R}_i}^{-1}(PD_i)$, $F_{\tilde{R}_i}^{-1}$ being the quantile function of $\tilde{R}_i$. The portfolio setting can be summarized as follows (in this subsection, I drop the sector subscript j for simplicity):

$$PL := \sum_{i=1}^{n} L_i = \sum_{i=1}^{n} LGD_i \cdot \mathbf{1}\left(\tilde{R}_i \leq F_{\tilde{R}_i}^{-1}(PD_i)\right) \tag{6.33}$$

With regard to the distribution of the portfolio loss rate PL, I look for the Value at Risk at a pre-specified confidence level q (VaR_q) and for the Expected Shortfall (ES_q). VaR is commonly used in risk management and controlling as a measure of portfolio credit risk, although it is incoherent (not sub-additive in general; see Acerbi and Tasche, 2001). It quantifies the *minimum* portfolio loss in the worst $(1 - q) \times 100$ per cent of cases. $VaR_q(PL)$ equals the value of the quantile function of the random variable PL:

$$VaR_q(PL) := F_{PL}^{-1}(q) \tag{6.34}$$

ES is a coherent risk measure which quantifies the *expected* portfolio loss in the worst $(1 - q) \times 100$ per cent of cases. $ES_q(PL)$ equals the conditional tail expectation beyond the q-quantile of the portfolio loss distribution augmented by a discontinuity adjustment (see for example Acerbi and Tasche, 2001):

$$ES_q(PL) := E\big[PL \mid PL \geq VaR_q(PL)\big] + VaR_q(PL) \cdot \frac{1 - q - \Pr\{PL \geq VaR_q(PL)\}}{1 - q}.$$
$$\tag{6.35}$$

Portfolio loss rate distribution can be estimated by means of simulation. First, I sample standardized asset returns $\tilde{R}_{ji}$ according to sampling algorithm 1. On that basis, I calculate default indicators as

$$D_i := \mathbf{1}\left(\tilde{R}_i \leq F_{\tilde{R}_i}^{-1}(PD_i)\right). \tag{6.36}$$

To compute of the default barrier $F_{\tilde{R}_i}^{-1}(PD_i)$ within VCG settings, I use a fast Fourier transform algorithm implemented in R and invert the univariate VCG cf numerically.

After s simulation runs I compute Monte Carlo estimators for the portfolio loss distribution, VaR and ES given by:

$$\hat{F}_{PL}(x_q) \equiv \hat{q} = \frac{1}{s} \sum_{k=1}^{s} \mathbf{1}(PL^k \leq x_q),$$

$$\widehat{VaR}_q(PL) = \min\{x \in [0, 1] : \hat{F}_{PL}(x) \geq q\} = PL^s_{\lceil s \cdot q \rceil},$$

$$\widehat{ES}_q(PL) = \frac{\displaystyle\sum_{k=1}^{s} PL^k \, \mathbf{1}\big(PL^k > \widehat{VaR}_q(PL)\big)}{\displaystyle\sum_{k=1}^{s} \mathbf{1}\big(PL^k > \widehat{VaR}_q(PL)\big)}$$

$$+ \widehat{VaR}_q(PL) \frac{1 - \hat{q} - \frac{1}{s} \displaystyle\sum_{k=1}^{s} \mathbf{1}\big(PL^k > \widehat{VaR}_q(PL)\big)}{1 - \hat{q}}$$

respectively. Here $PL^s_{\lceil s \cdot q \rceil}$ represents the order statistic of the sample $\{PL^1, \ldots, PL^s\}$ which is either of order $s \cdot q$ or a larger order next to it.

Table 6.3 Structure of the small test portfolio.

Rating Category	PD(%)	Share in the Total Portfolio LGD(%)	Total # of Debtors
IG: Aa	0.064	35	10
IG: A	0.077	15	10
IG: Baa	0.301	15	25
SG: Ba	1.394	15	25
SG: B	4.477	15	25
SG: C	14.692	5	5

Note: Rating categories and the corresponding probabilities of default (PD) were obtained from Moody's (2006, p. 33). IG indicates investment-grade ratings and SG indicates speculative-grade ratings. The composition of the portfolio is the same as in Puzanova et al. (2009).

6.3.2 Test Portfolios

For the sake of comparability, I use the same two stylized portfolios as in Puzanova (2011) so that I can collate the results on the portfolio tail loss based on VCG settings with those for the Hierarchical Archimedean Copula (HAC) model[2]. Each portfolio consists of only two sub-portfolios corresponding to two sectors $j = 1, 2$.

The smaller portfolio comprises 100 credit exposures as summarized in Table 6.3. 65% of the portfolio LGD is attributed to investment-grade borrowers (IG, sector $j = 1$) and 35% is attributed to speculative-grade borrowers (SG, sector $j = 2$) according to Moody's rating grades/categories. The broad rating grades IG and SG serve in our example as two sectors with different sector-specific dependence parameters. In each rating category 80% of the total LGD is evenly distributed among 20% of the largest debtors. The remaining 20% of the LGD in each rating category is evenly distributed among the remaining debtors. The second, larger portfolio composed of 1,000 credit exposures has the identical PD-LGD structure to that represented in Table 6.3 and is obtained from the small portfolio by subdividing each credit exposure into 10 parts.

6.3.3 Parameter Setup

As mentioned before, I will compare two hierarchical modeling frameworks with lower-tail dependence (VCG and HAC) with a Gaussian model. In order to lay down a benchmark Gaussian specification, I modify the one-factor Gaussian model of the Vasicek type (Vasicek, 1987) accordingly. At the top, market (or portfolio) level of the hierarchy, all obligors in portfolio are related to each other through the systematic factor Z^{mrkt}, which specifies the inter-group covariation. At the lower level of the hierarchy, the sector-specific (or sub-portfolio-specific) systematic factors Y_j specify the additional intra-group covariation. The remaining variation of asset returns is attributed to an idiosyncratic component W_{ji}. To put it formally, the Gaussian model for standardized asset returns turns out to be:

$$\tilde{R}_{ji}^G = \sqrt{\rho_j - \rho_{mrkt}}\, Y_j + \sqrt{\rho_{mrkt}}\, Z^{mrkt} + \sqrt{1 - \rho_j}\, W_{ji}, \quad j = 1, 2. \qquad (6.37)$$

According to (6.37) the intra-sector correlation in the Gaussian setting equals ρ_j, whereas the inter-sector correlation is given by ρ_{mrkt}. These linear correlation coefficients are also binding for the other two portfolio models under consideration.

Table 6.4   Model parameters used in the simulation.

Model	Parameters	Estimates
Gauss	ρ_1	0.0321
	ρ_2	0.1212
	ρ_{mrkt}	0.0144
VCG/HAC	κ_{Y_1}	0.0214
	κ_{Y_2}	0.1309
	$\kappa_{Z_{mrkt}}$	0.0175
	μ_1	-0.9084
	μ_2	-0.9036

Note: The correlation parameters used in the simulation for the Gaussian model are set following Puzanova and Siddiqui (2005). The model parameters for the Variance Compound Gamma model (VCG) and Hierarchical Archimedean Copula (HAC) are calibrated accordingly in order to maintain the same linear correlation structure.

For the sake of comparability, I set the estimates of the kurtosis parameters $\kappa_{Z_{mrkt}}$ and κ_{Y_j} as given in Puzanova (2011). Furthermore, I simplify the issue of parameter calibration for the VCG model by using identical skewness parameters for obligors belonging to the same sector j, i.e. $\mu_{ji} \equiv \mu_j$. I set $\mu_j = \sqrt{\rho_j/(\kappa_{Z_{mrkt}} + \kappa_{Y_j})}$ (cf. (6.19)) to meet the required intra-group asset correlation. The inter-group asset correlation equals ρ_{mrkt}.[3] Table 6.4 lists all parameter values used in the simulation exercise.

6.3.4   Simulation Results

In this subsection I report the results of a Monte Carlo simulation study for two test portfolios under the VCG framework and compare them with the outcomes of the HAC and Gaussian models given in Puzanova (2011). In all simulations I generate $s = 1.5 \times 10^7$ realizations of the portfolio loss variable in order to achieve more precise results.[4]

Figure 6.9 demonstrates that the loss distribution based on the VCG has a heavier tail than the loss distribution arising from non-tail-dependent Gaussian risk factors. For the same dependence parameters $\kappa_{(\cdot)}$, the HAC model leads to even more probability mass in the tail of the portfolio loss distribution due to the stronger lower-tail dependence of the underlying asset returns. The difference between the three models is more pronounced in the case of the larger portfolio because the more debtors there are in the portfolio, the more combinations of joint defaults are possible and the greater effect the tail dependence takes.

As for the measures of the tail portfolio risk, the simulation results on VaR and ES at different levels q are presented in Table 6.5. In all cases the tail risk figures within the Gaussian setting are the lowest and those within the HAC setting are the highest, with the VCG figures lying in between. The absolute difference becomes more distinct the further we go in the tail. In relative terms, the tail risk under VCG (HAC) settings is about 20–25% (25–30%) higher than under Gaussian assumptions for the smaller test portfolio and about 45–55% (55–80%) higher for the larger portfolio. Therefore, the risk of VaR/ES underestimation if the assumption of zero lower tail dependence coefficient is wrong is more pronounced for the larger portfolio.

The results presented above demonstrate that, for the same linear correlation of asset returns, the model risk can be very considerable if the true distributions are skewed, heavy-tailed and/or exhibit lower-tail dependence.

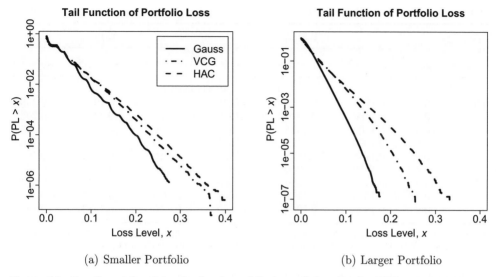

(a) Smaller Portfolio   (b) Larger Portfolio

Figure 6.9 Log-lin graphs of the simulated portfolio loss tail function for different model settings: Gaussian, Variance Compound Gamma (VCG) and Hierarchical Archimedean Copula (HAC). Results are given for two test portfolios containing 100 and 1,000 credit exposures.

The tail dependence properties of the underlying joint distribution of asset returns have a large influence on the tail behavior of the portfolio loss distribution. To illustrate the sensitivity of portfolio tail risk to the skewness and kurtosis parameters of the hierarchial VCG model, I report the VaR for the smaller portfolio for different parameter values in Table 6.6. Here, a simplified model setting is considered with $\kappa_{Y_j} = \kappa_Y$ and $\mu_j = \mu$ for $j = 1, 2$. The simulation results demonstrate the impact of the increasing (absolute) parameter values on the portfolio VaR.

Table 6.5 Comparison of VaR and ES for different settings.

q	$\widehat{VaR}_q$			$\widehat{ES}_q$		
	Gauss	VCG	HAC	Gauss	VCG	HAC
			Smaller portfolio			
0.9900	0.0955	0.1180	0.1210	0.1221	0.1433	0.1514
0.9950	0.1055	0.1355	0.1415	0.1335	0.1593	0.1712
0.9990	0.1455	0.1785	0.1875	0.1634	0.2030	0.2129
0.9995	0.1665	0.1930	0.2080	0.1921	0.2155	0.2330
0.9999	0.1985	0.2330	0.2485	0.2176	0.2582	0.2725
			Larger portfolio			
0.9900	0.0615	0.0905	0.0950	0.0734	0.1102	0.1214
0.9950	0.0695	0.1045	0.1125	0.0814	0.1248	0.1386
0.9990	0.0880	0.1340	0.1530	0.1010	0.1506	0.1781
0.9995	0.0960	0.1465	0.1695	0.1105	0.1650	0.1930
0.9999	0.1135	0.1725	0.2065	0.1256	0.1897	0.2269

Note: VaR and ES at different levels q estimated using simulation for various parameter settings and three different models: Gaussian, Variance Compound Gamma (VCG) and Hierarchical Archimedean Copula (HAC). Results are given for two test portfolios containing 100 and 1,000 credit exposures.

Table 6.6 Parameter sensitivity of the portfolio tail loss.

$\kappa_{Z^{mrkt}}$	μ	$\widehat{VaR}_{0.99}$			$\widehat{VaR}_{0.999}$		
		$\kappa_Y = 0.2$	$\kappa_Y = 0.5$	$\kappa_Y = 0.9$	$\kappa_Y = 0.2$	$\kappa_Y = 0.5$	$\kappa_Y = 0.9$
				VCG model			
0.01	−0.5	0.1055	0.1315	0.1575	0.1670	0.1975	0.2380
	−0.7	0.1180	0.1540	0.1950	0.1775	0.2355	0.2985
	−0.9	0.1300	0.1825	0.2590	0.2010	0.2825	0.3485
0.05	−0.5	0.1090	0.1325	0.1600	0.1730	0.2040	0.2465
	−0.7	0.1245	0.1575	0.1960	0.1915	0.2475	0.3035
	−0.9	0.1350	0.1860	0.2555	0.2110	0.2840	0.3500
0.10	−0.5	0.1165	0.1380	0.1605	0.1765	0.2120	0.2520
	−0.7	0.1300	0.1615	0.2000	0.2070	0.2515	0.3080
	−0.9	0.1455	0.1960	0.2660	0.2245	0.2980	0.3500

Note: Parameter sensitivity of the VaR at different levels q with respect to the parameters of the Variance Compound Gamma model (VCG). Only the small portfolio containing 100 credit exposures is considered.

Finally, I would like to touch on the issue of simulation efficiency for large portfolio losses. For the Monte Carlo simulation carried out in accordance with the sampling algorithm in Subsection 6.2.3, the CPU time needed for 1.5×10^7 simulation runs on the reference computer amounted to 21 min. (1.85 hours) for the VCG model in the case of the smaller (larger) portfolio. The long run times could be unacceptable for those practitioners who have to carry out many computations for large portfolios. Reducing the number of simulation runs would only shorten the computation time at the expense of precision. To avoid such an unfavorable trade off, I recommend always bearing in mind that Importance Sampling (IS) or another variance-reducing technique can be implemented. In the next section I derive a promising IS algorithm for the VCG portfolio model.

6.4 IMPORTANCE SAMPLING ALGORITHM

For the portfolio loss function within a Gaussian framework, a two-stage IS algorithm was introduced by Glasserman and Li (2005). Inspired by that paper, and using results from Kang and Shahabuddin (2005) and Merino and Nyfeler (2004), I work out a three-stage IS algorithm for the hierarchical VCG model based on the exponential tilting of the systematic factors and conditional portfolio loss distribution.

I begin with the transformation of the conditional portfolio loss distribution. The basic idea of the IS in this case is to shift the mean of the conditional loss distribution into the tail so that large losses will not be rare any more and VaR/ES can be estimated more efficiently. To achieve this, the number of default events should be increased in a meaningful way by scaling up conditional PDs.

The simulation approach I used in the previous section was to sample the VCG asset returns and to compute the default indicators (6.36). Alternatively, it is possible to calculate individual PDs *conditional* on the specific realization of the systematic factors (denoted by p)

$$p_{ji} = \Phi \left(\frac{F_{\tilde{R}_{ji}}^{-1}(PD_{ji}) + \mu_{ji} - \mu_{ji} \cdot (Z_j \mid Z^{mrkt})}{\sqrt{(Z_j \mid Z^{mrkt}) \cdot \left[1 - \mu_{ji}^2(\kappa_{Z^{mrkt}} + \kappa_{Y_j})\right]}} \right) \tag{6.38}$$

and to sample default indicators D_{ji} from mutually independent Bernoulli distributions with parameters p_{ji}.

As described in great detail in the literature mentioned at the beginning of this section, the exponential twisting of the conditional PDs will lead to the desirable transformation of the conditional loss distribution. The exponentially twisted conditional PDs are given as:

$$p_{ji}^*(\theta) := \frac{e^{L_{ji}\theta} p_{ji}}{1 - p_{ji} + e^{L_{ji}\theta} p_{ji}}, \tag{6.39}$$

where θ is a common twisting parameter which can be uniquely identified, as will be described later.

Sampling default indicators $D_{ji} \sim Be\left(p_{ji}^*(\theta)\right)$ biases the simulated portfolio loss distribution. The bias can be corrected, however, using, the likelihood ratio, which is the ratio of the original and the transformed conditional loss distributions. This likelihood ratio for the portfolio loss function conditional on the systematic factors $\mathbf{Z} = (Z_1, \ldots, Z_m)$ can be given as follows:

$$L(PL \mid \mathbf{Z}) = \exp\left(-\theta PL + \sum_{j=1}^{m} \sum_{i=1}^{n_j} \ln\left(1 - p_{ji} + e^{L_{ji}\theta} p_{ji}\right)\right). \tag{6.40}$$

The second term in brackets represents the cumulant generating function of the conditional loss distribution, which I denote $C_{PL|\mathbf{Z}}(\theta)$ in the following. The first derivative of this term equals the mean of the distribution. Thus, to shift the mean into the tail, I have to choose the twisting parameter θ such that the mean equals the desirable quantile x_q:

$$\theta_{x_q} := \left\{\theta : \left[C_{PL|\mathbf{Z}}(\theta)\right]' = x_q\right\}. \tag{6.41}$$

It is important to point out that, for practical purposes, there is no need to solve (6.41) repeatedly for different values of x_q. It is sufficient to choose one single value of x_q far in the tail but less than VaR_q. x_q can be chosen, for instance, on the basis of a quick preliminary Monte Carlo simulation. Its exact value does not considerably affect the simulation efficiency.

Let us now go on with the exponential twisting of the Gamma distributed systematic factors. Consider a Gamma variable with the shape parameter β and rate parameter λ. The corresponding exponentially twisted pdf at point x arises as a ratio of the original Gamma pdf and its moment generating function for a $\vartheta < \lambda$ multiplied by $e^{\vartheta x}$:

$$f_*(x; \vartheta) = \frac{e^{\vartheta x}}{(1 - \vartheta/\lambda)^{-\beta}} \cdot \frac{e^{-\lambda x}}{\Gamma(\beta)\lambda^{-\beta}} \cdot x^{\beta-1} = \frac{e^{-\lambda^*(\vartheta)x}}{\Gamma(\beta)(\lambda^*(\vartheta))^{-\beta}} \cdot x^{\beta-1},$$

which turns out to be a Gamma pdf with the parameters β and $\lambda^*(\vartheta) := \lambda - \vartheta$.

According to the above result, I use the Gamma distribution with the parameters $(1/\kappa_{Z^{mrkt}}, 1/\kappa_{Z^{mrkt}} - \vartheta)$ to sample the market-level factor Z^{mkrt}. As for the sector-specific systematic factors, these factors are independently Gamma-distributed conditional on a realization of the market-level factor $Z^{mkrt} = z^{mkrt}$. Thus, I sample the sector-specific factors from mutually independent Gamma distributions with parameters $\left(z^{mkrt}/\kappa_{Y_j}, 1/\kappa_{Y_j} - \vartheta_j\right)$. I will show in the following paragraphs how to select the twisting parameters ϑ and ϑ_j. But first, let us consider the likelihood ratios needed to correct the bias of sampling from the transformed distributions.

The likelihood ratio is always the ratio of the original distribution to the sampling distribution. For the twisted pdf of Z^{mrkt} it can be written as:

$$L(Z^{mrkt}) = \exp\left(-\vartheta Z^{mrkt} - \frac{1}{\kappa_{Z^{mrkt}}} \ln(1 - \kappa_{Z^{mrkt}} \vartheta)\right), \tag{6.42}$$

where the second term in brackets is the cumulant generating function of Z^{mrkt}, which I denote $C_{Z^{mrkt}}(\vartheta)$. For the twisted conditional variables $Z_j \mid Z^{mrkt}$, the likelihood ratio reads:

$$L(\mathbf{Z} \mid Z^{mrkt}) = \exp\left(-\sum_{j=1}^{m} \vartheta_j Z_j \mid Z^{mrkt} - \sum_{j=1}^{m} \frac{Z^{mrkt}}{\kappa_{Y_j}} \ln(1 - \kappa_{Y_j} \vartheta_j)\right). \tag{6.43}$$

I denote the sum of the cumulant generating functions (the second term in brackets) by $\sum_{j=1}^{m} C_{Z_j \mid Z^{mrkt}}(\vartheta_j)$. The overall likelihood ratio is just the product of (6.40), (6.42) and (6.43):

$$L(PL) = \exp\left(-\theta PL - \vartheta Z^{mrkt} - \sum_{j=1}^{m} \vartheta_j Z_j \mid Z^{mrkt}\right.$$

$$\left. + C_{PL \mid \mathbf{Z}}(\theta) + C_{Z^{mrkt}}(\vartheta) + \sum_{j=1}^{m} C_{Z_j \mid Z^{mrkt}}(\vartheta_j)\right). \tag{6.44}$$

In order to choose appropriate values for the twisting parameters ϑ and ϑ_j, I adopt theorem 1 in Bassamboo and Jain (2006, p. 743) for an asymptotically optimal IS algorithm. According to this theorem, and keeping in mind that conditional PDs stochastically increase in the systematic factors, I can set optimal twisting parameters ϑ^* and ϑ_j^* by solving the following optimization problem:

$$\sup_{z^{mrkt}; z_1, \ldots, z_m \in \mathbb{R}_+} \left[\inf_{\vartheta \in (0, 1/\kappa_{Z^{mrkt}})} (C_{Z^{mrkt}}(\vartheta) - \vartheta z^{mrkt}) \right. \tag{6.45}$$

$$\left. + \sum_{j=1}^{m} \inf_{\vartheta_j \in (0, 1/\kappa_{Y_j})} \left(C_{Z_j \mid Z^{mrkt}}(\vartheta_j) - \vartheta_j z_j\right) + \inf_{\theta \in \mathbb{R}_+} (C_{PL \mid \mathbf{Z}}(\theta) - \theta x_q) \right].$$

Expressed in words, I maximize simultaneously (i) the probability that realizations of the systematic factors Z^{mrkt} and $Z_j \mid Z^{mrkt}$ are greater than certain values and (ii) the probability that portfolio loss is greater than a desirable quantile.

In summary, I propose the following IS algorithm for the simulation of the portfolio loss distribution within the VCG setting:

Simulation algorithm 2: Importance Sampling for the VCG framework

- Solve (6.45) to define parameters ϑ^* and ϑ_j^*, $j = 1, \ldots, m$.
- Repeat the following simulation steps s times:
  - Sample $Z^{mrkt} \sim \Gamma(1/\kappa_{Z^{mrkt}}, 1/\kappa_{Z^{mrkt}} - \vartheta^*)$.
  - Sample $Z_j \mid Z^{mrkt}$, $j = 1, \ldots, m$ from independent Gamma distributions with parameters $(Z^{mrkt}/\kappa_{Y_j}, 1/\kappa_{Y_j} - \vartheta_j)$.
  - Compute conditional PDs p_{ji}, $i = 1, \ldots, n_j$, $j = 1, \ldots, m$ as in (6.38).
  - If $x_q \leq E[PL \mid \mathbf{Z}] = \sum_{j=1}^{m} \sum_{i=1}^{n_j} L_{ji} \cdot p_{ji}$, set $\theta_{x_q} = 0$. Otherwise define θ_{x_q} by solving (6.41).
  - Compute twisted conditional PDs $p_{ji}^*(\theta_{x_q})$ according to (6.39).

- Sample D_{ji} from independent Bernoulli distributions with parameters $p_{ji}^*(\theta_{x_q})$.
- Compute portfolio loss rate $PL^k = \sum_{j=1}^m \sum_{i=1}^{n_j} L_{ji} \cdot D_{ji}$ for the kth simulation run.
- Compute the corresponding likelihood ratio $L(PL^k)$ according to (6.44), setting $\theta := \theta_{x_q}$, $\vartheta_{ji} := \vartheta_{ji}^*$ and $\vartheta := \vartheta^*$.
- Compute IS estimators for the portfolio loss rate distribution, VaR and ES as follows:

$$\hat{F}_{PL}^{IS}(x_q) \equiv 1 - \hat{q}^{IS} = 1 - \frac{1}{s}\sum_{k=1}^s L(PL^k)\mathbf{1}(PL^k > x_q),$$

$$\widehat{VaR}_q^{IS}(PL) = \min\left\{x \in [0,1] : \hat{F}_{PL}^{IS}(x) \geq q\right\},$$

$$\widehat{ES}_q^{IS}(PL) = \frac{\sum_{k=1}^s PL^k \cdot L(PL^k)\mathbf{1}\left(PL^k > \widehat{VaR}_q^{IS}(PL)\right)}{\sum_{k=1}^s L(PL^k)\mathbf{1}\left(PL^k > \widehat{VaR}_q^{IS}(PL)\right)}$$

$$+ \widehat{VaR}_q^{IS}(PL)\frac{1 - \hat{q}^{IS} - \frac{1}{s}\sum_{k=1}^s L(PL^k)\mathbf{1}\left(PL^k > \widehat{VaR}_q^{IS}(PL)\right)}{1 - \hat{q}^{IS}}.$$

For the sake of completeness, I should mention that the complete IS procedure would be the following: (i) solving (6.45) for the beginning of the simulation; (ii) sampling Z^{mrkt} accordingly; (iii) solving

$$\sup_{z_1,\ldots,z_m \in \mathbb{R}_+} \left[\sum_{j=1}^m \inf_{\vartheta_j \in (0,1/\kappa_{Y_j})} (C_{Z_j|Z^{mrkt}}(\vartheta_j) - \vartheta_j z_j) + \inf_{\theta \in \mathbb{R}_+}(C_{PL|\mathbf{Z}}(\theta) - \theta x_q)\right] \quad (6.46)$$

to set ϑ_j^* conditionally on Z^{mrkt}; (iv) sampling $Z_j \mid Z^{mrkt}$ accordingly; (v) solving (6.41) to set θ_{x_q} conditional on $Z_j \mid Z^{mrkt}$; (vi) computing conditional PDs and sampling default indicators accordingly. However, the step of solving (6.46) for a particular realization of Z^{mrkt} can be skipped in order to speed up the simulation without any material loss of efficiency. Thus, it is only necessary to solve (6.45) for ϑ^* and ϑ_j^* once before beginning the simulation.

The simulation algorithm 2 leads to a considerable variance reduction of the estimated portfolio quantiles, ensuring stable results for VaR and ES. Table 6.7 clarifies this statement using an example. For both portfolios, I repeat the IS and Monte Carlo simulation scenarios 100 times in order to compute the respective sample variances of the VaR estimates. The results show that, even for as few as 10^3 simulation runs per scenario, the variation of the IS estimates for VaR at different levels q is 1 to 3 orders of magnitude smaller than the variation of Monte Carlo estimates based on 10^4 simulation runs, the CPU time elapsed being fairly comparable. It is noteworthy that IS delivers stable results for portfolio losses far in the tail where Monte Carlo simply fails to generate any sufficient number of realizations because, on average, it only generates $(1-q) \times s$ outcomes which lie beyond the q-quantile of the loss distribution: see Figure 6.10 for an illustration. Overall, I judge the gain in simulation efficiency when using the IS algorithm to be well worth the time needed to implement it into a suitable programming language.

Table 6.7   The variance reduction factor for VaR obtained via IS.

q	Variance Reduction Factor	
	Smaller Portfolio	Larger Portfolio
0.995	1.16	4.17
0.997	2.23	7.62
0.999	10.49	12.96
0.9995	25.87	15.60
0.9997	37.45	24.03
0.9999	140.66	54.54
0.99995	262.43	111.94
0.99997	375.51	129.60
CPU time: MC	1.62 min.	9.13 min.
CPU time: IS	1.73 min.	9.79 min.

Note: For Variance Compound Gamma settings the variance reduction factor for VaR estimation at different levels q is given. It is a ratio of the sample variance of VaR estimated via Monte Carlo (MC) to the sample variance of VaR estimated via Importance Sampling (IS). The sample variances were computed on the basis of 100 independent scenarios, each containing 10^4 simulation runs for MC and 10^3 simulation runs for IS. Also given is the CPU time elapsed. The results are presented for two test portfolios containing 100 and 1,000 credit exposures.

6.5 CONCLUSIONS

The Variance Compound Gamma (VCG) model introduced in this chapter can be useful for modeling asset returns both in univariate and multivariate settings. The underlying VCG process is a pure-jump Lévy process that arises from a two-stage Gamma-time change of a Brownian motion.

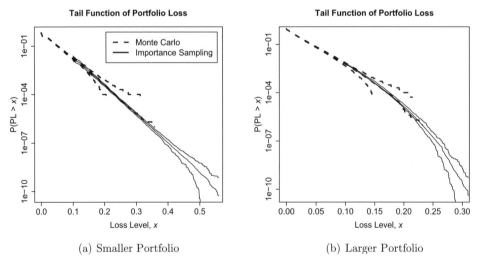

(a) Smaller Portfolio   (b) Larger Portfolio

Figure 6.10   Comparison of Monte Carlo and Importance Sampling simulation results with 10^4 and 10^3 replications respectively. The log-lin graphs of the tail function of the portfolio loss rate give the pointwise means and 95% confidence intervals calculated from 100 independent scenarios.

The *univariate* VCG process can be useful for the univariate modeling of stock returns, for the purposes of option or credit derivative pricing. This stochastic pure-jump process satisfies such important stylized facts about stock returns as asymmetry and excess kurtosis. Moreover, it overcomes the major shortcoming of Black–Scholes-type Gaussian models with continuous sample paths of asset returns and allows for unanticipated default events triggered by sudden asset price shocks. This last feature is crucial to the modeling of credit risk.

The *multivariate* VCG framework has several advantages in terms of modeling credit portfolios. The specific time-change procedure proposed generates a hierarchical dependence structure that allows for a stronger dependence within specified sectors or sub-portfolios and for a weaker dependence between them. The model is flexible enough for a differentiated treatment of sub-portfolios with respect to their tail dependence properties. It is worth noting that, although the copula function underlying the one-period, static VCG model cannot be given explicitly, a closed, copula-like representation of the joint characteristic function of asset returns exists. It is, in fact, the nested Archimedean copula, introduced in Puzanova (2011) and applied to marginal characteristic functions.

This chapter shows that the VCG copula family, which joins the asset returns of firms operating in one particular sector (or attributed to one particular sub-portfolio), is ordered with respect to each of its parameters. This result implies that higher absolute values of the skewness parameters of asset returns and/or of the variance parameters of the underlying stochastic times lead to the stronger dependence as given by the concordance measure known as Kendall's tau. The magnitude of tail dependence also increases in skewness parameters. By contrast, the grouped VCG copula, which joins the asset returns of firms operating in different sectors (or attributed to different sub-portfolios), does not exhibit tail dependence. This copula family is also ordered but has a lower Kendall's tau for comparable parameter values.

From a computational point of view the advantage of the VCG model is that simulation can be easily accomplished using pseudo-random number generators for normal and Gamma distributions which are standard components of mathematical and statistical packages. The variance-reducing Importance Sampling algorithm provided in this chapter increases simulation efficiency considerably.

From the perspective of the portfolio credit risk assessment, the main advantage of the multivariate VCG model over a Gaussian framework is that the stochastic time change applied gives rise to tail dependence of asset returns and, in turn, to clustering default events. Therefore, implementation of the suggested model could have far-reaching implications for risk controlling and banking regulation and, on a large scale, for financial stability. It would result in a more conservative assessment of portfolio credit risk and, consequently, higher capital requirements. Therefore, the model is able to counter the systematic underestimation of credit risk in banking sector – one of the underlying causes of the recent financial turmoil.

APPENDIX A: THE VCG PROBABILITY DISTRIBUTION FUNCTION

The pdf of VCG-distributed asset returns can only be given in its integral representation. Bearing in mind that (i) conditionally on a realization z_j of the sector-specific business time, the asset return of each single firm in sector j is normally distributed and (ii) conditionally on a realization z^{mrkt} of the market business time, the sector-specific subordinators are Gamma-distributed, the VCG pdf can be given as:

$$
f_{R_{ji}(t)}(x) = \int_0^\infty \int_0^\infty \frac{1}{\sigma_{ji}\sqrt{2\pi z_j}} \exp\left(-\frac{(x - \mu_{ji}z_j)^2}{2\sigma_{ji}^2 z_j}\right)
$$

$$
\times \frac{e^{-z_j/\kappa_{Y_j}}}{\Gamma(z^{mrkt}/\kappa_{Y_j})\kappa_{Y_j}^{z^{mrkt}/\kappa_{Y_j}}} z_j^{z^{mrkt}/\kappa_{Y_j}-1} \, dz_j
$$

$$
\times \frac{e^{-z^{mrkt}/\kappa_{Z_{mrkt}}}}{\Gamma(t/\kappa_{Z_{mrkt}})\kappa_{Z_{mrkt}}^{t/\kappa_{Z_{mrkt}}}} (z^{mrkt})^{t/\kappa_{Z_{mrkt}}-1} \, dz^{mrkt}
$$

$$
= \frac{2}{\sigma_{ji}\sqrt{2\pi}\, \Gamma(t/\kappa_{Z_{mrkt}})\kappa_{Z_{mrkt}}^{t/\kappa_{Z_{mrkt}}}} \exp\left(\frac{x\,\mu_{ji}}{\sigma_{ji}^2}\right)
$$

$$
\times \int_0^\infty \frac{e^{-z^{mrkt}/\kappa_{Z_{mrkt}}} \cdot (z^{mrkt})^{t/\kappa_{Z_{mrkt}}-1}}{\Gamma(z^{mrkt}/\kappa_{Y_j})\kappa_{Y_j}^{z^{mrkt}/\kappa_{Y_j}}} \left(\frac{|x|/\sigma_{ji}}{\sqrt{\mu_{ji}^2/\sigma_{ji}^2 + 2/\kappa_{Y_j}}}\right)^{z^{mrkt}/\kappa_{Y_j}-1/2}
$$

$$
\times K_{(z^{mrkt}/\kappa_{Y_j}-1/2)}\left(\frac{|x|}{\sigma_{ji}}\sqrt{\frac{\mu_{ji}^2}{\sigma_{ji}^2} + \frac{2}{\kappa_{Y_j}}}\right) \, dz^{mrkt}.
$$

$\Gamma(\cdot)$ is the gamma function and $K_{(\lambda)}(\cdot)$ denotes the modified Bessel function of the third kind with the index λ:

$$
K_{(\lambda)}(x) = \frac{1}{2}\int_0^\infty y^{\lambda-1} \exp\left[-\frac{x}{2}(y + y^{-1})\right] dy, \quad x > 0.
$$

The mean, variance, skewness and excess kurtosis of the VCG-distributed asset returns are as follows:

$$
E[R_{ji}(t)] = \mu_{ji}t, \tag{A.1}
$$

$$
\text{var}(R_{ji}(t)) = \left[\sigma_{ji}^2 + \mu_{ji}^2(\kappa_{Z_{mrkt}} + \kappa_{Y_j})\right]t, \tag{A.2}
$$

$$
\gamma_1(R_{ji}(t)) = \mu_{ji}(\kappa_{Z_{mrkt}} + \kappa_{Y_j})\frac{3\sigma_{ji}^2 + 2\mu_{ji}^2(\kappa_{Z_{mrkt}} + \kappa_{Y_j})}{\sqrt{t}\left[\sigma_{ji}^2 + \mu_{ji}^2(\kappa_{Z_{mrkt}} + \kappa_{Y_j})\right]^{3/2}}
$$

$$
-\frac{2\mu_{ji}^3\kappa_{Z_{mrkt}}\kappa_{Y_j}}{\sqrt{t}\left[\sigma_{ji}^2 + \mu_{ji}^2(\kappa_{Z_{mrkt}} + \kappa_{Y_j})\right]^{3/2}},
$$

$$
\gamma_2(R_{ji}(t)) = \frac{3(\kappa_{Z_{mrkt}} + \kappa_{Y_j})}{t}\left(2 - \frac{\sigma_{ji}^4}{\left[\sigma_{ji}^2 + \mu_{ji}^2(\kappa_{Z_{mrkt}} + \kappa_{Y_j})\right]^2}\right)
$$

$$
-\frac{\mu_{ji}^2\kappa_{Z_{mrkt}}\kappa_{Y_j}\left[6\sigma_{ji}^2 + \mu_{ji}^2(6\kappa_{Z_{mrkt}} + 7\kappa_{Y_j})\right]}{t\left[\sigma_{ji}^2 + \mu_{ji}^2(\kappa_{Z_{mrkt}} + \kappa_{Y_j})\right]^2}.
$$

The integral representation of the multivariate pdf of VCG-distributed asset returns can be given as follows (for $t = 1$, so the subscript t has been dropped):

$$
f_{\mathbf{R}(t)}(\mathbf{x}) = \frac{2^m}{(2\pi)^{n/2} |\Sigma|^{1/2} \Gamma(t/\kappa_{Z^{mrkt}}) \kappa_{Z^{mrkt}}^{t/\kappa_{Z^{mrkt}}}} \exp(\mathbf{x}' \Sigma^{-1} \boldsymbol{\mu})
$$

$$
\times \int_0^\infty \prod_{j=1}^m \frac{e^{-z^{mrkt}/\kappa_{Z^{mrkt}}} \cdot (z^{mrkt})^{t/\kappa_{Z^{mrkt}}-1}}{\Gamma(z^{mrkt}/\kappa_{Y_j}) \kappa_{Y_j}^{z^{mrkt}/\kappa_{Y_j}}} \left(\frac{\mathbf{Q}_j}{\sqrt{\boldsymbol{\mu}'_j \Sigma_j^{-1} \boldsymbol{\mu}_j + 2/\kappa_{Y_j}}} \right)^{z^{mrkt}/\kappa_{Y_j} - n_j/2}
$$

$$
\times K_{(z^{mrkt}/\kappa_{Y_j} - n_j/2)} \left(\mathbf{Q}_j \cdot \sqrt{\boldsymbol{\mu}'_j \Sigma_j^{-1} \boldsymbol{\mu}_j + \frac{2}{\kappa_{Y_j}}} \right) dz^{mrkt}.
$$

In the expression above I use $\mathbf{x}$, $\boldsymbol{\mu}$ and Σ to denote the vector of arguments of the distribution function, the vector of skewness parameters and the variance matrix of the Gaussian part respectively (all ordered with respect to sectors). The sub-vectors $\mathbf{x}_j$ and $\boldsymbol{\mu}_j$ and the submatrix Σ_j represent the corresponding parameters for sector j. $\mathbf{Q}_j = \sqrt{\mathbf{x}'_j \Sigma_j^{-1} \mathbf{x}_j}$ is the Mahalanobis distance between the elements of $\mathbf{x}_j$.

APPENDIX B: HAC REPRESENTATION FOR THE VCG FRAMEWORK

Starting from expression (6.17), which is based on the marginal *conditional* cfs, I derive in this appendix a copula representation of the joint cf of VCG-distributed asset returns, which is a function of *unconditional* marginal cfs:

$$
E_{Z^{mrkt}} \left[\prod_{j=1}^m E_{Z_j|Z^{mrkt}} \left[\prod_{i=1}^{n_j} \phi_{R_{ji}|Z_j}(\theta_{ji}) \right] \right] \tag{B.1}
$$

$$
= E_{Z^{mrkt}} \left[\prod_{j=1}^m E_{Z_j|Z^{mrkt}} \left[\exp\left(-Z_j \mid Z^{mrkt} \sum_{i=1}^{n_j} \varphi_{Z_j}^{-1} \circ \phi_{R_{ji}}(\theta_{ji}) \right) \right] \right]
$$

$$
= E_{Z^{mrkt}} \left[\prod_{j=1}^m \varphi_{Y_j}^{Z^{mrkt}} \left(\sum_{i=1}^{n_j} \varphi_{Z_j}^{-1} \circ \phi_{R_{ji}}(\theta_{ji}) \right) \right]
$$

$$
= E_{Z^{mrkt}} \left[\exp\left\{ -Z^{mrkt} \sum_{j=1}^m \varphi_{Z^{mrkt}}^{-1} \circ \varphi_{Z_j} \left(\sum_{i=1}^{n_j} \varphi_{Z_j}^{-1} \circ \phi_{R_{ji}}(\theta_{ji}) \right) \right\} \right]
$$

$$
= \varphi_{Z^{mrkt}} \left[\sum_{j=1}^m \varphi_{Z^{mrkt}}^{-1} \circ \varphi_{Z_j} \left(\sum_{i=1}^{n_j} \varphi_{Z_j}^{-1} \circ \phi_{R_{ji}}(\theta_{ji}) \right) \right].
$$

The aim of the transformation, accomplished after the first equality sign, is to proceed to a representation which incorporates unconditional marginal cfs of R_{ji}. To do so, I use the expression (6.12) that implies $\psi_{X_{ji}}(\theta) = -\varphi_{Z_j(t)}^{-1} \circ \phi_{R_{ji}}(\theta)$ by inversion. Conditionally on $Z_j \mid Z^{mrkt}$, the normally distributed idiosyncratic part of asset returns in (6.14) is the only random part. Taken together, these statements imply the following chain of transformations:

$$\phi_{R_{ji}|Z_j}(\theta) = E\left[\exp\left(i\theta\mu_{ji}\, Z_j \mid Z^{mrkt} + i\theta\sigma_{ji}\sqrt{Z_j \mid Z^{mrkt}}\, W_{ji}\right)\right]$$

$$= \exp\left(i\theta\mu_{ji}\, Z_j \mid Z^{mrkt} - \frac{1}{2}\theta^2\sigma_{ji}^2 Z_j \mid Z^{mrkt}\right)$$

$$= \exp\left(Z_j \mid Z^{mrkt} \cdot \psi_{X_{ji}}(\theta)\right)$$

$$= \exp\left(-Z_j \mid Z^{mrkt} \cdot \varphi_{Z_j}^{-1} \circ \phi_{R_{ji}}(\theta)\right)$$

Now, an expression in form $E_{Z_j|Z^{mrkt}}\left[\exp\left(-Z_j \mid Z^{mrkt}\theta_{ji}\right)\right]$ represents the LT of the conditional random variable $Z_j \mid Z^{mrkt}$, which is Gamma distributed. This LT equals the LT of the Gamma random variable Y_j to the power of Z^{mrkt}, which leads to the expression given after the second equality sign in (B.1).

Solving equation (6.9) for φ_{Y_j} and substituting $\varphi_{Y_j}^{Z^{mrkt}}$ by the resulting expression gives the representation after the fourth equality sign in (B.1).

Replacing the remaining expectation operator with the LT of Z^{mrkt} delivers the final line in (B.1). The HAC representation (6.26) follows from this last expression.

NOTES

1. Note that I do not use the term "grouped" copula in the sense of Daul et al. (2003), who introduced a meta t-distribution based on *comonotone* common factors.
2. Currently, the HAC model is only available in a static form, i.e. in contrast to the VCG model there is no HAC representation in terms of stochastic processes governing asset returns. The HAC has the same form as on the right-hand side of 6.17 when applied to probability-integral transforms of asset returns. In this chapter, the nested copula 6.17, however, links single cfs to the joint cf, which results in a joint distribution of asset returns whose hierarchical VCG copula can only be given implicitly.
3. I leave the issue of parameter estimation and further empirical investigations for future work.
4. $s = 1.5 \times 10^7$ corresponds to the Monte Carlo estimation of the small probability $1 - q = 0.0001$ (which is equivalent to the estimation of $VaR_{0.9999}$ in terms of simulation efficiency) with an estimation error of at most 5% at the 95% confidence level.

REFERENCES

Acerbi, C., Tasche, D., May 2001. Expected Shortfall: A Natural Coherent Alternative to Value at Risk, Working Paper.

Bassamboo, A., Jain, S., Dec. 2006. Efficient Importance Sampling for Reduced Form Models in Credit Risk. In: Perrone, L., Wieland, F., Liu, J., Lawson, B., Nicol, D., Fujimoto, R. (Eds), Proceedings of the 2006 Winter Simulation Conference. WSC, Monterey, pp. 741–748.

Bollerslev, T., Todorov, V., Li, S., 2011. Jump Tails, Extreme Dependencies, and the Distribution of Stock Returns, Working Paper.

Brillinger, D., 1969. The Calculation of Cumulants via Conditioning. Annals of the Institute of Statistical Mathematics 21(1), 215–218.

Cont, R., Tankov, P., 2003. Financial Modelling with Jump Processes. CRC Press: London.

Daul, S., De Giorgi, E., Lindskog, F., McNeil, A., 2003. The Grouped t-Copula with an Application to Credit Risk. Risk 16(11), 73–76.

Dubey, S., 1970. Compound Gamma, Beta and F Distributions. Metrika 16(1), 27–31.

Giese, G., 2004. Enhanced CreditRisk+. In: Gundlach, M., Lehrbass, F. (Eds), CreditRisk+ in the Banking Industry. Springer: Berlin, pp. 77–88.

Glasserman, P., Li, J., 2005. Importance Sampling for Portfolio Credit Risk. Management Science 51(11), 1643–1656.

Kang, W., Shahabuddin, P., Dec. 2005. Fast Simulation for Multifactor Portfolio Credit Risk in the *t*-Copula Model. In: Kuhl, M., Steiger, N., Armstrong, F., Joines, J. (Eds), Proceedings of the 2005 Winter Simulation Conference. ACM, Orlando, pp. 1859–1868.

Luciano, E., Schoutens, W., 2006. A Multivariate Jump-Driven Financial Asset Model. Quantitative Finance 6(5), 385–402.

Madan, D., Carr, P., Chang, E., 1998. The Variance Gamma Process and Option Pricing. European Finance Review 2(1), 79–105.

Merino, S., Nyfeler, M., 2004. Applying Importance Sampling for Estimating Coherent Risk Contributions. Quantitative Finance 4(2), 199–207.

Moody's, Jan. 2006. Default and Recovery Rates of Corporate Bond Issuers, 1920-2005. Special Comment, Moody's Investors Service, Global Credit Research.

Moosbrucker, T., Jan. 2006. Pricing CDOs with Correlated Variance Gamma Distributions, Working Paper.

Nelsen, R., 1999. An Introduction to Copulas. Springer Verlag: New York.

Puzanova, N., 2011. A Hierarchical Archimedean Copula for Portfolio Credit Risk Modelling, Deutsche Bundesbank, Discussion Paper, Series 2: Banking and Financial Studies 2011/14.

Puzanova, N., Siddiqui, S., 2005. Default Dependence Among Corporate Bond Issuers: Empirical Evidence from Time Series Data. Applied Financial Economics Letters 1(5), 297–302.

Puzanova, N., Siddiqui, S., Trede, M., 2009. Approximate Value-at-Risk Calculation for Heterogeneous Loan Portfolios: Possible Enhancements of the Basel II Methodology. Journal of Financial Stability 5(4), 374–392.

Sato, K.-I., 1999. Lévy Processes and Infinitely Divisible Distributions. Cambridge University Press: Cambridge.

Schmidt, R., Stadtmüller, U., 2006. Nonparametric Estimation of Tail Dependence. The Scandinavian Journal of Statistics 33(2), 307–335.

Schoutens, W., 2005. Lévy Processes in Finance: Pricing Financial Derivatives. Wiley Series in Probability and Statistics. Wiley: Chichester.

Vasicek, O., Feb. 1987. Probability of Loss on Loan Portfolio, KMV Corporation.

Wang, S., 1999. Discussion on: "Understanding Relationships Using Copulas" by E. Frees and E. Valdez, Jan. 1998. North American Actuarial Journal 3(1), 137–141.

7

Monte Carlo Methods for Portfolio Credit Risk

Tim J. Brereton[1], Dirk P. Kroese[1] and Joshua C. Chan[2]

[1]*The University of Queensland*
[2]*Australian National University*

7.1 INTRODUCTION

The financial crisis of 2007–2009 began with a major failure in the credit markets. The causes of this failure stretch far beyond inadequate mathematical modeling (see Donnelly and Embrechts (2010) and Brigo et al. (2009) for detailed discussions from a mathematical finance perspective). Nevertheless, it is clear that some of the more popular models of credit risk were shown to be flawed. Many of these models were and are popular because they are mathematically tractable, allowing easy computation of various risk measures. More realistic (and complex) models come at a significant computational cost, often requiring *Monte Carlo methods* to estimate quantities of interest.

The purpose of this chapter is to survey the Monte Carlo techniques that are used in portfolio credit risk modeling. We discuss various approaches for modeling the dependencies between individual components of a portfolio and focus on two principal risk measures: Value at Risk (VaR) and Expected Shortfall (ES).

The efficient estimation of credit risk measures is often computationally expensive, as it involves the estimation of small quantiles. Rare-event simulation techniques such as importance sampling can significantly reduce the computational burden, but the choice of a good importance sampling distribution can be a difficult mathematical problem.

Recent simulation techniques such as the cross-entropy method (Rubinstein and Kroese, 2004) have greatly enhanced the applicability of importance sampling techniques by adaptively choosing the importance sampling distribution, based on samples from the original simulation model.

The remainder of this chapter is organized as follows. In Section 7.2 we describe the general model framework for credit portfolio loss. Section 7.3 discusses the crude and importance sampling approaches to estimating risk measures via the Monte Carlo method. Various applications to specific models (including Bernoulli mixture models, factor models, copula models and intensity models) are given in Section 7.4. Many of these models capture empirical features of credit risk, such as default clustering, that are not captured by the standard Gaussian models. Finally, the Appendix contains the essentials on rare-event simulation and adaptive importance sampling.

7.2 MODELING CREDIT PORTFOLIO LOSSES

Portfolio credit risk is usually evaluated in a *static* setting, whereby the loss of a portfolio is modeled via a single random variable L representing the sum of the losses incurred by the individual components of the portfolio; that is,

$$L = \text{Loss}_1 + \cdots + \text{Loss}_n.$$

If the individual losses are independent, the problem of describing the distribution of L reduces to the problem of describing the marginal distribution of each individual loss. However, in practice the individual losses tend to be dependent on each other. It is therefore important to appropriately model the dependence between the $\{\text{Loss}_i\}$.

Losses can result from changes in credit quality as well as from default. For simplicity we will only consider default events. We write each individual loss as the product of the loss incurred if the individual component defaults and a Bernoulli (that is, indicator) random variable that takes the value 1 when a default occurs and 0 otherwise. Thus, our model is given by

$$L = l_1 D_1 + \cdots + l_n D_n, \tag{7.1}$$

where the $\{l_i\}$ are the magnitudes of individual losses and the $\{D_i\}$ are Bernoulli variables modeling the default events. The $\{l_i\}$ can be random or deterministic. The empirical evidence suggests a strong relation between the magnitudes of losses and the number of defaults. However, many popular credit risk models assume independence between the $\{l_i\}$ and $\{D_i\}$. We will focus on modeling only the default events $\{D_i\}$, though some of the models given below can be modified to incorporate dependence between losses and numbers of defaults.

7.2.1 Risk Measures

The distribution of L – often called the *loss distribution* and denoted as F_L – is the central object of credit risk modeling. F_L is typically not available in closed form. Instead, certain risk measures are used to describe its key features, particularly its tail behavior. The most widely used risk measure in credit risk is *Value at Risk* (VaR), which describes the quantiles of the loss distribution. For example, the 99% VaR of a portfolio is the value of the loss variable L such that a greater loss would only occur 1% of the time. The VaR for confidence level α is given by

$$v_\alpha = F_L^{-1}(\alpha),$$

where F_L^{-1} is the generalized inverse of F_L:

$$F_L^{-1}(\alpha) = \inf\{l : F_L(l) \geq \alpha\}. \tag{7.2}$$

Common values for α are 0.95, 0.99, 0.995 and 0.999. The use of VaR as a risk measure has been the subject of significant criticism (see Bluhm et al. (2010) and McNeil et al. (2005) for discussions). In particular, it has the counter-intuitive feature that it is not sub-additive: the VaR of two portfolios might be larger than the sum of the VaRs of the individual portfolios. In other words, the VaR of a portfolio is not necessarily reduced through diversification. This led Artzner et al. (1999) to propose a class of *coherent risk measures*, which satisfy certain "natural" requirements, including sub-additivity. One of the most popular of these is the *Expected Shortfall* (ES), also known as *Conditional Value at Risk* (CVaR). The α expected shortfall is given by

$$c_\alpha = \mathbb{E}\left[L \mid L \geqslant v_\alpha\right].$$

Expected shortfall is also an example of a spectral risk measure, see Bluhm et al. (2010).

7.2.2 Modeling Dependency

The key challenge in modeling portfolio credit risk lies in describing the relationship between default events. Defaults do not occur independently of one another, but rather tend to cluster. These default clusters could occur as the result of sector-specific conditions, such as a downturn in a particular industry or market, or as a result of broader macroeconomic factors. A major failing of credit models in the financial crisis of 2007–2009 was that they failed to adequately model the possibility that a large number of defaults could occur simultaneously. In order to discuss this limitation, we need to introduce a number of different *dependency measures* that describe the relationship between random variables.

The simplest measure of dependency between two random variables X and Y is given by their pairwise linear correlation $\rho(X, Y) = \text{Cov}(X, Y)/\sqrt{\text{Var}(X)\text{Var}(Y)}$. Its multivariate analog is the correlation matrix. The dependency structure of random vector $\mathbf{X}$ is completely specified by its correlation matrix if and only if $\mathbf{X}$ has an *elliptical* distribution; see McNeil et al. (2005). Important special cases are the multivariate normal and multivariate Student-t distributions.

A drawback of linear correlation (and other correlation measures, such as rank correlation) is that it describes the average joint behavior of random variables. In risk management it is *extremal* events, rather than typical events, that are of primary interest. Two dependency measures that describe extremal behavior are the coefficients of upper and lower tail dependence. Specifically, given two random variables X and Y, with distributions F_X and F_Y, we define the coefficient of upper tail dependence as

$$\lambda_u = \lim_{q \uparrow 1} \mathbb{P}\left(Y > F_Y^{-1}(q) \mid X > F_X^{-1}(q)\right),$$

and the coefficient of lower tail dependence as

$$\lambda_l = \lim_{q \downarrow 0} \mathbb{P}\left(Y \leqslant F_Y^{-1}(q) \mid X \leqslant F_X^{-1}(q)\right).$$

These measures describe the relationship between variables in the tails of distributions. A joint distribution is said to have upper (lower) tail independence if $\lambda_u = 0$ ($\lambda_d = 0$). Some of the most popular models of credit risk – in particular, the various Gaussian copula models – exhibit tail independence in both tails. This is clearly not a desirable feature in risk models, as empirical evidence tends to indicate that both defaults and risk factors tend to become more correlated in extreme settings. With the exception of the canonical Gaussian models, all of the models described in the following sections possess tail dependence.

7.3 ESTIMATING RISK MEASURES VIA MONTE CARLO

For a general loss distribution F_L, analytic calculation of the various risk measures described in the last section is usually impossible. Often the only feasible approach is to estimate these risk measures using Monte Carlo methods. To proceed, we need a method for drawing independent and identically distributed (iid) replicates of the random variable L and a method for estimating risk measures, given an iid sample $L_1, \ldots, L_N$. The methodology for estimating risk measures is largely model independent, and is the focus of this section.

The Monte Carlo estimation of VaR turns out to be somewhat more difficult than the traditional problem of estimating an expectation. In particular, VaR estimators are non-linear functions of the sample. Many classical Monte Carlo methods cannot be applied to VaR estimation or need to be modified to work well. In addition, it is typically difficult to find confidence intervals for VaR estimators.

7.3.1 Crude Monte Carlo Estimators

The *Crude Monte Carlo* (CMC) estimator of VaR is the quantile estimator of classical statistics; see van der Vaart (1998) for a discussion of its properties in a statistical context. It replaces the unknown distribution function of L, F_L, in the definition of VaR in 7.2 with the empirical distribution function $\hat{F}_L$. That is, we estimate VaR using

$$\hat{v}_\alpha = \inf \left\{ l : \hat{F}_L(l) \geqslant \alpha \right\},$$

where

$$\hat{F}_L(l) = \frac{1}{N} \sum_{i=1}^{N} \mathbb{I}(L_i \leqslant l) \tag{7.3}$$

is the empirical distribution function of the iid sample $L_1, \ldots, L_N$. Note that $\hat{F}_L$ is a step function. Consequently, the CMC quantile estimator can be easily obtained by ordering the $\{L_i\}$ as $L_{(1)} \leqslant \cdots \leqslant L_{(N)}$ and finding the $\lceil \alpha N \rceil$th largest value.

Algorithm 7.3.1   (CMC VaR Estimator)

1. *Generate an iid sample $L_1, \ldots, L_N$.*
2. *Order the sample from smallest to largest as $L_{(1)} \leqslant \cdots \leqslant L_{(N)}$.*
3. *Return $\hat{v}_\alpha = L_{(\lceil \alpha N \rceil)}$.*

The CMC estimator for the ES is more straightforward, as the ES is simply an expectation. The estimator is given by

$$\hat{c}_\alpha = \frac{1}{N(1-\alpha)} \sum_{i=1}^{N} L_i \, \mathbb{I}(L_i \geqslant \hat{v}_\alpha).$$

The variance of the VaR estimator is difficult to evaluate, because the estimator is not an average of iid random variables. However, the following central limit theorems, given with references in Hong and Liu (2011), show that the VaR and ES estimators have asymptotically normal distributions.

Theorem 7.3.1   (Central Limit Theorems for the CMC VaR and ES Estimators) *If $\mathbb{E}L^2 < \infty$ and the density of L, f_L, is positive and continuously differentiable in a neighborhood of v_α, then, as $N \to \infty$*

1. $\sqrt{N}(\hat{v}_\alpha - v_\alpha) \xrightarrow{D} \frac{\sqrt{\alpha(1-\alpha)}}{f_L(v_\alpha)} Z_1$,

2. $\sqrt{N}(\hat{c}_\alpha - c_\alpha) \xrightarrow{D} \frac{\sqrt{\mathrm{Var}(L\mathbb{I}(L > v_\alpha))}}{(1-\alpha)} Z_2$,

where Z_1 and Z_2 are standard normal random variables and $\xrightarrow{D}$ denotes convergence in distribution.

7.3.2   Importance Sampling

The CMC VaR and ES estimators generally require a very large sample size in order to achieve an acceptable level of accuracy. This is because the estimators are focused on the relatively "rare" event $\{L > v_\alpha\}$. There is a substantial body of theory devoted to efficient Monte Carlo methods for rare events. This theory has mainly been developed in the context of estimating rare-event probabilities of the form $\ell = \mathbb{P}(S(\mathbf{X}) > \gamma)$ for some real-valued function S, threshold γ and random vector $\mathbf{X}$. Some key concepts and techniques of rare-event simulation are discussed in the Appendix. The following discussion will assume familiarity with these concepts.

The importance sampling approach to quantile estimation was suggested in Glynn (1996). We replace the CMC estimator of the empirical distribution function with the IS estimator

$$\hat{F}_L^{\text{IS}}(l) = 1 - \frac{1}{N} \sum_{i=1}^{N} W(L_i)\mathbb{I}(L_i > l),$$

where the $\{L_i\}$ are drawn from the IS density g and $W(l) = f_L(l)/g(l)$ is the likelihood ratio. Note that this estimator focuses on the right tail of the distribution – see Glynn (1996) for a motivation. This then leads to the IS VaR estimator

$$\hat{v}_\alpha^{\text{IS}} = \inf\left\{l : \hat{F}_L^{\text{IS}}(l) \geqslant \alpha\right\}. \tag{7.4}$$

The corresponding ES estimator is

$$\hat{c}_\alpha^{\text{IS}} = \frac{1}{N(1-\alpha)} \sum_{i=1}^{N} W(L_i)L_i\mathbb{I}\left(L_i \geqslant \hat{v}_\alpha^{\text{IS}}\right), \tag{7.5}$$

where the L_i are drawn from g. If g is chosen such that draws from the right tail of L happen more frequently, this estimator could provide considerably better performance than the CMC estimator. In practice, the IS VaR estimator is calculated as follows

Algorithm 7.3.2   (IS VaR Estimation)

1. *Draw $L_1, \ldots, L_N$ from the IS density g.*
2. *Calculate the likelihood ratios $W(L_1), \ldots, W(L_N)$.*
3. *Order the $\{L_i\}$ as $L_{(1)} \leqslant \cdots \leqslant L_{(N)}$.*
4. *Find $N^* = \sup\{n : \frac{1}{N} \sum_{i=n}^{N} W(L_{(i)}) \geqslant 1 - \alpha\}$.*
5. *Return $v_\alpha^{\text{IS}} = L_{(N^*)}$.*

So far we have taken g as given. The following central limit theorems, given in Hong and Liu (2011) and Sun and Hong (2010), suggest a good choice of g.

Theorem 7.3.2   (Central Limit Theorem for the IS VaR Estimator) *If L has a positive and differentiable density f_L in a neighborhood of v_α and there exists an $\epsilon > 0$ such that $W(l)$ is bounded for all $l \in (v_\alpha - \epsilon, v_\alpha + \epsilon)$ and $\mathbb{E}_g\mathbb{I}(L \geqslant v_\alpha - \epsilon)(W(L))^p$ is finite for some $p > 2$, then as $N \to \infty$*

1. $\sqrt{N}(\hat{v}_\alpha^{\text{IS}} - v_\alpha) \xrightarrow{D} \dfrac{\sqrt{\text{Var}_g(W(L)\mathbb{I}(L \geqslant v_\alpha))}}{f_L(v_\alpha)} Z_1,$

2. $\sqrt{N}(\hat{c}_\alpha^{\text{IS}} - c_\alpha) \xrightarrow{D} \dfrac{\sqrt{\text{Var}_g(W(L)L\mathbb{I}(L > v_\alpha))}}{(1-\alpha)} Z_2,$

where Z_1 and Z_2 are standard normal random variables and $\xrightarrow{D}$ denotes convergence in distribution.

This suggests that a good choice of g, at least asymptotically, is one that minimizes $\mathrm{Var}_g(W(L)\mathbb{I}(L \geqslant v_\alpha))$. This is equivalent to finding the density g that minimizes the variance of

$$\hat{\ell}^{\mathrm{IS}} = \frac{1}{N} \sum_{i=1}^{N} W(L_i)\mathbb{I}(L_i > v_\alpha),$$

where the L_i are drawn from g. This is the standard IS estimator for

$$\ell = \mathbb{P}(L > v_\alpha).$$

Of course, the computation of $\hat{\ell}^{\mathrm{IS}}$ involves v_α, which is the unknown quantity we seek to estimate. However, a rough estimate of v_α can often be obtained, either through an approximation or by doing an initial simulation using the CMC VaR estimator. Importance sampling estimators for VaR and ES will often provide very large efficiency gains, even in settings where the initial estimate of v_α is quite inaccurate.

Another complication is that we usually do not know f_L, the density of L. Thus, we cannot apply importance sampling to the $\{L_i\}$ directly. Instead, we seek to represent L as a function S of either a random vector $\mathbf{X}$ with known density $f_{\mathbf{X}}$ or a vector-valued stochastic process $\mathbf{X} = (\mathbf{X}(t), 0 \leqslant t \leqslant T)$, to which we can apply importance sampling.

In practice, the procedure for applying importance sampling is as follows.

Algorithm 7.3.3   (Importance Sampling Estimation for VaR and ES) *Given a representation $L = S(\mathbf{X})$,*

1. *Calculate an initial estimate of v_α, denoted as $\hat{v}_\alpha$.*
2. *Find an appropriate importance sampling density for estimating $\mathbb{P}(L > \hat{v}_\alpha)$.*
3. *Generate $L_1 = S(\mathbf{X}_1), \dots, L_N = S(\mathbf{X}_N)$ under the IS density and calculate the corresponding likelihood ratios $W(\mathbf{X}_1), \dots, W(\mathbf{X}_N)$.*
4. *Calculate the VaR estimate as in 7.4 and the ES estimate as in 7.5.*

7.3.2.1   Adaptive Importance Sampling

Because credit risk models are generally complicated, it may be difficult (or even impossible) to find *a priori* a good importance sampling density g. Adaptive importance sampling methods aim to avoid difficult theoretical and computational issues by "learning" a good density from the data. We assume here that f_L, the density of L, is not known and that a representation of the form $L = S(\mathbf{X})$, where $\mathbf{X}$ has density $f_{\mathbf{X}}$, can be used instead. We apply importance sampling to the $\mathbf{X}$. Given a prespecified IS density $g_{\boldsymbol{\theta}}$ parameterized by $\boldsymbol{\theta}$, the idea is to take an initial sample $\mathbf{X}_1, \dots, \mathbf{X}_M$ and try to learn the optimal parameters using this sample. If the initial sample $\mathbf{X}_1, \dots, \mathbf{X}_M$ can be sampled directly from the zero-variance density $g^*(\mathbf{x}) = f(\mathbf{x} \mid S(\mathbf{x}) > v_\alpha)$, then the parameters can be chosen either to minimize the CE distance to g^*,

$$\hat{\boldsymbol{\theta}}^*_{\mathrm{CE}} = \operatorname*{argmax}_{\boldsymbol{\theta}} \frac{1}{M} \sum_{i=1}^{M} \log\left(g_{\boldsymbol{\theta}}(\mathbf{X}_i)\right),$$

or to minimize the variance of the estimator

$$\hat{\boldsymbol{\theta}}^*_{\text{VM}} = \operatorname*{argmin}_{\boldsymbol{\theta}} \frac{1}{M} \sum_{i=1}^{M} W_{\boldsymbol{\theta}}(\mathbf{X}_i).$$

In some settings, g^* is sampled from using Markov Chain Monte Carlo methods (see Kroese et al. (2011) for an introduction). However, because the probability of a loss greater than v_α is not too small, we can often use a more direct acceptance–rejection method here.

Algorithm 7.3.4   (Sampling Approximately from g^*)

1. *Generate a sample $L_1, \ldots, L_M$.*
2. *Order the sample from smallest to largest as $L_{(1)} \leqslant \cdots \leqslant L_{(M)}$.*
3. *Choose $L_{(\lceil \alpha M \rceil)}, \ldots, L_{(M)}$ as an approximate sample from g^*.*

A very small sample is usually sufficient to find very good CE or VM parameters. The additional computational cost of the trial is generally small compared to the overall costs of the simulation. Indeed, there is hardly any overhead compared with non-adaptive methods for quantile estimation, as such methods use trial runs to find an initial estimate of v_α. A similar adaptive approach is taken in Reitan and Aas (2010). For an alternative method, where the parameters are updated during the primary sampling phase, see Egloff and Leippold (2010).

7.4   SPECIFIC MODELS

In this section we discuss four specific classes of credit risk model: Bernoulli mixture models, factor models, copula models and intensity models. Although each of these models is based on the general framework 7.1, they use different mathematical structures to model the dependencies between the default variables $\{D_i\}$. As a result, each model requires a different Monte Carlo approach to efficiently estimate the VaR and ES.

7.4.1   The Bernoulli Mixture Model

Bernoulli mixture models are a fundamental class of credit risk models because many credit risk models can be represented as a mixture model. It is straightforward to apply importance sampling to these models.

In a Bernoulli mixture model, the Bernoulli default variables $D_1, \ldots, D_n$ are conditionally independent given a vector of default probabilities $\mathbf{P} = (P_1, \ldots, P_n)$. It is assumed that these default probabilities are of the form $\mathbf{P}(\boldsymbol{\Psi})$, where $\boldsymbol{\Psi}$ is a random vector with a known density $f_{\boldsymbol{\Psi}}$. Conditional on $\mathbf{P}$, calculating L reduces to calculating a weighted sum of independent light-tailed random variables.

It is quite straightforward to sample from a Bernoulli mixture model.

Algorithm 7.4.1   (Sampling from a Bernoulli Mixture Model)

1. *Generate a vector of success probabilities $\mathbf{P} = (P_1, \ldots, P_n)$.*
2. *Given $\mathbf{P}$, generate $D_1 \sim \text{Ber}(P_1), \ldots, D_n \sim \text{Ber}(P_n)$.*

7.4.1.1 One-step Importance Sampling

It is usually not possible to directly apply importance sampling to L, as the distribution of L is often unavailable in closed form. Instead we can apply importance sampling to drawing either $\mathbf{P}$ or the $D_1, \ldots, D_n$ conditional on $\mathbf{P}$. It is simplest to apply importance sampling in the second case. If we assume that $l_1, \ldots, l_n$ are constants, then, conditional on $\mathbf{P}$,

$$L = l_1 D_1 + \cdots + l_n D_n$$

is the sum of independent random variables, with the ith variable taking the value l_i with probability P_i and 0 otherwise. We exponentially twist each of these variables so that the default probability for the ith component is given by

$$\widetilde{P_i} = \frac{P_i \exp(\theta\, l_i)}{P_i \exp(\theta\, l_i) + 1 - P_i}.$$

The unique "asymptotically efficient" choice of θ is the solution to $\kappa_n(\theta^* \mid \mathbf{P}) = v_\alpha$, where

$$\kappa_n(\theta \mid \mathbf{P}) = \sum_{i=1}^{n} \log \left[P_i \exp(\theta\, l_i) + 1 - P_i \right] \tag{7.6}$$

is the joint cumulant generating function of the $\{l_i D_i\}$ conditional on $\mathbf{P}$.

Algorithm 7.4.2   (One-Step Importance Sampling for a Mixture Model)

1. *Generate* $\mathbf{P} = (P_1, \ldots, P_n)$.
2. *Find* θ^*, *the solution to* $\kappa_n'(\theta) = v_\alpha$. *(This step usually needs to be done numerically.)*
3. *If* $\theta^* < 0$, *set* $\theta^* = 0$.
4. *Calculate* $\widetilde{P_i} = \frac{P_i \exp(\theta^* l_i)}{P_i \exp(\theta^* l_i) + 1 - P_i}$, $i = 1, \ldots, n$.
5. *Given* $\widetilde{P_1}, \ldots, \widetilde{P_n}$, *generate* $D_i \sim \mathrm{Ber}(\widetilde{P_i})$, $i = 1, \ldots, n$.
6. *Return* $L = l_1 D_1 + \cdots + l_n D_n$ *and the corresponding likelihood ratio*

$$W(L) = \exp(\kappa_n(\theta^* \mid \mathbf{P}) - \theta^* L).$$

Unfortunately, this approach may not give an asymptotically efficient estimator for $\ell = \mathbb{P}(L > v_\alpha)$. This is because $\mathbf{P}$ can play a critical role in driving the dynamics of the rare event. For example, in the context of Gaussian factor models, Glasserman and Li (2005) show that asymptotic efficiency can only be achieved if the correlation between the defaults decreases (at some rate) as $n \to \infty$ and $v_\alpha \to \infty$.

7.4.1.2 Two-step Importance Sampling

A potentially more effective importance sampling scheme involves importance sampling in generating $\mathbf{P}$ as well as $D_1, \ldots, D_n$. We can decompose the variance of $\hat{\ell}$ as

$$\mathrm{Var}(\hat{\ell}) = \mathbb{E}\left(\mathrm{Var}\left(\hat{\ell} \mid \mathbf{P}\right)\right) + \mathrm{Var}\left(\mathbb{E}\left(\hat{\ell} \mid \mathbf{P}\right)\right).$$

The one-step importance sampling procedure detailed above minimizes $\mathrm{Var}(\hat{\ell} \mid \mathbf{P})$. Regarding sampling $\mathbf{P}$, we aim to minimize $\mathrm{Var}(\mathbb{E}(\hat{\ell} \mid \mathbf{P}))$. This is equivalent to minimizing the variance of $\hat{z}$, the CMC estimator of

$$z = \mathbb{P}\left(L > v_\alpha \mid \mathbf{P}(\boldsymbol{\Psi})\right).$$

The zero-variance density g^* for such a problem is given by

$$g^*_{\boldsymbol{\psi}}(\boldsymbol{\psi}) \propto \mathbb{P}(L > v_\alpha \mid \mathbf{P}(\boldsymbol{\psi})) f_{\boldsymbol{\psi}}(\boldsymbol{\psi}).$$

The normalizing constant is the unknown ℓ, so this is not a practical IS density.

There are two common approaches to finding a good IS density. One approach uses a density $g_{\boldsymbol{\psi}}$ whose mean is set equal to the mode of $g^*_{\boldsymbol{\psi}}$. This mode is the solution to a generally intractable optimization problem.

Given $g_{\boldsymbol{\psi}}$, the two-step importance sampling scheme is summarized as follows.

Algorithm 7.4.3   (Two-Step Importance Sampling for a Mixture Model)

1. *Draw* $\boldsymbol{\Psi}$ *from* $g_{\boldsymbol{\psi}}$.
2. *Generate* $\mathbf{P} = \mathbf{P}(\boldsymbol{\Psi})$.
3. *Find* θ^*, *the solution to* $\kappa'_n(\theta) = v_\alpha$.
4. *Calculate* $\widetilde{P}_i = \frac{P_i \exp(l_i \theta^*)}{P_i \exp(l_i \theta^*) + 1 - P_i}$, $i = 1, \ldots, n$.
5. *Given* $\widetilde{P}_1, \ldots, \widetilde{P}_n$, *generate* $D_i \sim \mathsf{Ber}(\widetilde{P}_i)$, $i = 1, \ldots, n$.
6. *Return* $L = l_1 D_1 + \cdots + l_n D_n$ *and the corresponding likelihood ratio*

$$W(L) = \frac{f_{\boldsymbol{\psi}}(\boldsymbol{\Psi})}{g_{\boldsymbol{\psi}}(\boldsymbol{\Psi})} \exp\left(\kappa_n(\theta^* \mid \mathbf{P}) - \theta^* L\right).$$

7.4.1.3   *Worked Example: A Bernoulli Mixture Model with Beta Probabilities*

We consider a simple Bernoulli mixture model for a portfolio with $n = 1,000$ components, with $l_1 = \cdots = l_n = 1$. The default probabilities are all equal, with $P \sim \mathsf{Beta}(0.5, 9)$. We consider three approaches: CMC, CE and one-step importance sampling. The CE approach finds the outcomes of P corresponding to the highest $N(1 - \alpha)$ samples of L. It then computes the MLEs for a Beta distribution numerically. For the IS approach, $\kappa_n(\theta \mid P) = \hat{v}_\alpha$ can be solved analytically. However, for this problem, the dynamics of L are largely driven by P. Thus, the IS estimator performs very poorly. Each estimator was used to calculate 100 estimates. The means and standard deviations of these estimators are reported. For IS, the first 10% of the sample was used to calculate a rough estimate of $\hat{v}_\alpha$. For CE, the first 10% of the sample was used to learn the parameters.

7.4.2   Factor Models

In *factor models*, the ith component defaults when a corresponding random variable X_i crosses a preset threshold ρ_i. That is,

$$D_i = \mathbb{I}\left(X_i > \rho_i\right), \quad i = 1, \ldots, n.$$

The variable X_i can sometimes be thought of as corresponding to a default time, as in the Li copula model (see Li (2000)), though this need not be the case. The relationship between the $\{D_i\}$ is imposed by having the $\{X_i\}$ all depend on a vector of common factors, $\boldsymbol{\Psi}$. A model with one factor is called a *single factor* model; a model with more than one factor is referred to as a *multi-factor* model. These factors may correspond to macroeconomic or industry-specific factors, though they need not have an economic interpretation. In the simplest case of a *linear factor model*, each X_i is a weighted sum of the factors and another random variable, $\mathcal{E}_i$ which represents the component-specific *idiosyncratic* risk. Conditional on $\boldsymbol{\Psi}$, factor models are Bernoulli mixture models.

The most popular factor models are based on the normal and Student-t distributions. We focus on three specific factor models.

- In the *Gaussian factor model*, each X_i has the representation

$$X_i = a_{i1} Z_1 + \cdots + a_{im} Z_m + a_i \mathcal{E}_i,$$

where the $\{Z_j\}$ and $\{\mathcal{E}_i\}$ are independent standard normal random variables and the coefficients are chosen such that the marginal distribution of each X_i is standard normal. Here, conditional on $Z_1 = z_1, \ldots, Z_m = z_m$ (thus, $\boldsymbol{\Psi} = \mathbf{Z}$), the default probability for the ith component is

$$
\begin{aligned}
P_i &= \mathbb{P}\left(\mathcal{E}_i > \frac{\rho_i - (a_{i1} z_1 + \cdots + a_{im} z_m)}{a_i} \right) \\
&= \Phi\left(\frac{(a_{i1} z_1 + \cdots + a_{im} z_m) - \rho_i}{a_i} \right).
\end{aligned}
$$

- In the *Student-t factor model*, each X_i is a weighted sum of Student-t random variables. Usually, the Student-t factor model is chosen such that each X_i has the following representation

$$X_i = \sqrt{\frac{r}{V}} \left(a_{i1} Z_1 + \cdots + a_{im} Z_m + a_i \mathcal{E}_i \right),$$

where the $\{Z_j\}$ are standard normals and V has a chi-squared distribution with r degrees of freedom. Here, conditional on $Z_1 = z_1, \ldots, Z_m = z_m$ and $V = v$ (thus, $\boldsymbol{\Psi} = (\mathbf{Z}, V)$), the default probability is

$$
\begin{aligned}
P_i &= \mathbb{P}\left(\mathcal{E}_i > \frac{\sqrt{v/r}\, \rho_i - (a_{i1} z_1 + \cdots + a_{im} z_m)}{a_i} \right) \\
&= \Phi\left(\frac{(a_{i1} z_1 + \cdots + a_{im} z_m) - \sqrt{v/r}\, \rho_i}{a_i} \right).
\end{aligned}
$$

- A more general single factor model with heavy tails and tail dependence is introduced in Bassamboo et al. (2008). It is an extension of the normal mean-variance mixture models described in Frey and McNeil (2001). Here, each X_i is of the form

$$X_i = \frac{\alpha_i Z + \sqrt{1 - \alpha_i^2}\, \mathcal{E}_i}{W},$$

where the $\{\mathcal{E}_i\}$ are iid random variables independent of the random variable Z, and W is a random variable independent of Z and the $\{\mathcal{E}_i\}$, with a density f_W that satisfies

$$f_W(w) = \lambda w^{\nu-1} + o(w^{\nu-1}) \quad \text{as } w \downarrow 0. \tag{7.7}$$

This model includes that single factor Student-t model as a special case, as the chi-squared distribution satisfies 7.7. Conditional on $Z = z$ and $W = w$ (thus, $\Psi = (Z, W)$) the default probabilities are

$$P_i = \mathbb{P}\left(\mathcal{E}_i > \frac{w\rho_i - \alpha_i z}{\sqrt{1 - \alpha_i^2}}\right).$$

It is usually straightforward to sample from a factor model.

Algorithm 7.4.4   (Sampling from a Factor Model)

1. *Draw the common factors* Ψ *and the idiosyncratic risks* $\mathcal{E}_1, \ldots, \mathcal{E}_n$.
2. *Calculate* $X_1, \ldots, X_n$ *as per the model.*
3. *Calculate* $L = l_1 \mathbb{I}(X_1 > \rho_1) + \cdots + l_n \mathbb{I}(X_n > \rho_n).$

7.4.2.1   *Importance Sampling*

Factor models are usually Bernoulli mixture models. Thus, importance sampling can be applied as above. It is usually necessary to use a two-step importance sampling scheme, as in Subsection 7.4.1.2. The difficulty lies in choosing g_Ψ, the IS density for the common factors Ψ.

In the case of Gaussian factor models, where $\Psi = \mathbf{Z}$, Glasserman and Li (2005) use a multivariate normal density $N(\boldsymbol{\mu}, I)$ with the mean vector $\boldsymbol{\mu}$ set equal to the mode of $g_\mathbf{Z}^*$. The mode, in turn, can be obtained as the solution to the optimization problem

$$\boldsymbol{\mu}^* = \underset{\mathbf{z}}{\operatorname{argmax}} \, \mathbb{P}\left(L > v_\alpha \mid \mathbf{Z} = \mathbf{z}\right) \exp(-\mathbf{z}^\mathsf{T}\mathbf{z}/2). \tag{7.8}$$

Glasserman and Li suggest a number of approximations that simplify this problem. One approach is the *constant approximation*, where L is replaced by $\mathbb{E}[L \mid \mathbf{Z} = \mathbf{z}]$ and $\mathbb{P}(L > v_\alpha \mid \mathbf{Z} = \mathbf{z})$ is replaced by $\mathbb{I}(\mathbb{E}[L \mid \mathbf{Z} = \mathbf{z}] > v_\alpha)$. In this case, (7.8) becomes

$$\underset{\mathbf{z}}{\operatorname{argmin}} \left\{\mathbf{z}^\mathsf{T}\mathbf{z} : \mathbb{E}\left[L \mid \mathbf{Z} = \mathbf{z}\right] > v_\alpha\right\}. \tag{7.9}$$

Another approach is the *tail bound approximation*, which is shown to be asymptotically optimal for the case of a homogeneous single factor portfolio. This approach approximates $\mathbb{P}(L > v_\alpha \mid \mathbf{Z} = \mathbf{z})$ by its upper bound, and 7.8 becomes

$$\underset{\mathbf{z}}{\operatorname{argmax}} \left\{\kappa_n(\theta_{v_\alpha} \mid \mathbf{z}) - \theta_{v_\alpha} v_\alpha - \mathbf{z}^\mathsf{T}\mathbf{z}/2\right\},$$

where $\theta_{v_\alpha} = \theta_{v_\alpha}(\mathbf{z})$ is the solution to $\kappa_n'(\theta \mid \mathbf{z}) = v_\alpha$ and κ_n is given in 7.6.

In a multi-factor setting, the problem of finding a good approximation of g^* becomes much more difficult. This is because more than one combination of factors can cause a loss larger than v_α. Glasserman et al. (2008) propose an approach which essentially attempts to partition the rare event $\{L > v_\alpha\}$ into different sub-events; each sub-event corresponds to a particular set of factors taking large values, and they solve (7.9) for each of these events. This approach is shown to be asymptotically efficient in certain settings. As far as we are aware, this is the only method given in the existing literature that deals adequately with the problem of possibly infinite variance in a multifactor setting.

In the Student-t factor model setting given above, Kang and Shahabuddin (2005) propose first sampling V, then $Z_1, \ldots, Z_m$. Given V, they proceed as in Glasserman et al. (2008). They propose exponentially twisting V by a parameter which is again the solution of a constrained optimization problem. Note that this approach is very computationally expensive, as it requires multiple numerical optimization procedures per sample. Kang and Shahabuddin (2005) suggest using a stratified sampling scheme to minimize this cost.

For the general single-factor model, Bassamboo et al. (2008) introduce two methods. In the first, they propose exponentially twisting W and find a good twisting parameter θ by minimizing the upper bound on the likelihood ratio. This approach gives bounded relative error under some technical conditions. In the second, they apply hazard-rate twisting to $V = 1/W$, see Juneja and Shahabuddin (2006) for a discussion of this method. Again, they choose the twisting parameter to minimize the upper bound on the likelihood ratio. Under some technical conditions, the resulting estimator is shown to be asymptotically efficient.

Another method for applying variance reduction to Student-t factor models is given in Chan and Kroese (2010). In this approach, VaR can be estimated by calculating the expectations of truncated gamma random variables.

7.4.2.2 Worked Example: A Gaussian Factor Model

We consider an example suggested in Glasserman and Li (2005). In this example, the portfolio is of size $n = 1,000$, with $l_i = (\lceil 5i/n \rceil)^2$. The barriers are given by $\rho_i = \Phi^{-1}(1 - P_i)$, where $P_i = 0.01 * (1 + \sin(16\pi i/n))$. The $m = 10$ factor loadings, $\{a_{ij}\}$, are drawn uniformly on $(0, 1/\sqrt{m})$.

We calculate the VaR and ES using three different methods: CMC, Glasserman and Li's method and Cross Entropy (CE). For Glasserman and Li's algorithm, we only apply importance sampling to the $\{Z_i\}$, as twisting the $\{D_i\}$ does not make a substantial difference in this case, and takes considerably more time. We draw the $\{Z_i\}$ from a N(μ, I) distribution, with μ the solution of 7.4.2.1 found via numerical root-finding. In the CE approach, we set the means of the $\{Z_i\}$ and the mean of the $\{\mathcal{E}_i\}$ equal to the sample means of the $\{Z_i\}$ and $\{\mathcal{E}_i\}$ corresponding to the $\lfloor N(1 - \alpha) \rfloor$ highest values of L.

Table 7.2 gives the numerical results. The estimators were calculated 100 times each and their means and standard deviations are reported. The Glasserman and Li estimator uses the

Table 7.1 Estimated VaR and ES for a Bernoulli Mixture Model.

Estimator	$\hat{v}_\alpha$	Std($\hat{v}_\alpha$)	$\hat{c}_\alpha$	Std($\hat{c}_\alpha$)
$\alpha = 0.95$	$N = 10^4$			
CMC	197.5	3.3	270.0	4.3
CE	197.6	1.4	269.9	5.3
IS	197.5	3.2	269.7	4.8
$\alpha = 0.99$	$N = 10^4$			
CMC	316	7.7	382.9	10.0
CE	314.9	3.2	375.6	8.3
IS	316.2	9.3	378.2	9.8
$\alpha = 0.995$	$N = 10^4$			
CMC	363.3	9.9	430.6	10.5
CE	362.6	2.7	421.9	6.6
IS	363.4	9.3	413.0	27.0

Table 7.2   Estimated VaR and ES for a Gaussian factor model.

Estimator	$\hat{v}_\alpha$	Std($\hat{v}_\alpha$)	$\hat{c}_\alpha$	Std($\hat{c}_\alpha$)
$\alpha = 0.95$	$N = 10^4$			
CMC	215	7	488	19
CE	217	3	469	3
GL	216	3	469	3
$\alpha = 0.99$	$N = 10^5$			
CMC	595	31	988	58
CE	600	13	987	12
GL	599	6	987	5
$\alpha = 0.995$	$N = 10^5$			
CMC	833	17	1,267	28
CE	837	2	1,274	2
GL	837	2	1,274	2

first 10% of the sample to find an initial estimate of $\hat{v}_\alpha$. The CE estimator uses the first 10% of the sample to learn good parameters. Note that the CE and Glasserman and Li estimators performing better relative to the CMC estimator as α gets larger. Running times are not given here, as they are implementation-specific, but we note that the Glasserman Li approach is considerably slower than the CE approach in our implementation.

7.4.3   Copula Models

One of the most popular ways of expressing dependency in credit risk models is to use copulas. A copula is simply a multivariate distribution function with uniform marginals:

$$C(u_1, \ldots, u_n) : [0, 1]^n \to [0, 1].$$

Copulas describe the dependency structure between uniform random variables $U_1, \ldots, U_n$. These can be transformed into random variables $X_1, \ldots, X_n$, with arbitrary distributions $F_1, \ldots, F_n$, by setting $X_1 = F_1^{-1}(U_1), \ldots, X_n = F_n^{-1}(U_n)$. This means that the dependency structure of the $\{X_i\}$ can be modeled separately from their marginal distributions. It can be shown that the dependency structure of any distribution can be defined via a copula (see Nelsen (2006)). Often, the X_i are taken to be default times as, for example, in the Li model, see Li (2000). However, this need not be the case. If each D_i is of the form $D_i = \mathbb{I}(X_i > \rho_i)$, then the model is said to be a *threshold model*.

We focus on the Gaussian, Student-t and Archimedean copulas, as these are the most popular copulas in credit risk modeling. The Gaussian copula has tail independence. An attractive feature of the other models is that they exhibit tail dependence.

- The *Gaussian copula*, popularized in Li (2000), is of the form

$$C_G(u_1, \ldots, u_n) = \Phi_\Gamma \left(\Phi^{-1}(u_1), \ldots, \Phi^{-1}(u_n) \right),$$

where $\Phi_\Gamma(\cdot)$ is the multivariate normal distribution function with mean vector $\mathbf{0}$ and correlation matrix Γ. The Gaussian factor model, described above, can be interpreted as a Gaussian copula.

- The *Student-t copula* is of the form

$$C_T(u_1, \ldots, u_n) = T_{\nu, \Gamma}\left(T_\nu^{-1}(u_1), \ldots, T_\nu^{-1}(u_n)\right),$$

where $T_{\nu, \Gamma}$ is the multivariate Student-t distribution function with ν degrees of freedom, mean vector $\mathbf{0}$ and correlation matrix Γ. The Student-t factor model can be interpreted as a Student-t copula. The Student-t copula has tail dependence in both tails.

- *Archimedean copulas* are of the form

$$C_\psi(u_1, \ldots, u_n) = \psi^{-1}(\psi(u_1) + \cdots + \psi(u_n)),$$

where the *generator* of the copula is a function $\psi : [0, 1] \to [0, \infty]$ that satisfies the following conditions:

1. It is strictly decreasing.
2. $\psi(0) = \infty$ and $\psi(1) = 0$.
3. ψ^{-1} is completely monotonic, meaning $(-1)^k \frac{d^k}{du^k} \psi^{-1}(u) \geq 0$, $\quad \forall k \in \mathbb{N}$ and $u \in [0, \infty]$.

The class of Archimedean copulas includes the *Gumbel copula*, where $\psi_\eta(u) = (-\log u)^\eta$, and the *Clayton copula*, where $\psi_\eta(u) = u^{-\eta} - 1$. The Gumbel copula has upper tail dependence and the Clayton copula has lower tail dependence.

7.4.3.1 *Sampling from a General Copula*

In theory, it is possible to sample from any copula $C(u_1, \ldots, u_n)$. The approach, given in Cherubini et al. (2004), is as follows. Let $C_i(u_1, \ldots, u_i) = C(u_1, \ldots, u_i, 1, \ldots, 1), i = 1, \ldots, n$. The conditional distribution of the copula C_i is

$$C_i(u_i \mid u_1, \ldots, u_{i-1}) = \mathbb{P}(U_i \leq u_i \mid U_1 = u_1, \ldots, U_{i-1} = u_{i-1})$$

$$= \frac{\frac{\partial^{i-1}}{\partial u_1, \ldots, \partial u_{i-1}} C_i(u_1, \ldots, u_i)}{\frac{\partial^{i-1}}{\partial u_1, \ldots, \partial u_{i-1}} C_{i-1}(u_1, \ldots, u_{i-1})}.$$

We can then decompose $C(u_1, \ldots, u_n)$ as follows

$$C(u_1, \ldots, u_n) = \mathbb{P}(U_1 < u_1) C_2(u_2 \mid u_1) \cdots C_n(u_n \mid u_1, \ldots, u_{n-1}).$$

Algorithm 7.4.5 (Sampling from a General Copula)

1. *Draw U_1 uniformly on $(0, 1)$.*
2. *Draw U_i from the distribution $C_i(\cdot \mid u_1, \ldots, u_{i-1})$, for $i = 2, \ldots, n$.*

In general, $C_i(\cdot \mid u_1, \ldots, u_{i-1})$ has to be sampled via the inverse transform method (see Kroese et al. (2011)). This involves drawing a uniform random variable V, and solving $V = C_i(u_i \mid u_1, \ldots, u_{i-1})$ for u_i. This usually needs to be done using a numerical root-finding procedure. In practice, this tends to make sampling from an arbitrary copula too expensive to be feasible.

7.4.3.2 *Sampling from Gaussian and Student-t Copulas*

The Gaussian and Student-t copulas are *implicit copulas*. That is, they are copulas implied by the multivariate normal and Student-t distributions. Hence, drawing from these copulas is simply a case of drawing from their respective multivariate distribution. Algorithms for drawing from these distributions are given in Kroese et al. (2011).

Algorithm 7.4.6 (Sampling from a Gaussian Copula)

1. *Draw* $\mathbf{Z} = (Z_1, \ldots, Z_n) \sim \mathsf{N}(0, \Sigma)$.
2. *Return* $U_1 = \Phi(Z_1), \ldots, U_n = \Phi(Z_n)$.

Algorithm 7.4.7 (Sampling from a Student-t Copula)

1. *Draw* $\mathbf{Y}$ *from a multivariate Student-t distribution with* v *degrees of freedom and correlation matrix* Γ.
2. *Return* $U_1 = T_v(Z_1), \ldots, U_n = T_v(Z_n)$.

7.4.3.3 Sampling from Archimedean Copulas

Archimedean copulas are particularly easy to sample from. The approach below uses Bernstein's theorem, which states that if ψ satisfies the conditions for an Archimedean generator, then ψ^{-1} is of the form

$$\psi^{-1}(u) = \int_0^\infty e^{-u\lambda} \, dF_\Lambda(\lambda).$$

That is, $\psi^{-1}(u)$ is the Laplace transform of some distribution F_Λ. It is easily verified that, if Λ is drawn from F_Λ and $X_1, \ldots, X_n$ are iid and $\mathsf{U}(0, 1)$ distributed, then

$$U_1 = \psi^{-1}\left(\frac{-\log X_1}{\Lambda}\right), \ldots, U_n = \psi^{-1}\left(\frac{-\log X_n}{\Lambda}\right)$$

have the distribution given by the Archimedean copula. Thus, if we know F_Λ, we have the following algorithm for sampling from an Archimedean copula.

Algorithm 7.4.8 (Sampling from an Archimedean Copula)

1. *Draw* Λ *from the distribution* F_Λ.
2. *Draw iid standard uniform random variables* $X_1, \ldots, X_n$.
3. *Return*

$$U_1 = \psi^{-1}\left(\frac{-\log X_1}{\Lambda}\right), \ldots, U_n = \psi^{-1}\left(\frac{-\log X_n}{\Lambda}\right).$$

Given an arbitrary generator, ψ, F_Λ may not be a known distribution, or one that can be sampled from in a straightforward manner. However, F_Λ is known for both the Gumbel and Clayton copulas. For the Gumbel copula, Λ has a stable distribution $\mathsf{St}(1/\eta, 1, \gamma, \eta)$, where $\gamma = (\cos(\pi\eta/2))^\eta$. In the case of the Clayton copula, Λ is $\mathsf{Gam}(1/\eta, 1)$ distributed.

7.4.3.4 Importance Sampling

Importance sampling is straightforward for Gaussian and Student-t copula models, as it can be applied directly to the multivariate densities.

Table 7.3   Estimated VaR and ES for a Clayton Copula model.

Estimator	$\hat{v}_\alpha$	Std($\hat{v}_\alpha$)	$\hat{c}_\alpha$	Std($\hat{c}_\alpha$)
$\alpha = 0.95$	$N = 10^3$			
CMC	72	4.9	89.9	2.4
CE	73	5.2	86.5	9.6
IS	73.5	5.4	86.8	4.8
$\alpha = 0.95$	$N = 10^4$			
CMC	72.7	1.6	88.9	0.8
CE	72.9	0.3	88.7	0.1
IS	72.8	1.5	88.5	0.9
$\alpha = 0.99$	$N = 10^4$			
CMC	97.5	0.6	100.1	0.2
CE	97.6	0.5	99	0.5
IS	97.6	0.6	98.7	0.4

In an Archimedean copula model, $U_1, \ldots, U_n$ are independent conditional on Λ. If $D_1, \ldots, D_n$ are generated using a threshold approach, we can represent such a model as a Bernoulli mixture model. This is because,

$$\mathbb{P}(U_i > \rho_i) = \mathbb{P}\left(\psi^{-1}\left(\frac{-\log X_i}{\Lambda}\right) > \rho_i\right) = 1 - \exp\{-\Lambda\psi(\rho_i)\}. \qquad (7.10)$$

Thus, we can apply importance sampling as in the Bernoulli mixture model case given above.

7.4.3.5 Worked Example: A Clayton Copula Model

We consider the case where exponentially distributed default times are generated using a Clayton copula. Uniform random variables $U_1, \ldots, U_n$ are drawn from a Clayton copula with parameter $\eta = 1.5$. These are transformed into exponential random variables with parameter $\lambda = 0.1$ by setting

$$X_i = -\frac{\log U_i}{\lambda}.$$

Each D_i is then generated as $\mathbb{I}(X_i < 1)$. VaR and CVaR are both estimated using CMC, CE and one-step importance sampling. In all three cases, the Clayton copula is sampled from via the Laplace transform method detailed above. In the CE case, Λ is sampled from a Gamma distribution with parameters estimated from the elite sample. In the one-step IS case, the importance sampling is applied by twisting the default probabilities $P_1, \ldots, P_n$, which are calculated as in 7.10. For the CE estimator, the first 10% of the sample is used for learning phase. For the IS estimator, the first 10% of the sample is used as to get a rough estimate of $\hat{v}$. The results are given in the following table. Note that the CE estimator gives significant variance reduction provided that the sample size is large enough to estimate good parameters in the learning phase. The one-step importance sampling estimator performs not much better than CMC, as the value of L is very dependent on the realization of Λ.

7.4.4   Intensity Models

In intensity models, the default times of the n components, $\tau_1, \ldots, \tau_n$, are modeled by the arrival times of point processes. Denoting by T the time at which the portfolio is assessed, the Bernoulli default variables are given by $D_1 = \mathbb{I}(\tau_1 < T), \ldots, D_n = \mathbb{I}(\tau_n < T)$. In a *top-down* approach, the defaults are modeled as the arrivals of a single point process. The intensity of this process is given without reference to the portfolio constituents. In a *bottom-up* approach, each component of the portfolio is modeled separately. We will focus on this approach, and refer the reader to Giesecke (2008) for further discussion of modeling approaches. We model each τ_i as corresponding to the arrival time of an indicator process $(N_i(t), t \geqslant 0)$. Such a process has a stochastic intensity $\lambda_i(t), t \geqslant 0$, which is equal to 0 after the first arrival. Intuitively, $\lambda_i(t)$ is the rate at which arrivals occur at time t, conditional on the filtration (that is, the history) of the process up to time t. The default probability for the ith component is given by

$$P_i = 1 - \mathbb{P}(\tau_i < T) = 1 - \mathbb{E}\left[\exp\left\{-\int_0^T \lambda_i(s)\,\mathrm{d}s\right\}\right].$$

Dependency between defaults can be induced by assuming that each intensity λ_i is a function of a common process $(X(t), t \geqslant 0)$ and an idiosyncratic process $(X_i(t), t \geqslant 0)$; for example, $\lambda_i(t) = X(t) + X_i(t)$. A popular modeling choice for the process $(X(t))$ is that it satisfies a stochastic differential equation with jumps:

$$\mathrm{d}X(t) = \mu(X(t))\,\mathrm{d}t + \sigma(X(t))\,\mathrm{d}B(t) + \Delta J(t), \tag{7.11}$$

where $(B(t), t \geqslant 0)$ is a standard Brownian motion, $(\Delta J(t), t \geqslant 0)$ is a jump process, and both μ and σ are deterministic functions. The idiosyncratic processes $(X_i(t), t \geqslant 0), i = 1, \ldots, n$ can be modeled in a similar way. If μ and σ are affine functions, then under certain assumptions, the default probabilities $P_1, \ldots, P_n$ can be found by solving a system of ODEs (see Duffie et al. (2003) and Duffie (2005)).

One appeal of intensity models is that they can capture the empirical phenomenon of *contagion*, where defaults tend to happen in clusters. A popular model of contagion is the *generalized Hawke's process*, where the point process $(N(t), t \geqslant 0)$ has a stochastic intensity that satisfies

$$\mathrm{d}\lambda(t) = \kappa(\mu - \lambda(t))\,\mathrm{d}t + \sigma\sqrt{\lambda(t)}\,\mathrm{d}B(t) + \Delta N(t).$$

Point processes in which the intensity depends on the number of arrivals are called *self-exciting*. Intensity models can also capture dependency between credit losses and the default process. A general introduction of using point process models in credit risk is given in Giesecke (2004). For the relevant background on stochastic differential equations see, for example, Protter (2005).

7.4.4.1   *Sampling from Intensity Models*

In practice, though each portfolio component is modeled by a separate point process, we only simulate a single point process. This point process has intensity $\lambda(t) = \sum_{i=1}^n \lambda_i(t)$. On the event of a default, the ith component of the portfolio is chosen to default with probability $\lambda_i(t)/\lambda(t)$. The choice of algorithm for simulating from a stochastic intensity model depends on whether the intensity $\lambda(t)$ can be bounded between jumps. If the intensity can be bounded between jumps and it is straightforward to determine $\lambda(t)$ for an arbitrary t, then a thinning method due to Ogata (1981) can be used. At each jump, a piecewise constant process ($\lambda^*(t)$) is identified such that $\lambda(t) < \lambda^*(t)$ almost surely so long as no other jumps occur. A Poisson process with intensity function $\lambda^*(t)$ is simulated, and points are accepted with probability $\lambda(t)/\lambda^*(t)$. This gives the following algorithm.

Algorithm 7.4.9 (Sampling from a point process via thinning)

1. *Set $i = 0$ and $\tau_0 = 0$.*
2. *Find λ_i^*, the upper bound of $\lambda(t)$, $\tau_i \leqslant t \leqslant T$ given the history of the process up until time τ_i.*
3. *Simulate arrival times $\tilde{\tau}_1, \dots \tilde{\tau}_n$ for a homogeneous Poisson process with intensity λ^*. Accept each arrival with probability $\lambda_i(\tau)/\lambda_i^*$. Stop after the first arrival time $\tilde{\tau}_i^*$ is accepted.*
4. *Set $\tau_i = \tilde{\tau}_i^* + \tau_{i-1}$.*
5. *Set $i = i + 1$ and repeat from step 2 until $\tau_i > T$.*

There is a general method of sampling from a point process driven by a stochastic intensity. If the compensator $\Lambda(t) \to \infty$ as $t \to \infty$ then $(N(t))$ is a standard Poisson process under the time change defined by $(\Lambda(t))$, with inter-arrival times given by $\mathsf{Exp}(1)$ random variables (see Giesecke et al. (2011)). The arrival times of the original process can be found by inverting $\Lambda(t)$. That is, given a sequence $Y_1, \dots, Y_n$ of $\mathsf{Exp}(1)$ random variables representing the interarrival times of the time-changed process, the nth arrival time of the original process, τ_n, can be found by solving,

$$\tau_n = \inf_{t \geqslant 0} \left\{ \int_0^t \lambda(s)\, \mathrm{d}s \geqslant \sum_{i=1}^n Y_i \right\}.$$

This suggests the following algorithm.

Algorithm 7.4.10 (Sampling from a point process via a time change)

1. *Set $i = 1$.*
2. *Draw Y_i from an $\mathsf{Exp}(1)$ distribution.*
3. *Return τ_i, the time at which $\Lambda(t)$ hits $\sum_{j=1}^i Y_j$.*
4. *Set $i = i + 1$ and repeat from step 2 until $\tau_i > T$.*

This method is usually very computationally expensive, as the integral process $\Lambda(t) = \int_0^t \lambda(s)\, \mathrm{d}s, t \geqslant 0$ needs to be approximated on a discrete grid. The conditional distributions of $\Lambda(t)$ may also be unknown, in which case the process may only be approximately sampled at the grid points. An alternative method, that does not require simulating the intensity between jumps is suggested in Giesecke et al. (2011). However, this method may be difficult or impossible to apply in some settings.

7.4.4.2 Importance Sampling

Importance sampling can be applied to intensity models in a number of different ways. For example, it can be observed that the events $\{N(t) > \gamma\}$ and $\{\sum_{i-1}^n N_i(t) > \gamma\}$ can both be written in the form $\{S_{\lceil \gamma \rceil} < T\}$, where S_k is the sum of k random variables, representing the first k arrival times. In this setting, exponential twisting can be applied to S_k. Unfortunately, this is often not possible, as the distribution of the S_k is usually either unknown or intractable – see Giesecke and Shkolnik (2011) for a discussion. However, in this setting, standard large deviations techniques can be applied to find good twisting parameters.

Another method is to apply a change of measure to the point process itself. This is the approach taken in Zhang et al. (2009), which considers a generalized Hawke's process. In the approach given in Giesecke and Shkolnik (2011), the change of measure is applied to the intensity processes instead.

If indicator processes are independent of one another conditional on some common factors $\mathbf{X}_t$, then they have a Bernoulli mixture model structure. The techniques described in Section 7.4 can therefore be applied. In the particular case where intensities are of the form $\lambda_i(t) = X(t) + X_i(t)$ driven by 7.11, and the random factors are affine processes, Bassamboo and Jain (2006) propose applying an exponential change of measure to the processes, with a parameter θ that minimizes the upper bound on the likelihood ratio.

7.4.5 An Example Point Process Model

In this model, taken from Giesecke and Shkolnik (2011), the individual component intensities are given by

$$\lambda_i(t) = (w_i X_0(t) + X_i(t))(1 - N_i(t)),$$

where each $X_i(t)$ satisfies the SDE

$$dX_i(t) = \kappa_i \left(\bar{X}_i(t) - X_i(t) \right) dt + \sigma_i \sqrt{X_i(t)} \, dB_i(t) + \delta_i \, dJ_i(t).$$

Here, $J_i(t) = \Delta_1 N_1(t) + \cdots + \Delta_n N_n(t)$ and the $(B_i(t), t \geqslant 0), i = 1, \ldots, n$ are standard Brownian motions. The $\{\kappa_i\}$ are drawn uniformly on $(0.5, 1.5)$. The $\{\bar{X}_i\}$ are drawn uniformly on $(0.001, 0.051)$ and each σ_i is equal to $\min(\sqrt{2\kappa_i \bar{X}_i}, \bar{\sigma}_i)$, where the $\{\bar{\sigma}_i\}$ are drawn uniformly on $(0, 0.2)$. Each factor weight w_i is drawn uniformly on $(0, 1)$. The $\{\Delta_i\}$ are drawn uniformly on $(0, 2/n)$ and the $\{\delta_i\}$ are drawn uniformly on $(0, 2)$. We compare the CMC algorithm with one of the two algorithms given in Giesecke and Shkolnik (2011).

In the CMC approach, the process $(N_t, t \geqslant 0)$ is generated using the time-change algorithm (Algorithm 7.4.10). A single point process is generated with intensity $\lambda(t) = \sum_{i=1}^n \lambda_i(t)$. The intensity processes $\lambda_1(t), \ldots, \lambda_n(t)$ are square-root processes, so they can be simulated exactly on a mesh using non-central chi-squared random variables (see Glasserman (2004)). A mesh of 1,000 points is used and the integral $\int_0^t \lambda(s) \, ds$ is evaluated via the trapezoidal rule. On the event of the kth default, the ith component of the portfolio is selected to default with probability $\lambda_i(\tau_k)/\lambda(\tau_k)$.

The IS algorithm replaces the point process $(N(t))$ with a Poisson process with intensity $\lambda = \hat{v}_\alpha$. The number of defaults, N, is drawn from a Poisson distribution with mean $\hat{v}_\alpha$. The default times $\tau_1, \ldots, \tau_N$ are N ordered uniform random variables on the interval $[0, 1]$. At time T, the Radon–Nikodym derivative for this change of measure is given by

$$M(T) = \exp\{\hat{v}_\alpha \tau_N - N(T) \log(\hat{v}_\alpha)\} + \sum_{k=1}^N \log(\lambda(\tau_k)) - \int_0^{\tau_N} \lambda(s) \, ds.$$

The dynamics of $(\lambda_i(t), t \geqslant 0), i = 1, \ldots, n$ remain unchanged between defaults. A great advantage of this method is a reduction in computational effort, as $\lambda_i(t)$ only needs to be calculated up until the final default time.

Table 7.4 Estimated VaR and ES for an intensity model.

Estimator	$\hat{v}_\alpha$	Std($\hat{v}_\alpha$)	$\hat{c}_\alpha$	Std($\hat{c}_\alpha$)
$\alpha = 0.95$	$N = 10^3$			
CMC	20	0.0	23.0	0.6
IS	20	0.0	22.6	0.6
$\alpha = 0.99$	$N = 10^3$			
CMC	24.4	0.8	29.5	1.3
IS	24.2	0.4	26.7	0.5
$\alpha = 0.995$	$N = 10^3$			
CMC	26.1	1.0	33.1	1.3
IS	25.8	0.4	27.8	0.7

The following numerical results are based on a portfolio of size $n = 100$, with each $l_i = 1$. A sample size of $N = 10^3$ was used. The CMC and IS algorithms appear to give different values for c_α. However, for larger sample sizes, the CMC estimates of c_α get closer to the IS estimates. For the importance sampling algorithm, the first 20% of the sample is used to get a rough estimate of $\hat{v}_\alpha$.

APPENDIX A: A PRIMER ON RARE-EVENT SIMULATION

The problem of finding good estimators for risk measures such as VaR and ES can, to a large extent, be reduced to the problem of finding good estimators for rare-event probabilities. This is a much better understood problem, and one which has given rise to a large number of effective Monte Carlo techniques. The vast majority of the literature on VaR and ES estimation has focused on a variance reduction method known as *importance sampling* and has used methods from the theory of rare-event simulation to find good classes of importance sampling estimators. These methods can be roughly split into two classes: (1) methods based primarily on large deviations asymptotics, and (2) adaptive methods, which "learn" good estimators. In this appendix, we review the basics of rare-event probability estimation and discuss a number of approaches that work well in the credit risk context. There is an extensive literature on rare-event simulation; we mention, in particular, Bucklew (2004), Rubino and Tuffin (2009), Asmussen and Glynn (2007) and Kroese et al. (2011).

A fundamental problem of rare-event simulation is to estimate $\ell = \mathbb{P}(S(\mathbf{X}) > \gamma)$, when ℓ is very small. Here, S is a real-valued function, $\mathbf{X}$ is a random vector with density f, and γ is a constant. The *Crude Monte Carlo* (CMC) estimator of ℓ is defined as

$$\hat{\ell} = \frac{1}{N} \sum_{i=1}^{N} \mathbb{I}(S(\mathbf{X}_i) > \gamma), \tag{7.12}$$

where the $\{\mathbf{X}_i\}$ are iid draws from f. This estimator performs very well when ℓ is large, but works very badly as $\ell \to 0$. This is because the event of interest $\{S(\mathbf{X}) > \gamma\}$, which is rare by nature, must happen a large number of times in order to get an accurate estimate. The aim of rare event simulation is to find better estimators in such settings.

7.A.1 Efficiency

The accuracy of a rare-event estimator is often measured by its *relative error*. This is the normalized standard deviation of the estimator. We can usually think of a rare-event estimator as an average of iid replicates of a random variable, which we will label Z. For example, the CMC estimator is an average of iid replicates of $Z = \mathbb{I}(S(\mathbf{X}) > \gamma)$. The relative error is then defined as

$$\mathrm{RE} = \frac{\sqrt{\mathrm{Var}(Z)}}{\ell \sqrt{N}}.$$

The relative error of the CMC estimator of ℓ is given by

$$\frac{\sqrt{\ell(1-\ell)}}{\ell \sqrt{N}} \approx \frac{1}{\sqrt{N}\sqrt{\ell}}$$

for small ℓ. This means that a very large sample size is required in order to achieve a low error. For example, estimating a probability of order 10^{-6} to a relative error of 0.01 requires a sample size of approximately 10^{10}. If an estimator is unbiased, its variance is given by

$$\mathrm{Var}(Z) = \mathbb{E}Z^2 - (\mathbb{E}Z)^2 = \mathbb{E}Z^2 - \ell^2 \stackrel{\text{def}}{=} M - \ell^2.$$

This means that the variance of an unbiased estimator is entirely determined by $M = \mathbb{E}Z^2$, the second moment of the random variable Z.

Rare-event estimators are often evaluated in terms of their asymptotic performance. To do this, we embed the rare event of interest in a family of increasingly rare events indexed by a rarity parameter γ. For example, we might consider what happens to estimators of $\ell = \mathbb{P}(S(\mathbf{X}) > \gamma)$ as $\gamma \to \infty$. The most common notion of asymptotic efficiency is *logarithmic efficiency*. An estimator is said to be logarithmically or asymptotically efficient if

$$\liminf_{\gamma \to \infty} \frac{|\log M|}{\left|\log \ell^2\right|} \geqslant 1.$$

By Jensen's inequality, $M \geqslant \ell^2$. Logarithmic efficiency means that asymptotically the estimator attains this lower bound on a log scale.

7.A.2 Importance Sampling

Importance sampling is a variance reduction method that is particularly well suited to rare-event problems. The idea is to improve upon the efficiency of the CMC estimator by using a different probability measure, under which the rare event is more likely. To do this, we observe that an expectation with respect to some density f can be rewritten as an expectation with respect to another density g, so long as $f(\mathbf{x}) = 0$ when $g(\mathbf{x}) = 0$. We write

$$\mathbb{E}_f \mathbb{I}(S(\mathbf{X}) > \gamma) = \int \mathbb{I}(S(\mathbf{X}) > \gamma) f(\mathbf{x}) \, d\mathbf{x}$$

$$= \int \frac{f(\mathbf{x})}{g(\mathbf{x})} \mathbb{I}(S(\mathbf{X}) > \gamma) g(\mathbf{x}) \, d\mathbf{x} = \mathbb{E}_g W(\mathbf{X}) \mathbb{I}(S(\mathbf{X}) > \gamma),$$

where $W(\mathbf{x}) = f(\mathbf{x})/g(\mathbf{x})$ is the *likelihood ratio*. This allows us to replace the CMC estimator 7.12 of ℓ with the *Importance Sampling* (IS) estimator

$$\hat{\ell}_{IS} = \frac{1}{N} \sum_{i=1}^{N} W(\mathbf{X}_i) \mathbb{I}(S(\mathbf{X}_i) > \gamma),$$

where the $\{\mathbf{X}_i\}$ are now drawn from g rather than f. The second moment of the IS estimator is

$$M_{IS} = \mathbb{E}_g \left(\frac{f(\mathbf{X})}{g(\mathbf{X})} \right)^2 \mathbb{I}(S(\mathbf{X}) > \gamma) = \mathbb{E}_f \frac{f(\mathbf{X})}{g(\mathbf{X})} \mathbb{I}(S(\mathbf{X}) > \gamma) = \mathbb{E} W(\mathbf{X}) \mathbb{I}(S(\mathbf{X}) > \gamma).$$

An importance sampling estimator will have smaller variance than the CMC estimator if $M_{IS} < \mathbb{E}\hat{\ell}^2$, that is, if

$$\mathbb{E}_f \frac{f(\mathbf{X})}{g(\mathbf{X})} \mathbb{I}(S(\mathbf{X}) > \gamma) < \mathbb{E}_f \mathbb{I}(S(\mathbf{X}) > \gamma).$$

The optimal IS density is the density that minimizes M_{IS}. It turns out that this density, g^*, actually gives an estimator with zero variance. The zero-variance density is given by

$$g^*(\mathbf{x}) = \operatorname*{argmin}_{g \in \mathcal{G}} \mathbb{E}_f \frac{f(\mathbf{X})}{g(\mathbf{X})} \mathbb{I}(S(\mathbf{x}) > \gamma) = \frac{f(\mathbf{x}) \mathbb{I}(S(\mathbf{x}) > \gamma)}{\ell},$$

where $\mathcal{G}$ contains all permissible densities (those such that $g(\mathbf{x}) = 0 \Rightarrow f(\mathbf{x}) = 0$). Unfortunately, the normalizing constant of g^* is ℓ, the estimand, so it is not a practical IS density. However, it provides valuable insight into the structure of good IS densities. In particular, note that,

$$\frac{f(\mathbf{x}) \mathbb{I}(S(\mathbf{x}) > \gamma)}{\ell} = f(\mathbf{x} \mid S(\mathbf{x}) > \gamma).$$

In other words, the optimal IS density, g^* is the original density conditioned on the rare event of interest having occurred. In practice, we usually restrict the IS density g to be a member of a parameterized family of densities $\{g(\mathbf{x}; \boldsymbol{\theta}) : \boldsymbol{\theta} \in \Theta\}$. This replaces the infinite-dimensional optimization problem of finding an optimal density with the simpler finite-dimensional problem of finding an optimal vector of parameters $\boldsymbol{\theta}^*$. Even so, it is generally difficult to find a closed-form solution to the *Variance Minimization* (VM) problem

$$\operatorname*{argmin}_{\boldsymbol{\theta} \in \Theta} \mathbb{E}_f \frac{f(\mathbf{X})}{g(\mathbf{X}; \boldsymbol{\theta})} \mathbb{I}(S(\mathbf{X}) > \gamma).$$

Instead of solving the VM problem directly, we usually aim to either solve a simpler problem, often using large deviations asymptotics, or to "learn" a good density adaptively.

7.A.3   The Choice of g

The choice of a good importance sampling density g is highly dependent on the distribution of $\mathbf{X}$ and the properties of the set $\{S(\mathbf{X}) > \gamma\}$. The tail behavior of the $S(\mathbf{X})$ plays an important role in determining the appropriate importance sampling density. A random variable Y is said to be *light-tailed* if $\mathbb{E}e^{\theta Y} < \infty$ for some $\theta > 0$. Light-tailed random variables have tails that decay at least exponentially fast. A random variable that is not light-tailed is said to be *heavy-tailed*. The rare-event behavior of heavy-tailed random variables is considerably different from the behavior of light-tailed random variables. The theory of rare-event simulation for heavy tails is reviewed in Asmussen and Glynn (2007) and Blanchet and Lam (2011).

Sometimes rare events can happen in more than one way. In this case, choosing a g that increases the likelihood of the rare event happening in a certain way may decrease the likelihood of the rare event happening in another way. This means that the likelihood ratio can take extreme values. In the worst case scenarios, this can even lead to estimators with asymptotically infinite variance, as shown in Glasserman and Wang (1997). In such cases, the appropriate importance sampling density may be a mixture distribution. The use of a mixture distribution may be necessary in some multi-factor models, see Glasserman et al. (2007) for a discussion.

In a light-tailed setting, the best importance sampling density is often an *exponentially twisted* density, f_θ, derived from the original density f. This density, f_θ is defined as

$$f_\theta(\mathbf{x}) = \exp\left\{\boldsymbol{\theta}^\mathsf{T}\mathbf{x} - \kappa(\boldsymbol{\theta})\right\} f(\mathbf{x}),$$

where

$$\kappa(\boldsymbol{\theta}) = \log \mathbb{E}\exp\left\{\boldsymbol{\theta}^\mathsf{T}\mathbf{X}\right\}$$

is the *cumulant generating function* of $\mathbf{X}$. The likelihood ratio of an exponentially twisted density is given by

$$W(\mathbf{x}) = \exp\left\{\kappa(\boldsymbol{\theta}) - \boldsymbol{\theta}^\mathsf{T}\mathbf{x}\right\}.$$

Dembo and Zeitouni (2010) and Bucklew (2004) summarize the many attractive properties of likelihood ratios of this form. For example, if there exists an $\boldsymbol{\nu}$ such that

$$\exp\left\{\kappa(\boldsymbol{\theta}) - \boldsymbol{\theta}^\mathsf{T}\mathbf{x}\right\} < \exp\left\{\kappa(\boldsymbol{\theta}) - \boldsymbol{\theta}^\mathsf{T}\boldsymbol{\nu}\right\}$$

for all $\boldsymbol{\theta}$ and all $\mathbf{x}$ such that $S(\mathbf{x}) > \gamma$, then this is a uniform bound on the likelihood ratio. The parameter $\boldsymbol{\theta}$ can then be chosen to minimize this upper bound, often leading to asymptotically efficient estimators; see, for example, Bucklew (2004).

7.A.4   Adaptive Importance Sampling

As discussed, the choice of a good importance sampling density is typically model-specific and often involves heavy analysis. It is therefore desirable to have an effective way to locate a good importance sampling density in an automatic fashion. In this section we introduce a popular adaptive importance sampling technique for rare-event probability estimation, namely, the Cross Entropy (CE) method. A book-length treatment of the CE method can be found in Rubinstein and Kroese (2004), and a recent review is given in Kroese (2011). An improved variant that shows better performance in various high-dimensional settings is recently proposed in Chan and Kroese (2011). See also Chan, Glynn and Kroese (2011) for a comparison between the CE and VM methods.

To motivate the CE method, recall that the zero-variance IS density for estimating ℓ is the conditional density given the rare event, i.e.:

$$g^*(\mathbf{x}) = \ell^{-1} f(\mathbf{x})\mathbb{I}(S(\mathbf{x}) > \gamma).$$

This suggests a practical way to obtain a good importance sampling density. Specifically, if g is chosen to be "close enough" to g^* so that both behave similarly, the resulting importance sampling estimator should have reasonable accuracy. Therefore, our goal is to locate a convenient density that is, in a well-defined sense, "close" to g^*.

Now, we formalize this strategy as an optimization problem as follows. Consider the family of density function $\mathcal{G} = \{g(\mathbf{x}; \boldsymbol{\theta})\}$ indexed by the parameter vector $\boldsymbol{\theta}$ within which to obtain the optimal IS density g. One particularly convenient directed divergence measure of densities g_1 and g_2 is the *Kullback–Leibler divergence*, or *cross entropy distance*:

$$\mathcal{D}(g_1, g_2) = \int g_1(\mathbf{x}) \log \frac{g_1(\mathbf{x})}{g_2(\mathbf{x})} d\mathbf{x}.$$

We locate the density g such that $\mathcal{D}(g^*, g)$ is minimized. Since every density in $\mathcal{G}$ can be represented as $g(\cdot; \boldsymbol{\theta})$ for some $\boldsymbol{\theta}$, the problem of obtaining the optimal IS reduces to the following parametric minimization problem:

$$\boldsymbol{\theta}^*_{ce} = \underset{\boldsymbol{\theta}}{\operatorname{argmin}}\, \mathcal{D}(g^*, g(\cdot; \boldsymbol{\theta})).$$

Further, it can be shown that solving the CE minimization problem is equivalent to finding

$$\boldsymbol{\theta}^*_{ce} = \underset{\boldsymbol{\theta}}{\operatorname{argmax}}\, \mathbb{E}\, f(\mathbf{X})\mathbb{I}(S(\mathbf{X}) \geqslant \gamma) \log g(\mathbf{X}; \boldsymbol{\theta}). \tag{7.13}$$

The deterministic problem 7.13 typically does not have an explicit solution. Instead, we can estimate $\boldsymbol{\theta}^*_{ce}$ by finding

$$\widehat{\boldsymbol{\theta}}^*_{ce} = \underset{\boldsymbol{\theta}}{\operatorname{argmax}}\, \frac{1}{N} \sum_{i=1}^{N} \mathbb{I}(S(\mathbf{X}_i) \geqslant \gamma) \log g(\mathbf{X}_i; \boldsymbol{\theta}), \tag{7.14}$$

where $\mathbf{X}_1, \ldots, \mathbf{X}_N$ are draws from f. If we are able to draw approximately from g^* – e.g. via Markov Chain Monte Carlo methods – we can instead find

$$\widehat{\boldsymbol{\theta}}^*_{ce} = \underset{\boldsymbol{\theta}}{\operatorname{argmax}}\, \frac{1}{N} \sum_{i=1}^{N} \log g(\mathbf{X}_i; \boldsymbol{\theta}), \tag{7.15}$$

where $\mathbf{X}_1, \ldots, \mathbf{X}_N$ are drawn approximately from g^*.

7.A.5 Importance Sampling for Stochastic Processes

Importance sampling is easily extended to a discrete stochastic process, $\mathbf{X} = \{X_n, n = 0, \ldots, N\}$, as long as the conditional densities $f(x_n \mid x_1, \ldots, x_{n-1}), n = 1, 2, \ldots$ are known. A natural importance sampling approach is to simply replace these conditional densities with other conditional densities $g(x_n \mid x_1, \ldots, x_{n-1}), n = 1, 2, \ldots$. The likelihood ratio is then given by

$$W(\mathbf{x}) = \prod_{n=1}^{N} \frac{f(x_n \mid x_1, \ldots, x_{n-1})}{g(x_n \mid x_1, \ldots, x_{n-1})}.$$

It is less straightforward to apply importance sampling to a continuous-time process, $\mathbf{X} = \{X_t, 0 \leqslant t \leqslant T\}$. The idea is to use the identity

$$\mathbb{E}_{\mathbb{P}} S(\mathbf{X}) = \mathbb{E}_{\mathbb{Q}} \frac{d\mathbb{P}}{d\mathbb{Q}} S(\mathbf{X}),$$

where $d\mathbb{P}/d\mathbb{Q}$ is the *Radon–Nikodym derivative*, S is an arbitrary real-valued function and $\mathbb{P}$ and $\mathbb{Q}$ are equivalent measures. This allows us to affect a change of measure similar to that used in discrete setting importance sampling. We note that the stochastic process $\{(d\mathbb{P}/d\mathbb{Q})_t, 0 \leqslant t \leqslant T\}$ is a positive martingale. Often, instead of defining $\mathbb{Q}$ explicitly, a positive martingale $\{M_t, 0 \leqslant t \leqslant T\}$ is specified instead. This induces a new measure $\mathbb{Q}$ via Girsanov's theorem. See, for example, Protter (2005) for an in-depth treatment. Examples of specifying a positive martingale and working out the corresponding dynamics of $\mathbb{Q}$ can be found in Bassamboo and Jain (2006), Zhang et al. (2009) and Giesecke and Shkolnik (2011). A discussion of change of measure for affine jump diffusions, which are of particular importance in credit risk modeling, can be found in Duffie et al. (2000).

REFERENCES

Artzner, P., Delbaen, F., Eber, J., Heath, D., 1999. Coherent measures of risk. Mathematical Finance 9(3), 203–228.

Asmussen, S., Glynn, P. W., 2007. Stochastic Simulation. Springer-Verlag, New York.

Bassamboo, A., Jain, S., 2006. Efficient importance sampling for reduced form models in credit risk. In: Perrone, L. F., Wieland, F. P., Liu, J., Lawson, B. G., Nicol, D. M., Fujimoto, R. M. (Eds), Proceedings of the 2006 Winter Simulation Conference. Institute of Electrical and Electronics Engineers, Inc.

Bassamboo, A., Juneja, S., Zeevi, A., 2008. Portfolio credit risk with extremal depdendence: Asymptotic analysis and efficient simulation. Operations Research 56(3), 593–606.

Blanchet, J., Lam, H., 2011. Rare event simulation techniques. In: Jain, S., Creasey, R. R., Himmelspach, J., White, K. P., Fu, M. (Eds.), Proceedings of the 2011 Winter Simulation Conference. Institute of Electrical and Electronics Engineers, Inc., pp. 146–160.

Bluhm, C., Overbeck, L., Wagner, C., 2010. Introduction to Credit Risk Modeling: Second Edition. Chapman & Hall/CRC financial mathematics series, Boca Raton.

Brigo, D., Pallavicini, A., Torresetti, R., 2009. Credit models and the crisis, or: How I learned to stop worrying and love the CDOs. Working paper, Imperial College, London. http://ssrn.com/abstract=1529498

Bucklew, J. A., 2004. Introduction to Rare Event Simulation. Springer-Verlag, New York.

Chan, J. C. C., Glynn, P. W., Kroese, D. P., 2011. A comparison of cross-entropy and variance minimization strategies. Journal of Applied Probability 48A, 183–194.

Chan, J. C. C., Kroese, D. P., 2010. Efficient estimation of large portfolio loss probabilities in t-copula models. European Journal of Operational Research 205(2), 361–367.

Chan, J. C. C., Kroese, D. P., 2011. Improved cross-entropy method for estimation. Statistics and Computing 22(5), 1031–1040.

Cherubini, U., Luciano, E., Vecchiato, W., 2004. Copula Methods in Finance. John Wiley & Sons, Chichester, England.

Dembo, A., Zeitouni, O., 2010. Large Deviations Techniques and Applications: 2nd Edition. Springer-Verlag, New York.

Donnelly, C., Embrechts, P., 2010. The devil is in the tails: actuarial mathematics and the subprime mortgage crisis. ASTIN Bulletin 40(1), 1–33.

Duffie, D., 2005. Credit risk modeling with affine processes. Journal of Banking and Finance 29, 2751–2802.

Duffie, D., Filipovic, D., Schachermayer, W., 2003. Affine processes and applications in finance. The Annals of Applied Probability 13(3), 984–1053.

Duffie, D., Pan, J., Singleton, K., 2000. Transform analysis and asset pricing for affine jump diffusions. Econometrica 68(6), 1343–1376.

Egloff, D., Leippold, M., 2010. Quantile estimation with adaptive importance sampling. Annals of Statistics 37, 451–457.

Frey, R., McNeil, A. J., 2001. Modelling depedent defaults. Working paper, ETH Zentrum. http://e-collection.ethbib. ethz.ch/show?type=bericht&nr=273

Giesecke, K., 2004. Credit risk modeling and valuation: An introduction. In: Shimko, D. (Ed.), Credit Risk Models and Management, Vol. 2. John Wiley & Sons, New York.

Giesecke, K., 2008. Portfolio credit risk: Top down vs. bottom up approaches. In: Cont, R. (Ed.), Frontiers in Quantitative Finance: Credit Risk and Volatility Modeling. John Wiley & Sons.

Giesecke, K., Kakavand, H., Mousavi, M., 2011. Exact simulation of point processes with stochastic intensities. Operations Research 59(5), 1233–1245.

Giesecke, K., Shkolnik, A., 2011. Importance sampling for event timing models. Working Paper, Stanford. www.stanford.edu/dept/MSandE/cgi-bin/people/faculty/giesecke/pdfs/is.pdf

Glasserman, P., 2004. Monte Carlo Methods in Financial Engineering. Springer-Verlag, New York.

Glasserman, P., Kang, W., Shahabuddin, P., 2007. Large deviations of multifactor portfolio credit risk. Mathematical Finance 17, 345–379.

Glasserman, P., Kang, W., Shahabuddin, P., 2008. Fast simulation of multifactor portfolio credit risk. Operations Research 56(5), 1200–1217.

Glasserman, P., Li, J., 2005. Importance sampling for portfolio credit risk. Management Science 51(11), 1643–1656.

Glasserman, P., Wang, Y., 1997. Counterexamples in importance sampling for large deviations probabilities. Annals of Applied Probability 7(3), 731–746.

Glynn, P. W., 1996. Importance sampling for Monte Carlo estimation of quantiles. In: Proceedings of the Second International Workshop on Mathematical Methods in Stochastic Simulation and Experimental Design. pp. 180–185.

Hong, L. J., Liu, G., 2011. Monte Carlo estimation of value-at-risk, conditional value-at-risk and their sensitivities. In: Jain, S., Creasey, R. R., Himmelspach, J., White, K. P., Fu, M. (Eds), Proceedings of the 2011 Winter Simulation Conference. Institute of Electrical and Electronics Engineers, Inc., pp. 95–107.

Juneja, S., Shahabuddin, P., 2006. Rare-event simulation techniques: An introduction and recent advances. In: Henderson, S. G., Nelson, B. L. (Eds), Handbook in Operations Research and Management Science, Vol. 13. North-Holland.

Kang, W., Shahabuddin, P., 2005. Fast simulation for multifactor portfolio credit risk in the t-copula model. In: Armstrong, M. E. K. N. M. S. F. B., Joines, J. A. (Eds), Proceedings of the 2005 Winter Simulation Conference. Institute of Electrical and Electronics Engineers, Inc., pp. 1859–1868.

Kroese, D. P., 2011. The cross-entropy method. In: Wiley Encyclopedia of Operations Research and Management Science.

Kroese, D. P., Taimre, T., Botev, Z. I., 2011. Handbook of Monte Carlo Methods. John Wiley & Sons, New York.

Li, D. X., 2000. On default correlation: A copula function approach. Journal of Fixed Income 9(4), 43–54.

McNeil, A. J., Frey, R., Embrechts, P., 2005. Quantitative Risk Management: Concepts, Techniques, Tools. Princeton University Press/Princeton Series in Finance, Princeton.

Nelsen, R. B., 2006. An Introduction to Copulas: Second Edition. Springer-Verlag, New York.

Ogata, Y., 1981. On Lewis' simulation method for point processes. IEEE Transactions on Information Theory 27(1), 23–31.

Protter, P. E., 2005. Stochastic Integration and Differential Equations: 2nd Edition. Springer-Verlag, New York.

Reitan, T., Aas, K., 2010. A new robust importance-sampling method for measuring value-at-risk and expected shortfall allocations for credit portfolios. Journal of Credit Risk 6(4), 113–149.

Rubino, G., Tuffin, B. (Eds), 2009. Rare Event Simulation using Monte Carlo Methods. John Wiley & Sons, New York.

Rubinstein, R. Y., Kroese, D. P., 2004. The Cross-Entropy Method: A Unified Approach to Combinatorial Optimization Monte-Carlo Simulation, and Machine Learning. Springer-Verlag, New York.

Sun, L., Hong, L. J., 2010. Asymptotic representations for importance-sampling estimators of value-at-risk and conditional value-at-risk. Operations Research Letters 38(4), 246–251.

van der Vaart, A. W., 1998. Asymptotic Statistics. Cambridge University Press, Cambridge.

Zhang, X., Glynn, P., Giesecke, K., Blanchet, J., 2009. Rare event simulation for a generalized Hawkes process. In: Rossetti, M. D., Hill, R. R., Johansson, B., Dunkin, A., Ingalls, R. G. (Eds), Proceedings of the 2009 Winter Simulation Conference. Institute of Electrical and Electronics Engineers, Inc.

8

Credit Portfolio Risk and Diversification

Rudi Schäfer[1], Alexander F. R. Koivusalo[2] and Thomas Guhr[1]

[1] *University of Duisburg-Essen*
[2] *Koivusalo Capital, Malmö*

8.1 INTRODUCTION

The present financial crisis illustrates in a dramatic fashion that a deeper understanding of portfolio credit risk is needed. While defaults are rare events, the ensuing losses can be substantial and have a serious impact on the entire financial sector and the economy as a whole. We can distinguish two conceptually different approaches to credit risk modeling: structural and reduced-form approaches. The structural models go back to Black and Scholes (1973) and Merton (1974). The Merton model assumes that a company has a certain amount of zero-coupon debt which becomes due at a fixed maturity date. The market value of the company is modeled by a stochastic process. A possible default and the associated recovery rate are determined directly from this market value at maturity. In the reduced-form approach default probabilities and recovery rates are described independently by stochastic models. These models aim to reproduce the dependence of these quantities on common covariates or risk factors. For some well known examples of reduced-form models see, e.g., Jarrow and Turnbull (1995), Jarrow et al. (1997), Duffie and Singleton (1999), Hull and White (2000) and Schönbucher (2003). First passage models were first introduced by Black and Cox (1976) and constitute a mixed approach. As in the Merton model, the market value of a company is modeled as a stochastic process. Default occurs as soon as the market value falls below a certain threshold. In contrast to the Merton model, default can occur at any time. In this approach, the recovery rate is not determined by the underlying process for the market value. Instead recovery rates are modeled independently, for example, by a reduced-form approach (see, e.g., Asvanunt and Staal (2009a, b)). The independent modeling of default and recovery rates can lead to a serious underestimation of large losses, as pointed out, e.g., in Chava et al. (2008), Bade et al. (2011) and Koivusalo and Schäfer (2011).

Here we take a step back, historically, and revisit the Merton model, where defaults and recoveries are both determined by an underlying process. Hence, they are intrinsically connected. In Monte Carlo simulations we study the influence which correlations and the number of credits in the portfolio have on the tail behavior of the portfolio loss distribution. Even for small correlations we observe a fast convergence to the large portfolio limit, which can be calculated analytically. In other words, diversification has only a very limited effect on the tail risk of credit portfolios. Here we recapitulate the calculation in Schäfer and Koivusalo (2011), which yields a functional relation between recovery rates and default probability. In Monte Carlo simulations we find that the same functional dependence also holds for other processes. We discuss how to incorporate this relation into reduced-form models, in order to restore essential structural information which is usually neglected in the reduced-form approach.

This chapter is organized as follows. We give a short introduction to the Merton model in Section 8.2. In Section 8.3 we consider the case of independent asset value processes. In Section 8.4 we present Monte Carlo results for correlated diffusion processes, and we discuss the dependence of tail risk on correlation strength and portfolio size. In Section 8.5 we treat the diffusion case analytically in the large portfolio limit, and we compare the results to Monte Carlo simulations of finite portfolios. Furthermore, we present numerical results for correlated GARCH processes. In Section 8.6 we discuss the applicability of the structural recovery rate beyond the Merton model. We summarize our findings in Section 8.7.

8.2 MODEL SETUP

We follow the presentation in Schäfer et al. (2007) and Guhr and Schäfer (2012). As in the original paper of Merton (1974), we assume that a company k has a certain amount of zero-coupon debt; this debt has the face value F_k and will become due at maturity time T. A default of the zero-coupon bond occurs if the value $V_k(T)$ of the company's assets at time T is less than the face value, i.e. if $V_k(T) < F_k$. The recovery rate is then $R_k = V_k(T)/F_k$ and the normalized loss given default is

$$L_k = 1 - R_k = \frac{F_k - V_k(T)}{F_k}. \tag{8.1}$$

In this structural model, defaults and losses – and hence also recoveries – are directly determined by the asset value at maturity. Therefore, the stochastic modeling of the asset value $V_k(t)$ of a company allows assessment of its credit risk. Let $\widetilde{p}_k$ be the probability density function (PDF) of the asset value $V_k(T)$ at maturity. To simplify the notation, we will write V_k instead of $V_k(T)$ in integral expressions. Then the default probability is given by

$$P_{Dk} = \int_0^{F_k} \widetilde{p}_k(V_k)\,dV_k\,, \tag{8.2}$$

the expected recovery rate can be calculated as

$$\langle R_k \rangle = \frac{1}{P_{Dk}} \int_0^{F_k} \frac{V_k}{F_k}\,\widetilde{p}_k(V_k)\,dV_k\,, \tag{8.3}$$

and the expected loss given default is

$$\langle L_k \rangle = \frac{1}{P_{Dk}} \int_0^{F_k} \frac{F_k - V_k}{F_k}\,\widetilde{p}_k(V_k)\,dV_k \tag{8.4}$$

$$= \int_0^1 L_k\,p_k(L_k)\,dL_k\,, \tag{8.5}$$

where p_k is the PDF of the loss given default.

The loss for a portfolio of K contracts is the sum of the non-normalized losses $F_k - V_k(T)$, normalized to the sum of all face values,

$$L = \frac{\sum_{k=1}^{K}(F_k - V_k(T))\,\Theta(F_k - V_k(T))}{\sum_{l=1}^{K} F_l}\,. \tag{8.6}$$

Here we use the Heaviside function Θ as a default indicator,

$$\Theta(F_k - V_k(T)) = \begin{cases} 1 , & \text{if} \quad V_k(T) \leq F_k \quad \text{(default)} \\ 0 , & \text{if} \quad V_k(T) > F_k \quad \text{(no default)} \end{cases} . \tag{8.7}$$

We notice that the portfolio loss (8.6) is normalized such that $0 \leq L \leq 1$. Introducing the dimensionless fractional face values

$$f_k = \frac{F_k}{\sum_{l=1}^{K} F_l} \tag{8.8}$$

and using $L_k = (F_k - V_k(T))/F_k$ according to definition 8.1, we can cast the portfolio loss into the form

$$L = \sum_{k=1}^{K} f_k L_k \, \Theta(F_k - V_k(T)). \tag{8.9}$$

In the special case of a homogenous portfolio with identical face values for all companies, the fractional face values become $f_k = 1/K$ and the portfolio loss is the arithmetic mean

$$L = \frac{1}{K} \sum_{k=1}^{K} L_k \, \Theta(F_k - V_k(T)) , \qquad \text{if all } F_k \text{ are equal.} \tag{8.10}$$

The distribution $p(L)$ of the portfolio loss is the main quantity of interest. Since the portfolio loss is functionally dependent on the asset values at maturity, $V_k(T)$, we can calculate the portfolio loss distribution using a filter integral,

$$p(L) = \int_0^\infty dV_1 \cdots \int_0^\infty dV_K \, \tilde{p}(V_1, \ldots, V_K) \, \delta \left(L - \sum_{k=1}^{K} f_k L_k \, \Theta(F_k - V_k) \right). \tag{8.11}$$

We notice the subtle difference between the loss distribution and the distribution of the loss given default. This difference is best understood by considering Equation (8.11) for $K = 1$, which yields

$$p(L) = (1 - P_{D1})\delta(L) + P_{D1} p_1(L). \tag{8.12}$$

This is the weighted sum of the distribution $\delta(L)$ in the case of no default, and the distribution $p_1(L)$ in the case of default.

8.3 INDEPENDENT ASSET VALUES

Let us first consider the case of independent asset value processes. Then the multivariate PDF of the asset values, $\tilde{p}(V_1, \ldots, V_K)$, factorizes and we can write the portfolio loss distribution (8.11) as

$$p(L) = \int_0^\infty dV_1 \, \tilde{p}_1(V_1) \cdots \int_0^\infty dV_K \, \tilde{p}(V_K) \, \delta \left(L - \sum_{k=1}^{K} f_k L_k \, \Theta(F_k - V_k) \right). \tag{8.13}$$

For the expected loss we find

$$\langle L \rangle = \sum_{k=1}^{K} f_k \langle L_k \Theta(F_k - V_k) \rangle = \sum_{k=1}^{K} f_k \langle L_k \rangle P_{\mathrm{D}k}. \tag{8.14}$$

To check the form of the loss distribution around the expected loss, we consider the skewness and the kurtosis excess. They are combinations of the centered moments

$$m_\nu = \langle (L - \langle L \rangle)^\nu \rangle. \tag{8.15}$$

The skewness is the third centered moment, normalized by the standard deviation to the third power,

$$\gamma_1 = \frac{m_3}{m_2^{3/2}} = \frac{\langle (L - \langle L \rangle)^3 \rangle}{\langle (L - \langle L \rangle)^2 \rangle^{3/2}}. \tag{8.16}$$

It is zero for a symmetric distribution and it is the larger the more asymmetric the distribution is. The kurtosis excess is defined as

$$\gamma_2 = \frac{m_4}{m_2^2} - 3 = \frac{\langle (L - \langle L \rangle)^4 \rangle}{\langle (L - \langle L \rangle)^2 \rangle^2} - 3 \tag{8.17}$$

which is zero for a Gaussian and larger the fatter the tails.

Equation (8.13) yields for the second and third central moment

$$m_2 = \sum_{k=1}^{K} f_k^2 P_{\mathrm{D}k} \left(\langle L_k^2 \rangle - P_{\mathrm{D}k} \langle L_k \rangle^2 \right),$$

$$m_3 = \sum_{k=1}^{K} f_k^3 P_{\mathrm{D}k} \left(\langle L_k^3 \rangle - 3 P_{\mathrm{D}k} \langle L_k^2 \rangle \langle L_k \rangle + 2 P_{\mathrm{D}k}^2 \langle L_k \rangle^3 \right). \tag{8.18}$$

Because of $m_3 \neq 0$, the portfolio loss distribution is asymmetric. How does this asymmetry depend on the number of companies K? We assume that the face values F_k are all of the same order which implies $f_k \sim 1/K$ according to Equation (8.8). Furthermore, we assume that the parameters of the stochastic processes, and thus the individual default probabilities $P_{\mathrm{D}k}$ and moments $\langle L_k^\nu \rangle$, are also similar for the different companies. Then the second and the third centered moments are of order $1/K$ and $1/K^2$, respectively. This yields the estimate

$$\gamma_1 \sim \frac{1}{\sqrt{K}} \tag{8.19}$$

for the K dependence of the skewness. The skewness vanishes rather slowly as a function of K. Even for a large number of companies, the portfolio loss distribution is asymmetric. Similarly, we can consider the kurtosis excess and find

$$\gamma_2 \sim \frac{1}{K} \tag{8.20}$$

for its K dependence.

To further study the shape of the portfolio loss distribution as a function of K, we carry out a $1/K$ expansion, cf. Schäfer et al. (2007). We work with the characteristic function $\varphi(\omega)$ where

$$p(L) = \frac{1}{2\pi} \int_{-\infty}^{+\infty} \varphi(\omega) \exp(-i\omega L) d\omega \qquad \text{and} \qquad \varphi(\omega) = \int_{0}^{1} p(L) \exp(i\omega L) dL. \quad (8.21)$$

Equation (8.13) yields

$$\varphi(\omega) = \prod_{k=1}^{K} \int_{0}^{\infty} dV_k \, \tilde{p}_k(V_k) \exp(i\omega f_k L_k \Theta(F_k - V_k))$$

$$= \prod_{k=1}^{K} \left(\int_{F_k}^{\infty} dV_k \, \tilde{p}_k(V_k) + \int_{0}^{F_k} dV_k \, \tilde{p}_k(V_k) \exp(i\omega f_k L_k) \right)$$

$$= \prod_{k=1}^{K} \left((1 - P_{Dk}) + P_{Dk} \int_{0}^{1} dL_k \, p_k(L_k) \exp(i\omega f_k L_k) \right)$$

$$= \prod_{k=1}^{K} \left((1 - P_{Dk}) + P_{Dk} \varphi_k(\omega f_k) \right)$$

$$= \exp \left(\sum_{k=1}^{K} \ln \left(1 + P_{Dk}(\varphi_k(\omega f_k) - 1) \right) \right). \quad (8.22)$$

In the second last step, we introduced the characteristic function of the individual loss given default distribution,

$$\varphi_k(\omega_k) = \int_{0}^{1} p_k(L_k) \exp(i\omega_k L_k) dL_k. \quad (8.23)$$

We notice that it appears in Equation (8.22) with argument ωf_k. We recall that $f_k \sim 1/K$ if the face values are not too different in size. To derive an approximation for the portfolio loss distribution, we make this assumption. We may then view the argument ωf_k as small and expand the characteristic function. We find

$$\varphi(\omega f_k) = 1 + i\omega f_k \langle L_k \rangle - \frac{\omega^2}{2} f_k^2 \langle L_k^2 \rangle - \frac{i\omega^3}{6} f_k^3 \langle L_k^3 \rangle + \mathcal{O}\left(\frac{1}{K^4}\right) \quad (8.24)$$

up to third order in $1/K$ where $\langle L_k^\nu \rangle$ is the ν–th moment of the individual loss given default. We insert the expansion (8.24) into the last of the Equations (8.22) and also expand the logarithm up to third order in $1/K$. Collecting everything, we find

$$\varphi(\omega) = \exp \left(i \langle L \rangle \omega - \frac{m_2}{2} \omega^2 - i \frac{m_3}{6} \omega^3 + \mathcal{O}\left(\frac{1}{K^3}\right) \right). \quad (8.25)$$

The exact mean value $\langle L \rangle$ as given in Equation (8.14) and the exact centered moments m_2 and m_3 as given in Equation (8.18) occur. This yields for the portfolio loss distribution

$$p(L) = \frac{1}{2\pi} \int_{-\infty}^{+\infty} \exp\left(-i(L - \langle L \rangle)\omega - \frac{m_2}{2}\omega^2 - i\frac{m_3}{6}\omega^3 + \mathcal{O}\left(\frac{1}{K^3}\right)\right) d\omega \quad (8.26)$$

up to order $1/K^2$. If we settle with an approximation to first order $1/K$, we may drop the term involving m_3 and find the Gaussian

$$p(L) \simeq \frac{1}{\sqrt{2\pi m_2}} \exp\left(-\frac{(L - \langle L \rangle)^2}{2m_2}\right) \quad (8.27)$$

with variance m_2. The reason for the appearance of this Gaussian is, of course, the Central Limit Theorem. We convinced ourselves that the third centered moment m_3 is the next to leading term in a $1/K$ expansion. We thereby also showed the importance of the skewness γ_1 and the slowness of the convergence to a symmetric, that is, Gaussian form.

However, there is a severe drawback in the asymptotic approximations (8.26) and (8.27), because they cannot account for an important non-analytic contribution. There is always a contribution of a δ–function at $L = 0$ stemming from the probability that no default occurs. This contribution is often not included in graphical representations of the loss distribution.

A better approximation of the portfolio loss distribution is possible if we restrict ourselves to homogenous portfolios. Then we can rewrite Equation (8.13) as a combinatorial sum

$$p(L) = \sum_{j=0}^{K} \binom{K}{j} (1 - P_{\mathrm{D}})^{K-j} P_{\mathrm{D}}^{j} F_j(L) \quad (8.28)$$

where we define the function $F_j(L)$ as

$$F_j(L) = \int_0^1 dL_1 p_1(L_1) \cdots \int_0^1 dL_j p_j(L_j) \, \delta\left(L - \frac{1}{K}\sum_{k=1}^{j} L_k\right)$$

$$\approx \frac{1}{2\pi} \int_{-\infty}^{\infty} d\omega \exp\left(-i\omega\left(L - \frac{j}{K}\langle L_k \rangle\right)\right)$$

$$\exp\left(-\frac{\omega^2 j}{2K^2}\left(\langle L_k^2 \rangle - \langle L_k \rangle^2\right) - \frac{i\omega^3 j}{6K^3}\left(\langle L_k^3 \rangle - 3\langle L_k \rangle\langle L_k^2 \rangle + 2\langle L_k \rangle^3\right)\right).$$

The approximation for $F_j(L)$ follows the same line of arguing as above. For details see Schäfer et al. (2007). Note that each term of the sum in Equation (8.28) corresponds to the event that exactly j defaults occur. In particular, for $j = 0$ the delta peak $(1 - P_{\mathrm{D}})^K \delta(L)$ is obtained exactly in this approximation.

Of course, independent asset values are not realistic. However, when we study the influence of correlations, it will be helpful to contrast those results with the independent case. Furthermore, we can apply our insights for independent processes to derive analytical results for the correlated case in the large portfolio limit.

8.4 CORRELATED ASSET VALUES

While our considerations for independent asset values are valid for any stochastic process with finite moments, we are now going to consider a specific process for the asset values. We model their time evolution by a stochastic differential equation of the form

$$\frac{\mathrm{d}V_k}{V_k} = \mu\mathrm{d}t + \sqrt{c}\,\sigma\mathrm{d}W_\mathrm{m} + \sqrt{1-c}\,\sigma\mathrm{d}W_k. \tag{8.29}$$

This is a correlated diffusion process with a deterministic term $\mu\mathrm{d}t$ and a linearly correlated diffusion. The Wiener processes $\mathrm{d}W_k$ and $\mathrm{d}W_\mathrm{m}$ describe the idiosyncratic and the market fluctuations, respectively. For simplicity, we choose the same drift μ, volatility σ and correlation coefficient c for all companies.

In the Monte Carlo simulations we consider the stochastic process in Equation (8.29) for discrete time increments $\Delta t = T/N$, where the time to maturity T is divided into N steps. The market value of company k at maturity is then given by

$$V_k(T) = V_k(0) \prod_{t=1}^{N} \left(1 + \mu\Delta t + \sqrt{c}\,\sigma\eta_{\mathrm{m},t}\sqrt{\Delta t} + \sqrt{1-c}\,\sigma\varepsilon_{k,t}\sqrt{\Delta t}\right). \tag{8.30}$$

The random variables $\eta_{\mathrm{m},t}$ and $\varepsilon_{k,t}$ are independent and are drawn from a normal distribution. It is not difficult to carry out numerical simulations for arbitrary sets of input parameters. However, to study the generic behavior, it is helpful to reduce the number of free parameters in the model. We restrict our study to a homogeneous portfolio where the parameters for the asset value processes (8.30) are the same for all companies and all bonds have the same face value and maturity. We make these choices to prevent a competition of effects due to variations in these parameters with those features that we wish to focus on, namely the dependence of the loss distribution on the number of companies K and on the correlations. The parameters for the diffusion process are $\mu = 0.05$ and $\sigma = 0.15$. The initial asset value is set to $V_0 = 100$, the face value of the zero-coupon bonds is $F = 75$ with maturity time $T = 1$.

We begin with the simplest case in which correlations are absent, $c = 0$. In Figure 8.1, the simulated loss distributions are displayed for $K = 100$ and for $K = 1,000$ companies. While the strong non-Gaussian shape was to be expected for $K = 100$, it is remarkable that the loss distribution still has a small asymmetry for $K = 1,000$ and thus deviates from Gaussian form.

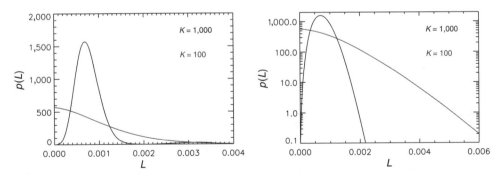

Figure 8.1   The portfolio loss distribution $p(L)$ for $K = 100$ and for $K = 1,000$ contracts, in the absence of correlations. $p(L)$ is shown on a linear scale (left), and on a logarithmic scale (right). The contribution proportional to $\delta(L)$ is not shown.

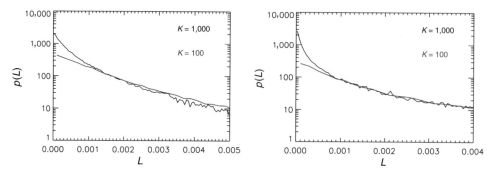

Figure 8.2 The portfolio loss distribution $p(L)$ for $K = 100$ and for $K = 1,000$ contracts, where the correlations are specified by $c = 0.2$ (left) and $c = 0.5$ (right). The contribution proportional to $\delta(L)$ is not shown.

This demonstrates once more that the Central Limit Theorem is for the loss distribution valid only for extremely large K. We can numerically check the $1/K$ behavior of skewness and kurtosis excess as predicted in Equations (8.19) and (8.20).

We proceed by switching on the correlations. The loss distributions resulting for $c = 0.2$ and $c = 0.5$ are displayed in Figure 8.2. The results differ considerably from the uncorrelated case, because they are much further away from Gaussian shape. In particular, we observe that the tails of the loss distributions are nearly identical for $K = 100$ and $K = 1,000$. That means the probability of large losses could not be reduced by increasing the number of contracts in the portfolio. How does this behavior depend on the correlation coefficient c? To answer this question, we examine two risk measures which capture the tail behavior of the portfolio loss distribution, the Value at Risk (VaR) and the Expected Tail Loss (ETL). Both measures are commonly used in credit risk management, see, e.g., Artzner et al. (1997), Frey and McNeil (2002) and Yamai and Yoshiba (2005). Figure 8.3 shows the Value at Risk and the Expected Tail Loss for the 99.9% confidence level. The results are shown for $K = 10$, $K = 100$ and $K = 1,000$ companies as a function of the correlation coefficient c. Importantly, already at a correlation coefficient of $c = 0.25$ or so, the three curves merge. Hence, for larger c, the tail behavior does not depend on the number K of companies anymore; the system behaves as if the effective number of companies were the same. Figures 8.2 and 8.3 demonstrate that

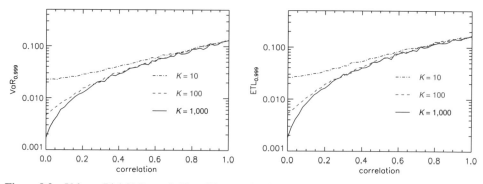

Figure 8.3 Value at Risk $\text{VaR}_{0.999}$ (left) and Expected Tail Loss $\text{ETL}_{0.999}$ (right) for $K = 10, 100, 1,000$ (solid, dashed, dotted line, respectively) as function of the correlation coefficient c. The scale on the vertical axis is logarithmic.

diversification does not reduce credit risk if the correlations are too large. This result is of high practical relevance, because correlation coefficients of 0.25 or larger are not at all uncommon in market data.

8.5 LARGE PORTFOLIO LIMIT

In the previous section we have seen the numerical results of the structural credit risk model with correlated asset value processes. The correlations had a profound effect on the tail behavior of the portfolio loss distribution. Increasing the number of contracts K in a portfolio has only a very limited effect on the risk of large portfolio losses. Even for rather small correlations, the portfolio loss distribution approaches very quickly an asymptotic limit for $K \to \infty$. Our goal in this section is to describe this limiting distribution analytically. In addition we will derive a functional relation between expected recovery rate and default probability, cf. Schäfer and Koivusalo (2011).

In the structural model defaults and losses are directly determined by the asset value at maturity. Therefore, the stochastic modeling of the asset value $V_k(t)$ of a company allows assessment of its credit risk. We consider a portfolio of K credit contracts, where the asset value of each company k is correlated to one or more covariates. Conditioned on the values of the covariates we obtain different values for default probability $P_{\mathrm{D}k}$ and expected recovery rate $\langle R_k \rangle = 1 - \langle L_k \rangle$. In fact, we find a functional dependence between these two quantities, which is in stark contrast to many reduced form models which assume their independence.

8.5.1 Correlated Diffusion

We consider a homogeneous portfolio of size K with the same parameters for each asset value process, and with the same face values, $F_k = F$, and initial asset values, $V_k(0) = V_0$. For discrete time increments $\Delta t = T/N$, we arrive at the discrete formulation of the asset value of company k at maturity,

$$V_k(T) = V_0 \prod_{t=1}^{N} \left(1 + \mu \Delta t + \sqrt{c}\,\sigma \eta_{\mathrm{m},t} \sqrt{\Delta t} + \sqrt{1-c}\,\sigma \varepsilon_{k,t} \sqrt{\Delta t} \right). \quad (8.31)$$

We define the market return X_{m} as the average return of all single companies k over the time horizon up to maturity,

$$X_{\mathrm{m}} = \frac{1}{K} \sum_{k=1}^{K} \left(\frac{V_k(T)}{V_0} - 1 \right)$$

$$= \frac{1}{K} \sum_{k=1}^{K} \prod_{t=1}^{N} \left(1 + \mu \Delta t + \sqrt{c}\,\sigma \eta_{\mathrm{m},t} \sqrt{\Delta t} + \sqrt{1-c}\,\sigma \varepsilon_{k,t} \sqrt{\Delta t} \right) - 1. \quad (8.32)$$

For $K \to \infty$ we can express the average over k as the expectation value for $\varepsilon_{k,t}$, which is zero. This leads us to the expression

$$\ln (X_{\mathrm{m}} + 1) = \sum_{t=1}^{N} \ln \left(1 + \mu \Delta t + \sqrt{c}\,\sigma \eta_{\mathrm{m},t} \sqrt{\Delta t} \right)$$

$$\approx \left(\mu - \frac{c\sigma^2}{2} \right) T + \sigma \sqrt{cT} \frac{1}{\sqrt{N}} \sum_{t=1}^{N} \eta_{\mathrm{m},t}. \quad (8.33)$$

In the last step of the calculation we expanded the logarithm up to first order in Δt. The random variables $\eta_{m,t}$ are standard normal distributed. Therefore the variable $\ln(X_m + 1)$ is normal distributed with mean $\mu T - \frac{1}{2}c\sigma^2 T$ and variance $c\sigma^2 T$, according to Itō's lemma. This implies a shifted log-normal distribution for the market return itself,

$$\overline{p}(X_m) = \frac{1}{(X_m + 1)\sqrt{2\pi c\sigma^2 T}} \exp\left(-\frac{\left(\ln(X_m + 1) - \mu T + \frac{1}{2}c\sigma^2 T\right)^2}{2c\sigma^2 T}\right). \quad (8.34)$$

Similarly, we can write for a single company k

$$\ln\frac{V_k(T)}{V_0} \approx \ln(X_m + 1) - \frac{(1-c)\sigma^2}{2}T + \sigma\sqrt{(1-c)T}\frac{1}{\sqrt{N}}\sum_{t=1}^{N}\varepsilon_{k,t}. \quad (8.35)$$

Conditioned on a fixed value for the market return X_m, all variables $V_k(T)$ are independent and the variable $\ln V_k(T)/V_0$ is normal distributed with mean $\ln(X_m + 1) - \frac{1}{2}(1-c)\sigma^2 T$ and variance $(1-c)\sigma^2 T$. Hence, the probability density function for the asset value $V_k(T)$ is given by

$$\widetilde{p}(V_k(T)) = \frac{1}{V_k(T)\sqrt{2\pi(1-c)\sigma^2 T}} \exp\left(-\frac{\left(\ln\frac{V_k(T)}{V_0} - \ln(X_m + 1) + \frac{1}{2}(1-c)\sigma^2 T\right)^2}{2(1-c)\sigma^2 T}\right). \quad (8.36)$$

We introduce the function

$$A(X_m) = \ln\frac{F}{V_0} - \ln(X_m + 1) \quad (8.37)$$

and the compound parameter

$$B = \sqrt{(1-c)\sigma^2 T}. \quad (8.38)$$

For $c = 0$ this parameter B is equal to the volatility on the time horizon T; for $c > 0$ it has a reduced value. With $A(X_m)$ and B we can express the individual default probability as

$$P_D(X_m) = \int_0^F \widetilde{p}(V_k)\,dV_k = \Phi\left(\frac{A(X_m) + \frac{1}{2}B^2}{B}\right), \quad (8.39)$$

where Φ is the cumulative standard normal distribution. The expectation value for the individual loss given default reads

$$\langle L_k(X_m)\rangle = \frac{1}{P_D(X_m)}\int_0^F\left(1 - \frac{V_k}{F}\right)\widetilde{p}(V_k)\,dV_k$$

$$= \frac{1}{P_D(X_m)}\left[\Phi\left(\frac{A(X_m) + \frac{1}{2}B^2}{B}\right) - e^{-A(X_m)}\Phi\left(\frac{A(X_m) - \frac{1}{2}B^2}{B}\right)\right]. \quad (8.40)$$

This leads to the expected recovery rate

$$\langle R(X_m)\rangle = e^{-A(X_m)} \Phi\left(\frac{A(X_m) - \frac{1}{2}B^2}{B}\right) \bigg/ \Phi\left(\frac{A(X_m) + \frac{1}{2}B^2}{B}\right). \qquad (8.41)$$

The portfolio loss for a homogeneous portfolio, or simply the average loss, is then given as

$$\langle L(X_m)\rangle = P_D(X_m)\langle L_k(X_m)\rangle. \qquad (8.42)$$

Conditioned on the market return, the single asset value processes are independent. Hence, we know from Section 8.3 that the variance of portfolio losses will be zero in the limit $K \to \infty$. We can therefore substitute the portfolio loss $L(X_m)$ by its expectation value and obtain from Equations (8.40) and (8.42)

$$L(X_m) = \Phi\left(\frac{A(X_m) + \frac{1}{2}B^2}{B}\right) - e^{-A(X_m)} \Phi\left(\frac{A(X_m) - \frac{1}{2}B^2}{B}\right). \qquad (8.43)$$

We can eliminate $A(X_m)$ from Equations (8.39) and (8.41) and arrive at a functional dependence of recovery rate and default probability,

$$\langle R(P_D)\rangle = \frac{1}{P_D} \exp\left(-B\,\Phi^{-1}(P_D) + \frac{1}{2}B^2\right) \Phi\left(\Phi^{-1}(P_D) - B\right). \qquad (8.44)$$

This functional relation depends only on a single parameter B. In Figure 8.4 we demonstrate this parameter dependence by showing $\langle R(P_D)\rangle$ for a set of parameter values. Larger values for B lead to an overall decrease of recovery rates. In addition the dependence on P_D becomes steeper. From Equation (8.44) we obtain the functional relation of portfolio losses and default probabilities,

$$L(P_D) = P_D - \exp\left(-B\,\Phi^{-1}(P_D) + \frac{1}{2}B^2\right) \Phi\left(\Phi^{-1}(P_D) - B\right). \qquad (8.45)$$

The parameter dependence of this relation is also shown in Figure 8.4.

In the Monte Carlo simulation we consider the stochastic process in Equation (8.31) for discrete time increments, and with the same parameters of the individual processes as in

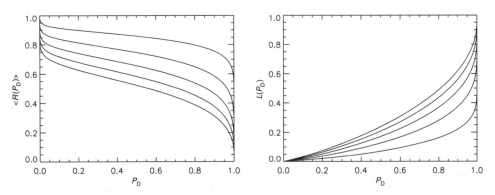

Figure 8.4   Parameter dependence of the functional relations $\langle R(P_D)\rangle$ (left plot) and $L(P_D)$ (right plot). The parameter values are $B = 0.2, 0.4, 0.6, 0.8$ and 1.0 (top to bottom in left plot, and bottom to top in right plot).

Section 8.4. As a correlation coefficient we choose $c = 0.5$. The simulation is run with an inner loop and an outer loop. In the inner loop we simulate $K = 500$ different realizations of $\varepsilon_{k,t}$ for a single realization of the market fluctuations $\eta_{m,t}$ with $t = 1, \ldots, N$. The inner loop can be interpreted as a homogeneous portfolio of size K, or simply as an average over the idiosyncratic part of the process. In each run of the inner loop, we calculate the market return X_m, the number of defaults $N_D(X_m)$ and the average recovery rate $\langle R(X_m) \rangle$. The number of defaults $N_D(X_m)$ counts how many times the condition $V_k(T) < F$ is fulfilled. We can estimate the default probability as

$$P_D(X_m) \approx N_D(X_m)/K. \tag{8.46}$$

We obtain the portfolio loss as

$$L(X_m) = \frac{1}{K} \sum_{k=1}^{K} \frac{F - V_k(T)}{F} \Theta(F - V_k(T)). \tag{8.47}$$

The outer loop runs over 10^6 realizations of the market terms, where we obtain different values for the market return X_m and, consequently, the number of defaults $N_D(X_m)$, the default probability $P_D(X_m)$ and the average recovery rate $\langle R(X_m) \rangle$.

Figure 8.5 shows the dependence of recovery rates $\langle R(X_m) \rangle$ on default probabilities $P_D(X_m)$ in one plot, and the dependence of portfolio losses $L(X_m)$ on default probabilities $P_D(X_m)$ in a second plot. In both cases we observe a very good agreement between the Monte Carlo simulations and the analytical results in Equations (8.44) and (8.45), respectively. Deviations from the average values are smaller for higher default probabilities. Low default probabilities correspond to positive or small negative market returns X_m. In this case defaults and recoveries are mostly influenced by the idiosyncratic part of the process and the correlation to the market plays only a minor role. This is why we observe a much broader range of recovery rates for low default probabilities.

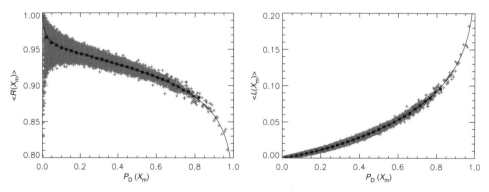

Figure 8.5 Dependence on default probabilities P_D for the diffusion process. The left plot shows the dependence of recovery rates $\langle R(X_m) \rangle$ on default probabilities $P_D(X_m)$. The right plot shows the dependence of portfolio losses $\langle L(X_m) \rangle$ on default probabilities $P_D(X_m)$. The Monte Carlo results for the diffusion process (grey symbols) are compared to the analytical results (solid line). Black star symbols indicate local average values of the simulation results. The parameter $B = \sqrt{(1 - c)\sigma^2 T}$ is determined from the simulation parameters.

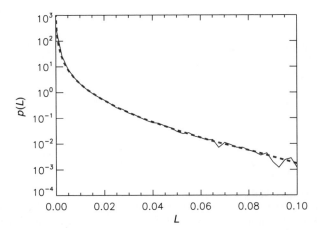

Figure 8.6   The portfolio loss distribution $p(L)$ for the correlated diffusion with $c = 0.5$. The black solid line corresponds to the simulation results. The grey dashed line shows the analytical results.

Given the functional relation (8.43) between portfolio loss L and market return X_m we can transform the PDF of market returns into the PDF of portfolio losses,

$$p(L) = \frac{1}{|L'(X_m)|} \, \overline{p}(X_m). \tag{8.48}$$

A comparison to the Monte Carlo result for the portfolio loss distribution is given in Figure 8.6. We observe an excellent agreement, even for large portfolio losses.

As we have seen in the numerical results in Section 8.4, even small correlations lead to a fast convergence of the portfolio loss PDF to the large portfolio limit. Let us now calculate the Value at Risk and Expected Tail Loss in this limit.

We start from the PDF of market returns (8.34) and calculate its quantile function as

$$\bar{F}^{-1}(\alpha) = \exp\left(\sqrt{c\sigma^2 T} \, \Phi^{-1}(\alpha) + \mu T - \frac{1}{2}c\sigma^2 T \right) - 1. \tag{8.49}$$

We can express the Value at Risk at confidence level α as

$$\text{VaR}_\alpha = L\left(\bar{F}^{-1}(1 - \alpha) \right), \tag{8.50}$$

where the function L is given by Equation (8.43). The Expected Tail Loss is the expectation value of portfolio losses which are larger than the Value at Risk,

$$\text{ETL}_\alpha = \frac{1}{1-\alpha} \int\limits_{\text{VaR}_\alpha}^{1} L\, p(L)\, dL = \frac{1}{1-\alpha} \int\limits_{-1}^{\bar{F}^{-1}(1-\alpha)} L(X_m)\, \overline{p}(X_m)\, dX_m. \tag{8.51}$$

It is straightforward to evaluate this integral numerically. Figure 8.7 shows Value at Risk and Expected Tail Loss for a 99.9% confidence interval, in dependence of the correlation coefficient c. Expressions (8.50) and (8.51) are valid in the large portfolio limit, $K \to \infty$. These results are compared to the simulations for finite K. We observe that the tail risk for $K = 1,000$ has reached the large portfolio limit even for very small correlations.

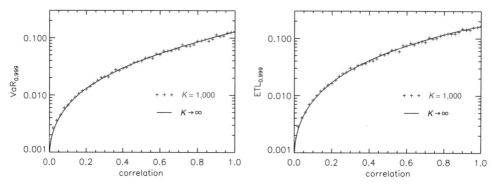

Figure 8.7 Value at Risk $\mathrm{VaR}_{0.999}$ (left) and Expected Tail Loss $\mathrm{ETL}_{0.999}$ (right) as function of the correlation coefficient c. The solid lines correspond to the analytical result for $K \to \infty$, while the grey symbols show the simulation result for $K = 1{,}000$. The scale on the vertical axis is logarithmic.

8.5.2   Correlated GARCH Process

Let us now consider the Merton model with a GARCH(1,1) model for the underlying asset value process. The GARCH model was first introduced by Bollerslev (1986). It is able to reproduce many of the stylized facts found in empirical financial time series. In particular, it exhibits volatility clustering and fat-tailed return distributions. The GARCH(1,1) model is a discrete time process with an autoregressive volatility. The return at time t reads

$$r_{k,t} = \sigma_{k,t} \left(\sqrt{c}\, \eta_t + \sqrt{1 - c}\, \varepsilon_{k,t} \right)$$
$$\sigma_{k,t}^2 = \alpha_0 + \alpha_1\, r_{k,t-1}^2 + \beta_1\, \sigma_{k,t-1}^2. \tag{8.52}$$

where η_t and $\varepsilon_{k,t}$ are independent normal distributed random variables. The parameters α_0, α_1 and β_1 are chosen in order to mimic the behavior of a typical empirical time series of daily returns. The initial values for the volatilities have been set homogeneously as $\sigma_{k,0} = \sigma \sqrt{\Delta t}$, where $\sigma = 0.15$ is the same value used in the diffusion case. However, the volatility does not remain the same for all k as t evolves, since $\sigma_{k,t}$ also depends on the idiosyncratic random part in $r_{k,t-1}$. Thus, the homogeneity of the portfolio is lost to some degree. Instead the process covers a wide range of volatilities both within one realization of the market terms, i.e. within one portfolio, and also over different market realizations. The GARCH process is therefore the most general case we examine here. It can provide a good indication of how broadly our analytical results for the diffusion case can be applied.

For the GARCH process the market value of company k at maturity reads

$$V_k(T) = V_0 \prod_{t=1}^{N} \left(1 + \mu \Delta t + r_{k,t} \right). \tag{8.53}$$

The deterministic drift term can also be included in Equation (8.52) instead. Then the parameters α_0, α_1 and β_1 have to be adjusted accordingly. The drift constant is again set to $\mu = 0.05$.

As in the diffusion case we simulate 10^6 portfolios of size $K = 500$. For each portfolio we calculate the market return X_m, the number of defaults $N_\mathrm{D}(X_\mathrm{m})$, the default probabilities $P_\mathrm{D}(X_\mathrm{m})$ and the expected recovery rate $\langle R(X_\mathrm{m}) \rangle$.

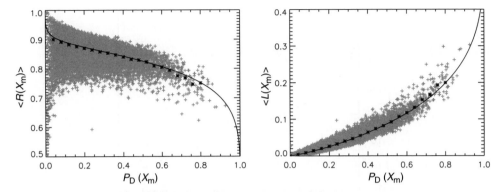

Figure 8.8 Dependence on default probabilities P_D for the GARCH process. The left plot shows the dependence of recovery rates $\langle R(X_m)\rangle$ on default probabilities $P_D(X_m)$. The right plot shows the dependence of portfolio losses $\langle L(X_m)\rangle$ on default probabilities $P_D(X_m)$. The Monte Carlo results for the GARCH process (grey symbols) are compared to the analytical results for the diffusion (solid line). The parameter B was fitted to the data.

In Figure 8.8 we present the Monte Carlo results for the P_D dependence of the GARCH process. One plot shows the dependence of recovery rates $\langle R(X_m)\rangle$ on default probabilities $P_D(X_m)$, a second plot shows the dependence of portfolio losses $\langle L(X_m)\rangle$ on default probabilities $P_D(X_m)$. First, we observe a much broader range of the individual results than in the diffusion case. This is to be expected because the fluctuating volatilities lead to pronounced fat tails in the return distribution of individual companies. While the returns are correlated in the GARCH(1,1) model, volatilities are rather uncorrelated, see Schäfer and Guhr (2010). Thus for the market return the fluctuations of individual volatilities average out to some degree. This is why we scarcely observe very high default probabilities in the simulations. The situation is different for empirical stock return time series, where volatilities are also strongly correlated.

It is a rather remarkable result that the average behavior of the GARCH simulation is so well described by the analytical results for the diffusion, see Equations (8.44) and (8.45), respectively. The parameter B has been fitted to the simulation data.

As demonstrated in Schäfer and Koivusalo (2011), the dependence of default probabilities and portfolio losses on the market return is completely different for the GARCH model. However, given the functional relation (8.45) between portfolio loss L and default probability P_D we can transform the PDF of default probabilities into the PDF of portfolio losses,

$$p(L) = \frac{1}{|L'(P_D)|}\,\hat{p}(P_D). \tag{8.54}$$

A comparison to the Monte Carlo result for the portfolio loss distribution is presented in Figure 8.9. We observe a very good agreement, even for extremely large losses.

Our results demonstrate that the functional dependence of recovery rates on default probabilities does not depend on the underlying process. The analytical result for the diffusion process describes also other underlying processes in the Merton model. Hence we call Equation (8.44) the *structural recovery rate*. Using this structural recovery rate we can describe the loss distribution if we have knowledge of the distribution of default probabilities.

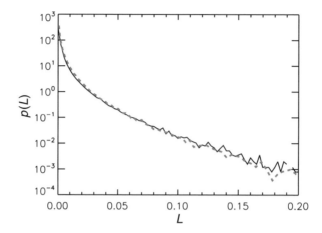

Figure 8.9   The portfolio loss distribution $p(L)$ for the correlated GARCH process. The black solid line corresponds to the simulation results. The grey dashed line shows the analytical results, where the PDF of default probabilities is transformed.

8.6   APPLICATIONS OF THE STRUCTURAL RECOVERY RATE

In a recent study Altman et al. (2005) find a strong negative correlation between default probabilities and recovery rates in empirical data. The structural recovery rate entails such a negative relation between default and recovery rates. It correctly describes the case of zero-coupon bonds for various underlying processes, but may even be applicable to a more general debt structure. An indication for this is given by Chen and Panjer (2003) who show that the Merton model with jump-diffusion can be calibrated to provide the same yield spreads as reduced-form models.

Reduced-form models are also able to reproduce negative correlations between default and recovery rates, if the default model and the recovery model depend on a single common covariate, see Chava et al. (2008) and Bade et al. (2011). Compared to the structural recovery rate, however, the reduced-form recovery introduces more parameters and lacks a deeper motivation.

In first passage models as described in Giesecke (2004), default may occur before maturity if the market value of the company falls below a default barrier. If defaults before maturity dominate in this model, recovery rates are independent of default rates. The average recovery rate is then constant and does not resemble the negative relation mentioned above. However, if defaults occur mostly at maturity, the structural recovery rate is recovered.

Finally, there is empirical evidence that the structural recovery rate is indeed applicable in a realistic setting. Becker et al. (2012) conduct a detailed study of Moody's Default and Recovery Database and find that the empirical dependence of default and recovery rates is well described by the structural recovery model. This is remarkable, as the Merton model makes many unrealistic assumptions: It neglects coupon payments, relies on a simple capital structure of the debtors, and does not allow for defaults prior to maturity. However, the strong empirical support for the structural recovery model makes it worthwhile to incorporate it into current credit risk models.

8.7 CONCLUSIONS

We revisited the Merton model as a structural model for credit risk. In Monte Carlo simulations we studied the influence of correlations and the number of contracts on the risk of large portfolio losses. We demonstrate that the presence of correlations diminishes the diversification effect in credit portfolios. In fact, the tail of the loss distribution converges quickly to the large portfolio limit. This limiting distribution exhibits fat tails even for small correlations. For the correlated diffusion, the large portfolio limit can be calculated analytically and yields a functional dependence of recovery rate and default probability. This *functional recovery rate* is very robust with respect to the underlying asset value process. Here, we showed results for correlated GARCH processes and find the same relation between default and recovery rates. Recent empirical evidence supports the applicability of the structural recovery model even in a realistic setting, where the assumptions of the Merton model are no longer valid. This makes it worthwhile to use the structural recovery rate in addition to first passage models or any other model for default probabilities.

REFERENCES

Altman, E. I., Brady, B., Resti, A., Sironi, A., 2005. The link between default and recovery rates: Theory, empirical evidence, and implications. Journal of Business 78(6), 2203–2228.

Artzner, P., Delbaen, F., Eber, J.-M., Heath, D., 1997. Thinking coherently. Risk 10, 68–71.

Asvanunt, A., Staal, A., April 2009a. The Corporate Default Probability model in Barclays Capital POINT platform (POINT CDP). Portfolio Modeling, Barclays Capital.

Asvanunt, A., Staal, A., August 2009b. The POINT Conditional Recovery Rate (CRR) Model. Portfolio Modeling, Barclays Capital.

Bade, B., Rösch, D., Scheule, H., 2011. Default and Recovery Risk Dependencies in a Simple Credit Risk Model. European Financial Management 17(1), 120–144.

Becker, A., Koivusalo, A. F. R., Schäfer, R., 2012. Empirical evidence for the structural recovery model. Preprint, arXiv:1203.3188.

Black, F., Cox, J. C., 1976. Valuing corporate securities: Some effects of bond indenture provisions. Journal of Finance 31, 351–367.

Black, F., Scholes, M., 1973. The pricing of options and corporate liabilities. Journal of Political Economy 81(3), 637.

Bollerslev, T., 1986. Generalized autoregressive conditional heteroskedasticity. Journal of Econometrics 31, 307–327.

Chava, S., Stefanescu, C., Turnbull, S., 2008. Modeling The Loss Distribution, Working Paper.

Chen, C.-J., Panjer, H., 2003. Unifying discrete structural models and reduced-form models in credit risk using a jump-diffusion process. Insurance: Mathematics and Economics 33(2), 357–380.

Duffie, D., Singleton, K., 1999. Modeling the term structure of defaultable bonds. Review of Financial Studies 12, 687–720.

Frey, R., McNeil, A. J., 2002. Var and expected shortfall in portfolios of dependent credit risks: Conceptual and practical insights. Journal of Banking & Finance 26(7), 1317–1334.

Giesecke, K., 2004. Credit Risk Modeling and Valuation: An Introduction, 2nd Edition. Credit Risk: Models and Management. Risk Books, Ch. 16, p. 487.

Guhr, T., Schäfer, R., 2012. Lecture Notes on Econophysics. University of Duisburg-Essen.

Hull, J. C., White, A., 2000. Valuing credit default swaps I: No counterparty default risk. Journal of Derivatives 8(1), 29–40.

Jarrow, R. A., Lando, D., Turnbull, S. M., 1997. A markov model for the term structure of credit risk spreads. Review of Financial Studies 10(2), 481–523.

Jarrow, R. A., Turnbull, S. M., 1995. Pricing derivatives on financial securities subject to default risk. Journal of Finance 50, 53–86.

Koivusalo, A. F. R., Schäfer, R., 2011. Calibration of structural and reduced-form recovery models. Preprint, arXiv:1102.4864.

Merton, R. C., 1974. On the pricing of corporate dept: The risk structure of interest rates. Journal of Finance 29, 449–470.

Schäfer, R., Guhr, T., 2010. Local normalization: Uncovering correlations in non-stationary financial time series. Physica A 389(18), 3856–3865.

Schäfer, R., Koivusalo, A. F. R., 2011. Dependence of defaults and recoveries in structural credit risk models. Preprint, arXiv:1102.3150.

Schäfer, R., Sjölin, M., Sundin, A., Wolanski, M., Guhr, T., 2007. Credit risk — a structural model with jumps and correlations. Physica A 383(2), 533.

Schönbucher, P. J., 2003. Credit Derivatives Pricing Models. John Wiley & Sons, New Jersey.

Yamai, Y., Yoshiba, T., 2005. Value-at-risk versus expected shortfall: A practical perspective. Journal of Banking & Finance 29(4), 997–1015.

Part III
Credit Portfolio Risk Securitization
and Tranching

Differences in Tranching Methods: Some Results and Implications*

Ashish Das and Roger M. Stein

Moody's Analytics and Moody's Corporation

9.1 INTRODUCTION[†]

We review the mathematics of evaluating the credit risk of tranches of structured transactions with simple loss-priority structure using two common tranching approaches: PD-based tranching where the probability of default of a tranche is the quantity of interest; and EL-based tranching where the expected loss on a tranche is the quantity of interest.[1] These approaches are used to either evaluate the credit quality of an exogenously defined tranche or to determine the theoretically appropriate attachment and detachment points for a tranche to meet an exogenously defined target PD or EL. We compare the attributes of different tranching approaches.

We also examine the relative conservatism of different approaches to tranching. We define tranching framework X as more "conservative" than tranching framework Y in a specific setting if, in that setting, tranche credit enhancement (CE) levels are higher when using framework X than when using framework Y. For our discussions, we assume that the "target" or idealized levels of EL and PD are exogenously defined.

We collect a series of sometimes disparate observations that follow simply from the mathematics of calculating PD and EL for a given tranche. Though these observations follow logically, a number of results may appear counter-intuitive. To illustrate, we use stylized collateral loss distributions, though the results hold for more realistic loss distributions as well. Our goal is to provide more transparency into the credit risk analytics of structured transactions as well as to provide some clear mathematical results and implications that market participants can use in thinking about these risks.

We show that (a) neither approach results in uniformly more or less conservative tranche levels; (b) for a fixed detachment (attachment) point of a tranche, lowering the attachment (detachment) point necessarily increases the EL of the tranche, even if the tranche is made thicker by this move and regardless of the probability distribution of the underlying collateral; (c) because different organizations use different target PD and EL levels for determining risk grades and use different assumptions in generating these targets, it is typically unclear (without

---

*Moody's Investors Service, Inc. Reproduced by permission of Moody's Investors Service.

†We are grateful to John Hull, Alan White, David Lando, Jordan Mann, Yufeng Ding and Aziz Lookman for extensive comments on earlier drafts of this chapter. We also thank all of the members of Moody's Academic Research and Advisory Committee for useful discussions during presentations of this work at MAARC meetings. We wish to thank Shirish Chinchalkar for extensive programming work to generate the numerical examples and for his comments. All errors are, of course, our own. This chapter was written while both authors were at Moody's Research Labs. Finally, the views presented here are those of the authors and do not represent the views of our current or former employers.

reference to the underlying loss distribution) which tranching method will imply higher CE levels in any given instance; (d) there is generally no constant LGD assumption (including 100% LGD) that can be made on *collateral* to translate a PD-based tranche into an EL-based tranche; (e) assuming a monotonically decreasing density of the loss distribution in the tail, the upper bound on the LGD of the most senior tranche is 50% under EL-based tranching (in practice, for loss distributions often used by market participants, the LGD of the senior-most tranche may be much lower); (f) in the EL-based approach, it may be impossible to create a tranche with a target EL, given a specific capital structure and loss distribution; this will occur whenever the PD of the tranche above is higher than the target EL of the given tranche.

Note that neither approach results in uniformly more or less conservative tranche levels. Rather, analyses that focus on EL vs. PD answer different questions, both of which are of interest to investors. Provided the analyses are used in the manner defined (i.e. as either an EL or a PD), there is no inconsistency.

The remainder of this chapter is organized as follows: Section 9.2 outlines terminology. Section 9.3 briefly discusses the basic mathematics of tranching and some implications, including the observation that EL-based and PD-based tranching approaches do not produce similar attachment and detachment points for any tranche in the capital structure. Section 9.4 shows that, for a fixed detachment (attachment) point of a tranche, lowering the attachment (detachment) point necessarily increases the EL of the tranche regardless of the probability distribution of the collateral. Section 9.5 presents the upper-bound for the LGD on the senior-most tranche. Section 9.6 illustrates why some tranches with a target EL are unattainable under the EL-based tranching approach, even though they can exist under the PD-based approach.

9.2 DEFINING A TRANCHE

A tranche is specified by *attachment* and *detachment* points. These points partition losses on the underlying collateral such that losses below the attachment point do not affect the tranche, losses above the attachment point and below the detachment point are absorbed entirely by holders of the tranche, and in states of the world in which losses exceed the detachment point, the tranche has lost everything.

Tranching is the structured finance analog to the use by a corporation of multiple classes of liabilities. In both cases, the mechanism seeks to provide different liability holders with different liens on the assets supporting the liabilities should the issuer default. The function of tranching is to apportion losses in the underlying collateral loss distribution among tranche holders in a manner that provides more or less risk of loss to the holders of the different tranches. The most common tranching methods target a specific PD (PD-based tranching) or a specific EL (EL-based tranching) for the tranche and then set the attachment and detachment points to achieve the targeted value in order to appeal to investors with a specific risk preference. Clearly, in the settings above, tranche attachment and detachment points depend critically on the assumptions of the collateral loss distribution.[2]

Conversely, given a set of *exogenously* defined tranches and a loss distribution for the collateral, one can use the same analytic machinery to determine the PD or EL for a tranche. This is often done in the rating process where the capital structure of a transaction is defined by bankers or other structurers and ratings are then determined by raters, based on the credit enhancement implicit in the capital structure of the transaction (e.g. Lucas, Goodman and Fabozzi (2006)).

For the purposes of our discussion here, we consider tranching in a very simple setting, similar to what is done for synthetic transactions, by assuming no cash flow waterfall and a simple loss-priority approach. Assuming no waterfall simplifies the analysis but it ignores some features of cashflow timing that can affect tranching for cashflow transactions. Despite this limitation, many of our results carry over to the waterfall case. (Mahadevan, et al. (2006), for example, provides an overview of some typical securitization structures.)

The mathematics of tranching is relatively simple and involves only basic calculus and probability theory that can be found in any undergraduate textbook on probability (e.g. Feller (1978)). However, the subtlety lies primarily in the interpretation and the logical consequences of these results. In the next section we review the mathematical machinery in detail before going on to explore these consequences.

9.3   THE MATHEMATICS OF TRANCHING

We examine two approaches to evaluating tranches defined by attachment point, A, and a detachment point, D. Under both approaches, when the collateral pool underlying a transaction experiences a loss (L) that is less than A, the tranche experiences zero loss, whereas the tranche is wiped out if the pool losses exceed D. For simplicity, we assume that the pdf of the collateral loss distribution is given.

9.3.1   PD-based Tranching

Tranche PD is the probability of collateral losses exceeding the attachment point. A tranche meets a given PD target if the tranche PD is less than an exogenously defined value, PD_T:

$$Tranche\ PD = P(L > A) = \int_A^1 f(L) \cdot dL \le PD_T \tag{9.1}$$

where

$A \equiv$ the tranche attachment point,
$L \equiv$ the percentage loss on the portfolio,
$f(\cdot) \equiv$ the pdf of the percentage loss on the portfolio,
$PD_T \equiv$ predefined target default rate for a tranche.

PD-based credit enhancement (CE or *subordination*) is equal to the collateral portfolio credit VaR (e.g. Bohn and Stein, 2009) with $\alpha = PD_T$.

Note that the tranche width, $(D - A)$, does not appear anywhere in this expression, underscoring the insensitivity of the PD-based approach to the width of the tranche (or the severity of losses on it). Thus a very thick tranche and a very thin tranche, with the same attachment point, would have the same credit quality under the PD-based tranching approach. This implies that the required subordination to achieve a given target PD is the same for all variations on the size of the tranche and configuration capital structure of the transaction.[3]

In the PD-based tranching approach, tranche credit enhancements can be calculated simply by determining the 1-PD_Tth quantile of the loss distribution.[4]

9.3.2 EL-based Tranching

For EL-based tranching the EL of the tranche is calculated. This calculation is more involved as it depends not only on the underlying loss distribution but also on the width of the tranche. Consider two tranches with identical attachment points but different detachment points. These tranches will experience different percentage losses for each dollar lost, since the loss will represent a different percentage of the total size of the respective tranches.

As in the case of PD-based tranching, whenever the pool experiences losses less than A, the tranche is unaffected. If losses are greater than D, the tranche is completely wiped out, i.e. it experiences its maximum loss, $D - A$. However, when the losses are between A and D, the measure is affected differentially: in absolute terms, the tranche loss increases linearly from 0 (at A) to $D - A$ (at D), or, in percentage terms, relative to the tranche par, from 0% at A to 100% at D. This can be expressed as

$$Percentage\ Tranche\ Loss = \min \left[1, \max \left(\left(\frac{L - A}{D - A} \right), 0 \right) \right].$$

The expected loss of this tranche, relative to the tranche width $(D - A)$, can be expressed (cf., Pykhtin (2004)), using the pdf of the collateral loss distribution, as

$$Tranche\ EL = \int_0^1 Percentage\ Tranche\ Loss \cdot f_L(L)\, dL$$

$$= \int_0^1 \min \left[1, \max \left(\left(\frac{L - A}{D - A} \right), 0 \right) \right] \cdot f_L(L)\, dL \qquad (9.2)$$

where the terms are defined as above and

$L \equiv$ percentage loss on the portfolio,
$f_L(\cdot) \equiv$ pdf of the loss on the portfolio.

Note that the tranche width, $(D - A)$, is explicit in this expression, underscoring the sensitivity of the EL-based approach to the width of the tranche (and the severity of losses on it). It can be shown that, for the same attachment point, A, the smaller the width of the tranche (the closer we make D to A), the higher the tranche EL.

We can also use (9.2) to define a tranche, rather than to evaluate the credit quality of an exogenously defined tranche, in an iterative process. The process starts with the most senior tranche in the capital structure and repeats iteratively to the lowest rated tranche as follows:

First, the subordination level for the senior-most tranche is determined based on a desired target expected loss, EL_{Sr}. Because the senior-most tranche, by definition, is at the top of the capital structure, the detachment point, D, for that tranche is defined as 100%. Therefore, the above formula for the senior-most tranche EL, with pool loss expressed as percent, can be used to define the Credit Enhancement for the senior-most tranche:

$$CE_{Sr} = \min \left\{ A \Big| \left[EL_{Sr} \geq \int_0^1 \min \left[1, \max \left(\left(\frac{L - A}{1 - A} \right), 0 \right) \right] f_L(L) dL \right] \right\}.$$

We can easily use numerical methods to solve for lowest value of A that satisfies the above equation. This value of A is the credit enhancement, CE_{Sr}, which satisfies the credit quality criterion EL_{Sr}.

If there is an additional tranche subordinated to the senior-most tranche, we can now determine the subordination required for this tranche (Senior Subordinated) to achieve its desired target EL, EL_{SrSub}. The detachment point for the Senior Subordinated tranche is equal to the attachment point of the senior-most tranche. Thus, we obtain the Senior Subordinated attachment point by solving for lowest value of B that satisfies the expression below:

$$CE_{SrSub} = \min \left\{ B \, \middle| \, \left[EL_{SrSub} \geq \int_0^1 \min \left[1, \max \left(\left(\frac{L-B}{CE_{Sr} - B} \right), 0 \right) \right] \cdot f_L(L) dL \right] \right\}.$$

This process is repeated until all desired tranche levels are determined.

Unlike PD-based tranching, an attachment and detachment point cannot be found for every arbitrary EL target. In some cases, the shape of the distribution is such that some EL targets cannot be achieved through subordination without reducing the size of (or eliminating) tranches above.

Note also that from equation (9.2) it is clear that assumptions about the LGD of the *collateral* (LGD_c), do not translate linearly into assumptions about the *tranche EL LGD_t*).

Also note that setting $LGD_c = 1$ (which makes the loss distribution equivalent to a default distribution) does *not* convert an EL-based tranching approach to a PD-based tranching approach. Two tranches with identical attachment points but different detachment points will have the same tranche PD but different *tranche ELs* even if they are both based on the identical loss distribution and even if $LGD_c = 1$.

9.4 THE EL OF A TRANCHE NECESSARILY INCREASES WHEN EITHER THE ATTACHMENT POINT OR THE DETACHMENT POINT IS DECREASED

In this section, we show that, regardless of the probability density function of the underlying collateral, lowering the attachment point of a tranche while keeping the detachment point fixed necessarily increases the tranche EL.[5] We later show that decreasing the detachment point similarly necessarily increases the tranche EL.

Some observers erroneously reason that even though lowering the attachment point increases the PD, the tranche LGD could decrease since the new tranche is now thicker due to the new lower attachment point. In fact, there is some empirical evidence supporting the negative correlation between tranche size and tranche LGD (Tung, Hu and Cantor (2006)). Thus, they reason, it is not obvious whether EL would increase or decrease. This reasoning turns out to be incorrect.

We now show that *regardless of the probability distribution of the collateral losses*, decreasing the attachment point or the detachment point necessarily increases the tranche EL. Although this argument can be made entirely geometrically (see Figure 9.1 and Figure 9.2) we will prove it analytically after making the geometric argument. First, we show that for a fixed detachment point, D, lowering the attachment point, A, increases EL.

In Figure 9.1, the horizontal axis shows the percentage collateral loss for a hypothetical loss distribution. Note that the horizontal axis should go from 0% to (not shown above) 100%.

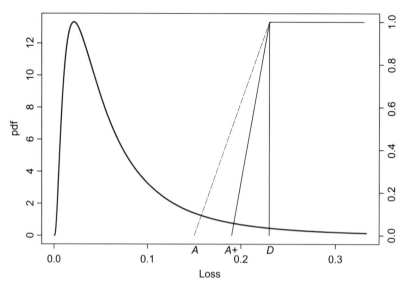

Figure 9.1   Decreasing the attachment point increases the tranche expected loss.

The left vertical axis shows the probability density function of the collateral losses while the right vertical axis shows the percentage loss on the tranche from 0 to 100%. In this figure, D denotes the detachment point of a tranche.

Consider two different cases of tranching for the same collateral pool: (1) when the attachment point, A^+, is higher (the plus superscript is used to remind us that this attachment point is above attachment point A) and (2) when the attachment point is A.

The dashed line starting at A is the graph of percentage loss on the tranche as a function of collateral loss if A is the attachment point, and the solid line starting from A^+ is the graph of percentage loss on the tranche as a function of collateral loss if A^+ is the attachment point. We will show that, given a fixed detachment point, D, the EL for the tranche with attachment point, A, (case 2) is always as high as or higher than the EL for the tranche with attachment point, A^+, (case 1) regardless of the pdf of the collateral loss.

We now compute the EL for each case. For case 1 where the attachment point is A^+, the higher of the two attachment points, the tranche EL using Equation (9.2) is:

$$Tranche\ EL_{A^+,D} = \int_0^A 0 \cdot f_L(L)dL + \int_A^{A^+} 0 \cdot f_L(L)dL + \int_{A^+}^D \left(\frac{L - A^+}{D - A^+}\right) \cdot f_L(L)dL + \int_D^1 1 \cdot f_L(L)dL$$

$$= \int_{A^+}^D \left(\frac{L - A^+}{D - A^+}\right) \cdot f_L(L)dL + [1 - F(D)] \tag{9.3}$$

where

$L \equiv$ the percentage loss on the collateral,
$F(D) \equiv$ the cumulative distribution function of the losses on the collateral,
and other terms are as previously defined.

Similarly for case 2, where the attachment point is A, the lower of the two attachment points, the tranche EL is given as:

$$Tranche\ EL_{A,D} = \int_0^A 0 \cdot f_L(L)dL + \int_A^{A^+} \left(\frac{L-A}{D-A}\right) \cdot f_L(L)dL + \int_{A^+}^D \left(\frac{L-A}{D-A}\right) \cdot f_L(L)dL$$

$$+ \int_D^1 1 \cdot f_L(L)dL$$

$$= \int_A^{A^+} \left(\frac{L-A}{D-A}\right) \cdot f_L(L)dL + \int_{A^+}^D \left(\frac{L-A}{D-A}\right) \cdot f_L(L)dL + [1 - F(D)]. \quad (9.4)$$

Comparing Equations (9.3) and (9.4) we see that the last term is the same and the first term in (9.4) is non-negative. Hence, in order to show that the EL in (9.4) is higher than EL in (9.3), it is sufficient to show that

$$\int_{A^+}^D \frac{L-A}{D-A} \cdot f_L(L)dL \geq \int_{A^+}^D \frac{L-A^+}{D-A^+} \cdot f_L(L)dL.$$

Since the pdf is non-negative, it is sufficient to show that

$$\left(\frac{L-A}{D-A}\right) \geq \left(\frac{L-A^+}{D-A^+}\right) \quad \text{for } L \in [A^+, D].$$

These two fractions are simply the percentage loss on the tranche in each case. Thus, we can prove the inequality by showing that the *percentage* tranche loss is as large or larger when the attachment point is A as it is when the attachment point is A^+. It is obvious from Figure 9.1 that the percentage tranche loss case 1 (shown in dotted lines) is as high or higher than that for case 2 everywhere. While the figure shows this geometrically, we can prove the inequality analytically by rewriting the first term of the above inequality as below and arguing that this term decreases as A increases

$$\left(\frac{L-A}{D-A}\right) = 1 - \left(\frac{D-L}{D-A}\right).$$

Thus, we have shown that, for a fixed detachment point lowering the attachment point necessarily increases the EL of the tranche.

Using similar arguments to those just given, it is straightforward to see that as the detachment point, D, of a tranche is decreased but the attachment point, A, is kept constant, EL of the tranche increases as well. This is because the percentage losses on the tranche with lower detachment point, D, are as high or higher than that for the tranche with the higher detachment point, $D+$, regardless of the level of the collateral loss. This can be easily seen in Figure 9.2.

Thus, using similar arguments to those used in the case of the attachment point, it can be shown that regardless of the probability distribution of the collateral, lowering the detachment point necessarily increases the EL of the tranche.

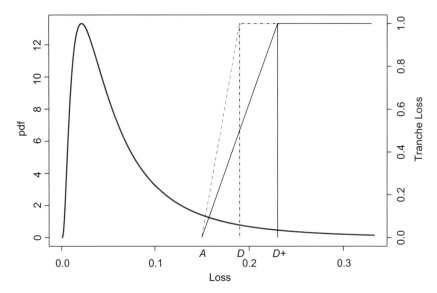

Figure 9.2   Decreasing the detachment point increases the tranche expected loss.

An implication of this result is that simply "thickening" a tranche does not necessarily make it less risky from an expected loss perspective.

9.5   UPPER BOUND ON TRANCHE EXPECTED LGD (LGD_t) ASSUMPTION GIVEN EL-BASED TRANCHES

Consider now the *expected loss given default*[6] of a tranche with attachment point A and detachment point D. For losses between A and D, the percentage loss to the tranche is the probability weighted value of the tranche loss $(L - A)$ as a percentage of the tranche size $(D - A)$. Since we only consider losses above A, LGD_t is calculated by normalizing by the probability distribution in the region above A (the PD of the tranche) only. Finally, for collateral losses above D, the tranche loss is 100%, so the LGD contribution from this region is just 1 times the probability of losses above D, again normalized by the probability of losses above A. Mathematically, this can be written as:

$$
LGD_t = \frac{\displaystyle\int_A^D \left(\frac{L - A}{D - A}\right) \cdot f_L(L)dL + \int_D^1 1 \cdot f_L(L)dL}{\displaystyle\int_A^D f_L(L)dL + \int_D^1 f_L(L)dL}.
$$
(9.5)

First consider the LGD_t of a tranche which is not the senior-most. It is obvious that in the limit when the tranche is infinitesimally thin (D is very close to A), LGD_t becomes 1 since the first terms in both the numerator and the denominator collapse to zero. Similarly, as the tranche becomes wider the expected LGD of the tranche decreases from 1.

Now consider LGD_t for the senior-most tranche. As the detachment point is 1, Equation (9.5) can be simplified to:

$$LGD_{Aaa} = \frac{\int_A^1 \left(\frac{L-A}{1-A}\right) \cdot f_L(L)dL}{\int_A^1 f_L(L)dL}. \tag{9.6}$$

The tranche expected LGD for the senior-most tranche will depend on the probability density function of the collateral loss distribution in the region to the right of the attachment point for the senior-most tranche. Under most realistic assumptions the probability density function of the collateral loss value is non-increasing with extreme losses (i.e. for very large losses, the probability of a specific loss decreases as the losses get larger and larger).[7] Under these plausible conditions, we show that the upper bound for expected LGD is 0.5.

Consider the case in which the pdf of the collateral loss value is constant beyond the attachment point. This represents the upper bound on the mass in the tail, given our assumption of a non-increasing tail. In this case, $f_L(L)$ equals $f_L(A)$ for $L \geq A$. Now (9.6) becomes:

$$LGD_{Sr} = \frac{\int_A^1 \left(\frac{L-A}{1-A}\right) \cdot f_L(A)dL}{\int_A^1 f_L(A)dL} = \frac{\int_A^1 \left(\frac{L-A}{1-A}\right) \cdot dL}{\int_A^1 dL} = \frac{1}{(1-A)^2} \cdot \int_A^1 (L-A) \cdot dL = 0.5.$$

Thus, for non-increasing tails, the maximum possible mass in the tail results in $LGD_t = 0.5$. Note again that we have assumed the maximum possible non-increasing tail here. In many collateral loss distributions the LGD_t value would be much smaller than 0.5 since the tail decreases and is convex.[8]

We illustrate the magnitude of tranche LGDs in the tail using a hypothetical loss distribution modeled as a t-copula with degrees of freedom equal to 4 (Cherubini (2004)). Note that we do not necessarily advocate the use of this assumption, and only use it to illustrate our results.

Table 9.1 gives some examples of senior tranche expected LGDs under this loss distribution assumption. (This first step is similar in some ways to Gregoriou and C. Hoppe (2008).) The table shows sample loss distributions using PD estimates for the collateral asset of 50, 100 and 200 bps and correlation assumptions of 5, 15 and 25%. For this example, we assume the target tranche EL, EL_{Sr}, is equal to 5 bps.

From the table, it is clear that, under a variety of parameterizations of the collateral loss distribution, tranche expected LGDs are well below the 50% upper bound. For corporate issuers, there is empirical evidence of a positive relationship between PD and LGD (e.g. Meng et al. (2006)). However, in Table 9.1, we have imposed the condition that the EL of the senior tranche is constant at 5 bp. Since EL is the product of PD and LGD, the typical PD-LGD relationship is reversed and the tranche PDs vary inversely with expected LGD levels.

Conceptually, the lower the consequences of default (in terms of investor losses), the more default risk is tolerable given a constant target EL. This is reflected in attachment points that increase with the tranche expected LGD as well. We can contrast this with the PD-based

Table 9.1   Examples of senior tranche expected LGDs.

PD (bp)	Rho	Sr Tranche Attachment Point (%)	Sr Tranche PD (bp)	Sr Tranche Expected LGD (%)
50	0.05	14.74	61	8.21
100	0.05	20.90	59	8.46
200	0.05	27.26	58	8.65
50	0.15	19.25	45	11.19
100	0.15	27.35	42	11.99
200	0.15	35.98	39	12.95
50	0.25	24.55	33	14.97
100	0.25	35.27	29	17.36
200	0.25	45.85	28	18.18

approach which imposes the same PD assumption regardless of whether the risk in default to the investor is very high or very low.

An EL-based tranche will be less conservative (lower credit enhancement) than the PD-based tranche if the EL-based target is derived by taking the target PD (from a PD-based approach) and multiplying it by an LGD that is in the range ([tranche LGD], 1]. This relationship is formally shown below.

$$\text{Tranche } PD_{PD\text{-}based} \cdot LGD_{PD\_to\_EL\_multiplier} \equiv \text{Tranche } EL_{EL\text{-}based}$$

$$= \text{Tranche } PD_{EL\text{-}based} \cdot \text{Tranche expected } LGD_{EL\text{-}based}$$

$$\text{Now, if } LGD_{PD\_to\_EL\_multiplier} > \text{Tranche expected } LED_{EL\text{-}based}$$

$$\Rightarrow \text{Tranche } PD_{EL\text{-}based} = \frac{\text{Tranche } PD_{PD\text{-}based} \cdot LGD_{PD\_to\_EL\_multiplier}}{\text{Tranche expected } LGD_{EL\text{-}based}} > \text{Tranche } PD_{PD\text{-}based}$$

$$\Rightarrow \text{Tranche } CE_{EL\text{-}based} < \text{Tranche } CE_{PD\text{-}based}.$$

In practice EL targets are not set by simply taking the PD targets and multiplying them with a constant LGD. In fact, industry practice is to use different target levels based on rating grades. These levels are provided by rating agencies and other market providers.

Thus if, for the same credit grade, organization A defines a target PD of 15 bps for its PD-based tranching approach, while organization B uses a target EL of 1.5 bp, the relative conservatism of the approaches is unclear without reference to the actual loss distribution. In this case, for distributions in which the LGD of the tranche (either PD-based or EL-based) turns out to be less than 10%, the CE implied under the PD-based approach will be higher than the CE implied under the EL approach. However, for all other cases (i.e. where the LGD of the tranche is greater than 10%), the EL-based tranching approach will produce higher CE-levels.

9.6 "SKIPPING" OF SOME TRANCHES IN THE EL-BASED APPROACH

Given a specific capital structure and loss distribution, under the EL-based approach, it may be impossible to create a tranche with a target EL; this will occur whenever the PD of the tranche above is higher than the target EL of the given tranche. To see this, consider Equation (9.3) (reproduced here for convenience)

$$Tranche\ EL_{A^+,D} = \int_0^A 0 \cdot f_L(L)dL + \int_A^{A^+} 0 \cdot f_L(L)dL + \int_{A^+}^D \left(\frac{L - A^+}{D - A^+}\right) \cdot f_L(L)dL + \int_D^1 1 \cdot f_L(L)dL$$

$$= \int_{A^+}^D \left(\frac{L - A^+}{D - A^+}\right) \cdot f_L(L)dL + [1 - F(D)].$$

Here, since the first term is non-negative, it is impossible to find an attachment point, A, such that tranche EL is less than the target EL *whenever* the term $[1 - F(D)]$ is higher than the target EL. The term $[1 - F(D)]$ can be interpreted as the PD of the tranche (say, senior) immediately above the one of interest (say, senior subordinated). This follows naturally since, in such a case, the loss of the senior subordinated tranche is 100% if the pool losses are higher than the detachment point of this tranche.

In words, this can be rewritten as:

$$Tranche\ EL_{A,D} = [\text{contribution between } A \text{ and } D] + [PD \text{ of tranche above} \times 1].$$

Conceptually, the EL for the tranche is the portion due to defaults and partial losses given default between A and D plus the total loss in the part beyond D. Thus, if the PD of the senior tranche is higher than the target EL of the senior subordinated tranche, it is impossible to find an attachment point, A, that will make the EL of the tranche lower than the idealized EL since the portion of the EL defined by mass *above* the detachment point of the target tranche is *already* higher than the full target EL for the tranche.

For example, imagine that, in addition to creating a senior-most tranche targeting investors seeking an instrument with an EL (credit quality) of 5 bps, the banker originating this transaction also wished to create a senior subordinated tranche, below the senior tranche, to appeal to investors seeking a target EL of EL_{SrSub}. In this example, assume that $EL_{SrSub} = 10$ bps. Assume further that the collateral loss distribution was the one shown in the first row of Table 9.1. Looking at the first row pool in Table 9.1, we see that the PD of the senior-most tranche is 61 bps. In this case, it would not be possible for this pool to support a structure with an EL of 10bp since the PD of the senior-most tranche is already higher than the 10 bps and the loss for the senior subordinated tranche beyond the senior-most tranche attachment point is always 100%. Thus, a tranche targeting investors seeking this target EL would not be feasible without reducing the size of the senior-most tranche.

9.7 CONCLUSION

In this short chapter, we focused on the mathematics of tranching and its implications under both the PD- and EL-based tranching approaches. We showed that (a) because different organizations use different target PD and EL levels for determining risk grades, it is typically unclear (without reference to the underlying loss distribution) which tranching method will imply higher CE levels; (b) for a fixed detachment (attachment) point of a tranche, lowering the attachment (detachment) point will necessarily increase the EL of the tranche regardless of the probability distribution of the underlying collateral; (c) there is generally no constant LGD assumption that can be made on collateral to translate a PD-based tranche into an EL-based tranche; (d) in the EL-based approach, it can often happen that it is impossible to create a tranche with a target EL, given a specific capital structure and loss distribution; this will occur whenever the PD of the tranche above is higher than the idealized EL of the given tranche and (e) the upper bound on the LGD of the senior-most tranche under many distributions of collateral is 50%. In many models commonly used in practice the LGD of the senior-most tranche will be lower than 50%.

Many of these observations lead naturally from our examination of tranche LGD, which itself follows from the width of the tranche. Simply put, the PD-based approach is not sensitive to the LGD of the tranche and is thus not sensitive to the size of the tranche. All equal, the credit enhancement under the PD approach will be the same, regardless of how thin the tranche is.

It is instructive to consider the differences in tranching approaches and which measures should appeal for which types of applications. First, we note that neither measure is "too conservative" nor "too liberal". By definition, each tranching approach delivers attachment points that are consistent with its objectives and definition. Further, because organizations that use these measures define their targets differently, it is typically unclear which will imply a higher credit enhancement level.

Finally, these measures should appeal to different users for different applications. For users concerned with never experiencing a default (even a default with *de minimus* economic impact) the PD-based measure is a more natural one. For users focused on managing economic loss, the EL measure may be more appropriate. For users concerned with conservatism, the choice is less clear since either measure may produce a more conservative estimate depending on the capital structure, collateral loss distribution, tranche of interest and definition of the target measure.

NOTES

1. Please note that we abuse the notation a bit to use probability of default (PD) to denote the probability of an economic loss on the tranche since default for a tranche as a legal or contractual term may not be very well-defined.
2. The discussion of *which* distributional assumptions are appropriate for which assets and of *how* to parameterize these distributions is a widely debated topic that is beyond the scope of this article. For our purposes, we assume a collateral loss distribution that is given and may have been calculated analytically, through simulation, empirically or otherwise.
3. Recently, there has been much attention focused on so-called "thin tranches" that span only a small region of the loss distribution. These tranches are viewed by some as being more risky than traditional tranches since when they default, they can be completely wiped out very quickly. The PD approach treats thin tranches and thicker tranches the same with respect to subordination levels.
4. For some distributions, this can be done analytically. For empirical distributions, it can be done non-parametrically by simply choosing the quantile.
5. Throughout this chapter we will make a rather innocuous technical assumption that the pdf of the collateral loss is continuous and positive everywhere. This allows us to make statements like "EL will necessarily increase" as opposed to "weakly increase," which will be true for any collateral loss pdf.
6. Tranche LGD here is not the same thing as LGD in the context of a corporate bond. With a corporate (or sovereign or municipal) bond, a default is a legally or contractually defined event, and an estimate of the monetary loss is made given that such an event occurs. Here, the tranche LGD is the estimate of the loss not conditional on a legal event but conditional on there being any loss at all to the tranche.

7. Admittedly this assumption may be questioned. For instance, one can imagine a distribution in which losses decline monotonically in the tail up to a point, but then spike for some reason. In such a setting, the results in this section would not hold.

8. Note that the higher the convexity of the pdf in the region to the right of the attachment point, A, the lower the LGD of the tranche.

REFERENCES

Bohn, J. R., Stein, R. M., 2009, Active Credit Portfolio Management in Practice. John Wiley and Sons.

Cherubini, U., Luciano, E., Vecchiato, W., 2004. Copula Methods in Finance. John Wiley & Sons.

Feller, W., 1978. An Introduction to Probability Theory and its Applications. John Wiley and Sons.

Gregoriou, G. N., Hoppe, C., 2008. The Handbook of Credit Portfolio Management. McGraw-Hill Finance and Investing, pp. 140–141.

Lucas, J. L., Goodman, L. S., Fabozzi, F. J., 2006. Collateralized Debt Obligations – Structures and Analysis. John Wiley & Sons.

Mahadevan, S., Polanskyj, P., Tirupattur, V., Onur, P., Sheets, A., 2006. Structured Credit Insights – Instruments, Valuation, and Strategies. Morgan Stanley.

Meng, Q., Levy, A., Kaplin, A., Wang, Y., Hu, Z., 2010. Implications of PD-LGD Correlation in a Portfolio Setting. Modeling Methodology, Moody's KMV.

Pykhtin, M., 2004. Asymptotic Model for Economic Capital for Securitisations. In: Structured Credit Products: Pricing, Rating, Risk Management, and Basel II. Perraudin, W. (Ed.): Risk Books, pp. 215–244.

Tung, J., Hu, J., Cantor., R., 2006. Measuring Loss-Given-Default for Structured Finance Securities: An Update. Moody's Special Comment, December 2006.

10

Global Structured Finance Rating

Henrik Jönsson[1], Francesca Di Girolamo[1,2], Wim Schoutens[2] and
Francesca Campolongo[1]

[1] *European Commission*
[2] *K.U. Leuven*

10.1 INTRODUCTION

Asset-backed securities (ABSs) are securities created through a securitization process whose value and income payments are backed by a specific pool of underlying assets. Illiquid assets that cannot be sold individually are pooled together by the originator (Issuer) and transferred to a shell entity specially created to be bankruptcy remote, (a so-called Special Purpose Vehicle (SPV)). The SPV issues notes (liabilities) to investors with distinct risk return profiles and different maturities: senior, mezzanine and junior notes. This technique is called tranching of the liability. Cash flows generated by the underlying assets are used to service the notes; the risk of the underlying assets as a result are diversified because each security now represents a fraction of the total pool value.

A securitization credit rating is an assessment of the credit risk of a securitization transaction, addressing how well the credit risk of the assets is mitigated by the structure. The rating process is based on both quantitative assessment and a qualitative analysis of how the transaction mitigates losses due to defaults. For the quantitative assessment, different default scenarios combined with other assumptions, for example, pre-payments, are generated using more or less sophisticated models. Typically the input parameters to this assessment are unknown and estimated from historical data or given by expert opinions. In either case, the values used for the parameters are uncertain and these uncertainties propagate through the model and generate uncertainty in the rating output. This introduces uncertainty into the assessment and it therefore becomes important to understand the rating parameter sensitivity. For an introduction to ABS, the rating methodologies and some aspects of model risk and parameter sensitivity, see Campolongo et al. (2013), Jönsson and Schoutens (2010) and Jönsson et al. (2009).

There was increased attention paid to the rating of asset-backed securities during the credit crisis 2007–2008 due to the enormous losses anticipated by investors and the large number of downgrades among structured finance products. Rating agencies have been encouraged to sharpen their methodologies and to provide more clarity to the limitations of their ratings and the sensitivity of those ratings to the risk factors accounted for in their rating methodologies (see, for example, IMF's Global Stability Report, April 2008, IMF (2008)).

Moody's, for example, introduced two concepts in Moody's (2009), V Scores and Parameter Sensitivity. Moody's V Scores provide a relative assessment of the quality of available credit information and the potential variability around the various inputs to rating determination. The intention of the V Scores is to rank transactions by the potential for rating changes owing to uncertainty around the assumptions. Moody's parameter sensitivity provides a quantitative calculation of the number of rating notches that a rated structured finance security may vary by, if certain input parameters used differ.

The objectives of this chapter are twofold. Firstly, we advocate the use of uncertainty and sensitivity analysis techniques to enhance the understanding of the variability of the ratings due to the uncertainty in the input parameters. Uncertainty analysis quantifies the variability in the output of interest due to the variability in the inputs. Global sensitivity analysis assesses how the uncertainty in the output can be allocated to its different sources. Through global sensitivity analysis, we quantify the percentage of output variance that each input or combination of inputs accounts for.

Secondly, we propose a novel rating approach called global rating, that takes this uncertainty in the output into account when assigning ratings to tranches. The global ratings should therefore become more stable and reduce the risk of cliff effects, that is, that a small change in one or several of the input assumptions generates a dramatic change in the rating. The global rating methodology proposed gives one way forward for the rating of structure finance products.

The rest of the chapter is outlined as follows. In the next section, we introduce the ABS structure we are going to use an example: we describe the basic steps of modeling the cash flows produced by the asset pool, we point out how these cash flows are distributed to the liabilities and we outline the procedure to get ratings. A description of the general elements of global sensitivity analysis is provided in Section 10.3, with particular attention to the techniques used in this chapter. In Section 10.4, we apply uncertainty and global sensitivity analysis techniques to the ratings exercise of the example structure. The *global rating*, introduced in Section 10.5, is an attempt to take into account the uncertainty in the ratings process when assigning credit ratings to ABSs. The paper ends with conclusions.

This paper is based on results first presented in Di Girolamo et al. (2012).

10.2 ASSET-BACKED SECURITIES

10.2.1 The ABS Structure for the Experiment

Throughout the paper we assume that the pool is homogeneous, i.e., that all the constituents of the pool are identical with respect to initial amount, maturity, coupon, amortization and payment frequency, see Table 10.1, and with respect to risk profile (i.e. probability of default). This implies that all the assets in the pool are assumed to behave as the average of the assets in the pool. We also assume the pool to be static, i.e. no replenishment is made, and that the assets do not prepay.

Table 10.1 Collateral characteristics.

Collateral	
Number of loans	2,000
Initial principal amount	100,000,000
Weighted average maturity	5 years
Weighted average coupon (per annum)	9%
Amortization	Level-Pay
Payment frequency	Monthly

Table 10.2 Liability and structural characteristics.

		Liabilities	
Class of Notes	Initial Principal Amount	Interest Rate (per annum)	Credit Enhance-ment (%)
A	80,000,000	1%	20%
B	14,000,000	2%	6%
C	6,000,000	4%	0%

General Features	
Final maturity	10 years
Payment frequency	Monthly
Principal allocation	Sequential
Shortfall rate (per annum)	Applicable note coupon

Senior Expenses	
Senior fees ($i_f^{(Sr)}$)	2% of outstanding pool balance
Payment frequency	Monthly
Shortfall rate (per annum) ($r_{SF}^{(Sr)}$)	20%

Reserve Account	
Target amount ($q_{Targ}^{(CR)}$)	1.0% of outstanding pool balance
Interest rate ($r^{(CR)}$)	1.0%
Initial balance	0

This collateral pool backs three classes of notes: A (senior), B (mezzanine) and C (junior). The details of the notes are given in Table 10.2 together with other structural characteristics. To this basic liability structure we have added a cash reserve account. The reserve account balance is initially zero and is funded by excess spread.

The payment priority of the structure, the waterfall, is presented in Table 10.3. The waterfall is a so-called combined waterfall, where the available funds at each payment date constitute both interest and principal collections.

10.2.2 Cash Flow Modeling

We denote by t_m, $m = 0, 1, \ldots, M$ the payment date at the end of month m, with $t_0 = 0$ being the closing date of the deal and $t_M = T$ being the final legal maturity date.

The cash collection each month from the asset pool consist of interest payments and principal collections (scheduled repayments) which together with the principal balance of the reserve account constitute available funds.

10.2.2.1 Asset Behavior

We begin by modeling the asset behavior for the current month, say m. The number of performing loans in the pool at the end of month m will be denoted by $N(m)$. We denote

Table 10.3   The waterfall used in the analysis.

Waterfall	
Level	Basic Amortization
1)	Senior expenses
2)	Class A interest
3)	Class B interest
4)	Class A principal
5)	Class B principal
6)	Reserve account reimburs.
7)	Class C interest
8)	Class C principal
9)	Class C additional returns

by $n_D(m)$ the number of defaulted loans in month m. The following relation holds true for all m:

$$N(m) = N(m-1) - n_D(m). \tag{10.1}$$

The outstanding principal amount of an individual loan at the end of month m, after any amortization, is denoted by $B(m)$. This amount is carried forward to the next month and is, therefore, the current outstanding principal balance at the beginning of (and during) month $m + 1$. Denote by $B_A(m)$ the scheduled principal amount repaid (A stands for amortized) in month m. The outstanding principal amount at the end of month m:

$$B(m) = B(m-1) - B_A(m). \tag{10.2}$$

Defaulted principal is based on the previous month's ending principal balance times the number of defaulted loans in current month:

$$P_D(m) = B(m-1) \cdot n_D(m). \tag{10.3}$$

We will recover a fraction of the defaulted principal after a time lag, T_{RL}, the recovery lag:

$$P_{Rec}(m) = P_D(m - T_{RL}) \cdot RR(m - T_{RL}), \tag{10.4}$$

where RR is the Recovery Rate.

Interest collected in month m is calculated on performing loans:

$$I(m) = (N(m-1) - n_D(m)) \cdot B(m) \cdot r_L, \tag{10.5}$$

where r_L is the loan interest rate. It is assumed that defaulted loans pay neither interest nor principal.

Scheduled repayments are based on the performing loans from the end of previous month less defaulted loans:

$$P_{SR}(m) = (N(m-1) - n_D(m)) \cdot B_A(m). \tag{10.6}$$

The available funds in each month, assuming that total principal balance of the cash reserve account (B_{CR}) is added, is:

$$A_F(m) = I(m) + P_{SR}(m) + P_{Rec}(m) + B_{CR}(m). \qquad (10.7)$$

The total outstanding principal amount on the asset pool has decreased with:

$$P_{Red}(m) = P_D(m) + P_{SR}(m), \qquad (10.8)$$

and to make sure that the notes remain fully collateralized, we have to reduce the outstanding principal amount of the notes with this amount.

10.2.2.2 Payment Waterfall

The cash flows from the collateral pool (i.e. the available funds in (10.7)) is distributed to the transaction parties and the note investors according to a payment waterfall. The waterfall we are assuming in our simple example is presented in Table 10.3.

The senior expenses represent payments to transaction parties, e.g. the issuer and the servicer, that are necessary for the structure to function properly. The senior expenses due to be paid are based on the outstanding pool balance during the current month (plus any unpaid fees from previous month times a shortfall interest rate).

After payment of the senior expenses, the available funds are updated:

$$A_F^{(1)}(m) = \max\left(0, A_F(m) - I_P^{(Sr)}(m)\right), \qquad (10.9)$$

where $I_P^{(Sr)}(m)$ is the senior expenses paid. We use the superscript (1) in $A_F^{(1)}(m)$ to indicate that it is the available funds after item 1 in the waterfall.

The interest due to be paid to the class A notes is based on the current outstanding principal balance of the A notes at the beginning of month m, i.e. before any principal redemption. Denote by $B_C^{(A)}(m-1)$ the outstanding balance at the end of month $m-1$, after any principal redemption. This amount is carried forward and is, therefore, the current outstanding balance at the beginning of (and during) month m. To this amount, we add any shortfall from the previous month. The interest due to be paid is:

$$I_{Due}^{(A)}(m) = B_C^{(A)}(m-1) \cdot r^{(A)} + I_{SF}^{(A)}(m-1) \cdot \left(1 + r^{(A)}\right), \qquad (10.10)$$

where $I_{SF}^{(A)}(m-1)$ is any interest shortfall from month $m-1$ and $r^{(A)}$ is the fixed interest rate for the A notes. We assume the interest rate on shortfalls is the same as the note interest rate.

The interest paid to the A notes depends of course on the amount of available funds:

$$I_P^{(A)}(m) = \min\left(I_{Due}^{(A)}(m), A_F^{(1)}(m)\right). \qquad (10.11)$$

If the available funds are not enough to cover the interest due we get a shortfall that is carried forward to the next month:

$$I_{SF}^{(A)}(m) = \max\left(I_{Due}^{(A)}(m) - I_P^{(A)}(m), 0\right). \qquad (10.12)$$

After class A interest payments, the available funds are updated:

$$A_F^{(2)}(m) = \max\left(0, A_F^{(1)}(m) - I_P^{(A)}(m)\right). \qquad (10.13)$$

The interest payments to the B and C notes are calculated identically.

The principal payments to the notes are based on the total principal reduction of the collateral pool $P_{Red}(m)$ calculated in (10.8). The allocation of principal due to be paid to the notes is supposed to be done sequentially, which means that principal due is allocated in order of seniority. In the beginning, principal due is allocated to the Class A notes. Until the Class A notes have been fully redeemed no principal is paid out to the the other classes of notes. After the Class A notes are fully redeemed, the Class B notes start to be redeemed, and so on.

Note that we are here discussing the calculation of principal due to be paid. The actual amount of principal paid to the different notes depends on the available funds at the relevant level of the waterfall.

That is:

$$P_{Due}^{(A)}(m) = \min\left(B_C^{(A)}(m-1),\ P_{Red}(m) + P_{SF}^{(A)}(m-1) \right), \tag{10.14}$$

where $P_{SF}^{(A)}(m-1)$ is principal shortfall from previous month.

And the amount paid:

$$P_P^{(A)}(m) = \min\left(P_{Due}^{(A)}(m-1),\ A_F^{(3)}(m) \right). \tag{10.15}$$

Finally, we have to update the outstanding balance after the principal redemption:

$$B_C^{(A)}(m) = B_C^{(A)}(m-1) - P_P^{(A)}(m), \tag{10.16}$$

and available funds:

$$A_F^{(4)}(m) = \max\left(0,\ A_F^{(3)}(m) - P_P^{(A)}(m) \right). \tag{10.17}$$

The principal payment to the B and C notes are calculated in a similar manner. Since we apply a sequential allocation of principal due, no principal will be paid to the B and C notes until the A notes are fully redeemed.

See Di Girolamo et al. (2012) for a more detailed description of the payment waterfall.

10.2.3 Modeling and Simulating Defaults

We model defaults in the asset pool using the Logistic model:

$$F(t) = \frac{a}{1 + be^{-c(t-t_0)}},\quad 0 \le t \le T, \tag{10.18}$$

where a, b, c and t_0 are positive constants. Parameter a controls the right endpoint of the curve.

The Logistic model can easily be combined with a Monte Carlo based scenario generator to generate default scenarios by sampling a value for a from a given default distribution. In this paper, the Normal Inverse distribution will be used to describe the cumulative portfolio default rate (PDR) distribution at the maturity of the structure:

$$F_{PDR}(y) = P[PDR < y] = \Phi\left(\frac{\sqrt{1-\rho}\,\Phi^{-1}(y) - K^d(T)}{\sqrt{\rho}} \right) \tag{10.19}$$

where $0\% \le y \le 100\%$ and $K^d(T) = \Phi^{-1}(p(T))$. The default distribution in (10.19) is a function of the obligor correlation, ρ, and the default probability, $p(T)$, which are unknown and unobservable. Instead of using these parameters as inputs, it is common to fit the mean and standard deviation of the distribution to the mean and standard deviation estimated from historical data.

To perform the sensitivity analysis we need to run our rating algorithm multiple times with different parameter settings, as will be explained in Section 10.4. Each run of the rating algorithm is rather time-consuming as expected loss and the expected average life of the notes are calculated based on Monte Carlo simulation. Thus, in order to speed up the sensitivity analysis experiment, we make use of Quasi-Monte Carlo simulations based on Sobol sequences.[1] (See Kucherenko (2008), Kucherenko et al. (2011), Kucherenko (2007), and Kucherenko et al. (2009) for more information on Sobol sequences and their applications.)

10.2.4   Expected Loss Rating

Credit ratings are based on assessments of either expected loss or probability of default. The expected loss assessment incorporates assessments of both the likelihood of default and the loss severity, given default. The probability of default approach assesses the likelihood of full and timely payment of interest and the ultimate payment of principal no later than the legal final maturity. In this paper, the expected loss rating approach under the assumption of a large, granular portfolio, is being used, following Moody's (2006).

The ratings are based on cumulative expected loss (EL) and expected weighted average life (EWAL). Expected loss is based on the relative net present value loss (RPVL). The EL and EWAL are estimated using Monte Carlo simulations.

The present value of the cash flows under the A note, for a given scenario ω_j, is:

$$PVCF_A(\omega_j) = \sum_{m=1}^{m_T} \frac{\left(I_P^{(A)}(m;\omega_j) + P_P^{(A)}(m;\omega_j)\right)}{(1+r_A/12)^{m/12}}, \tag{10.20}$$

where $I_P^{(A)}(m;\omega_j)$ and $P_P^{(A)}(m;\omega_j)$ is the interest and principal payment received, respectively, in month m under scenario ω_j. We have included ω_j in the expressions to emphasize that these quantities depend on the scenario.

Thus, for the A note, the relative present value loss under scenario ω_j is given by:

$$RPVL_A(\omega_j) = \frac{B_0^{(A)} - PVCF_A(\omega_j)}{B_0^{(A)}}, \tag{10.21}$$

where $B_0^{(A)}$ is the initial nominal amount of the A tranche.

The expected loss estimate using M number of scenarios is:

$$\widehat{EL}_A = \frac{1}{M} \sum_{j=1}^{M} RPVL_A(\omega_j). \tag{10.22}$$

The weighted average life $WAL_A(\omega_j)$ for the A notes (in years) is defined as:

$$WAL_A(\omega_j) = \frac{1}{12 B_0^{(A)}} \left(\sum_{m=1}^{m_T} m P_P^{(A)}(m;\omega_j) + m_T B_C^{(A)}(m_T;\omega_j) \right), \tag{10.23}$$

where $B_C^{(A)}(m_T;\omega_j)$ is the current outstanding amount of the A notes at maturity (month m_T) after any amortization. Thus, we assume that if the notes are not fully amortized after the legal maturity, any outstanding balance is amortized at maturity. Since we assume monthly payments, the factor $\frac{1}{12}$ is used to express WAL in years.

As was the case with the expected loss, we apply Monte Carlo simulations to estimate the EWAL:

$$\widehat{EWAL}_A = \frac{1}{M} \sum_{j=1}^{M} WAL_A(\omega_j). \tag{10.24}$$

10.3 GLOBAL SENSITIVITY ANALYSIS

Sensitivity analysis (SA) is the study of how the variation (uncertainty) in the output of a statistical model can be attributed to different variations in the input of the model. In other words, it is a technique for systematically changing input variables in a model to determine the effects of such changes. In most instances, the sensitivity measure is chosen to be a partial derivative and inputs are allowed only small variations around a nominal value (local sensitivity analysis). However, when the additivity of the model is not known *a priori* and interactions among the inputs cannot be excluded, an analysis of this kind is unreliable. In contrast to the local approach, global sensitivity analysis does not focus on the model sensitivity around a single point, but aims at exploring the sensitivity across the whole input space. Usually global sensitivity analysis is performed by allowing simultaneous variations of the inputs, thus also allowing the capture of potential interactions effects between the various inputs. For a general introduction to global sensitivity analysis, see Saltelli et al. (2004) and Saltelli et al. (2008).

In this section, we introduce the two sensitivity methods that we are going to apply to our rating exercise: the elementary effect method and the variance-based method.

The elementary effect method belongs to the class of screening methods. Screening methods are employed when the goal is to identify the subsets of influential inputs among the many contained in a model, relying on a small number of model evaluations.

The variance-based methods are more accurate but computationally more costly and therefore not always affordable. Through the variance-based methods, it is possible to identify the factors that contribute the most to the total variance in the output.

In our analysis we follow a two-step approach. Firstly, we apply the elementary effect method to identify the subset of input factors that can be viewed as non-influential. The non-influential factors will be given fixed values. Then, we apply the variance-based technique to quantify and distribute the uncertainty of our model output among the influential input parameters.

In the present section, we give a general description of the elementary effect method and the variance-based techniques. The notation adopted is the following:

We assume that there are k uncertain input parameters $X_1, X_2, \ldots, X_k$ (assumed to be independent) in our model, and denote by Y the output of our generic model, $Y(\mathbf{X}) = f(X_1, X_2, \ldots, X_k)$.

Examples of input parameters in our model are the mean and standard deviation of the default distribution. Examples of outputs are the expected loss and the expected weighted average life of a tranche.

We assign a range of variation and a statistical distribution to each input factor. For example, we could assume that X_1 is the mean of the default distribution and that it takes values in the range [5%, 30%] uniformly, that is, each of the values in the range is equally likely to be chosen. We could of course use non-uniform distributions as well, for example, an empirical distribution.

These input parameters and their ranges create an input space of all possible combinations of values for the input parameters.

10.3.1 Elementary Effects

The elementary effects method (EE method) is a very efficient method within the screening methods for identifying important inputs with few simulations. It is very simple, easy to implement and the results are clear for interpretation. It was introduced in Morris (1991) and has been refined by Campolongo et al. (2007). Because of the complexity of its structure, the ABS ratings exercise is computationally expensive and the EE method is very well suited to the sensitivity analysis of the ABS model's output.

The method starts with a one-at-a-time sensitivity analysis. It computes for each input parameter a local sensitivity measure, the so-called Elementary Effect (EE), which is defined as the ratio between the variation in the model output and the variation in the input itself, while the rest of the input parameters are kept fixed. Then, in order to obtain a global sensitivity measure, the one-at-a-time analysis is repeated several times for each input, each time under different settings of the other input parameters, and the sensitivity measures are calculated from the empirical distribution of the elementary effects.

In order to estimate the sensitivity measures, a number of elementary effects must be calculated for each input parameter. To compute r elementary effects, r trajectories in the input space are needed. Each trajectory is composed by $(k + 1)$ points in the input space such that each input changes value only once and two consecutive points differ only in one component.

Once a trajectory has been generated, the model is evaluated at each point of the trajectory and one elementary effect for each input can be computed. Let $\mathbf{X}^{(l)}$ and $\mathbf{X}^{(l+1)}$, with l in the set $\{1, 2, \ldots, k\}$, denote two points on the jth trajectory. If the ith component of $\mathbf{X}^{(l)}$ is increased by Δ, such that $\mathbf{X}^{(l+1)} = (X_1, X_2, \ldots, X_i + \Delta, \ldots, X_k)$, then the EE of input i is:

$$EE_i^j \left(\mathbf{X}^{(l)}\right) = \frac{Y\left(\mathbf{X}^{(l+1)}\right) - Y\left(\mathbf{X}^{(l)}\right)}{\Delta}, \qquad (10.25)$$

and

$$EE_i^j \left(\mathbf{X}^{(l+1)}\right) = \frac{Y\left(\mathbf{X}^{(l)}\right) - Y\left(\mathbf{X}^{(l+1)}\right)}{\Delta} \qquad (10.26)$$

if the ith component of $\mathbf{X}^{(l)}$ is decreased by Δ.

By randomly sampling r trajectories, r elementary effects can be estimated for each input, one per trajectory. The number of trajectories (r) depends on the number of inputs and on the computational cost of the model. Typical values of r are between 4 and 10. The number of levels across which each input is varied is chosen by the analyst (see Morris (1991) and Campolongo et al. (2007)).

We are applying the sensitivity measure introduced in Campolongo et al. (2007), which is defined as the mean of the absolute value of the elementary effects of each input:

$$\mu_i^* = \frac{\sum_{j=1}^{r} |EE_i^j|}{r}. \qquad (10.27)$$

See Campolongo et al. (2007) for all the details about the design that builds the r trajectories of $(k + 1)$ points in the input space.

Section 10.4.2.1 presents the results obtained by applying the EE methodology to the ABS model. Results do not depend on the choice of strategy employed to compute the elementary effects.

10.3.2   Variance-based Method

We begin our discussion on variance-based methods by noting that the variance of our generic output, $V(Y)$, can be decomposed into a main effect and a residual effect:

$$V(Y) = V_{X_i}(E_{X_{\sim i}}(Y|X_i)) + E_{X_i}(V_{X_{\sim i}}(Y|X_i)). \tag{10.28}$$

Here, $E_{X_{\sim i}}(Y|X_i)$ is the conditional expectation given X_i, calculated over all input factors except X_i, and V_{X_i} denotes the variance calculated with respect to X_i. Equivalently, $V_{X_{\sim i}}(Y|X_i)$ is the variance with respect to all factors except X_i, conditional on X_i.

The first term in (10.28) is of most interest to us. It tells us how much the mean of the output varies when one of the input factors (X_i) is fixed. A large value of $V(E(Y|X_i))$ indicates that X_i is an important factor contributing to the output variance. When we divide this variance by the unconditional variance $V(Y)$, we obtain the first-order sensitivity index with respect to factor i:

$$S_i = \frac{V_{X_i}(E_{X_{\sim i}}(Y|X_i))}{V(Y)}. \tag{10.29}$$

These first order sensitivity indices represent the main effect contribution of each input factor. When $\sum_{i=1}^k S_i = 1$, the inputs do not interact and the model is purely additive.

However, when $\sum_{i=1}^k S_i < 1$, the interactions between the inputs play a role in explaining the output variance.

For instance, the Second Order Sensitivity Index, $S_{i,j}$, quantifies the extra amount of the variance corresponding to the interaction between inputs i and j that is not explained by the sum of their individual effects. The second order sensitivity index is

$$S_{i,j} = \frac{V_{X_i,X_j}(E_{X_{\sim i,j}}(Y|X_i, X_j)) - V_{X_i}(E_{X_{\sim i}}(Y|X_i)) - V_{X_j}(E_{X_{\sim j}}(Y|X_j))}{V(Y)}. \tag{10.30}$$

In general, for a model output depending on k inputs, the following relation has been shown to hold:

$$\sum_{i=1}^k S_i + \sum_i \sum_{j>i} S_{i,j} + \cdots + S_{1,2,\ldots,k} = 1, \tag{10.31}$$

where S_i are the first order sensitivity indices, $S_{i,j}$ are the second order sensitivity indices, and so on until $S_{1,2,\ldots,k}$, which is the kth order sensitivity index.

For more details, see Saltelli (2002), Saltelli et al. (2004), Saltelli et al. (2008) and Sobol' (1993). For the computation of the Sensitivity Indices see Saltelli et al. (2010) and Ratto and Pagano (2010). Results of our experiment are presented and discussed in Section 10.4.2.2.

10.4   GLOBAL SENSITIVITY ANALYSIS RESULTS

The sensitivity analysis (SA) is performed on the structure presented in Section 10.2.1–10.2.2 and the default model presented in Section 10.2.3. The fundamental output in our study is the rating of the ABSs. These ratings are derived from the expected average life and the expected loss of the notes. Because of that, these two quantities are the outputs the SA should investigate in order to assess the influence of the unknown inputs in the ABS ratings.

Without loss of generality, the investor is assumed to be informed about the collateral pool's characteristics and the structural characteristics given in Table 10.1 and Table 10.2, respectively, and the waterfall in Table 10.3. These are treated as controllable input factors.

Assuming that the default distribution of the pool will follow a Normal Inverse distribution and the default curve is modeled by the Logistic model, the uncertain input factors in the SA are not related to the model choice, but to the parameters of the cumulative default rate distribution, the default timing (the Logistic function) and the recoveries: the mean (μ_{cd}) and the standard deviation (σ_{cd}) of the Normal Inverse distribution; b, c and t_0 of the Logistic Function; the recovery rate (RR) and the recovery lag (T_{RL}) in months.

The input ranges are summarized in Table 10.4. See Di Girolamo et al. (2012) for the motivations for our choice of ranges.

In this section we present the results on sensitivity analysis and we refer to Di Girolamo et al. (2012) for the full study.

10.4.1   Uncertainty Analysis

We want to explore the input space effectively in the sense of not only exploring the center of the input space but also its corners and edges. To achieve this, the sample points will be generated by the same method as the one used for the variance-based sensitivity analysis method, described in the following section. In total, 256 sample points were used.

For each combination of input values, we run the ABS model 2^{14} times to derive ratings for the tranches. The empirical distributions of the ratings of the tranches are shown in Figure 10.1.

All three histograms show evidence of dispersion in the rating outcomes. The dispersion is most significant for the mezzanine tranche. The ratings of the senior and the junior tranches behave in a more stable way: we get ratings with a low degree of risk, 78% of times for the A notes, and the C notes are unrated 51% of time.[2]

The uncertainty analysis highlights an important point: the uncertainty in the rating of the mezzanine tranche is very high.

Table 10.4   Ranges for the uncertain input factors.

Parameter	Range
μ_{cd}	[5%, 30%]
Coeff. Variation $\left(\frac{\sigma_{cd}}{\mu_{cd}}\right)$	[0.25, 1]
b	[0.5, 1.5]
c	[0.1, 0.5]
t_0	$[\frac{T}{3}, \frac{2T}{3}]$
T_{RL}	[6, 36]
RR	[5%, 50%]

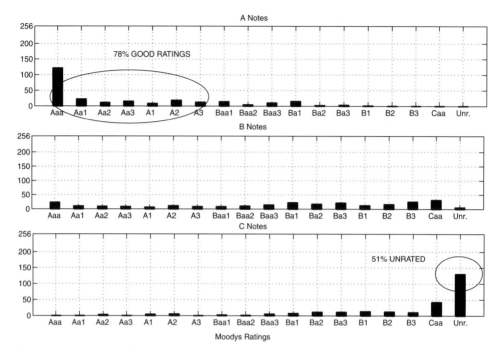

Figure 10.1   Empirical distribution of Moody's ratings obtained by 256 simulations.

As a measure of the ratings dispersion, we look at the interquartile range, which is defined as the difference between the 75th percentile and the 25th percentile. Ratings percentiles are provided in Table 10.5. It does not come as a surprise that the range is highest for the B notes, 9 notches, given the very dispersed empirical distribution shown in Figure 10.1. From Table 10.5, we can also conclude that the interquartile range is equal to five and three notches for the A notes and the C notes, respectively.

This dispersion in the rating distribution is of course a result of the uncertainty in the expected losses and expected average lives, which are used to derive the ratings of each note.

In the next section, we apply sensitivity analysis methods to assess which sources of uncertainty among the input factors are contributing most to the uncertainty in the outputs.

10.4.2   Sensitivity Analysis

We analyze six outputs: the expected loss and the expected weighted average life of each of the three classes of notes. Due to the fact that the ABS model is computationally

Table 10.5   Rating percentiles and interquartile ranges.

	Percentile						Interquartile Range
Note	25	50	75	80	90	95	Number of Notches
A	Aaa	Aa1	A2	A3	Baa3	Ba1	5
B	A2	Ba1	B2	B3	Caa	Caa	9
C	B2	N.R.	N.R.	N.R.	N.R.	N.R.	3

expensive, we will start our sensitivity analysis by using the elementary effect method to identify non-influential input factors. Each of the non-influential inputs will be fixed to a value within its range. After that, the variance-based method will be applied to quantify and to distribute the uncertainty of our model outputs among the input parameters identified to be influential.

The starting point for both methods is the selection of a number of settings of the input parameters. The number of SA evaluations to receive sensitivity analysis results depends on the technique used. In the elementary effect method, we select 80 settings of input parameters.[3] In the variance-based method, we select 2^8 settings of input parameters.[4] For each setting of the input parameters, the ABS model runs 2^{14} times to provide the outputs and the ratings.

10.4.2.1   Elementary Effects

For a specific output, the elementary effect method provides one sensitivity measure, μ_i^*, for each input factor. These sensitivity measures are used to rank each input factor in order of importance relative to the other inputs. The input factor with the highest μ_i^* value is ranked as the most important factor for the variation of the output under consideration. It is important to keep in mind that the ranking of the inputs is done for each output separately.

In Figure 10.2, Figure 10.3 and Figure 10.4, bar plots visually depict the rank of the input factors for each of the six outputs. The least influential factors across all outputs are the recovery

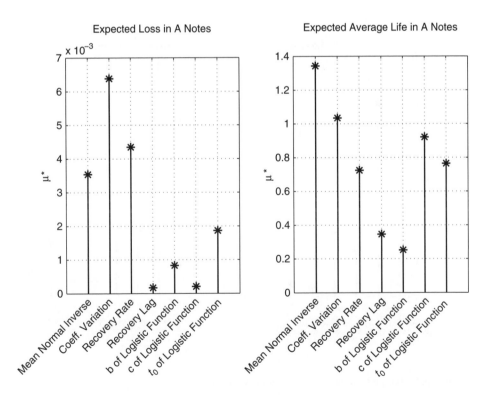

Figure 10.2   Bar plots of the μ^* values for the A notes.

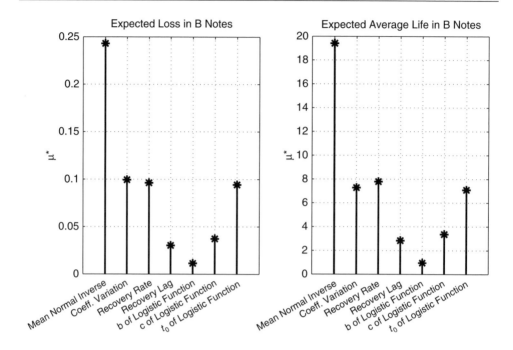

Figure 10.3   Bar plots of the μ^* values for the B notes.

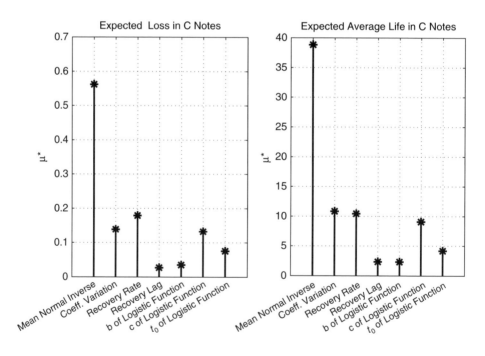

Figure 10.4   Bar plots of the μ^* values for the C notes.

lag and the Logistic function's b parameter. Hence they could be fixed without affecting the variance of the outputs of interest and therefore, the uncertainty in the ratings.

Among the other input parameters, the mean of the default distribution (μ_{cd}) is clearly the most important input parameter overall for all three notes. It is characterized by high μ^* values for both the expected loss and the expected average life of all the notes. This highlights the strong influence the mean default rate assumption has on the assessment of the ABSs. The only exception to ranking the mean default rate as the most influential input factor is the expected loss of the A notes. Here, the coefficient of variation is ranked the highest, with the recovery rate as second and the mean default rate as third.

10.4.2.2   Variance-based Methods

In the elementary effect analysis performed above, two out of seven input parameters were identified as non-influential. These two inputs can therefore be fixed to values within their ranges. We have chosen to let $b = 1$ and $T_{RL} = 18$ (months). For the other input factors, we are going to apply variance-based methods to quantify their contribution to the output variances.

We now select 2^8 settings of input parameters, we run our model for each of them and finally we obtain the sensitivity indices.

Figure 10.5 depicts a clear decomposition of the output variance highlighting the main contributions due to the individual input parameters (first order effects) and due to pairwise interactions between input parameters that are involved in the model (second order effects). For the B and C notes, the mean cumulative default rate, μ_{cd}, clearly contributes the most to the variance, accounting for approximately more than 60% and more than 70%, respectively. The uncertainty analysis performed earlier pointed out that the uncertainty in the rating of the mezzanine tranche is very high. The first order sensitivity indices indicate that improving the knowledge of μ_{cd}, can help to reduce the variability of the outputs. In fact, if we could know the value of μ_{cd} for certain, then the variance in expected loss and expected average life of the B notes could be reduced by more than 60%.

For the senior tranche, the first order indices indicate that μ_{cd} is the largest individual contributor to the variation in the expected loss of the A notes (17%), and that c is the largest individual contributor to the variation in expected average life of the A notes (24%). However, large parts of the variation in expected loss and expected average life of the A notes come from interaction between input factors. This indicates that the first order indices cannot solely be used to identify the most important inputs and that more sophisticated sensitivity measures must be used.

When interactions are involved in the model, we are unable to understand which input is the most influential by just using the first order effect contributions. Figure 10.5 depicts the decomposition of the variance, including explicitly the second order effect contributions due to the pairwise interactions between input parameters. From the partition of the expected loss of the A notes variance, we can clearly see that the interaction between μ_{cd} and the coefficient of variation and the interaction between μ_{cd} and RR significantly contribute to the total variance, with 15% and 10%, respectively. It is also indicated that 15% of the total variance originates from interactions among three or more inputs. For the other outputs, the first order indices are in most cases larger than the higher order effects.

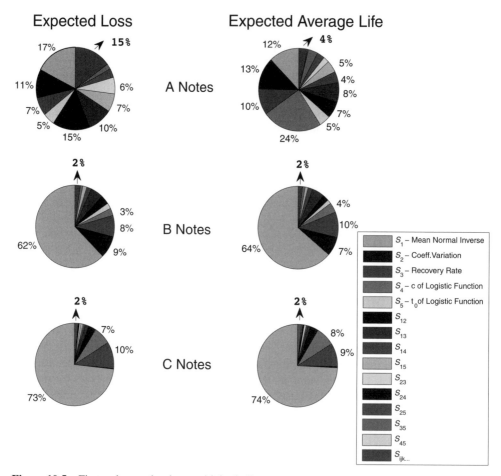

Figure 10.5   First and second order sensitivity indices.

10.5   GLOBAL RATING

In the previous section, we saw that the uncertainty in the input parameters propagates through the model and generates uncertainty in the outputs. The rating of the A notes, for example, shown in Figure 10.1, ranges from Aaa to Unrated. The question is how to pick the rating of the A notes if we have this variability?

By using sensitivity analysis, we have been able to quantify this uncertainty and identify its sources. If we knew the true value of the most important inputs, we could eliminate most of the variability in the model. In practice, these values are unknown to us. This implies that we have an intrinsic problem in the rating of ABSs.

In this section, we propose using a new rating approach that takes into account the uncertainty in the outputs when rating ABSs. This new approach should be more stable, reducing the risk of cliff effects when assigning ratings to tranches.[5] The idea is to assign the rating according to the uncertainty/dispersion of the credit risk. We call this new approach a *global rating*, because it explores the whole input space when generating the global scenarios.

The global rating procedure is basically the same as the one used for the uncertainty analysis and sensitivity analysis:

1. identify the uncertain input factors, their ranges and distributions,
2. generate N global scenarios, i.e., N different settings of the inputs, from the input space,
3. for each global scenario generate a rating of each note,
4. derive a rating for each note by a percentile mapping.

10.5.1   Methodology

The global approach derives the rating of a note from the empirical distribution of ratings generated from the global scenarios. An important fact is that this procedure is independent of which rating methodology is used to derive the rating of each global scenario, that is, if it is based on expected loss or probability of default.

We propose a global rating scale that reflects the dispersion of the credit risk of a tranche, taking into account the uncertainties that affect the rating process.

The global rating scale that we propose is superimposed on a rating scale used by a rating agency or by a financial institution. The global rating is based on a percentile mapping of the underlying rating scale, that is, a global rating is assigned to a tranche if a predetermined fraction of the ratings generated, using the uncertainty scenarios, is better than or equal to a given underlying rating.

To set up a global rating scale, we therefore first have to decide on the underlying rating scale. Imagine we use Moody's. A proposal for the global rating scale A−E is provided in Table 10.6. The global rating B in Table 10.6, for example, indicates that a substantial fraction of the ratings generated under different scenarios fall into Moody's rating scale Aaa−Baa3. This informs the potential investor that the tranche shows low credit risk for certain scenarios but that there are scenarios where the credit risk are at a medium level.

Secondly, we have to choose the fraction of rating outcomes that should lie in the credit risk range. As a first attempt, we have defined the global scale with respect to the 80th percentile of the local scale (in this case Moody's ratings). From the mapping in Table 10.6, one can see that to assign a global rating B, for example, at least 80% of the ratings must be better than or equal to Baa3.

Using the percentiles of the ratings in Table 10.5, we can derive the global ratings of the three notes. The global ratings based on the rating scale provided in Table 10.6 for different rating percentiles are shown in Table 10.7.

Table 10.6   A proposal of global rating scale and the corresponding ranges in Moody's rating scale.

Global Rating	Moody's
A	A3–Aaa
B	Baa3–Aaa
C	Ba3–Aaa
D	B3–Aaa
E	N.R.–Aaa

Table 10.7 Global ratings for different percentiles.

Note	Percentile		
	75%	80%	90%
A	A	**A**	B
B	D	**D**	E
C	E	**E**	E

The idea of basing ratings on percentiles is loosely related to the Standard and Poor's approach for assigning ratings to CDOs. For further information, see Standard and Poor's (2004), Standard and Poor's (2009), Standard and Poor's (2001) and Standard and Poor's (2010).

10.6 CONCLUSION

In this chapter, we have shown how global sensitivity analysis can be used to analyze the main sources of uncertainty in the ratings of asset-backed securities (ABSs). The global sensitivity analysis was applied to a test example consisting of a large homogeneous pool of assets, backing three classes of notes (senior, mezzanine and junior).

Due to the fact that deriving ratings for ABSs is computationally expensive, the elementary effect method was chosen for an initial analysis aiming to identify the non-influential input parameters. As a second step, variance-based methods were applied to quantify and to distribute the uncertainty of the outputs among the input parameters, identified to be influential.

The sensitivity analysis led to the conclusion that the least influential inputs across all outputs are the recovery lag and the Logistic function's b parameter. Hence, they could be fixed without affecting the variance of the outputs of interest and, therefore, the ratings.

The mean of the default distribution was found to be the most influential input parameter among all inputs for all three notes. For the mezzanine and the junior tranche, the mean cumulative default rate contributes the most to the variance, accounting for approximately more than 60% and more than 70%, respectively, of the total variance of the expected loss and the expected weighted average life of the tranches.

For the senior tranche, large parts of the variation in the outputs came from interactions between input parameters. This indicates that the first order indices cannot solely be used to identify the most important inputs and more sophisticated sensitivity measures must be used. Using both the first and second order sensitivity indices we detect the mean of the default distribution to be the most influential input parameter.

In the final section of this chapter, we proposed a new rating approach called *global rating*. The global rating approach takes into account that the uncertainty in the input parameters propagates through the model and generates uncertainty in the outputs. The global approach derives the rating of a tranche from the empirical distribution of ratings generated from the input scenarios. Each scenario is a unique combination of values of the input parameters. An important fact is that this procedure is independent of which rating methodology is used to derive the rating of each global scenario, that is, if it is based on expected loss or probability of default.

The global rating scale is chosen to reflect the dispersion of the credit risk of a tranche. This scale is superimposed on a rating scale used by a rating agency or financial institution. The scale is based on a percentile mapping of the underlying rating scale, that is, a global rating is assigned to a tranche if a predetermined fraction of the ratings generated using the uncertainty scenarios is better than or equal to a given underlying rating. The idea is to let the global rating reflect a range of possible credit risks.

ACKNOWLEDGMENT

This study was initiated in the framework of the research project "Quantitative analysis and analytical methods to price securitisation deals," sponsored by the European Investment Bank via the university research sponsorship programme EIBURS, and realized 2008–2010 at the international research institute EURANDOM (www.eurandom.nl). The authors acknowledge the intellectual support of the participants of the project.

NOTES

1. We have been using the "sobolset" class (with the "MatousekAffineOwen" scramble algorithm) and "RandStream" class (with the "mrg32k3a" generator algorithm) in MATLAB® for generating Sobol sequences and pseudo random numbers, respectively.
2. This is not surprising because losses are allocated to the notes in reverse order of seniority, it is the junior tranche that absorbs any losses first.
3. We apply the method by using $r = 10$ trajectories of 4 points. Having $k = 7$ input parameters, the total number of SA model evaluations is 80 ($N = r(k + 1)$). This choice has been demonstrated to produce valuable results in a general application of the sensitivity analysis.
4. This choice has been demonstrated to produce valuable results in a general application of the variance-based method (see Ratto and Pagano (2010)).
5. The cliff effect refers to the risk that a small change in one or several of the input assumptions generates a dramatic change in the rating.

REFERENCES

Campolongo, F., Cariboni, J., Saltelli, A., 2007. An effective screening design for sensitivity analysis of large models. Environmental Modelling & Software 22, 1509–1518.
Campolongo, F., Jönsson, H., Schoutens, W., 2013. Quantitative Assessment of Securitisation Deals, SpringerBriefs in Finance.
Di Girolamo, F., Jönsson, H., Campolongo, F., Schoutens, W., 2012. Sense and sensitivity: an input space odyssey for ABS ratings, International Journal of Financial Research, Vol. 3, No. 4.
IMF, 2008. Global Financial Stability Report, April.
Jönsson, H., Schoutens, W., 2010. Known and less known risks in asset-backed securities, in D. Wigan (Ed.) Credit Derivatives – The March to Maturity, IFR Market Intelligence.
Jönsson, H., Schoutens, W., van Damme, G., 2009. Modeling default and prepayment using Lévy processes: an application to asset backed securities, Radon Series on Computational and Applied Mathematics 8, 183–204, de Gruyter, Berlin.
Kucherenko, S., 2007. Application of global sensitivity indices for measuring the effectiveness of Quasi-Monte Carlo methods, Proc. of the Fifth International Conference on Sensitivity Analysis of Model Output.
Kucherenko, S., 2008. High dimensional Sobol's sequences and their application, Technical Report – www.broda.co.uk.
Kucherenko, S., Feil, B., Shah, N., Mauntz, W., 2011. The identification of model effective dimensions using global sensitivity analysis, Reliability Engineering and System Safety 96, 440–449.
Kucherenko, S., Rodriguez-Fernandez, M., Pantelides, C., Shah, N., 2009. Monte Carlo evaluation of derivative-based global sensitivity measures, Reliability Engineering and System Safety 94, 1135–1148.
Moody's Investor Service, 2006. Moody's ABSROM™ v 1.0 User Guide.

Moody's Investor Service, 2009. V Scores and Parameter Sensitivities in the EMA Small-to-Medium Enterprise ABS Sector, International Structured Finance, Rating Methodology.

Morris, M.D., 1991. Factorial sampling plans for preliminary computational experiments, Technometrics 33, nb. 2, 161–174.

Ratto, M., Pagano, A., 2010. Using recursive algorithms for the efficient identification of smoothing spline ANOVA models, Advances in Statistical Analysis 94, 367–388.

Saltelli, A., 2002. Making best use of model evaluations to compute sensitivity indices, Computer Physics Communications 145, 280–300.

Saltelli, A., Annoni, P., Azzini, I., Campolongo, F., Ratto, M., Tarantola, S., 2010. Variance based sensitivity analysis of model output. Design and estimator for the total sensitivity index, Computer Physics Communications 181, 259–270.

Saltelli, A., Ratto, M., Andres, T., Campolongo, F., Cariboni, J., Gatelli, D., Saisana, M., Tarantola, S., 2008. Global Sensitivity Analysis: The Primer, Wiley.

Saltelli, A., Tarantola, S., Campolongo, F., Ratto, M., 2004. Sensitivity Analysis in Practice, Wiley.

Sobol', I., 1993. Sensitivity analysis for non linear mathematical models, Mathematical Modelling and Computational Experiment 1, 407–414. Translated from Russian: Sobol', I., 1990. Sensitivity estimates for non linear mathematical models, Matematicheskoe Modelirovanie 2, 112–118.

Standard and Poor's, 2001. CDO Evaluator applies correlation and Monte Carlo simulation to determine portfolio quality.

Standard and Poor's, 2004. CDO Spotling: General cash flow analytics for CDO securitization.

Standard and Poor's, 2009. Update to global methodologies and assumptions for corporate cash flow and synthetic CDOs.

Standard and Poor's, 2010. CDO Evaluator System Version 5.1 – User Guide.

Part IV
Credit Derivatives

11

Analytic Dynamic Factor Copula Model*

Ken Jackson[1], Alex Kreinin[2] and Wanhe Zhang[3]

[1]*University of Toronto*
[2]*Risk Analytics, Business Analytics, IBM, Toronto*
[3]*Royal Bank of Canada, Toronto*

11.1 INTRODUCTION

Due to their computational efficiency, factor copula models are popular for pricing multi-name credit derivatives. Within this class of models, the Gaussian factor copula model is the market standard model. However, it cannot match market quotes consistently without violating the model assumptions as explained in Hull and White (2006) and Torresetti et al. (2006). For example, it has to use different correlation factor loadings for different tranches based on the same underlying portfolio. To better match the observable spreads, several modifications have been proposed based on the conditional independence framework. See, for example, Andersen and Sidenius (2004), Baxter (2007) and Hull and White (2008). Most of these approaches are static one-period models that generate a portfolio loss distribution at a fixed maturity. They may not be flexible enough to match market quotes or applicable for new products with strong time-dependent features, such as forward-starting tranches, tranche options and leveraged super-senior tranches as pointed out in Andersen (2006). Another popular approach to calibrate factor copula models is base correlation, as, for example, discussed in McGinty et al. (2004), which calibrates the correlation for the first loss tranche, i.e. the sum of all tranches up to a detachment point. Although it guarantees the existence of the correlation parameter, it is not arbitrage-free. For example, it is easy to construct a tranche with a negative spread using this method as noticed in Torresetti et al. (2006).

Another methodology for multi-name credit derivatives is the top-down approach, which models the portfolio loss directly. For example, Bennani (2005), Schönbucher (2005) and Sidenius et al. (2008) proposed similar frameworks to model the dynamics of the aggregate portfolio losses by modeling the forward loss rates. With these pool loss dynamics, the pricing of credit derivatives becomes straightforward. This approach has been further extended by many researchers, such as Giesecke, et al. (2011). However, these models require a large amount of data to calibrate and are currently speculative as explained in Andersen (2006).

It is tempting to see whether we can introduce dynamics into the factor copula model to combine its computational efficiency with the ability to calibrate more consistently against market quotes. The main challenge in developing such a dynamic factor copula model is that the arbitrage-free property and computational efficiency become more difficult to achieve,

*This research was supported in part by the Natural Sciences and Engineering Research Council (NSERC) of Canada.

as the number of state variables grows rapidly with the introduction of dynamics. Fingers (2000) proposed several extensions of one-period default models. However, they are not based on the factor copula approach. Therefore, only Monte Carlo simulation is available to implement these extensions. In addition, the correlation coefficients are not allowed to be time-dependent. Andersen (2006) and Sidenius (2007) introduced several "chaining" techniques to build multi-period factor copula models from one-period factor copula models. As these models must integrate over all the common factors, they require a multi-dimensional integration, which is usually computed by Monte Carlo simulation. This makes the model calibration extremely time-consuming. Except for some special cases, for example where the factors are the same for all periods, existing "chaining" methods cannot avoid multi-dimensional integration. Therefore, current multi-period models are hard to generalize to more than two periods.

In this chapter we develop a novel chaining method to build a multi-period factor copula model, which does not allow arbitrage opportunities and avoids multi-dimensional integration. Based on our model, the portfolio loss of a completely homogeneous pool possesses the Markov property, so we can compute its distribution across time by a recursive method instead of by Monte Carlo simulation. Numerical results demonstrate the accuracy, efficiency and flexibility of our model in calibrating against market quotes.

The rest of this chapter is organized as follows. Section 11.2 describes the pricing equations for synthetic CDOs. Section 11.3 reviews the widely used Gaussian factor copula model as an example of the conditional independence framework. Section 11.4 reviews existing "chaining" methods before introducing our new multi-period model. Section 11.5 discusses calibration. Section 11.6 presents the numerical results. Section 11.7 concludes the chapter and discusses future work.

11.2 PRICING EQUATIONS

In a synthetic CDO, the protection seller absorbs the pool loss specified by the tranche structure. That is, if the pool loss over $(0, T]$ is less than the tranche attachment point a, the seller does not suffer any loss; otherwise, the seller absorbs the loss up to the tranche size $S = b - a$. In return for the protection, the buyer pays periodic premia at specified times $t_1 < t_2 < \ldots < t_n = T$.

We consider a synthetic CDO containing K names with loss-given-default N_k for name k in the original pool. Assume that the recovery rates are constant. Let D_i denote the risk-free discount factors at time t_i, and d_i denote the expected value of D_i in a risk-neutral measure. Denote the pool loss up to time t_i by L_i. Then, the loss absorbed by the specified tranche is

$$\mathcal{L}_i = \min(S, (L_i - a)^+), \quad \text{where } x^+ = \max(x, 0). \tag{11.1}$$

We make the standard assumption that the discount factors D_i's and the pool losses L_i's are independent, whence D_i's and $\mathcal{L}_i$'s are also independent.

In general, valuation of a synthetic CDO tranche balances the expectation of the present values of the premium payments (premium leg) against the effective tranche losses (default leg), such that

$$\mathbb{E}\left[\sum_{i=1}^{n} s(S - \mathcal{L}_i)(T_i - T_{i-1})D_i\right] = \mathbb{E}\left[\sum_{i=1}^{n}(\mathcal{L}_i - \mathcal{L}_{i-1})D_i\right]. \tag{11.2}$$

The fair spread s is therefore given by

$$s = \frac{\mathbb{E}\left[\sum_{i=1}^{n}(\mathcal{L}_i - \mathcal{L}_{i-1})D_i\right]}{\mathbb{E}\left[\sum_{i=1}^{n}(S - \mathcal{L}_i)(T_i - T_{i-1})D_i\right]} = \frac{\sum_{i=1}^{n}(\mathbb{E}\mathcal{L}_i - \mathbb{E}\mathcal{L}_{i-1})d_i}{\sum_{i=1}^{n}(S - \mathbb{E}\mathcal{L}_i)(T_i - T_{i-1})d_i}. \tag{11.3}$$

In the last equality of (11.3), we use the fact that D_i and $\mathcal{L}_i$ ($\mathcal{L}_{i-1}$) are independent. Alternatively, if the spread is set, the value of the synthetic CDO is the difference between the two legs:

$$\sum_{i=1}^{n} s(S - \mathbb{E}\mathcal{L}_i)(T_i - T_{i-1})d_i - \sum_{i=1}^{n}(\mathbb{E}\mathcal{L}_i - \mathbb{E}\mathcal{L}_{i-1})d_i.$$

Therefore, the problem is reduced to the computation of the mean tranche losses, $\mathbb{E}\mathcal{L}_i$. To compute this expectation, we have to compute the portfolio loss L_i's distribution. Therefore, we need to specify the correlation structure of the portfolio defaults.

11.3 ONE-FACTOR COPULA MODEL

Due to their tractability, factor copula models are widely used to specify a joint distribution for default times consistent with their marginal distribution. A one-factor model was first introduced by Vasicek (1987) to evaluate the loan loss distribution, and the Gaussian copula was first applied to multi-name credit derivatives by Li (2000). After that, the model was generalized by Andersen et al. (2003), Hull and White (2004) and Laurent and Gregory (2005), to name just a few. In this section, we review the one-factor Gaussian copula model to illustrate the conditional independence framework.

Let τ_k be the default time of name k, where $\tau_k = \infty$ if name k never defaults. Assume the risk-neutral default probabilities

$$\pi_k(t) = \mathbb{P}(\tau_k \leq t), \quad k = 1, 2, \ldots, K$$

are known. In order to generate the dependence structure of default times, we introduce random variables U_k, such that

$$U_k = \beta_k X + \sqrt{1 - \beta_k^2}\varepsilon_k, \quad \text{for } k = 1, 2, \ldots, K \tag{11.4}$$

where X is the systematic risk factor; ε_k are idiosyncratic risk factors, which are independent of each other and also independent of X; and the constants $\beta_k \in [-1, 1]$.

The default times τ_k and the random variables U_k are connected by a percentile-to-percentile transformation, such that $\mathbb{P}(\tau_k \leq t) = \mathbb{P}(U_k \leq b_k(t))$, where each $b_k(t)$ can be viewed as a default barrier.

Models satisfying the assumptions above are said to be based on the conditional independence framework. If, in addition, we assume X and ε_k follow standard normal distributions, then we get a Gaussian factor copula model. In this case, each U_k also follows a standard normal distribution. Hence we have

$$b_k(t) = \Phi^{-1}(\pi_k(t)) \tag{11.5}$$

where Φ is the standard normal cumulative distribution function. Conditional on a particular value x of X, the risk-neutral default probabilities are defined as

$$\pi_k(t, x) \equiv \mathbb{P}(\tau_k \le t \mid X = x) = \mathbb{P}(U_k \le b_k(t) \mid X = x) = \Phi\left[\frac{\Phi^{-1}(\pi_k(t)) - \beta_k x}{\sqrt{1 - \beta_k^2}}\right]. \tag{11.6}$$

In this framework, the default events of the names are assumed to be conditionally independent. Thus the problem of correlated names is reduced to the problem of independent names. The pool losses L_i satisfy

$$\mathbb{P}(L_i = l) = \int_{-\infty}^{\infty} \mathbb{P}_x(L_i = l) d\Phi(x) \tag{11.7}$$

where $L_i = \sum_{k=1}^{K} N_k \mathbf{1}_{\{U_k \le b_k(t_i)\}}$, and $\mathbf{1}_{\{U_k \le b_k(t_i)\}}$ are mutually independent, conditional on $X = x$.[1] Therefore, if we know the conditional distributions of $\mathbf{1}_{\{U_k \le b_k(t_i)\}}$, the conditional distributions of L_i can be computed easily, as can $\mathbb{E}[\mathcal{L}_i]$. To approximate the integral (11.7), we use a quadrature rule. Thus the integral (11.7) reduces to

$$\mathbb{P}(L_i = l) \approx \sum_{m=1}^{M} w_m \mathbb{P}_{x_m}(L_i = l)$$

where the w_m and x_m are the quadrature weights and nodes, respectively.

A significant drawback of this model is that it does not allow the β_k's to be time-dependent, which is often required to calibrate the model effectively. If β_k is a function of time, $\pi_k(t, x)$ may be a decreasing function of time, which may lead to an arbitrage opportunity, as explained in the next section. More specifically, for $0 < t_1 < t_2$, to guarantee $\pi_k(t_1, x) \le \pi_k(t_2, x)$, or equivalently,

$$\Phi\left(\frac{b_k(t_1) - \beta_k(t_1)x}{\sqrt{1 - \beta_k(t_1)^2}}\right) \le \Phi\left(\frac{b_k(t_2) - \beta_k(t_2)x}{\sqrt{1 - \beta_k(t_2)^2}}\right)$$

we need

$$\frac{b_k(t_1) - \beta_k(t_1)x}{\sqrt{1 - \beta_k(t_1)^2}} \le \frac{b_k(t_2) - \beta_k(t_2)x}{\sqrt{1 - \beta_k(t_2)^2}}.$$

As x may be any real value, for any fixed $\beta_k(t_1) \ne \beta_k(t_2)$, it is easy to find an x to violate this inequality. For example, if $b_k(t_1) = -2$, $b_k(t_2) = -1.4$, $\beta_k(t_1) = 0.6$ and $\beta_k(t_2) = 0.8$, then

$$\pi_k(t_1, 2) = \mathbb{P}(\tau_k \le t_1 \mid X = 2) = \Phi(-4)$$
$$\pi_k(t_2, 2) = \mathbb{P}(\tau_k \le t_2 \mid X = 2) = \Phi(-5).$$

11.4 MULTI-PERIOD FACTOR COPULA MODELS

To overcome this drawback, Andersen (2006) and Sidenius (2007) pioneered the technique of "chaining" a series of one-period factor copula models to produce a multi-period factor copula model. However, their approaches must integrate over the multi-dimensional common factors to evaluate the portfolio loss distribution over time, requiring the evaluation of a high-dimensional integral, usually computed by Monte Carlo simulation. Therefore, their models are hard to generalize to more than two periods, except for some special, but possibly unrealistic, cases, such as, the common factors are the same for all periods. In this section, we first review the approaches of Andersen (2006) and Sidenius (2007). We then present our new model, which avoids multi-dimensional integration.

In general, the conditional independence framework, including one-period and multi-period factor copula models, has to satisfy two properties: consistency and no arbitrage. By consistency, we mean that the model has to match the marginal default probabilities of the underlyings, i.e.,

$$\mathbb{P}(\tau_k \leq t) = \int_{\mathcal{D}} \mathbb{P}(\tau_k \leq t \mid X^{(t)} = x) dF(x). \tag{11.8}$$

Here, $X^{(t)}$ represents the common factors up to time t (it may be a multiple dimensional random variable in the discrete case or a stochastic process in the continuous case); $\mathcal{D}$ is the domain of $X^{(t)}$; and $F(\cdot)$ is the cumulative distribution function of $X^{(t)}$. By no arbitrage, we mean that the pool loss distribution is a non-decreasing function of time, i.e.,

$$\mathbb{P}(L_i = l) \leq \mathbb{P}(L_j = l), \text{ for } t_i \leq t_j. \tag{11.9}$$

To satisfy this constraint in practice, we usually require a stronger condition: the conditional default probability of a single name is non-decreasing over time, i.e.,

$$\mathbb{P}(\tau_k \leq t_1 \mid X^{(t_1)} = x) \leq \mathbb{P}(\tau_k \leq t_2 \mid X^{(t_2)} = y), \text{ for } t_1 \leq t_2 \text{ and } x(t) = y(t), \text{ for } t \leq t_1 \tag{11.10}$$

where $x(t)$ means the value of x at time t. Obviously, if we satisfy condition (11.10), then the pool loss (11.9) is non-decreasing, which implies no arbitrage. Generally, the consistency property is easy to satisfy, but the no arbitrage property is not, as shown in the previous section.

In the rest of the chapter we extend the factor copula model to a discrete-time dynamic model. For each period $(t_{i-1}, t_i]$ and each name k, we associate a latent random variable

$$Y_{k,i} = \beta_{k,i} X_i + \sqrt{1 - \beta_{k,i}^2} \epsilon_{k,i} \tag{11.11}$$

where X_i is a random variable associated with the common factors for period $(t_{i-1}, t_i]$ and $\epsilon_{k,i}$ are mutually independent random variables associated with idiosyncratic factors for name k and period $(t_{i-1}, t_i]$. To guarantee the no arbitrage property, Andersen (2006) employed a discrete version of the first hitting time model to construct the conditional default probabilities. More specifically, he connected the default time τ_k and the latent random variables by

$$\mathbb{P}(\tau_k < t) = \mathbb{P}(Y_{k,1} \leq b_k(t_1)), \qquad\qquad\qquad t \leq t_1$$
$$\mathbb{P}(t_{i-1} < \tau_k \leq t) = \mathbb{P}(Y_{k,1} > b_k(t_1), \ldots, Y_{k,i-1} > b_k(t_{i-1}), Y_{k,i} \leq b_k(t_i)), \quad t \in (t_{i-1}, t_i].$$

Then the conditional default probability for $t \leq t_1$ is the same as that in the one-factor copula model. For $t \in (t_{i-1}, t_i]$, the conditional default probability satisfies

$$\mathbb{P}(t_{i-1} < \tau_k \leq t \mid X^{(i)} = x^{(i)}) = \mathbb{P}(Y_{k,1} > b_k(t_1), \ldots, Y_{k,i-1} > b_k(t_{i-1}),$$
$$Y_{k,i} \leq b_k(t_i) \mid X^{(i)} = x^{(i)}).$$

Here, $X^{(i)}$ is associated with the common factors for the periods up to t_i, or equivalently, $X^{(i)} = \{X_1, X_2, \ldots, X_i\}$.

Similar to the one-factor copula model, we must compute the boundary $b_k(t_i)$ satisfying the consistency property (11.8). For $t \leq t_1$, the computation is the same as that for the one-factor copula model. However, for $t \in (t_{i-1}, t_i]$, it appears that we must integrate the common factors up to t_i. The complexity of this multi-dimensional integration depends on the assumptions associated with the X_i's. Andersen (2006) showed two special cases: (1) X_i are the same and (2) a two-period model, where X are two dimensional random variables. Besides the computation of the default boundary, the multi-dimensional integration also arises when computing the unconditional portfolio loss distribution from the conditional loss distributions.

Sidenius (2007) attacked the no arbitrage problem by introducing conditional forward survival probabilities

$$\mathbb{P}(\tau_k > t \mid \tau_k > t_{i-1}, X^{(i)} = x^{(i)}) = \frac{\mathbb{P}(\tau_k > t \mid X^{(i)} = x^{(i)})}{\mathbb{P}(\tau_k > t_{i-1} \mid X^{(i)} = x^{(i)})}, \quad t \in (t_{i-1}, t_i].$$

Using this, he expressed the conditional survival probability for $t \in (t_{i-1}, t_i]$ as

$$\mathbb{P}(\tau_k > t \mid X^{(i)} = x^{(i)}) = \mathbb{P}(\tau_k > t \mid \tau_k > t_{i-1}, X^{(i)} = x^{(i)})\mathbb{P}(\tau_k > t_{i-1} \mid X^{(i-1)} = x^{(i-1)}).$$

For $t \leq t_1$, the conditional survival probability is the same as that in the one-factor copula model.

The model allows a conditional forward survival probability for each time period $(t_{i-1}, t_i]$ to be associated with each correlation factor, i.e. $\mathbb{P}(\tau_k > t \mid \tau_k > t_{i-1}, X^{(i)} = x^{(i)}) = \mathbb{P}(\tau_k > t \mid \tau_k > t_{i-1}, X_i = x_i)$. For example, if the X_i's associated with the latent random variables $Y_{k,i}$ in (11.11) are independent, then the conditional forward survival probability can be computed by

$$\mathbb{P}(\tau_k > t_i \mid \tau_k > t_{i-1}, X^{(i)} = x^{(i)}) = \frac{\mathbb{P}\left(\beta_{k,i}X_i + \sqrt{1 - \beta_{k,i}^2}\epsilon_{k,i} > b_k(t_i) \mid X_i = x_i\right)}{\mathbb{P}\left(\beta_{k,i}X_i + \sqrt{1 - \beta_{k,i}^2}\epsilon_{k,i} > b_k(t_{i-1}) \mid X_i = x_i\right)}.$$

Using the consistency property (11.8), we can calibrate the $b_k(t_i)$ recursively. However, it is impossible to preserve any tractability for general cases. Similarly, the multi-dimensional integration problem cannot be avoided, except in some special cases, such as where all X_i are the same.

To overcome the high-dimensional integration problem, we use a similar approach based on the same latent random variables (11.11), but we connect $Y_{k,i}$ and τ_k by the forward default probability

$$\mathbb{P}(Y_{k,i} \leq b_k(t_i)) = \mathbb{P}(\tau_k \in (t_{i-1}, t_i] \mid \tau_k > t_{i-1}) = \frac{\mathbb{P}(\tau_k \leq t_i) - \mathbb{P}(\tau_k \leq t_{i-1})}{1 - \mathbb{P}(\tau_k \leq t_{i-1})}.$$

If X_i and $\epsilon_{k,i}$ follow standard normal distributions, then each $Y_{k,i}$ also follows a standard normal distribution. Therefore, we can compute the conditional default boundary $b_k(t_i)$ by

$$b_k(t_i) = \Phi^{-1}\left(\mathbb{P}(\tau_k \in (t_{i-1}, t_i] \mid \tau_k > t_{i-1})\right).$$

We can also compute each conditional forward default probability by

$$\mathbb{P}\left(\tau_k \in (t_{i-1}, t_i] \mid \tau_k > t_{i-1}, X_i = x_i\right) = \Phi\left(\frac{b_k(t_i) - \beta_{k,i} x_i}{\sqrt{1 - \beta_{k,i}^2}}\right).$$

The idea of using forward default probabilities has been used for CDO analysis by Morokoff (2003). However, in Morokoff's model the correlation coefficients are constant and no analytical methods are available.

To compute the conditional pool loss distribution, we need to construct $\mathbb{P}(\tau_k \leq t_i \mid X_1 = x_1, \ldots, X_i = x_i)$ from $\mathbb{P}\left(\tau_k \in (t_{i-1}, t_i] \mid \tau_k > t_{i-1}, X_i = x_i\right)$. Based on the definitions of these terms, we have

$$\mathbb{P}(\tau_k \leq t_i \mid X_1 = x_1, \ldots, X_i = x_i)$$
$$= \mathbb{P}(\tau_k \leq t_{i-1} \mid X_1 = x_1, \ldots, X_{i-1} = x_{i-1}) + \mathbb{P}(\tau_k \in (t_{i-1}, t_i] \mid X_1 = x_1, \ldots, X_i = x_i)$$
$$= \mathbb{P}(\tau_k \leq t_{i-1} \mid X_1 = x_1, \ldots, X_{i-1} = x_{i-1})$$
$$+ \mathbb{P}(\tau_k > t_{i-1} \mid X_1 = x_1, \ldots, X_{i-1} = x_{i-1}) \cdot \mathbb{P}\left(\tau_k \in (t_{i-1}, t_i] \mid \tau_k > t_{i-1}, X_i = x_i\right).$$

For the rest of the chapter we denote $P(\tau_k \leq t_{i-1} \mid X_1 = x_1, \ldots, X_{i-1} = x_{i-1})$ by $q_{k,i-1}$ and $\mathbb{P}\left(\tau_k \in (t_{i-1}, t_i] \mid \tau_k > t_{i-1}, X_i = x_i\right)$ by $p_{k,i}$ for simplicity. If $q_{k,i}$ and $p_{k,i}$ are the same for all $k = 1, \ldots, K$, we denote them by q_i and p_i, respectively.

Using the conditional default probabilities $q_{k,i}$, we can compute efficiently the conditional distribution of the pool loss for a completely homogeneous pool, where $\beta_{k,i}$, $\pi_k(t)$ and N_k are the same for $k = 1, \ldots, K$. In this special, but important, case, the distribution of L_i can be computed by the distribution of number of defaults l_i, as $L_i = N_1 \sum_{k=1}^{K} \mathbf{1}_{\{\tau_k \leq t_i\}} = N_1 l_i$. Therefore, the conditional pool loss distribution of a completely homogeneous pool satisfies

$$\mathbb{P}\left(L_i = rN_1 \mid X_1 = x_1, \ldots, X_i = x_i\right) = \mathbb{P}\left(l_i = r \mid X_1 = x_1, \ldots, X_i = x_i\right)$$
$$= \binom{K}{r}\left(q_{i-1} + (1 - q_{i-1})p_i\right)^r\left((1 - q_{i-1})(1 - p_i)\right)^{K-r}$$
$$= \binom{K}{r}\left(\sum_{m=0}^{r}\binom{r}{m}q_{i-1}^m(1 - q_{i-1})^{r-m}p_i^{r-m}\right)(1 - q_{i-1})^{K-r}(1 - p_i)^{K-r}$$
$$= \sum_{m=0}^{r}\binom{K}{m}q_{i-1}^m(1 - q_{i-1})^{K-m} \cdot \binom{K-m}{r-m}p_i^{r-m}(1 - p_i)^{K-m-(r-m)}$$
$$= \sum_{m=0}^{r}\mathbb{P}\left(l_{i-1} = m \mid X_1 = x_1, \ldots, X_{i-1} = x_{i-1}\right)\mathbb{P}\left(\hat{l}_{(i-1,i]}^{K-m} = r - m \mid X_i = x_i\right) \quad (11.12)$$

where $\hat{l}_{(i-1,i]}^{K-m}$ is the number of defaults during $(t_{i-1}, t_i]$ with the pool size $K - m$, and its distribution is computed using the conditional forward default probability p_i.

To compute the tranche loss, we need to compute the unconditional pool loss distribution from the conditional ones, i.e. we need to integrate over the common factors X_i. Generally, this requires a multi-dimensional integration, for which Monte Carlo simulation is usually used. However, we can avoid the multi-dimensional integration in this special case by exploiting the independence of the X_i's:

$$\mathbb{P}\left(l_i = r\right) = \int_{-\infty}^{\infty} \cdots \int_{-\infty}^{\infty} \sum_{m=0}^{r} \mathbb{P}\left(l_{i-1} = m \mid X_1 = x_1, \ldots, X_{i-1} = x_{i-1}\right)$$

$$\cdot \mathbb{P}\left(\hat{l}_{(i-1,i]}^{K-m} = r - m \mid X_i = x_i\right) d\Phi(x_1) \ldots d\Phi(x_i)$$

$$= \sum_{m=0}^{r} \int_{-\infty}^{\infty} \cdots \int_{-\infty}^{\infty} \mathbb{P}\left(l_{i-1} = m \mid X_1 = x_1, \ldots, X_{i-1} = x_{i-1}\right) d\Phi(x_1) \ldots d\Phi(x_{i-1})$$

$$\cdot \int_{-\infty}^{\infty} \mathbb{P}\left(\hat{l}_{(i-1,i]}^{K-m} = r - m \mid X_i = x_i\right) d\Phi(x_i)$$

$$= \sum_{m=0}^{r} \mathbb{P}\left(l_{i-1} = m\right) \mathbb{P}\left(\hat{l}_{(i-1,i]}^{K-m} = r - m\right). \tag{11.13}$$

Therefore, the unconditional pool loss distribution possesses the Markovian property and can be computed recursively. Iscoe (2003) derived a similar Markovian property for the two name case of Morokoff's model in Morokoff (2003), where the correlation coefficients are constant. Our derivation is more general, and our model fixes the correlation decay of Morokoff's model as described in Iscoe (2003).

Remark   We need to assume that the X_i's are independent to derive the key formula (11.13), which enables us to avoid the costly multi-dimensional integration in computing the unconditional pool loss distribution from the conditional one. However, it is worth noting that this is the only place in this chapter where we need to assume that X_i and X_j are independent for all $i \neq j$. Therefore we could use more general processes for the X_i's if we do not need to compute the unconditional pool loss distribution from the conditional one or if we could replace (11.13) by another efficient formula to compute the unconditional pool loss distribution from the conditional one.

The difference between our approach and Andersen's approach in Andersen (2006) can be understood intuitively as follows. In Andersen's approach, the latent random variables Y_k, which reflect the healthiness of name k, are reset back to zero at the beginning of each period. Therefore the process forgets its previous position. The latent process of our model is also reset to zero at the beginning of each period. However, in our model it describes the healthiness of the forward default probability. The process for the default probability actually remembers its position at the end of the previous period: how the process evolves for the new period depends on the latent process of the forward default probability. In addition, as noted above, it appears that Andersen's approach requires a costly multi-dimensional integration to compute the unconditional pool loss distribution from the conditional one, except in some simple special cases. For a completely homogeneous pool, assuming that the X_i and X_j are independent for all $i \neq j$, our approach uses the much less costly recurrence (11.13) to compute the unconditional pool loss distribution from the conditional one.

For a more general pool[2] it still holds that the event that r defaults occur before t_i is equivalent to the event that m defaults occur before t_{i-1} and $r - m$ defaults occur during $(t_{i-1}, t_i]$, for $m = 0, \ldots r$. That is,

$$\mathbb{P}(l_i = r) = \sum_{m=0}^{r} \mathbb{P}(l_{i-1} = m, l_{(i-1,i]} = r - m)$$

$$= \sum_{m=0}^{r} P(l_{i-1} = m) \cdot \mathbb{P}(l_{(i-1,i]} = r - m \mid l_{i-1} = m).$$

Moreover, this relationship extends to the conditional probabilities:

$$\mathbb{P}(l_i = r \mid X_1 = x_1, \ldots, X_i = x_i) = \sum_{m=0}^{r} \mathbb{P}(l_{i-1} = m \mid X_1 = x_1, \ldots, X_{i-1} = x_{i-1})$$

$$\cdot \mathbb{P}(l_{(i-1,i]} = r - m \mid l_{i-1} = m, X_1 = x_1, \ldots, X_i = x_i).$$

Under the assumptions of our model, we can simplify the expression above using

$$\mathbb{P}(l_{(i-1,i]} = r - m \mid l_{i-1} = m, X_1 = x_1, \ldots, X_i = x_i)$$
$$= \mathbb{P}(l_{(i-1,i]} = r - m \mid l_{i-1} = m, X_i = x_i).$$

Therefore

$$\mathbb{P}(l_i = r \mid X_1 = x_1, \ldots, X_i = x_i) = \sum_{m=0}^{r} \mathbb{P}(l_{i-1} = m \mid X_1 = x_1, \ldots, X_{i-1} = x_{i-1})$$

$$\cdot \mathbb{P}(l_{(i-1,i]} = r - m \mid l_{i-1} = m, X_i = x_i).$$

To obtain the unconditional pool loss distribution, we need to integrate over the common factors, as we did in (11.13). Therefore, in our model, the Markov property holds for a general pool:

$$\mathbb{P}\left(l_i = r\right) = \sum_{m=0}^{r} \mathbb{P}\left(l_{i-1} = m\right) \cdot \mathbb{P}\left(l_{(i-1,i]}^{K-m} = r - m \mid l_{i-1} = m\right).$$

However, as the default probability of each name may be different in a general pool, we end up with another combinatorial problem: we need to consider all possible combinations of $l_{i-1} = m$.

Obviously, the completely homogeneous pool is a special case. However, it is of considerable practical importance, since such pools often arise in practice. Moreover, the pool loss of a general pool is generally approximated by the pool loss of a completely homogeneous one for computational efficiency in calibration and the valuation of bespoke contracts.

Remark   For simplicity, we used the Gaussian factor copula model to illustrate our new discrete dynamical multi-period factor copula model. However, it is important to note that our approach can be applied to construct a multi-period factor copula model from any one-factor copula model based on the conditional independence framework.

11.5 CALIBRATION

Our goal is to calibrate our model against the market tranche quotes on the same underlying pool. To illustrate our approach, we use the tranche quotes of the credit indexes, CDX and ITRAXX. As our model allows the correlation factor loadings to be time-dependent, we can introduce dynamics into the model by letting the correlation factor loadings follow particular dynamic processes. This added flexibility gives our dynamic model enough degrees of freedom to calibrate against market quotes.

We obtain the spread quotes for the indexes and tranches on CDX and ITRAXX from the Thomson Datastream. We approximate the default probabilities of a single name using the index spreads, which are the average spreads of the 125 names in CDX or ITRAXX. Due to the data availability and popularity, we calibrate our model against the four mezzanine tranches with maturities 5 years, 7 years and 10 years. We therefore have to fit 12 market tranche quotes on the same underlying pool.

To fit these 12 tranche quotes, we must incorporate sufficient degrees of freedom into our model. As the correlation factor loadings are time-dependent in our model, they can be any dynamic process within the range [0, 1]. Therefore, we can obtain sufficient degrees of freedom by constructing a suitable dynamic process for the correlation factor loadings. To illustrate our approach, we employ a binomial tree structure for the correlation factor loadings in our numerical examples. We assume that the correlation factor loading process is a piecewise constant function over time and each branch of the tree describes one possible path of the factor loading process. To compute the tranche prices, we only need to take the expectation of the tranche prices on each branch. Figure 11.1 illustrates an equally-spaced three-period[3] tree, where ρ_j is the value of the correlation factor loading and p_j is the probability of the process taking the upper branch. With this tree structure, the correlation factor loading process has four possible paths for a 10-year maturity contract. For example, for an annual payment tranche contract, one possible path for the $\beta_{k,i}$'s is $(\rho_0, \rho_0, \rho_0, \rho_1, \rho_1, \rho_1, \rho_3, \rho_3, \rho_3, \rho_3)$ with probability $p_0 p_1$. We can increase or decrease the degrees of freedom of the tree by adjusting the number of periods or the tree structure, e.g. constraining the general tree to be a binomial tree. Recently, Kaznady (2011) proposed an improved alternative multi-path parameterization of the correlation coefficients dynamics.

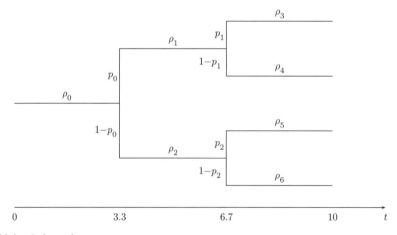

Figure 11.1   A dynamic tree structure.

Table 11.1   Risk-neutral cumulative default probabilities.

Time	1Y	2Y	3Y	4Y	5Y
Probability	0.0041	0.0052	0.0069	0.0217	0.0288

11.6 NUMERICAL EXAMPLES

We begin by comparing the results generated by the Monte Carlo method to those obtained by the recursion (11.13) on an example with arbitrarily chosen parameters. The numerical experiments are based on 5-year CDOs with 100 underlying names and annual premium payments. The tranche structure is the same as those of CDX, i.e. six tranches with attachment and detachment points, 0–3%, 3–7%, 7–10%, 10–15%, 15–30% and 30–100%. We assume a constant interest rate of 4% and a constant recovery rate of 40%. For simplicity, we assume that all $\beta_{k,i} = 0.6$. The risk-neutral cumulative default probabilities are listed in Table 11.1.

Each Monte Carlo simulation consists of 100,000 trials, and 100 runs (with different seeds) for each experiment are made. Based on the results of these 100 experiments, we calculate the mean and the 95% non-parametric confidence interval. Table 11.2 presents the risk premia for the CDOs. For our example, the running time of one Monte Carlo experiment with 100,000 trials is about 14 times that used by our recursive method. These results demonstrate that the recursive relationship (11.13) is accurate and efficient.

To calibrate against the market quotes, we employ the tree structure for the correlation factor loadings discussed in the previous section. In particular, we use an equally-spaced four-period tree. However, we add constraints by using the same growth rate μ_j and probability p_j for period j, as shown in the tree in Figure 11.2. Therefore, we have 7 parameters in total to calibrate against 12 tranche quotes. We compute the parameters by solving an associated optimization problem. For the objective function of the optimization problem, we could use either the absolute error in the spreads

$$f_{abs} = \sum (m_i - s_i)^2, \text{ for } i = 1, \ldots, 12$$

or the relative error in the spreads

$$f_{rel} = \sum (m_i - s_i)^2 / m_i^2, \text{ for } i = 1, \ldots, 12$$

where m_i is the market spread quote for tranche i and s_i is the model spread for tranche i.

Table 11.2   Tranche premia (bps).

Tranche	Monte Carlo	95% CI	Recursion
0–3%	953.40	[946.71, 960.62]	951.60
3–7%	182.09	[179.51, 184.81]	181.59
7–10%	58.95	[57.26, 60.33]	58.77
10–15%	22.21	[21.01, 23.39]	22.09
15–30%	3.47	[3.03, 3.78]	3.44
30–100%	0.07	[0.03, 0.09]	0.07

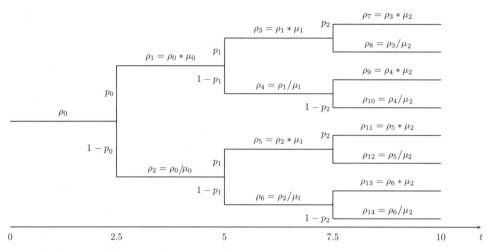

Figure 11.2   A particular dynamic tree example.

Table 11.3 lists the calibration result for the tranche quotes of CDX series 8 on April 4, 2007. The upper half of the table uses the absolute spread error as the objective function, while the lower half of the table uses the relative spread error as the objective function. In both cases, the rows "Parameter" display the values of the parameters in our model, in the order ρ_0, μ_0, p_0, μ_1, p_1, μ_2, p_2.

Table 11.4 lists the calibration results for the same data using the Gaussian factor copula model and the normal inverse Gaussian factor copula model in Kalemanova et al. (2007). In the table, "NIG(1)" means the normal inverse Gaussian factor copula model with one extra parameter for fat-tailness, and "NIG(2)" means the normal inverse Gaussian factor copula

Table 11.3   Calibration result of CDX 8 on April 4, 2007.

Maturity	5 yr			7 yr			10 yr		
Tranche	Market	Model	Abs Err	Market	Model	Abs Err	Market	Model	Abs Err
3–7	111.81	110.13	1.68	251.44	254.65	3.21	528.31	528.37	0.06
7–10	22.31	20.90	1.41	54.69	59.51	4.82	134.00	134.21	0.21
10–15	10.42	7.99	2.43	26.47	28.45	1.98	63.30	61.38	1.92
15–30	4.34	1.97	2.37	9.50	12.08	2.58	20.46	23.36	2.90
Parameter	0.73	0.43	0.98	0.32	0.57	0.11	0.63	$f_{abs} = 8.52$	
Tranche	Market	Model	Rel Err	Market	Model	Rel Err	Market	Model	Rel Err
3–7	111.81	109.88	1.73%	251.44	300.00	19.31%	528.31	560.57	6.11%
7–10	22.31	21.37	4.23%	54.69	54.00	1.26%	134.00	141.36	5.49%
10–15	10.42	10.79	3.57%	26.47	25.01	5.52%	63.30	60.20	4.90%
15–30	4.34	4.36	0.37%	9.50	9.86	3.79%	20.46	22.30	8.99%
Parameter	0.55	0.65	0.80	0.42	0.71	0.15	0.57	$f_{rel} = 25.01\%$	

Table 11.4 Calibration result of CDX 8 on April 4, 2007 by different models.

Maturity	5 yr				7 yr				10 yr			
Tranche	Market	Gaussian	NIG(1)	NIG(2)	Market	Gaussian	NIG(1)	NIG(2)	Market	Gaussian	NIG(1)	NIG(2)
3–7	111.81	149.77	84.48	92.12	251.44	379.65	240.59	240.36	528.31	653.48	537.32	536.43
7–10	22.31	14.61	32.42	33.21	54.69	80.52	62.03	64.61	134.00	248.90	154.68	148.07
10–15	10.42	1.51	21.42	19.71	26.47	14.80	36.18	35.30	63.30	77.84	66.95	65.44
15–30	4.34	0.02	12.28	9.36	9.50	0.49	19.02	16.18	20.46	5.49	29.00	26.38
Abs err		39.98	32.14	24.86		131.62	18.88	18.54		171.19	24.39	17.42
Parameter		Gaussian: 0.30				NIG(1): 0.46, 0.37				NIG(2): 0.44, 0.99, –0.61		
Tranche	Market	Gaussian	NIG(1)	NIG(2)	Market	Gaussian	NIG(1)	NIG(2)	Market	Gaussian	NIG(1)	NIG(2)
3–7	111.81	164.22	89.70	86.76	251.44	383.20	289.34	265.15	528.31	635.06	642.09	616.51
7–10	22.31	21.07	23.40	24.17	54.69	94.04	53.01	53.28	134.00	255.83	173.08	151.31
10–15	10.42	2.88	12.52	12.50	26.47	20.92	24.02	25.14	63.30	89.10	54.25	53.37
15–30	4.34	0.07	4.96	4.46	9.50	0.98	8.77	9.23	20.46	8.06	15.40	16.95
Rel err		130.96%	31.95%	31.26%		128.06%	19.53%	8.35%		118.37%	46.17%	31.39%
Parameter		Gaussian: 0.33				NIG(1): 0.34, 0.44				NIG(2): 0.35, 0.99, –0.63		

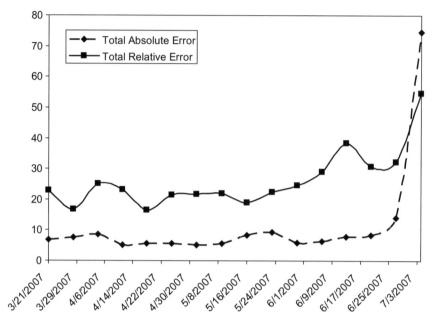

Figure 11.3 Weekly calibration result of CDX 8.

model with two extra parameters for skewness and fat-tailness. Our results in Table 11.3 are far superior to the results of the three models in Table 11.4.

In addition to the market data on a single day, we calibrate our model against market spreads of CDX series 8 on each Wednesday from March 23, 2007 to July 4, 2007. Figure 11.3 plots the absolute errors and relative errors of the 12 tranches using the four-period tree structure with 7 parameters. The unit of the absolute error is basis points and the unit of the relative error is percentage. For market data before the credit crunch (July 2007), our model is able to match the data quite well with 7 parameters. For market data after the credit crunch, the calibration error increases dramatically. We believe this is because the market quotes exhibit arbitrage due to the large demand and supply gap. As the financial crisis developed, traders tried to sell the credit derivatives they were holding, but no one wanted to buy them. For more numerical results about calibration of our model, refer to Kaznady (2011).

11.7 CONCLUSIONS

In this chapter we introduce a dynamic multi-period factor copula model which can be calibrated fairly easily and matches the market quotes quite well. Using the independence of the common factors and the forward default probability, we show that the loss of a completely homogeneous pool possesses the Markov property. We can therefore avoid the multi-dimensional integration that must be computed in the multi-period factor copula models. The calibration results demonstrate the flexibility of our model in fitting the market quotes. Most importantly, the method is a generic one: it can be applied to construct a multi-period factor copula model from any one-period factor copula model based on the conditional independence framework.

Our numerical results demonstrate that our multi-period factor copula model is able to calibrate consistently against market data. However, we have developed an efficient method for completely homogenous pools only using an independent latent process across time. Therefore, key open questions are how to extend the model to a general pool and a general latent process.

NOTES

1. As we assume constant recovery rates, the pool losses L_i are discrete random variables here. This approach can be extended to the continuous case with stochastic recovery rates.
2. There are two other types of underlying pools: (1) homogeneous pools, where all N_k are the same, for all $k = 1, \ldots, K$, and either $\beta_{k,i}$ or $\pi_k(t)$ are different for some k; (2) inhomogeneous pools, where N_k, $\beta_{k,i}$ and $\pi_k(t)$ are different for some k.
3. As illustrated in this example, the number of periods for the tree may be different from the number of periods of our model, which equals the number of premium payments.

REFERENCES

Andersen, L., 2006. Portfolio losses in factor models: Term structures and intertemporal loss dependence. Journal of Credit Risk 2(4), 3–31.

Andersen, L., Sidenius, J., 2004. Extensions to the Gaussian copula: Random recovery and random factor loadings. Journal of Credit Risk 1(1), 29–70.

Andersen, L., Sidenius, J., Basu, S., 2003. All your hedges in one basket. Risk 16(11), 67–72.

Baxter, M., 2007. Gamma process dynamic modelling of credit. Risk 20(10), 98–101.

Bennani, N., 2005. The forward loss model: A dynamic term structure approach for the pricing of portfolio credit derivatives, working paper, available at http://www.defaultrisk.com.

Fingers, C., 2000. A comparison of stochastic default rate models. RiskMetrics Journal 1(2), 49–73.

Giesecke, K., Goldberg, L., Ding, X., 2011. A top down approach to multi-name credit. Operations Research 59(2), 283–300.

Hull, J., White, A., 2004. Valuation of a CDO and an nth to default CDS without Monte Carlo simulation. Journal of Derivatives 12(2), 8–23.

Hull, J., White, A., 2006. Valuing credit derivatives using an implied copula approach. Journal of Derivatives 14(2), 8–28.

Hull, J., White, A., 2008. Dynamic models of portfolio credit risk: A simplified approach. Journal of Derivatives 15(4), 9–28.

Iscoe, I., 2003. Losing default correlation, step by step. Tech. rep., Algorithmics Inc.

Kalemanova, A., Schmid, B., Werner, R., 2007. The normal inverse Gaussian distribution for synthetic CDO pricing. Journal of Derivatives 14(3), 80–93.

Kaznady, M., 2011. Calibration of multi-period single-factor Gaussian copula models for CDO pricing. Master's thesis, University of Toronto, available at http://www.cs.toronto.edu/NA/reports.html.

Laurent, J.-P., Gregory, J., 2005. Basket default swaps, CDOs and factor copulas. Journal of Risk 7(4), 103–122.

Li, D., 2000. On default correlation: A copula approach. Journal of Fixed Income 9(4), 43–54.

McGinty, L., Beinstein, E., Ahluwalia, R., Watts, M., 2004. Credit correlation: A guide. Tech. rep., JP Morgan.

Morokoff, W., 2003. Simulation methods for risk analysis of collateralized debt obligations. Tech. rep., Moody's KMV.

Schönbucher, P., 2005. Portfolio losses and the term structure of loss transition rates: a new methodology for the pricing of portfolio credit derivatives, working paper, available at http://www.defaultrisk.com.

Sidenius, J., 2007. On the term structure of loss distributions — a forward model approach. International Journal of Theoretical and Applied Finance 10(4), 749–761.

Sidenius, J., Piterbarg, V., Andersen, L., 2008. A new framework for dynamic credit portfolio loss modeling. International Journal of Theoretical and Applied Finance 11(2), 163–197.

Torresetti, R., Brigo, D., Pallavicini, A., 2006. Implied correlation in CDO tranches: A paradigm to be handled with care, working paper, available at www.defaultrisk.com.

Vasicek, O., 1987. Probability of loss distribution. Tech. rep., KMV Corporation.

12

Dynamic Modeling of Credit Derivatives

Alfred Hamerle, Kilian Plank and Christian Scherr
University of Regensburg

12.1 INTRODUCTION

The integrative pricing of options and corresponding credit derivatives has recently been addressed extensively (see Carverhill and Luo (2011), Collin-Dufresne et al. (2012), Hamerle et al. (2012), Li and Zhao (2011)) in discussing the influential publication of Coval et al. (2009). In the present chapter, we do not want to restrict ourselves to the specific question of whether CDX tranches offered a risk premium comparable to S&P 500 index options. Rather, we provide a simple model with a small number of parameters and a high degree of analytical tractability for a general option-based pricing of credits derivatives. The comprehensive and (semi-)analytical[1] description of credit-related assets (firm values), as well as corresponding portfolios, are therefore in the center of focus.

In a certain sense, this corresponds to the notion of the CreditGrades model, originally presented by Finger et al. (2002) and Stamicar and Finger (2005). Within the CreditGrades model, equity and asset processes are linked by a particular formula that expresses asset volatility in terms of equity volatility, as well as equity and debt level. To overcome the main disadvantages of this approach, Sepp (2006) introduced two robust model extensions, taking account of both stochastic volatility and jump behavior. Ozeki et al. (2010) adapted the latter concept and transfer it into the more general setting of Lévy processes.

To construct a model offering maximum possible analyticity, and despite capturing the main empirical results by drawing only on a few parameters, we refer to a CAPM-like framework. Within this setting, we integrate equity and asset values, both following a double exponential process, by applying a beta factor that indicates the interaction of market and idiosyncratic risk. A main reasoning is that we wish to evaluate the model introduced by Kou (2002), which we use to describe the equity as well as the asset movements over the course of this chapter.

12.1.1 General Model Choice

Prior to describing the economic implications of our methodology, we justify our general modeling approach. For the sake of simplicity, we intend to modify the classical diffusion model just at a minimum. We can therefore introduce stochastic volatility (see Ball and Roma (1994), Heston (1997), Hull and White (1987), Scott (1997), Stein and Stein (1991)) or add jumps to the continuous component (see Chan (1999), Kou (2002), Merton (1976), Sepp and Skachkov (2003)).

Stochastic volatility models can reproduce many empirical phenomena, but fail to explain sudden changes in equity or asset values (see Cont and Tankov (2004b)). Especially the prices of short-term derivatives cannot be replicated by these processes. The fact that first passage time distributions are only available in the case of zero correlation between asset value and volatility process (see Sepp (2006)) reveals a further disadvantage, notably because this contradicts empirical observations. Finally, even within a simple CAPM-like framework, stochastic volatility models do not enable an analytical integration of equity and asset-value processes and thus seem unsuited for our purposes.

By contrast, amplifying the Brownian motion by an independent jump process enables us to capture sudden movements of the contemplated quantities, and as an immediate consequence, also the corresponding empirical phenomena. In the case of so-called spectrally negative Lévy processes,[2] several jump characteristics provide analytically known first passage time distributions (see Sato (1999) for details). Alternatively, one can adopt explicit solutions, for instance, existing with regard to the Kou model. Knowledge of the associated distribution facilitates an analytical calibration of first passage time models. Moreover, the fact that there are jump densities perserving this analyticity, despite setting up a CAPM-framework that comprises market and idiosyncratic movements, suggests that this type of extension to the standard model is well suited for our purposes.

12.1.2   Modeling Option Prices

Evaluating our option pricing model, we follow Kou (2002), who proposed four crucial criteria in discussing the so-called Kou or (asymmetric) double exponential jump-diffusion model.

Naturally, an option pricing model must first of all be able to reproduce the most important empirical phenomena. A systematic comparison of jump-diffusion models with the Black–Scholes model, reveals discontinuous modeling as superior in describing empirical observations and their modeling flexibility (see Cont and Tankov (2004b)). This is based on their affinity to empirically observed behavior patterns. Levels of stocks and stock indices not only diffuse smoothly, they also are exposed to instantaneous changes. The most classic example of this is the fact that Brownian motion cannot capture the empirically proved variability of equity returns (see Ball and Torous (1985), Cont and Tankov (2004a), Jorion (1988)), a phenomenon that is also referred to as heavy or fat tails of the return distribution. Within the Black–Scholes framework, this is directly related to the well known volatility smile or volatility skew. By definition, this artifical volatility serves exclusively as a fitting tool, without having any economic meaning. Otherwise, empirical phenomena such as the steep short-term skew extracted from index option markets soon after the 1987 crash, could not be reproduced. To maintain the concept of modeling equity by a geometric Brownian motion, the initially constant volatility parameter becomes a bivariate function of time and strike level.[3] This function, also denominated as local or implied volatility, is, according to Rebonato (1999), a wrong number which, plugged into the wrong formula, gives the right answer. By contrast, in terms of Cont and Tankov (2004b), models incorporating jumps lead "generically to highly variable returns with realistic tail behavior, without the need for introducing non-stationarity" and, as stated in Runggaldier (2002), additionally have superior empirical replication properties. Performing a comparison within the class of jump-diffusion models, Ramezani and Zeng (2007) suggested that the model introduced by Merton (1976) does not achieve the fitting quality of Kou's (asymmetric) double exponential model.

Secondly, a pricing model must not permit arbitrage. Otherwise, the fundamental theorem of asset pricing will no longer be applicable and thus, in general, martingale theory can no longer be adopted. Yet, martingale theory constitutes the fundamental pricing rule when applying risk-neutral measurements and, as a consequence, prices in general can no longer be determined by referring to risk-neutral probabilities. Contrary to fractal Brownian motions[4] for example, arbitrage is prohibited by the double exponential jump-diffusion model.

Thirdly, the model should offer a closed-form pricing formula, at least for European options. The great success of the Black–Scholes model depends crucially on the fact that prices can be evaluated using an analytical formula and therefore within a fraction of a second. The determination of prices using standard simulation tools not only proves to be very time-consuming, but also tends to exhibit significant bias, which only disappears very slowly (see Broadie and Kaya (2006)). Models not offering analytical pricing tools are thus avoided by practitioners. The Kou model belongs to the class of exponential affine models, which are treated extensively in Duffie, Pan and Singleton (2000). Basically, analytical pricing formulas can be found for the members of this class solving related differential equations and performing a Fourier transform. Separately, Kou (2002) developed a closed-form pricing formula in the manner of Black–Scholes, by generalizing the cumulative normal distribution function. In this regard, not only the pricing of European options can be performed analytically, but also that of path-dependent options, such as barrier, lookback and perpetual American options.

Fourthly, the building blocks of the model should yield an economic interpretation. The 1987 crash empirically revealed the danger of a sudden breakdown of equity values ("crashphobia"). Since then, empirical surveys confirm the jump fear of market participants and its effects on pricing options (see Bates (2000), Rubinstein (1994)). The asymmetric double exponential jump-diffusion model captures this fear and additionally depicts excessive reaction behavior. Whereas the diffusion component models information continuously reaching the markets, the jump part expresses the eventuality of the equity value suddenly changing. Merton (1976) stated several economic reasons for continuously modeled price movements, namely temporary imbalances between supply and demand, changes in capitalization rates, and changes in the economic outlook. "Abnormal" vibrations in prices are caused by information arriving only at arbitrary and discrete points of time. Once such important information has reached the market, both upwards and downwards movements can be initiated, but of course with different intensities. A compound process therefore reveals the best candidate for capturing these empirically documented observations; the Poisson part images the randomness, and the distribution part reproduces the way such information is handled by the markets. In this regard, markets often do not behave logically, tending to react in an exaggerated manner. The jump part of the Kou model applied in this paper incorporates all these economic aspects, because it is specified as a compound process with an asymmetric double exponential jump distribution. The latter has high peaks and heavy tails and thus generally captures both market over and underreaction with respect to "discontinuous" information.

12.1.3 Modeling Credit Risk

In the context of credit risk modeling, one basically refers to the reduced-form and the structural approach. Reduced-form models are characterized by their purely probabilistic nature and treat a default as an unpredictable Poisson event.[5] Within this framework, a variety of credit spread curves can be fitted, but the economic mechanism driving the corresponding default process is not specified. Departing from the firm value process thus entails the interrelation between the capital structure of a firm and its default risk not being readily evident. Furthermore, according to Duffie and Singelton (1999) there are certain conditions in which the model parameters might become unstable. Not only because a central objective of our paper entails the robust estimation of parameters, but also because of its explanatory power, we adopt the structural approach. This approach was introduced by Merton (1974) and explicitly indicates the behavior of the total value of a firm's assets and is therefore also known as the value-of-the-firm approach. With this methodology, economic fundamentals, namely the portions of equity and debt of a company, are applied to model credit events. Thus the structural approach provides sufficient insights into the economic coherences of default risk. One crucial drawback of the Merton model is its static nature, because only the asset value at maturity determines the default behavior of the modeled firm. On the one hand, this assumption entails a very easy mathematical treatment of credit risk, yet on the other hand, Shreve (2009) claimed, "It can not capture a delicate tradeoff that involves time to expiration, because the model does not evolve in time." A realistic description of a company's economic state must take into account that, in general, credit events occur during the credit period.

In order to provide an approach that is closer to reality, we therefore refer to the class of first passage time models defining the default event as the first touching or crossing of some predetermined barrier. This type of modeling was pioneered by Black and Cox (1976), and further research was conducted by Collin-Dufresne and Goldstein (2001) and Longstaff and Schwartz (1995).

Following Chen and Kou (2009) and Zhou (2001), several empirical facts can be reproduced, if the asset value is modeled by a jump-diffusion process.

Bond prices often exhibit unexpected downward jumps prior to or at the time of default (see Duffie and Lando (2001)). In this regard, Duffie and Lando (2001) selected incomplete accounting information as a central research theme. However, incomplete or insufficient information suddenly reaching the markets in a cumulative manner constitutes only one reason why jumps can be observed. Due to the fact that pricing contingent claims generally involves expectation values, this inevitably causes jumps. As soon as the uncertainty subsides, the expectation value becomes deterministic. Consider, for example, a company with a pending lawsuit. Until the judges announce their verdict, the associated financial impact is generally priced in terms of expectations. However, the moment the judgment becomes legally binding, the expected financial impact is substituted by its actual impact, provoking a corresponding jump. Comparable to this scenario, one can also specify unanticipated measures by the central bank as a special source of jump movements. Further factors inherently inducing a significant and instant increase or decrease of the firm's asset values include changing of political power relations and associated legislation, default of a major customer, sudden retirement of a member of the directorial board, unexpected decisions of the general shareholders' meeting, e.g. regarding the amount of dividend payments, and similar events.

Contrary to the so-called predictability of default within a diffusion-based model framework, empirical data do not reveal vanishing credit spreads even in the case of very short maturities (see Lando (2004)). Sepp (2006) provided an explanation of this phenomenon. If the asset value follows a pure diffusion and exhibits a sufficient distance to the predefined default barrier at the starting time, the probability of a credit event converges to zero as the maturity approaches zero. Knowledge of the difference between the contemporaneous asset value level and the level of default, also referred to as distance to default, enables a reliable statement to be made on whether or not the firm is likely to default. Since a diffusion simply needs time to reach the default barrier, an asset-value process that is far from this barrier cannot trigger a default event within a short period of time. This causes related spreads to vanish. Without using jumps, which have the inherent explanatory power to image the empirical fact of non-dissolving spreads, term structure effects cannot be reproduced appropriately.

The term structures of credit spreads reveal a broad variety of shapes – upward, downward and humped. The credit spreads of high-rated bonds normally slope upwards, whereas Fons (1994), He et al. (2000) and Sarig and Warga (1989) suggested downward and humped shapes for speculative corporate credits. Chen and Kou (2009) used the double exponential jump-diffusion model and demonstrate its goodness of fit in many cases. Even limiting to a one-sided model does not substantially change the features with regard to credit spreads.

Having now specified the basic economic framework, we briefly outline the remainder of the chapter. Section 12.2 provides an outline of the contemplated credit derivatives and the underlying mechanism. The adopted modeling techniques are described in Section 12.3. In Section 12.4, we present the empirical properties of the model. A conclusion is given in Section 12.5. Due to space limitations, we refrain from attaching an appendix and thus refer interested readers to the detailed explanations in Scherr (2012).

12.2 PORTFOLIO CREDIT DERIVATIVES

Portfolio credit derivatives or securitizations like CDOs purchase a pool of claims, for instance bonds, loans, credit default swaps, etc., financed by issuing a set of securities called "tranches." By structuring the cash flows of the pool, it is possible to create securities of different seniorities, which may be sold to different classes of investors. Similar to corporate liabilities, this results in senior, mezzanine and equity claims.

Securitizations can be classified into cash and synthetic transactions, among others. Cash transactions acquire the claims in the pool directly. Cash flows arising from the pool comprise interest and principal, and are usually allocated to the tranches in order of seniority, i.e. from senior to equity. Losses are assigned in reverse order.

By contrast, synthetic transactions collect a pool of credit default swaps (CDS) referenced on other claims, such as corporate bonds. Hence, the issued tranches are also usually synthetic, which means that no principal is exchanged. Instead, the tranche investor guarantees pool losses within a certain range and obtains interest payments for this form of insurance. Subsequently, we consider a simple synthetic transaction with strict loss prioritization.

Let L_t denote the cumulative loss in the pool at time t, i.e. the relative number of swaps with a triggered default event, weighted with the contractual default payment. The loss of tranche k with attachment point a_k, $0 \leq a_k < a_{k+1} < 1$ and $k = 1, \ldots, K$, is then given by

$$L_{k,t}^{tr} := \frac{\min(a_{k+1}, L_t) - \min(a_k, L_t)}{a_{k+1} - a_k}. \tag{12.1}$$

Thus, for $L_t \leq a_k$, tranche k does not incur losses and has a 100% loss for $L_t \geq a_{k+1}$. As an example of portfolio credit derivatives, in the remainder of this chapter, we focus on the iTraxx credit default swap index and the associated tranches. The European iTraxx and its North American counterpart CDX.NA.IG are synthetic transactions, which are traded on the market. The iTraxx Europe is an index of credit default swaps, referencing the top 125 European corporates with the highest CDS trading volume. A new series is issued every six months, which allows for changes in the trading volume or defaults. The buyer of the index receives the contractual credit spread on his invested notional and has to pay compensation in the case of default. Subsequent spreads are then paid on a notional reduced by $\frac{1}{125}$.

The index is also the reference for synthetic tranches with a standard maturity of five years. These tranches cover the loss ranges $0-3\%, 3-6\%, 6-9\%, 9-12\%, 12-22\%$, and $22-100\%$, with strict loss prioritization. The tranche spread is always paid on the remaining notional after deduction of losses.

Furthermore, let $\Delta_j := t_j - t_{j-1}$ denote the time between two payment dates t_j and t_{j-1} $(j = 1, \cdots, m)$ and τ_i the default time of the reference name underlying CDS i. In a simplified version, the spread of this swap is then given by

$$s_i := \frac{LGD \cdot \sum_{j=1}^{m} e^{-rt_j} \cdot \mathbb{P}\left(t_{j-1} < \tau_i \leq t_j\right)}{\sum_{j=1}^{m} \Delta_j \cdot e^{-rt_j} \cdot \mathbb{P}\left(\tau_i > t_j\right)}, \tag{12.2}$$

where LGD names the loss given default and r the risk-free rate. In this context, all expectation values are calculated with respect to a risk-neutral measure $\mathbb{Q}$. The spread of a CDS index with n equally weighted names can be evaluated as follows:

$$s^{\text{index}} := \frac{LGD \cdot \sum_{i=1}^{n} \sum_{j=1}^{m} e^{-rt_j} \cdot \mathbb{P}\left(t_{j-1} < \tau_i \leq t_j\right)}{\sum_{i=1}^{n} \sum_{j=1}^{m} \Delta_j \cdot e^{-rt_j} \cdot \mathbb{P}\left(\tau_i > t_j\right)}. \tag{12.3}$$

Finally, the spread of tranche k is specified by

$$s_k^{tr} := \frac{\sum_{j=1}^{m} e^{-rt_j} \cdot \left[\mathbb{E}\left(L_{k,t_j}^{tr}\right) - \mathbb{E}\left(L_{k,t_{j-1}}^{tr}\right)\right]}{\sum_{j=1}^{m} \Delta_j \cdot e^{-rt_j} \cdot \left[1 - \mathbb{E}\left(L_{k,t_j}^{tr}\right)\right]}. \tag{12.4}$$

12.3 MODELING ASSET DYNAMICS

12.3.1 The Market Model

The model presented in this section is applied to capture the dynamics of stock indices that serve as a proxy for the dynamics of the represented markets. These dynamics are again part of our CAPM-like firm value model for determining the risk characterics of a homogenous CDS pool.

To depict the dynamics of a stock index, we adopt the model introduced by Kou (2002). According to this model, the value $S(t)$ of the index follows the risk-neutral dynamic

$$\frac{dS(t)}{S(t-)} = (\tilde{r} - \lambda \zeta) \, dt + \sigma \, dB(t) + d\left[\sum_{i=1}^{N(t)} (V_i - 1)\right], \tag{12.5}$$

where $B(t)$ specifies a standard Brownian motion, $N(t)$ denotes a Poisson process with jump rate λ and $(V_i)_{i \in \{1,\dots,N(t)\}}$ is a sequence of independent, identically distributed (i.i.d.) non-negative random variables. All these random components are assumed to be independent. The modified interest rate[6] $\tilde{r}$, the volatility σ and the jump rate λ are constants within this model. Furthermore, the density assigned to the V_i is chosen such that $Y_i := \ln(V_i)$, $i \in \mathbb{N}$, offers an asymmetric double exponential distribution:

$$f_{Y_i}(y) = p \cdot \eta_1 e^{-\eta_1 y} \mathbf{1}_{y \geq 0} + q \cdot \eta_2 e^{\eta_2 y} \mathbf{1}_{y < 0}, \quad \eta_1 > 1, \ \eta_2 > 0. \tag{12.6}$$

The probabilities of jumps upwards and downwards are thus given by $p, q \geq 0$, $p + q = 1$, and the random variable Y_i can be specified by

$$Y_i \overset{\mathrm{d}}{=} \begin{cases} \xi^+, & \text{with probability } p \\ -\xi^-, & \text{with probability } q. \end{cases} \tag{12.7}$$

ξ^+ and ξ^- are exponential random variables with parameters η_1 and η_2.

The dynamics of the modeled return process $\frac{dS(t)}{S(t-)}$ are therefore split into three elementary components: the drift $\tilde{r} - \lambda \zeta$, the diffusion $\sigma B(t)$, and the jump part $\sum_{i=1}^{N(t)} (V_i - 1)$. Within the drift component, the term $\lambda \zeta$ has a special meaning. This term is referred to as the compensator of the jump process and is defined as:

$$\lambda \zeta := \mathbb{E}\left[\sum_{i=1}^{N(t)} (V_i - 1) \right]. \tag{12.8}$$

Rearranging the compensator to the jump part yields:

$$\frac{dS(t)}{S(t-)} = \tilde{r}dt + \sigma dB(t) + \left\{ d\left[\sum_{i=1}^{N(t)} (V_i - 1) \right] - \lambda \zeta dt \right\}. \tag{12.9}$$

The dynamics of the return process are thus described by a deterministic part with growth rate $\tilde{r}$ and a stochastic part containing two sources of randomness. Firstly, a diffusion with zero expectation and constant volatility, and secondly, a jump process also with constant volatility and, due to the compensator, zero expectation again.

By reasons of this choice concerning parameters and model characteristics, the stochastic differential equation (12.5) can easily be solved:

$$S(t) = S(0) \exp\left[\left(\tilde{r} - \frac{1}{2}\sigma^2 - \lambda\zeta \right) t + \sigma B(t) \right] \prod_{i=1}^{N(t)} V_i. \tag{12.10}$$

For simplicity, but without loss of generality, $S(0)$ is set to 1 in the sequel. The computations in this article are thus based on

$$S(t) = \exp\left[\left(\tilde{r} - \frac{1}{2}\sigma^2 - \lambda\zeta \right) t + \sigma B(t) \right] \prod_{i=1}^{N(t)} V_i. \tag{12.11}$$

The log-return process $(Z_t)_{t \geq 0} =: Z(t)$, with

$$Z_t := \ln(S_t), \tag{12.12}$$

can be derived directly from (12.11):

$$Z_t = \ln(S_t) = \ln\left\{ \exp\left[(\tilde{r} - \tfrac{1}{2}\sigma^2 - \lambda\zeta) t + \sigma B(t) \right] \prod_{i=1}^{N(t)} V_i \right\} \tag{12.13}$$

$$= (\tilde{r} - \tfrac{1}{2}\sigma^2 - \lambda\zeta) t + \sigma B(t) + \sum_{i=1}^{N(t)} \ln(V_i). \tag{12.14}$$

Defining

$$\mu := \left(\tilde{r} - \frac{1}{2}\sigma^2 - \lambda\zeta \right) \tag{12.15}$$

the log-return process is given by:

$$Z_t = \mu t + \sigma B(t) + \sum_{i=1}^{N(t)} Y_i. \tag{12.16}$$

12.3.1.1   Closed-form Option Pricing

The independence of the randomness parts in (12.16) and their additive assembling entail $Z(t)$ being a Lévy process. The high degree of analytical tractability of Lévy processes and the specific memoryless property of the exponential jump part in (12.16) enable the derivation of a formula with respect to the probability of the terminal value Z_T exceeding a certain level a:

$$\mathbb{P}(Z_T \geq a) = \Upsilon(\mu, \sigma, \lambda, p, \eta_1, \eta_2; a, T). \tag{12.17}$$

Because of its complexity, we do not cite the explicit functional dependence of Υ with respect to its input variables. For these details, readers are referred to Scherr (2012).

Based on the analytically known distribution properties of Z_T, Kou (2002) devised a closed-form pricing formula for European call options. The monotonicity feature of the exponential function constitutes a crucial condition for this derivation, because it entails the following relation:

$$Z_T \geq a \quad \Leftrightarrow \quad S_T \geq \exp(a). \tag{12.18}$$

Given the maturity T and the strike level K, the actual price $C(K, T)$ of a European call option written on an asset following (12.5) can be determined analytically:

$$C(K, T) = \Upsilon\left(\tilde{r} + \tfrac{1}{2}\sigma^2 - \lambda\zeta, \sigma, \tilde{\lambda}, \tilde{p}, \tilde{\eta}_1, \tilde{\eta}_2; \ln(K), T\right) \tag{12.19}$$

$$-K \exp(-rT) \cdot \Upsilon\left(\tilde{r} - \tfrac{1}{2}\sigma^2 - \lambda\zeta, \sigma, \lambda, p, \eta_1, \eta_2; \ln(K), T\right), \tag{12.20}$$

where

$$\tilde{p} = \frac{p}{1+\zeta} \cdot \frac{\eta_1}{\eta_1 - 1}, \quad \tilde{\eta}_1 = \eta_1 - 1, \quad \tilde{\eta}_2 = \eta_2 + 1, \quad \tilde{\lambda} = \lambda(\zeta + 1). \tag{12.21}$$

The weighted average of the pooled equity values or, in other words, the related index level corresponds to the asset value that we are depicting by applying this double exponential jump-diffusion model. The dynamics $S(t)$ of the stock index are thus described by the stochastic process specified in (12.5). As mentioned before, throughout this chapter, we assess $S(0)$ as 1. The level of the contemplated index thus always equals 1 at the starting time. In this context, rescaling the level reduces complexity only and does not induce a bias in the results.

In the calculations so far, the model parameters were always assumed implicitly to be given. Of course, this requirement is not fullfilled in general. Conversely, a fundamental challenge in capturing the dynamics of the contemplated stock index or, more generally, the related market, is to identify reliable parameter values.

12.3.1.2 Model Calibration and Relative Entropy

Two methods are commonly combined to fix these values. Firstly, the parameters are simply set to exogenous values or chosen to satisfy exogenous constraints. Secondly, a calibration procedure is conducted to back out parameter sets that are associated with certain optimality features. A quantity that is frequently optimized within such a calibration procedure is the sum of the in-sample quadratic pricing errors:

$$S(\theta) = \sum_{i=1}^{N} [C(K_i, T; \theta) - C_i]^2 . \tag{12.22}$$

Here, θ denotes the vector containing the model parameters. The optimization procedure reveals the parameter set θ_0 that minimizes the sum of quadratic differences between model prices $C(K_i, T; \theta)$ and observed market prices C_i. This procedure is called least-squares calibration. For a given day, we thus extract a parameter vector θ_0 enabling – in the sense of least squares – the best fit of the model-based option prices to the quoted prices. Repeating the calibration procedure for all observation dates in our data set, we obtain time series of the model parameters. These time series are essential in terms of our objective – the pricing of credit derivatives – because they contain the required information on the market dynamics. These market dynamics are again used to generate dependence among the individual asset-value processes of the firms on which the corresponding reference pool is built.

Cont and Tankov (2004a) developed a method not only to find the best fit, but also regarding the time stability of parameters. For this purpose, the objective function $S(\theta)$ is complemented by a penalty function $\mathcal{F}$, reflecting the "distance" between the measure $\mathbb{Q}_\theta$ associated with θ and a given measure $\mathbb{P}$:

$$\mathcal{G}(\theta) = \sum_{i=1}^{N} [C(K_i, T; \theta) - C_i]^2 + \alpha \mathcal{F}(\mathbb{Q}_\theta, \mathbb{P}). \tag{12.23}$$

Here, we chose $\mathcal{F}$ to be represented by the so-called relative entropy introduced by Kullback and Leibler (1951):

$$\mathcal{E}(\mathbb{Q}, \mathbb{P}) = \mathbb{E}^{\mathbb{Q}} \left[\ln \left(\frac{d\mathbb{Q}}{d\mathbb{P}} \right) \right] = \mathbb{E}^{\mathbb{P}} \left[\frac{d\mathbb{Q}}{d\mathbb{P}} \ln \left(\frac{d\mathbb{Q}}{d\mathbb{P}} \right) \right], \tag{12.24}$$

$\frac{d\mathbb{Q}}{d\mathbb{P}}$ denoting the Radon–Nikodym derivative of $\mathbb{Q}$ with respect to $\mathbb{P}$.

In the case of the double exponential model, the relative entropy can be calculated as

$$T^{-1} \mathcal{E}(\mathbb{Q}, \mathbb{P}) = \frac{1}{2\sigma^2} \left(b^{\mathbb{Q}} - b^{\mathbb{P}} \right)^2 + \frac{p^{\mathbb{Q}}}{\eta_1^{\mathbb{Q}}} \ln \left(\frac{p^{\mathbb{Q}}}{p^{\mathbb{P}}} \right) - p^{\mathbb{Q}} \frac{\eta_1^{\mathbb{Q}} - \eta_1^{\mathbb{P}}}{\left(\eta_1^{\mathbb{Q}} \right)^2} + \frac{p^{\mathbb{P}}}{\eta_1^{\mathbb{P}}} - \frac{p^{\mathbb{Q}}}{\eta_1^{\mathbb{Q}}}$$
$$+ \frac{q^{\mathbb{Q}}}{\eta_2^{\mathbb{Q}}} \ln \left(\frac{q^{\mathbb{Q}}}{q^{\mathbb{P}}} \right) - q^{\mathbb{Q}} \frac{\eta_2^{\mathbb{Q}} - \eta_2^{\mathbb{P}}}{\left(\eta_2^{\mathbb{Q}} \right)^2} + \frac{q^{\mathbb{P}}}{\eta_2^{\mathbb{P}}} - \frac{q^{\mathbb{Q}}}{\eta_2^{\mathbb{Q}}}, \tag{12.25}$$

whereby $b^{\mathbb{Q}}$ and $b^{\mathbb{P}}$ represent truncated versions of the drift. Details of the properties of the relative entropy and the derivation of its functional form for double exponential Lévy processes are presented in Scherr (2012).

12.3.2 The Asset-value Model

In order to describe the development of the asset values on which the contemplated portfolio is built, we also use the double exponential jump-diffusion model:

$$\frac{dA(t)}{A(t-)} = (r - \lambda\zeta_A)\,dt + \sigma_A dB(t) + d\left[\sum_{i=1}^{N_A(t)} (V_{A,i} - 1)\right]. \tag{12.26}$$

There are two main reasons for this choice. Firstly, due to the formal analogy, it offers a convenient means of including information about market dynamics. This means integrating market and idiosyncratic risk dynamics, and therefore producing a dependence structure among the pooled asset values. Secondly, there is an analytically known first passage time distribution of the process

$$X_t = \left(r - \frac{1}{2}\sigma_A^2 - \lambda\zeta_A\right)t + \sigma_A B(t) + \sum_{i=1}^{N_A(t)} \ln\left(V_{A,i}\right) \tag{12.27}$$

with respect to a constant logarithmic default barrier b. Analogous to Section 12.3.1, the process $X(t)$ represents the logarithmic version of $A(t)$, $A(0) := 1$. Due to the relationship

$$X_t \leq b \quad \Leftrightarrow \quad A_t \leq e^b = D \tag{12.28}$$

we can image the default behavior of the modeled firm values by a first passage time model according to Black and Cox (1976). Thus a default event is caused if the asset value falls to or below the value of debt for the first time. The value of debt is assumed to be constant. Mathematically, the default time is defined by

$$\tau := \inf\{t \mid A_t \leq D\}. \tag{12.29}$$

τ thus represents the first passage time of the asset-value process $A(t)$ with respect to the barrier D. From an economic point of view, this refers to the moment the company's value of assets deceeds the value of debt and, therefore, it is no longer possible to meet all financial obligations. An immediate consequence is that a default event is triggered.

12.3.2.1 First Passage Time Distribution

The first passage time or default time τ depends primarily on the behavior of the stochastic process $A(t)$, and therefore constitutes a random variable. The identical random variable can be obtained, if one observes the behavior of the logarithmic version of $S(t)$ and the logarithmic default boundary b:

$$\tau = \inf\{t \mid A_t \leq D\} = \inf\{t \mid \ln(A_t) \leq \ln(D)\} = \inf\{t \mid X_t \leq b\}. \tag{12.30}$$

Several papers deal with analytical formulas for the distribution of τ. Based on the so-called Wiener–Hopf factorization, Boyarchenko and Levendorskii (2002) discussed solutions for general jump-diffusion processes with two-sided jumps. Kou and Wang (2003) calculated the first passage time distribution with respect to an upper boundary, using both martingales and differential equations. Lipton (2002) adopted fluctuation identities to reveal a closed-form formula for a constant boundary. These formulas are crucial for our analysis, because, according to (12.2) and (12.3), the distribution function of τ completely determines CDS and CDS index spreads, if we are dealing with a fixed LGD level.

In order to formulate an analytic expression for $\mathbb{P}\,(t \leq \tau_b)$, we thus apply the moment-generating function of X_t:

$$\Phi\,(k, t) := \mathbb{E}\left(e^{k \cdot X_t}\right) = \exp\left[G\,(k) \cdot t\right], \qquad (12.31)$$

with

$$G\,(x) := x\mu + \frac{1}{2}x^2\sigma^2 + \lambda\left(\frac{p\eta_1}{\eta_1 - x} + \frac{q\eta_2}{\eta_2 + x}\right). \qquad (12.32)$$

As shown at large in Scherr (2012), based on the zeros of

$$G\,(x) - \alpha, \quad \alpha \in \mathbb{R}, \qquad (12.33)$$

the Laplace transform of the cumulative distribution function $F_\tau(t)$, regarding the first passage time, can be evaluated analytically.

Therefore, given the parameters of the double exponential model, the maturity T and the constant LGD, we can calculate the spread of a CDS contract, subject to the default barrier D, by simply performing a Laplace inversion.[7] Assuming a homogenous portfolio, the model's calibration to the quoted index spread can be conducded by a numerical algorithm very quickly and with great accuracy. This is one of the major advantages of the approach presented.

12.3.2.2   Integrative Modeling

The comprehensive analytical tractability of the double exponential model with respect to option pricing, which means capturing market dynamics, and first passage time properties motivates and enables an integrative pricing of option markets and CDS indices. Assuming a homogenous portfolio, the market dynamics backed out are used to produce a dependence structure among the pooled CDS contracts. Therefore we state that within a CAPM-like framework, the diffusion motion of the market influences that of the firm value process by a factor β. The diffusion component of the asset-value process thus encompasses two independent parts: market-induced diffusion $\beta\sigma_M B_M$ and idiosyncratic diffusion $\sigma_I B_I$. The sum of two independent Gaussian distributed random variables again constitutes a Gaussian random variable:

$$\beta\sigma_M B_M + \sigma_I B_I \sim \mathcal{N}\left(0, \beta^2\sigma_M^2 + \sigma_I^2\right) = \mathcal{N}\left(0, \sigma_A^2\right), \qquad (12.34)$$

where σ_A is given externally in the empirical section of this chapter.

Concerning the jumps, we follow Hull (2006) and thus omit idiosyncratic jumps. This approach is based on the conjecture that idiosyncratic upwards and downwards jumps cancel out over the long run.[8] Jumps in the asset value are thus caused exclusively by jumps in the market dynamics. With respect to the distribution of these jumps, we again adopt the factor β:

$$Y_A := \beta \cdot Y_M. \qquad (12.35)$$

Hence, jumps in the market dynamics cause jumps in the asset value, but weakened. Because the debt level of the companies modeled is assumed to be constant, and therefore does not yield any reaction to market jumps, only the equity part is exposed to the market. As a result, the characteristics of the asset movements are consistently reflected by the model. An exponentially distributed random variable remains exponentially distributed, if multiplied by a scalar. This property ensures that the asset-value dynamics modeled within this CAPM-framework still conform to the Kou model:

$$dX_t = \left(r - \lambda\zeta_A - \frac{\sigma_A^2}{2} \right) dt + \sigma_A dB(t) + \sum_{i=1}^{N_A(t)} Y_{A,i}, \quad \lambda\zeta_A := \mathbb{E}\left[\sum_{i=1}^{N_A(t)} \left(V_{A,i} - 1 \right) \right],$$

(12.36)

and thus provide integrated pricing as well as analytical calibration.

12.4 EMPIRICAL ANALYSIS

12.4.1 Elementary Data

The elementary data used in our empirical analysis comprise EuroSTOXX 50 option prices, spreads of the iTraxx Europe, and risk-free interest rates. To obtain information about the options and the credit index, we applied Thomson Reuters Datastream. Interest rates for the European area are drawn from the webpage of the European Central Bank. Because the pre-crisis and crisis periods had been treated extensively in the past, and because above all a model should capture contemporary empirical facts, we chose the first section of the iTraxx Europe Series 16 to serve as the reference period of 39 days. The options written on the EuroSTOXX 50 cover different strike levels and different maturities. Because the EuroSTOXX 50 is generally available as a price index, for each strike level and maturity pair, both the price of the call option and the corresponding put option are necessary to determine the implicit dividend rate δ, by applying the put-call-parity. Of course, given the dividend dynamics and assuming an absence of arbitrage, this data set exhibits redundancies regarding the parameters determining the market value process. With respect to the adopted time series and the aim of demonstrating the validity of our model, we integrate options expiring in December 2015, as well as those maturing in December 2016. Thus we are able to prove the good fit and the capability of predicting option prices.

However, the evaluation of an option pricing model is not central to our analysis. The market model serves as building block of an asset-value model designed to determine the behavior of the companies pooled in the iTraxx Europe. As an immediate consequence, after calibrating to the index spread with a certain maturity, tranche spreads written on the index can be evaluated and, again for the purpose of demonstrating the model's reliability, index spreads for different maturities can be calculated. Therefore, we consider iTraxx Europe index spreads with five year maturity, as well as those with seven and ten years to expiry. Because all the introduced evaluations of prices involve discounting future cash flows, knowledge of the level of interest rates is necessary to perform the corresponding calculations. The European Central Bank offers spot rates for AAA-rated bonds on a monthly basis, spreading from one month to thirty years. Based on this data set, the associated interest rates are chosen to discount future cash flows accurately.

12.4.2 Implied Dividends

As a preliminary step with regard to our market model, we have to back out the implied dividend dynamics by applying the put-call parity:

$$c + Ke^{-rT} = p + S_0 e^{-\delta T}.$$

(12.37)

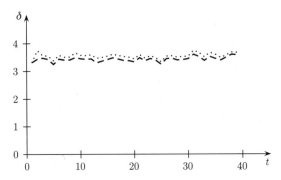

Figure 12.1 Time series of implied dividend rates δ (quoted in percent) depicted on a daily basis. The dotted line refers to the options expiring on December 18, 2015, the dashed line to those reaching maturity on December 16, 2016.

Rewriting this formula yields:

$$\delta = \log \left\{ \frac{S_0}{c + K e^{-rT} - p} \right\} \cdot T^{-1}. \tag{12.38}$$

Given put and call prices for a fixed interest rate r, maturity T and stock price S_0, one can extract the implied dividend rate δ as a function of the strike level K.

From a theoretical perspective, this function should be a constant. Performing the calculation reveals only marginal differences between the implied dividends throughout different strike levels and thus confirms the assumption of a liquid and arbitrage free option market. With respect to further analysis, we calculate the mean dividend rate for each day in our data set. The results are depicted in Figure 12.1.

12.4.3 Market Dynamics

Initially, we fix the $\sigma = \sigma_M$ of the continuous market value process at 0.05. At first glance, this choice might suggest a far too low level of volatility, but one has to take into account that the total volatility of the process also depends on the volatility of the jump part. A check for robustness reveals the insensitivity of the overall volatility level with respect to the value of σ within the interval [0.05, 0.1].

After specifying σ, just two parameters have to be estimated within the calibration procedure: the jump intensity λ and the jump parameter $\eta := \eta_2$. We therefore restrict the Kou model to the special case of a spectrally negative Lévy process and set the probability of jumping upwards to zero. The reasoning for the choice is given, on the one hand, by the fact that within a risk-neutral environment, market participants exhibit asymmetric expectations of future developments. As stated before, the existence of "crashphobia" is well known, but there is no evidence of the existence of "boomphobia." On the other hand, we intend to develop a model capturing the most important empirical phenomena, despite featuring only a sparse number of parameters. A diffusion process enlarged by a negative exponential jump component should be well suited for this task. Nevertheless, a model comprising upward jumps of course offers more flexibility and constitutes a topic worthy of future research.

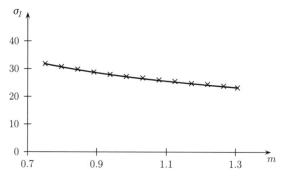

Figure 12.2   Implied volatility σ_I (quoted in percent) of our market model (solid line) based on options expiring on December 18, 2015 and reference date September 20, 2011 (crosses).

For the purpose of evaluation and without loss of generality, we restrict ourselves to European call options. The MATLAB optimization algorithm `lsqnonlin` is used to reveal the parameter set (λ, η) that minimizes the $\mathcal{G}$-function defined in (12.23). The number of strike levels is denoted by N. In the course of our analysis, we consider the strike levels spreading from €1700 to €2900, whereas the increments are chosen to be 100. N thus equals 13. The optimization of $\mathcal{G}$ reveals the tupel $(\lambda_{opt}, \eta_{opt})$ that minimizes the quadratic differences between the market prices and the model prices. Figure 12.2 shows the high degree of coincidence between observed and fitted option prices, with the reference date September 20, 2011, for contracts expiring on December 18, 2015. The cited quantity moneyness is given by the quotient of the strike level K and the current stock price S_0:

$$m := \frac{K}{S_0}. \tag{12.39}$$

By applying the technique of relative entropy, the parameters reveal extensive time stability and synchronism with the observed market prices. The time series for λ exhibits $\mu_\lambda = 1.25$ and $\sigma_\lambda = 0.0321$, whereas the corresponding quantities regarding η are $\mu_\eta = 5.83$ and $\sigma_\eta = 0.202$. This confirms the economic validity of the model, that can capture market dynamics by drawing only on the two degrees of freedom.

The major driver of general model complexity and the associated increment of parameters is due to the aim of capturing and explaining the empirically observed equity characteristic depicted by the so-called volatility surface. Here, we are primarily interested in developing a model that offers reliable out-of-time properties regarding long-term maturities. In our analysis, we therefore calibrate our market model to the prices of options expiring on December 18, 2015 and use the corresponding model specification to evaluate the prices for contracts maturing on December 16, 2016. The average relative pricing error of this procedure amounts to 0.017, with a standard deviation of 0.0098. These numbers illustrate the reliability as well as the out-of-time performance of the chosen market model.

Extracting the associated risk-neutral density from both a static or dynamic approach generally requires the numerically calculated second derivative of the call price with respect to the strike level. However, this again shows the tremendous advantage of using Lévy processes. According to the so-called Lévy–Khinchin representation logarithmic, the market-return

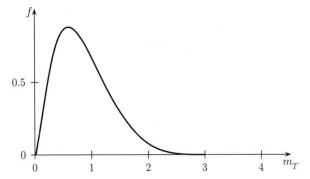

Figure 12.3 Risk-neutral density f of the terminal moneyness level M_T on December 16, 2016 implied by options expiring on December 18, 2015 and reference date September 20, 2011.

distribution can be expressed by a closed-form formula, depending on the interest rate r, maturity T, dividend rate δ, volatility σ and the two jump-part parameters λ and η. Applying the transformation formula to this return distribution enables an evaluation of the terminal moneyness level distribution with reference date September 20, 2011 as shown in Figure 12.3.

12.4.4 Asset Value Model

Capturing the market dynamics through applying an option pricing model, we are able to specify the systematic part of our asset-value process. In order to establish the complete asset dynamics within a CAPM-framwork, two topics must still be discussed; firstly, the coupling parameter β and secondly, the calibration of the default boundary.

The proposed model integrates equity and asset dynamics in a twofold manner. The continuous movements of the market affect those of the asset values by a factor of 0.8. Fixing this value is again due to our aim of presenting a simple and robust model for pricing credit derivatives. The level of this quantity captures the main results of a regression performed by Collin-Dufresne, Goldstein and Yang (2012), who extract equity and debt betas. These values are subsequently aggregated to form asset betas by using the corresponding leverage ratios. We fix the value of the entire continuous asset volatility at 0.25. This choice ensures the total asset volatility being comparable to that quoted by Coval et al. (2009). Within the framework of our model, jump movements in the company's asset value are incited, if and only if, jumps in the corresponding market can be observed. Even in such extreme scenarios, asset values do not behave in an identical manner to equity, due to the existence of debt. We take account of this fact by setting the the jump parameter η_A to $\frac{\eta}{0.8}$ and thus reducing the expected decline in the logarithmic return from $\frac{1}{\eta}$ to $\frac{0.8}{\eta}$. This reflects the economic fact that in crisis situations asset values generally do not react identically to equity values, but of course they are similar. Beyond the economic coherences, preserving the analytical tractability is the main reason for this approach. The superposition of two independent Brownian motions again turns out to be a member of this class and an exponentially distributed random variable stays exponentially distributed, if multiplied by a scalar. Altogether, this enables an analytical calibration of our model or, more precisely, the determination of a default boundary. For our calibration, we choose the five-year iTraxx Europe index spread, because in the sequel, among others, we

wish to evaluate the pure out-of-time projection quality of our asset pool model. Applying the
MATLAB algorithm `fzero` to the function

$$\mathcal{D}(b) = s^{model}(b) - s^{empiric}, \tag{12.40}$$

whereas s denotes the spread and b the default boundary, enables a very fast determination of the associated time series. The resulting marginal fluctuations of this series
($\mu_b = -1.21$, $\sigma_b = 0.01$) entail the logarithmic default boundary not serving only as a fitting
parameter, but in fact having an economic meaning. It therefore can be seen as a measurement of the creditworthiness of the companies modeled. Within the considered short period of
time, the level of financial standing should not change radically, except in the event of market
turmoil.

12.4.5 Tranche Pricing

After specifying the dynamics of the pooled assets, one can adopt them to derive the tranche
spreads by performing a Monte Carlo simulation. In this regard, the proposed model offers
another important advantage. Namely, knowledge of the first passage time distribution, and
therefore the term structure of expected losses, enables a sound testing of the simulation
technique. Given the analytically determined default boundary, and therefore the crucial input
parameter, the simulation implied bias can be detected. In the case of significant differences,
it is necessary to enlarge the computational effort to the point that model and market values
coincide. As a further consequence of this procedure, the evaluated tranche spreads can
be regarded as solid and reliable, at least from a technical point of view. The diagrams in
Figure 12.4 show the five-year tranche spreads that were calculated using market information
from options expiring on December 18, 2015. It becomes obvious that, due to the high level
of the index spread, tranche spreads rise dramatically. Moreover, the fact that even spreads of
more senior tranches exceed the index spread causes confusion.

Besides the potential effects implied by our model, analyzing empirical data helps to resolve
this puzzle. In 2008, when iTraxx tranches were still being traded, senior spreads also reached
the magnitude of associated index values of about 150 bps. This coherence emerged all the more
as the index spreads increased. Taking into account that this level, on average, were lower than
the level of iTraxx Europe quoted at the beginning of Series 16, a further amplification of the
observed interrelation seems reasonable. This conjecture is supported by the fact that in 2008,
the CDX.NA.IG temporarily also offered index spreads of about 200 bps, whereas the spreads
of the 10−15% tranche simultaneously rose to 250 bps. In this light, the puzzle is resolved.

12.4.6 Out-of-time Application

So far, we have primarily considered, heuristically speaking, cross-sectional properties of our
model, because we focused on the characteristics of tranches and their modeling. However, we
also wish to present longitudinal features. For this purpose, we use the model based on four-year
option prices and five-year index spreads, to make an out-of-time forecast of the index spreads
with seven and ten-year maturity. At this point, the main advantage of dynamic modeling
becomes obvious. Specifying a continuous-time model entails the associated distributions and
properties at all times already being embedded in the definition of the process. Adopting the
identical parameter set used for the pricing of five-year tranches, we thus only change the
expiry date of the credit derivative and by this means can gather the requested values. This

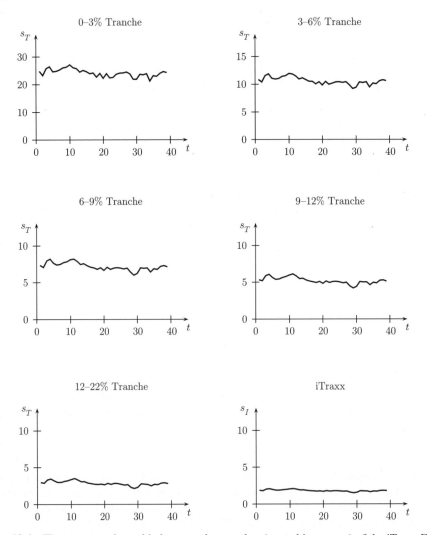

Figure 12.4   Five-year tranche and index spreads s_T and s_I (quoted in percent) of the iTraxx Europe
Series 16 evaluated by applying Monte Carlo simulations.

reflects the general idea behind dynamic modeling. In contrast to econometric or static models,
dynamic models can capture the entire development of asset values regarding arbitrary and
not only several or even just one point of time. Therefore, our calibrated model can easily be
applied to yield spreads with respect to maturities of seven and ten years. The resulting time
series are depicted in Figures 12.5 and 12.6.

   The analysis of the differences between computed and empiric values reveals the model's
ability to capture the principal market dynamics. Obviously, however, there appears to be a
systematic bias. A potential cause of this deviation might be the way interest rates are handled
within our model. For simplicity, as well as for analytical tractability, we omit the time
dependence of r and instead fix its value to the spot rate of AAA-rated bonds with identical
maturity. In addition, the lack of more comparable long-term information may constitute a

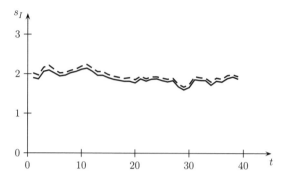

Figure 12.5 Time series of model-based (dashed line) and empirically observed (solid line) index spreads s_I (quoted in percent) of the iTraxx Europe Series 16 with seven years up to expiry.

further reason. Yet, at the same time, the relative pricing error can on average be assigned to 0.04 and 0.05, respectively. Bearing in mind that there are only three fitting parameters and that the proposed procedure is purely out-of-time, these results can be regarded as highly satisfactory, thus confirming the validity of the proposed model.

12.5 CONCLUSION

In this article, we present a structual approach for the dynamics of credit-related assets within a CAPM-like framework. This setting enables the pricing of general single- and multi-name credit derivatives, whereas we exemplarily focus on CDS and CDS indices. The main advantages of the approach are its economic validity, analytical tractability and the sparse number of parameters. This can be achieved by modeling market and idiosyncratic movements through a spectrally negative Lévy process, which constitutes a special case of the well-known double exponential jump-diffusion model. The probabilistic features inherent to the diffusion and jump part and the selected method of coupling result in the emerging asset-value process also constituting a member of this class. Due to the simplicity and concurrent flexibility of this approach, a further generalization seems to be a worthwile topic for further research.

Based on empirical data for the EuroSTOXX 50 and the iTraxx Europe Series 16, we demonstrate the most important features of the applied modeling techniques. We therefore

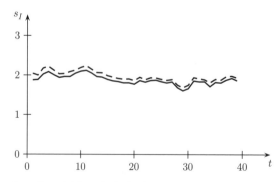

Figure 12.6 Time series of model-based (dashed line) and empirically observed (solid line) index spreads s_I (quoted in percent) of the iTraxx Europe Series 16 with ten years up to expiry.

perform an analytical calibration to market data, including both option prices and index spreads, and also calculate the prices of associated tranches. Moreover, by evaluating seven- and ten-year index spreads using only data for financial instruments with shorter maturities, we convincingly demonstrate the out-of-time properties of our dynamic model.

NOTES

1. This term subsumes combinations of analytical and simulation-based techniques.
2. This denomination refers to Lévy processes with the additional restriction that jumps are almost surely negative.
3. A remarkable citation of Fisher Black should not be omitted in this context: "Is it reasonable to take that volatility as constant over time. I think not."
4. For technical details, we refer to Rogers (1997).
5. A comprehensive treatment of reduced-form models can be found in Duffie and Singelton (1999), Jarrow et al. (1997) and Madan and Unal (1998).
6. This rate accounts for dividends paid on the underlying equity: $\tilde{r} := r - \delta$, where r denotes the risk-free interest rate and δ the rate of a continously distributed dividend.
7. Details on this issue are outlined in Kou and Wang (2003)
8. A model also incorporating idiosyncratic jumps of course offers a greater variety of features. Here, however, we wish to keep the model setting as simple as possible, but further research should consider such generalization.

REFERENCES

Ball, C., Roma, A., 1994. Stochastic volatility option pricing. Journal of Financial and Quantitative Analysis 29, 589–607.

Ball, C., Torous, W., 1985. On jumps in common stock prices and their impact on call option pricing. Journal of Finance 40, 155–173.

Bates, D., 2000. Post-'87 crash fears in the S&P 500 futures option market. Journal of Econometrics 94, 181–238.

Black, F., Cox, J., 1976. Valuing corporate securities: Some effects of bond indenture provisions. Journal of Finance 31, 351–367.

Boyarchenko, S., Levendorskii, S., 2002. Barrier options and touch-and-out options under regular Lévy processes of exponential type. The Annals of Applied Probability 12, 1261–1298.

Broadie, M., Kaya, O., 2006. Exact simulation of stochastic volatility and other affine jump diffusion processes. Operations Research 54, 217–231.

Carverhill, A., Luo, D., 2011. Pricing and integration of CDX tranches in the financial market. Working Paper, University of Hong Kong.

Chan, T., 1999. Pricing contingent claims on stocks driven by Lévy processes. Annals of Applied Probability 9, 504–528.

Chen, N., Kou, S., 2009. Credit spreads, optimal capital structure, and implied volatility with endogenous default and jump risk. Mathematical Finance 19, 343–378.

Collin-Dufresne, P., Goldstein, R., 2001. Do credit spreads reflect stationary leverage ratios? Journal of Finance 56, 1929–1957.

Collin-Dufresne, P., Goldstein, R., Yang, F., 2012. On the relative pricing of long maturity S&P 500 index options and CDX tranches. Journal of Finance (forthcoming).

Cont, R., Tankov, P., 2004a. Calibration of jump-diffusion option pricing models: A robust non-parametric approach. Journal of Computational Finance 7, 1–49.

Cont, R., Tankov, P., 2004b. Financial Modelling with Jump Processes. Chapman & Hall/CRC, Boca Raton, FL.

Coval, J., Jurek, J., Stafford, E., 2009. Economic catastrophe bonds. American Economic Review 99, 628–666.

Duffie, D., Lando, D., 2001. Term structures of credit spreads with incomplete accounting information. Econometrica 69, 599–632.

Duffie, D., Pan, J., Singleton, K., 2000. Transform analysis and asset pricing for affine jump-diffusions. Econometrica 68, 1343–1376.

Duffie, D., Singelton, K., 1999. Modeling term structures of defaultable bonds. Review of Financial Studies 12, 687–720.

Finger, C., Finkelstein, V., Pan, G., Lardy, J.-P., Ta, T., Tierney, J., 2002. CreditGrades technical document. RiskMetrics Group.

Fons, J., 1994. Using default rates to model the term structure of credit risk. Financial Analysts 50, 25–32.

Hamerle, A., Igl, A., Plank, K., 2012. Correlation smile, volatility skew and systematic risk sensitivity of tranches. Journal of Derivatives (forthcoming).

He, J., Hu, W., Lang, L., 2000. Credit Spread Curves and Credit Ratings. Working Paper, Chinese University of Hong Kong.

Heston, S., 1997. A closed-form solution for options with stochastic volatility with applications to bond and currency options. Review of Financial Studies 6, 327–343.

Hull, J., 2006. Options, Futures, and Other Derivatives, 6th Edition. Pearson/Prentice Hall, Upper Saddle River, NJ.

Hull, J., White, A., 1987. The pricing of options on assets with stochastic volatilites. Journal of Finance 42, 281–300.

Jarrow, R., Lando, D., Turnbull, S., 1997. A markov model for the term structure of credit spreads. Review of Financial Studies 10, 481–523.

Jorion, P., 1988. On jump processes in the foreign exchange and stock markets. Review of Financial Studies 1, 427–445.

Kou, S., 2002. A jump-diffusion model for option pricing. Management Science 48, 1086–1101.

Kou, S., Wang, H., 2003. First passage times of a jump diffusion process. Advances in Applied Probability 35, 504–531.

Kullback, S., Leibler, R., 1951. On information and sufficiency. The Annals of Mathematical Statistics 22, 79–86.

Lando, D., 2004. Credit Risk Modeling: Theory and Applications. Princeton University Press, Princeton, NJ.

Li, H., Zhao, F., 2011. Economic catastrophe bonds: Inefficient market or inadequate model? Working Paper, University of Michigan.

Lipton, A., 2002. Assets with jumps. Risk 15, 149–153.

Longstaff, F., Schwartz, E., 1995. A simple approach to valuing risky fixed and floating rate debt. Journal of Finance 50, 789–819.

Madan, D., Unal, H., 1998. Pricing the risks of default. Review of Derivatives Research 2, 121–160.

Merton, R., 1974. On the pricing of corporate debt: The risk structure of interest rates. Journal of Finance 29, 449–470.

Merton, R., 1976. Option pricing when underlying stock returns are discontinuous. Journal of Financial Econometrics 3, 125–144.

Ozeki, T., Umezawa, Y., Yamazaki, A., Yoshikawa, D., 2010. An extension of CreditGrades model approach with Lévy processes. Quantitative Finance 10, 1–13.

Ramezani, C., Zeng, Y., 2007. Maximum likelihood estimation of the double exponential jump-diffusion process. Annals of Finance 3, 487–507.

Rebonato, R., 1999. Volatility and Correlation in the Pricing of Equity, FX and Interest Rate Options. John Wiley, Chichester, UK.

Rogers, L., 1997. Arbitrage with fractional brownian motion. Mathematical Finance 7, 95–105.

Rubinstein, M., 1994. Implied binomial trees. Journal of Finance 49, 771–818.

Runggaldier, W., 2002. Jump-diffusion models. Università di Padova.

Sarig, O., Warga, A., 1989. Some empirical estimates of the risk structure of interest rates. Journal of Finance 44, 1351–1360.

Sato, K.-I., 1999. Lévy Processes and Infinitely Divisible Distributions. Cambridge University Press, Cambridge, UK.

Scherr, C., 2012. A Semianalytic Approach to the Dynamic Modeling of Credit Derivatives. Working Paper, University of Regensburg.

Scott, L., 1997. Pricing stock options in a jump-diffusion model with stochastic volatility and interest rates: Applications of Fourier inversion methods. Mathematical Finance 7, 413–426.

Sepp, A., 2006. Extended CreditGrades model with stochastic volatility and jumps. Wilmott Magazine 2006, 50–62.

Sepp, A., Skachkov, I., 2003. Option pricing with jumps. Willmott Magazine 2003, 50–58.

Shreve, S., 2009. Did faulty mathematical models cause the financial fiasco? Analytics 2009, 6–7.

Stamicar, R., Finger, C., 2005. Incorporating equity derivatives into the CreditGrades model. RiskMetrics Group.

Stein, E., Stein, J., 1991. Stock price distributions with stochastic volatility: An analytical approach. Review of Financial Studies 4, 727–752.

Zhou, C., 2001. The term structure of credit spreads with jump risk. Journal of Banking & Finance 25, 2015–2040.

13

Pricing and Calibration in Market Models

Frank Gehmlich[1], Zorana Grbac[2],* and Thorsten Schmidt[3]

[1]*Chemnitz University of Technology*
[2]*University of Evry Val d'Essonne*
[3]*Chemnitz University of Technology*

13.1 INTRODUCTION

A credit portfolio consists of a number of different credit names (obligors). Modeling of credit portfolio risk is a challenging task which relies on the adequate quantification of the two main sources of risk. The first one is market risk, which is the risk stemming from the changes in interest rates and changes in the credit quality of the single credit names in the portfolio. The second is correlation risk (also known as default correlation) among these credit names. A good model for credit portfolio risk should incorporate both sources of risk.

The main purpose of credit portfolio risk modeling is valuation and hedging of various contingent claims on a portfolio. In general, securities whose value and payments depend on a portfolio of underlying assets are termed asset-backed securities. For an overview and detailed descriptions of different types of asset-backed securities we refer to Part I of this book. Credit portfolio risk tranching is discussed in Part III.

In the literature two main approaches can be found for credit portfolio models: the bottom-up approach, where the default intensities of each credit name in the portfolio are modeled, and the top-down approach, where the modeling object is the aggregate loss process of the portfolio. Both approaches have been studied in numerous recent papers; we refer to Lipton and Rennie (2011) and Bielecki et al. (2010) for a detailed overview. Since in this article we focus on the top-down approach, we mention some of the recent papers where this approach is studied: Schönbucher (2005), Sidenius et al. (2008), Ehlers and Schönbucher (2006, 2009), Arnsdorf and Halperin (2008), Longstaff and Rajan (2008), Errais et al. (2010), Filipović et al. (2011) and Cont and Minca (2011).

In this article we develop a dynamic market model in the top-down setting, similar in spirit to Eberlein et al. (2012). As discussed in that paper, the market model framework has a number of advantages in comparison to the HJM approach for credit portfolio modeling. Similarly to Filipović et al. (2011) we utilize (T, x)-bonds to build an arbitrage-free model. However, we consider only a set of finitely many maturities which are indeed traded in the market. Considering instead a continuum of maturities as in the HJM approach puts unnecessary restrictions on the model. In particular, this is reflected in the drift condition which must be satisfied for all maturities. Taking into account only the traded maturities, one gains an additional degree of freedom in the specification of arbitrage-free models. For example, this allows various additional types of contagion as shown in Eberlein et al. (2012). As a consequence, a tractable affine specification of our model which includes contagion can be

*The research of Zorana Grbac benefited from the support of the "Chaire Risque de crédit" and Fédération Bancaire Française.

obtained. Needless to say contagion effects are of particular importance in the current credit and sovereign crises and a tractable model with contagion is practically highly relevant.

The dynamics of (T_k, x)-forward prices is driven by time-inhomogeneous Lévy processes as proposed in Eberlein et al. (2012). This allows for two types of jumps in the forward price dynamics: the jumps driven by the default dates of the credit names in the portfolio, as well as the jumps triggered by external macroeconomic events; see Cont and Kan (2011).

Finally, the practical relevance of the model is illustrated by its ability to provide a good fit to the market data. We use the iTraxx data from August 2006 to August 2010 and calibrate the model to the full data set of four years. This goes beyond the usual calibration practice, where the models are calibrated to data from one day (cf. Cont et al. (2010) for an overview). The calibration is done by applying an EM-algorithm together with an extended Kalman filter to a two-factor affine diffusion specification of our model, as proposed in Eksi and Filipović (2012). Already this simple specification provides a very good fit across *different tranches* and *maturities*.

The chapter is organized as follows. In Section 13.2 we introduce the basic building blocks for credit portfolio market models. In Section 13.3 the model for the dynamics of the forward (T_k, x)-prices is presented and conditions for the absence of arbitrage are derived. Section 13.4 is a tractable affine specification of the model. In Section 13.5 we present valuation formulas for single tranche CDOs and call options on STCDOs. Section 13.6 is dedicated to the calibration of a two-factor affine diffusion market model to data from the iTraxx series.

13.2 BASIC NOTIONS

Consider a fixed time horizon $T^* > 0$ and a complete stochastic basis $(\Omega, \mathcal{G}, \mathbb{G}, \mathbb{Q}_{T^*})$, where $\mathcal{G} = \mathcal{G}_{T^*}$. $\mathbb{G} = (\mathcal{G}_t)_{0 \leq t \leq T^*}$ satisfies the usual conditions. The filtration $\mathbb{G}$ represents the full market filtration and all price and interest rate processes in the sequel are adapted to it. We set $\mathbb{Q}^* := \mathbb{Q}_{T^*}$ and denote the expectation with respect to $\mathbb{Q}^*$ by $\mathbb{E}^*$.

Following the market model approach we consider a tenor structure containing finitely many maturities, denoted by $0 = T_0 < T_1 < \ldots < T_n = T^*$. Set $\delta_k := T_{k+1} - T_k$, for $k = 0, \ldots, n - 1$.

The studied credit risky market consists of a *pool* of credit risky assets. As laid out in the introduction, we follow the *top-down* approach and directly study the aggregated losses. In this regard, denote by $L = (L_t)_{t \geq 0}$ the non-decreasing *aggregate loss process*. Assume that the total volume is normalized to 1 and denote by $\mathcal{I} := [0, 1]$ the set of loss fractions such that L takes values in $\mathcal{I}$. We assume

(A1) $L_t = \sum_{s \leq t} \Delta L_s$ is an $\mathcal{I}$-valued, non-decreasing marked point process, which admits an absolutely continuous compensator

$$\nu^L(dt, dy) = F_t^L(dy)dt.$$

As shown in Filipović et al. (2011, Lemma 3.1), under (A1), the indicator process $(\mathbf{1}_{\{L_t \leq x\}})_{t \geq 0}$ is càdlàg with intensity process

$$\lambda(t, x) = F_t^L((x - L_t, 1] \cap \mathcal{I}).$$

In particular, this yields that the process M^x given by

$$M_t^x = \mathbf{1}_{\{L_t \leq x\}} + \int_0^t \mathbf{1}_{\{L_s \leq x\}} \lambda(s, x) \mathrm{d}s \qquad (13.1)$$

is a $\mathbb{Q}^*$-martingale.

The basic instruments are the (T_k, x)-bonds introduced in Filipović et al. (2011). They are simple securities and prices for more complex products such as CDOs can be derived from them in a model-free way, see Proposition 13.5.1.

Definition 13.2.1   A security which pays $\mathbf{1}_{\{L_{T_k} \leq x\}}$ at maturity T_k is called (T_k, x)-*bond*. Its price at time $t \leq T_k$ is denoted by $P(t, T_k, x)$.

If the market is free of arbitrage, $P(t, T_k, x)$ is non-decreasing in x and

$$P(t, T_k, 1) = P(t, T_k), \qquad (13.2)$$

where $P(t, T_k)$ denotes a time-t price of a default-free zero coupon bond with maturity T_k. Moreover, if L already crossed the level x, the (T_k, x)-bond price is zero, i.e. on the set $\{L_t > x\}$ it holds $P(t, T_k, x) = 0$.

In Filipović et al. (2011) a forward rate model for (T, x)-bonds has been analyzed under the assumption that (T, x)-bonds are traded for all maturities $T \in [0, T^*]$. This assumption imposes unnecessary restrictions to the model, since in practice the set of traded maturities is only finite. The market model approach takes this fact into account, see Eberlein et al. (2012) for a detailed discussion. Here, we follow the framework introduced in that paper with slight modifications. The main ingredients in market models are the (T_k, x)-forward bond prices defined below.

Definition 13.2.2   The (T_k, x)-forward price is given by

$$F(t, T_k, x) := \frac{P(t, T_k, x)}{P(t, T_k)} \qquad (13.3)$$

for $0 \leq t \leq T_k$.

The (T_k, x)-forward prices actually give the distribution of L_{T_k} under the $\mathbb{Q}_{T_k}$-forward measure defined later in (13.8). More precisely, if we take $P(\cdot, T_k)$ as a numeraire we obtain

$$\mathbb{Q}_{T_k}\left(L_{T_k} \leq x | \mathcal{G}_t\right) = \frac{1}{P(t, T_k)} P(t, T_k) \mathbb{E}_{\mathbb{Q}_{T_k}}\left(\mathbf{1}_{\{L_{T_k} \leq x\}} | \mathcal{G}_t\right)$$

$$= \frac{P(t, T_k, x)}{P(t, T_k)} = F(t, T_k, x).$$

13.3 THE MODEL

13.3.1 Modeling Assumptions

Let X be an $\mathbb{R}^d$-valued time-inhomogeneous Lévy process on the given stochastic basis $(\Omega, \mathcal{G}, \mathbb{G}, \mathbb{Q}_{T^*})$ with $X_0 = 0$ and Lévy–Itô decomposition

$$X_t = W_t + \int_0^t \int_{\mathbb{R}^d} x(\mu - v)(\mathrm{d}x, \mathrm{d}s), \tag{13.4}$$

where W is a d-dimensional Wiener process with respect to $\mathbb{Q}^*$, μ is the random measure of jumps of X with its $\mathbb{Q}^*$-compensator $v(\mathrm{d}x, \mathrm{d}t) = F_t(\mathrm{d}x)\mathrm{d}t$. Note that the canonical representation (13.4) is justified if X has a finite first moment. This is guaranteed by the following assumption which implies the existence of exponential moments of X, compare Eberlein and Kluge (2006, Lemma 6).

(A2) There are constants $\tilde{C}, \varepsilon > 0$ such that for every $u \in [-(1 + \varepsilon)\tilde{C}, (1 + \varepsilon)\tilde{C}]^d$

$$\sup_{0 \le t \le T^*} \left(\int_{|x|>1} \exp\langle u, x \rangle F_t(\mathrm{d}y) \right) < \infty.$$

The main ingredient of the approach studied here is the dynamics of the (T_k, x)-forward prices. We assume throughout that

$$F(t, T_k, x) = \mathbf{1}_{\{L_t \le x\}} G(t, T_k, x), \tag{13.5}$$

where

$$G(t, T_k, x) = G(0, T_k, x) \exp \left(\int_0^t a(s, T_k, x)ds + \int_0^t b(s, T_k, x)dX_s \right.$$

$$\left. + \int_0^t \int_{\mathcal{I}} c(s, T_k, x; y)\mu^L(ds, dy) \right). \tag{13.6}$$

Remark 13.3.1   Note that the above specification of G allows both for jumps due to defaults in the portfolio via L, as well as jumps due to external market forces via X. The former allows for direct contagion effects; when $\Delta L_t \ne 0$, Assumption (A5) below gives that $\Delta G(t, T_k, x) = c(t, T_k, x; \Delta L_t)$.

Remark 13.3.2   This approach is similar in spirit to Eberlein et al. (2012). However, note that in that paper the forward spreads are modeled, whereas here we decide to model directly the (T_k, x)-forward prices which simplifies calibration of the model. As we shall see later on, the market model framework allows a very general specification for the dynamics of the loss process. We will study an affine special case which includes contagion and provides a highly tractable framework. This is a major advantage of the market approach in contrast to the HJM framework, where the risky short rate is directly connected to the intensity of the loss process. For a detailed discussion of this issue we refer to Eberlein et al. (2012, Section 1 and Remark 5.3).

We make the following assumptions.

(A3) For all T_k there is an $\mathbb{R}$-valued function $c(s, T_k, x; y)$, which is called the *contagion parameter* and which as a function of $(s, x, y) \mapsto c(s, T_k, x; y)$ is $\mathcal{P} \otimes \mathcal{B}(\mathcal{I}) \otimes \mathcal{B}(\mathcal{I})$-measurable. We also assume

$$\sup_{s \leq T_k, x, y \in \mathcal{I}, \omega \in \Omega} |c(s, T_k, x; y)| < \infty$$

and $c(s, T_k, x; y) = 0$ for $s > T_k$.

(A4) For all T_k there is an $\mathbb{R}_+^d$-valued function $b(s, T_k, x)$, which as a function of $(s, x) \mapsto b(s, T_k, x)$ is $\mathcal{P} \otimes \mathcal{B}(\mathcal{I})$-measurable. Moreover,

$$\sup_{s \leq T_k, x \in \mathcal{I}, \omega \in \Omega} b(s, T_k, x) \leq \tilde{C},$$

where $\tilde{C} > 0$ is the constant from Assumption (A2). If $s > T_k$, then $b(s, T_k, x) = 0$.

(A5) $[L, X]_t = 0$ for all $t \geq 0$.

The drift term $a(\cdot, T_k, \cdot)$, for every T_k, is an $\mathbb{R}$-valued, $\mathcal{O} \otimes \mathcal{B}(\mathcal{I})$-measurable process such that $a(s, T_k, x) = 0$, for $s > T_k$, that will be specified later. Here $\mathcal{O}$ and $\mathcal{P}$ denote respectively the optional and the predictable σ-algebra on $\Omega \times [0, T^*]$

The technical assumptions (A3) and (A4) ensure measurability of the subsequent operations. Assumption (A5) states that jumps in L influence F only through c and not via a direct dependence of L and X, which is natural from a modeling point of view.

13.3.2   Absence of Arbitrage

From discussion in Section 5 of Eberlein et al. (2012) it follows that the market of (T_k, x)-bonds is free of arbitrage, if for each $k, i = 2, \ldots, n$ the process

$$\left(\frac{P(t, T_k, x)}{P(t, T_i)} \right)_{0 \leq t \leq T_i \wedge T_{k-1}} \tag{13.7}$$

is a $\mathbb{Q}_{T_i}$-local martingale. The forward measure $\mathbb{Q}_{T_k}$ is defined on $(\Omega, \mathcal{G}_{T_k})$ by its Radon-Nikodym derivative with respect to the terminal forward measure $\mathbb{Q}_{T_n} = \mathbb{Q}^*$, i.e.

$$\left. \frac{d\mathbb{Q}_{T_k}}{d\mathbb{Q}_{T_n}} \right|_{\mathcal{G}_t} = \frac{P(0, T_n)}{P(0, T_k)} \frac{P(t, T_k)}{P(t, T_n)}. \tag{13.8}$$

We assume that this density has the following expression as stochastic exponential

$$\left. \frac{d\mathbb{Q}_{T_k}}{d\mathbb{Q}_{T_n}} \right|_{\mathcal{G}_t} = \mathcal{E}_t \left(\int_0^{\cdot} \alpha(s, T_k) dW_s + \int_0^{\cdot} \int_{\mathbb{R}^d} (\beta(s, T_k, y) - 1)(\mu - \nu)(ds, dy) \right),$$

where $\alpha \in L(W)$ and $\beta \in G_{\mathrm{loc}}(\mu)$, see Theorem III.7.23 in Jacod and Shiryaev (2003), as well as pages 207 and 72 for defininitions of $L(W)$ and $G_{\mathrm{loc}}(\mu)$, respectively. Moreover, under $\mathbb{Q}_{T_k}$ the process

$$W_t^{T_k} := W_t - \int_0^t \alpha(s, T_k) ds \tag{13.9}$$

is a d-dimensional standard Brownian motion and

$$\nu^{T_k}(\mathrm{d}s, \mathrm{d}y) := \beta(s, T_k, y)\nu(\mathrm{d}s, \mathrm{d}y) = F_s^{T_k}(\mathrm{d}y)\mathrm{d}s, \qquad (13.10)$$

is the compensator of μ; see Theorem III.3.24 in Jacod and Shiryaev (2003).

The compensator of the random measure μ^L of the jumps in the loss process under $\mathbb{Q}_{T_k}$ is denoted by $\nu^{L,T_k}(\mathrm{d}t, \mathrm{d}x) = F_t^{L,T_k}(\mathrm{d}x)\mathrm{d}t$.

Set

$$
\begin{aligned}
D(t, T_k, x) := \; & a(t, T_k, x) + \frac{1}{2}\parallel b(t, T_k, x) \parallel^2 \\
& + \Big\langle b(t, T_k, x), \alpha(t, T_k) \Big\rangle \\
& + \int_{\mathbb{R}^d} \Big(e^{\langle b(t, T_k, x), y\rangle} - 1 - \Big\langle b(t, T_k, x), y \Big\rangle \beta(t, T_k, y)^{-1} \Big) F_t^{T_k}(\mathrm{d}y).
\end{aligned}
\qquad (13.11)
$$

The following result gives conditions which provide an arbitrage-free specification of the studied model. More precisely, we obtain necessary and sufficient conditions for (13.7) to hold, or equivalently conditions for the (T_k, x)-forward price process $F(\cdot, T_k, x)$ being a local martingale under the forward measure $\mathbb{Q}_{T_k}$, for $k = 2, \ldots, n$; cf. Lemma 5.1 in Eberlein et al. (2012).

Theorem 13.3.1   *Suppose that* **(A1) – (A5)** *hold and let $k \in \{2, \ldots, n\}$, $x \in \mathcal{I}$. Then the process $(F(t, T_k, x))_{0 \le t \le T_{k-1}}$ given by (13.5) is a $\mathbb{Q}_{T_k}$-local martingale if and only if*

$$D(t, T_k, x) = \lambda^{T_k}(t, x) - \int_{\mathcal{I}} \Big(e^{c(t, T_k, x; y)} - 1 \Big) \mathbf{1}_{\{L_{t-}+y\le x\}} F_t^{L,T_k}(\mathrm{d}y) \qquad (13.12)$$

on the set $\{L_t \le x\}$, $\lambda^1 \otimes \mathbb{Q}_{T_k}$-a.s., where λ^1 denotes the Lebesgue measure on $\mathbb{R}$ and $\lambda^{T_k}(t, x) := F_t^{L,T_k}((x - L_t, 1] \cap \mathcal{I})$.

Proof   The proof follows along the same lines as the proof of Theorem 5.2 in Eberlein et al. (2012). Since the specification of the dynamics of the (T_k, x)-forward prices is different in this chapter, we include the proof here for the sake of completeness.

Using integration by parts yields

$$\mathrm{d}F(t, T_k, x) = G(t-, T_k, x)\mathrm{d}\mathbf{1}_{\{L_t \le x\}} + \mathbf{1}_{\{L_{t-}\le x\}}\mathrm{d}G(t, T_k, x) + \mathrm{d}\big[G(\cdot, T_k, x), \mathbf{1}_{\{L_.\le x\}} \big]_t.$$

Firstly, note that analogously to (13.1),

$$M_t^{x, T_k} := \mathbf{1}_{\{L_t \le x\}} + \int_0^t \mathbf{1}_{\{L_s \le x\}} \lambda^{T_k}(s, x)\mathrm{d}s \qquad (13.13)$$

is a $\mathbb{Q}_{T_k}$-martingale with $\lambda^{T_k}(t, x) := F_t^{L,T_k}((x - L_t, 1] \cap \mathcal{I})$. Hence,

$$
\begin{aligned}
\mathrm{d}\mathbf{1}_{\{L_t \le x\}} &= \mathrm{d}M_t^{x, T_k} - \mathbf{1}_{\{L_t \le x\}} \lambda^{T_k}(t, x)\mathrm{d}t \\
&= \mathbf{1}_{\{L_{t-}\le x\}} \Big(\mathrm{d}M_t^{x, T_k} - \lambda^{T_k}(t, x)\mathrm{d}t \Big),
\end{aligned}
$$

since $dM_t^{x,T_k} = \mathbf{1}_{\{L_{t-}\leq x\}}dM_t^{x,T_k}$, and we obtain

$$G(t-, T_k, x)d\mathbf{1}_{\{L_t \leq x\}} = G(t-, T_k, x)\mathbf{1}_{\{L_{t-}\leq x\}}\left(dM_t^{x,T_k} - \lambda^{T_k}(t, x)dt\right)$$
$$= F(t-, T_k, x)\left(dM_t^{x,T_k} - \lambda^{T_k}(t, x)dt\right).$$

Secondly, we have

$$dG(t, T_k, x) = G(t-, T_k, x)\left(\left(a(t, T_k, x) + \frac{1}{2}\|b(t, T_k, x)\|^2\right)dt\right.$$

$$+ \int_{\mathcal{I}}\left(e^{c(t,T_k,x;y)} - 1\right)\mu^L(dt, dy)$$

$$+ \int_{\mathbb{R}^d}\left(e^{\langle b(t,T_k,x),\tilde{x}\rangle} - 1 - \langle b(t, T_k, x), \tilde{x}\rangle\right)\mu(dt, d\tilde{x})$$

$$\left.+ \int_{\mathbb{R}^d}\langle b(t, T_k, x), \tilde{x}\rangle(\mu - \nu)(dt, d\tilde{x}) + b(t, T_k, x)dW_t\right),$$

where we have used the integration by parts formula, Assumption **(A5)** and Itô's formula for semimartingales. Now we use the representation of X under $\mathbb{Q}_{T_k}$ given via (13.9) and (13.10) which leads to

$$dG(t, T_k, x) = G(t-, T_k, x)\left(\left(a(t, T_k, x) + \frac{1}{2}\|b(t, T_k, x)\|^2 + \langle b(t, T_k, x), \alpha(t, T_k)\rangle\right)dt\right.$$

$$+ b(t, T_k, x)dW_t^{T_k}$$

$$+ \int_{\mathcal{I}}\left(e^{c(t,T_k,x;y)} - 1\right)F_t^{L,T_k}(dy)dt$$

$$+ \int_{\mathcal{I}}\left(e^{c(t,T_k,x;y)} - 1\right)(\mu^L - \nu^{L,T_k})(dt, dy)$$

$$+ \int_{\mathbb{R}^d}(e^{\langle b(t,T_k,x),\tilde{x}\rangle} - 1)(\mu - \nu^{T_k})(dt, d\tilde{x})$$

$$\left.+ \int_{\mathbb{R}^d}\left(e^{\langle b(t,T_k,x),\tilde{x}\rangle} - 1 - \langle b(t, T_k, x), \tilde{x}\rangle\right)\beta^{-1}(t, T_k, \tilde{x})F_t^{T_k}(d\tilde{x})dt\right). \quad (13.14)$$

Finally, the covariation between G and $\mathbf{1}_{\{L.\leq x\}}$ is given by

$$\left[G(\cdot, T_k, x), \mathbf{1}_{\{L.\leq x\}}\right]_t = \sum_{s\leq t}\Delta\mathbf{1}_{\{L_s\leq x\}}\Delta G(s, T_k, x).$$

Since $\mathbf{1}_{\{L.\leq x\}}$ drops from 1 to 0 as L crosses the barrier x,

$$\Delta\mathbf{1}_{\{L_s\leq x\}} = -\mathbf{1}_{\{L_{s-}\leq x, L_s > x\}} = -\mathbf{1}_{\{L_{s-}\leq x, L_{s-}+\Delta L_s > x\}}$$

$$= -\int_{\mathcal{I}}\mathbf{1}_{\{L_{s-}\leq x\}}\mathbf{1}_{\{L_{s-}+y>x\}}\mu^L(\{s\}, dy).$$

Using this together with (13.14) and Assumption (**A5**) leads to

$$d\left[G(\cdot, T_k, x), \mathbf{1}_{\{L \leq x\}}\right]_t = -G(t-, T_k, x) \int_{\mathcal{I}} \mathbf{1}_{\{L_{t-} \leq x\}} \mathbf{1}_{\{L_{t-} + y > x\}} \left(e^{c(t, T_k, x; y)} - 1\right) \mu^L(dt, dy).$$

Collecting all the summands we obtain the desired result.   □

13.4 AN AFFINE SPECIFICATION

Up to now, the presented framework was very general. In this section, an affine factor model is studied in more detail. Affine factor models are a subclass of Markovian factor models which are used frequently in practice because of their high degree of tractability. The following section on calibration will show that a simple two-factor affine model provides an excellent fit to market data.

For simplicity, we study affine diffusion models only, i.e. affine models driven by a Brownian motion. The extension to Lévy processes as drivers can be done following the path laid out here. Consider a d-dimensional Brownian motion W and let μ and σ be functions from $\mathcal{Z}$ to $\mathbb{R}^d$ and $\mathbb{R}^{d \times d}$ satisfying

$$\mu(z) = \mu_0 + \sum_{i=1}^{d} \mu_i \, z_i, \quad \frac{1}{2}\sigma(z)^\top \sigma(z) = v_0 + \sum_{i=1}^{d} v_i \, z_i$$

for some vectors $\mu_i \in \mathbb{R}^d$ and matrices $v_i \in \mathbb{R}^{d \times d}$, $i = 0, \ldots, d$. Note that because of $\sigma(z)^\top \sigma(z)$ also v_i, $i = 0, \ldots, d$ are symmetric matrices. We assume that for any $z \in \mathcal{Z}$, $Z = Z^z$ is the continuous, unique strong solution of

$$dZ_t = \mu(Z_t)dt + \sigma(Z_t)^\top dW_t, \quad Z_0 = z \in \mathcal{Z}.$$

We specify G in the following variant of an affine specification. Let

$$G(t, T_k, x) = \exp\left(A(t, T_k, x) + B(t, T_k, x)^\top Z_t + \int_0^t \int_{\mathcal{I}} c(s, T_k, x, L_{s-}; y)\mu^L(ds, dy) \right.$$
$$\left. + \int_0^t d(s, T_k, x, L_{s-}, Z_s)ds \right), \tag{13.15}$$

for $t \leq T_k$. Here A, B, c and d are deterministic functions which have to be specified in an appropriate way to guarantee absence of arbitrage. Note that while G has an (exponential)-affine dependence on Z its dependence on the loss process via the function c is much more general. It is precisely this extension of the affine framework which allows the introduction of contagion in an arbitrage-free model as we will show in the sequel.

Finally, we assume that the compensator of the loss process has the following affine structure: assume that $F_t^L(dy) = m(t, L_{t-}, Z_t, dy)$ where

$$m(t, l, z, dy) := m_0(t, l, dy) + \sum_{i=1}^{d} m_i(t, l, dy)z_i. \tag{13.16}$$

We assume that $m(t, l, z, dy)$ is a Borel measure, in particular $m(\cdot, A) \geq 0$, for every $A \in \mathcal{B}(\mathcal{I})$. This gives a restriction on m_i depending on the state space: consider, for example, the state space $\mathcal{Z} = \mathbb{R}^{d_1} \times (\mathbb{R}_{\geq 0})^{d_2}$, where $d_1 + d_2 = d$ and $d_1 > 0$. This implies that $m_1 = \cdots = m_{d_1} \equiv 0$, as otherwise m would attain negative values. We assume that $m_i(t, l, z, \mathcal{I}) < \infty$, $i = 1, \dots, d$ (finite activity).

All appearing functions are assumed to be càdlàg in each variable. Furthermore we assume a flat interest rate structure, i.e. $P(t, T_k) = 1$ for all $0 \leq t \leq T_k$, so that the $\mathbb{Q}_{T_k}$-forward measures coincide. This can be extended in a straightforward manner to the setup where risk-free bond prices are independent of X and L, as we only use the fact that the semimartingale characteristics of the driving processes coincide under all forward measures.

Proposition 13.4.1   *Assume G is given by (13.15). Moreover, assume that*

$$d(t, T_k, x, l, z) = d_0(t, T_k, x, l) + \sum_{i=1}^{d} d_i(t, T_k, x, l)z_i$$

and

$$d_i(t, T_k, x, l) = m_i(t, l, \mathcal{I}) - \int_{\mathcal{I}} e^{c(t, T_k, x, l; y)} \mathbf{1}_{\{y \leq x - l\}} m_i(t, l, dy), \qquad (13.17)$$

$i = 0, \dots, d$. *If A and B satisfy the following system of differential equations*

$$-\partial_t A(t, T_k, x) = B(t, T_k, x)^\top \mu_0 + \frac{1}{2} B(t, T_k, x)^\top v_0 B(t, T_k, x) \qquad (13.18)$$

$$-\partial_t B(t, T_k, x)_j = B(t, T_k, x)^\top \mu_j + \frac{1}{2} B(t, T_k, x)^\top v_j B(t, T_k, x) \qquad (13.19)$$

then the model given by (13.5) is free of arbitrage.

Proof   In order to verify absence of arbitrage we analyze the drift condition (13.12). As in the proof of Theorem 13.3.1 we obtain the dynamics of the forward rates

$$\frac{dF(t, T_k, x)}{F(t-, T_k, x)} = \left(-\lambda(t, x) + D(t, T_k, x) + \int_{\mathcal{I}} \left(e^{c(t, T_k, x, L_{t-}; y)} - 1 \right) F_t^L(dy) \right) dt$$

$$- \int_{\mathcal{I}} \left(e^{c(t, T_k, x, L_{t-}; y)} - 1 \right) \mathbf{1}_{\{L_{t-} + y > x\}} F_t^L(dy) dt + d\tilde{M}_t$$

where $D(t, T_k, x)$ is given by

$$D(t, T_k, x) = \partial_t A(t, T_k, x) + \partial_t B(t, T_k, x)Z_t$$

$$+ \langle B(t, T_k, x), \mu(Z_t) \rangle + \frac{1}{2} \| B(t, T_k, x)\sigma(Z_t) \|^2 + d(t, T_k, x, L_{t-}, Z_t)$$

and $\tilde{M}$ is a local martingale. In order to ensure absence of arbitrage, the forward price processes need to be local martingales and hence the drift terms need to vanish. Note that

$$\lambda(t, x) - \int_{\mathcal{I}} \left(e^{c(t, T_k, x, L_{t-}; y)} - 1 \right) \mathbf{1}_{\{y \leq x - L_{t-}\}} F_t^L(dy)$$

$$= \lambda(t, 0) - \sum_{i=0}^{d} (Z_t)_i \int_{\mathcal{I}} e^{c(t, T_k, x, L_{t-}; y)} \mathbf{1}_{\{y \leq x - L_{t-}\}} m_i(t, L_{t-}, dy)$$

$$= -\sum_{i=0}^{d} (Z_t)_i \left(\int_{\mathcal{I}} e^{c(t, T_k, x, L_{t-}; y)} \mathbf{1}_{\{y \leq x - L_{t-}\}} - 1 \right) m_i(t, L_{t-}, dy) \qquad (13.20)$$

where we set $(Z_t)_0 := 1$ to simplify the notation. In the following we consider the drift for all possible values $L_{t-} = l \in \mathcal{I}$ and $Z_t = z \in \mathcal{Z}$. Observe that (13.20) at values $L_{t-} = l$ and $Z_t = z$ reads

$$-\sum_{i=0}^{d} z_i \left(\int_{\mathcal{I}} e^{c(t,T_k,x,l;y)} \mathbf{1}_{\{y \leq x-l\}} m_i(t,l,dy) - m_i(t,l,\mathcal{I}) \right) = \sum_{i=0}^{d} z_i d_i(t,T_k,x,l),$$

where the equality is implied by assumption (13.17). On the other hand, the remaining terms of $D(t,T_k,x)$, considered at values $L_{t-} = l$ and $Z_t = z$ are given by

$$\partial_t A(t,T_k,x) + \partial_t B(t,T_k,x)^\top z + \sum_{i=0}^{d} B(t,T_k,x)^\top \mu_i z_i$$

$$+ \frac{1}{2} \sum_{i=0}^{d} z_i B(t,T_k,x)^\top v_i B(t,T_k,x).$$

Observe that this sum is zero if the following two equations are satisfied:

$$-\partial_t A(t,T_k,x) = B(t,T_k,x)^\top \mu_0 + \frac{1}{2} B(t,T_k,x)^\top v_0 B(t,T_k,x)$$

$$-\partial_t B(t,T_k,x)_i = B(t,T_k,x)^\top \mu_i + \frac{1}{2} B(t,T_k,x)^\top v_i B(t,T_k,x),$$

and hence, the drift term in the dynamics of the forward price vanishes.   □

It is important to note that, in the spirit of the market model approach, we do not have to satisfy boundary conditions for the Riccati equations. Of course one typically would nevertheless choose $B(T_k,T_k,x)_i = A(T_k,T_k,x) = 0$.

13.5 PRICING

The aim of this section is to discuss the pricing of credit portfolio derivatives in the market model framework. A single tranche CDO (STCDO) is a typical example of such a derivative and it is a standard market instrument for investment in a pool of credits. For a detailed overview on credit portfolio risk tranching we refer to Chapter 3 of this book.

We consider here a STCDO which is specified as follows: $0 < T_1 < \cdots < \cdots T_m$ denotes a collection of future payment dates and $x_1 < x_2$ in $[0,1]$ are called lower and upper detachment points. The fixed spread is denoted by S. An investor in the STCDO receives premium payments in exchange for payments at defaults: the *premium leg* consists of a series of payments equal to

$$S[(x_2 - L_{T_k})^+ - (x_1 - L_{T_k})^+] =: Sf(L_{T_k}), \tag{13.21}$$

received at T_k, $k = 1, \ldots, m-1$. The function f is defined by

$$f(x) := (x_2 - x)^+ - (x_1 - x)^+ = \int_{x_1}^{x_2} \mathbf{1}_{\{x \leq y\}} dy. \tag{13.22}$$

The *default leg* consists of a series of payments at tenor dates T_{k+1}, $k = 1, \ldots, m-1$, given by

$$f(L_{T_k}) - f(L_{T_{k+1}}). \tag{13.23}$$

This payment is non-zero only if $\Delta L_t \neq 0$ for some $t \in (T_k, T_{k+1}]$. For alternative payment schemes we refer to Filipović et al. (2011). Note that

$$(13.23) = \int_{x_1}^{x_2} \left[\mathbf{1}_{\{L_{T_k} \leq y\}} - \mathbf{1}_{\{L_{T_{k+1}} \leq y\}} \right] dy = \int_{x_1}^{x_2} \mathbf{1}_{\{L_{T_k} \leq y, L_{T_{k+1}} > y\}} dy.$$

Similarly to Eberlein et al. (2012, Section 8.1), it is convenient to replace the forward measures $\mathbb{Q}_{T_k}$ by (T_k, x)-forward measures defined below. In order to do so, we assume henceforth that the processes $(F(t, T_k, x))_{0 \leq t \leq T_{k-1}}$, are *true* $\mathbb{Q}_{T_k}$-martingales for every $k = 2, \ldots, n$ and $x \in \mathcal{I}$. Moreover, $(F(t, T_1, x))_{0 \leq t \leq T_1}$ is a *true* $\mathbb{Q}_{T_1}$-martingale. For $x \in [0, 1]$ and $k \in \{1, \ldots, m-1\}$, the (T_k, x)-*forward measure* $\mathbb{Q}_{T_k,x}$ on $(\Omega, \mathcal{G}_{T_k})$ is defined by its Radon–Nikodym derivative

$$\frac{d\mathbb{Q}_{T_k,x}}{d\mathbb{Q}_{T_k}} := \frac{F(T_{k-1}, T_k, x)}{\mathbb{E}_{\mathbb{Q}_{T_k}}[F(T_{k-1}, T_k, x)]} = \frac{F(T_{k-1}, T_k, x)}{F(0, T_k, x)}$$

and the corresponding density process is given by

$$\left. \frac{d\mathbb{Q}_{T_k,x}}{d\mathbb{Q}_{T_k}} \right|_{\mathcal{G}_t} = \frac{F(t, T_k, x)}{F(0, T_k, x)}.$$

Note that $\mathbb{Q}_{T_k,x}$ is not equivalent to $\mathbb{Q}_{T_k}$ if $\mathbb{Q}_{T_k}(L_{T_{k-1}} > x) > 0$, but it is absolutely continuous with respect to $\mathbb{Q}_{T_k}$. Similar measure changes – yielding so-called defaultable forward measures – have been introduced and applied in the pricing of credit derivatives in Schönbucher (2000) and Eberlein et al. (2006).

Proposition 13.5.1 *The value of the STCDO at time $t \leq T_1$ is*

$$\pi^{STCDO}(t, S) = \int_{x_1}^{x_2} \left(\sum_{k=1}^{m} c_k P(t, T_k, y) - \sum_{k=1}^{m-1} P(t, T_{k+1}, y) v(t, T_{k+1}, y) \right) dy, \tag{13.24}$$

where $c_1 = S$, $c_k = 1 + S$, for $2 \leq k \leq m - 1$, $c_m = 1$ and

$$v(t, T_{k+1}, y) := \mathbb{E}_{\mathbb{Q}_{T_{k+1},y}} \left(G(T_k, T_{k+1}, y)^{-1} | \mathcal{G}_t \right)$$

with $G(\cdot, T_{k+1}, x)$ specified in (13.6). The STCDO spread S_t^* at time t, i.e. the spread which makes the value of the STCDO at time t equal to zero, is given by

$$S_t^* = \frac{\displaystyle\sum_{k=1}^{m-1} \int_{x_1}^{x_2} P(t, T_{k+1}, y) (v(t, T_{k+1}, y) - 1) \, dy}{\displaystyle\sum_{k=1}^{m-1} \int_{x_1}^{x_2} P(t, T_k, y) dy}. \tag{13.25}$$

Proof   The premium $Sf(L_{T_k})$ is paid at tenor dates $T_1, \ldots, T_{m-1}$ and thus the value of the premium leg at time t equals

$$\sum_{k=1}^{m-1} P(t, T_k) \mathbb{E}_{\mathbb{Q}_{T_k}}(Sf(L_{T_k})|\mathcal{G}_t) = \sum_{k=1}^{m-1} SP(t, T_k) \int_{x_1}^{x_2} \mathbb{E}_{\mathbb{Q}_{T_k}}(\mathbf{1}_{\{L_{T_k} \leq y\}}|\mathcal{G}_t)dy$$

$$= S \sum_{k=1}^{m-1} \int_{x_1}^{x_2} P(t, T_k, y)dy,$$

where we have used

$$P(t, T_{k+1}, y) = P(t, T_{k+1}) \mathbb{E}_{\mathbb{Q}_{T_{k+1}}} \left(\mathbf{1}_{\{L_{T_{k+1}} \leq y\}}|\mathcal{G}_t\right)$$

for the last equality.

The default payments are given by $f(L_{T_k}) - f(L_{T_{k+1}})$ at tenor dates $T_{k+1}, k = 1, \ldots, m-1$. For each k the value at time t of this payment is

$$P(t, T_{k+1}) \mathbb{E}_{\mathbb{Q}_{T_{k+1}}}(f(L_{T_k}) - f(L_{T_{k+1}})|\mathcal{G}_t)$$

$$= P(t, T_{k+1}) \mathbb{E}_{\mathbb{Q}_{T_{k+1}}} \left(\int_{x_1}^{x_2} \left(\mathbf{1}_{\{L_{T_k} \leq y\}} - \mathbf{1}_{\{L_{T_{k+1}} \leq y\}}\right) dy \, \Big| \, \mathcal{G}_t\right)$$

$$= \int_{x_1}^{x_2} P(t, T_{k+1}) \mathbb{E}_{\mathbb{Q}_{T_{k+1}}} \left(\mathbf{1}_{\{L_{T_k} \leq y\}} - \mathbf{1}_{\{L_{T_{k+1}} \leq y\}} \, \Big| \, \mathcal{G}_t\right) dy$$

$$= \int_{x_1}^{x_2} \left(P(t, T_{k+1}) \mathbb{E}_{\mathbb{Q}_{T_{k+1}}} \left(\mathbf{1}_{\{L_{T_k} \leq y\}} \, \Big| \, \mathcal{G}_t\right) - P(t, T_{k+1}, y)\right) dy. \qquad (13.26)$$

It remains to calculate the conditional expectation $\mathbb{E}_{\mathbb{Q}_{T_{k+1}}}\left(\mathbf{1}_{\{L_{T_k} \leq y\}} \, \big| \, \mathcal{G}_t\right)$. We have

$$\mathbb{E}_{\mathbb{Q}_{T_{k+1}}}\left(\mathbf{1}_{\{L_{T_k} \leq y\}}|\mathcal{G}_t\right)$$

$$= \mathbb{E}_{\mathbb{Q}_{T_{k+1}}}\left(\mathbf{1}_{\{L_{T_k} \leq y\}} G(T_k, T_{k+1}, y) G(T_k, T_{k+1}, y)^{-1}\Big|\mathcal{G}_t\right)$$

$$= \mathbb{E}_{\mathbb{Q}_{T_{k+1}}}\left(F(T_k, T_{k+1}, y) G(T_k, T_{k+1}, y)^{-1}\Big|\mathcal{G}_t\right)$$

$$= F(t, T_{k+1}, y) \mathbb{E}_{\mathbb{Q}_{T_{k+1},y}}\left(G(T_k, T_{k+1}, y)^{-1}\Big|\mathcal{G}_t\right),$$

where the last equality follows by changing the measure to $\mathbb{Q}_{T_{k+1},y}$. Denoting

$$v(t, T_{k+1}, y) := \mathbb{E}_{\mathbb{Q}_{T_{k+1},y}}\left(G(T_k, T_{k+1}, y)^{-1}\Big|\mathcal{G}_t\right),$$

the value of the default leg at time t is given by

$$\sum_{k=1}^{m-1} \int_{x_1}^{x_2} (P(t, T_{k+1}, y)v(t, T_{k+1}, y) - P(t, T_{k+1}, y)) dy.$$

Finally, the value of the STCDO is the difference of the time-t values of the payment leg and of the default leg. Thus we obtain (13.24). Solving $\pi^{STCDO}(t, S) = 0$ in S yields the spread S_t^*.   □

In Section 13.4 the constant risk-free term structure assumption is imposed, i.e. it is assumed $P(t, T_k) = 1$, for every T_k and $t \le T_k$. In this case the previous result takes the following form.

Corollary 13.5.1 *Under the constant risk-free term structure assumption, the value at time $t \le T_1$ of the STCDO is given by*

$$\pi^{STCDO}(t, S) = \int_{x_1}^{x_2} \left(\sum_{k=1}^{m-1} S F(t, T_k, y) + F(t, T_m, y) - F(t, T_1, y) \right) dy. \quad (13.27)$$

The STCDO spread S_t^* at time t is equal to

$$S_t^* = \frac{\displaystyle\int_{x_1}^{x_2} (F(t, T_1, y) - F(t, T_m, y)) dy}{\displaystyle\sum_{k=1}^{m-1} \int_{x_1}^{x_2} F(t, T_k, y) dy}.$$

Proof The result follows by inspection of the previous proof whilst noting that

$$\mathbb{E}_{\mathbb{Q}_{T_{k+1}}} \left(1_{\{L_{T_k} \le y\}} | \mathcal{G}_t \right) = \mathbb{E}_{\mathbb{Q}^*} \left(1_{\{L_{T_k} \le y\}} | \mathcal{G}_t \right) = P(t, T_k, y) = F(t, T_k, y),$$

since $P(t, T_k) = 1$ and all forward measures coincide. Hence,

$$v(t, T_{k+1}, y) = \frac{F(t, T_k, y)}{F(t, T_{k+1}, y)}$$

and the corollary is proved.   □

We conclude this section by studying an option on the STCDO defined above. This option gives the right to enter into such a contract at time T_1 at a pre-specified spread S. Its payoff is given by

$$\left(\pi^{STCDO}(T_1, S) \right)^+$$

at T_1.

The assumption of the constant risk-free term structure is still in force. We further assume $G(0, T_k, y)$, $a(t, T_k, y)$, $b(t, T_k, y)$ and $c(t, T_k, y; z)$ are constant in y between x_1 and x_2. For simplicity we denote $a(t, T_k, y) = a(t, T_k, x_1)$ by $a(t, T_k)$ and similarly for the other quantities.

Proposition 13.5.2 *The value of the option at time $t \le T_1$, denoted by $\pi^{call}(t, S)$, is*

$$\pi^{call}(t, S) = \mathbb{E}_{\mathbb{Q}^*} \left(f(L_{T_1}) \left(\tilde{d}_1 + \sum_{k=2}^{m} \tilde{d}_k \exp \left(\int_0^{T_1} a(t, T_k) dt \right. \right. \right.$$

$$\left. \left. \left. + \int_0^{T_1} b(t, T_k) dX_t + \int_0^{T_1} \int_{\mathcal{I}} c(t, T_k; z) \mu^L(dt, dz) \right) \right)^+ \middle| \mathcal{G}_t \right),$$

where $\tilde{d}_1 = (S-1)G(0, T_1)$, $\tilde{d}_k = SG(0, T_k)$, for $2 \leq k \leq m-1$, and $\tilde{d}_m = G(0, T_m)$. If in addition X, $a(\cdot, T_k)$ and $b(\cdot, T_k)$ are conditionally independent of L given $\mathcal{G}_t$, then

$$\pi^{call}(t, S) = \mathbb{E}_{\mathbb{Q}^*}\left(f(L_{T_1})\right) \mathbb{E}_{\mathbb{Q}^*}\left(\left(\tilde{d}_1 + \sum_{k=2}^{m} \tilde{d}_k \exp\left(\int_0^{T_1} a(t, T_k)dt\right.\right.\right.$$
$$\left.\left.\left. + \int_0^{T_1} b(t, T_k)dX_t + \int_0^{T_1}\int_{\mathcal{I}} c(t, T_k; z)\mu^L(dt, dz)\right)\right)^+ \Big| \mathcal{G}_t\right),$$

where

$$\mathbb{E}_{\mathbb{Q}^*}\left(f(L_{T_1})|\mathcal{G}_t\right) = x_2 \mathbb{Q}^*\left(L_{T_1} \leq x_2|\mathcal{G}_t\right) - x_1 \mathbb{Q}^*\left(L_{T_1} \leq x_1|\mathcal{G}_t\right)$$
$$- \mathbb{E}_{\mathbb{Q}^*}\left(L_{T_1}\mathbf{1}_{\{x_1 < L_{T_1} \leq x_2\}}|\mathcal{G}_t\right).$$

Proof The value of the option at time $t \leq T_1$ is given by the conditional expectation

$$\pi^{call}(t, S) = \mathbb{E}_{\mathbb{Q}^*}\left(\left(\pi^{STCDO}(T_1, S)\right)^+ | \mathcal{G}_t\right)$$
$$= \mathbb{E}_{\mathbb{Q}^*}\left(\left(\int_{x_1}^{x_2}\left(\sum_{k=1}^{m-1} SF(T_1, T_k, y) + F(T_1, T_m, y) - F(T_1, T_1, y)\right)dy\right)^+ \Big| \mathcal{G}_t\right),$$

where we have used Corollary 13.5.1. Now the result follows by inserting (13.5) and (13.6). The second result is obvious by conditional independence and definition of f. $\qquad\square$

13.6 CALIBRATION

This section is devoted to the detailed description of the calibration of a two-factor affine diffusion model. The method which turned out to provide the best results utilizes the EM-algorithm together with an unscented Kalman filter. In contrast to typical calibration approaches, where the models are fit to one or two single days (see Cont et al. (2010) for overview and comparison), we calibrate the model to the full observation period which encompasses four years of observed data from the iTraxx Europe. The model is able to provide a very good fit throughout all tranches and maturities. In the calibration methodology we follow the scheme suggested in Eksi and Filipović (2012). As discussed previously, the considered affine market model includes a direct contagion effect which improves the calibration results.

The data consists of implied *zero-coupon spreads* of the iTraxx Europe from 30 August 2006 to 3 August 2010. In contrast to Eberlein et al. (2012) we also incorporate data from 2006 and 2007, which are characterized by steady spread movements at an extremely low level. It will turn out that the fit to this time period is not as good as the fit to the more volatile period starting in the year 2008. This suggests a structural break starting from the credit crisis, which is very reasonable.

The implied zero-coupon spreads are observed at detachment points $\{x_1, \ldots, x_J\}$ which equal $\{0, 0.03, 0.06, 0.09, 0.12, 0.22, 1\}$. They are obtained by computing the spread of quoted STCDO premiums over the risk-free interest yield over the same period, in our notation

Figure 13.1 The iTraxx Europe zero-coupon index spread for the period August 2006 to August 2010. The different graphs refer to the time to maturity of 3, 5, 7 and 10 years.

given by

$$R(t, \tau, j) := -\frac{1}{\tau} \log \left(\frac{1}{x_{j+1} - x_j} \int_{x_j}^{x_{j+1}} F(t, t + \tau, x) dx \right). \tag{13.28}$$

Here $\tau := T - t$ denotes time to maturity and the observed values are $\{3, 5, 7, 10\}$. It is important to remark that there was no default in the underlying pool in the observation period. The realized index spreads are shown in Figure 13.1. With the beginning of the credit crisis volatility, as well as levels of credit spreads, rose to levels never seen before. After a period of stabilization, from early 2010 onwards the spread levels started again to rise to higher levels as the European debt crises evolved. This heterogeneous data set makes the calibration very difficult.

Figure 13.2 shows STCDOs spread premiums over different maturities and tranches. It is remarkable that curves for different maturities look quite similar, which makes it plausible to capture the observed dynamics with a low number of factors. The principal component analysis performed in Eksi and Filipović (2012) reveals that two factors already explain 88.3% of the realized variance and we therefore consider a two-factor affine model.

More precisely, we consider the following two-dimensional affine diffusion Z with values in the state space $\mathcal{Z} := \mathbb{R}^+ \times \mathbb{R}^+$. We assume that Z solves the SDEs

$$dZ_t^1 = \kappa_1 \left(Z_t^2 - Z_t^1 \right) dt + \sigma_1 \sqrt{Z_t^1} dW_t^1 \tag{13.29}$$

$$dZ_t^2 = \kappa_2 \left(\theta_2 - Z_t^2 \right) dt + \sigma_2 \sqrt{Z_t^2} dW_t^2, \tag{13.30}$$

with $Z_0 = (z_1, z_2)^\top \in \mathcal{Z}$. Here $\kappa_1, \kappa_2, \theta_2, \sigma_1, \sigma_2$ are positive constants and W^1 and W^2 are two independent standard Brownian motions under the objective probability measure $\mathbb{P}$. In this formulation, Z^2 is a Feller square-root process and Z^1 is a non-negative process with stochastic mean reversion level Z^2. Then, (Z^1, Z^2) is a time-homogeneous process. As a consequence, the functions A and B given in equations (13.18) and (13.19), respectively, do not depend on t and T, but on the difference $T - t$ only. In the following we write $A(t, T, x) = A(T - t, x)$ and $B(t, T, x) = B(T - t, x)$.

Pricing is done under a risk-neutral measure $\mathbb{Q}^*$ and we chose a class of equivalent measures which preserve the affine structure of Z. This is done by considering the market prices of risk

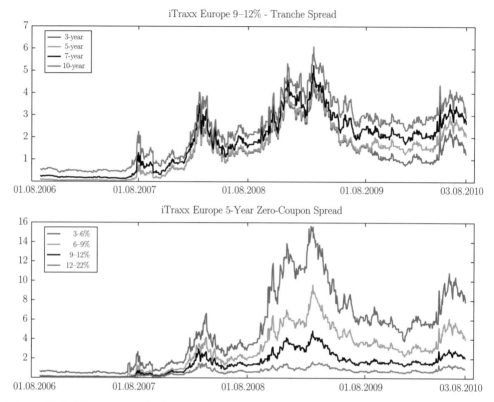

Figure 13.2   The upper graph shows the iTraxx Europe 9–12% tranche spread from August 2006 to August 2010 for different maturities. The lower graph illustrates the iTraxx Europe tranche spreads from August 2006 to August 2010 for a fixed maturity of five years.

λ^1 and λ^2, given by

$$\lambda_t^i = \frac{\lambda_i \sqrt{Z_t^i}}{\sigma_i},$$

with some constants $\lambda_1, \lambda_2 \in \mathbb{R}$. Applying Girsanov's theorem, we change to the equivalent probability measure $\mathbb{Q}^*$ where $\tilde{W}_t^i = W_t^i + \int_0^t \lambda_s^i ds$, $i = 1, 2$ are independent standard $\mathbb{Q}^*$-Brownian motions. Then, under $\mathbb{Q}^*$, Z is again affine and satisfies the following SDEs; see Cheridito et al. (2010):

$$dZ_t^1 = (\kappa_1 + \lambda_1)\left(\frac{\kappa_1}{\kappa_1 + \lambda_1}Z_t^2 - Z_t^1\right)dt + \sigma_1\sqrt{Z_t^1}d\tilde{W}_t^1, \tag{13.31}$$

$$dZ_t^2 = (\kappa_2 + \lambda_2)\left(\frac{\kappa_2}{\kappa_2 + \lambda_2}\theta_2 - Z_t^2\right)dt + \sigma_2\sqrt{Z_t^2}d\tilde{W}_t^2. \tag{13.32}$$

This is the starting point to apply the results from Section 13.4. Additionally to the factor process, we need to specify the compensator of the loss process. We chose the following affine specification

$$m(t, l, z, dy) = m_0(t, l, dy) + m_1(t, l, dy)z_1,$$

where the jump distributions $m_i(t, l, \cdot)$ are chosen from the Beta family. This in turn gives

$$m(t, l, z, dy) = \frac{1}{B(a_1, b_1)} y^{a_1-1}(1-y)^{b_1-1}dy + \frac{z_1}{B(a_2, b_2)} y^{a_2-1}(1-y)^{b_2-1}dy,$$

where all coefficients are positive. Finally, the contagion term is assumed to be linear in the loss level, i.e.

$$c(t, T_k, x, L_{t-}; y) = cy(T_k - t). \tag{13.33}$$

One reason for this choice is that due to a lack of defaults in the observation period, a precise estimation of a non-linear relation does not seem reasonable. Finally, we consider F as in (13.5) and G as in (13.15). Together with (13.18) and (13.19) this yields an arbitrage-free model.

13.6.1   Calibration Procedure

For the calibration of the model we follow the ideas in Eksi and Filipović (2012) and utilize the EM-algorithm together with Kalman filter techniques for the estimation of the (unobserved) factor process Z from the observed STCDO prices.

For the calibration procedure itself we make the following two assumptions: firstly, we assume that tranche spreads are piecewise constant between the detachment points, i.e.

$$G(t, T_k, x) = G(t, T_k, x_{i+1}), \quad \text{for } x \in [x_i, x_{i+1}). \tag{13.34}$$

As previously, $F(t, T_k, x) = 1_{\{L_t \leq x\}} G(t, T_k, x)$. Secondly, we assume that observed prices are model prices plus an additive measurement error. More precisely, we consider observation times $0 = t_0, t_1, t_2, \ldots$ and assume that

$$R(t_k, \tau, j) = -\frac{1}{\tau} \log \left(\frac{1}{x_{j+1} - x_j} \int_{x_j}^{x_{j+1}} F(t_k, t_k + \tau, x) \, dx \right) + \varepsilon(k, \tau, j + 1)$$

The error terms $\varepsilon(k, \tau, j)$ are assumed to be independent and normally distributed random variables with zero mean and tranche dependent variance σ_j^2. Moreover, they are independent of Z and L.

Considering equation (13.18), our two-factor affine specification (13.31) and (13.32) yields that $v_0 = 0$ as well as $\mu_0 = (0, \kappa_2\theta_2)^\top$. Letting $\tau = T_k - t$ we obtain

$$A(\tau, x) = \kappa_2\theta_2 \int_0^\tau B(s, x)_1 ds + \int_0^\tau C_0(s, x; l) ds - \tau.$$

Integrating this term w.r.t. x gives, using (13.34), that

$$\int_{x_j}^{x_{j+1}} e^{A(\tau, x)} dx = e^{\kappa_2\theta_2 \int_0^\tau B(s, x_{j+1})_1 ds - \tau} \cdot \int_{x_j}^{x_{j+1}} e^{\int_0^\tau C_0(s, x; l) ds} dx.$$

We obtain the following representation for the observed spreads:

$$R(t_k, \tau, j) = \frac{1}{\tau} \log(x_{j+1} - x_j) - \frac{1}{\tau} \kappa_2 \theta_2 \int_0^\tau B(s, x_{j+1})_1 ds + 1 - \frac{1}{\tau} B(\tau, x_{j+1})^\top Z_t$$

$$- \frac{1}{\tau} \log \left(\int_{x_j}^{x_{j+1}} e^{\int_0^\tau C_0(s, x; l) ds} \, dx \right) + \varepsilon(t_k, \tau, j)$$

$$=: K(\tau, x_{j+1}) - \frac{1}{\tau} B(\tau, x_{j+1})^\top Z_t + \varepsilon(t_k, \tau, j) \tag{13.35}$$

for all tranches $j \in \{1, \ldots, J-1\}$ and maturities $\tau \in \{3, 5, 7, 10\}$. As R is a linear function of Z, it may be represented by

$$R_{t_k} := (R(t_k, \tau_1, 1), \ldots, R(t_k, \tau_4, J-1))^\top = f(Z_{t_k}) + \epsilon_k$$

with error vector $\epsilon_k := (\epsilon(t_k, \tau_1, 1), \ldots, \epsilon(t_k, \tau_4, J-1))^\top$.

Following the quasi-maximum likelihood procedure, we approximate the transition density of this equation by a normal density where we match the first and the second conditional moments. Taking into account the dependence structure of the process, we approximate the conditional distribution of Z_{t_k} given $Z_{t_{k-1}}$ by a normal distribution with mean $g(Z_{t_{k-1}})$ and covariance matrix Q_{k-1}. The computations of g and Q are relegated to the appendix, see Proposition A.1. Essentially, the affine structure allows to derive the conditional Fourier transform in tractable form which gives the conditional moments.

The EM-algorithm basically requires two iterative steps, namely filtering (expectation step) and the maximization of the likelihood (maximization step). The most difficult step in our setup is the expectation step which we approach with an extended Kalman filter.

The linearity of the functions $f(z) =: f_0 + f_1^\top z$ and $g(z) = g_0 + g_1^\top z$ makes it straightforward to compute the moments required for the Kalman filter as we show now. Let $\mathcal{F}_t^R := \sigma(R_s : s \leq t)$. Denote $\mathbf{m}_k := \mathbb{E}(Z_{t_k} | \mathcal{F}_{t_k}^R)$ and $\mathbf{m}_k^- := \mathbb{E}(Z_{t_k} | \mathcal{F}_{t_{k-1}}^R)$. Analogously, denote by $\mathbf{P}_k$ and $\mathbf{P}_k^-$ the conditional variance of Z_{t_k} given $\mathcal{F}_{t_k}^R$ and $\mathcal{F}_{t_{k-1}}^R$, respectively.

In the *prediction step*, we compute $\mathbf{m}_k^-$ and $\mathbf{P}_k^-$ which gives

$$\mathbf{m}_k^- = \mathbb{E}(Z_{t_k} | \mathcal{F}_{t_{k-1}}^R) = f_0 + f_1^\top \mathbf{m}_{k-1}$$
$$\mathbf{P}_k^- = f_1 \mathbf{P}_{k-1} f_1^\top + Q_{k-1}.$$

The *updating step* incorporates the new information given by R_{t_k}. By $\mathrm{Cov}(X, Y)$ for two random vectors X and Y we denote the variance-covariance matrix and $\mathrm{Var}(X) := \mathrm{Cov}(X, X)$. We obtain

$$\mathbf{r}_k^- = \mathbb{E}\left(R_k | \mathcal{F}_{t_{k-1}}^R\right) = g(\mathbf{m}_k^-) = g_0 + g_1^\top \mathbf{m}_k^-$$
$$\mathbf{F}_k = \mathrm{Var}\left(R_k | \mathcal{F}_{t_{k-1}}^R\right) = g_1 \mathbf{P}_k^- g_1^\top + \Sigma$$
$$\mathbf{S}_k = \mathrm{Cov}\left(Z_{t_k}, R_k | \mathcal{F}_{t_{k-1}}^R\right) = \mathbf{P}_k^- g_1;$$

Table 13.1   Estimated parameter values.

θ_2	κ_1	κ_2	λ_1	λ_2	σ_1^2	σ_2^2	c	a_1	b_1	a_2	b_2
1.8178	2.0639	6.6046	−0.6444	−6.7376	0.7734	0.2685	−0.0690	0.7318	6.1632	0.2938	23.1966

here Σ denotes the diagonal matrix with entries $\sigma_1^2, \ldots, \sigma_{J-1}^2$. Furthermore, we set

$$\mathbf{K}_k := \mathbf{S}_k \mathbf{F}_k^{-1}$$
$$\mathbf{m}_k := \mathbf{m}_k^- + \mathbf{K}_k (R_k - \mathbf{r}_k^-)$$
$$\mathbf{P}_k := \mathbf{P}_k^- - \mathbf{K}_k \mathbf{F}_k \mathbf{K}_k^\top.$$

Here, $\mathbf{K}_k$ is the so-called Kalman gain and $R_k - \mathbf{r}_k^-$ the innovation. For further details on Kalman filtering we refer to the book of Grewal and Andrews (1993).

To initialize the filter we use the unconditional moment and the unconditional covariance matrix given in the earlier Corollary A.1. Starting from $\xi = (\kappa_1, \kappa_2, \theta_2, \sigma_1, \sigma_2, \lambda_1, \lambda_2, c, a_1, b_1, a_2, b_2)$, an initial parameter vector, the Kalman filter computes recursively an estimation of the unobserved factor process with approximate likelihood function given by

$$L(R_1, \ldots, R_n; \xi) = -\frac{n}{2} \log 2\pi - \frac{1}{2} \sum_{k=1}^{n} \log |\mathbf{F}_k| - \frac{1}{2} \sum_{k=1}^{n} (\mathbf{r}_k^- - R_k)^\top \mathbf{F}_k^{-1} (\mathbf{r}_k^- - R_k).$$

The EM-algorithm proceeds iteratively between filtering and maximization until a prescribed precision is obtained.

13.6.2   Calibration Results

Using the calibration methodology described above we fit the model to the full data set from August 2006 to August 2010. Table 13.1 gives the parameter values obtained by the calibration.

The contagion parameter c is negative, implying that (upward) jumps in the loss process lead to downward jumps in the forward price, i.e. a loss in (T, x)-bond prices, which is very intuitive. Note that in Eksi and Filipović (2012) a two-factor affine model together with a catastrophic component was used to obtain a good fit even to super-senior spreads. The two-factor affine market model considered here, however, is able to obtain a fairly good fit without this catastrophic component. Figures 13.3 and 13.4 illustrate the results of our calibration example. As can be seen, the proposed model is able to capture the market dynamics across all tranches and maturities even though there is a structural break in the observed spread data.

Finally, it needs to be remarked, that a good fit of the calibration per se does not yet imply a good hedging performance. Therefore a detailed analysis of the model for further applications is required. Hedging in affine models can be studied along the lines of Filipović and Schmidt (2010). This, however, is beyond the scope of this chapter. Nevertheless, the hedging analysis in Eksi and Filipović (2012) suggests that affine factor models which show a good fit over a long observation period perform very well for hedging purposes.

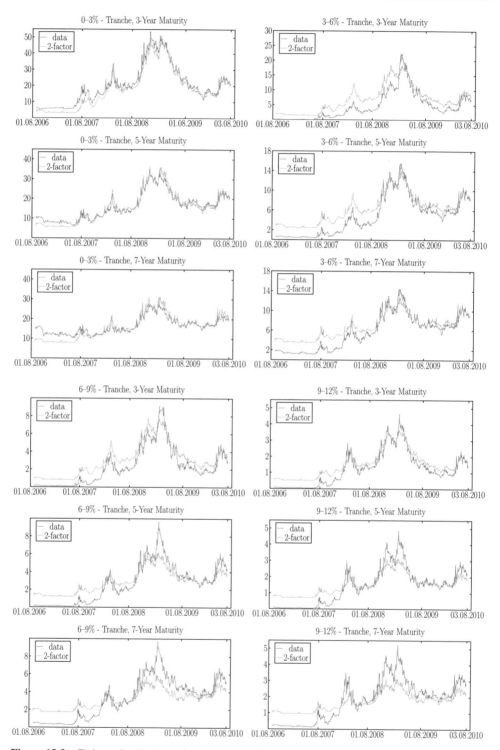

Figure 13.3   Estimated and observed spreads – part 1.

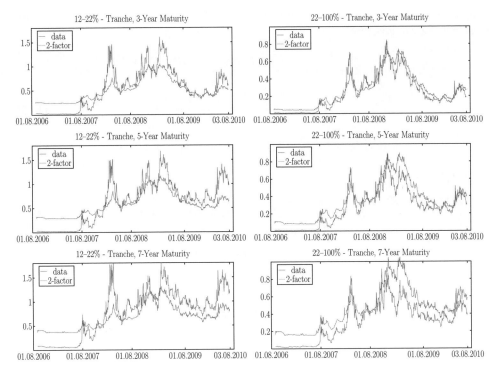

Figure 13.4   Estimated and observed spreads – part 2.

APPENDIX A: COMPUTATIONS

As shown in Keller-Ressel et al. (2011) stochastically continuous, time-homogeneous affine processes on the canonical state space are always regular. Thus, the process Z given by (13.29) and (13.30) possesses an exponentially-affine characteristic function

$$\mathbb{E}(e^{\langle u, Z_T \rangle} | \mathcal{G}_t) = \exp(\phi(T - t, u) + \psi(T - t, u)Z_t) \quad \forall t \leq T,$$

where $\phi(t, u)$, $\psi(t, u)$ are sufficiently differentiable, $\mathbb{C}$-, respectively $\mathbb{C}^d$-valued functions. The moments, as derivatives of the characteristic function evaluated at zero, are of polynomial order. We write

$$m_k(T - t, z_1, z_2) := \mathbb{E}\left((Z_T^1)^{k_1}(Z_T^2)^{k_2} | Z_t^1 = z_1, Z_t^2 = z_2\right), \quad k_1, k_2 \in \mathbb{N}, k_1 + k_2 = k,$$

for the k-th conditional moment. Observe that $m_k(\tau, z_1, z_2)$ has to be a local martingale thus an application of Itô's formula yields

$$\frac{\partial}{\partial \tau} m_k(\tau, z_1, z_2) = \kappa_1(z_2 - z_1)\frac{\partial m_k}{\partial z_1} + \kappa_2(\theta_2 - z_2)\frac{\partial m_k}{\partial z_2} + \frac{1}{2}\sigma_1^2 z_1 \frac{\partial^2 m_k}{\partial z_1^2} + \frac{1}{2}\sigma_2^2 z_2 \frac{\partial^2 m_k}{\partial z_2^2}$$

$$m_k(0, z_1, z_2) = z_1^{k_1} z_2^{k_2}.$$

Proposition A.1   *Assume Z is given by (13.29) and (13.30). Then the $\mathbb{P}$-conditional first moments of Z are given by*

$$\mathbb{E}\left(Z_t^1 | Z_0^1 = z_1, Z_0^2 = z_2\right) = -\frac{\left(-\kappa_1 + \kappa_1 e^{-\kappa_2 t} - e^{-\kappa_1 t}\kappa_2 + \kappa_2\right)\theta_2}{\kappa_1 - \kappa_2} + e^{-\kappa_1 t}z_1$$

$$-\frac{\kappa_1\left(e^{-t(\kappa_1 - \kappa_2)} - 1\right)e^{-\kappa_2 t}}{\kappa_1 - \kappa_2}z_2. \tag{13.36}$$

$$\mathbb{E}\left(Z_t^2 | Z_0^1 = z_1, Z_0^2 = z_2\right) = -\left(e^{-\kappa_2 t} - 1\right)\theta_2 + e^{-\kappa_2 t}z_2. \tag{13.37}$$

Furthermore,

$$\text{Var}\left(Z_t^1 | Z_0^1 = z_1, Z_0^2 = z_2\right) = \frac{1}{2}\frac{1}{(\kappa_1 - \kappa_2)^2 \kappa_2 \kappa_1 (2\kappa_1 - \kappa_2)(\kappa_1 + \kappa_2)}$$
$$\left(4\kappa_1^2\kappa_2\sigma_2^2(2\kappa_1 - \kappa_2)(\kappa_1 z - \theta_2\kappa_2 + \kappa_2 z)e^{-(\kappa_1 + \kappa_2)t}\right.$$
$$- \kappa_2(\kappa_1 + \kappa_2)\left(4\kappa_1^3 y\sigma_1^2 + 2\kappa_1^3 z\sigma_2^2 - 2\kappa_1^3 z\sigma_1^2 + \kappa_1^2\kappa_2\sigma_1^2\theta_2\right.$$
$$+ 4\kappa_1^2 z\kappa_2\sigma_1^2 - \kappa_1^2\kappa_2\sigma_2^2\theta_2 - 10\kappa_1^2\kappa_2 y\sigma_1^2 - 2\kappa_1 z\kappa_2^2\sigma_1^2$$
$$\left.- 2\kappa_1\kappa_2^2\sigma_1^2\theta_2 + 8\kappa_1\kappa_2^2 y\sigma_1^2 + \kappa_2^3\sigma_1^2\theta_2 - 2\kappa_2^3 y\sigma_1^2\right)e^{-2\kappa_1 t}$$
$$+ 2\kappa_1^2(\kappa_1 - \kappa_2)(\kappa_1 + \kappa_2)\left(2\kappa_2\kappa_1 + 2\sigma_2^2\kappa_1 - 2\sigma_2^2\kappa_2\right.$$
$$\left.- \kappa_2^2 + \kappa_2\sigma_1^2\right)(z - \theta_2)e^{-\kappa_2 t} + 2\kappa_2(\kappa_1 + \sigma_1^2)$$
$$(\kappa_1 - \kappa_2)(2\kappa_1 - \kappa_2)(\kappa_1 + \kappa_2)(-z\kappa_1 + y\kappa_1 + \theta_2\kappa_2 - \kappa_2 y)e^{-\kappa_1 t}$$
$$+ \theta_2(2\kappa_1 - \kappa_2)(\kappa_1 - \kappa_2)^2$$
$$\left(2\kappa_2\kappa_1^2 + \kappa_1^2\sigma_2^2 + 2\kappa_2^2\kappa_1 + \kappa_1\kappa_2\sigma_1^2 + \kappa_2^2\sigma_1^2\right)) \tag{13.38}$$

$$\text{Var}\left(Z_t^2 | Z_0^1 = z_1, Z_0^2 = z_2\right) = \frac{1}{2}\frac{1}{(\kappa_1 - \kappa_2)\kappa_2}\left(2\kappa_2(-z\kappa_1 + y\kappa_1 + \theta_2\kappa_2 - \kappa_2 y)e^{-\kappa_1 t}\right.$$
$$- \sigma_2^2(2z - \theta_2)(\kappa_1 - \kappa_2)e^{-2\kappa_2 t}$$
$$+ 2(-\theta_2 + z)\left(\sigma_2^2\kappa_1 - \sigma_2^2\kappa_2 + \kappa_2\kappa_1\right)e^{-\kappa_2 t}$$
$$\left.+ \theta_2\left(\sigma_2^2 + 2\kappa_2\right)(\kappa_1 - \kappa_2)\right) \tag{13.39}$$

$$\text{Cov}\left(Z_t^1 Z_t^2 | Z_0^1 = z_1, Z_0^2 = z_2\right) = \frac{1}{2\kappa_2\left(\kappa_1^2 - \kappa_2^2\right)}\left(2\kappa_2\sigma_2^2(\kappa_2 z - \theta_2\kappa_2 + z\kappa_1)e^{-(\kappa_1 + \kappa_2)t}\right.$$
$$- \kappa_1\sigma_2^2(2z - \theta_2)(\kappa_1 + \kappa_2)e^{-2\kappa_2 t}$$
$$+ 2(\kappa_1 + \kappa_2)\left(\sigma_2^2\kappa_1 + \kappa_2\kappa_1 - \sigma_2^2\kappa_2\right)(z - \theta_2)e^{-\kappa_2 t}$$
$$+ 2\kappa_2(\kappa_1 + \kappa_2)(-z\kappa_1 + y\kappa_1 + \theta_2\kappa_2 - \kappa_2 y)e^{-\kappa_1 t}$$
$$\left.+ \theta_2(\kappa_1 - \kappa_2)\left(2\kappa_2\kappa_1 + \sigma_2^2\kappa_1 + 2\kappa_2^2\right)\right) \tag{13.40}$$

such that the conditional covariance is given by

$$Q_{t_k} = \begin{pmatrix} \text{Var}\left(Z_{t_k}^1 | Z_{t_{k-1}}^1, Z_{t_{k-1}}^2\right) & \text{Cov}\left(Z_{t_k}^1 Z_{t_k}^2 | Z_{t_{k-1}}^1, Z_{t_{k-1}}^2\right) \\ \text{Cov}\left(Z_{t_k}^1 Z_{t_k}^2 | Z_{t_{k-1}}^1, Z_{t_{k-1}}^2\right) & \text{Var}\left(Z_{t_k}^2 | Z_{t_{k-1}}^1, Z_{t_{k-1}}^2\right) \end{pmatrix}.$$

Proof Denote $\mathbb{E}(Z_t^1 | Z_0^1 = z_1, Z_0^2 = z_2) =: h(t, z_1, z_2)$. The Kolmogorov backward equation implies that

$$\partial_t h = \kappa_1(z_2 - z_1)\partial_{z_1}h + \kappa_2(\theta_2 - z_2)\partial_{z_2}h + \frac{1}{2}\sigma_1^2 z_1 \partial_{z_1 z_1} h + \frac{1}{2}\sigma_2^2 z_2 \partial_{z_2 z_2} h.$$

Thus, inserting the polynomial property of moments yields

$$\frac{d}{dt}h_0 + \frac{d}{dt}h_{z_1}z_1 + \frac{d}{dt}h_{z_2}z_2 = \kappa_1(z_2 - z_1)h_{z_1} + \kappa_2(\theta_2 - z_2)h_{z_2}, \tag{13.41}$$

for some functions h_0, h_{z_1} and h_{z_2} which fulfill the following system of ordinary differential equations

$$\frac{d}{dt}h_0 = \kappa_2\theta_2 h_{z_2}$$

$$\frac{d}{dt}h_{z_1} = -\kappa_1 h_{z_1}$$

$$\frac{d}{dt}h_{z_2} = \kappa_1 h_{z_1} - \kappa_2 h_{z_2}$$

with respect to the boundary conditions $h_0(0) = h_{z_2}(0) = 0$, $h_{z_1}(0) = 1$. The solution to this system is given by

$$h_0(t) = -\frac{\left(-\kappa_1 + \kappa_1 e^{-\kappa_2 t} - e^{-\kappa_1 t}\kappa_2 + \kappa_2\right)\theta_2}{\kappa_1 - \kappa_2}$$

$$h_{z_1}(t) = e^{-\kappa_1 t}$$

$$h_{z_2}(t) = -\frac{\kappa_1\left(e^{-t(\kappa_1 - \kappa_2)} - 1\right)e^{-\kappa_2 t}}{\kappa_1 - \kappa_2}$$

which yields the first assertion (13.36). Regarding $\mathbb{E}(Z_t^2 | Z_0^1 = z_1, Z_0^2 = z_2) =: h(t, z_1, z_1)$, we get a system of ordinary differential equations with the modified boundary condition $h_0(0) = h_{z_1}(0) = 0$, $h_{z_2}(0) = 1$ in an analogous way. Its solution is given by

$$h_0(t) = -\left(e^{-\kappa_2 t} - 1\right)\theta_2$$

$$h_{z_1}(t) = 0$$

$$h_{z_2}(t) = e^{-\kappa_2 t}$$

which yields (13.37).

For $\mathbb{E}(Z_t^1 Z_t^2 | Z_0^1 = z_1, Z_0^2 = z_2) =: h(t, z_1, z_2)$ we consider terms of second order, i.e.

$$\frac{d}{dt}h_0 + \frac{d}{dt}h_{z_1}z_1 + \frac{d}{dt}h_{z_2}z_2 + \frac{d}{dt}h_{z_1 z_2}z_1 z_2 + \frac{d}{dt}h_{z_1^2}z_1^2 + \frac{d}{dt}h_{z_2^2}z_2^2$$

$$= \kappa_1(z_2 - z_1)(h_{z_1} + 2h_{z_1^2}z_1 + h_{z_1 z_2}z_2) + \kappa_2(\theta_2 - z_2)(h_{z_2} + h_{z_1 z_2}z_1 + 2h_{z_2^2}z_2) + \sigma_1^2 z_1 h_{z_1^2} + \sigma_2^2 z_2 h_{z_2^2}$$

for some functions $h_0 \ldots, h_{z_2^2}$ which solve following system of ordinary differential equations

$$\frac{d}{dt}h_0 = \kappa_2\theta_2 h_{z_2}$$

$$\frac{d}{dt}h_{z_1} = -\kappa_1 h_{z_1} + \kappa_2\theta_2 h_{z_1 z_2} + \sigma_1^2 h_{z_1^2}$$

$$\frac{d}{dt}h_{z_2} = \kappa_1 h_{z_1} - \kappa_2 h_{z_2} + \left(2\kappa_2\theta_2 + \sigma_2^2\right)h_{z_2^2}$$

$$\frac{d}{dt}h_{z_1 z_2} = 2\kappa_1 h_{z_1^2} - (\kappa_1 + \kappa_2)h_{z_1 z_2}$$

$$\frac{d}{dt}h_{z_1^2} = -2\kappa_1 h_{z_1^2}$$

$$\frac{d}{dt}h_{z_2^2} = \kappa_1 h_{z_1 z_2} - 2\kappa_2 h_{z_2^2}$$

with respect to the boundary condition $h_0(0) = h_{z_1}(0) = h_{z_2}(0) = h_{z_1^2}(0) = h_{z_2^2}(0) = 0$, $h_{z_1 z_2}(0) = 1$. The solution to this system is given by

$$
\begin{aligned}
h_0(t) = {} & \frac{1}{2}\frac{\theta_2 e^{-t(2\kappa_2 + \kappa_1)}}{\left(\kappa_1^2 - \kappa_2^2\right)\kappa_2}\left(e^{\kappa_1 t}\kappa_1\left(2\theta_2\kappa_2 + \sigma_2^2\right)(\kappa_1 + \kappa_2)\right.\\
& - 2e^{\kappa_1 t}\kappa_2^2\left(\theta_2\kappa_1 + \sigma_2^2 + \theta_2\kappa_2\right) + 2e^{2\kappa_2 t}\kappa_2^2\left(\theta_2 + 1\right)(\kappa_1 + \kappa_2)\\
& - \left(2\left(\kappa_1 + \kappa_2\right)\left(2\theta_2\kappa_2\kappa_1 + \kappa_2\kappa_1 + \sigma_2^2\kappa_1 - \sigma_2^2\kappa_2 - \theta_2\kappa_2^2\right)e^{(\kappa_1 + \kappa_2)t}\right.\\
& \left.+ (\kappa_1 - \kappa_2)\left(\sigma_2^2\kappa_1 + 2\kappa_2\kappa_1 + 2\theta_2\kappa_2\kappa_1 + 2\kappa_2^2 + 2\theta_2\kappa_2^2\right)e^{t(2\kappa_2 + \kappa_1)}\right)\\
h_{z_1}(t) = {} & -e^{-\kappa_1 t}\left(\theta_2 e^{-\kappa_2 t} - \theta_2 - 1\right)\\
h_{z_2}(t) = {} & -\frac{\left(2\theta_2\kappa_2\kappa_1 + \sigma_2^2\kappa_1\right)e^{-2\kappa_2 t}}{(\kappa_1 - \kappa_2)\kappa_2} - \frac{e^{-\kappa_2 t}}{(\kappa_1 - \kappa_2)\kappa_2}\left(\kappa_2\left(\theta_2\kappa_1 + \sigma_2^2 + \theta_2\kappa_2\right)e^{-\kappa_1 t}\right.\\
& \left. - \kappa_1\kappa_2\left(\theta_2 + 1\right)e^{-t(\kappa_1 - \kappa_2)} + 2\theta_2\kappa_2\kappa_1 - \kappa_2\kappa_1 - \sigma_2^2\kappa_1 + \sigma_2^2\kappa_2 + \theta_2\kappa_2^2\right)\\
h_{z_1 z_2}(t) = {} & e^{-(\kappa_1 + \kappa_2)t}\\
h_{z_1^2}(t) = {} & 0\\
h_{z_2^2}(t) = {} & \frac{\left(e^{-2\kappa_2 t} - e^{-(\kappa_1 + \kappa_2)t}\right)\kappa_1}{\kappa_1 - \kappa_2}
\end{aligned}
$$

which yields

$$\mathbb{E}(Z_t^1 Z_t^2 | Z_0^1 = z_1, Z_0^2 = z_2) = h_0(t) + h_{z_1}(t)z_1 + h_{z_2}(t)z_2 + h_{z_1 z_2}(t)z_1 z_2 + h_{z_1^2}(t)z_1^2 + h_{z_2^2}(t)z_2^2.$$

Analogously we compute $\mathbb{E}\left((Z_t^1)^2 | Z_0^1 = z_1, Z_0^2 = z_2\right) =: h(t, z_1, z_2)$ with boundary condition $h_0(0) = h_{z_1}(0) = h_{z_2}(0) = h_{z_1 z_2}(0) = h_{z_2^1}(0) = 0$, $h_{z_1^2}(0) = 1$.
The solution is given by

$$
\begin{aligned}
h_0(t) = {} & \frac{1}{2}\frac{e^{-2(\kappa_1 + \kappa_2)t}\theta_2^2}{(\kappa_1 + \kappa_2)}\left(2e^{2\kappa_2 t}\kappa_1\kappa_2^{\,3}(\kappa_1 + \kappa_2)(2\kappa_1 - \kappa_2) + 2\kappa_1^3\kappa_2(\kappa_1 + \kappa_2)(2\kappa_1 - \kappa_2)e^{2\kappa_1 t}\right.\\
& - 4\kappa_1^2\kappa_2^2(\kappa_1 + \kappa_2)(2\kappa_1 - \kappa_2)e^{(\kappa_1 + \kappa_2)t} - 4\kappa_2\kappa_1^2(\kappa_1 - \kappa_2)(2\kappa_1 - \kappa_2)(\kappa_1 + \kappa_2)e^{t(2\kappa_1 + \kappa_2)}\\
& + 4\kappa_2^2\kappa_1(\kappa_1 - \kappa_2)(2\kappa_1 - \kappa_2)(\kappa_1 + \kappa_2)e^{t(2\kappa_2 + \kappa_1)}\\
& \left. + 2\kappa_1\kappa_2(\kappa_1 + \kappa_2)(2\kappa_1 - \kappa_2)(\kappa_1 - \kappa_2)^2 e^{2(\kappa_1 + \kappa_2)t}\right)\\
& + \frac{1}{2}\frac{e^{-2(\kappa_1 + \kappa_2)t}\theta_2}{(\kappa_1 + \kappa_2)}\left(-\kappa_2^2(\kappa_1 + \kappa_2)(-\kappa_1\sigma_2 + \kappa_1\sigma_1 - \kappa_2\sigma_1)(\kappa_1\sigma_2 + \kappa_1\sigma_1 - \kappa_2\sigma_1)e^{2\kappa_2 t}\right.\\
& + \kappa_1^3\sigma_2^2(\kappa_1 + \kappa_2)(2\kappa_1 - \kappa_2)e^{2\kappa_1 t} - 4\kappa_1^2\kappa_2^2\sigma_2^2(2\kappa_1 - \kappa_2)e^{(\kappa_1 + \kappa_2)t}\\
& - 2\kappa_1^2(\kappa_1 - \kappa_2)(\kappa_1 + \kappa_2)\left(2\kappa_2\kappa_1 + 2\sigma_2^2\kappa_1 - \kappa_2^2 + \kappa_2\sigma_1^2 - 2\sigma_2^2\kappa_2\right)e^{t(2\kappa_1 + \kappa_2)}\\
& + 2\kappa_2^2\left(\kappa_1 + \sigma_1^2\right)(\kappa_1 - \kappa_2)(2\kappa_1 - \kappa_2)(\kappa_1 + \kappa_2)e^{t(2\kappa_2 + \kappa_1)}\\
& \left. + (2\kappa_1 - \kappa_2)(\kappa_1 - \kappa_2)^2\left(\kappa_1^2\sigma_2^2 + 2\kappa_2\kappa_1^2 + \kappa_2\sigma_1^2\kappa_1 + 2\kappa_2^2\kappa_1 + \kappa_2^2\sigma_1^2\right)e^{2(\kappa_1 + \kappa_2)t}\right)
\end{aligned}
$$

$$h_{z_1}(t) = \frac{\left(-\kappa_1 \sigma_1^2 + 2\theta_2 \kappa_2 \kappa_1 + \kappa_2 \sigma_1^2\right)\left(e^{-\kappa_1 t}\right)^2}{(\kappa_1 - \kappa_2)\kappa_1}$$
$$+ \frac{\left(\kappa_1^2 + 2\kappa_1^2 \theta_2 - 2\kappa_1^2 \theta_2 e^{-\kappa_2 t} - 2\theta_2 \kappa_2 \kappa_1 - \kappa_2 \kappa_1 + \kappa_1 \sigma_1^2 - \kappa_2 \sigma_1^2\right)e^{-\kappa_1 t}}{(\kappa_1 - \kappa_2)\kappa_1}$$

$$h_{z_2}(t) = \frac{e^{-\kappa_2 t}}{\kappa_2(\kappa_1 - \kappa_2)^2 (2\kappa_1 - \kappa_2)} \left(2\kappa_2 \kappa_1 (2\kappa_1 - \kappa_2)\left(\kappa_1 \theta_2 + \sigma_2^2 + \theta_2 \kappa_2\right)e^{-\kappa_1 t}\right.$$
$$- \kappa_2 \left(4\kappa_2 \kappa_1^2 \theta_2 - \kappa_1^2 \sigma_1^2 + \kappa_1^2 \sigma_2^2 - 2\kappa_2^2 \kappa_1 \theta_2 + 2\kappa_2 \sigma_1^2 \kappa_1 - \kappa_2^2 \sigma_1^2\right)e^{-t(2\kappa_1 - \kappa_2)}$$
$$- \kappa_1^2 \left(2\theta_2 \kappa_2 + \sigma_2^2\right)(2\kappa_1 - \kappa_2)e^{-\kappa_2 t}$$
$$- \kappa_2(2\kappa_1 - \kappa_2)(\kappa_1 - \kappa_2)\left(\kappa_1 + 2\kappa_1 \theta_2 + \sigma_1^2\right)e^{-t(\kappa_1 - \kappa_2)}$$
$$\left. + \kappa_1(\kappa_1 - \kappa_2)\left(4\theta_2 \kappa_2 \kappa_1 + 2\kappa_2 \kappa_1 + 2\sigma_2^2 \kappa_1 - 2\theta_2 \kappa_2^2 - \kappa_2^2 + \kappa_2 \sigma_1^2 - 2\sigma_2^2 \kappa_2\right)\right)$$

$$h_{z_1^2}(t) = e^{-2\kappa_1 t}$$

$$h_{z_1 z_2}(t) = 2\frac{\kappa_1 \left(e^{-(\kappa_1 + \kappa_2)t} - e^{-2\kappa_1 t}\right)}{\kappa_1 - \kappa_2}$$

$$h_{z_2^2}(t) = \frac{\left(e^{-2\kappa_1 t} - 2e^{-(\kappa_1 + \kappa_2)t} + e^{-2\kappa_2 t}\right)\kappa_1^2}{(\kappa_1 - \kappa_2)^2}.$$

Finally, observe that for $\mathbb{E}\left((Z_t^2)^2 | Z_0^1 = z_1, Z_0^2 = z_2\right) =: h(t, z_1, z_2)$ with boundary condition $h_0(0) = h_{z_1}(0) = h_{z_2}(0) = h_{z_1 z_2}(0) = h_{z_1^2}(0) = 0, h_{z_2^2}(0) = 1$, we obtain the solution

$$h_0(t) = \frac{1}{2}\frac{\theta_2 e^{-t(2\kappa_2 + \kappa_1)}}{(\kappa_1 - \kappa_2)\kappa_2}\left(\left(2\theta_2 \kappa_2 + \sigma_2^2\right)(\kappa_1 - \kappa_2)e^{\kappa_1 t}\right.$$
$$+ \left(2\theta_2 \kappa_2 + 2\kappa_2 + \sigma_2^2\right)(\kappa_1 - \kappa_2)e^{t(2\kappa_2 + \kappa_1)}$$
$$\left. + \left(-2\sigma_2^2 \kappa_1 - 4\theta_2 \kappa_2 \kappa_1 - 2\kappa_2 \kappa_1 + 2\sigma_2^2 \kappa_2 + 4\theta_2 \kappa_2^2\right)e^{(\kappa_1 + \kappa_2)t} + \kappa_2^2 e^{2\kappa_2 t}\right)$$

$$h_{z_1}(t) = e^{-\kappa_1 t}$$

$$h_{z_2}(t) = \frac{e^{-\kappa_2 t}}{\kappa_2(\kappa_1 - \kappa_2)}\left(\sigma_2^2 \kappa_1 + 2\theta_2 \kappa_2 \kappa_1 + \kappa_2 \kappa_1 - \sigma_2^2 \kappa_2 - 2\theta_2 \kappa_2^2 - \kappa_1 \kappa_2 e^{-t(\kappa_1 - \kappa_2)}\right)$$
$$+ \frac{\left(2\theta_2 \kappa_2 + \sigma_2^2\right)e^{-2\kappa_2 t}}{\kappa_2}$$

$$h_{z_1 z_2}(t) = 0$$
$$h_{z_1^2}(t) = 0$$
$$h_{z_2^2}(t) = e^{-2\kappa_2 t}.$$

$\square$

It is an easy exercise to derive the unconditional moments from the above result by taking the limit $t \to \infty$, and we give the result in the next corollary.

Corollary A.1. *Assume Z is given by (13.29) and (13.30). The unconditional moments of Z up to order two are given by*

$$\mathbb{E}\left(Z_t^1\right) = \theta_2$$
$$\mathbb{E}\left(Z_t^2\right) = \theta_2$$

$$\text{Var}\left(Z_t^1\right) = \frac{1}{2} \frac{\theta_2 \left(2\kappa_2\kappa_1^2 + \kappa_1^2\sigma_2^2 + 2\kappa_2^2\kappa_1 + \kappa_1\kappa_2\sigma_1^2 + \kappa_2^2\sigma_1^2\right)}{\kappa_2\kappa_1\left(\kappa_1 + \kappa_2\right)}$$

$$\text{Var}\left(Z_t^2\right) = \frac{1}{2} \frac{\theta_2 \left(\sigma_2^2 + 2\kappa_2\right)}{\kappa_2}$$

$$\text{Cov}\left(Z_t^1 Z_t^2\right) = \frac{1}{2} \frac{\left(2\kappa_2\kappa_1 + \sigma_2^2\kappa_1 + 2\kappa_2^2\right)\theta_2}{\left(\kappa_1 + \kappa_2\right)\kappa_2}.$$

REFERENCES

Arnsdorf, M., Halperin, I., 2008. BSLP: Markovian bivariate spread-loss model for portfolio credit derivatives. Journal of Computational Finance 12, 77–107.

Bielecki, T. R., Crépey, S., Jeanblanc, M., 2010. Up and down credit risk. Quantitative Finance 10, 1137–1151.

Cheridito, P., Filipović, D., Kimmel, R. L., 2010. A note on the Dai-Singleton canonical representation of affine term structure models. Mathematical Finance 20(3), 509–519.

Cont, R., Deguest, R., Kan, Y. H., 2010. Default intensities implied by CDO spreads: inversion formula and model calibration. SIAM Journal on Financial Mathematics 1, 555–585.

Cont, R., Kan, Y. H., 2011. Dynamic hedging of portfolio credit derivatives. SIAM Journal on Financial Mathematics 2, 112–140.

Cont, R., Minca, A., 2011. Recovering portfolio default intensities implied by CDO quotes. Mathematical Finance. DOI:10.1111lj.1467-9965.2011.00491.x.

Eberlein, E., Grbac, Z., Schmidt, T., 2012. Market models for credit risky portfolios driven by time-inhomogeneous Lévy processes, submitted.

Eberlein, E., Kluge, W., 2006. Exact pricing formulae for caps and swaptions in a Lévy term structure model. Journal of Computational Finance 9(2), 99–125.

Eberlein, E., Kluge, W., Schönbucher, P. J., 2006. The Lévy Libor model with default risk. Journal of Credit Risk 2(2), 3–42.

Ehlers, P., Schönbucher, P., 2006. Pricing interest rate-sensitive credit portfolio derivatives. Working Paper, ETH Zurich.

Ehlers, P., Schönbucher, P., 2009. Background filtrations and canonical loss processes for top-down models of portfolio credit risk. Finance and Stochastics 13, 79–103.

Eksi, Z., Filipović, D., 2012. A dynamic affine factor model for the pricing of CDOs. Working paper.

Errais, E., Giesecke, K., Goldberg, L. R., 2010. Affine point processes and portfolio credit risk. SIAM Journal on Financial Mathematics 1, 642–665.

Filipović, D., Overbeck, L., Schmidt, T., 2011. Dynamic CDO term structure modelling. Mathematical Finance 21, 53–71.

Filipović, D., Schmidt, T., 2010. Pricing and hedging of CDOs: A top-down approach. In Chiarella, C., Novikov, A. (Eds), Contemporary Quantitative Finance, pp. 231–254. Springer.

Grewal, M. S., Andrews, A. P., 1993. Kalman Filtering: Theory and Practice. Prentice-Hall.

Jacod, J., Shiryaev, A. N., 2003. Limit Theorems for Stochastic Processes (2nd ed.). Springer.

Keller-Ressel, M., Schachermayer, W., Teichmann, J., 2011. Affine processes are regular. Probability Theory and Related Fields 151(3-4), 591–611.

Lipton, A., Rennie, A. (Eds), 2011. The Oxford Handbook of Credit Derivatives. Oxford University Press, London.

Longstaff, F., Rajan, A., 2008. An empirical analysis of collateralized debt obligations. The Journal of Finance 63, 529–563.

Schönbucher, P. J., 2000. A Libor Market Model with Default Risk. Working Paper, University of Bonn.

Schönbucher, P. J., 2005. Portfolio losses and the term structure of loss transition rates: a new methodology for the pricing of portfolio credit derivatives. Working paper.

Sidenius, J., Piterbarg, V., Andersen, L., 2008. A new framework for dynamic credit portfolio loss modelling. International Journal of Theoretical and Applied Finance 11, 163–197.

14

Counterparty Credit Risk and Clearing of Derivatives – From the Perspective of an Industrial Corporate with a Focus on Commodity Markets

Frank Lehrbass
RWE Supply and Trading

14.1 INTRODUCTION*

The materialization of credit risk is nothing new to the non-financial industry. The insolvency of Enron in 2001 is one prominent case which made the non-financial industry learn lessons. These "lessons learned" helped to manage the Global Financial Crisis (GFC), e.g. netting and margining techniques minimized losses from Lehman's insolvency. As credit risk remains a relevant topic it pays to have a closer look at the various types of credit exposures encountered in the commodity markets, the available tools for credit risk management and the hedging and pricing of transactions. The specifics of the commodity markets make this chapter a special one as there is not always a one-to-one applicability of techniques from the financial industry. This chapter is written from the perspective of an industrial corporate involved in the commodity markets. Readers interested in corporate risk management in general are referred to the book by Crouhy et al. (2006).

Broadly speaking one encounters two types of credit portfolio in the industrial commodity business and it is important to be aware of their relative magnitudes of credit risk. On the one hand there are the portfolios made up of trading positions, which are typically held by trading houses like Glencore and the like. Trading positions are usually liquid and short-term. This allows the application of counterparty credit risk mitigation techniques as they have already been established in banking. The commodity industry has adapted these techniques in the aftermath of the Enron insolvency and the one of TXU Europe in 2002. These techniques comprise the use of Master Agreements like the ones published by ISDA (International Swaps and Derivatives Association) or EFET (European Federation of Energy Traders), which allow netting and thereby prevent cherry picking of the insolvency administrator; and the use of Credit Support Annexes, which define how margining is done between the counterparties. In essence this leads to cash collateralization of the bulk of the Mark-to-Market (MtM) of the positions and reduces credit losses to relatively small amounts. More on these techniques will follow in the relevant sections.

---

* The content of this chapter represents the authors' personal opinions and does not necessarily reflect the views of RWE Supply & Trading or its staff.

The G-20 leaders announced in September 2009 that all standardized OTC derivative contracts should be cleared through central counterparties. Therefore the credit risk management for trading portfolios will be covered rather briefly and put into one section on "Clearing via a Central Counterparty."

On the other hand there are the portfolios of commodity positions due to the traditional business of procuring and selling commodities. The procurement of commodities usually means buying long term from an upstream commodity producer (e.g. oil from Exxon). As these counterparties are usually of a higher credit quality than the normal industrial corporate, credit risk is no pressing topic.[1] Nevertheless it can happen that a top-notch entity all of a sudden deteriorates in quality, as the example of BP during the Gulf of Mexico oil spill in 2010 showed. This could be taken as a motivation to hedge these exposures using Credit Derivatives. But it would be hard to explain to the shareholders of a, say, single A rated commodity company, why all better rated "suppliers" are hedged with single name Credit Default Swaps (CDS). The most that could be defended in practical terms seems to be a "First-to-Default CDS" referenced on a basket of suppliers. Hence, neither the trading portfolios nor the procurement side are a huge challenge in terms of credit risk.

But there is the sale side of the commodity portfolio. Here one finds the main challenge, because as a rule the mitigation techniques applied to the trading portfolio cannot be used to a significant degree. This is due to the fact that the commodity positions can be rather illiquid[2] and that the counterparties are not sufficiently cash rich to handle margin calls, which can become huge.[3] The counterparties buying commodities from a commodity firm are usually lower rated and therefore banks are hesitant to commit huge liquidity lines. So the typical sales customer neither has the cash at hand nor a liquidity line in the back. Therefore margining cannot be applied. What can be done is explained after a short description of the types of credit exposure as they arise in commodity business. The focus is on practically relevant techniques according to the experience of the author.

The sections are ordered along the following line of thought:

- Become aware of the credit risk (exposure concepts).
- Try to bring down the exposure before deal closing (exposure-reducing techniques).
- Try to reduce the remaining risk (*ex ante* risk-reducing techniques).
- Once the credit position is assumed, check when it is time to transfer or share the risk (*ex post* risk-reducing techniques).
- Try to reach a holistic view by looking at the whole portfolio and all relevant risk factors involved. Connect your insights with actions.

Thus a section on pricing, management and portfolio modeling concludes this chapter. Since we necessarily have to cover a lot of contractual topics, it must be stated explicitly that this chapter does not provide legal advice.

14.2   CREDIT EXPOSURES IN COMMODITY BUSINESS

We now introduce credit exposure concepts, which have turned out to be of practical relevance.

14.2.1   Settlement Exposure

The simplest concept is the "settlement exposure" (SE), which is defined as the potential loss in case of default of the counterparty. It arises from the amount of commodities already delivered but not yet paid for. Thus the SE measures what is at stake in terms of "unpaid invoices."[4] The SE is determined as "quantity times price" in light of the specifics of the collection procedures, which are applied to overdue payments. Even if a one month payment in arrears has been agreed, the sales unit is not allowed to terminate delivery instantaneously and start collection procedures but has to remind the overdue customer and take other steps, which are required by the country-specific laws and industry-specific regulations. Usually this makes the SE the size of two or three monthly invoice amounts rather than just one. The SE becomes variable if a deterministically varying delivery amount has been agreed and stochastic if a floating price has been agreed or options are included (e.g. the option for the counterparty to deviate up to +/− 10% from the agreed base amount of delivery).

Such a situation gives rise to the concept of "projected SE." As with every "moving target," various methods of quantification of a single number are applicable. Some define the projected SE as a kind of maximum value of all potential future SE or choose a certain quantile value of the distribution of potential SE. Others choose the SE as it derives from application of the forward curve and expectations on the option exercise.

For a fixed price deal the SE is usually dominated by another credit exposure element related to MtM. Therefore we move on to this next concept and remind the reader that for the "bread and butter" business of a fixed price contract the SE is a deterministic figure (in this case, agreed quantity times fixed price).

14.2.2 Performance Exposure

The commercially most relevant exposure concept is the "performance exposure" (PE). It is measured as the replacement costs of a contract that have to be spent in the event of the counterparty being no longer able or willing to fulfill its obligations. There are various approaches to measure PE, three of which will be introduced in this section. To keep the focus on credit risk matters, the legal risk of an "unwilling" counterparty is left aside.[5]

It is clear that the replacement costs of a contract can also become negative, i.e. one would be happy not to have the contract on the books. But the insolvency of a counterparty does not present an opportunity to achieve that, because the administrator of the insolvent counterparty normally will insist on performance. Therefore a default of the counterparty does not represent an upside but only a downside, if commodity price movements have brought our contract in the money. The degree of "being in the money" is measured by the MtM of the contract and it might be positive or negative depending on how the terms and conditions of the contract compare to current market rates.

14.2.2.1 *PE Measured as Potential Future Exposure*

Typically the MtM of a contract at initiation is rather small but can change significantly over time. On top of the current MtM there is a potential increase, which has to be factored into a measure of "potential future exposure" (PFE). The PFE tries to quantify the answer to the "question 'What is the most I could lose to this counterparty with some degree of confidence' and is useful for limit setting and stress testing" (Burger et al. 2007, p. 267). A commonly used level of confidence is 95% and this will be used in all our examples.

In order to have price certainty on the input side corporate "end customers" usually prefer fixed price contracts (e.g. buying Belgian gas at Zeebrugge hub at a fixed price in contrast to a floating price indexed to Zeebrugge index, TTF or another commodity price like oil). It should be no surprise that the PFE of fixed price contracts can get large, if the contract refers to the delivery of a large amount of the commodity and/or covers a long period, say beyond 10 years.

In the next section we give an example for the PFE calculation of a fixed price contract and devote the subsequent section to a floating price contract, which usually does not have a significant PFE – but details matter, as the worked-out example will show.

14.2.3   Example of Fixed Price Deal with Performance Exposure

We assume that we are a sales company, which has sold 1 MWh of electrical power to a counterparty for delivery in exactly one years' time at a fixed price of 50 EUR/MWh that has to be paid at delivery. We assume that there is a forward wholesale contract that allows purchasing the power sold.

To calculate the MtM of the sales contract we have to look at the price of this forward contract. To keep the focus on the credit risk involved in the sales contract we assume that we can buy the power at the same price of 50 EUR/MWh but from a "nearly default free" counterparty, e.g. via a central counterparty.

To calculate the PFE we assume that the power forward contract price follows a Geometric Brownian motion and that the annualized volatility is 16%. It is obvious that our sales contract gets in the money if wholesale power prices drop below 50 EUR/MWh. To determine the PFE at a confidence level of 95% we have to estimate that level of power prices which is exceeded with 95% probability in one year's time. We find this answer by setting the parameter k to 1.64 in the following formula[6] (time horizon $\tau=1$, volatility $\eta=0.16$):

$$S_{down\ quantile} = S_0 e^{-\kappa\eta\sqrt{\tau}-0.5\eta^2\tau}. \tag{14.1}$$

Hence, the "5% worst case" from a credit perspective is a price decline to 38 EUR/MWh. If the counterparty goes into insolvency in such a market situation and the insolvency administrator decides not to honor the contract, we are forced to sell to the market at a lower level to replace the sales contract.[7] It is very probable that the insolvency administrator will not honor the contract as it is out of the money from her or his perspective. On the other hand, if prices end up above 50 EUR/MWh, the insolvency administrator would insist on our performance to realize the best for the creditors of the insolvent company.

Hence, the level of MtM, which is exceeded with only 5% probability, amounts to 12 EUR/MWh (=50–38 EUR/MWh).

14.2.3.1   PE Measured as Expected Positive Exposure

Beside the PFE of 12 EUR/MWh we can also calculate the "expected positive exposure" (EPE). Recall that our exposure is never a negative MtM, but only the positive ones, i.e. max(0; MtM). Hence, the EPE is the value of a call option on the MtM with strike zero. Using the well-known Black-Scholes formula (1973) with an interest rate of zero results in an EPE of 3 EUR for this example.

Summing up, the PE can be calculated as PFE or alternatively EPE. For the sake of limit setting the PFE is usually used, whereas for other purposes the EPE might be more useful. For example, in a simultaneous consideration of all credit exposures of a company it might be an overly conservative assumption that all exposures are at their 95% worst case levels.

Especially if the portfolio consists of long and short positions, it is simply impossible that the exposures to those counterparties where we have sold and those where we have bought from materialize at their PFE levels at the same time.

14.2.4   Example of a Floating Price Deal with Performance Exposure

As before, the sales and procurement position are analyzed simultaneously. We assume that we have agreed some time ago to deliver 500k metric tons (mt) of coal of quality as defined in the index API2 (= All Publications Index, see Burger et al., (2007, p. 21) for more details) by ship to our counterparty on a monthly basis for a period of two years. The USD price per metric ton is to be at 90.9 USD/mt and a flat forward curve is assumed.[8] The coal is "Delivered Ex Ship" (DES) in a Non-European port specified by our counterparty at a premium to API2 of 110%. This makes the "all in" sales price 100 USD/mt.

It is assumed that delivery of the coal is monthly by one ship and that invoices are sent immediately at month end. Given a 10-day payment period and special collection procedures lasting at most 14 days, no more than two cargoes should be at risk. In other words, a non-payment for one cargo results in closing out the contract before the third cargo arrives at the port. Worst case is that two cargoes have been unloaded but not paid for. This makes the Settlement Exposure the size of two monthly invoices. This yields a SE, projected along the – flat – forward curve, of 200 USD/mt.

Let us assume that the highest PE occurs in exactly one year's time to keep the calculations easy. Hence, the then outstanding amount of coal to be delivered is 12 times 500k, which is six million mt.

The coal is procured at market and the pricing is therefore also related to API2. This coal is then shipped to the ports specified by the counterparty. The contractual agreement on DES requires us to pay for the transport, i.e. vessel loading, costs of voyage and cargo insurance, because "under DES, the risk of damage is transferred when the goods are made available to the buyer on board the ship, uncleared for import at the port of destination. The buyer is responsible for custom clearance" (Coyle et al., 2003, p. 390). This brings in the costs of freight, which are assumed to be fixed at 5 USD/mt.

Although the indexation on both sides of the portfolio is to API2, the difference in detail generates some performance exposure. The size of the credit exposure is based on the MtM per metric ton, which reads as follows:

$$110\% \text{ API2} - (\text{API2} + 5) \tag{14.2}$$

This can be simplified to:

$$10\% \text{ API2} - 5 \tag{14.3}$$

This shows that even in indexed transactions a performance exposure can arise. Again the Geometric Brownian Motion (GBM) is a sensible model for the coal price dynamics (Burger et al., 2007, p. 130). The PFE for the sales side is found by inserting that level of API2 into formula (14.3) that is exceeded with 5% probability in one year's time. Before we use formula (14.1) again, we have to recognize that this time it is an up move in the market for API2 coal that will increase the MtM as given by (14.3). To make efficient use of formula (14.1) we arrive at the "up quantile" by setting the parameter k to −1.64 and $\tau = 1$. As the underlying commodity is coal we choose a volatility of $\eta = 0.12$. The PFE per mt of coal as based on (14.3) is as follows:

$$10\% * 90.9 * \exp(1.64 * 0.12 - 0.5 * 0.12^2) - 5 = 6 \qquad (14.4)$$

Multiplied by the six million mt of coal still outstanding to be delivered in one years' time, this generates a PFE figure of USD 36 mn (6 USD times 6 mn). It should be noted that according to (14.3) and with a level of API2 being today at 90.9 USD/mt the contract already has some positive MtM from coal price moves since initiation amounting to 4.09 USD/mt and a total of EUR 24.5 mn, which is already included in the PFE figure.

It should be clear that the PFE depends on the future point in time that we look at. Thus we could repeat the application of formula (14.4) for various future points in time like in one month, quarter etc. For purposes of limit setting one often looks at the maximum of all those PFE values per contract and adds the relevant SE, which is USD 100 mn (200 EUR times 500k).

For other purposes the EPE might be more interesting. The EPE is the expectation of the positive MtM, i.e. EPE = max(10% API2 – 5; 0). This can be calculated via the Black–Scholes formula by setting the interest rate to zero, the spot to 10% API2 and the strike to 5 USD.

That the PE measured as PFE is lower than the SE is the normal situation for floating price deals. Both figures show that credit exposures can reach significant sizes. A coal trading company being hit at the wrong time by an insolvency of the coal purchasing customer will certainly feel the impact in its P&L.

14.2.5 General Remarks on Credit Exposure Concepts

So far the stochastic levels of MtM have been put into a single number via usage of the expectation operator (EPE) and "Value at Risk" like quantile concepts (PFE). What has not been mentioned so far is a concept like "Expected Shortfall" (ES), which measures the average exposure if markets move beyond worst case levels. The following chart (Figure 14.1) shows these three PE profiles in comparison. The hump curve shape is typical for contracts that contain an equal amount of delivery per month. The shape is due to two counteracting factors. On the one hand the physical amount to be delivered decreases but on the other hand the volatility increases, e.g. with square root of time in the case of geometric Brownian motion.

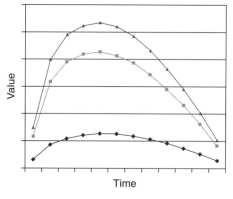

> **ES** – Average exposure above PFE

> **PFE** – the positive value of a contract that will not be exceeded with a certain probability (the confidence level)

> **EPE** – the expected value of all positive realization of the contract value

Figure 14.1   Performance exposure concepts.

The peak of the PFE curve is referred to as "Maximum Potential Future Exposure." Whatever concept is chosen from the menu for quantification of PE, the SE must not be forgotten.

One more remarkable difference between these two concepts is that SE is rather one-sided, which impacts on the party delivering the commodity, while PE is relevant for both parties to the contract. Exceptions to this rule arise, e.g. where prepayment is agreed (the prepayment of the buyer counts as SE for the buyer).

It is clear that real-life contracts can become so complex that the exposures can no longer be calculated analytically but simulation techniques become unavoidable. Another push in this direction comes from more realistic models for the commodity price dynamics, which are touched upon below.

14.3 *EX ANTE* EXPOSURE-REDUCING TECHNIQUES

14.3.1 Payment Terms

The SE hinges upon the payment terms, as we have seen in the definition. Usually a counterparty will try to diversify its sources of credit. Hence, it is interested in getting good credit terms beside what it gets from the banks. Also competition and tradition force a commodity company to grant at least some payment windows to its customers. Usually these windows are shortened if the counterparty deteriorates in creditworthiness but whether this is really enforceable depends on the contractual and bargaining position. As the SE measures what is at stake in terms of "unpaid invoices" the simplest way to reduce the SE is to agree prepayment for at least some percentage of upcoming deliveries. For counterparties with a very weak credit standing, e.g. in an insolvency situation, full prepayment is a usual technique to manage the SE.

14.3.2 Material Adverse Change Clauses

This section is devoted to clauses that are negotiated into commodity contracts, to prepare the counterparties for situations where the creditworthiness of one party has changed materially in an adverse direction. Such clauses are among the traditional instruments of the credit officers of a bank and are known as "financial covenants." Of course these clauses can be used by anyone negotiating a contract.

In such a financial covenant, certain metrics are defined to measure the creditworthiness of the bank's client in an objective way, e.g. via measuring the tangible net worth (TNW) based on the most recent annual report or by looking at the external rating, and linked to consequences.

For well rated utilities it is also possible to insist on such one-sided covenants from lower-rated counterparties which want to do business. Thus a material adverse change (MAC) clause also applies some metrics and trigger levels. If a metric hits a trigger level (e.g. TNW of the counterparty below trigger), the utility may ask the counterparty for collateral in form of cash or a letter of credit (LC, more detail follows in a subsequent section). It is clear that this request for collateral hits the counterparty in an already demanding situation. Therefore a MAC can also be seen as a lever to start re-negotiations of the contract and the triggers are set at levels which are hit before things get too demanding for the counterparty. The specification of the algorithm to determine the amount of collateral that can be requested is usually also part of the original contract negotiations.

In wholesale business "among equals" one encounters symmetrical MACs, where both sides put themselves under the metrics and triggers. Hence, it can happen that counterparty A is requesting collateral from B and vice versa.

Beside these "hard" MAC clauses there are also "soft" MAC clauses such as termination of a control and profit transfer agreement or an impaired ability to perform. Especially with respect to the latter clause there is always the issue of enforceability.

14.3.3   Master Agreements

Already in the year 2000 the European Federation of Energy Traders (EFET) published the first version of a Master Trading Agreement, which has been developed and extended further since then in terms of coverage of products and jurisdictions. To handle the thereby arising specifics, appendices are available to tailor the EFET Master to the requirements of a certain location and market for a specific product (e.g. for gas traded at the Netherland's TTF Hub). As the ISDA Master is well known, it is not discussed here. Details can be found in the book by Harding et al. (2002). What is important is how beneficial the technique of using Master Agreements has proven itself to be during the crisis. Take as an example the insolvency of Lehman. Counterparties of Lehman had two types of positions. On the one hand were those that were in the money, i.e. Lehman owed the counterparty something. On the other hand were those that were out of the money. As a rule, in the Western world the insolvency codes grant the administrator the right to cherrypick. This means that the administrator insists on a 100% performance of the contracts that are out of the money, whereas the ones in the money are honored only with the insolvency quota (usually way below 100%). This is avoided by using a Master Agreement, where one finds what is called the "single agreement concept." It says that all trades done under the Master form a single contract and not a multitude. Hence, the Master Agreement acts as one empty umbrella, covering all subsequent transactions with the counterparty, and there is no menu to choose from for the administrator.

The Master Agreement also clarifies how the values of the trades are netted to one single figure. Thus counterparties of Lehman could deduct the values they owed Lehman from the in the money positions. The net result constituted the claim to the insolvency estate. That way Master Agreements helped to mitigate losses significantly during the crisis. Therefore the next section is dedicated to netting.

A short overview on other master agreements concludes this section. The ISDA agreement has not been designed for physical commodity trades. Hence, it is no surprise that the ISDA is only one of many master agreements used in the industry, among which the most prominent EFET already has been mentioned. For the UK physical power market there is the Grid Trading Master Agreement (GTMA). The Emission Trading Master Agreement (ETMA) was introduced by the IETA (International Emission Trading Association) in the year 2003. Cross Product Master Netting Agreements (CPMA) as published by the Bond Market Association are the next higher dimension of Master Agreements as they try to serve as an umbrella for ISDA, EFET and other Master Agreements in order to extend the "netting"[9] potential to the maximum.

14.3.4   Netting

In the preceding section the most important type of netting was introduced, which is known as "close out netting" (ISDA Master, 2002, p. 11). Other types of netting like payment netting (i.e. only the balance of payments is wired and not each position) are interesting under good weather conditions, and this is not what credit is about. Therefore we keep our focus on "close out netting" and call it simply "netting" henceforth. Netting applies to SE as well, as the subsequent example illustrates.

In the above example the insolvency of Lehman constituted a reason for early termination and this led to the calculation of the so-called "close out amount," which quantifies the replacement costs (or "economic equivalent," ISDA Master, 2002, p. 22). If this close out amount turns out positive, it is what Lehman owes the counterparty. Hence, it will be recorded in the register run by the insolvency administrator and compensated with the insolvency quota. This netting of positions, applied while calculating the "close out amount," is called "close out netting." The possibly large differences are illustrated in one more example.

We look at a company that has been transacting a commodity with a marketer, which has gone into insolvency. At the time of default, the company had two deals outstanding with the marketer. The deals were documented under a Master Agreement and per deal the outstanding claims are (i.e. essentially the sum of unpaid invoices + MtM + default interest) as follows: for a 3-year power purchase contract EUR +2 mn and for a 6-month natural gas swap EUR −1.8 mn. The close out amount nets to EUR 200k. Without netting the administrator would insist on our performance under the gas swap and pay us the insolvency quota on the power purchase contract value. For a marketer a low insolvency quota of 10% can be reasonably assumed. With this information at hand we can compare the outcomes with and without netting. With netting we get rid of the gas swap and end our relationship to the marketer at a balance of 10% of 200k, which is EUR 20k. A loss of EUR 180k results.

Without netting we have to continue with the swap and keep our negative MtM of EUR −1.8 mn and get 10% of 2 mn, which is EUR 200k. Summing up, without netting we have a balance of EUR −1.6 mn.

The example has also illustrated what is called "cross commodity netting." Just as the ISDA Master can cover equity, interest rate, FX, commodity and credit derivatives transactions, the same is possible for the other Master Agreements which are used in the industry. If a master agreement does not allow for this, conclusion of a CPMA between the counterparties can achieve it.

It should not be forgotten that there are jurisdictions in which netting is not legally enforceable (see the ISDA homepage for a list of countries where netting works) or where netting depends on the type of counterparties involved. This is especially important if one is interested in "cross affiliate netting," whereby one attempts to put different legal entities under one umbrella. With a larger pool of business entities, more transactions would be in the "netting" set – thus providing more potential for offsetting "signs" in front of the individual amounts (i.e. the +/− in the example).

14.3.5 Margining

In the preceding section on MAC we saw a technique to receive collateral like cash from our counterparty if it is getting too weak in terms of credit. As the world is full of surprises (e.g. Lehman was rated investment grade up to its insolvency) the natural extension of the MAC concept is to do a more frequent collateralization of exposures. Indeed this technique also helped to keep the losses from the Lehman insolvency small for some market participants. So how does it work?

Contractually the most widespread implementation works with the ISDA Credit Support Annex[10] (CSA), which is signed on top of the ISDA Master. Details can be found in the book by Harding et al. (2002).

For very weak counterparties one can agree an "Independent Amount" in the CSA, which quantifies the value of collateral, which is given by the weak counterparty as "initial margin" to the more creditworthy counterparty. "Independent" means that this has to be done before any transactions are concluded. In the extreme it could happen that the creditworthy counterparty is sitting on collateral and does not have a current credit exposure to the weak one at all. But that would be a waste of resources by the weak counterparty. Therefore we assume that trading starts between the two. In the CSA one also agrees on a "Threshold," which is the level of MtM of one's positions below which a call for collateral cannot be made. For the weak counterparty, a "Threshold" of zero would be the natural choice. This means that as soon as the MtM on the side of the creditworthy counterparty becomes positive, a margin call is sent to the weak counterparty. To simplify the exchange of collateral one can also agree "Minimum Transfer Amounts"[11] and "Rounding" conventions but we ignore these details to keep the focus and encourage the reader to consult Harding et al. (2002) for more detail.

Having received the margin call the weak counterparty normally transfers the cash collateral the following business day to the creditworthy counterparty. Thus, the MtM of the previous day is cash collateralized and if the weak counterparty goes into insolvency after the payment day the only remaining exposure is the additional MtM if any.[12]

The same logic applies if the weak counterparty does not want or cannot deliver collateral. In reality it cannot be figured out quickly which of the two situations applies. Both situations initially feel the same and are sometimes intermingled with "Disputes" around the margin call (e.g. the weak counterparty may shed doubt on the calculations of the MtM of the creditworthy counterparty). To keep things compact there are normally not more than two weeks where the collateralization is not working. This is due to a strict timeline for handling disputes, which is spelled out in the ISDA documents. In the extreme the ISDA rules allow early termination of the contract and close out. This will lead to one more credit exposure category, which is discussed in the next section.

So far we have not spoken about the "Threshold" for the creditworthy counterparty. Naturally it will be a strictly positive amount, say EUR 10 mn. As long as the MtM on the side of the weak counterparty stays below EUR 10 mn, it has no right to send margin calls to the creditworthy counterparty. As soon as the MtM exceeds the "Threshold" it is allowed to ask for margins but only up to the amount exceeding the "Threshold," e.g. if the MtM is 15 mn it may ask for 5 mn collateral. Therefore the "Threshold" is a key element of the still missing new exposure concept, which is subsequently introduced as "close out exposure."

The daily exchanges of collateral in dependence of the agreed "Thresholds" and market driven variations of MtM are called "Variation Margins." It is clear that a CSA among equally creditworthy counterparties would look different than in the case above. As a rule there would be no independent amount and the "Thresholds" would be equal and strictly positive.

The CSA cannot only be linked to an ISDA Master but also to an EFET or a CPMA. As a final word an important conceptual difference should be noted. The CPMA works with the concept of "set-off" whereas in each Master there is only one "net amount." Basically the CPMA sets off the net amounts from the various Master Agreements.

14.3.6 Close Out Exposure and Threshold

The "close out exposure" (COE) represents the potential increase in uncollateralized PE between the last successful margin call and the close out of the contracts subsequent to a default event (note that non-delivery of collateral is also a default event). Under an EFET CSA there is effectively a close out period of 10 business days. Hence, the COE can be calculated like the PE but for a fixed time horizon of ten days (i.e. $\tau = 10/250$ in formula (14.1)).

On top of the COE there is the exposure below the "Threshold," which is not collateralized by agreement. An *ex ante* exposure-reducing technique is to agree on automatic "Threshold" reductions triggered by rating downgrades. An agreement whereby a positive "Threshold" goes to zero as soon as the counterparty gets downgraded to below investment grade or close to this stage is common.

To conclude, even under daily margining there can be significant credit exposures if we encounter high levels of "Thresholds" and/or high volatilities and large transactions.

14.4   *EX ANTE* RISK-REDUCING TECHNIQUES

This section is devoted to risk management techniques, which can be applied from the start of a transaction. It is an exception to the rule if these techniques are brought in retrospectively – but it is sometimes possible.

14.4.1   Credit Enhancements in General

Whenever you encounter a counterparty – willing to do business with you – that is simply too weak on its own, it pays to look out for "friends and family." The latter means that stronger parts of the corporate family – if it exists – function as "Guarantor." The former means that "business friends" may assume this role or step in if credit losses materialize, e.g. as an "Insurer."

14.4.2   Parent Company Guarantees

A "Parent Company Guarantee" (PCG) spreads creditworthiness within a corporate family from a higher level to a lower level. Typically, within a group there is a specialized subsidiary for procuring commodities or trading them. Imagine an industrial customer group that wants to buy power and delegates that task to one entity – say, "Power Purchase Ltd." – within the group. Although the group owns the entity in full its liability for the entity is limited – as the name says. Assume now that the entity has bought power at a fixed price for ten years and that power prices have decreased since then. To get rid of this out of the money position in the group the easiest way is to let the entity go insolvent. As a "Limited" usually has little equity, the net benefit to the group is significant. Synthetically it has created a call on power prices. If prices go up, it keeps the entity alive, if not, it lets it go into insolvency.

To avoid such situations it is usually required that stronger parents guarantee the weaker members of the family via a PCG. Usually such a PCG is irrevocable, on first demand and unconditional (which means that there is no need for the beneficiary to prove any loss). The "Guarantor" (parent company) is obliged severally and not jointly. Of course the value of a guarantee is dependent on the strength of the "Guarantor." In reality it can happen that the parent is weaker than the subsidiary, e.g. as was the case with Sal. Oppenheim and BHF Bank in Germany. In this case a PCG does not help. In fact family ties can even become endangering, be it via cash pooling or granting a loan to the parental company.

Beside the PCG there are other weaker attempts to spread the creditworthiness of the parent or any other stronger credit. For example, there are parent company letters called a letter of comfort, letter of intent or letter of responsibility, issued to reassure a subsidiary's counterparty that it will support the subsidiary in the case of financial difficulties. It hinges on the fine print whether such an assurance constitutes a binding contract or only a moral obligation; a letter of comfort may only express that the parent company will keep an eye on the entire business of the subsidiary. Other letters can express the intent to keep a level of equity at the subsidiary or the willingness to defer internal debt or to assume debt of the subsidiary. It is obvious that the PCG stands out as unique among the family relations.

14.4.3 Letters of Credit

A documentary "Letter of Credit" is abbreviated as Doc LC,[13] and may also be referred to as a documentary credit. The latter refers to the essential logic of a Doc LC (henceforth LC). Once the beneficiary of the LC presents the documents complying with the terms and conditions of the LC to the issuing bank, it is obliged to honor it irrespective of anything else. Thus the bank deals in documents with no further interest in the commodities or activities of the counterparties.

The former example with the coal delivery via ship has already put us in the world of international trade, where the LC is a common payment method and works as follows:

- "The buyer arranges for its bank to issue the seller a LC in the sale amount.
- The buyer's bank places the amount in the seller's bank.
- The seller prepares a draft against the deposit and attaches the draft to the following documents: clean, negotiable bill of lading, certificate of insurance, seller's invoice and LC.
- The seller endorses the order bill of lading to the bank and receives the money.
- The seller's bank endorses the bill of lading to the buyer's bank.
- The buyer's bank endorses the bill of lading to the buyer.
- The buyer takes the bill of lading to the carrier and picks up the shipment" (Coyle et al., 2003, p. 388).

The example illustrates the essential risk-reducing steps: as soon as the seller has received the LC he can trust that he will be paid if he delivers as contractually agreed. He does not have to worry about the fate of his counterparty. Of course the credit quality of the LC issuing bank is as important as that of the "Guarantor" in the preceding section.

If the seller gets uncomfortable with the credit of the issuing bank, a request can be made for the LC to be confirmed by a top-notch bank, who then takes over the responsibility for making payments.

As concerns the quality of the wording, there are for instance the "Uniform Customs and Practices" (UCP) published by the International Chamber of Commerce (ICC), which can be referred to in the LC (e.g. ICC Publication No. 600). Unless explicitly stated, a LC is irrevocable.

Comparable to the PCG is the "Standby LC" (SLC). This is not intended to serve as a means of payment, but can be drawn down if the counterparty defaults on its contractual obligations. Such SLC are also often used as "Bid, Prepayment, Completion/Performance or Warranty Bonds." Obviously the term "Bond" does not mean a "Straight Coupon Bond" or any other security but a special type of SLC. SLCs guarantee the performance of our counterparty on its contractual obligations in a tender ("Bid Bond"), credit enhance an advance payment, protect us financially if the counterparty does not complete construction work or whatever its performance obligation is, or help us financially to warrant the agreed quality of goods and services ("Warranty Bond").

Hence, Letters of Credit in many forms help an industrial corporate not only to reduce its risk in export business (e.g. shipping coal), but also to protect itself against contractual defaults of a counterparty in many forms of business relations (e.g. EPC contract for a new production site, Service/Maintenance Contracts, Rental or Lease Agreements).

14.4.4 Credit Insurance

Credit insurance (CI) follows the structure of conventional insurance policies. The insurance buyer pays the underwriter a premium for which the insurer promises to compensate the buyer for losses resulting from pre-defined events within a pool of counterparties.[14] In the case of CI, the event is a payment default by a counterparty.

Compared to cash bond or CDS spreads, the CI pricing levels[15] appear surprisingly low, but nevertheless enable profitable business, as the annual reports of the credit insurers reveal – even during the GFC. The solution to this "miracle" can be found in the fine print of the policies.

First, CI typically insures SE and not PE. Second, the premium is often quoted on the basis of annual turnover. Assume that the SE is at most a quarter of the annual invoices. One therefore has to multiply the premium by four to get a more instructive figure for the purposes of comparison to, for example, CDS. Third, the maximum payout by the insurer is limited to a fixed multiple of the premium paid. Fourth, one has to follow strict procedural rules in handling overdue payments to qualify for a payout in case of an eventual loss. Fifth, the insurer usually covers only 90% of each credit loss to keep incentives aligned, i.e. to avoid moral hazard. Sixth, the insurer might be allowed to cancel coverage at any time and – in the case of a portfolio policy – to decline it from the very beginning for a certain fraction of total applications for coverage.

As a result, doing business with a professional insurer can lead to a situation where all credit-risky industry sectors are excluded from the policy and for the remaining industry sectors the most credit-risky names do not get coverage at all. If counterparties become weak one should not be surprised to see the insurer withdrawing coverage. So it is no surprise that the premium for insurance is much lower than levels seen on the CDS market.

14.4.5 Clearing via a Central Counterparty[16]

As a response to the GFC the G-20 leaders announced in September 2009 that "all standardized OTC derivative contracts should be traded on exchanges or electronic trading platforms, where appropriate, and cleared through central counterparties (=CCP) by end-2012." This results in the combination of the *ex ante* exposure-reducing technique "Margining" with a move to a "top-notch" counterparty. This decision has led to the Dodd–Frank Act in the US and the European Markets Infrastructure Regulation (EMIR). Both are intended to promote counterparty risk mitigation. In the words of EMIR, the CCP "legally interposes itself between the counterparties to the contracts traded within one or more financial markets, becoming the buyer to every seller and the seller to every buyer and which is responsible for the operation of a clearing system."

To keep the focus, we apply a European perspective and note that Europe in principle seems to follow the developments in the US. We describe what regulation can be expected to come, what the benefits of a CCP are, and potential implications for the marketplace and the setup of credit functions.

14.4.5.1   What Regulation can be Expected to Come?

By September 2012 the ESMA (European Securities and Markets Authority) published the "Final Report" on the draft of technical standards by which an obligation to move to a CCP will be determined. Such moves are expected to happen stepwise starting mid of 2013. I.e. it will not be the case that already in 2012 an anouncement like "All TTF[17] gas deals have to go on APX Endex[18] as CCP" will come. To come to such a clearing obligation, the bottom up approach will presumably be the prevailing one: The CCP points out to the national regulator that it is ready for being CCP for a product. This can be expected for the first half of 2013. The national regulator – if convinced – authorizes a CCP to clear a class of OTC derivatives and informs ESMA. From that point in time any market participant should be aware that deals done from then on might have to be moved to a CCP retrospectively. Up to that point in time grandfathering of existing deals is hoped for. ESMA is expected to decide within six months on regulator's request. It can be guessed that mandatory clearing for ESMA's resulting list of clearable derivatives is live at the end of 2013. The entities in scope of the clearing obligation are investment firms according to MiFID[19], credit institutions, (re-) insurance companies (each under relevant directives), other financial firms and non-financial counterparties (NFC) exceeding the "Clearing Threshold" (CT). The CT is compared with the amount of derivative positions at an NFC and discounts "commercial hedging" (= derivative positions taken with an objectively measurable risk reducing effect directly related to the commercial activity, including proxy hedging) and presumably intra-Group transactions from the measurement. To measure the CT, five asset classes are considered, which are credit derivatives, equity derivatives, interest rate, foreign exchange, and commodity or others derivative contracts. If the CT of presumably EUR 3 bn in gross notional value (EUR 1 bn for equity and credit each) is exceeded for at least one asset class, all deals fall under the clearing obligation. This matter of fact will be especially important for the Treasury operations of an NFC, as the margin requirements can become big all of a sudden. It can be expected that one has to comply with the clearing obligation within few months. Non-compliance with the clearing obligation will presumably leave the existing contracts legally valid. As concerns business between two NFC the clearing obligation only arises, if both are above the CT. Thus a lot of business between NFC still can stay uncleared, but the derivative business of an NFC with a bank will have to be cleared, if the CT has been crossed by the NFC.

14.4.5.2   What are the Benefits of a CCP?

Keeping the European focus we look a bit deeper into the working of a CCP according to the dominant "Principal to Principal" (P2P) model. Suppose an industrial corporate wants to sign a standardized derivative contract, which has been declared to be under a clearing obligation at a specified CCP. Seen from the perspective of this industrial corporate, which we call the Non-Clearing Member (NCM), the CCP becomes visible only through intermediation of a Clearing Member (CM), which forms a conduit to get the deals into the CCP.

Hence, the first P2P relation is between NCM and CM, i.e. these two do the deal. In the next step the CM enters into a back-to-back trade with the CCP. To make the CCP the ultimate credit risk from the perspective of the industrial corporate, the margins are transferred by the CM to the CCP via full title transfer and thus are owned by the CCP. The industrial corporate gets a security interest over the right of the Clearing Member (CM) to receive amounts that are left over after closing out positions in case a CM defaults. If CM defaults, all transactions and collateral are ported to another CM by the CCP.

It becomes evident that the CCP is now the point of focus. The lines of defense of the CCP to cover the financial consequences of the default of a CM can be ordered as follows:[20]

1. use of margins paid in by CM,
2. the contributions to the clearing fund of the affected CM,
3. any remaining contributions of the affected CM to the clearing fund,
4. the reserves of the CCP,
5. the contributions of all non-affected CM on pro rata basis,
6. contingent capital from all non-affected CM.

Effectively the NCM is exposed to the CCP in a "7th loss position." This is much more senior than in traditional bilateral margined transactions under a Master Agreement. But as the GFC has taught us, a senior position can turn into a mezzanine all of a sudden if systemic risk materializes.

Therefore, on top of these multiple lines of defense there is the perception of a CCP as a systemically relevant institution. Thus credit monitoring is done by the supervisors, who are paid for monitoring and managing systemic risk. In the words of EMIR: "Furthermore, as the use of CCPs becomes compulsory under EU-law, they must be subject to rigorous organizational, conduct of business and prudential requirements."

14.4.5.3   What Could it Mean for the Marketplace?

Market forces will presumably lead to few CCP.[21] As a further downside, on top of this oligopolistic market structure it might happen that netting sets have to be torn apart because one leg of a spread position has to go on CCP1, whereas the other is now ordered to go to CCP2. Of course, one can try to stitch this back together with CPMA, but whether and how this will work has to be seen.

Formerly non-margined positions will have to be margined.[22] As the amount of available high quality collateral rather shrinks than grows, the supply side of collateral goes down, whereas the demand side moves sky high. It is evident that this can lead to a general collateral squeeze. In the words of the IMF:

> The shrinking set of assets perceived as safe, now limited to mostly high-quality sovereign debt, coupled with growing demand, can have negative implications for global financial stability. It will increase the price of safety and compel investors to move down the safety scale as they scramble to obtain scarce assets. Safe asset scarcity could lead to more short-term volatility jumps, herding behavior, and runs on sovereign debt.
>
> —IMF, 2012, p. 1

But when a problem of system-wide importance is approaching, one can start to react:

> Indeed, one CCP has already decided that high-grade corporate bonds will be accepted as initial margin for swap trades as a result of a shortage of high-quality assets
>
> —IMF, 2012, p. 15

We also might see a repetition of central banks' behavior during the crisis, i.e.

> central banks could and actually did act as a backstop by temporarily exchanging riskier assets with safer ones (central bank money), in part via an expansion of eligible collateral types, with more frequent open market operations to a broader range of counterparties and at longer maturities
>
> —IMF, 2012, p. 30

Looking at the set of CMs and "house banks" involved with each CCP, it will turn out that often one and the same small set of banks are around the few CCP, i.e. these underlying risk driving entities link the fate of the CCP.[23] In addition these banks might already play an important role in helping many smaller banks in their derivative business. But much more important is their service for the CCP: As committed lines of credit are employed by the CCP as one form of liquidity, a CM gets even more important than just playing its role in the lines of defense.

Combining this with a general collateral squeeze scenario yields an interesting exercise in credit risk measurement in a portfolio context. It could happen that the whole system now shows a higher concentration of credit risk than before. On top, there are various feedback loops: if markets get stressed the calls for initial margins will go up, the haircuts on non-cash collateral get bigger, the credit lines smaller etc. (for much more detail see IMF, 2012). Obviously the well-known pro-cyclicality of the Basel banking regulations boosts the threatening potential to the system.

Without the clearing obligation we could choose from a multitude of counterparties and just do margining with zero or very low thresholds. This step turns the bulk of the credit risk entangled in a deal between two industrial entities or a bank into margin at risk. Thus a significant improvement in system stability can be achieved by making margining obligatory for a defined set of products and business relations. It is understandable that the supervisors need central evidence of the OTC business. An obligation to report all trades into Trade Repositories (TR) can achieve this.

These two obligations alone would achieve a lot. But now it seems as if one were also obliged to contribute to a risk concentration exercise. In order not to spend too much time on systemic risk issues, we neglect these potential downsides of increased systemic risk and conclude that – with a pinch of salt – the effect of a move to a CCP is that it turns credit risk into margin at risk.

14.4.5.4   What Could It Mean for the Setup of Credit Functions?

As there is much less credit-related threatening potential from a CCP, the measurement of Credit Value at Risk (CVaR) should be replaced by measuring "Margin at Risk." The latter quantifies a future "worst case" margin call and is solely driven by market prices, whereby the challenge in risk measurement lies less with the negligible credit risk of the CCP but more in a state-of-the-art modeling of commodity prices and funding conditions.

Making too conservative estimations of future liquidity needs results in the risk of paying too much to the banks – via commitment fees for potentially abundant liquidity lines – or simply holding too much cash.

The last aspect points to a general optimization of collateral. A Treasury-like function should have a say in what collateral is accepted and granted. It should try to maximize the value of collateral received and minimize the value of collateral given. The banks will try the same and they might be inclined to ask for a bit more collateral than the CCP does. As concerns cash collateral a proper choice of currency and interest rate would be part of the task. It is advisable that the function approves all CSA.

The function should also risk-manage collateral taken: is there too much of one type of collateral (e.g. mostly bonds from one issuer)? Is there wrong way exposure, e.g. Italian customers offering Italian government bonds as collateral? Or Italian customers offering guarantees from Italian banks sitting on big positions of Italian government bonds? Are there filing requirements when taking collateral or recharacterization risk?[24]

For collateral which is transferred via full title transfer, an active use of collateral is commercially reasonable, as already done by the banks. Bonds could be sold in combination with a repurchase agreement and provide another form of secured funding. By the same token the sale of the bond would underline the full title transfer and minimize recharacterization risk.

To simplify the management of collateral it is advisable to streamline the Master Agreements and CSAs. This also ensures that hedging relations are not broken up at disparate times when there is a default under one Master but nowhere else. This streamlining could also form an opportunity to shorten the time horizon for close outs and to bring down thresholds or transform them into Minimum Transfer Amounts if that appears more sensible. It should be noted that this section has only provided a first glance at the potential consequences.

14.5   *EX POST* RISK-REDUCING TECHNIQUES

14.5.1   Factoring

Factoring is often used synonymously with "Accounts Receivable Financing." As a consequence of the GFC, banks were reluctant to grant credit to industrial corporates and put them in a situation where they had to raise cash via alternative routes. One such route is to sell "Accounts Receivable" to a factor, which is a company specialized in the purchase of receivables.

Thus the industrial corporate is no longer dependent on the conversion of "Accounts Receivable" to actual cash payment from their counterparties. This is an advantage in terms of time and reliability. But of course this does not come for free, as there is the factor's fee. This fee varies with the fine print of the factoring agreement and is highest in the case of "Non-Recourse Factoring." This is the traditional method of factoring and puts the risk of non-payment fully with the factor. If the counterparty cannot pay the invoice due to insolvency, it becomes the risk of the factor. The factor cannot seek payment of the receivable from the seller. So it is clear that the factor will only purchase "solid" invoices and often turns away lesser credit qualities or buys them only at very significant discounts, which impairs the financing function.

As even a weak industrial corporate can generate good quality receivables, factoring is more easily attainable than traditional bank and equity financing. Other forms of factoring, where the factor can make recourse to the seller, are of no importance in the context of credit risk-reducing techniques.

14.5.2   Novation

Novation means that one of the existing counterparties in a contract is exchanged for a new one through a trilateral agreement, i.e. the two "old" counterparties and the "new" one agree on this replacement. To give an example, assume that we are an industrial corporate and have bought "financial coal" from Lehman, i.e. we have agreed on a swap where we pay fix and receive the index API2. Now we feel uncomfortable with Lehman as counterparty and want to move to a CCP. Normally we are not a member of the clearinghouse and therefore need a clearing broker. The clearing broker typically is a bank and we assume that it is our favorite top-notch bank B. We three agree now that Lehman is replaced by B. Next B, Lehman and the CCP agree to put the trade on the clearinghouse. Thus both banks face the clearinghouse as new counterparty and we face B instead of Lehman.

14.5.3 Risk-reducing Trades

One example has been already given in the section on novation. By replacing a weak counterparty with a stronger one, credit risk can be reduced, i.e. the probability of a credit loss can be decreased while the credit exposure stays the same, since the commodity nature of the deal did not change.

Inserting a stronger middle man into a business relation is called "Sleeving." The "Sleeve" is an entity that both original counterparties accept as their new counterparty. For taking on two additional credit risk positions, the sleeve earns a spread between the purchase and selling price.

Putting existing transactions on a clearinghouse is one form of "Sleeving." In the GFC "Sleeving" was also done in the traditional format using other market participants as "Sleeves."

The step preceding "Sleeving" and carrying out other costly risk-mitigating measures should always be the minimization of credit exposures subject to keeping the desired positions in the commodity markets.

The easiest step is to check whether "Master Agreements" or "CPMA" can be negotiated ex post, which allow (more) netting (offsets in the case of CPMA). If not, it pays to check whether there are entities within a group with offsetting commodity positions. Assume that one part of the group has bought oil and the other has sold exactly the same specification and amount to exactly the same external counterparty. In this case the physical position is flat but the group carries two redundant credit exposures. Unwinding these deals externally and setting up intra-group replacement trades is a worthwhile exercise, even if the contracts do not offset each other completely.

Now imagine a situation where three counterparties have created the following "Triangle": A has sold commodity X to B, who has sold to C, where A has bought from. Physically A is flat in commodity X but carries two redundant credit exposures to B and C. Of course only one of the two deals can be in the money at one point in time but that should be a big enough concern for A to look for such "Triangles." As a rule A knows about its trades to B and C but not about the trade between B and C. There are now professional service providers like the company "TriOptima," who help to discover redundant credit exposures and propose them for unwinding to all counterparties, who agreed to participate in such exposure compressions, which are executed in what are called "cycles." This is usually more efficient than exploring the marketplace oneself for triangular relations. Such risk-reducing trade "cycles" were being carried out before the insolvency of Lehman. This is therefore one of the more modern techniques of risk reduction.

14.5.4 Hedging with CDS

If you were a bond portfolio manager you could manage your exposures either by selling the bond, hedging it with a credit default swap (CDS), through a collateralized bond obligation (CBO) or by referencing it in a synthetic collateralized debt obligation (CDO). These instruments and techniques are explained in the books by Felsenheimer et al. (2006) and Schönbucher (2003). As the latter two markets (CBO & CDO) have dried out during the financial crisis, we are left with the CDS. The buyer of a CDS receives protection against losses arising from a credit event from the referenced entity, e.g. a particular corporate customer. The size of protection is determined by the notional of the CDS contract. For a bond investor holding USD 10 mn of a bond issued by the referenced entity a perfect hedge would be to buy exactly that notional amount using a CDS with the same tenor and seniority as the bond. For that, she or he has to pay a running premium to the CDS counterparty. If the credit event occurs, the premium payment stops and the CDS counterparty has to pay an amount of "(100% minus recovery rate) times notional" to the CDS buyer. The recovery rate is determined through an auction for the bonds issued by the referenced entity. For more details we refer the reader to the literature quoted.

In most Western countries the contractual claims from commodity contracts rank equally with outstanding debt in an insolvency situation. Therefore the CDS is a potential instrument for managing the credit risk in a commodity portfolio. As there are roughly more than thousand names traded in the CDS market worldwide, there is a chance that the corporate customer under consideration can be hedged with a CDS. But even if a CDS is not yet traded on a certain name it is worthwhile to check whether that corporate has issued a bond because that would enable a standard CDS to be written on that name. And even if no bonds were outstanding one could go for a CDS with a fixed recovery rate, where the rate is pre-agreed by both counterparties of the CDS. There are thus many ways in which the bulk of credit risk can be externalized. As a rule the most efficient one is the standard single name CDS. We are then left with the CDS counterparty risk, but as highlighted above that can be brought down to lower levels by bilateral margining.

The CDS can therefore be a useful tool for hedging credit risk as soon as one is able to quantify the right amount of protection notional and is willing to accept some basis risks, which will be discussed subsequently. For example, hedging the PFE is not only costly but would presumably raise questions by the auditor, why there are such huge CDS positions on the book of an industrial corporate while the "hedged" positions show only a small, current MtM. One attempt to provide a more suited hedging tool is the C-CDS. Before we discuss C-CDS, we highlight the basis risks already involved in standard CDS.

The basis risks evolve because the following questions defining a CDS are answered differently in a commodity contract than under standard CDS terms.

14.5.4.1 *What Company is Referenced?*

As a rule commodities are often traded with subsidiaries of larger groups (see also the section on PCG). The reference entity that is quoted in the CDS market is usually not the same one that one trades with. Unless there is an explicit link between our counterparty and the reference entity there is a basis risk. In certain cases it can be tailored away, e.g. via PCG.

14.5.4.2 *Where do you Look at to Find Credit Events?*

The standard CDS is not triggered by commodity contracts but is referring to debt in the wide sense of bonds issued by the Reference Entity or loans taken. The behavior of the Reference Entity under a commodity contract is irrelevant.

14.5.4.3 *What Obligations are Usable?*

The receivable from the commodity contract is not a deliverable obligation under standard CDS terms. Instead only certain senior unsecured bonds go into an auction after a credit event has happened to determine the loss via the difference between the secondary market value (determined by auction) and par. In most jurisdictions, the receivable from the commodity contract ranks equally with the senior unsecured bond. The mismatch arises due to the timeline of cashing in the value from the receivable. Whereas the holder of a senior unsecured bond gets the cash as soon as the auction has happened, one has to go through the work-out process with the receivable, which is rather lengthy. It might even happen that the counterparty to the commodity contract has not gone into insolvency but only the reference entity.

14.5.5   Hedging with Contingent-CDS

In a C-CDS the notional of the CDS is dynamic and equal to the MtM of a referenced (in our case: commodity) position. All other terms are those of the standard single name CDS as we know it. In order to avoid the misunderstanding that the C-CDS is the ultimate solution we point to the mismatches described above for the plain vanilla CDS.

The view of the protection seller as to whether he or she can set up decent hedging positions in the underlying credit and commodity markets determines the availability of C-CDS. As concerns the specifics of the commodity markets we discuss them in a subsequent section. With respect to the credit markets, it can be assumed that the C-CDS will not cover more names than the standard CDS. As it can be considered a necessary condition for a corporate customer to be "hedgeable" via standard CDS to have an external rating, the potential coverage via CDS will turn out rather limited.

In fact C-CDS have occasionally been seen related to the MtM of Interest Rate Swaps but so far never related to a commodity price-driven MtM.

14.5.6   Hedging with Puts on Equity

If the counterparty's shares are liquidly traded, one might ponder hedging with an out of the money put on their stock price.[25] In fact, out of the money puts on equity and CDS are very similar products and the difference is rather in terms of tenor. Whereas the put is a product typically covering short term (at the money options are liquidly traded up to one year), the CDS typically gives coverage for 5 years. What is needed to make this workable is a model that relates equity and credit. Typically this can be done via so-called "structural models" (see Schönbucher, 2003). Although these models have been criticized for not being able to explain credit spreads, recent research shows that this has to be differentiated. Structural models are capable of performing at least as good as reduced-form models, as long as similar initial conditions are provided (Gündüz and Uhrig-Homburg, 2011). But any hedging with equity derivatives needs fundamental credit analysis to set the model parameters in order to avoid too much mismatch risk. For further information the reader is referred to the quoted literature.

14.6   *EX POST* WORK OUT CONSIDERATIONS

How far the *ex ante* exposure-reducing techniques hold up in an insolvency situation depends on the relevant insolvency code(s). The plural comes in because as a rule we have at least three locations with potentially different codes to face: the country of each counterparty and the country where the collateral sits. We only highlight some big points in light of the limitations of this chapter: in the preceding sections it has become evident that the function of collateral is to "mop up" the rest of exposure after netting. Using established contractual frameworks makes this a very effective tool in real life and it has helped to limit the losses from Lehman and the like. But one is not always in the comfortable situation of holding collateral and to benefit from netting. Therefore a bit more effort might be needed and, in general, granting the work out managers the ability to act based on good judgment, reliable information about the existing exposure, and the commercial situation of the insolvent counterparty is the road to loss minimization.

Generally speaking a work out strategy starts with summarizing the alternatives for action and can be designed before the insolvency, at the point when the counterparty is getting weaker and weaker. What can be done in light of the contract (e.g. use a MAC in advance to an insolvency)[26] and based on national legislation (e.g. similar clauses in trade law) defines the set of alternatives. A game theoretic approach can help to check how these alternatives are considered from the angle of the various "participants in the game," for example the willingness of the counterparty to cooperate might be judged by estimating the inclination to whitewash assets or guessing the strategic importance of an uninterrupted production for the counterparties' group. Once insolvency is reached, the (preliminary) insolvency administrator becomes an additional participant and the other creditors, each with a specific target function. Continuation of the delivery of the commodity has to be decided from day to day under risk and return considerations. It pays to be able to have a good understanding of the willingness and ability to pay. Changes in the conditions for delivery are common, because now an absolutely weak counterparty has to be served. Prepayment and shortening of risk horizons (e.g. fixing quantities and prices only for the next month) might become advisable. As every case is very specific, there are no "one size fits all" approaches.

14.7 PRACTICAL CREDIT RISK MANAGEMENT AND PRICING

If traders or salesmen are not able to earn the cost of credit of their business then the challenging question arises: why does one not buy a bond from that corporate customer instead or write a CDS on that name?

Simple as it seems, the line of reasoning goes astray in the latter part as neither the bond nor the CDS would provide a perfect hedge for a commodity-driven exposure. The perfect hedge would be a C-CDS. The C-CDS would not only hedge a credit event but also cover the MtM moves. The line of reasoning would be correct if the costs of credit were based on C-CDS quotes and the C-CDS would not suffer from the mismatches already known from the standard CDS.

Hence, we have to be modest and face the fact that PE cannot be perfectly hedged and that there is no market price for this part of credit risk readily available. More hope is with the SE. The SE can be hedged via CI or CDS but in case of CI we have had a glance at the potential fine print and should not underrate the credit exposure to the insurer itself. This leaves us with very small subsets of counterparties and credit exposures which we can put a market price tag on. As an industrial corporate cannot restrict its business to that intersection of two small subsets it is forced to behave as an internal credit insurer if it wants to put a price tag on risks taken.

Crouhy et al. (2006) give some guidance on that in general and make clear how the pricing of credit risk fits into the context of shareholder value (their chapter 2) and related RAROC approaches (chapters 2 and 15), which go back to Zaik et al. (1996).

Here we list some specific steps to get an efficient set-up of this internal credit insurance operation. As credit risk management is not the core business of an industrial corporate, efficiency is the key in order to avoid losing business from credit risk price tags being too high.

The first step is the minimization of credit exposures per se with the various techniques that we have discussed. "Close Out Netting" is one prominent example and there are industrial corporates, which have achieved negotiation of Master Agreements with their counterparties in significant number.

The second step is the risk mitigation *ex ante* and *ex post*. *Ex ante*, the Front Office functions should explore what they can get easily from their counterparties (e.g. a PCG or short payment terms). Middle Office functions should be able to guide the Front Office to risk-reducing trades.

Both steps aim at minimizing the need for internal insurance, because the risk-bearing capacity of a corporate is a scarce resource and credit costs should be as low as possible. Therefore the existence of an internal insurer does not preclude external insurance (CI) or hedging with CDS if that is cheaper. In times of "risk-on mode" (i.e. risk-seeking markets) in the financial markets it can happen that there is little work for the internal insurer in terms of underwriting but more work in transferring risk to the outside world via CDS or maybe even CLO like structures if that is cheaper than CI, which effectively is similar to a mezzanine tranche of a CLO.[27]

The third step is the active management of the insurance portfolio. "Active" implies watching out for early warning signals and having lively communication between Front Office and the supporting insurance entities – not only at times of work out. Management means that the usual control cycle of measuring, reporting and action is implemented (see again Crouhy et al. 2006). It is clear that the internally calculated credit charges are the correct costs of credit as there are no others. To avoid that the Fornt Office is being overcharged by the monopolistic internal insurer, an independent risk-controlling function is essential.

The pricing principle is that of an insurer, i.e. the price is made up of a charge for "Expected Losses" and the costs for "Credit Risk Capital" (CRC). With IFRS 9 a correction of asset values for "Expected Losses" will come under the name of "Credit Value Adjustments." Thus for an industrial corporate it is no longer only a matter of good governance to have credit risk awareness in place.

In a subsequent section it is sketched how CRC can be measured in light of the commodity specifics we now turn to. It will become clear that negligence of the peculiarities can lead to mispricing of credit risk.

14.8 PECULIARITIES OF COMMODITY MARKETS

The stochastic nature of the credit exposures is also encountered in a bank that manages the counterparty risk in its trading book. But the dependence between commodity and credit dynamics gives rise to some differences. To give an example, assume that we have "time chartered" vessels at a fixed price from a carrier for a period of two years. In the GFC the charter rates went down as well as the creditworthiness of the carriers. Hence, the "Probability of Default" (PD) increased while at the same time the MtM went to negative numbers making our credit exposure zero. Determination of the credit costs without acknowledging this dependence would lead to overcharging the Front Office. What we face here is a so-called "Right Way Exposure." The opposite can be found in the sales business of commodities. If you sell power to corporate customers at a fixed price and prices go down with the economy, the PD goes up as the PE does. Modeling of credit risk in a commodity context should take into account "Wrong Way Exposures" in order not to underrate the CRC, and also "Right Way Exposures" in order not to waste risk-bearing capacity.

These two peculiarities get an additional push in significance due to the high volatilities, which one can encounter in the commodity markets. The high volatilities push up the PE as we have seen and also impact the SE in floating price deals. For the COE the short term behavior is especially relevant. Note that we encounter the so-called "Samuelson Effect" in commodity markets: Samuelson (1965) claimed that the volatility of forward price returns increases as time to maturity decreases. He argued that the most important information was revealed close to maturity of the contract. Thus short-term price movements are expected to revert back towards a long-run mean. This implies that long-dated contracts experience lower volatility than short-dated contracts.

Following Burger et al., a headline summary of the stylized facts of power prices (2007, 114) is:

• seasonal patterns and periodicities,
• price spikes,
• mean reversion,
• price dependent volatilities,
• long-term non-stationarity.

In principle all features also apply to other commodities. For instance, look at weather, which also impacts the demand for gas, oil and coal to say the least. If we move to longer forecast horizons, our best expectation about the future is the long term mean.

Mean reversion is also related to commercial adaptation processes. If the price for oil is high, more drilling will take place and all wet wells will contribute to future oil supply and bring down the oil price *ceteris paribus*. This explains why the mean reversion times for other commodities are longer than for power.

Price spikes also occur for other commodities. The price of oil is sharply driven by statements of the OPEC or individual oil-producing countries. The price for carbon (CO_2 emission rights) can move sharply in light of surprising political action or statements by politicians.

The political nature of commodity markets is another important special feature. As commodities are closely related to basic needs of the population, it is no surprise that the political influence is much bigger than in the financial markets. In terms of riskiness, commodity markets can easily compete with the financial markets – not only in terms of volatility as already discussed. The failure of a bank is clearly outpaced by a nuclear power plant failing. The most recent example is related to the catastrophe in Fukushima, Japan, on March 11, 2011, where nuclear power plants got out of control after a tsunami. On March 14, 2011 the German government issued the "Atom Moratorium" and in June 2011 the "Energiewende" was announced. Effectively these two measures led to an immediate shut down ("Moratorium") of 8 GW nuclear capacities and shortened the lifetime of the remaining nuclear power plants considerably with the goal to get completely rid of nuclear power by 2022 in Germany. The interesting fact is not only that it shows how "political" commodity markets can become, but also how special the information processing is. Interestingly, the forward prices reacted in March 2011 with a price increase, but the spot market for power did not. Such a behavior is unknown from equity markets. If information about the future of a company is published, the stock price reacts and forward prices move in tandem. More specifically in light of, say, bad news on the whole economy the future on the relevant equity index is shortened and puts pressure via arbitrage on the spot market too. That spot and forward can move independently, as in the case of German power, is due to the fact that power is basically non-storable.[28] Recent research has even shown that "forward prices cannot be explained by the spot (i.e. the historical filtration) alone" (Biegler-Koenig et al., 2011).

As concerns information processing in the crude oil futures market, recent research again shows some properties special to these markets, for example, "the reaction to news is significantly more pronounced in contango than in backwardation markets" (Borovkova, 2011). The two basic shapes of the forward curve, i.e. upward-sloping contango and downward-sloping backwardation, are also something special. Without high levels of dividend yields an equity forward curve would always be in contango due to positive financing costs.

Another feature is the fragmentation of commodity markets. Crude oil is traded in various specifications (Brent, West Texas Intermediate, Louisiana Light Sweet, etc.) and the same applies to all other commodities. For a detailed overview see Burger et al. (2007, p. 4). A common feature of non-storable power and the storable commodities is that it very much matters when and where the commodity is needed. This makes the network connections very important. For instance, even with LNG vessels now being bookable to transport gas to the most lucrative markets, the port and pipeline network still dictates where gas can be delivered eventually. It is evident that floating storage entails significant physical risk (e.g. vessel is damaged).

Physical risk comprises the loss potential due to the physical breakdown of important components, for example electricity lines might not be able to transport the agreed amount of electricity due to extreme weather conditions (sudden ice on the lines making them break) or congestion. It is clear that such breakdowns lead to spikes in market prices. Other examples are accidents like a burning storage for wooden pellets or the sudden shutdown of a power plant for technical reasons (i.e. outages). However, such events may have no impact at all on the market prices if the market is sufficiently big.

Cartea and Figueroa (2005) note that "two distinctive features are present in energy markets in general, and are very evident in electricity markets in particular: the mean reverting nature of spot prices and the existence of jumps or spikes in the prices." As a consequence they "present a mean-reverting jump diffusion model for the electricity spot price." Thereby they extend the model of Clewlow and Strickland (1999) towards fat-tailed distributions. Although we have not mentioned spot price models so far in detail, we do it here, because below we use the model of Clewlow and Strickland (1999).

In light of what has been highlighted so far it should be no surprise that the inter-market dependency structures are not stable. We try to take this fact into account below.

14.9   PECULIARITIES OF COMMODITY RELATED CREDIT PORTFOLIOS

We now turn to peculiarities of the credit portfolios related to commodity markets. As a logical consequence of the physical nature of the business, the set of knowledgeable counterparties is small per definition. This leads to concentration risk. The same results from the fact that the upstream markets exhibit rather oligopolistic structures. The concentration risk around CCP has already been mentioned. Another unavoidable concentration risk arises from the fact that there are only few suppliers of crucial components for power plants and other equipment needed in the industry (e.g. specialized vessels to build offshore wind turbines).

As concerns the credit quality of commodity producers, it is essentially capped at the rating of the domicile country. As substantial amounts of coal, oil and gas are produced outside of the G-20 countries this is an important issue for credit risk management.[29] On top of that, local financial standards and the quality of commercially relevant law are not always akin to what you know from the G-20.

The peculiarities of "Wrong and Right Way Exposure" have been mentioned already. Through being exposed to one and the same commodity for a subset of specialized market participants, challenging risk dependencies emerge.

An instructive example is as follows. Assume falling power prices. These impact the credit-worthiness of the few utilities in a national market simultaneously by lowering their earnings for the part of the production which has not been sold fixed forward and bringing their fixed price power sales contracts in the money, which means that rising credit exposures meet a shrinking risk-bearing capacity.

Looking at the products that are underlying the credit exposures in a commodity related portfolio, a lot of embedded options come to the light, which can push the effect of commodity volatility beyond linearity. Two prominent examples are "Swing Options" and "Extension Options." Only the former needs an explanation: the buyer of a commodity purchases a minimum amount unconditionally at a fixed price (forward) and gets the option to top up the amount up to an agreed maximum amount (call option with strike = fixed price). Thus he or she can swing between the minimum take and the maximum take.

Sometimes the industry offers so-called "Contracting Services," where for instance a power plant is built tailored to the needs of one single counterparty. As the design and location of the production site is tailored, an insolvency of the counterparty creates a much more challenging work out situation than for a standard product that can easily be sold to the market.

14.10   CREDIT RISK CAPITAL FOR A COMMODITY RELATED PORTFOLIO – MEASURED WITH AN EXTENSION OF CREDITMETRICS

The value of assigning CRC to the business units is twofold: in a static perspective it is done to honor the usage of the scarce resource "Risk-Bearing Capacity." Seen from a dynamic angle, the allocation of CRC should incentivize a move of the whole organization towards an optimal portfolio in the sense of RAROC. In the following we present a worked out example case for a very simplified gas portfolio and apply the usual credit risk horizon of one year. CRC is measured as CVaR (Credit Value at Risk) minus Expected Loss.

By now it should be clear that credit and commodity price risk have to be looked at simultaneously, which requires some more thought on the modeling of commodity dynamics. Gruber et al. (2007, 130) state that certain commodities can be modeled "via geometric Brownian motion." But as Gruber et al. state, this is only a starting point. State of the art models are rather multi-factor models of the forward curve (e.g. as described in Blanco and Pierce, 2012), which fit given market curves by construction and capture the dynamics of curve shape and level. In this context one should note the caution towards "perfect fit" as expressed by Schoutens, Simons and Tistaert (2003). Although many models can be fitted accurately to market prices for plain vanilla products, they still might lead to very different pricing and hedging as concerns more complex products. Unfortunately in real life complex products are rather the rule.

For reasons of convenience we sketch the simplest version of an arbitrage free commodity price model as introduced by Clewlow and Strickland (1999), which is a one-factor model. For this the two authors claim that their approach "can be seen as an extension of the first model of Schwartz (1997), in the same way that the Heath, Jarrow and Morton (1992) framework can be viewed as an extension of, say, the Vasicek (1977) model. The volatility structure of forward prices is the same, and reflects the mean reverting nature of energy prices, but the initial forward curve can be whatever the market dictates – unlike the Schwartz model where the curve is endogenously determined." For a simultaneous study of commodity and credit dynamics with the Schwartz model applied to "Structured Commodity Finance" see for example Kluge and Lehrbass (2003). As the approach by Clewlow and Strickland is superior, we use their one-factor model and apply it to natural gas traded at the "Title Transfer Facility" in the Netherlands (TTF).

The TTF forward price F(t,T) at maturity T and time t is assumed to be generated by:

$$\frac{dF(t, T)}{F(t, T)} = \sigma e^{-\alpha(T-t)} dz(t). \tag{14.5}$$

The parameter σ is the TTF spot price volatility, z(t) a standard Wiener process without drift and α stands for the constant force of mean reversion. Clewlow and Strickland show that the implied process for the spot price generates a log-normal distribution for the spot price at a future point in time. Thus European options on the spot can be priced by the Black–Scholes formula but with a "lengthier" expression for the volatility.

Another consequence is that the forward curve at any future time is simply a function of the spot price at that time, the initial forward curve and the two volatility function parameters. The forward is also log-normally distributed and option pricing along the lines of Black–Scholes is applicable again.

We consider a stylized gas contract for delivery of one MW of natural gas at TTF at a fixed price of 25 EUR for the full year ahead, say for the full year 2013. TTF gas is quoted per energy content in MWh and, to get a feeling for this amount, it is noted that a gas-fired power plant needs roughly 2 MWh of gas to produce one MWh of power.

As we consider a year contract this makes the total amount of gas to be delivered 365 days times 24 hours, i.e. 8,760 MWh. To keep things tractable we discuss the contract per 1 MW and note that we can hedge this contract by transacting 1 MW year ahead forward immediately, which also is assumed to trade at 25 EUR/MWh.

To calculate the exposure figures we need an assumption on the TTF year ahead forward price dynamics and assume it to be log-normal as in formula (14.1), which is legitimate in light of the results by Clewlow and Strickland. Inspired by the recent work of Korn et al. (2011) we set a volatility of 0.3 close to implied volatility levels, as it has turned out that implied volatilities contain superior information for risk management purposes. Especially with respect to the GFC, it has proven beneficial to move from backward looking historical volatilities to forward looking ones.

We determine the PFE by setting $\tau = 1$, $\eta = 0.3$ in formula (14.1). The risk horizon is one year, followed by a full year of delivery. We assume this for tractability and one can imagine the timeline as if today is 1 Jan 2012 and the time horizon for CRC measurement is one year, i.e. ends in Dec 2012, and the year ahead forward covers 2013. We assume that the last month, in which the forward is traded, is Dec 2012. We ignore the SE as it is not relevant within the risk horizon.[30]

Application of formula (14.1) yields that the level of gas prices, which is exceeded with 95% probability, is 15 EUR. Hence, the 95% PFE for a sales contract amounts to 10 EUR (25 − 10). As gas prices are floored at zero but not to the upside, the PFE for a purchase contract is higher, i.e. 14 EUR.

The EPE is 3 EUR and results again from an application of the Black–Scholes put formula for a strike of 25 EUR in case of a fixed price sales contract. Note that the EPE for a purchase contract is at the same level.

Of course we will not use these static PFE and EPE figures as an input into a standard credit portfolio model, because that would neglect the peculiarities of the commodity markets (i.e. setting EAD = LGD * PFE or EPE and using a credit portfolio model with deterministic exposures).[31]

Instead we look for a credit portfolio model which can be combined with the commodity dynamics. We apply a "state-of-the-art CreditMetrics-type portfolio model" (Duellmann and Kick, 2011), which is essentially the model introduced by Vasicek (2002). It models default as being triggered by an insufficient asset value, i.e. a counterparty defaults if its asset value falls below some default threshold. This threshold is set such that the given PD per counterparty is met for the time horizon under consideration. Let X_i be the asset return of counterparty i over the time horizon τ. Let $U, Y, Z_1, Z_2, \ldots, Z_n$ be mutually independent standard normal variables, which represent systematic and idiosyncratic risk factors. If we set

$$X_i = Y\sqrt{\rho} + Z_i\sqrt{1 - \rho} \qquad (14.6)$$

the asset returns of counterparties i and j will be correlated with a degree of ρ. This correlation parameter is termed the asset correlation. The spot price of gas at the time horizon τ is assumed to be log-normally distributed around today's forward level and the gas price log-return G consequently is a normal random variable with the following standard deviation:

$$Stdev(G) = \eta\sqrt{\tau} \qquad (14.7)$$

The dependence between commodity and asset returns is generated by constructing G as follows:

$$G = -0.5\eta^2\tau + \eta\sqrt{\tau}(\theta Y + \sqrt{1 - \theta^2}U) \qquad (14.8)$$

The systematic asset value Y and gas price returns are correlated with a degree of θ. Looking at empirical data one finds that this parameter is not constant. We model it as a normal random variable with a mean of 12% and standard deviation of 18%, where the levels are roughly motivated by a tentative analysis of the correlation between the returns of the German equity index DAX as a representative of "asset value" and of TTF prices.

We call this combination of a "CreditMetrics-type portfolio model" with log-normal dynamics for the commodity price and stochastic correlation a "three stochastic factor model" (3SFM).

It is noted that there are better ways to model correlation (e.g. the square root process by Emmerich, 2006), because drawings of θ could be outside the interval of −100% and +100%, but in the 10k simulation runs that we applied, no value of θ occurred outside of the mentioned interval.

It should also be noted that although on average returns over all asset classes tend be positively correlated, special situations can occur, where exactly the opposite happens.

For instance if, like in the two oil crises in the 1970's, rising commodity prices impact GDP growth and bring down stock prices. This flipping of correlation between negative and positive values is already captured by the simple assumption of the correlation to be normally distributed and therefore used in what follows. The asset correlation is kept constant. For a credit portfolio model with stochastic asset correlation see Roesch (2011).

It is clear that, following Korn et al. (2011), it would be good to apply implied parameters wherever possible. Unfortunately we can do this only for the TTF volatility as there is a liquid derivatives markets but not for the correlation parameters.

We consider a portfolio of 100 counterparties and investigate not only the case of having sold gas but also the other two extreme cases of having bought from our counterparties and nothing sold and the case of 50 short and 50 long positions.

We can color the nature of the three cases: a balanced portfolio arises if the industrial corporate has ordered its sales units to do one-to-one hedges immediately after signing the sales contracts. For proprietary trading, balanced portfolios are rather the exception than the rule. For trading, a weekly or monthly flipping between long and short portfolios can be expected.

Now we have to set the asset correlation parameter, which is assumed to be fixed at $\rho = 0.15$. Empirical research has shown that typical values are around zero. "The highest asset correlation ... is found in the German construction sector, with about 2.1%" (Hamerle et al., 2003). Nevertheless the banking world parameterization according to Basel II is centered on a value of 20% because "by assuming conservative values for the correlations, model risk should be absorbed as much as possible" (Hamerle et al., 2003). Obviously we try to stay in some middle area with our choice of parameter value.

To abstract from differences in rating and industry sector, only one type of counterparty is considered. To keep the results easily tractable a (uniform) one-year PD of 1% and a LGD of 100% are used.

We note that this stands in contrast to what has been elaborated so far. One could imagine big differences between the credit qualities of the buy and sell side. For example, buying all gas from a company like Statoil (rated AA) and selling it to other corporate customers would lead to a credit portfolio which is not balanced in terms of credit quality. As there are not that many AA or higher rated corporates, the buyers would be of lesser quality than our supplier. The same applies to the concentration risk topics, which are not reflected in our example case.

But the uniform counterparty assumption has some advantages: it is convenient and easy to follow and the experienced reader can guess easily where variations will lead, e.g. leaving the average PD the same but using differing values for different counterparties will regularly lead to a reduction in CRC. This has been elaborated by Broeker (2002).

Before we present the results from the simulations, we provide ourselves with an expectation for the figures by looking at the case of independence of commodity and default dynamics (asset correlation is nevertheless pegged to 0.15).

One can calculate the "Expected Loss" (EL) of the portfolio easily for the case of independence. The EPE per MWh is 3 EUR. This figure times the annual quantity times the number of counterparties (100) times the PD gives 26,280 EUR. The results from the simulation model with on average positive correlation between commodity and credit dynamics are shown in Table 14.1:

Table 14.1 Results for the simulation model with on average positive correlation between commodity and credit dynamics.

Expected Loss/Case (EUR)	All Short	Balanced	All Long
Expected Loss	28,965	25,166	20,876

As the mean level of the correlation θ is 12%, a pure sales portfolio (All short) exhibits a higher EL than in the case of independence due to the – on average – "Wrong Way Exposure" effect and a pure purchase portfolio (All long) benefits from the "Right Way Exposure."

Now we turn to the CRC measures, where we speak about the near and far tail of the distribution. Here the PFE helps to get a bit of orientation. We start with the number of defaults in the portfolio. The expected absolute number is 1 (1% of 100) and does not depend on the asset correlation of 0.15. There are 7 respectively 16 defaults corresponding to the quantiles at levels of 99% and 99.99%.

For the pure short (long) portfolio, all exposures move in parallel and multiplication with the PFE at level of 95% gives an estimate for potential Credit Value at Risk figures for levels beyond 99% when assuming the case of independence between commodity and credit dynamics. The PFE per MWh sold (bought) is 10 (14) EUR. This figure times the annual quantity times the number of counterparties defaulting at the 99% level gives EUR 613,200 (858,480). To get an analogous orientation for potential Credit Value at Risk figures for levels beyond 99.99% we do the same exercise and get EUR 1,401,600 (1.962.240). We call these figures "conservative estimates of CVaR."

It should be noted that these values for CVaR would result, if we used a standard credit portfolio model and feed in fixed exposures at the PFE level, i.e. ignore all what has been elaborated on the dependencies so far.

As one more refinement to the "three stochastic factor model" (3SFM) we now allow default at any time up to the risk horizon (e.g. a semi-dynamic model as in Schönbucher, 2003, p. 345). Now we need the dynamics of the commodity prices not only for a single point in time but at varying, stochastic default times.

Therefore we combine a semi-dynamic model as in Schönbucher (2003) with commodity dynamics according to a one-factor Clewlow Strickland model, where the rate of mean reversion α is chosen very close to zero (i.e. 0.000001) and the spot volatility σ to be 0.3. This choice of parameters makes the setting comparable to the 3SFM.

Schönbucher (2003, 345) describes a "static copula default risk model," which allows drawing the default times based on a given fixed default intensity per counterparty. We choose a Gaussian copula model and set the intensities to 0.01, which means that the expected time of default is 100 years. We get varying default times in the 10k runs. For each default time we generate a spot commodity price and take the relevant forward price from the thereby also stochastic term structure. As delivery starts at the end of the risk horizon of one year, it is always the same forward contract under consideration but now seen from varying (default) times. The modeling of the correlation is not changed. We call this dynamic model "three stochastic factor semi-dynamic model" (3SFSDM). All other settings of the example remain unchanged (flat forward curve at 25 EUR/MWh, 1% PD corresponds to a default intensity of 0.01).

Table 14.2   Credit value at risk under various modeling approaches.

Method	CVaR/Case (EUR)	All Short	Balanced	All Long	Percentage Changes		
Conservative Estimates	CVaR 99%	613,200	735,840	858,480			
	CVaR 99.99%	1,401,600	1,681,920	1,962,240			
3SFM	CVaR 99%	378,578	287,249	348,084	−38.26%	−60.96%	−59.45%
	CVaR 99.99%	1,523,168	913,900	1,332,642	8.67%	−45.66%	−32.09%
3SFSDM	CVaR 99%	321,236	217,039	230,554	−47.61%	−70.50%	−73.14%
	CVaR 99.99%	1,116,082	905,663	1,544,532	−20.37%	−46.15%	−21.29%

Table 14.2 shows the results for all three approaches and gives the percentage changes induced by moving to an increasingly refined modeling approach.

The highest decrease in risk capital appears for the CVaR 99%, amounting to a capital reduction of 73% for the "all long" portfolio. Although we have generated fat tails through the introduction of stochastic correlation, we only rarely get above the "conservative estimates of CVaR."

With a more realistic setting for the rate of mean reversion α and the spot volatility σ we would also be able to effectively incorporate the Samuelson effect. Instead of providing more glimpses at other refinements we close by hinting at the following case study, where an analytical credit portfolio model is briefly discussed. This analytical model can be considered a "starter kit" as a "free software" is available on the web and as it does not require setting up a Monte Carlo engine and forward and volatility surface fitting like in the models discussed so far.

14.11   CASE STUDY: CREDITRISK$^+$ APPLIED TO A COMMODITY RELATED CREDIT PORTFOLIO

The model CreditRisk$^+$ was published by Credit Suisse (Credit Suisse Financial Products, 1997) and is well known and established in the financial industry (see Gundlach and Lehrbass, 2004). Therefore we do not provide an introduction but refer to the literature. Since CreditRisk$^+$ is an analytical model, the portfolio loss distribution for real-life portfolios can be calculated within seconds. This feature makes the model attractive for practitioners and also makes it worthwhile to see how far one can get for a commodity portfolio with little effort. Therefore we put the example from above into a CreditRisk$^+$ setting.

First, we parameterize CreditRisk$^+$ such that the number of defaults at confidence levels of 99% and 99.99% are 7 respectively 16 defaults (corresponding to an asset correlation of 15%). Given the uniform PD of 1% we set the "Variability of the Default Rate" (Credit Suisse Financial Products, 1997) to match the quantiles of the default number distribution. We express this "Variability" as multiple of the PD (the resulting figure is the standard deviation of the total expected rate of default). We get a figure of 1.32 and resulting quantile levels of 7 respectively 16.6 defaults. As the latter value is a bit higher behind the decimal point we can

Table 14.3   Results for case study.

Method	CVaR/Case (EUR)	All Short	Balanced	All Long	Percentage Changes		
EAD pegged to PFE	CVaR 99%	613,200	735,840	858,480			
	CVaR 99.99%	1,489,156	1,786,656	2,084,156			
EAD pegged to EPE	CVaR 99%	184,099	184,099	184,099	−69.98%	−74.98%	−78.56%
	CVaR 99.99%	447,056	447,056	447,056	−69.98%	−74.98%	−78.55%
EAD lognormal shock a la BKW	CVaR 99%	263,555	277,506	289,780	−57.02%	−62.29%	−66.24%
	CVaR 99.99%	1,050,145	1,218,245	1,382,260	−29.48%	−31.81%	−33.68%

expect slightly higher CVaR figures. For the purpose of this case study this level of precision appears sufficient.

Having calibrated this way, we now can add the exposure data to make CreditRisk$^+$ calculate the portfolio loss distribution. With an LGD of 100% we can set the exposures at the level of PFE per MWh sold (bought) amounting to 10 (14) EUR. Alternatively we can choose the EPE, which is 3 EUR in both cases. The results (again for a year ahead contract, i.e. 8760 hours) are shown in Table 14.3. The method leading to the results in the last lines is explained subsequently:

There is the enriched version of CreditRisk$^+$ by Bürgisser, Kurth and Wagner (BKW, 2001), where the exposures are shocked stochastically up and down by a lognormal scaling factor with volatility v and mean of 1. Since we consider only one product (gas), we make use of their results "for a Single Segment" incorporating only "Systematic Default and Severity Variation," i.e. we keep the "Variability of the Default Rate" (the default correlations) as calibrated and shock all exposures simultaneously up and down. It should be noted that this setting results still in an analytical model.

In the case of the pure sales portfolio ("all short") we know that the PFE is 3.33 times the EPE. We set v such that the multiplicative shock has its 95% quantile at 3.33. The resulting v is 0.73. We set the exposures to be shocked at the level of the EPE and get the CVaR values as in the table. For a long portfolio we do it analogously and for the mixed one we take the average of the multiplicator between EPE and PFE. More explicitly we get for the "all long" $v = 0.94$ and for "balanced" $v = 0.84$.

The EPE-based results are more realistic than the PFE-based ones, because we get rid of the assumption that all counterparties default at their worst case exposure levels. In contrast, sometimes they might default when the contracts are not so much in the money. This is captured by the application of the BKW model.

It should be pointed out that independence between default and commodity dynamics is still assumed. Hence, the wrong way exposure feature as seen above in the sales contracts is not reflected as evidenced in the lower CVaR figures. It also becomes evident that this approach is rather limited to portfolios with homogeneous contracts (i.e. where the ratio EPE to PFE is rather uniform) and that one can be far off from the values generated by the extended CreditMetrics model.

14.12 OUTLOOK

As a rule existing credit functions are centered on credit analysis and follow a traditional commercial banking style approach. But there is change to come as a source from the industry spells out with a focus on trading portfolios:

> In line with the move to more exchange trading and clearing of OTC derivatives, energy credit teams may also find that assessing counterparty credit risk becomes less important. Instead, forecasting margin requirements and optimizing company credit lines and OTC capacity will come to the fore as companies attempt to remain on the right side of new regulations without stretching their balance sheets too far when it comes to posting collateral
>
> —Reitman and McCallion, 2011

The new focus would put less emphasis on the negligible credit risk of CCPs and more on a state-of-the-art modeling of credit and commodity prices as well as funding conditions. Another aspect is the optimization of OTC capacity, which not only requires traditional tools of risk mitigation but also includes innovative work on credit risk hedging strategies using CDS or insurance. A state-of-the-art modeling of credit, commodity and other important factors is a prerequisite to this.

On the other hand there are the sales portfolios, which require significant risk bearing capacity. Here one will see structured deals that will need to continue off the exchange and non-standard deals that have physical optionality in them. Thus know-how from commercial banking and commodity trade finance is highly relevant and the existing credit functions will not run out of work. A joint view on credit and commodity dynamics is worthwhile again. But there is no "one size fits all" approach. Ideally the set-up, workflows and model implementations are adapted to the prevailing business needs (e.g. are most deals exchange traded or OTC?, what are the relevant risk factors?) and have to balance resources and rewards.[32] The "rewards to resources" ratio gets especially low if high-cost controls in low-risk areas are in place. In the extreme not only risk increasing actions by Front Office need prior approval by controlling units but also risk-reducing (i.e. instead of low risk even lowering risk is heavily controlled). A checklist for balancing resources and rewards might look like (Reitman and McCallion, 2011):

- "Past loss data: how many losses have historically been experienced relating to this process or business?
- Audit findings: was the control introduced in response to a specific issue, or are thematic findings evident elsewhere in the process or business that is relevant to the analysis?
- External feeds: is further industry or political, economic, sociological, technological, legal or environmental data available that enables a more informed assessment of the associated risks?
- Loss modeling: what is the expected impact on future losses if these controls are reduced or removed?
- Failure cost: what is the anticipated worst-case impact arising from the removal of the control?"

The first question could be answered assuming a commonsense approach without going back too far in history. It is generally agreed that with respect to global financial markets we have seen worst case scenarios during the GFC. Thus a look at the realized losses over the last years gives good guidance.

In general this chapter has shown that there is no "ideal solution" and provided some thought on credit-related matters in a wide sense. Thereby we have reached the insight that future research will not run out of challenging topics!

NOTES

1. This may sound like an outdated statement, because credit portfolio models have taught us that even top-notch counterparties can become a concentration risk. With a pinch of salt this holds true only at very high levels of confidence for the Credit Value at Risk, e.g. a top-notch upstream company with their way 'above-average' exposures may well impact the 99.99 level but not those lower levels like 99% or 95% that are usually of interest for an industrial corporate.
2. A sales contract can reach out far beyond 3 years, which makes determination of the MtM rather difficult.
3. Imagine the potential size of the MtM of a 10-year contract, where a MtM is done by extrapolation of the forward curve.
4. For accounting purposes one could also differentiate between receivables and accruals according to whether an invoice has been sent or not.
5. The risk management tool for this eventuality is to employ capable legals and to operate in sound jurisdictions.
6. This value corresponds to the 95% quantile of a standard normal distribution.
7. We implicitly assume an insolvency quota of 0% for the sake of exposition.
8. For storable commodities like coal a flat forward curve could open up arbitrage opportunities if the financing rate is not equal to the convenience yield, which rarely is the case. We assume it to keep the calculations tractable. For more details see Burger et al., 2007, p. 48.
9. Netting is put in quotation marks as the CPMA makes use of set-off and not of netting. The difference will become clear subsequently. Both concepts are related but distinct.
10. For this chapter CSA signifies the English Law CSA whereby collateral is transferred with full title. This stands in contrast to the English Law Credit Support Deed (CSD) whereby merely a security interest in the collateral is evidenced. As a consequence under a CSD no use of collateral is permitted, e.g. it is not possible to sell a bond, which was received as collateral. The New York Law CSA seems to stand in the middle conceptually. Although it creates a security interest in the collateral it allows re-use (rehypothecation).
11. Note that only at first glance does "Minimum Transfer Amount" (MTA) seem to be equal to a "Threshold" (TH). The difference becomes evident once the level is exceeded. In the first case exposure up to the MTA is collateralized whereas in the second there remains an unsecured exposure amounting to the TH.
12. The determination of MtM for an illiquid contract can be agreed in advance but needs some creativity. For example, the forward curve for the liquid years can be extrapolated to allow MtM for a longer term deal. The agreement is on the method of extrapolation.
13. "Letter of Credit" can also be abbreviated as L/C or LOC. The qualifiers before the L are important, so a Doc LC is very different from a Standby LC, as we will see.
14. One can also get cover for a single name. However, for the purposes of this chapter paper we focus on portfolio policies.
15. Essentially all of these instruments refer to the same credit risk.
16. This section is partially based on insights from the ISDA conference "New Regulatory Environment for Commodity Trading and ISDA Commodity Definitions," March 2012.
17. TTF = Title Transfer Facility. TTF is a virtual hub and has established itself as the benchmark for gas traded in continental Europe.
18. APX Endex is a Dutch energy exchange. A transfer of TTF products to ICE seems to be under consideration.

19. MiFID = Markets in Financial Instruments Directive.
20. The wording to name the lines of defense is close to the one used by the European Exchange (Eurex). In fact the wording differs a bit from CCP to CCP.
21. The "winner takes it all" applies here, as maximum netting potential can be offered. The crucial competitive parameters are initial margin, fees and performance.
22. "The higher demand would arise from an upfront initial margin that typically is not posted on bilateral interdealer trades, and from contributions to guarantee funds at the CCP, with the size of contributions depending on the amount of cleared contracts." (IMF, 2012, p. 16). Moreover, the IMF mentions reductions in the overall potential to re-use collateral for the supply side, increased demand due to the Basel III Liquidity Coverage Ratio and Solvency II.
23. Interoperability (IO) of CCPs is another factor contributing to linking the CCP. IO means an arrangement between two or more CCPs that involves a cross-system execution of transactions.
24. This happens when a full title transfer is retrospectively re-interpreted by a court to be only a security interest over the collateral. If the security interest has not been perfected then the collateral is no longer accessible as full title is gone and the pledge has not been perfected.
25. This long vega trade can also be done by buying a call and shorting the shares. If the implied vola appears too expensive or if the derivative is simply not available, a replicating strategy might be pondered. An application to sovereigns can be found in Lehrbass (2000), where sovereign bonds are delta hedged via the national stock market indices.
26. The claw back periods should be kept in mind, which again shows that knowledge of the national insolvency codes is important.
27. This results from the structural features of CI. The possibility to decline coverage establishes seniority.
28. Pumped storage and storage via electrical mobility in cars are not significant enough to change that fact.
29. This also holds true on the demand side: for instance, the decarbonization of the developed countries and the hunger for energy and the absence of a carbon charge in the emerging markets/frontier markets will lead to a corresponding re-routing of coal: less coal burned in Europe, more in Asia.
30. No delivery within the year, thus no SE arises. Due to the time horizon of our risk analysis there is no need to include a jump component into the commodity price dynamics as proposed by Cartea and Figueroa (2005). This is more valid for short horizons.
31. We use the established abbreviations: EAD = Exposure at Default, LGD = Loss given Default, percentage figure showing what share of exposure is lost eventually. LGD is equivalent to 100% minus Recovery Rate. The latter corresponds roughly to the "insolvency quota".
32. Reward means the rewards from having controls in place, e.g. knowing/measuring positions, risk and performance, being able to optimize and manage.

REFERENCES*

Biegler-Koenig, R., Benth, F. E. Kiesel, R. 2011. An Empirical Study of the Information Premium on Electricity Markets. Presentation at the 12th Symposium on Finance, Banking, and Insurance, December 15–16, Karlsruhe Institute of Technology, Germany.
Black, F., Scholes, M. 1973. The pricing of options and corporate liabilities. Journal of Political Economy 81, 637–659.
Blanco, C., Pierce, M. 2012. Multi-Factor Forward Curve Models for Energy Risk Management, Energy-Risk, April.
Borovkova, S., 2011. News Analytics for Energy Futures, Presentation at the 12th Symposium on Finance, Banking, and Insurance, December 15–16, Karlsruhe Institute of Technology, Germany.
Burger, M., Graeber, B., Schindlmayr, G. 2007. Managing Energy Risk. Chichester: John Wiley & Sons.
Burgisser, A. Kurth, A. Wagner, 2001. Incorporating severity variations into credit risk. Journal of Risk, 3(4), 5–31.

*Conference presentations can be requested from the conference organizers. As a rule the presentations are related to working papers, which can be found on the web.

Broeker, F., 2002. Rating Quality and Capital Charge. Dresdner Bank discussion paper.

Cartea, A., Figueroa, M. G. 2005. Pricing in Electricity Markets: A Mean Reverting Jump Diffusion Model with Seasonality. Applied Mathematical Finance, 12, 313–335.

Clewlow, L., Strickland, C. 1999. Valuing Energy Options in a One Factor Model Fitted to Forward Prices. Working Paper, University of Technology, Sydney.

Coyle, J. J., Bardi, E. J., Langley, C. J., Jr. 2003. The Management of Business Logistics: A Supply Chain Perspective. Mason: South-Western.

Credit Suisse Financial Products, 1997. CreditRisk$^+$ – A Credit Risk Management Framework.

Crouhy, M., Galai, D., Mark, R. 2006. The Essentials of Risk Management. New York: McGraw-Hill.

Duellmann, K, Kick, T. K. 2011. Stress Testing German Banks Against a Global Credit Crunch, Presentation at the 12th Symposium on Finance, Banking, and Insurance, December 15–16. Karlsruhe Institute of Technology, Germany.

Emmerich, C. van, 2006. Modelling Correlation as a Stochastic Process. Technical Report. University of Wuppertal.

Felsenheimer, J., Gisdakis, P., Zaiser, M. 2006. Active Credit Portfolio Management. Chichester: John Wiley & Sons.

Gundlach, M., Lehrbass, F. Credit Risk$^+$ in the Banking Industry. Berlin: Springer.

Hamerle, A., Liebig, T., Roesch, D. 2003. Benchmarking asset correlations. RISK, November.

Gündüz, Y., Uhrig-Homburg, M. 2011. Does modeling framework matter? A comparative study of structural and reduced-form models, Discussion Paper No 05/2011. Deutsche Bundesbank.

Harding, P. C., Johnson, C. A. (eds.), 2002. Mastering Collateral Management and Documentation. Harlow: Pearson Education Ltd.

Heath, D., Jarrow, R., Morton, A. 1992. Bond Pricing and the Term Structure of Interest Rates: A New Methodology for Contingent Claim Valuation. Econometrica, 60, 77–105.

International Monetary Fund, 2012. Global Financial Stability Report – The Quest for Lasting Stability, April.

Kluge, D., Lehrbass, F. 2003. Default Probabilities in Structured Commodity Finance, in: Credit Risk. Heidelberg: Physica.

Korn, O., Kempf, A., Sassning, S. 2011. A Fully Implied Approach to Find the Global Minimum Variance Portfolio, Presentation at the 12th Symposium on Finance, Banking, and Insurance, December 15–16, Karlsruhe Institute of Technology, Germany.

Le Couteur, I., Weal, R. 2011. Cost of control: balancing risk and expense. RISK, September.

Lehrbass, F., 2000. A Simple Approach to Country Risk. In: Measuring Risk in Complex Stochastic Systems. Berlin: Springer.

Reitman, A., McCallion, P. 2011. The evolving credit function. Energy Risk, August 2011.

Roesch, D., 2011. Securitization Risk Measurement. Presentation at the International Conference on Credit Analysis and Risk Management, July 21–23, Oakland University, Rochester, Michigan, USA.

Samuelson, P., 1965. Rational theory of warrant pricing. Industrial Management Review 6, 13–32.

Schönbucher, P., 2003. Credit Derivatives Pricing Models. Chichester: John Wiley & Sons.

Schoutens, W., Simons, E., Tistaert, J. 2003. A Perfect Calibration! Now What? Working Paper, Catholic University of Leuven, Leuven and Brussels.

Schwartz, E. S., 1997. The stochastic behaviour of commodity prices: Implications for pricing and hedging. Journal of Finance 52, 923–973.

Vasicek, O. A., 1977. An equilibrium characterisation of the term structure. Journal of Financial Economics 5, 177–188.

Vasicek, O. A., 2002. The Distribution of Loan Portfolio Value. RISK, December.

Zaik, E. W., Walter, J., Kelling, G. 1996. RAROC at Bank of America: From theory to practice. Journal of Applied Corporate Finance Vol. 9, 83–93.

CDS Industrial Sector Indices, Credit and Liquidity Risk

Monica Billio[1], Massimiliano Caporin[2], Loriana Pelizzon[1]
and Domenico Sartore[1]

[1]Università Ca' Foscari Venezia
[2]Università di Padova

15.1 INTRODUCTION

Is sector credit risk primarily an industry-specific type of risk? Or is sector credit risk driven primarily by common factors? How stable is this relationship? Understanding the nature of industrial sector's credit risk is of key importance given the large and rapidly increasing size of the corporate bond and CDS markets. Furthermore, the nature of the industrial sector's credit risk directly affects the ability of financial market participants to diversify the risk of debt portfolios.

However, despite the importance of CDS in the financial markets, relatively little research about the sources of commonality of these financial products has appeared in the literature.

This chapter investigates these issues using four different methodologies. We first perform a simple dynamic correlation analysis. Second, we use principal component analysis to estimate the number and importance of common factors driving the changes in the CDS indexes. Third, we consider the Exceedence Correlation (EC) of Longin and Solnik (2001) to investigate the heterogeneity of the exposures to different observable factors. Fourth, we perform a quantile regression to investigate the heterogeneity of the exposures among different states of the common factors. We use an extensive database of Credit Derivatives Swap of US Industrial Sector Indices.

A Credit Derivatives Swap (CDS) contract is similar to an insurance contract: it obliges the seller of the CDS to compensate the buyer in the event of loan default. It is a swap because, generally, the agreement is that in the event of default the buyer of the CDS receives money (usually the face value of the bond), and the seller of the CDS receives the defaulted bond. Therefore, this contract is able to measure precisely the credit risk embedded in a corporate bond.

Inspired by the studies of Pan and Singleton (2008), Fontana and Scheicher (2010), Ang and Longstaff (2011) and Longstaff et al. (2011), we consider as observable factors ten different financial variables that are able to capture common exposure to (i) market risk, (ii) credit risk, (iii) liquidity risk and (iv) interest rate risk.

Three important results emerge from the analysis. First, the simple correlation analysis highlights that CDS industrial sector indexes co-move but with different intensity through time. Second, the co-movements are largely characterized by the common exposure to a single risk factor, that explains on average 82% of the changes of the 18-CDS indexes. However, this exposure changes a lot through time (from 33 to 96%) indicating that the relationship is not stable and not linear. Third, the exposure to credit risk and interest rate risk is non-linear, and is larger when the high yield bond spread and the interest rates face large changes. This means that there are some amplifying mechanisms in the transmission of credit and interest rate risks. These results indicate that diversification among sectors might collapse when credit and liquidity events hit the market. The information extracted from CDS market could thus provide relevant information for sector allocation strategies.

The remainder of the chapter is organized as follows. Section 15.2 describes the data. Section 15.3 presents the different approaches used to investigate the linearity of the relation across CDS and its stability and the results. Section 15.5 concludes.

15.2   THE DATA

The data for the five-year CDS of US Industrial indexes used in this study are obtained from Datastream and are based on CDS market quotation data from industry sources. The sample covers the period from January 2004 until December 2011.

We have considered the CDS Indexes of 18 economic sectors: Automobile (AUTOMOB), Banking (BANKING), Basic Resouces (BASICRES), Chemical (CHEMIC), Construction and materials (CONSTMAT), Financial services (FINSERV), Food and beverage (FOOD-BEV), Health care (HEALTCARE), Industrial goods and Services (INDLGDS), Insurance (INSURAN), Media (MEDIASEC), Oil and Gas (OILEGAS), Personal and Household Goods (PSNLHSLD), Retail (RETAILSEC), Technology (TECHNOL), Telecomunication (TELECOM), Travel and Leisure (TRAVLEI) and Utilities (UTILITIES). The beginning of this sample period is dictated by the availability of liquid CDS data.

Table 15.1 provides summary information for the daily CDS Indexes. All CDS Indexes are denominated in basis points and are, therefore, free of units of account for the CDS swap contracts. The average values of the CDS range widely across industries. The lowest average is 94.93 basis points for Banking; the highest average is 758 basis points for the Automobile sector. Both the standard deviations and the minimum/maximum values indicate that there are significant time-series variation in sovereign CDS premiums.

Table 15.1 also reports the summary statistics of the daily changes in sovereign CDS premiums. In Figure 15.1, we report the dynamic of the changes in the CDS spreads over time.

Table 15.2 provides additional descriptive statistics, and reports the correlation matrix of daily changes in the five-year CDS Index spreads. Table 15.2 shows that, while there is clearly significant cross-sectional correlation in spreads, the correlations are far from perfect. Most of the correlations are less than 0.7, and a few are negative. The average correlation across the 18 sectors is 0.25.

Since there is virtually an unlimited number of variables that could be related to Industry credit risk, it is important to be selective in their choice. We define the relevant common factors selecting variables used in previous studies to explain CDS variations; see Pan and Singleton (2008), Fontana and Scheicher (2010), Ang and Longstaff (2011) and Longstaff et al. (2011).

Table 15.1 Summary statistics.

Sector CDS Levels					
	Mean	Standard Deviation	Minimum	Maximum	Median
AUTOMOB	758.84	1160.16	139.7	8717.72	420.31
BANKING	94.93	85.34	10.2	595.99	94.3
BASICRES	232.66	362.56	44.14	4066.7	137.98
CHEMIC	156.94	221.83	44.88	3155.08	104.99
CONSTMAT	178.28	120.13	31.72	610.51	155.74
FINSERV	306.72	355.13	21.36	2015.21	199.03
FOODBEV	108.69	70.51	29.38	394.57	93.15
HEALTCARE	108.09	58.6	34.2	322.43	107.03
INDLGDS	126.52	91.83	48.55	754.15	103.33
INSURAN	345.88	401.54	17.24	3182.45	141.44
MEDIASEC	465.31	826.82	56	5981.22	225.7
OILEGAS	128.44	76.01	42.98	406.42	107.56
PSNLHSLD	222.49	153.28	46.51	926.71	225.44
RETAILSEC	184.67	135.82	41.61	949.58	157.43
TECHNOL	200.39	132.46	70.95	863.13	163.6
TELECOM	182.9	109.56	47.96	707.32	176.5
TRAVLEI	521.69	433.76	96.32	2458.63	369.01
UTILITIES	169.48	102.11	38.62	452.15	134.48

Change in Sector CDS Levels					
	Mean	Standard Deviation	Minimum	Maximum	Median
AUTOMOB	0.15	176.36	−5000.98	2568.11	−0.07
BANKING	0.1	11.64	−283.17	187.35	−0.02
BASICRES	0.11	99.67	−1722.25	1877.41	0
CHEMIC	0.03	60.53	−1076.7	1828.61	−0.03
CONSTMAT	0.13	5.83	−29.1	67.54	−0.02
FINSERV	0.24	46.02	−1361.87	754.63	−0.04
FOODBEV	0.05	3.13	−25.95	47.79	−0.02
HEALTCARE	0.06	2.78	−18.68	35.39	−0.04
INDLGDS	0.06	9.91	−314.88	230.78	−0.06
INSURAN	0.14	81.23	−2752.8	1191.93	−0.01
MEDIASEC	0.12	122.85	−2553.91	1857.08	0.01
OILEGAS	0.06	4.39	−54.66	57.61	−0.05
PSNLHSLD	0.23	10.44	−78.15	190.74	−0.01
RETAILSEC	0.12	7.56	−82.49	112.66	−0.05
TECHNOL	0.08	9.42	−111.02	92.14	−0.09
TELECOM	0.1	8.15	−132.1	175.33	−0.07
TRAVLEI	0.16	36.83	−650.47	338.76	−0.31
UTILITIES	0.12	4.65	−24.29	36.58	−0.06

This table presents summary statistics for daily 5 year CDS spreads and daily changes in CDS spreads for the 18 industrial sectors. The sample period considered is January 2004 to December 2011.

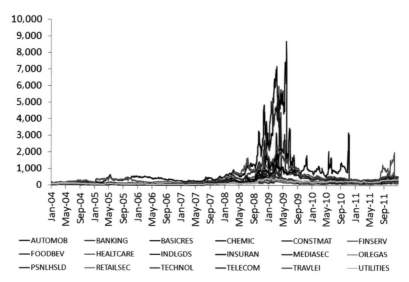

Figure 15.1   CDS levels across the economic sectors.

We use the daily return on the NYSE index (log-return) and the daily change in the VIX volatility index from the financial stock market.

From the bond market, we use the changes in the spreads of US investment-grade and high-yield corporate bonds. Specifically, we include the change in the spreads between five-year BBB- and AAA-rated bonds and between five-year BB and BBB-rated bonds. The former captures the range of variation in investment-grade bond yields, while the latter reflects the variation in the spreads of high-yield bonds.

From the government bond market, we use the "term spread" calculated as the difference between the yield to maturity of the 10-year Treasury bond and the 13-week TBill rate.

Moreover, recent research on corporate credit spreads suggests that these spreads may include premiums for bearing risks such as jump-to-default risk, recovery risk, the risk of variation in spreads or distress risk, liquidity risk, etc. As a proxy for the variation in the equity risk premium, we use monthly changes in the earnings-price ratio for the S&P 100 index. As another risk premium proxy, we use monthly changes in the spreads between implied and realized volatility for index options. We use monthly changes in the expected excess returns of five-year Treasury bonds as a proxy for changes in the term premium.

Liquidity risk is captured using two variables: the change in the difference between the US REPO rate and the 13-week TBill rate, and the change in the difference between Libor and the 13-week TBill rate.

Table 15.3 provides summary statistics of these 10 variables, while Table 15.4 reports the correlations between the changes in the CDS Indexes and the conditioning variables. As Table 15.4 shows, the correlations of the different CDS indexes and the common factors are quite different; however, the sign of the correlations are almost the same for all the different sectors.

Table 15.2 Correlations.

Correlation Matrix

	AUTOMOB	BANKING	BASICRES	CHEMIC	CONSTMAT	FINSERV	FOODBEV	HEALTCARE	INDLGDS	INSURAN	MEDIASEC	OILEGAS	PSNLHSLD	RETAILSEC	TECHNOL	TELECOM	TRAVLEI	UTILITIES
AUTOMOB	1																	
BANKING	0.11	1																
BASICRES	0.00	0.04	1															
CHEMIC	0.030	0.05	0.02	1														
CONSTMAT	0.23	0.30	0.06	0.06	1													
FINSERV	0.09	0.11	0.07	0.01	0.28	1												
FOODBEV	0.17	0.26	0.07	0.06	0.66	0.22	1											
HEALTCARE	0.18	0.28	0.05	0.09	0.69	0.2	0.72	1										
INDLGDS	0.07	0.14	0.01	0.04	0.28	0.12	0.28	0.29	1									
INSURAN	0.05	0.07	0.00	0.02	0.13	0.07	0.09	0.1	0.04	1								
MEDIASEC	0.08	0.01	-0.13	0.19	0.09	0.03	0.08	0.09	0.06	0.01	1							
OILEGAS	0.17	0.26	0.06	0.06	0.65	0.22	0.63	0.63	0.26	0.1	0.07	1						
PSNLHSLD	0.24	0.29	0.11	0.18	0.58	0.24	0.53	0.52	0.21	0.1	0.11	0.49	1					
RETAILSEC	0.33	0.28	0.05	0.11	0.66	0.23	0.63	0.61	0.22	0.11	0.16	0.53	0.65	1				
TECHNOL	0.23	0.25	0.09	0.06	0.57	0.23	0.51	0.53	0.21	0.09	0.11	0.48	0.46	0.53	1			
TELECOM	0.17	0.27	0.04	0.07	0.59	0.2	0.6	0.63	0.26	0.1	0.07	0.53	0.51	0.53	0.48	1		
TRAVLEI	0.1	0.13	-0.02	0.02	0.31	0.24	0.3	0.27	0.1	0.07	0.11	0.27	0.23	0.32	0.3	0.24	1	
UTILITIES	0.21	0.28	0.08	0.08	0.68	0.25	0.65	0.68	0.28	0.11	0.09	0.7	0.53	0.57	0.53	0.58	0.27	1

This table reports the correlation matrix of daily CDS index changes. The sample consists of daily observations for January 2004 to December 2011.

Table 15.3   Summary statistics of conditioning variables.

	Conditioning Variables Levels				
	Mean	St.Dev.	Min	Max	Median
BB-BBB	1.78	0.99	0.52	6.37	1.47
BBB-AAA	1.49	0.9	0.5	4.73	1.41
LIQRISK	0.21	0.19	−0.1	1.72	0.15
NYSE	7649.92	1220.64	4226.31	10311.6	7484.5
RISK-APP	3.14	4	−23.76	26.18	2.92
SP100-PE	19.94	5.5	12.57	40.57	18.5
TBOND5RATE	3.14	1.2	0.79	5.23	3.18
TED	0.51	1.55	−2.04	5.14	0.68
TS	1.89	1.33	−0.62	3.85	2.17
VIX	21.16	10.69	9.89	80.86	18

	Changes in Conditioning Variables				
	Mean	St.Dev.	Min	Max	Median
BB-BBB	0.00	0.07	−0.57	0.6	0
BBB-AAA	0.00	0.06	−1.52	1.53	0
LIQRISK	0.00	0.07	−0.94	0.58	0
NYSE	0.5	99.52	−686.36	696.83	4.13
RISK-APP	0.00	2.5	−26.43	18.67	0.06
SP100-PE	−0.01	0.49	−10.31	4.55	0
TBOND5RATE	0.00	0.07	−0.46	0.34	0
TED	0.00	0.07	−0.75	0.82	0
TS	0.00	0.08	−0.49	0.73	0
VIX	0.00	1.96	−17.36	16.54	−0.07

This table presents summary statistics for the conditioning variables. The sample period considered is January 2004 to December 2011.

15.3   METHODOLOGY AND RESULTS

15.3.1   Preliminary Analysis

As a first evaluation of the linearity of the relation across CDS and its stability we consider the rolling evaluation of the linear correlation. We calculate correlation between changes in CDS spreads considering 60 observations, roughly equivalent to one quarter. The rolling correlation (average across the 18 sectors correlations) is plotted in Figure 15.2 from March 2004 through December 2011. This figure shows overall high values of the correlation between changes in the CDS Indexes (generally between 0.13 and 0.88). Furthermore, we observe that the correlations across the Industries change greatly through the sample. Starting from December 2008, it increased from 0.30 to 0.80. Looking to the last part of the sample, it seems that the overall correlation among the different countries has been reduced. However, this is not the case for all the Industries. For example, in the last part of the sample the correlation with Utilities and almost all the other Industries has increased (the rolling window correlations among the sector indices are available upon request).

Increased commonality among CDS Sector Indexes can be empirically detected by using principal components analysis (PCA), a technique in which the changes of the CDS Indexes

Table 15.4 Correlations between conditioning variables and Sector CDS.

	BB-BBB	BBB-AAA	LIQRISK	NYSE	RISK-APP	SP100-PE	TBOND5RATE	TED	TS	VIX
AUTOMOB	0.16	0	0.03	-0.1	0.06	0	-0.08	0.03	-0.05	0.07
BANKING	0.21	-0.03	0.05	-0.24	0.18	-0.01	-0.11	0.06	-0.06	0.2
BASICRES	0.07	0	0	-0.05	0.01	0.05	-0.05	0	-0.02	0.01
CHEMIC	0.05	-0.04	0.05	-0.02	-0.01	-0.01	-0.04	0.03	-0.01	0.02
CONSTMAT	0.55	0.06	0.08	-0.44	0.3	-0.02	-0.26	0.11	-0.13	0.42
FINSERV	0.23	-0.04	0.04	-0.16	0.13	0.01	-0.12	0.06	-0.07	0.15
FOODBEV	0.47	0.08	0.07	-0.36	0.19	-0.02	-0.21	0.1	-0.08	0.31
HEALTCARE	0.52	0.07	0.06	-0.34	0.22	-0.04	-0.22	0.12	-0.08	0.31
INDLGDS	0.21	0.05	0.03	-0.12	0.08	0.02	-0.11	0.03	-0.06	0.09
INSURAN	0.11	-0.01	0.03	-0.1	0.1	0.08	-0.05	0.03	-0.02	0.11
MEDIASEC	0.07	-0.02	0.02	0.01	0	-0.03	-0.03	0.02	0	0.01
OILEGAS	0.48	0.09	0.02	-0.32	0.17	0.01	-0.19	0.07	-0.11	0.28
PSNLHSLD	0.41	-0.02	0.05	-0.34	0.22	-0.03	-0.18	0.07	-0.09	0.29
RETAILSEC	0.5	0.01	0.08	-0.37	0.28	-0.05	-0.25	0.09	-0.1	0.33
TECHNOL	0.4	0.02	0.08	-0.26	0.19	-0.04	-0.16	0.11	-0.02	0.25
TELECOM	0.45	0	0.06	-0.31	0.25	-0.05	-0.18	0.11	-0.06	0.33
TRAVLEI	0.23	0	-0.01	-0.12	0.09	-0.02	-0.06	0.02	-0.03	0.13
UTILITIES	0.51	0.07	0.07	-0.36	0.22	-0.01	-0.22	0.14	-0.08	0.31

This table presents the correlations between the changes in the conditioning variables and the changes in the Sector CDS. The sample period considered is January 2004 to December 2011.

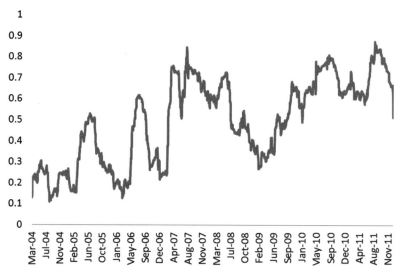

Figure 15.2   Average rolling correlations.

are decomposed into orthogonal factors of decreasing explanatory power (see Muirhead, 1982 for an exposition of PCA).

The time-series results for the Cumulative Risk Fraction (i.e. eigenvalues) is presented in Figure 15.3. The time-series graph of eigenvalues for the most important principal components (PC1, PC2, PC3 and PC4) shows that the first principal component captures the majority of changes in CDS during the whole sample, but the relative importance of these groupings varies considerably. Periods in which the first principal component explains a larger percentage of total variation are largely associated with the last part of the sample. In particular, Figure 15.3

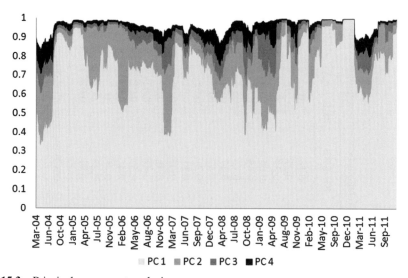

Figure 15.3   Principal component analysis.

shows that the first principal component is very dynamic, it captures from 33 to 99% of CDS variation, increasing significantly during crisis periods. The PC1 eigenvalue increases from the beginning of the sample, peaking at 96% in 2004, and subsequently decreases. The PC1 eigenvalue starts to increase in 2005 during the GM/Ford crisis, declines slightly in 2006, increases again in 2007 and then subsequently decreases. In 2009, it continues to increase in line with the Sovereign European crisis. As a result, the first principal component explains 82% of CDS variation over 2010–2011. The results show that there is strong commonality in the behavior of CDS Industrial Indexes.

As a further analysis, we consider the exceedence correlation (EC) of Longin and Solnik (2001). EC is a conditional correlation measure across two time series. It takes into account only those observations when the two time series are both above or below a given empirical quantile. In formulae, if we consider the quantile or order α, and focus on two economic sectors i and j, EC is computed as follows:

$$EC^- = Corr\left[\Delta CDS_{i,t}, \Delta CDS_{j,t} | F_i\left(\Delta CDS_{i,t}\right) < q, F_j\left(\Delta CDS_{j,t}\right) < q\right], \quad (15.1)$$

$$EC^+ = Corr\left[\Delta CDS_{i,t}, \Delta CDS_{j,t} | F_i\left(\Delta CDS_{i,t}\right) > 1 - q, F_j\left(\Delta CDS_{j,t}\right) > 1 - q\right]. \quad (15.2)$$

where F_i and F_j are the cumulative density functions of the corresponding CDS variations. Therefore, EC is represented by two values, EC^- measures the correlation in the lower quantiles α, while EC^+ considers observations above $1 - \alpha$. EC is generally measured for several values of α. By convention, the graphs report at the center (for $\alpha = 0.5$) the full sample standard correlation, while on the two sides, we have EC^- (on the left) and EC^+ (on the right).

Table 15.5 presents the summary statistics of the exceedence we have calcualted among the different sectors. We report the exceedence correlations by reporting in the middle the full sample standard correlation, while on the left and right sides, we report EC^- and EC^+, respectively. As the mean, the min, the maximum and the different percentiles show, in

Table 15.5 Descriptive statistics of exceedence correlations within CDS sectors.

	MIN	MEAN	MEDIAN	MAX	25%	75%	5%	95%
0.05	−0.26	0.13	0.11	0.77	−0.04	0.25	−0.15	0.50
0.10	−0.09	0.20	0.15	0.69	0.04	0.35	−0.03	0.56
0.20	0.01	0.27	0.21	0.74	0.13	0.42	0.05	0.60
0.30	0.02	0.31	0.25	0.78	0.16	0.47	0.08	0.62
0.40	0.04	0.33	0.27	0.79	0.17	0.51	0.09	0.66
0.50	0.05	0.34	0.28	0.71	0.18	0.53	0.10	0.68
Corr.	−0.13	0.25	0.20	0.72	0.08	0.31	0.01	0.65
0.50	0.03	0.35	0.34	0.74	0.20	0.49	0.08	0.67
0.60	0.02	0.33	0.31	0.73	0.19	0.46	0.07	0.65
0.70	0.02	0.31	0.28	0.75	0.16	0.46	0.06	0.61
0.80	0.00	0.28	0.24	0.75	0.13	0.40	0.04	0.58
0.90	−0.08	0.21	0.17	0.75	0.07	0.34	−0.02	0.54
0.95	−0.26	0.16	0.12	0.81	0.01	0.31	−0.12	0.51

This table reports the descriptive statistics of the exceedence correlations across the changes in the CDS sector indices. The central line is based on full sample correlations, the upper part of the table focuses on EC^- while the lower part on EC^+. The sample period considered is January 2004 to December 2011.

most cases, the exceedence correlation EC^+ decreases as q decreases. This suggests that large positive CDS changes correspond to lower correlation across sectors (note that EC^+ considers the correlation above the quantile $1 - q$). The same for EC^-: for large negative CDS changes, the correlation across sectors tends to decrease (in most cases). This result indicates that the relation across CDS sectors is not linear: it is higher when there are small positive or negative changes, but for large changes in the CDS of one sector, the relationship is quite low and in some cases is negative.

15.3.2 Common Factor Analysis

15.3.2.1 Covariates Impact at Exceedence

The relation between the covariates and each economic sector is evaluated using the Exceedence measure and the Quantile Regressions.

Regarding the Exceedence measure, we considered the conditional correlation measure across the CDS Sector $\Delta CDS_{i,t}$ and the covariate variable $\Delta X_{j,t}$.

In formulae, if we consider the quantile of order α, EC is computed as follows:

$$EC^- = Corr\left[\Delta CDS_{i,t}, \Delta X_{j,t} | F_i\left(\Delta CDS_{i,t}\right) < q, F_j\left(\Delta X_{j,t}\right) < q\right], \qquad (15.3)$$

$$EC^+ = Corr\left[\Delta CDS_{i,t}, \Delta X_{j,t} | F_i\left(\Delta CDS_{i,t}\right) > 1 - q, F_j\left(\Delta X_{j,t}\right) > 1 - q\right]. \qquad (15.4)$$

where F_i and F_j are the cumulative density functions of the corresponding CDS and X variations.

Table 15.6 presents exceedence correlation averages among the different sectors. As the table shows, the exceedence correlation EC^+ decreases as q decreases. The same is true for the opposite: for large negative CDS changes, the correlation among sectors and covariates decreases, suggesting that large positive or negative CDS changes correspond to lower exposures to covariates. This result confirms those obtained in the previous section: the relation across CDS sectors is not linear and is largely driven by common factors that are relevant in normal times, but not when there is turbulence in the market. In fact, the linkages are large and the first principal component is able to explain more than 80% of the variability of all the sectors when the market is in normal time. During the other periods, we have that the linkages are low (sometimes negative) and the first principal component is able to explain only 35% of the variability of all the sectors. This pattern is well represented by Figures 15.4 and 15.5 that report average exceedence correlations within CDS sector indices and between the indices and the covariates.

15.3.2.2 Covariates Impact at Quantiles

The analysis performed above concentrates on pairwise relationships. Quantile regression offers a systematic strategy for examining how variables influence the location, scale and shape of the entire response distribution. The advantage is that quantile regressions are a particularly efficient way to estimate a linear relation that can vary across quantiles. This is a flexible way to detect the presence of relation asymmetries in the data.

Table 15.6 Average exceedence correlations between CDS sectors and covariates.

Quantile	BB_BBB	BBB_AAA	TS	REPO-TBILL	RISK_APP	TED	NYSE	TBOND5RATE	VIX	SP100_PE
0.050	0.266	0.225	0.090	−0.197	0.041	0.051	0.001	0.137	0.002	0.174
0.100	0.267	0.244	0.145	0.069	0.166	0.116	0.123	0.139	0.124	0.026
0.200	0.340	0.244	0.125	0.089	0.180	0.110	0.270	0.117	0.172	0.033
0.300	0.340	0.285	0.168	0.102	0.195	0.125	0.295	0.135	0.183	0.042
0.400	0.341	0.300	0.193	0.112	0.220	0.122	0.289	0.134	0.207	0.037
0.500	0.355	0.311	0.182	0.112	0.230	0.124	0.254	0.135	0.226	0.039
Corr.	0.314	0.016	0.044	−0.223	0.148	−0.009	−0.141	0.066	−0.061	0.200
0.500	0.395	0.222	0.154	0.106	0.381	0.119	0.229	0.090	0.382	0.071
0.600	0.389	0.201	0.124	0.080	0.350	0.126	0.221	0.101	0.370	0.072
0.700	0.369	0.189	0.126	0.056	0.320	0.095	0.198	0.058	0.342	0.069
0.800	0.347	0.175	0.117	0.033	0.278	0.065	0.155	0.043	0.297	0.062
0.900	0.401	0.135	0.015	0.006	0.217	0.040	0.053	−0.141	0.233	0.171
0.950	0.362	0.131	0.046	−0.077	0.207	0.207	0.007	0.026	0.137	−0.101

This table reports the average exceedence correlations between the changes in the CDS sector indices and the covariates. The central line is based on full sample correlations, the upper part of the table focuses on EC^- and the lower part on EC^+. The sample period considered is January 2004 to December 2011.

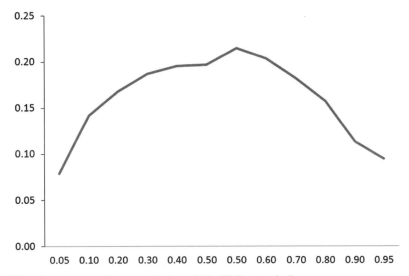

Figure 15.4 Average exceedence correlation within CDS sector indices.

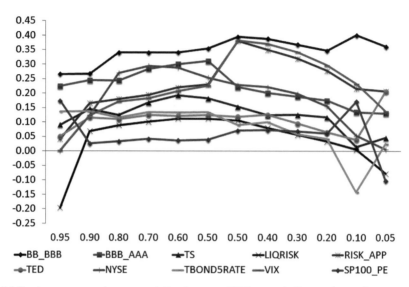

Figure 15.5   Average exceedence correlation between CDS sector indices and covariates.

We group the covariates in the vector X_t and are interested in monitoring the contemporaneous impact of changes in X_t on the changes in the sector CDS. The Quantile Regression coefficients are estimated by solving the following minimization problem

$$min_{\beta_0,\beta_1} \sum_{t=1}^{T} \rho_\alpha \left(\Delta CDS_{i,t} - \beta_0 - \beta_1' X_t \right)$$ (15.5)

where $\rho_\tau(a)$ is the *check* function for quantile α defined as $\rho_\alpha(X) = X \times (\alpha - I(X < 0))$ and β_1 is the vector of coefficients linking the covariates to the sector CDS index. Given the estimated coefficients, the α quantile for $\Delta CDS_{i,t}$ is given as

$$Q_t(\alpha) = \widehat{\beta}_{\alpha,0} + \widehat{\beta}'_{\alpha,1} X_t$$ (15.6)

where the hat denotes estimated values while the α highlights that the estimated coefficients are quantile-specific. To evaluate the coefficient standard errors we resort to the bootstrap-based procedure of Kocherginsky et al. (2005). Such a choice strengthens the results with respect to the possible presence of heteroskedasticity. Readers interested in further details on quantile regression should refer to Koenker (2005).

The impact of covariates clearly depends on the chosen quantile level α. To evaluate the changes in the correlation between covariates and sector CDS indices across different quantiles, we estimate the model in (15.5) for the following quantile levels: 0.01, 0.015, 0.02, 0.025, 0.05, 0.1, 0.2, 0.3, 0.4, 0.5, 0.6, 0.7, 0.8, 0.9, 0.95, 0.975, 0.98, 0.985, 0.99. The estimated coefficients can be graphically represented together with the corresponding standard errors to evaluate the stability of the relation at different quantiles.

Table 15.7 reports the estimated coefficients and the t-statistic for all the 18 sectors of the ten covariates respectively for the 0.05, 0.50 and 0.95 quantiles. Figure 15.6 indicates the number of significant coefficients for each covariate. Table 15.7 and Figure 15.6 show that the significant covariate for all the quintiles is the spreads of high-yield bonds portfolio. This

Table 15.7 Coefficients of the covariates at different quantiles.

Covariates	Quantile	AUTOMOB	BANKING	BASICRES	CHEMIC	CONSTMAT	FINSERV	FOODBEV	HEALTCARE	INDLGDS	INSURAN	MEDIASEC	OILGAS	PSNLHSLD	RETAILSEC	TECHNOL	TELECOM	TRAVLEI	UTILITIES
BB-BBB	0.05	1.86	0.21	—	0.26	0.39	0.93	0.22	0.23	0.29	0.99	1.04	0.31	0.56	0.46	0.48	0.58	1.62	0.34
	0.50	1.55	0.18	0.26	0.25	0.38	0.48	0.17	0.18	0.31	0.42	0.57	0.28	0.48	0.42	0.49	0.52	1.01	0.31
	0.95	3.78	0.27	0.41	0.30	0.49	1.42	0.23	0.26	0.38	1.02	1.36	0.35	0.73	0.62	0.65	0.61	1.53	0.41
BBB-AAA	0.05	—	—	—	—	—	—	—	—	—	—	0.60	—	—	—	—	—	—	—
	0.50	1.29	—	0.18	—	—	—	—	—	—	—	0.24	—	—	—	—	—	—	—
	0.95	—	—	—	—	—	—	—	—	—	—	—	—	—	—	—	—	—	—
TS	0.05	-4.33	—	-0.73	-0.34	-0.21	-1.51	-0.11	—	—	—	—	—	—	—	—	—	—	—
	0.50	0.40	—	—	0.06	—	—	0.05	0.05	0.02	-1.63	-1.27	—	—	—	—	—	—	—
	0.95	5.78	—	1.23	0.73	—	—	0.23	—	—	—	2.03	—	—	—	—	—	—	—
LIQRISK	0.05	—	—	—	—	—	—	—	—	—	—	—	—	—	—	—	—	—	—
	0.50	—	—	—	—	—	—	—	—	—	—	—	—	—	—	—	—	—	—
	0.95	—	—	—	—	—	—	—	—	—	—	—	0.18	0.57	0.62	0.68	0.14	1.76	-0.10
RISK-APP	0.05	—	0.01	—	—	—	—	—	—	—	—	—	—	—	—	—	—	—	—
	0.50	—	—	0.00	—	0.00	—	0.00	0.00	—	—	-0.04	0.00	—	—	—	—	—	0.00
	0.95	—	—	-0.02	—	—	-0.02	-0.01	0.00	—	—	-0.01	-0.01	—	—	—	—	—	-0.01
TED	0.05	5.06	0.44	0.87	0.45	—	1.77	0.16	—	0.31	—	1.27	—	—	—	0.33	—	—	0.28
	0.50	—	—	—	—	—	—	—	—	—	—	—	—	—	—	—	—	—	—
	0.95	—	—	—	—	—	—	—	—	—	—	—	—	—	—	—	—	—	—
NYSE	0.05	-7.00	—	-1.49	-0.74	—	—	-0.28	—	-0.28	—	-2.62	-0.21	-0.60	-0.68	-0.70	—	-2.36	—
	0.50	-0.04	-0.03	—	-0.01	-0.01	-0.01	—	—	—	-0.05	—	-0.01	-0.02	-0.01	-0.02	-0.01	-0.02	-0.01
	0.95	-0.03	-0.01	—	-0.02	-0.01	—	—	—	—	-0.01	—	0.00	-0.01	-0.01	-0.01	-0.01	—	-0.01
TBOND5RATE	0.05	4.10	—	0.76	0.40	0.34	1.58	0.22	0.10	0.31	1.79	1.18	0.24	0.41	0.41	0.40	0.57	0.40	0.27
	0.50	0.30	—	0.10	0.05	0.14	0.17	—	—	0.11	0.15	0.20	0.11	0.17	0.14	0.13	0.24	0.40	0.09
	0.95	—	-0.30	-0.95	-0.52	—	—	-0.15	—	—	—	-1.32	—	—	-0.40	—	—	—	—
VIX	0.05	—	—	—	—	—	—	—	—	—	—	—	—	—	—	—	—	—	—
	0.50	—	-0.01	0.00	—	0.01	—	0.01	0.00	—	0.01	—	0.00	—	—	—	0.00	—	0.00
	0.95	—	—	—	—	—	—	—	0.00	—	—	—	0.01	—	—	—	—	—	0.00
SP100-PE	0.05	—	—	—	—	—	—	—	—	—	—	—	—	0.01	—	—	—	—	—
	0.50	—	-0.01	—	—	0.01	—	0.01	—	—	—	—	0.01	—	—	—	—	—	—
	0.95	—	—	—	—	—	—	—	—	—	—	—	—	—	—	—	-0.01	—	0.01

This table presents the quantile regression coefficients of each sector CDS index with respect to the covariates reported in the first column. The table includes only the statistically significant coefficients at the 5% confidence level. Quantile levels are reported in the second column. The sample period considered is January 2004 to December 2011.

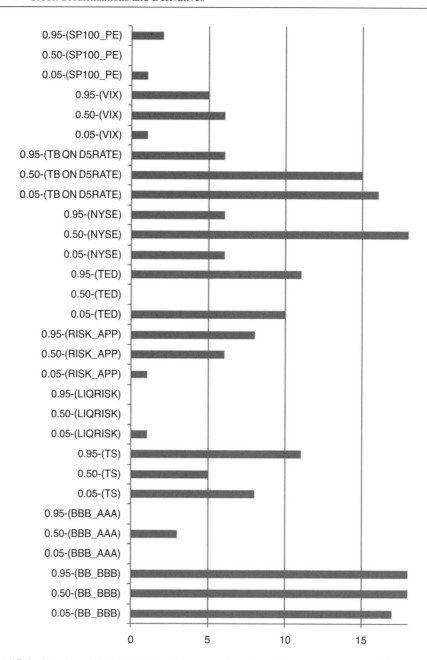

Figure 15.6   Number of statistically significant covariates impact across CDS sector indices.

variable is significant for all the sectors for the 0.95 and 0.50 quantiles and for 17 sectors for the 0.05 quantile. This means that the most important common factor is the spread of the high-yield bonds portofolio, i.e. credit risk. Table 15.7 shows that this factor has the same sign of impact across quantiles. This result indicates that the credit risk of all the sectors is largely driven by a common factor that characterizes the probability of default. The spread of the investment grade portfolio is instead significant for only three sectors and only for the 0.50 quantile. There is only one other factor that is significant for all the different sectors, but only in the 0.50 percentile: the change in the NYSE. Therefore, the equity market negatively affects the different sector CDSs: an increase in the NYSE reduces the probability of default of the different firms and therefore the CDS reduces. This second common factor indicates that, when there is a reduction in the equity market, the credit risk (and therefore the probability of default) of all the different sectors is larger.

The 5 year Treasury Bond rate factor is common for 16 out of 18 sectors for the 0.95 quantile and for 15 out of 18 for the 0.50 quantile. The coefficient is positive for all the sectors. This factor is largely related to the business cycle, i.e. when the Treasury Bond rate is high, the economy is booming and the probability of default of all the sectors is lower.

The three variables that are related to liquidity risk are VIX, TED spread, REPO-TBill rate. Among them, the one which is mostly relevant is the TED spread with a significant impact in different ways when the CDS increases and when CDS decreases over lower and higher quantiles. An increase of the TED spread turns into a further increase of the CDS low quantile and a reduction on CDS high quantile. This result is explained by the fact that when the TED spread increases credit risk also increases and therefore the two phenomena should be interpreted together.

The other common factors are significant for a number of sectors that ranges from zero to 11. More specifically, P/E is not relevant, an increase in the risk appetite leads to a lower CDS change and is significant only for half of the sectors.

The term spread impacts in different ways: increases in term spread turn into a further decrease of CDS for upper quantiles; and an increase in term spread provides a further increase of CDS for the lower quantile.

15.4 STABILITY OF RELATIONS

Beside the graphical comparison, some tests might be considered to verify the stability of the covariates' impact on the CDS indices.

We take into account two tests. At first, we consider the equality of coefficients across the highest quantiles and verify the following null hypothesis: $H_0 : \widehat{\beta}_{0.90,1} = \widehat{\beta}_{0.95,1} = \widehat{\beta}_{0.99,1}$ and $H_0 : \widehat{\beta}_{0.95,1} = \widehat{\beta}_{0.98,1} = \widehat{\beta}_{0.985,1} = \widehat{\beta}_{0.99,1}$. The test was proposed by Koenker and Basset (1982), and is a Wald-type test. Under the null, the test statistic follows a chi-square distribution, where the degrees of freedom depend on the number of covariates entering the equation. When the covariates are K, the degrees of freedom are $2K$ in the first test, and $3K$ in the second case.

Table 15.8 shows that the null hypothesis of no differences among quantile exposures is rejected in most of the cases. Therefore, this analysis shows that the exposure to common factors is different when CDS presents positive or negative changes or when changes are large or small.

Table 15.8   Tests for the equality of quantile regression coefficient across time.

	2004–2011 vs. 2007–2011 P-value	2004–2011 vs. 2009–2011 P-value	2007–2011 vs. 2009–2011 P-value
S_AUTOMOB	0.000	0.000	0.003
S_BANKING	0.000	0.008	0.001
S_BASICRES	0.009	0.166	0.038
S_CHEMIC	0.001	0.000	0.047
S_CONSTMAT	0.064	0.993	0.252
S_FINSERV	0.000	0.002	0.000
S_FOODBEV	0.001	0.000	0.047
S_HEALTCARE	0.037	0.460	0.000
S_INDLGDS	0.003	0.027	0.013
S_INSURAN	0.000	0.005	0.676
S_MEDIASEC	0.000	0.000	0.432
S_OILEGAS	0.019	0.436	0.021
S_PSNLHSLD	0.013	0.842	0.352
S_RETAILSEC	0.000	0.189	0.002
S_TECHNOL	0.010	0.018	0.003
S_TELECOM	0.116	0.465	0.000
S_TRAVLEI	0.158	0.224	0.014
S_UTILITIES	0.003	0.002	0.000

The table reports the P-value of the test for the equality of quantile coefficients across time.

We also proceed to verify the stability of coefficients across time. For this purpose we create a step dummy, D_t which assumes value 1 after date m (and zero before). Then, we estimate the following quantile regression:

$$min_{\beta_0,\beta_1} \sum_{t=1}^{T} \rho_\alpha \left(\Delta CDS_{i,t} - \beta_0 - \beta_1' X_t - \delta' X_t D_t \right). \tag{15.7}$$

The null hypothesis of coefficients equivalence in the two subsamples 1 to m and $m + 1$ to T is equivalent to $H_0 : \delta = 0$ and corresponds to a standard Wald-type test for linear restrictions in the quantile regression framework.

We have considered two subsamples: 2007–2011 and 2009–2011. In all the cases (i.e. 2004–2011 vs. 2007–2011, 2004–2011 vs. 2009–2011, 2007–2011 vs. 2009–2011) we find that the null hypothesis of stability of the parameters has been rejected. This confirms the results of the different approaches we have used: the relationship between CDS indexes and common risk factors are largely unstable through time and heterogeneous among quantiles.

15.5   CONCLUSIONS

We studied the nature of sectors' credit risk using credit default swap data for 18 Industrial Sectors. We showed that credit risk is more largely a global common factor than a sector-specific phenomena. Our results suggest that the source of these higher correlations is the dependence of sector credit spreads on a common set of global market factors, risk premiums and liquidity patterns. Specifically, we found that the Sector CDS spreads are driven primarily by high-yield factors and the Treasury 5 year Bond Rate. However, this relation is not linear and is not stable through time. Nevertheless, there is strong evidence that common factors are able to explain most of the changes of CDS Industrial Sector Indices.

REFERENCES

Ang A., Longstaff, F., 2011. Systemic Sovereign Credit Risk: Lessons from the U.S. and Europe, Columbia Working Paper.

Duffie, D., 1999. Credit swap valuation. Financial Analysts Journal, 55(1), 73–87.

Eichengreen, B., Mody, A., 2000. What Explains Changing Spreads on Emerging-Market Debt? In: Edwards, S. (Ed.) The Economics of International Capital Flows, University of Chicago Press, Chicago, IL.

Fontana, A., Scheicher, M., 2010. An Analysis of Euro Area Sovereign CDS and their Relation with Government Bonds, ECB Working Paper 1271.

Longstaff, F. A., Pan, J., Pedersen, L. H., Singleton, K. J., 2011. How sovereign is sovereign credit risk?, American Economic Journal: Macroeconomics, forthcoming.

Kamin, S., von Kleist, K., 1999. The Evolution and Determinants of Emerging Market Credit Spreads in the 1990s, Working paper No. 68, Bank for International Settlements.

Koenker, R., Bassett, G., Jr., 1982. Robust Tests for Heteroskedasticity Based on Regression Quantiles, Econometrica, 50(1), 43–62.

Koenker, R., 2005. Quantile Regression, Econometric Society Monographs, n. 38, Cambridge University Press, New York.

Koenker, R., Zhao, Q., 1996. Conditional Quantile Estimation and Inference for ARCH Models, Econometric Theory, 12, 793–813.

Longin, F. M., Solnik, B., 2001. Extreme correlation of international equity markets, Journal of Finance 56, 649–676.

Mauro, P., Sussman, N., Yafeh Y., 2002. Emerging market spreads: Then versus now, Quarterly Journal of Economics 117, 695–733.

Muirhead, R. J., 1982. Aspects of Multivariate Statistical Theory. John Wiley & Sons, New York.

Pan, J., Singleton, K. J., 2008. Default and recovery implicit in the term structure of sovereign CDS spreads, Journal of Finance 63, 2345–2384.

Risk Transfer and Pricing of Illiquid Assets with Loan CDS

Michael Schwalba, Matthias Korn and Konstantin Müller

16.1 INTRODUCTION

The shipping industry as a whole is going through a significant downturn in charter rates due to an overcapacity in transportation capacities, especially container, created to a great extent by the financial crisis. It is now a major undertaking to estimate the fair value of ships and the respective loans secured on them.

It is common practice in banking to base one's risk assessment on the usually statistically derived properties: probability of default (PD) and recovery rates (RR). Once these key figures have been calculated, expected loss (EL) can be obtained and the minimum margin a bank has to charge on a loan to such entities is known. The actual margin will have to cover additional costs such as liquidity, capital and other operations.

The Basel II regulatory framework includes the so-called internal rating-based approach, which forms the basis for a fair margin calculation. It uses transition matrices that are then used for a "real-world" parameterization, which cannot be interpreted as risk-neutral. The credit risk modeling approach used in this context will vary depending on the banks' sophistication and regulatory requirements. Popular modeling approaches are based on Gupton, Finger and Bhatia (1997) and CSFB (1997). All of these modeling approaches are used to compute the loss distribution. Once it is known the required economic capital is defined by a risk measure like Value at Risk (VaR) or Expected Shortfall. The capital allocated to each loan has to earn a return which also needs to be charged to the debtor. This method applies the concept of RAROC (risk-adjusted return on capital). As such, the RAROC approach attempts to distribute aggregate risk costs directly to individual loans in relation to the bank's debt and equity costs. Finally, the gross margin has to cover all other costs like funding costs.

Unfortunately, the RAROC approach is not arbitrage-free, nor does it allow a relative value assessment between these assets. Recent developments in the market have expected this weakness in various ways.

Capital requirements for European banks have been tightened up over the last 18 months resulting in a requirement for all banks regulated by the European Banking Authoritiy (EBA) to hold 9% core Tier 1 capital by 30 June 2012. In order to get the new requirements, banks can either shrink their risk-weighted assets (RWA) or raise fresh capital in the market. In this situation, portfolios usually have much lower margins than currently traded in the market, making the successful placement of those a difficult task. Based on these "distressed" market prices a sole risk-adjusted pricing is unable to form the basis for a sufficient tool of active portfolio management.

Coming back to the introductory comments on the shipping industry, the current market environment seems to make it difficult for banks to act as long-term credit lenders on their own balance sheet anymore. However, the distressed state of the market should offer plenty of attractive investment opportunities. We therefore need to have a closer look at the global shipping market and outline some of its specific characteristics to develop a robust framework for LCDS on shipping loans.

16.2 SHIPPING MARKET

One of the industry's characteristic features is its distinctive mobility. In principle, a shipowner is free to charter out his vessel on any spot market in the world at the same price. This is why merchant shipping is regarded as truly global business. Apart from a very few exceptions, there are no local markets less affected by changes in global demand for seaborne trade. As a consequence, merchant shipping as a whole is directly concerned with market cycles making it a very cyclical business.

This strong cyclical nature is accelerated by long design and construction periods that may mean three to four years from ordering a new vessel to its actual delivery. This complicates the timing of investment decisions and makes the so-called asset play another important role in merchant shipping. The analysis of past shipping cycles has shown that orders tend to increase at the beginning or near the top of economic cycles. Due to long construction periods, deliveries often do not increase until the economy is already cooling off. That means that capacities are still increasing while demand for transportation is already weakening. Together, those interacting phases of booming business followed by exacerbating decline create a highly speculative market environment.

Despite broad acceptance of the mechanics described here, shipping markets seem to have changed little over the centuries, leading to a strong demand for risk management approaches. Those needs are reflected in the evolution of the freight derivatives markets.

In freight derivatives markets, contracts are traded that are settled against an agreed future value of a freight market index. Trading started in 1985 on the Baltic Exchange in London with standard future contracts settled against the Baltic Freight Index (BFI). This index was designed as a weighted average of 11 trade routes collected daily from a panel of brokers. To provide a more accurate reflection of the risks of different cargoes and transportation routes, the single index was replaced by four dry cargo indices in 2001. Besides the Baltic Exchange Capesize Index (BCI), the Baltic Exchange Panamax Index (BPI), Baltic Exchange Handymax Index (BHMI) and the Baltic Dry Index was also introduced. All indices are based on weighted averages of estimated freight rates on representative routes provided by independent shipbrokers.

The need for more accurate hedging instruments was not restricted to diversification in settlement indices, but also led to the introduction of bespoke forward freight agreements (FFAs), which started to take over in the late 1990s. Today, FFAs are the main form of freight derivative, traded mostly over the counter. As principal-to-principal contracts, they are usually arranged by brokers and can be tailor-made with customized cargo size and settlement dates.

Several other shipping derivatives exist in addition to FFAs, but FFAs are the most liquid traded instruments. For this reason, we will demonstrate in Section 16.4.2.1 how a liquid FFA market can be used for hedging second-hand vessel prices, which is essential for our valuation framework. Before that, we will first clarify the terms and mechanics of LCDS contracts in the following section.

16.3 LOAN CREDIT DEFAULT SWAPS

Loan CDS contracts are very similar to standard unsecured CDS contracts on bonds. They differ in just two features, namely the reference obligation and the termination. While the reference obligation of most CDS contracts is a senior unsecured bond, the reference obligation of a LCDS contract must be a syndicated loan. These loans are always senior, often secured, frequently come with covenants and are callable. If a such a loan is prepaid, it is no longer available as reference obligation. In this situation, the relevant LCDS contract is cancelled – the second major difference from a standard CDS contract.

As mentioned before, LCDS contracts are almost identical to standard CDS contracts. Nevertheless, we will summarize the terms and mechanics to illustrate the general requirements a robust pricing framework must fulfill.

A LCDS is an OTC credit derivative arranged between two counterparties. The one counterparty – the protection buyer – pays a fixed quarterly premium to the other counterparty – the protection seller. These premiums or spreads are generally quoted on an annual basis or combined with upfront payments. The spread payments continue until either the maturity date of the contract or a credit or termination event. Credit events in LCDS contracts do not differ from those in standard CDS contracts. They are clarified in the ISDA standard documentation and a matter of the concrete documentation of the terms. For our model, we will think of a credit event as a default, i.e. bankruptcy and failure to pay. Restructuring is quite common in the shipping lender business and would lead to many unnecessary defaults in a matter of sufficient future cash-flows.

If a credit event occurs, the contract terminates early and the protection seller receives the proportional premium for the period between the last payment date and the effective credit event. Beyond that, no further spread payments are due. Simultaneously the protection seller makes a payment to the protection buyer to cover his losses resulting from the relevant credit event. As in standard CDS contracts, this payment can be defined as a physical settlement or cash settlement.

Under a physical settlement, the protection buyer delivers adequate obligations. In exchange, the protection seller pays par value of the outstanding notional.

Under cash settlement, the protection seller directly compensates the protection buyer for his resulting losses due to the credit event. Therefore a price for the distressed obligation is determined via an auction held among a number of credit default swap dealers shortly after the credit event. This number is often expressed as a fraction of the outstanding notional determines the recovery rate, R. The contract is finally settled when the seller pays the buyer the loss given default $L = (1 - R)N$.

Termination events can occur of different varieties and depend on the reference obligation and contractual framework. For our purposes, we will think of termination as the disappearance of suitable reference obligations, typically because the obligator has called the relevant loan. In case of a termination event, the contract ends and no further spread or compensation payments are made except for the accrued premium.

16.3.1 LCDS Pricing

In OTC deals, the contractual LCDS spread is usually set such that the contract is at par. That means no initial adjustment payment of one counterparty has to be made. Given that, the clean price is zero and contracts are usually quoted in terms of their spread.

From a modeling perspective, it is often convenient to express the price of CDS and LCDS in terms of its two legs, namely the premium leg and default leg. Before we can explain this in more mathematical terms, we will first clarify the common notations:

- T_1: default time of the reference obligation,
- T_2: cancellation time of the LCDS contract,
- T: maturity of LCDS contract,
- R: recovery rate,
- $B(t, t_i)$: risk-free discount factor at time t_i,
- t_i: premium payments dates for $i = 1, \ldots, m$,
- Δ_i: day count fraction for premium period i,
- N: notional of the contract,
- s_t: fair LCDS spread at time t, which equates the premium leg and default leg.

To start with the valuation of the premium leg, we recall that it consists of a stream of payments $s_t \Delta_i N$ at dates t_i until either a credit event occurs, the contract is cancelled or its maturity is reached. With

$$\tau = \min(T_1, T_2)$$

the value of the premium leg is therefore given by

$$V_t^{PL} = s_t \, \mathbb{E}_t^Q \left[\sum_{t_i \geq t} \Delta_i \, N \, B(t, t_i) \, \mathbb{1}_{\{\tau > t_i\}} \right], \tag{16.1}$$

where expectations $\mathbb{E}_t^Q[\cdot] = \mathbb{E}[\cdot \mid \mathcal{G}_t]$ are taken under the pricing measure Q conditional on the current market information $\mathcal{G}_t$.

This equation so far neglects the proportional premium amount to be paid for the received protection between the last payment time and the possible occurance of a default or termination event. The value of such accrued premium is given by

$$V_t^{AP} = s_t \, \mathbb{E}_t^Q \left[\sum_{t_i \geq t} \frac{\tau - t_{i-1}}{t_i - t_{i-1}} \Delta_i \, N \, B(t, \tau) \, \mathbb{1}_{\{t \vee t_{i-1} < \tau \leq t_i\}} \right]. \tag{16.2}$$

In analogy with the CDS pricing methodology the value of the default leg is calculated as the present value of the expected default payments in case of a credit event, which is

$$V_t^{DL} = \mathbb{E}_t^Q \left[N(1 - R) \, B(t, T_1) \, \mathbb{1}_{\{T_1 < \min(T_2, T)\}} \right]. \tag{16.3}$$

In terms of its two legs, the condition of the fair spread is therefore given by

$$V_t^{PL} + V_t^{AP} = V_t^{DL}. \tag{16.4}$$

This condition together with (16.1), (16.2) and (16.3) is generally valid. But to begin the actual calculation, the dynamics of T_1, T_2, $B(\cdot, \cdot)$ and even R have to be further specified.

The modeling of the risk-neutral default dynamics in particular is a crucial point in any valuation framework and has been subject to extensive research. In today's credit derivatives literature, there are two main modeling approaches: the intensity-based approach and the structural approach. Although we chose a structural model for our valuation framework, we will briefly summarize the intensity-based approach which can be regarded as the market standard for liquidly traded asset classes.

16.3.2 Modeling LCDS Under the Intensity-based Model

In this section, we give a short introduction to the intensity-based or reduced-form models. Under the intensity-based approach, the default dynamics are described exogenously by a definition of a so-called intensity process under the risk-neutral probability measure Q. For application to LCDS specifically, we refer to Wei (2007).

After the above presentation, we shall work on the pricing space $(\Omega, \mathcal{G}, \mathbb{F}, Q)$ directly where no arbitrage is allowed under the risk-neutral measure Q. Let T_1 and T_2 be defined as $\mathbb{F}$-stopping times, so that

$$N_t^1 = \mathbb{1}_{\{T_1 \leq t\}} \quad \text{and} \quad N_t^2 = \mathbb{1}_{\{T_2 \leq t\}}$$

indicates the occurence of the credit and the cancellation event.

As N^1 and N^2 are defined as non-explosive, adapted counting processes, the well-known result from Doob–Meyer guarantuees a representation via their intensity processes. That means processes λ^1 and λ^2 exist such that $(N_t^i - \int_0^t \lambda_s^i ds)_t$ is a local martingale.

Within CDS definitions, where only T_1 and therefore λ^1 have to be modeled, the intensity is often called the *hazard rate*. This is why the presented modeling framework is also known as the hazard rate approach. One of the great advantages of the intensity-based approach is that it can be adapted to various situations and real-life problems. This is basically done by choosing an appropriate parametric form for λ^1 and λ^2. The most flexible choice in this connection is to make N^1 and N^2 doubly stochastic.

In a doubly stochastic setup, the intensity is allowed to be random but in such a way that conditioning on a particular realization $\lambda^i_\cdot(\omega)$ of the intensity, the counting process becomes a inhomogeneous Poisson process with intensity $\{s \mapsto \lambda_s^i(\omega)\}$.

Using the law of iterated expectations, we get the following key relationship:

$$\begin{aligned}
Q_t(T_i > s) &= Q[N_s^i - N_t^i = 0 \,|\, \mathcal{G}_t] \\
&= \mathbb{E}\left[Q[N_s^i - N_t^i = 0 |(\lambda_u)_{t \leq u \leq s}] \,|\, \mathcal{G}_t\right] \\
&= \mathbb{E}_t\left[e^{-\int_t^s \lambda_u^i du}\right]
\end{aligned}$$

where we implicitly assume that that the background filtration $\mathbb{G}$ is generated by both λ^i and the jump times T_i. With this, we have specified the probabilities for either a credit event or a termination event up to time s. Given that we are regarding a setup where both cases may occur simultaneously, we have to go one step further with determining the joint distribution of T_1 and T_2. Here, we assume that at time t, conditional on the paths of λ^1 and λ^2, N^1 and N^2 are independent. It is worth mentioning that a dependency between the default and termination dynamic can still be modeled by incorporating a suitable dependency structure among λ^1 and λ^2. It follows that for $s, v \geq t$, we have

$$Q_t(T_1 > s, T_2 > v) = \mathbb{E}_t\left[e^{-\int_t^s \lambda_u^2 du - \int_t^v \lambda_u^2 du}\right]. \tag{16.5}$$

For the probability at time t that the contract will "survive" until $s \geq t$, we then have

$$Q_t(\tau > s) = Q_t(T_1 > s, T_2 > s) = \mathbb{E}_t\left[e^{-\int_t^s \lambda_u^1 + \lambda_u^2 du}\right]. \tag{16.6}$$

We now assume that the default-free term structure of interest rates is given by a spot rate process r. The risk-free discount factor for a payment at time $s \geq t$ is then given by

$$B(t, s) = e^{-\int_t^s r_u du}.$$

Under suitable technical conditions concerning r, we can write

$$V_t^{PL} = s_t \sum_{t_i \geq t} \Delta_i \, N \, e^{-\int_t^{t_i} (r_u + \lambda_u^1 + \lambda_u^2) du}. \tag{16.7}$$

The calculation of the present value of the accrued premium is a bit more challenging since it requires the specification of the distribution of τ:

$$V_t^{AP} = s_t \, \mathbb{E}_t^Q \left[\sum_{t_i \geq t} \frac{\tau - t_{i-1}}{t_i - t_{i-1}} \Delta_i \, N \, B(t, \tau) \, \mathbb{1}_{\{t \vee t_{i-1} < \tau \leq t_i\}} \right] \tag{16.8}$$

$$= s_t \sum_{t_i \geq t} \frac{\Delta_i \, N}{t_i - t_{i-1}} \int_{t \vee t_{i-1}}^{t_i} B(t, u) \, (u - t_{i-1}) d Q_t(\tau \leq u). \tag{16.9}$$

To calculate the default leg, we make use of the simplifying assumption that the recovery rate R is independent of T_1 and T_2 and has expected value $\bar{R}$ under the pricing measure Q:

$$V_t^{DL} = \mathbb{E}_t^Q \left[N(1 - R) \, B(t, T_1) \, \mathbb{1}_{\{T_1 < \min(T_2, T)\}} \right] \tag{16.10}$$

$$= N(1 - \bar{R}) \int_t^T \int_t^{v \wedge T} B(t, u) \frac{\partial^2 Q_t(T_1 > u, T_2 > v)}{\partial u \partial v} du dv. \tag{16.11}$$

Before the derived setup can be used for actual numerical calculation, the dynamics of λ^1, λ^2 and r have to be specified. In practice this is often done under simplifying assumptions like deterministic intensities, for the sake of analytical tractability.

Besides choosing a parametrical form of λ^1, λ^2, one crucial point in building a robust valuation framework is fitting the model with a suitable data. For liquid asset classes, namely corporates, λ^1 can be fitted to available bond or CDS spreads. This is done by running the model backwards. That means a fair spread is observed and one runs the CDS pricing formula for the intensity λ^1 that reproduces that spread. In the LCDS context, we have to take into account the termination dynamics, i.e. we need to calibrate λ^2. In the absence of any securities from which one could extract an implied intensity, in practice, historical estimates for this parameter are used.

In illiquid asset classes like shipping, where available market-data of traded securities is generally scarce, the only available data is often based on internal rating or credit risk models as mentioned above. Therefore the intensity model is frequently calibrated to historical rating migration and default data. In our view, that contradicts the general no-arbitrage principle, where dynamics have to be modeled under the pricing measure Q, while using historical data implies the usage of the statistical or real-world measure P.

To overcome these inconsistencies we propose a new pricing methodology in the following section.

16.4   VALUATION FRAMEWORK FOR LCDS

As we described in the above section, the scarcity of available market-data entails a modified valuation approach for LCDS on illiquid asset classes. In this context, we find that a structural modeling approach is suitable to meet some of the special features coming across in shipping finance. For this reason, we recall the basic ideas behind the structural or firm value approach which goes back on the seminal work of Black and Scholes (1973) and Merton (1974).

16.4.1   The Structural Approach

The basic idea behind the structural approach is to adopt the Black and Scholes (1973) option pricing model to value corporate liabilities. To meet the requirements of the Black–Scholes model, several assumptions have to be made. In the original setup by Merton (1974), the value V of the firm's assets is described by a geometrical Brownian motion

$$dV_t = \mu_V V_t dt + \sigma_V V_t d\tilde{W}_t, \tag{16.12}$$

where $\tilde{W}$ is a standard Brownian motion under the physical probability measure P and the mean rate of return μ_V and the asset volatility σ_V are constant parameters.

To apply the principles of risk-neutral valuation, Merton (1974) adopts further assumptions like the lack of transaction costs or taxes, the unrestricted divisibility of assets, continuous time trading and unrestricted borrowing and lending at a constant interest rate r. Furthermore, it is supposed that the company produces no cash flows before a given time T. It is assumed that the company's capital structure comprises only equity shares and a zero-coupon bond with maturity T and face value D. In this case, the firm's value V is given as the sum of equity and debt values. That means it can be constructed from traded securities so we can set its risk-neutral drift to r and (16.12) simplifies to

$$dV_t = r V_t dt + \sigma_V V_t dW_t, \tag{16.13}$$

where W is a standard Brownian motion under the risk-neutral measure Q.

Assuming that default can occur only at maturity of the zero-coupon T, equity represents a European call option on the firm's assets with maturity T and strike price D. Directly applying the well-known Black–Scholes pricing formula, the value of equity at time $t \leq T$ is given by

$$E_t = \mathcal{BS}(V_t, \sigma_V, T - t) \tag{16.14}$$
$$= V_t \Phi(d_1(V_t, T - t)) - De^{-r(T-t)}\Phi(d_2(V_t, T - 1))$$

where $\Phi(\cdot)$ is the distribution function of the standard normal distribution and $d_1(\cdot, \cdot)$ and $d_2(\cdot, \cdot)$ are given by

$$d_1(V_t, T - t) = \frac{\ln\left(\frac{e^{r(T-t)}V_t}{D}\right) + \frac{1}{2}\sigma_V^2(T - t)}{\sigma_V\sqrt{T - t}}$$
$$d_2(V_t, T - t) = d_1(V_t, T - t) - \sigma_V\sqrt{T - t}.$$

The probability of default can be calculated as

$$Q(V_T < D) = \Phi(-d_2) \tag{16.15}$$

and the value of the outstanding debt at time $t \leq T$ is given by

$$L_t = V_t - E_t. \tag{16.16}$$

Besides this very simple setup, several extensions have been proposed to apply the model to more realistic situations. As a natural extension we will relax the assumption that default can occur only at maturity date T. Instead, we assume that the firm's asset value must stay above a lower barrier over the whole lifetime of the outstanding debt. This basic assumptions refers to the general class of so-called first passage time models and admits of much more flexibility than the original setup.

According to Black and Cox (1976) the first passage time assumption may be justified by safety covenants in the issued debt. Formally, these covenants would allow the creditors to close down the company if its value V_t falls below a certain level $K(t)$. Hence, the time of default can be described as

$$T_1 = \inf\{t \geq 0 \mid V_t \leq K(t)\}. \tag{16.17}$$

Although (16.17) applies to the more realistic situation where default is not restricted to a fixed date, we need to make strong assumptions of the firm's overall capital structure. This may not seem adequate from a theoretical point of view and is also proven by practical implementation where firm value models have been of limited empirical success in explaining the price behavior of corporate debt instruments and their credit risk spreads.

Despite this, we propose a structural model for the given context. This is due to the fact that in our opinion many of the inadequacies in the valuation of corporate securities can be solved in the shipping finance context. That will be explained in further detail in the next section.

16.4.2 Credit Risk in Shipping Loans

As described in the above sections, the shipping market is quite unique in many aspects. This is also true for shipping finance, which significantly differentiates from usual corporate lending. In the following section, we will outline some general characteristics that qualify for a direct application of the structural approach.

Vessels are tradionally financed by a simple debt structure that is not very comparable with complex capital structure of corporations. After the breakdown of the high-yield bond and equity market sponsored by retail customers bank loans are the most important source of ship finance.

These loans are typically secured by a first preferred mortgage that uses the vessel as single asset collateral. The borrower is a one-ship company for fiscal reasons, often registered in remote legal jurisdictions like Liberia. In this structure, the actual shipowner holds shares in the one-ship company whereby the asset is isolated from any claims arising elsewhere in the owner's business. On the other hand, the shipowner will not issue a guarantee using his whole financial capability in case of loan-distress. This implies that all repayments of principal and interest must be made based on the operating income of the vessel if the shipowner is unwilling to inject additional equity.

In the following sections, we address these specific characteristics by applying a structural modeling framework. In doing so, we take up the idea that a borrower's default decision will directly be determined by the performance of the underlying asset, i.e. the concerning vessel.

One of the central premises of the structural approach, specifically the Black–Scholes framework, is the existence of a dynamic hedging portfolio. In particular, it must be possible to express bearish views by entering short positions in the relevant vessel or at least the corresponding vessel class at any given time t. In the following section, we give a simple argument for how the ship value can be hedged with actively traded derivatives. This is done for two reasons: to serve as a theoretical foundation for the applicability of the structural approach and also as a central building block for our valuation framework. While the knowledge of a possible hedging strategy for V_t gives further insight about the thus unknown asset volatility σ_V.

16.4.2.1 Hedging the Ship Value

As a starting point vessels can be seen as depreciating assets whose values are cyclical and uncertain especially in the current market situation. Although a ship must not have a limited technical life, its economic life ends when a sufficient positive net cash flow for the costs including debt service can no longer be generated.

Under normal market condtions, vessel prices will be marked somewhere between new-building and scrap prices on the secondary market. Given this cap and this floor, prices can fluctuate on a broad range.

There are different factors that determine the ship's value. Alongside age, inflation and shipyard orderbooks, current freight rates and shipowners' expectations about the future are the major influence on ship values. From a theoretical point of view, the value of a ship is the net present value of all the future expected cash flows of the vessel capped by the remaining operating life time plus its intrinsic scrap value. Therefore the theoretical ship value V_t can be written as

$$V_t = \sum_{\tau=t}^{T} \frac{\mathbb{E}_t[X_\tau - d_\tau]}{(1+\tilde{r}_\tau)^\tau} + \frac{\mathbb{E}_t[V_T]}{(1+\tilde{r}_T)^T}, \tag{16.18}$$

where X_τ is the instantaneous timecharter equivalent freight rate, d_τ is the operating cost and V_T is the intrinsic scrap value at the time T. All these quantities may be time-dependent and stochastic. That is why the expectations are taken under the real-world measure P. Therefore in our model the theoretical price of a vessel at time t is based on the assumptions about its expected operation revenue and the discount rate. In order for (16.18) to hold, the uncertainty about the vessel's future cashflow has to be incorporated in the discount factor $\tilde{r}$ in terms of a risk premium.

For the sake of simplicity, we first assume that operation costs d_τ and scrap value are deterministic. Due to these assumptions the ship value V_t at time t simplifies to

$$V_t = \sum_{\tau=t}^{T} \frac{\mathbb{E}_t[X_\tau] - d_\tau}{(1+\tilde{r}_\tau)^\tau} + \frac{S_T}{(1+\tilde{r}_\tau)^\tau}. \tag{16.19}$$

As we described in Section 16.2, future earnings can be estimated by forward freight agreements (FFA) covering the same period. The existence of a consistent hedging strategy implies that X_τ may also be described by its risk-neutral dynamics,

$$V_t = \sum_{\tau=t}^{T} \frac{\mathbb{E}_t^Q[X_\tau] - d_\tau}{(1+r_\tau)^\tau} + \frac{S_T}{(1+r_\tau)^\tau}, \tag{16.20}$$

where r describes the risk-free interest rate and expectations are now taken under the risk-neutral measure Q. Assuming that forward freight rates are unbiased predictors of future freight rates, we can rewrite (16.20) to

$$V_t = \sum_{\tau=t}^{T} \frac{F_\tau - d_\tau}{(1 + r_\tau)^\tau} + \frac{S_T}{(1 + r_\tau)^\tau}, \qquad (16.21)$$

allowing the ship value to be expressed as the discounted present value of a series of FFA contracts with maturities spread over n periods covering the remaining economic life time.

In the following sections we will assume that the ship value can be hedged using the simplifying argument of Equation (16.21). This will allow us to describe the ship value in its risk-neutral dynamics.

16.4.3   Valuation of LCDS on Shipping Loans

After establishing a hedging methodology for second-hand ship values, which gives a general foundation of the applicability of a structural modeling approach, we will now develop a consistent valuation framework for LCDS on shipping loans. For this purpose, we will outline the general requirements of such a modeling approach. Subsequently, we will discuss a mathematical implementation and give some simulation results for a (simplified) LCDS contract.

As a starting point, it is worth mentioning that a direct application of the concepts of Section 16.4.1 would imply that a rational ship owner defaults when the ship value drops below certain barrier, e.g. the market value of the concerning mortgage. This concept refers to a common market practice where the loan to value ratio (LTV) is often seen as a key indicator for the health of an outstanding obligation.

In our opinion, this argument disregards the specific income-producing properties of a vessel. For a shipowner using debt finance, wealth comes in two forms: cash flow (dividends) and capital gains. Although this idea was considered by Merton (1973) for the theory of stock prices, it had only a minor influence on the evolution of credit risk modeling. In terms of traditional option pricing methodology the value of delayed default to a shipowner comes not from the ability to "put" the ship to the financing bank when it is at its lowest value, but rather from the ability to extract positive cash flows from operations before negative capital gains must either be realized or "put" to the lender.

Thereafter, a borrower's default decision depends not only on the asset value (i.e. investor's equity) but also the liquidity (i.e. ship income). A rational borrower would not default when the ship's net cash flow is positive, even if the owner's equity position is negative.

In the next section, we will develop a LCDS pricing model that includes these considerations to properly reflect a rational borrower's default decision. Rather than assume a single default trigger based on asset value (measured by contemporaneous loan-to-value, LTV), our model incorporates a second trigger based on ship income (represented by contemporaneous debt service coverage, DSC). In this regard, we refer to the work of Goldberg and Capone (2002) and Tu and Eppli (2003) and others, who analyzed the impact of a double-trigger default modelling on multifamily and commercial mortgage pricing.

Besides explicit cash flow consideration, there are several other requirements a realistic default model for shipping loans should meet. For this purpose, we have summarized the typical terms and conditions of a (simplified) shipping loan contract in Table 16.1.

Table 16.1 Terms and conditions of a shipping loan.

Loan amount:	N
Maturity:	$T_n \leq T$
Repayment:	$n - 1$ regular installments of N_i paid quarterly, plus N_{T_n} balloon installment paid at maturity
Interest:	$s + r_i$ LIBOR plus spread paid quarterly
Security:	First preferred mortgage

Shipping loans are usually contracted floating over a reference interest rate, we consider this LIBOR. To reflect this, we will incorporate stochastic shortrate dynamics into our model. The second point we will explicitly take into consideration is the partially amortizing nature of shipping loans. That means that a balloon payment is due at loan maturity, which has to be funded by the shipowner. To adequately reflect the risks arising from scheduled balloon payments, we choose a Monte Carlo simulation approach. Although this causes some difficulties in pricing with potentially defined prepayment options, we abstain from adopting a backward numeric approach to fully recognize this important risk component.

16.4.4   Simulation Model

After discussing some general model requirements, we will proceed with further specifying our simulation approach. There are basically three state variables we will explicitly take into account, namely the interest rate dynamics, ship value and cash flow.

For the interest rate dynamics, we assume a mean reverting process introduced by Cox, Ingersoll and Ross (1985) which is described by

$$dr_t = \kappa(\theta - r_t)dt + \sigma_r \sqrt{r_t} dW_t^r, \tag{16.22}$$

where $\kappa \in \mathbb{R}_+$ determines the speed of mean reversion, $\theta \in \mathbb{R}$ is the long-term equilibrium rate, $\sigma_r \in \mathbb{R}_+$ is a constant volatility parameter and W^r is a standard Wiener process.

As a second state variable, we model the ship value using a lognormal diffusion process. To incorporate cash flow considerations we will assume that the ship value V can be described by

$$dV_t = (\alpha_V - \beta_V)V_t dt + \sigma_V V_t d\tilde{W}_t^V, \tag{16.23}$$

where α_V is the expected total return on the vessel, $\sigma_V \in \mathbb{R}_+$ is a constant volatility parameter and $\tilde{W}^V$ is a standard Wiener process. Cash flow considerations are incorporated by a continuous payout rate β_V.

Using the hedging argument of Section 16.4.2.1, we can apply the risk-neutral valuation principle. That means that we can describe the ship value under its risk-neutral dynamics given by

$$dV_t = (r_t - \beta_t)V_t dt + \sigma_V V_t dW_t^V, \tag{16.24}$$

where r is the riskless interest rate and W_t^V is a standard Wiener process under Q. We assume an instantaneous correlation $\rho_{rV} \in \mathbb{R}_+$ between W^r and W^V.

As we stated before, an important factor for the shipowner's default decision is the ability to extract positive cash flows from operating the vessel. In our model, these cash flows are determined by multiplying the ship value by the payout rate at distinctive dates over the contract's life time. For commercial mortgage context, Tu and Eppli (2003) specify the payout rate dynamics as

$$\beta_t = \lambda dr_t + \sigma_\beta dW_t^\beta, \tag{16.25}$$

where λ is an estimated parameter, r is the short rate, $\sigma_\beta \in \mathbb{R}_+$ is a constant volatility parameter and W^β is a standard Wiener process. Although there is some evidence in market practice that income demanded by shipowners may vary due to market conditions but is relatively stable in the long run, there is no empirical research on cash flow depository in shipping businesses. For our numerical analysis, we will therefore assume that the payout rate β is constant over time.

Given the specified state variables, the shipowner's default decision is modeled using both ship value and cash flow, as contemporaneous default triggers. As mentioned above, we will assume a rational borrower will not default as long as ship income is adequate to cover debt service. This income trigger event may be expressed via the debt service coverage falling below parity, i.e. DSC < 1.

On the other hand, it is unlikely that an initial debt service shortfall will cause an immediate default. The shipowner is more likely to fund the shortfall using a reserve account or other sources of equity as long as he perceives that the market will recover. Following the hedging argument that the ship value reflects the market's expectations about future earnings, we will assume that the owner will bridge cash flow deficiencies until the ship value falls below the value of outstanding debt, i.e. LTV > 1.

After specifying the dynamics of interest rate, ship value and cashflow, the borower's default behavior can be determined for each simulation path. In case of default, the lender who gains control over the vessel faces the decision to either sell it on the second-hand market or to scrap it. In both cases, it is assumed there are no transaction costs so that the obligation recovers with the maximum of the vessel's simulated market value and its intrinsic scrap value.

As mentioned before, we will restrict our analysis to the credit risk component of shipping LCDS contracts. For that reason, we will assume a non-callable shipping loan. Subject to that, the specification of the double-trigger default event is sufficient to simulate all cash flows for a stylized LCDS written on the relevant loan. In the next section, we will analyze the influence of different contractual specifications on the fair spread imposed by our modeling setup.

16.5 NUMERICAL RESULTS

In this section, we shall use our modeling framework to derive the fair spread of a (simplified) CDS contract.

As reference obligation we consider a loan originally provided to a one-ship company to fund the acquisition of a dry-bulk carrier. To highlight the effects of inherent credit risks, we will assume the loan to be non-callable. The vessel characteristics and the concerning loan terms are summarized in Table 16.2.

This data corresponds to the market situation observable in early 2007 when freight rates reached their all time high and new building as second-hand prices for merchant ships were escalating.

At first, we will consider the situation where the lender is already interested in transferring the inherent credit risk to an external investor at loan aquisition. For this purpose, we derive the fair spread of a LCDS contract for which contractual details are summarized in Table 16.3.

Table 16.2   Vessel characteristics and loan terms.

Vessel characteristics:	
Type:	Dry bulk carrier
Market value:	55,000,000 USD
Economic life:	25 years
DWT	75k (Panamax)
Scrap Value	12,000,000 USD
Loan terms:	
Loan amount:	38,500,000 USD
Advance ratio:	70%
Tenor:	15 years
Amortization:	60 regular installments of 481,250 USD paid quarterly, plus balloon installment of 9,625,000 USD paid at maturity
Pricing:	150 bps + LIBOR

As it is unlikely to find a counterparty who is willing to sell protection over the whole loan term, we will assume that the contract matures after 10 years.

By comparing the derived LCDS spread of 107 bps with the agreed loan spread of 150 bps it becomes obvious that the initial loan pricing provides a positive net margin.

As mentioned before, the assumed market data corresponds to the situation of thriving merchant shipping around the year 2007. During that prosperous market phase, commercial banks and specialized lenders also tried to benefit from steadily rising demand in shipping finance. As a consequence, numerous comparable deals with relatively low margins were made.

Since then, global shipping markets have been in decline. As such, the effects of weakening global demand for seaborne transportation are exacerbated by significant expansion of the world fleet. To properly reflect this ongoing development and to complete our numerical example, we consider the same loan to be kept on-balance for a period of 5 years. While the regular amortization schedule has decreased the outstanding loan amount by 25%, we assume that the vessel's market value has to dropped by more than 40%. The details of the changed conditions are summarized in Table 16.4.

While this represents only a cautious estimation of the current market situation, it is already obvious that the situation for the lender has dramatically worsened. To stress this, we consider a LCDS contract written on the same loan with a reduced maturity of five years.

Comparing the results summarized in Table 16.5 to the high level market phase, it becomes obvious that the spread level has significantly risen. Although the resulting negative net

Table 16.3   LCDS contract terms and conditions.

Contract specification:	
Face value:	USD 38,500,000
Maturity:	10 years
Initial LTV:	75 %
Fair spread	107 bps
Net margin:	+ 43 bps

Table 16.4 Vessel characteristics and loan terms.

Vessel characteristics:

Type:	Dry bulk carrier
Market value:	30,000,000 USD
Age:	5 years
Economic life:	25 years
DWT	75k (Panamax)
Scrap value	12,000,000 USD

Loan terms:

Loan amount:	28,875,000 USD
Advance ratio:	96%
Tenor:	15 years
Amortization:	40 regular installments of USD 481,250 paid quarterly, plus balloon installment of USD 9,625,000 paid at maturity
Pricing:	150 bps + LIBOR

margin of -580 bps seems significantly high, this result is not unrealistic under current market conditions in shipping finance.

Referencing the starting point, that shipping credit exposure is illiquid and future outlook is hard to predict, the given example shows a significant increase in the fair spread level over time from the market top level regarding charter rates in 2007 to the crisis levels today. Assuming that the normal yield of the shipping business for the shipowner is 10–11%, it is tough to handle such fair spread levels.

16.6 CONCLUSION

The first results of the proposed heuristic are promising. It seems possible to generate plausible fair spread levels for assumed LCDS contracts on bank shipping loans. As mentioned above, generating this is not trivial especially in a continuously declining market. The combination of asset value, cash flow and the interest rate development could lead to good predictor of default probability on a spread basis. From this point of view, it seems possible to distinguish between relatively good and bad investments. In taking an investment chance during such a crisis, at least the relative value approach seems to be adequate in times where the absolute value is too uncertain to be determined. This chapter gives a starting point for this approach.

Table 16.5 LCDS contract terms and conditions.

Contract specification:

Face value:	28,875,000 USD
Maturity:	5 years
Initial LTV:	96%
Fair spread	730 bps
Net margin:	−580 bps

APPENDIX A: MONTE CARLO PARAMETERIZATION

Table 16.6   Parameterization of Monte Carlo simulation.

Parameter	Value
Short Rate:	
Long-term equilibrium θ_r	0.04
Reversion speed κ_r	0.25
Volatility σ_r	0.1
Initial spot rate r_0	0.02
Ship Value:	
Asset volatility σ_V	0.2
Payout rate β_V	0.05
Instantaneous correlation ρ_{rV}	0

REFERENCES

Alizaldeh, A., Nomikos, N., 2009. Shipping Derivatives and Risk Management, Basingstoke, Palgrave Macmillan.

Black, F., Cox, J., 1976. Valuing Corporate Securities: Some Effects of Bind Indenture Provisions. Journal of Finance, 351–367.

Black, F., Scholes, M., 1973. The Pricing of Options and Corporate Liabilities, Journal of Political Economy, 18(3) 637–654.

Cox, J. C., Ingersoll, J. E., Ross, S. A., 1985. A Theory of the Term Structure of Interest Rates, Econometrica 53, 385–407.

CSFB, 1997. CreditRisk+: A Credit Risk Management Framework, Working Paper.

Goldberg, L., Capone, C. A., 2002. A Dynamic Double-Trigger Model of Multifamily Mortgage Default, Real Estate Economics 30(1), 85–113.

Gubton, G. M., Finger, C., Bhatia, M., 1997. CreditMetrics – Technical Document, Working Paper, Morgan Guaranty Trust Co.

Merton, R. C., 1974. On the Pricing of Corporate Debt: The Risk Structure of Interest Rates, Journal of Finance 29, 449–470.

Tu, C. C., Eppli, M., 2003. Term Default, Balloon Risk, and Credit Risk in Commercial Mortgages, Journal of Fixed Income 13, 42–52.

Wei, Z., 2007. Valuation of Loan CDS Under Intensity Based Model, Working Paper.

Part V
Regulation

17

Regulatory Capital Requirements
for Securitizations

Kristina Lützenkirchen[1], Daniel Rösch[1] and Harald Scheule[2]

[1]*Leibniz University of Hannover*
[2]*University of Technology, Sydney*

17.1 REGULATORY APPROACHES FOR SECURITIZATIONS

Asset securitizations are one of the most significant developments in financial intermediation in recent years. Financial institutions use vehicles such as asset-backed securities (ABSs), collateralized debt obligations (CDOs) or mortgage-backed securities (MBSs) to restructure the asset risks of their portfolios and transfer these to investors. Thus asset securitizations enable financial institutions to liquidate assets, transfer risk and consequently release capital. The Basel Committee on Banking Supervision develops capital adequacy rules for deposit-taking financial institutions and provides a capital relief for institutions which transfer credit risk to other investors. In a standard structure, the credit portfolio risk is partially transferred and partially retained. As a result, a deposit-taking institution, which partially transfers credit portfolio risk, may partially release regulatory capital. Under regulations which are currently implemented, banks may apply the following three approaches: at present two different ways for financial institutions that have received the approval to use the IRB Approach to determine regulatory capital for securitized assets are provided: the Ratings Based Approach (RBA) and Supervisory Formula Approach (SFA). Non-IRB banks (banks that use the Standardized Approach for their calculations of regulatory capital for their credit exposures) are required to apply the Standardized Approach (SA) to calculate capital requirements for their securitization exposures. The Standardized Approach is also based on external ratings but is less sophisticated than the RBA approach. The three approaches RBA, SFA and SA are described in the following sections.

17.1.1 Ratings Based Approach (RBA)

The RBA is based on an analytical model for calculating capital charges for tranches of securitized large portfolios (so-called "pools") by Pykhtin and Dev (2002, 2003). The model is related to a single-factor model for individual asset returns by Merton (1974), which is also known as the "Gaussian one-factor copula model."[1] The basic concept suggests capital charges for securitization exposures to be calculated via the Value at Risk (VaR) methodology, which is in line with the approach of regulatory capital calculation for credit exposures. However, using the VaR concept for securitization exposures is computationally challenging. The authors show that under certain conditions the expected loss of a tranche conditional on the realization of a macroeconomic risk factor equals the marginal Value at Risk for the tranche.

The Pyktin–Dev model has been employed to calibrate risk weights for tranches of structured financial instruments in order to develop a simple industry standard (compare Peretyatkin and Perraudin, 2004). A further major contribution to the final determination of the risk weights in the Basel documents has been provided by analysts of the Federal Reserve Board and the Bank of England.

A bank is obliged to apply the RBA for securitization exposures if a credit rating is available. Ratings-based regulatory capital requirements rely on the quality of the rating from external rating agencies as the unique parameter. The RBA for securitizations is attractive for its simplicity. It consists of two look-up tables displaying risk weights for long-term and short-term rated securitization tranches. The risk weights for the tranches vary according to the external rating grade, the seniority of a specific tranche, the granularity of the underlying pool and whether assets include securitizations (i.e. transaction is a resecuritization). Each of the tables for long-term and short-term rated tranches comprises five columns: three for securitization exposures: (i) Senior, Granular (ii) Non-senior, Granular and (iii) Non-granular and two for resecuritization exposures: (i) Senior and (ii) Non-senior. The resecuritization risk weights were added in the year 2009 as a response to the Global Financial Crisis (GFC).

A bank's portfolio is assumed to be granular if the sizes of individual loans in a credit portfolio are sufficiently small. Sufficiency is based on the effective number of exposures, which reflects the concentration risk of a credit portfolio and is defined by the Basel Committee on Banking Supervision (see Basel Committee on Banking Supervision, 2006) as follows:

$$N = \frac{\left(\sum_i EAD_i\right)^2}{\sum_i EAD_i^2} \tag{17.1}$$

where EAD represents the exposure-at-default for the ith instrument in the pool. Exposures from the same obligor must be treated as a single instrument. The formula implies that the number of effective exposures is equal to the absolute number of exposures if all exposures have an equal size. If N is equal to or greater than 6 the portfolio is considered to be "Granular" and Column 1 or 2 has to be applied. If N is less than 6 the portfolio is considered to be "Non-granular" (Column 3).

A tranche is considered to be a senior tranche if its position entitles a first claim on the assets or the cash flows in the portfolio. All tranches rated below BBB demand the same risk weights regardless of their classification as either "Senior, Granular", "Non-senior, Granular" and "Non-granular".

According to the Basel Committee on Banking Supervision (2009), a resecuritization structure is in existence if at least one of the underlying assets in the pooled portfolio is a securitization exposure. If one or more of the underlying assets is already a resecuritization exposure the entire structure is also regarded as a resecuritization. In addition, all standardized Asset-Backed-Commercial-Paper-Programs (ABCP-Programs) are treated as resecuritization exposures.

A resecuritization qualifies as "Senior" if the exposure is in a senior position and if none of the underlying assets is a resecuritization exposure itself. If any element in the pooled reference portfolio is to be considered as a resecuritized asset then the entire exposure qualifies as "Non-senior."

Table 17.1   Risk weights for long-term rated securitization tranches in the Ratings Based Approach.

Long-term Rating	Securitization Exposures			Resecuritization Exposures	
	Senior, Granular	Non-senior, Granular	Non-granular	Senior	Non-senior
AAA	7	12	20	20	30
AA	8	15	25	25	40
A+	10	18	35	35	50
A	12	20	35	40	65
A−	20	35	35	60	100
BBB+	35	50	50	100	150
BBB	60	75	75	150	225
BBB−	100	100	100	200	350
BB+	250	250	250	300	500
BB	425	425	425	500	650
BB−	650	650	650	750	850
Below			Deduction		

This table shows that risk weights are higher for lower credit ratings, non-senior, non granular and resecuritization exposures.

The tranche capital according to the RBA (C^{Tr}_{RBA}) is calculated as follows:

$$C^{Tr}_{RBA} = RW \cdot 0.08 \cdot T \tag{17.2}$$

where RW denotes the appropriate risk weight and T the thickness of the particular tranche. The thickness of a tranche is defined by a percentage of the total securitization that a specific tranche comprises given its lower and upper attachment levels.

The Tables 17.1 and 17.2 display the risk weights for long-term and short-term rated tranches provided by the Basel Committee on Banking Supervision (2009).

The floor for AAA rated tranches amounts to 7%. Note "Deduction" indicates a risk weight of 1,250% and implies that the whole securitization tranche has to be funded by capital as the required capital to risk-weighted assets is 8% (1,250%*8% = 100%).

Table 17.2   Risk weights for short-term rated securitization tranches in the Ratings Based Approach.

Long-term Rating	Securitization Exposures			Resecuritization Exposures	
	Senior, Granular	Non-senior, Granular	Non-granular	Senior	Non-senior
A1	7	12	20	20	30
A2	12	20	35	40	65
A3	60	75	75	150	225
Below			Deduction		

This table shows that risk weights are higher for lower credit ratings, non-senior, non granular and resecuritization exposures.

17.1.2 Supervisory Formula Approach (SFA)

The SFA has been introduced by the Basel Committee on Banking Supervision for instances where no external credit rating is available. The preferential application of the RBA implicitly supports external ratings for securitizations. However, an alternative approach for calculating capital charges for unrated securitization exposures was needed. A major consideration in designing the SFA was to ensure that capital requirements under both methodologies are consistent, avoiding incentives for regulatory arbitrage.

The SFA has been developed by Gordy and Jones (2003) and Gordy (2004). The essential feature of the formula is a bottom-up approach where capital is a function of characteristics of the pool and properties of the tranche. The model is based on a set of assumptions such as an asymptotic single risk factor, the granularity of the portfolio and a stochastic element for the loss distribution. Regulatory capital requirements are calculated based on a supervisory formula which requires certain input parameters determined by the bank. The parameters used in the model are (i) the capital requirement prior to securitization (K_{IRB}), (ii) the weighted average loss given default of the underlying pool (LGD), (iii) the effective number of exposures in the pool (N), (iv) the thickness of the tranches (T) and (v) the attachment level (L). Thus the model completely relies on internal credit risk information of the bank.

The capital requirement prior to securitization (K_{IRB}) is the core component of the formula and is defined as the sum of expected loss (provisions) and unexpected loss (capital) which is a measure for credit portfolio risk and is given for corporate loan portfolios by:[2]

$$K_{IRB} = \left(LGD \cdot \Phi\left(\frac{\Phi^{-1}(PD) + \sqrt{\rho}\Phi^{-1}(0.999)}{\sqrt{1-\rho}} \right) \right) \cdot MA \qquad (17.3)$$

with:

$$\rho = 0.12 \cdot \left(\frac{1 - \exp(-50PD)}{1 - \exp(-50)} \right) + 0.24 \cdot \left(1 - \frac{1 - \exp(-50PD)}{1 - \exp(-50)} \right). \qquad (17.4)$$

The asset correlation ρ is a measure for the degree of the dependency between assets in the portfolio and is defined as a decreasing function of the probability of default (PD). MA denotes the maturity adjustment for corporate loan exposures and is defined by the Basel Committee on Banking Supervision (2005) as a function of the PD and the maturity M:

$$MA = \frac{1 + (M - 2.5) \cdot b(PD)}{1 - 1.5 \cdot b(PD)} \qquad (17.5)$$

with $b(PD) = (0.11852 - 0.05478 \cdot \log(PD))^2$. The weighted average loss given default (LGD) is expressed by the following term:

$$LGD = \frac{\sum_i LGD_i \cdot EAD_i}{\sum_i EAD_i} \qquad (17.6)$$

where LGD_i denotes the average LGD associated with all exposures to the ith obligor.[3]

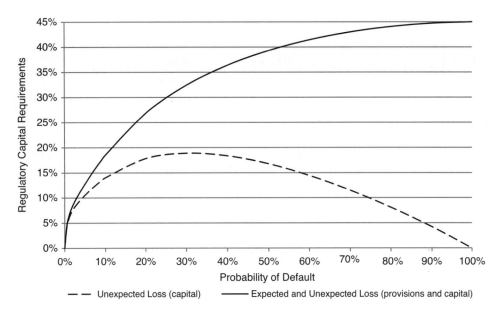

Figure 17.1   Regulatory capital: expected and unexpected losses.
Notes: This figure shows that the unexpected loss follows an inverse U-shape, while the sum of expected and unexpected loss increases with the probability of default in a monotone fashion.

Unlike capital requirements for securitizations, capital requirements for credit exposures (IRB Approach) are based on unexpected losses, assuming that the expected loss ($PD * LGD$) is covered by general and/or specific provisions. Therefore, the expected loss is subtracted from the unexpected loss.

$$ IRB = \left(\left(LGD \cdot \Phi \left(\frac{\Phi^{-1}(PD) + \sqrt{\rho}\Phi^{-1}(0.999)}{\sqrt{1-\rho}} \right) \right) - PD \cdot LGD \right) \cdot MA. \qquad (17.7) $$

Figure 17.1 shows the difference between regulatory capital requirements based on expected and unexpected losses and capital requirements based on unexpected losses only.

The figure illustrates that for higher PD values, capital based on unexpected losses (*IRB*) may not necessarily increase because higher PDs result in higher expected losses and therefore in higher provisions which are deducted. Capital requirements based on expected and unexpected losses (K_{IRB}) are monotonically increasing with higher PD values. Note that both graphs are based on the assumption that LGD is equal to 45%.

The effective number of exposures (N) is measured according to Equation (17.1). The thickness of the tranches (T) and the attachment levels of the tranches are determined pursuant the definition given in Section 17.1.1. The capital charge for a particular tranche is given by the following expression:

$$ max\{0.0056\, T,\, S(L+T) - S(L)\} \qquad (17.8) $$

with $S(.)$ denoting the Supervisory Formula which is defined as follows:

$$S(L) = \begin{cases} L, & \text{when } L \le K_{IRB} \\ K_{IRB} + K(L) - K(K_{IRB}) + \dfrac{dK_{IRB}}{\omega}\left(1 - \exp\left[\omega\dfrac{K_{IRB} - L}{K_{IRB}}\right]\right), & \text{when } L > K_{IRB} \end{cases}$$

(17.9)

where

$$h = \left(\frac{1 - K_{IRB}}{LGD}\right)^N$$

(17.10)

$$c = \frac{K_{IRB}}{(1 - h)}$$

(17.11)

$$\upsilon = \frac{1}{N}\big((LGD - K_{IRB})K_{IRB} + 0.25(1 - LGD)K_{IRB}\big)$$

(17.12)

$$f = \left(\frac{\upsilon + K_{IRB}^2}{1 - h} - c^2\right) + \frac{(1 - K_{IRB})K_{IRB} - \upsilon}{(1 - h)\tau}$$

(17.13)

$$g = \frac{(1 - c)c}{f} - 1$$

(17.14)

$$a = g \cdot c$$

(17.15)

$$b = g \cdot (1 - c)$$

(17.16)

$$d = 1 - (1 - h)(1 - Beta(K_{IRB}; a, b))$$

(17.17)

$$K(L) = (1 - h)\big((1 - Beta(L; a, b))L + Beta(L; a + 1, b)c\big).$$

(17.18)

$Beta(L; a, b)$ denotes the cumulative beta distribution with parameters a and b evaluated at L. The parameter τ is set to $\tau = 1,000$ and the parameter ω is set to $\omega = 20$.

The lower boundary for SFA capital requirements is set to 0.56% of the nominal exposure (Equation 17.8) which corresponds to a risk weight of 7% in the RBA. First loss tranches involve a capital requirement of 100% if the upper attachment level is below K_{IRB}.

In order to demonstrate the functionality of the Supervisory Formula, the impacts of certain risk characteristics on the tranches and the total regulatory capital requirements will be illustrated by analyzing the sensitivity of the SFA capital requirements to the effective number of exposures in the pool (N), to the probability of default (PD) and to the loss given default (LGD). The assumption is made that the originating and investing legal entities are regulated under the Basel II/III proposals. However, it can be shown that an incentive may exist for transferring the credit portfolio risk outside the banking sector (e.g. to unregulated investors such as hedge funds) and for releasing capital in aggregate terms if investors are not required to maintain regulatory capital at the same level as banks.

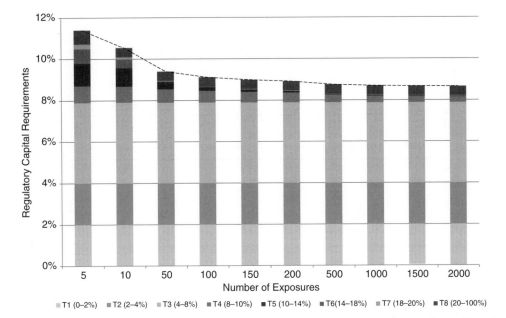

Figure 17.2 Regulatory capital requirements for securitization tranches dependent on the number of exposures in the pool.
Notes: This figure shows that the capital decreases with the number of exposures. Note that tranches with a detachment level below the capital requirement before securitization require a complete funding by equity.

Figure 17.2 shows the development of regulatory capital requirements for securitization tranches dependent on the number of exposures in the pool.

The following assumptions are made: the maturity of the underlying corporate loans is one year, the portfolio probability of default amounts to 1.5%, the LGD equals 45% and the portfolio is securitized into eight tranches (one junior tranche, six mezzanine tranches and one senior tranche) with appropriate attachment levels: $T1$: 0−2%, $T2$: 2−4%, $T3$: 4−8%, $T4$: 8−10%, $T5$: 10−14%, $T6$: 14−18%, $T7$: 18−20% and $T8$: 20−100%. The tranching structure will remain the same throughout the sensitivity analysis. The figure illustrates that the total regulatory capital requirements are decreasing (dashed line) for an increasing effective number of exposures in the pool (N). Hence, securitization exposures based on highly granular portfolios require a lower amount of regulatory capital.

The figure also shows that the tranches $T1$ and $T2$ are entirely funded by capital regardless of the effective number of exposures in the pool. Also the tranche $T3$ requires almost a full capital coverage. Capital charges for the tranches $T4−T8$ are more sensitive to an increase in the number of exposures.

Figure 17.3 illustrates the regulatory capital requirements before and after securitization dependent on the number of exposures in the pool and the difference in capital requirements as a ratio $(SFA_{capital}/K_{IRB})$.

Capital requirements prior to securitization are not affected by the number of exposures in the pool (solid black line). Accordingly, the ratio decreases for a higher portfolio granularity (solid grey line).

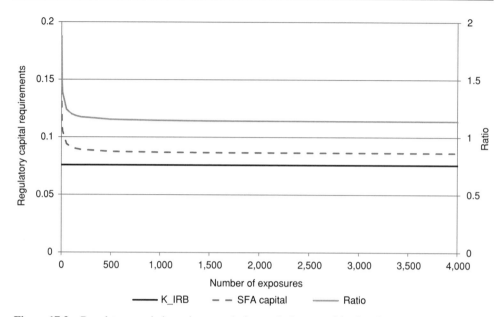

Figure 17.3   Regulatory capital requirements before and after securitization dependent on the number of exposures in the pool.
Notes: This figure shows that the SFA capital requirement exceeds the capital requirement before securitization. This difference decreases with the number of exposures.

Figure 17.4 shows the regulatory capital requirements for securitization tranches dependent on the portfolio probability of default.

Given a default probability of 0.5% the two lowest tranches $T1$ and $T2$ are required to be fully covered by regulatory capital. At this low level of default probability the more senior tranches ($T4-T8$) are to be covered by the product of the lower boundary (0.56%) and the thickness of the respective tranche according to Equation (17.8). In general, the coverage of all tranches (execpt $T1$ and $T2$) is increasing with higher PDs until a particular tranche has reached a coverage of 100%. For example, for a PD of 10% the whole tranche $T6$ has to be funded by capital.

Figure 17.5 illustrates the regulatory capital requirements before and after securitization dependent on the portfolio probability of default and the difference in capital requirements as a ratio ($SFA_{capital}/K_{IRB}$).

The figure shows that regulatory capital requirements after securitization (dashed line) are slightly higher than prior to securitization (solid black line). Note that this observation refers to the aggregate capital level where the risk is transferred to entities which are subject to the Basel requirements. In contrast, transferring risk to unregulated investors (e.g. institutions that are not subject to the Basel minimum capital requirements) would imply a capital release on aggregate.

Figure 17.6 shows regulatory capital requirements for securitization tranches dependent on an increasing loss given default.

The capital coverage of the tranches is increasing with higher LGDs until a particular tranche has reached a coverage of 100%.

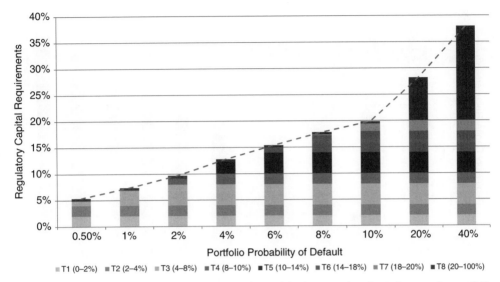

Figure 17.4   Regulatory capital requirements for securitization tranches dependent on the portfolio probability of default.
Notes: This figure shows that the capital increases with the portfolio probability of default. Note that tranches with a detachment level below the capital requirement before securitization require a complete funding by equity.

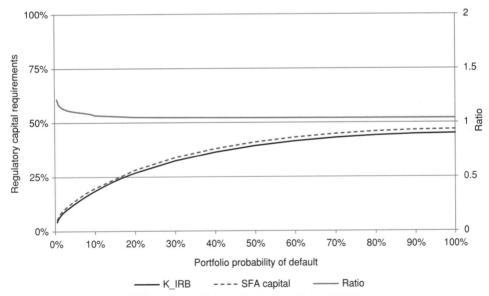

Figure 17.5   Regulatory capital requirements before and after securitization dependent on the portfolio probability of default.
Notes: This figure shows that the SFA capital requirement exceeds the capital requirement before securitization. This difference decreases with the portfolio probability of default.

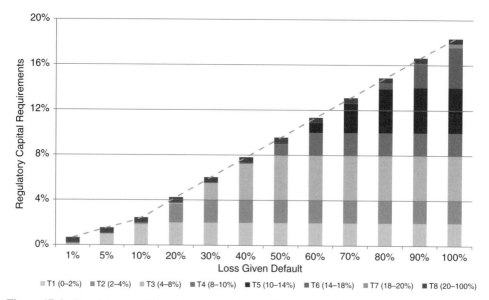

Figure 17.6 Regulatory capital requirements for securitization tranches dependent on the loss given default.
Notes: This figure shows that the capital increases linearly with the loss given default. Note that tranches with a detachment level below the capital requirement before securitization require a complete funding by equity.

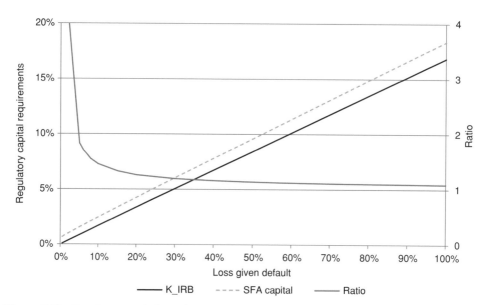

Figure 17.7 Regulatory capital requirements before and after securitization dependent on the loss given default.
Notes: This figure shows that the SFA capital requirement exceeds the capital requirement before securitization. This difference decreases with the loss given default.

Table 17.3 Risk weights for long-term rated securitization tranches in the Standardized Approach.

Long-term Rating	Securitization Exposures	Resecuritization Exposures
AAA to AA−	20	40
A+ to A−	50	100
BBB+ to BBB−	100	225
BB+ to BB−	350	650
B+ and below or unrated	Deduction	

This table shows that risk weights are higher for lower credit ratings and resecuritization exposures.

Figure 17.7 illustrates the regulatory capital requirements before and after securitization dependent on the loss given default and the difference in capital requirements as a ratio $(SFA_{capital}/K_{IRB})$.

The ratio is higher for lower LGDs (solid grey line). This fact may be interesting for mortgage-backed security markets where loans are collateralized by real estate, typically implying low LGDs (e.g. 10%).

17.1.3 Standardized Approach (SA)

Banks that use the Standardized Approach for the credit risk of their underlying exposures are also required to apply the Standardized Approach for securitization exposures. The risk weights presented in Table 17.3 and 17.4 have to be used under the Standardized Approach.

As with the RBA there are specific tables for short-term and long-term rated tranches respectively. However, the classification is less detailed compared to the classification in the RBA. In general, all risk weights are well above the risk weights given in the RBA tables.

17.2 POST-CRISIS REVISIONS TO THE BASEL FRAMEWORK

In July 2009 the Basel Committee on Banking Supervision introduced some enhancements to the existing Basel Framework as a response to the large losses of these assets during the GFC.[4] In the area of securitizations, enhancements to Pillar 1 were basically related to resecuritizations. Two columns were added in the IRB approach to the risk weight tables providing higher risk weights for Senior respectively Non-senior resecuritization exposures. The floor for resecuritization exposures has been set to 20% (senior resecuritization exposures).

Table 17.4 Risk weights for short-term rated securitization tranches in the Standardized Approach.

Short-term Rating	Securitization Exposures	Resecuritization Exposures
A-1/P-1	20	40
A-2/P-2	50	100
A-3/P-3	100	225
All other ratings or unrated	Deduction	

This table shows that risk weights are higher for lower credit ratings and resecuritization exposures.

The aim was to ensure the consistency of the RBA and SFA, which mitigates potential incentives for regulatory arbitrage.

Following the same rationale for applying higher risk weights for resecuritizations under the IRB Approach, the Standardized Approach has been revised as well by adding two additional columns for resecuritization exposures. The floor here has been set to 40% as a result of quantitative impact studies, conducted by the Committee for assessing resecuritization exposures.

In addition, the Basel Committee permitted banks to use external ratings where the evaluation of a tranche is based on a guarantee provided by the bank itself. In response to the crisis, banks are asked to collect detailed information about the underlying portfolio, have a better understanding of the type of risk and ensure a permanent access to the performance development of the underlying assets.

Finally, the credit conversion factor (CCF) for liquidity facilities (in the framework of securitizations such commitments are basically related to ABCP programs) has been increased to 50% for commitments with a maturity below one year under the Standardized Approach. This CCF is now consistent with the one for the long maturities. Furthermore, the treatment of liquidity facilities under the IRB has been clarified for senior securitization exposures and a favorable exception regarding liquidity facilities in the case of a general market disruption has been eliminated.

There is a broad discussion as to whether the described approaches by the Basel regulatory framework (Basel II/III) ensure sufficient capital charges to cover securitization exposures. Rösch and Scheule (2012) analyze the capital adequacy for RBA and SFA based on a comprehensive data set on asset securitization comprising more than 200,000 annual US tranche observations for the period 1997 to 2008. The authors find that regulatory capital for the two approaches is insufficient during economic downturns such as the GFC for certain risk segments. Beyond that, their empirical study indicates that the RBA results in a lower capital requirement than the SFA. These differences may provide an incentive for regulatory capital arbitrage and to solicit external credit ratings.

The quality issue of external ratings has been extensively discussed by academics and practitioners. A major concern is the conflict of interest between the issuers and the credit rating agencies. The issuer has an incentive to pick the credit rating agency offering the most optimistic rating ("rating-shopping") because the rating agencies are directly paid by the issuer ("Paid-by-Originator-Approach").[5] Bar-Isaac and Shapiro (2010) find that credit ratings for securitizations are more likely to understate the credit risk in booms rather than in recessions. Heitfield (2009) argues that credit ratings do not sufficiently distinguish the performance of structured exposures under different macroeconomic risk conditions, which is exacerbated by the fact that securitization exposures are to a large degree exposed to changes in the business cycle.[6]

17.3 OUTLOOK

Asset securitizations are still considered an attractive instrument to the financial industry. Risk intermediation, balance sheet management and fund-raising are regarded as major benefits. Consequently, the Group of Twenty (G-20), the Financial Stability Board (FSB) and other international organizations are supporting the re-establishment of sustainable securitization markets.

As a response to the issues discussed in Section 17.2 the following main targets are derived from the Basel Committee on Banking Supervision (2011):

- avoidance of misaligned incentives within securitization chain,
- increase of transparency of the securitization structure,
- reduction of regulatory reliance on ratings.

The following initiatives have been proposed by the Basel Committee on Banking Supervision (2011) in order to address these targets:

- increase of risk retention of originators,
- improvement of information about underlying assets and performance of securitizations and standardization of documents,
- release of new regulations on credit rating agencies including stricter disclosure requirements.

Furthermore, the Basel Committee on Banking Supervision currently discusses whether the risk weights under the RBA should be recalibrated for all securitization exposures. In addition, a simplification of highly complex products is contemplated.

This research was supported by the Centre for International Finance and Regulation (project number E001) which is funded by the Commonwealth and NSW Governments and supported by other Consortium members (see www.cifr.edu.au). We would like to thank the Centre for International Finance and Regulation and the Hong Kong Institute for Monetary Research for their support.

NOTES

1. Compare also Vasicek (1987), Gordy (2000) and Gordy and Howells (2006).
2. Similar formulas exist for retail loan exposures (i.e. real estate backed loans, qualifying revolving loans and other retail loans).
3. See Basel Committee on Banking Supervision (2006).
4. Compare Basel Committee on Banking Supervision (2009).
5. Compare Bolton et al. (2012).
6. Compare Claußen et al. (2010).

REFERENCES

Bar-Isaac, H., Shapiro, J., 2010. Ratings Quality over The Business Cycle. Working Paper, New York University and Oxford University.

Basel Committee on Banking Supervision, 2005. An explanatory note on the Basel II irb risk weight functions.

Basel Committee on Banking Supervision, 2006. International convergence of capital measurement and capital standards: A revised framework.

Basel Committee on Banking Supervision, July 2009. Enhancements to the Basel II framework.

Basel Committee on Banking Supervision, July 2011. Report on asset securitisation incentives.

Bolton, P., Freixas, X., Shapiro, J., 2012. The credit ratings game. Journal of Finance 67(1), 85–112.

Claußen, A., Löhr, S., Rösch, D., 2010. An Analytical Approach for Systematic Risk Sensitivity of Structured Products. Working Paper, Leibniz Universität Hannover.

Gordy, M., 2000. A comparative anatomy of credit risk models. Journal of Banking and Finance 24, 119–149.

Gordy, M., 2004. Model Foundations for the Supervisory Formula Approach. Structured Credit Products: Pricing, Rating, Risk Management and Basel II, (William Perraudin (Eds)), 307–328.

Gordy, M., Howells, B., 2006. Procyclicality in Basel II: Can we treat the disease without killing the patient? Journal of Financial Intermediation 15, 395–417.

Gordy, M. B., Jones, D., 2003. Random tranches. Risk 16(3), 78–83.

Heitfield, E., 2009. The past as prologue: Lessons learned from the crisis in mortgage-backed structured securities. Federal Reserve Board, Working Paper.

Merton, R. C., 1974. On the pricing of corporate debt: The risk structure of interest rates. Journal of Finance 29, 449–470.

Peretyatkin, V., Perraudin, W., 2004. Capital for Structured Products. Structured Credit Products: Pricing, Rating, Risk Management and Basel II, (William Perraudin (Eds)), 329–362.

Pykhtin, M., Dev, A., May 2002. Credit risk in asset securitizations: an analytical model. Risk 15(5), 16–20.

Pykhtin, M., Dev, A., January 2003. Coarse-grained CDOs. Risk 16(1), 113–116.

Rösch, D., Scheule, H., 2012. Capital incentives and adequacy for securitizations. Journal of Banking and Finance 36(3), 733–748.

Vasicek, O., 1987. Probability of Loss on Loan Portfolio. Working Paper, KMV Corporation.

18

Regulating OTC Derivatives*

Viral V. Acharya, Or Shachar and Marti Subrahmanyam[†]

18.1 OVERVIEW

Over-the-counter (OTC) derivatives account for a significant proportion of overall banking and intermediation activity. On the one hand, they enable end users like corporations, including industrial and financial firms, to hedge their underlying risk exposures in a customized manner. For example, an airline may hedge the price of its future commitments to buy jet fuel or a mutual fund may reduce its portfolio's exposure to exchange rate movements using such products. On the other hand, they enable banks and other financial intermediaries – the providers of hedging services to end users – to earn profits, as they in turn hedge the customized OTC products they sell, either by diversifying the risk across different end users or by shedding the risk to other intermediaries via liquid markets for standardized derivatives. The profit earned by the intermediaries is, in part, a compensation for the mismatch between the risks of the standardized and the customized products. It is clear that there is value to the economy from trading in derivatives, which enables users to hedge and transfer risk by altering the patterns of their cash flows. Interest rate swaps, for example, are the largest segment of OTC derivative markets and have contributed remarkably to the management of interest rate risk on corporate and commercial bank balance sheets. It is not surprising, therefore, that the use of derivatives has grown drastically in many countries, covering equity, interest rate, foreign exchange, commodity and credit markets.

The financial crisis of 2007 to 2009 has, however, highlighted two aspects of the OTC derivatives market that deserve attention and potential reform. The first aspect is that, while financial innovation – the design of new, customized products – typically occurs in the OTC space, this is also the arena in which banks can tailor their own risk taking and leverage buildup, since some of these positions are not reflected on their balance sheets either from a regulatory or statutory disclosure perspective. This is especially true since, thus far, regulatory capital requirements have not been suitably adjusted to reflect all aspects of OTC exposures, such as their illiquidity and their counterparty and systemic risks. The lack of such adjustment implies that risk taking is often more attractive for banks through off-balance-sheet OTC derivatives than via on-balance-sheet or exchange-traded products. For instance, the so-called toxic derivative assets (such as synthetic credit default swaps bought and sold on mortgage pools of dubious quality) that brought down many banks and insurance firms required, in retrospect, far too little regulatory capital relative to the risks incurred.

*Chapter 13 in Viral V. Acharya, Cooley, Thomas F., Richardson, Matthew P., and Ingo Walter, *Regulating Wall Street: The Dodd-Frank Act and the New Architecture of Global Finance*, John Wiley, 2010. Reprinted with permission of John Wiley & Sons, Inc.

†We received useful inputs and comments on earlier drafts from Menachem Brenner, Rob Engle, Steve Figlewski, Matt Richardson and Raghu Sundaram. We are also grateful to Darrell Duffie, Pablo Salame of Goldman Sachs and Til Schuermann of the Federal Reserve Bank of New York for useful discussions. Opinions expressed herein are entirely our own.

The second aspect that deserves attention concerns the opacity of exposures in OTC derivatives. By definition, an OTC derivative market does not have a central marketplace where all trades occur. This contrasts with exchange-traded derivatives, which are both traded on an exchange and cleared through a clearinghouse. Unlike cleared derivatives, where the clearinghouse monitors the risk of the positions of the various participants and imposes margins and other risk-mitigating devices, the risk-monitoring function in OTC markets is left to the individual counterparties. Since, for the most part thus far, OTC derivatives have not been centrally cleared, neither market participants nor regulators have accurate knowledge of the full range of the exposures and interconnections of the various market participants. This leads to a *counterparty risk externality* (see Acharya and Engle 2009; Acharya and Bisin 2010) that while each trade's counterparty risk is affected by other trades that are being done by the counterparties, this information is not visible. This prevents adequate risk controls against counterparty risk and a suitable conditioning of contract terms on precise measures of counterparty risk, and thereby results in a greater risk of leverage buildup *ex ante* and uncertainty about fallout of a counterparty's default *ex post*.

Primary concerns surrounding the failures or near failures of Bear Stearns, Lehman Brothers and American International Group (AIG) all had to do with uncertainty about how counterparty risk would spread through the web of OTC connections, particularly in the market for credit default swaps (CDSs), and in the case of AIG, how so much counterparty risk got built up in the first place. In the end, all this presented a fait accompli to regulators to engage in massive government bailouts of two of these three corporations. Indeed, much of the dislocation of the global economy after the financial crisis in 2008 can be traced to these spectacular failures.

The task of the Dodd–Frank Wall Street Reform and Consumer Protection Act of 2010 as far as derivatives reform is concerned can thus be considered to address these issues of leverage and opacity in those derivatives that are traded over the counter. In this chapter, we provide a condensed version of the reforms legislated by the Act relating to derivatives (the original text of this section of the Act is more than 450 pages) and our overall assessment of the reforms, followed by a more detailed discussion and implications for the future.

18.2   THE WALL STREET TRANSPARENCY AND ACCOUNTABILITY PART OF THE DODD–FRANK ACT OF 2010

In the fall of 2009, the US House of Representatives Financial Services Committee chaired by Congressman Barney Frank approved a bill, the Wall Street Reform and Consumer Protection Act of 2009, to regulate the massive OTC derivatives business. The proposed legislation called for sweeping changes in the structure (centralized trading versus over-the-counter trading) and regulation (margin requirements and transparency) of derivatives, but with exemptions for commercial end users. Then, in the spring of 2010, the Restoring American Financial Stability Act, proposed by the US Senate Banking Committee under Senator Christopher Dodd, required similar reforms of the derivatives markets targeted at improving their transparency and accountability.

In a controversial move, however, the revised Senate bill, the Wall Street Transparency and Accountability Act of 2010 (approved April 21, 2010), proposed prohibiting US federal assistance, including Federal Reserve advances and access to the discount window, as well as emergency liquidity or debt guarantee program assistance, to any dealer, major market participant, exchange or clearing organization in connection with derivatives or other activities (with limited exceptions for hedging activities by banks and derivatives involving certain financial asset classes). This provision would potentially have spurred financial institutions to separate their derivatives businesses from their US bank or US branch office in order for the bank or branch to be eligible for these forms of federal assistance. Such separation was, in fact, explicitly proposed in Senator Blanche Lincoln's amendment, which would remove government-backed financial firms (notably, the commercial banks) from any derivatives markets. As per the Lincoln Amendment, the affected institutions could still hold swaps and other derivatives, but they would have to be contained in separate legal entities that could not be used to fund or manage their banking businesses. Equally important, the affected lenders could not use their bank capital reserves to provide a backstop for their derivatives businesses.

While the clearing and transparency proposals of the House and the Senate bills were considered relatively uncontroversial, the restricted federal assistance and the Lincoln Amendment were both unexpected twists, and the conference version of the Dodd–Frank Act was keenly awaited to clarify the final legislation on these two issues. Unfortunately, the Act leaves key aspects of implementation to be determined by the Securities and Exchange Commission (SEC), the Commodity Futures Trading Commission (CFTC) and other financial regulators, with substantial scope for interpretation in the coming years.

What follows is a summary of the Wall Street Transparency and Accountability Act of 2010 – the part of the Dodd–Frank Wall Street Reform and Consumer Protection Act that deals with the derivatives markets. In this description, we follow closely the original language of the Act to minimize subjective translation of any of the provisions. The Act covers several key aspects: which derivatives will be affected; clearing, transparency and reporting requirements; bankruptcy-related issues; trading and risk mitigation; and extraterritorial enforcement and international coordination.

18.2.1 Which Derivatives Will Be Affected?

1. Coverage of derivatives: The Act repeals the provision under the Gramm–Leach–Bliley Act (GLBA), also known as the Financial Services Modernization Act of 1999, that prohibited the regulation of OTC derivatives. In this sense, it expands the scope of regulation for the first time to the completely unregulated OTC market. There is, however, an important exception being considered: The foreign exchange (FX) derivatives (forwards and swaps, among others) could be excluded based on the decision of the Treasury secretary. Specifically, "He/she may exempt FX swaps based on a) systemic risk, opacity, leverage, evasion and their consequences, b) whether existing regulations are sufficient, c) bank regulators can do the job, d) other effects." The Treasury secretary will be required to report to Congress within a year if and why FX derivatives are different from others, and if and why they should be exempted from the Act.[1] The Act also contains a specific clause that states that derivative contracts ("swaps") are not "insurance" contracts and precludes them being regulated as such.

18.2.2 Clearing

2. Clearing requirements: The default treatment of derivatives under the Act will be that they remain uncleared. Nevertheless, the exemption process to this default treatment has been clearly laid out with the intention that several plain-vanilla products will, over time, in fact be centrally cleared. In particular, the Act requires that within a year from its enactment, the "Commission" (the SEC and the CFTC[2]) shall adopt rules for reviewing a derivatives clearing organization's bid for the kind of derivatives it seeks to accept for clearing. If a set of derivatives is to be allowed for central clearing (based on outstanding interest, liquidity, pricing, trading infrastructure, mitigation of systemic risk taking account of the size of the market and clearing resources, the effect on competition and clarity on resolution of insolvency of the clearing agency), then the Commission will allow a 30-day comment period before the clearing commences. Further, there will be periodic reviews of derivatives that are cleared and of those that remain uncleared to assess whether clearing of some products needs to be stayed and whether other derivatives should be brought into the space of cleared derivatives.

An important issue concerns how the clearing requirements will be imposed on existing positions in a product viewed as "to be cleared." The Act clarifies that all positions, existing and new, need to be reported to a "swap data repository." Subject to this requirement, however, existing contracts need not be cleared if they are reported within specified time frames. Also, the clearing requirement will not be imposed on positions for which "one of the counterparties to the swap: (i) is not a financial entity;[3] (ii) is using swaps to hedge or mitigate commercial risk; and (iii) notifies the Commission, in a manner set forth by the Commission, how it generally meets its financial obligations associated with entering into uncleared swaps." The Act, however, permits regulators to consider further extending the exemption to small banks, savings associations, farm credit system institutions, and credit unions, including those with less than $10 billion of total assets.

3. Clearinghouse management: The Act recognizes that clearinghouses must be approved and reviewed based on their ability to provide needed financial resources for clearing as well as operational expertise. It requires the clearinghouses to provide public disclosure of contract terms, fees, margin methods, daily prices, volumes, open interest, governance structure, conflicts of interest and so on, for the products they clear. The Act also stipulates that a "clearinghouse will have adequate collateral to cover the default by a member/participant creating the largest financial exposure for that organization in extreme but plausible conditions (plus operational costs on a rolling basis for each year)." To this end, clearinghouses will have to ensure required record keeping of positions, conduct monitoring and daily credit risk assessment of all counterparties, and impose risk-based margins that provide coverage of their exposures in normal times.

The Act charges the clearinghouses with keeping collateral funds with minimum market, credit and liquidity risks. This recognizes the excessive counterparty credit risk created by some large swap counterparties that deployed the collateral backing their bilateral contracts for investments in risky securities. While the exact collateral-sharing rules across clearinghouses in case of a counterparty's insolvency are not clearly laid out (and presumably left to evolution of such practices in due course), the Act contains specific language to rule out counterparty risk across clearinghouses from each other's insolvency: "In order to minimize systemic risk, under no circumstances shall a derivatives clearing organization be compelled to accept the counterparty credit risk of another clearing organization."

Finally, the Act provides for the usual governance requirements of centrally cleared products pertaining to the regulation of insider trading, incentives for whistle-blowers and containment of conflicts of interest at the clearinghouse management level. On the latter, the Act requires the Commission to adopt numerical limits on the control or the voting rights of clearinghouses by any one institution, singling out systemically important financial firms.

4. Uncleared swaps: This is the default option for a derivative under the Act. Uncleared swaps will, however, be regulated for the first time. In particular, they may be subject to *margin* *and collateral requirements* in order to offset the risks they pose, and will also be subject to *transparency requirements* (outlined below in point 5). Furthermore, the Act explicitly recognizes that regulatory arbitrage – trading in uncleared clones to avoid clearing or trading in derivatives outside of the United States – may undermine the intended purpose of the Act. Hence, it allows regulators to take corrective actions to prevent such behavior. In fact, the Act gives unrestricted rights to the Commission and prudential regulators to require adequate margin on clones and abusive swaps that are used to evade clearing requirements; the required margins may be in line with, if not identical to, their cleared counterparts. The exact actions available to the Commission and the prudential regulators are not detailed in the Act.

18.2.3   Transparency and Reporting Requirements

5. Transparency: First and foremost, the Act requires that all existing derivative positions (both cleared and uncleared swaps) be reported to a swap data repository[4] within 180 days of its enactment, and all new positions (both cleared and uncleared) starting 90 days after the enactment (or an alternative legislated period). The repository, as the recipient of the trade information, will be tasked with providing data to the regulatory agencies (including foreign and international agencies, if applicable), to minimize systemic risk and to publish certain aggregate market information (trading and clearing in major swap categories and participants and developments in new products) to the public twice a year. In addition to this transparency at the position level, the Act requires *real-time public reporting*, meaning "to report data relating to a swap transaction, including price and volume, as soon as technologically practicable after the time at which the transaction has been executed." Such public reporting will, however, not include counterparty or customer information, and will also have a delay exemption for "block trades" (to be defined by the Commission for particular markets and contracts), taking account of the likely impact of disclosure of such trades on market liquidity.

18.2.4   Bankruptcy-Related Issues

6. Bankruptcy exemption: Under the Act, a security-based swap is treated as a sale and repurchase transaction in case of bankruptcy of one of the counterparties. Thus, derivatives contracts will continue to enjoy the exemption from bankruptcy of counterparties – as in the case of sale and repurchase transactions (repos) – as far as netting arrangements and segregation of collateral are concerned.

7. Collateral segregation: For cleared derivatives transactions, the Act requires both segregation of a counterparty's collateral and prohibition of commingling of such collateral with own funds, effectively requiring that a customer's collateral be treated, dealt with and accounted for strictly as belonging only to the customer. For uncleared derivative transactions, the Act requires the segregation of initial margin, but not of variation margin payments (i.e., daily margin requirements based on mark-to-market changes), upon request of a counterparty. If a counterparty does not ask for its collateral to be segregated in an uncleared derivative transaction, the Act requires a swap dealer[5] or a major swap participant[6] to report on a quarterly basis regarding the back-office procedures of the swap dealer or major swap participant in compliance with the agreement between the parties with respect to the handling of collateral. Also, there is no requirement that a counterparty request to segregate margin be made at the time the swap is executed.

18.2.5   Trading and Risk Mitigation

8. Systemically important institutions in derivatives markets: Major swap participants and swap dealers will be required to register with the Commission, which, in turn, will define what constitutes a "substantial position," that is, the threshold that the Commission determines to be prudent for the effective monitoring, management and oversight of entities that are systemically important or that can significantly impact the US financial system. In addition, major swap participants and swap dealers must meet periodic reporting requirements, minimum capital requirements, minimum initial and variation margin requirements (which, in certain instances, may include noncash collateral) and business conduct standards. In particular, major swap participants and swap dealers will be subject to capital requirements based on their total risk – including their uncleared transactions – by a prudential regulator (or by the Commission in the absence of a prudential regulator).

Unlike some of the prior versions of the legislation, the Act does not provide an explicit exemption from the margin requirement for end users. Nonetheless, in a letter from Chairs Christopher Dodd and Blanche Lincoln to Chairs Barney Frank and Colin Peterson (June 30, 2010), Senators Dodd and Lincoln expressed their view that the legislation was not intended to impose margin requirements on end users.

9. Position limits, position accountability and large trade reporting: The Act requires the Commission to establish limits, taking account of the hedge-exemption provisions, on the size of a position in any swap that may be held by any person or institution. In establishing such limits, the Commission is authorized to aggregate positions in (1) any security or loan or group of securities or loans on which the swap is based, or (2) any security or group or index of securities, the price, yield, value or volatility of which, or of which any interest therein, is the basis for a material term of such swap and related group or index of securities. The Commission may exempt, conditionally or unconditionally, any person or class of persons, any swap or class of swaps, or any transaction or class of transactions from the prescribed position limits. In addition to limits that may be established by the Commission, the Act also requires self-regulatory organizations to establish and enforce position limits or position accountability requirements in any security-based swap that may be held by their members.

10. De minimis investment requirement: It should be noted that derivatives trading activity does not necessarily qualify as "proprietary trading" as far as the Volcker Rule is concerned. Under this rule, banks retain the right to engage in hedge fund and private equity fund investments subject to a cap limiting those investments to 3 percent of the funds' capital and no more than 3 percent of the banks' Tier 1 capital. Importantly, the banking entity is prohibited from bailing out these investment funds in case of their insolvency.[7] Since derivatives are not necessarily included in the activities restricted by this *de minimis* investment requirement, they are also not subject to the additional capital requirements, nor to the quantitative limits applicable to proprietary trading under the Act (unless the appropriate federal bank agency, the SEC or the CFTC, determines that such additional requirements or limitations are appropriate to protect the safety and soundness of the banking entities engaged in such activities). Of course, derivative positions are subject to the requirements stipulated under the derivatives reforms, as described earlier.

11. Leverage limitation requirement: The Act requires the Federal Reserve to impose a maximum debt-to-equity leverage ratio of 15:1 on any financial company that the Council determines poses a "grave threat" to the US financial stability. The leverage and risk-based capital requirements applicable to insured depository institutions, depository institution holding companies, and systemically important nonbank financial companies must be not "less than" the "generally applicable risk-based capital requirements" and the "generally applicable leverage capital requirements," and not "quantitatively lower than" the requirements that were in effect for insured depository institutions as of the date the Act was enacted. However, it is unclear how leverage undertaken through derivatives contracts will affect the adoption of the maximum debt-to-equity ratio of 15:1 for systemically important firms.[8] The Act does not specify how the implicit leverage in derivatives contracts would be taken into account in the calculation of the overall leverage ratio.

12. The Lincoln Amendment (Section 716): The originally proposed Lincoln Amendment would have prevented insured depository institutions from engaging in derivatives activity by requiring them to spin off this activity. The Dodd–Frank Act enacts a diluted version that allows insured depository institutions to engage in "bona fide hedging and traditional bank activities" on their books – that is, hedging transactions and positions in plain-vanilla interest rate, FX and centrally cleared CDSs. All other derivatives activity can be managed by the depository institutions only in independent and well-capitalized "swap entities" as affiliates (swap dealers, major swap participants, exchanges and clearinghouses).

13. Prohibition on lender of last resort support:[9] This aspect of the Act constitutes the most far-reaching implication in terms of the resolution of derivatives exposures in case of insolvency. The Act imposes that from two years after the Act becomes effective (with some flexibility for extension up to one additional year) "no Federal assistance (e.g., advances from any Federal Reserve credit facility or discount window, FDIC insurance, or guarantees) may be provided to any swaps entity with respect to any of its activities." However, the Financial Stability Oversight Council can override the prohibition on Federal Reserve assistance with a two-thirds majority vote. Another important exception is made for affiliates of insured depository institutions: "The prohibition on Federal assistance contained does not apply to and shall not prevent an insured depository institution from having or establishing an affiliate which is a swaps entity, as long as such insured depository institution is part of a bank holding company, or savings and loan holding company, that is supervised by the Federal Reserve and such swaps entity affiliate complies with sections 23A and 23B of the Federal Reserve Act and such other requirements as the CFTC or the SEC, as appropriate, and the Board of Governors of the Federal Reserve System, may determine to be necessary and appropriate." To be eligible for such assistance, however, the insured depository institution must be engaged in only "bona fide hedging and traditional bank activities" (see point 12). The Lincoln Amendment (Section 716), besides allowing insured depository institutions to engage in bona fide hedging and traditional bank activities, also permits them to engage in separately well-capitalized swap entities as affiliates. The federal assistance to insured institutions, however, requires such affiliates, if any, to be spun off, but allows the insured depository institution up to 24 months to divest the swaps entity or cease the activities that require registration as a swaps entity.[10]

18.2.6   Extraterritorial Enforcement and International Coordination

14. Foreign platforms (boards of trade): The Act provides the Commission authority to require registration of foreign boards of trade that provide direct access to US market participants to their electronic trading and order matching system. In adopting specific rules and regulations, the Commission is directed to consider whether comparable regulation exists in the foreign board of trade's home country. If offering linked contracts, which are contracts that are priced against a contract that is traded on a US exchange, for which the Commission has not granted direct access permission, a foreign board of trade must adopt daily trading information requirements, record keeping, position limits and oversight requirements that are comparable to those on US exchanges. In addition, foreign boards of trade would be required to have the authority to liquidate or reduce market positions to protect against market manipulation and must notify the Commission should it adjust its reporting requirements or position limits or any other area of interest to the Commission.

15. International harmonization: The Act provides for the right levels of international harmonization in terms of setting standards for the regulation of derivatives and information sharing about derivatives positions: "In order to promote effective and consistent global regulation of swaps and security-based swaps, the Commodity Futures Trading Commission, the Securities and Exchange Commission, and the prudential regulators, as appropriate, shall consult and coordinate with foreign regulatory authorities on the establishment of consistent international standards with respect to the regulation (including fees) of swaps, security-based swaps, swap entities, and security-based swap entities and may agree to such information-sharing arrangements as may be deemed to be necessary or appropriate in the public interest or for the protection of investors, swap counterparties, and security-based swap counterparties."

In addition to these main issues, the Act requires studies to be conducted on the effectiveness of position limits as a regulatory tool, international harmonization of margining standards for swaps, and the possibility of developing algorithmic language to standardize electronic reporting of derivatives, among others. These are listed in detail in Appendix A, along with a table providing a time line of these future studies.

18.3   EVALUATION OF PROPOSED REFORMS

The main market failures in the OTC derivatives market are the buildup of excess leverage, opacity and difficulties of resolution when a large counterparty gets into trouble. Does the Wall Street Transparency and Accountability part of the Dodd–Frank Act on financial reforms address these issues? Our overall assessment is that while there are a lot of positives, a measured evaluation can be made only after specific details of implementation of the reforms are laid out by regulators over the next few years.

It should be noted at the outset that there are several aspects of the Dodd–Frank Act that seek to contain risk taking by systemically important institutions, not all of which are directly aimed at derivatives activity (for example, the Volcker Rule and leverage limitation described in Section 18.2, points 10 and 11). Clearly, hedge funds, as a group, have a significant presence in the derivatives markets. Hence, for some banking firms, such as Goldman Sachs, which has significant investments in hedge funds, the *de minimis* investment restrictions under the Volcker Rule could have a major impact on their aggregate level of derivatives exposure. If estimated correctly, the leverage limitation requirement of 15:1 would also restrict overall derivatives exposure of banks.

We focus our discussion, however, on those aspects of the Act that *directly* address derivatives activity that would remain on banks' books even after passage of the Act. These are: (1) derivatives that are standardized and have reasonable trading volumes would be considered for central clearing, and those that continue to trade OTC would be regulated in a "comparable" manner (points 1 through 4, 8 and 9); (2) transparency of all derivatives trades (point 5); and (3) bankruptcy issues relating to derivatives, the modified Lincoln Amendment, and the restriction of federal assistance for swap entities (points 6, 7, 12 and 13). The Act's proposals concerning international harmonization (points 14 and 15) are, by and large, reasonable, and we discuss them only briefly in concluding remarks.

First and foremost, many important details concerning clearing requirements for derivatives remain unspecified and subject to further examination by various regulators, including the SEC, the CFTC and the secretary of the Treasury. Over the next year or so, regulators will decide the particular types of derivatives that would be required to be centrally cleared. At one level, these tasks require detailed market knowledge and are not suitable for congressional debate and legislation. At another level, however, they will require significant human resources to be allocated to the relevant regulators (especially the CFTC) and will enlarge the gray area of regulatory discretion, which will inevitably lead to significant lobbying efforts from the industry. Hence, the new legislation places a great deal of faith in – and burden on – the prudential regulators to get it right. Given the existing pressures facing regulators and the substantial new burden imposed on them under the Act, it is not obvious how they will carry out their responsibilities. Furthermore, the challenges of recruiting appropriate talent to discharge these duties remain daunting.

The exact implementation of clearing provisions should be such that it contains the moral hazard of the clearinghouses, given their systemic importance. This moral hazard may arise when clearinghouses would take risks for their own private profit; as they become more systemically important, we run the risk of a replay of the recent crisis should the clearinghouses become the future government-sponsored enterprises (GSEs). Therefore, although their limited risk choices relative to private institutions make the moral hazard issue easier to deal with, given their systemic importance it is critical that their risk standards be constantly maintained. A consistent margin requirement across clearinghouses is also critical for avoiding a competitive race to the bottom. Otherwise, risky counterparties could migrate to clearinghouses that have the least stringent requirements; this would have the undesirable effect of concentrating systemic risk, rather than distributing it across multiple clearinghouses.

At the very outset, however, exception is potentially provided for not expanding the scope of the derivatives reform to FX derivatives. The exact guiding principle behind this exception is not spelled out, but the proposal presumably reflects the fact that banks deal in FX derivatives primarily to help their customers manage their business risks. Whether to regulate these derivatives is to be decided by the secretary of the Treasury after a detailed evaluation of the risks involved. Still, it is unclear why FX derivatives have been singled out, since a similar argument – that they aid hedging risks for ultimate users who have an offsetting business risk – could be made for a large fraction of overall positions in interest rate and commodity derivatives.

Concerning the Act's exemption for hedging transactions, we will provide direct evidence in this chapter that the primary systemic risk in the OTC derivatives market lies with dealers and not with end users. Hence, we endorse the Act's separate treatment of end-user positions. The Act, however, leaves out one rather important detail. The exempted positions must demonstrably be so for hedging purposes, and this should be verified on a regular basis through an audit procedure by the regulators, combined with the ability to penalize in case of unsatisfactory audit results (what we call the "audit and penalize" principle). Recognizing the limits to efficacy of such auditing in the case of large and complex organizations, we recommend that large swap participants, even in the end-user space, be subject to similar transparency requirements as dealers to avoid regulatory arbitrage of large scale and dimensions.

The Act relies heavily on margin requirements as the first line of defense against the buildup of leverage through derivatives. In particular, clearinghouses are required to charge margins such that they can withstand the failure of their largest exposure among the various members. Potentially, this is a sound way of determining margin requirements – rather than requiring that margins be raised uniformly across all positions on the clearinghouse. The simple rationale is that the Act will effectively require clearinghouses to ask members to fully collateralize their largest exposure in a given risk class (e.g., the largest exposure in single-name CDSs). Assuming that it is highly unlikely that two single names will default on the same day, this would mean the clearinghouse is reasonably well protected most of the time, and yet offers substantial collateral efficiency to its members. Indeed, requiring fully collateralized largest exposures might be a better way of imposing position limits (which the Act recommends for consideration following an evaluation study of their potential efficacy). The implicit position limit in this case is based on members' ability to generate collateral rather than an exogenous quantity restriction.

Recognizing the scope for creation of OTC clones simply to get around clearing requirements, the Act requires the regulators to charge margins for OTC positions also, in a manner that would be similar – even if not identical – for cleared varieties of these positions, and also empowers them to take adequate actions against evasive positions. However, there are likely to be several OTC products that are customized and without any similar cleared products. On this front, expecting regulators to get the margins right for each product's risk is likely to meet disappointment. It will also give rise to a "catch me if you can" game between industry and the regulators, not to mention the substantial workload on the regulators to react to changes in derivative positions of individual dealers in a timely manner.

Here, transparency in the OTC derivatives space could play a vital role. Fortunately, the Act does well on this front. *The Act's biggest strength lies in legislating counterparty-level transparency for the regulators, price-volume-level transparency for all market participants, and aggregated transparency of positions and players in different derivatives markets (twice a year).* By requiring that this transparency standard be applied right away to all OTC derivatives and not just to centrally cleared ones, the Act helps ensure that regulators will have the required information on interconnectedness of financial institutions in future systemic crises. Also, the time delay between execution and reporting of "block trades" that the Act permits is reasonable, as it will allow market makers sufficient time to unwind a position before the information about that position becomes public and will not deter them from supplying liquidity to the market.[11] Nevertheless, the transparency standard could be improved (as we will explain in detail) by gathering information on: (1) collateral backing different contracts (so as to ascertain the counterparty risk "exposure"), (2) potential exposures in stress scenarios rather than just current exposures that tend to be small in good times, and (3) the largest such potential exposures of a derivatives player to different counterparties. Some aggregated versions but at the level of each institution (that is, the largest potential uncollateralized exposures of each institution without revealing names of its counterparties or customers) should be made available to all market participants. In principle, with such a transparency standard, the counterparty risk externality could be mitigated and each derivative contract would better reflect – through price and collateral requirements – the counterparty risk arising from other trades and exposures of the involved parties.[12]

Consider next the modified Lincoln Amendment. The underlying rationale for requiring derivatives to be separately capitalized is to ease the resolution of the bank holding company that gets into trouble: The derivatives affiliate could simply be spun off, given its adequate capitalization. The rationale for exempting plain-vanilla interest rate, FX and credit derivatives from being separately capitalized is that these products are currently employed in significant quantities by banks for the purpose of hedging risks on their books – of loans, global transactions and counterparty risk in bilateral contracts. However, there is no explicit recognition of this hedging motive, and thus no recognition of its natural corollary that regulators "audit" over time, "penalizing" abuses and requiring that nonhedging transactions be better capitalized or moved to the well-capitalized subsidiary. *Not requiring – or even recommending – "audit and penalize" treatment of exemptions that are based on hedging motives is an important weakness of the Act.* It also raises the possibility of potential arbitrage by banks of the Act's intentions to contain leverage, for instance, by establishing large derivatives positions in the plain-vanilla segment on the bank's own balance sheet. And in case of a large bank's failure, if large uncollateralized exposures are discovered to be in this plain-vanilla space, the system may face a rerun of the Bear Stearns, Lehman and AIG episodes: Yes, there would be the well-capitalized derivatives subsidiary, but all the risk might in fact be on the bank's main book!

In our assessment, however, the Act's proposals for derivatives are the weakest in the area of bankruptcy resolution relating to derivatives and swap entities. There are three issues that raise concerns.

First, the restriction on federal assistance to swap entities, including clearinghouses, seems to rule out an important mechanism to deal *ex post* with systemic risk. The Act should recognize that once most derivative contracts move to centralized clearing platforms, clearinghouses will become important concentrations of systemic risk. While their capitalization levels can be monitored, there is always the small chance that those levels will prove inadequate when there is an unexpected shock to a large member or to several markets at once. In this case, there should be little hesitation to provide temporary liquidity assistance to the clearinghouse and resolve its situation in due course. But without such assistance, capital markets may freeze in the same way they froze when Bear Stearns, Lehman and AIG experienced problems. While the Act potentially allows for federal assistance to swap entities if the Council managing systemic risk approves so by a two-thirds vote, this is unnecessary discretionary uncertainty in the midst of a crisis and may cause costly delays in an emergency similar to September 2008.

Second, in the event that a clearinghouse gets to the point of insolvency, the Act explicitly prohibits its positions from being transferred to another clearinghouse. While every effort should be made to produce an orderly resolution, if there is a sufficiently healthy clearinghouse that manages similar products to those of the failing one, it might be far more orderly to have this clearinghouse deal with some – if not all – of the outstanding positions, especially the ones that may be difficult to liquidate or close out sufficiently quickly. Again, the Act seems to overly restrict *ex post* resolution options for stress scenarios at a clearinghouse. Even under more normal circumstances, transfer of positions across clearinghouses may in fact reduce systemic risk. Hence, a prohibition on such transfers may not be prudent.

Third, as we argue elsewhere in the book in the case of sale and repurchase agreements (repo markets), there is a case for softening the bankruptcy exemption for derivative transactions in scenarios where there is a systemically important counterparty that is going bankrupt.

By granting exemption from bankruptcy – primarily from automatic stay on a secured or collateralized part of the transaction – derivative counterparties effectively obtain a short-term, immediately demandable claim on the distressed firm. The derivatives positions then become equivalent to those of short-term creditors who join the run. In all systemic crises – the panics before the formation of the FDIC in 1934, the Continental Illinois failure of 1984, the collapse of Long-Term Capital Management in 1998 and the crisis of 2007 to 2009 – ultimately short-term creditors of distressed firms had to be stayed (respectively) through suspension of demandable deposits in commercial bank clearinghouse certificates, a government bailout, a Federal Reserve-orchestrated conversion of debt into equity, or a federal backstop. All this was to avoid fire-sale liquidations and liquidity dry-ups in markets. While the benefit of bankruptcy exemption is clear – it reduces counterparty risk and contagion risk, in turn generating greater liquidity for trades in good times – it comes at the expense of inducing more precipitous runs, and when these occur for systemically important firms, this invariably compromises taxpayer funds and entrenches the too-big-to-fail problem. A systemic exception to the bankruptcy exemption for derivatives for a prespecified period would buy the regulators some time to plan for orderly resolutions.

Leaving aside the uncertainty of exact implementation and the few critical weaknesses we have flagged, we believe that, in principle, many of the proposed changes have the potential to stabilize the derivatives markets and improve their functioning and their regulation over time. By requiring standardized products (which trade in large volumes and are sufficiently commoditized) to trade on exchanges or centralized clearinghouses (existing or newly formed), the Act makes progress on the front of containing leverage buildup through OTC derivatives positions. By requiring that not just cleared but even OTC derivatives be subject to high levels of transparency, the Act goes quite some distance in reducing the systemic risk of the OTC derivatives business and the systemic costs of bankruptcy of a major market participant. However, implementing these changes all at once may prove to be a major task. Hence, as a cautious step-by-step approach to getting the details right, *our overall recommendation is to start with applying changes to the credit derivatives market that was the primary source of OTC market stress in this crisis.* Following this, the costs and benefits of the migration from OTC to centralized clearing can be considered and evaluated for other markets, such as interest rate, FX and commodity derivatives. The main reason for this view is that the credit derivatives market is where most of the systemic consequences manifested themselves in the current crisis and where the underlying risk transfers are largely between financial firms, while other markets such as interest rate and FX derivatives were largely unaffected in the crisis and represent a larger amount of risk transfer between financial firms and end users.

Having provided our overall assessment of the derivatives reforms under the Dodd–Frank Act, we proceed as follows. In Section 18.4, we discuss the specifics of moving OTC markets to centralized exchanges or clearinghouses, the trade-off between relying on margin requirements versus transparency, why it is important to deal with the risk of dealers first and why the proposed reforms would help end users. In addition, we discuss the systemic risk that arises due to setting up centralized clearing platforms and whether the reforms adequately provide for dealing with this risk. We conclude in Section 18.5 with a look ahead at how the reforms may shape global derivatives arena in the future. In Appendix C, we also discuss the issue of sovereign credit derivatives and whether there is any need to ban them as has been called for in some parts of Europe.

18.4 CLEARING, MARGINS, TRANSPARENCY AND SYSTEMIC RISK OF CLEARINGHOUSES

18.4.1 Migration to Centralized Clearing Should Start with Credit Derivatives

The growth of OTC derivatives in recent years, particularly in the CDS market, makes them top candidates for proposed regulations.[13] A key issue with any derivative contract is that of collateral (or margin) requirements. If collateral requirements are too low, then counterparty risk issues manifest themselves; in contrast, if they are too high, they may remove any advantage of the derivative relative to managing risks simply by holding cash reserves. As such, setting the precise level of collateral requirements will ultimately be a practice that evolves over time in each exchange or clearinghouse (possibly also coordinated across exchanges and clearinghouses). However, some guidelines are necessary, especially as to how to margin the many customized CDSs that will continue to remain OTC.

We would like to stress that the risk exposure for credit derivatives is fundamentally of a different nature from that associated with traditional derivative products, such as interest rate swaps. Like other swaps, the mark-to-market value of a single-name CDS, a type of a credit derivative, fluctuates from day to day as the market's assessment of the underlying entity's credit risk varies. Although these daily fluctuations are similar to daily price movements for other derivatives and can be handled adequately within a standard margining system, the potential liability of the protection seller to its counterparty upon the occurrence of a credit event suddenly jumps to as much as 100 percent of the contract's notional principal. In nearly every case, this liability will greatly exceed the value of the collateral posted to cover daily margin flow variations and will leave the protection buyer exposed to significant counterparty risk.

Under central clearing, this *jump to default* liability would ultimately lie with the clearinghouse. One possible way to eliminate the counterparty risk, then, would be to require collateral equal to the full notional principal amount on all of a protection seller's swaps, but that would be prohibitively expensive. A more feasible and cheaper alternative that would also eliminate most of counterparty risk in the case of a credit event would be to require the protection seller to post margin equal to 100 percent of its single *largest* exposure to an individual reference entity. This additional margin would guarantee that the protection seller could always cover the potential liability from any *single* credit event that it has sold protection against. Only in the case of simultaneous defaults by multiple entities covered by the same protection seller would there be any residual counterparty risk. This margin requirement can be considered a *concentration charge* and would be in addition to posting the margin required to cover daily fluctuations in the values of all of the protection seller's open positions in the absence of a credit event.[14]

Another feature of CDS contracts that distinguishes them from other derivatives is that there are no obvious sellers of protection who are naturally hedged by other positions as end users. This is in contrast to FX and interest rate derivatives, where there could be end users whose positions are opposite to each other, so that the hedging activity actually reduces systemic risk. Furthermore, CDS trades inherently feature wrong-way exposures for protection buyers, as credit risk is tied to the macroeconomic cycle so that it materializes precisely when the counterparty (the protection seller) has also most likely become riskier. Hence, CDS regulation *must* move first, since the materialization of counterparty risk in CDSs, and potentially systemic risk in the financial sector, is likely to coincide with an economic downturn. A pragmatic approach for rolling out proposed regulation would be gradually to move single-name and index CDSs first to central clearing while adopting margin requirements, as discussed earlier for those CDSs that remain OTC. To minimize regulatory overload, other derivative markets could be added over time. Moreover, while CDS reforms are being put in place, regulators should require disclosures by the concerned parties to understand the quality of bilateral margining and risk management in interest rate, currency and commodities derivatives. Based on such information, policymakers would be able to better assess whether and what kind of additional regulation is needed in these markets.

18.4.2 Margin Requirements versus Transparency

Does the Act fully deal with the difficulty of opacity in OTC derivatives markets? The answer to this question is somewhat mixed. On the one hand, it is clear that single-name CDSs on corporations and sovereigns will likely move to central clearing platforms (as has already happened to some extent through industry-initiated efforts) and possibly over time move to exchanges. This would significantly reduce the opacity of these products. Nevertheless, since the bill requires transparency primarily for cleared derivatives, the status of uncleared derivatives markets remains open. Instead of requiring mandatory disclosures of these remaining OTC positions, the Act puts the burden on regulators to impose margins or capital requirements, hoping that they would be large enough to contain risks, and, wherever possible, to get trading to move to centrally cleared products.

Before discussing the Dodd–Frank Act's proposal to require margins for uncleared derivatives, let us review the current use of collateral by dealers to mitigate counterparty credit risks. The overall picture that emerges is that while there is clearly a substantial amount of collateral being posted on OTC derivative contracts between counterparties, the uncollateralized portions remain large enough to cause concern about counterparty risk and the attendant systemic risk issues.

More specific details on the state of collateral use in the OTC derivatives market emerge from the examination by the International Swaps and Derivatives Association (ISDA) of the state of the global marketplace for collateral in recent years. The ISDA conducted its first survey of collateral use in the OTC derivatives industry among its 67 member firms, including the top five banks – Goldman Sachs, Citigroup, JPMorgan Chase, Bank of America and Morgan Stanley – in 2000. Since that time, the reported number of collateral agreements in place has grown from about 12,000 to almost 151,000, while the estimated amount of collateral in circulation has grown from about $200 billion to an estimated $2.1 trillion at the end of 2008 and an estimated amount of almost $4 trillion at the end of 2009.

Not only has there been a continuing trend toward increased collateral coverage, in terms of both amount of credit exposure and the number of trades (Figures 18.1 and 18.2), but the use of cash collateral has also continued to grow in importance among most financial firms, and now stands at almost 84 percent of collateral received and 83 percent of collateral delivered, up from 78 percent and 83 percent, respectively, at the end of 2008. The use of government securities as collateral also grew. The increase in cash and government securities was balanced by a decline in the use of other forms of collateral, such as corporate bonds and equities. These trends are a reflection of the heightened demand for high-quality collateral post-Bear Stearns and especially after Lehman's collapse, while the supply of collateral has been reduced due to the hoarding of collateral as reserves by dealers (e.g., Goldman Sachs).[15] By some counts, according to an article in *Barron's*, fees earned on lending collateral contribute about a third of dealers' overall profits on derivatives trades.[16]

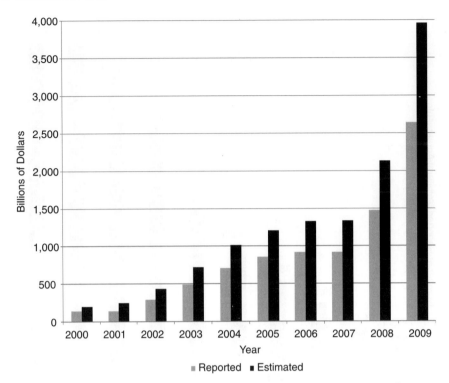

Figure 18.1   Growth of value of total reported and estimated collateral, 2000 to 2009 ($ billions).
Source: International Swaps and Derivatives Association, Margin Surveys 2000 to 2009.

When collateralized transactions are categorized by size, there is a significant variation in the counterparty mix relating to collateral arrangements (see Figure 18.3). Most collateral agreements among large firms are with hedge funds and institutional investors (50 percent), followed by corporations (15 percent), banks (13 percent) and other (21 percent). At the other extreme, small financial firms – the survey respondents with the least number of collateral agreements outstanding – deal mostly with other banks.[17] Approximately one-half of the collateral agreements at medium-sized financial firms are with other banks and corporations. Medium firms also deal with hedge funds and institutional investors, but to a relatively smaller extent than large firms. Other counterparties, which include commodity trading firms, special purpose vehicles, sovereigns, supranationals, private banking clients and municipalities, represent 21 percent of counterparties at large firms, 10 percent at medium firms and only 1 percent at small firms.

In addition to this substantial variation in the nature of counterparties involved in collateral arrangements, the percentage of trades subject to collateral arrangements varies across different types of underlying contracts (see Table 18.1). These differences are, in part, reflective of the variation in the risk of the underlying trades and counterparties, as well as the specific size of the market segment and its development. As illustrated, credit and fixed income are the most collateralized types of OTC derivative contracts (featuring 60 to 70 percent of trade volume and exposure that is collateralized), whereas FX, equity and commodities show less collateralization (between 45 and 50 percent of trade volume and exposure). This likely reflects

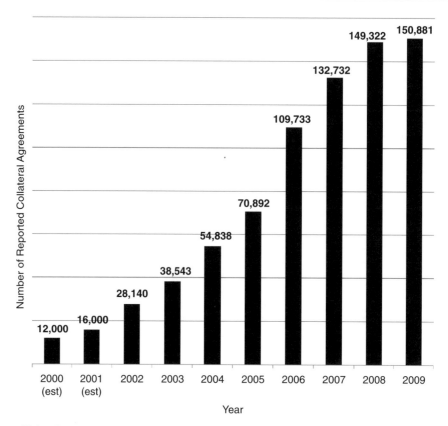

Figure 18.2   Growth of reported collateral agreements, 2000 to 2009.
Source: International Swaps and Derivatives Association, Margin Surveys 2000 to 2009.

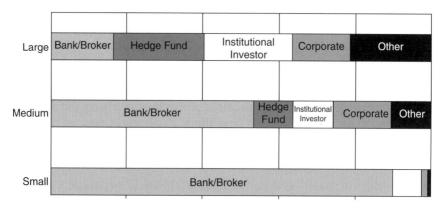

Figure 18.3   Counterparties of collateralized transactions.
Source: International Swaps and Derivatives Association, Margin Surveys 2000 to 2009.

Table 18.1   Trade volume and exposure collateralized, 2003–2009 survey.

	Trade Volume Requiring Collateral							Exposure Collateralized						
	2009	2008	2007	2006	2005	2004	2003	2009	2008	2007	2006	2005	2004	2003
OTC Derivatives	65	63	59	59	56	51	30	66	65	59	63	55	52	29
Fixed Income	63	68	62	57	58	58	53	71	66	65	57	58	55	48
FX	36	44	36	37	32	24	21	48	55	44	44	43	37	28
Equity	52	52	51	46	51	45	27	52	56	56	56	61	52	24
Metals	39	38	37	37	31	24	18	47	41	34	34	44	40	18
Energy	39	40	42	48	36	26	16	47	39	41	44	37	30	15
Credit	71	74	66	70	59	45	30	66	66	66	62	58	39	25

Source: International Swaps and Derivatives Association, Margin Surveys 2000 to 2009.

the fact that FX and commodities derivatives are used more often for hedging purposes and have end users as one counterparty, whereas fixed income and credit have a higher component of dealer-to-dealer trades. However, closer scrutiny of the detailed data, which unfortunately are not readily available today, would permit a more granular characterization of these major markets.

Given this evidence on collateralization of OTC derivatives, recent International Monetary Fund (IMF) research on the counterparty risk stemming from OTC derivatives finds that a large part of the counterparty risk in this market remains undercollateralized (i.e., up to $2 trillion) relative to the risk in the system.[18] This estimate is close to the $2 trillion net credit exposure figure presented by the Bank for International Settlements (BIS) in its semiannual derivatives survey,[19] but is higher than a recent ISDA survey cited by the BIS in its September 2009 quarterly review that puts the volume of undercollateralized derivatives at $1 trillion. Using information from the 10-Q quarterly statements, the IMF report estimates that the five key US banks mentioned before are jointly carrying almost $500 billion in OTC derivative payables exposure as of the third quarter of 2009. The five largest European banks – Deutsche Bank, Barclays, UBS, Royal Bank of Scotland (RBS) and Credit Suisse – had about $600 billion to $700 billion in undercollateralized risk (measured by residual derivative payables) as of December 2008.

This residual exposure arises for two reasons, according to the IMF report. First, sovereigns, as well as AAA-rated insurers, corporations, large banks and multilateral institutions "do not post adequate collateral since they are viewed by large complex financial institutions as privileged and (apparently) safe clients." Second, based on the bilateral nature of the contracts, dealers have agreed not to mandate adequate collateral for dealer-to-dealer positions. In fact, creditworthy dealers typically post no collateral to each other for these contracts.

It is estimated in the report that if the two-thirds of OTC contracts that are "standardized" were shifted into clearinghouses, as policymakers propose, banks would need to find over $200 billion in initial margins and guarantee funds: An extra $80 billion would be needed to cover clearing of CDSs; $40 billion to $50 billion for interest rate swaps; and $90 billion for equities, foreign exchanges and commodities. In addition, if regulators charged an ad hoc capital levy of 10 percent to 20 percent on the remaining third of (non-standard) OTC contracts retained by dealers on their own books, this would require the banks to hold an additional $70 billion to $140 billion of capital to reflect these risks adequately. Moreover, in such a scenario, non-standardized derivatives could no longer be netted against standardized ones, which implies that banks would need to hold even more capital against non-standardized contracts to immunize them against default. An estimate of the additional capital to be raised by banks would be in the range of $150 billion to $250 billion.

While some increase in initial collateral requirements seems unavoidable given the manifestations of counterparty risk witnessed in the recent crisis, the lack of adequate netting of collateral across different platforms and products raises the questions of whether margins or capital requirements are the best mechanism to deal with remaining OTC contracts and whether they can even be designed effectively. At one extreme, it is clear that the current undercollateralization of uncleared derivatives poses substantial systemic risk. At the other, where uncleared OTC positions are required to be fully collateralized, counterparties would most likely find it cheaper to take on basis risk by trading in standardized products that are cleared rather than the customized ones they desire.[20] Hence, if the goal is to shrink the size of opaque OTC markets, regulators can simply raise their margin requirements to prohibitive levels, effectively making these products unattractive to hedgers. In reality, in many cases, customized OTC products used for hedging by end users are unlikely to have any centrally cleared counterparts. How should the regulators deal with such products? We know that elsewhere in bank regulation, capital requirements designed by regulators have fallen woefully short of containing systemic risk and leverage, as they are too coarse and easily arbitraged. There is no reason to believe that the outcome here would be any different. A solution that does not pose large systemic risk, while at the same time making the use of customized OTC derivatives cost effective, is therefore required.

18.4.3   Toward a Transparency Standard

A better solution than increased margin requirements would therefore be to require transparency of the exposures of dealers and large swap players to all OTC products, not just centrally cleared ones, and at regular intervals. The information overhead can be minimized by requiring all dealers as well as large swap players to produce frequent risk reports on their OTC derivatives positions as follows:

- *Classification of exposures* into:
  - Product types (such as single-name or index CDSs, interest rate swaps, currency swaps, etc.).
  - Type of counterparty (bank, broker-dealer, corporation, monoline, etc.).
  - Maturity of contracts.
  - Credit rating of counterparties.
- *Size of exposures* should be reported:
  - As gross (maximum notional exposure).
  - As net (taking account of bilateral netting arrangements).
  - As uncollateralized net (recognizing collateral posted by counter parties).
  - In fair-value terms (to account for mark-to-market changes).
  - By major currency categories.
- Uncollateralized net exposures should be further modified and stated also as *potential exposures* based on stress tests that take account of replacement risk for the exposures, assuming severe market conditions such as replacement time of two to four weeks.
- *Concentration reports* should be provided, and detail the aforementioned information for the entity's largest counterparty exposures (say, the largest 5 or 10) that account for a substantial proportion of the total exposure, say 75 percent.

- *Margin call report* that lists the additional collateral liabilities of the firm as:
  - Total additional liability in case the firm experiences one, two, or more notch downgrades.
  - The largest such liabilities aggregated by different counterparties (e.g., the five largest).

Although this list appears to involve a large amount of information, the costs of such disclosure are not likely to be that onerous. Investment banks already maintain this information for internal risk management purposes; indeed, they publish some of it in their quarterly reports (see Appendix B for an overview of Goldman Sachs's and Citigroup's disclosure levels as of August 2010). Therefore, it would not be a huge additional burden for them to disclose this information to regulators in a standardized format at frequent intervals, say monthly. Some aggregated versions that respect customer confidentiality can then be made transparent to markets at large, for example on a quarterly basis, to help enhance market discipline against uncollateralized exposure buildup.[21] In particular, market transparency of counterparty exposures will create a tiering of financial firms in each OTC market, making it possible for new trades to be directed toward the least risky counterparty.

Overall, we recommend that the effective functioning of the OTC markets should rely more on transparency and less on rules designed by regulators, such as those based on capital, collateral or position limits, which could prove to be too rigid in some circumstances and could invite regulatory arbitrage.[22] This would be more in line with the spirit of market-based risk mitigation mechanisms that may be more flexible than regulation by fiat. However, even if regulators were to design margin requirements themselves, which may be less desirable, the proposed OTC transparency would still help. For instance, if regulators required that exposures to the (e.g., five) largest counterparties of each financial firm be sufficiently well collateralized, then they would have effectively mitigated a significant part of the systemic risk in OTC markets at a reasonable cost. And in case of failures, regulators would know the exposures with precision and could take anticipatory action to contain systemic contagion, since they would possess the necessary information ahead of time.

18.4.4   Deal with the Dealers First

The main participants in the overall derivatives landscape are large financial firms: commercial and investment banks, mutual funds, pension funds, hedge funds and insurance companies. For instance, in the United States, the derivatives market is dominated by the financial industry and five banks in particular. JPMorgan Chase, Bank of America, Goldman Sachs, Citigroup and Morgan Stanley account for more than 96 percent of the total industry notional amount and about 80 percent of industry net current credit exposure, as per Fitch Ratings' July 2009 report. Figure 18.4 depicts the shares of these top five banks in different markets and Figure 18.5 shows the outstanding notional amounts of derivative contracts by each bank, with JPMorgan Chase alone accounting for more than 30 percent of market trading volume.

It is clear from these numbers that reform of OTC derivatives should first and foremost be applied, and with some urgency, to these major dealer banks. Importantly, these banks not only serve as intermediaries and dealers in the derivatives market, but they also buy and sell derivatives to manage risks on their own balance sheets, and to undertake speculative positions in their proprietary trading desks. Furthermore, they directly or indirectly control several other investment vehicles, such as asset management/private banking entities, including hedge funds, which are likely to be significant users of OTC derivative products. Current reporting standards are insufficient to separate both the *proprietary and asset management*-based derivative trading

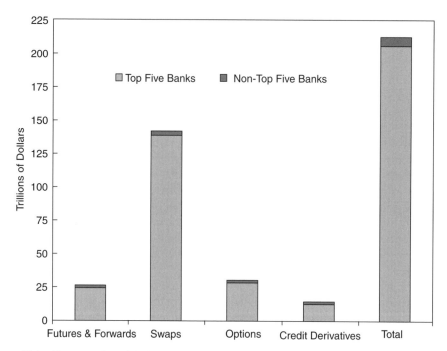

Figure 18.4   Concentration of derivative contracts – all commercial banks, 4Q09 ($ trillions)
Source: Call Reports, Office of the Comptroller of the Currency, 4Q09.

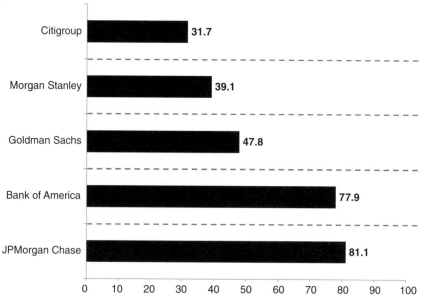

Figure 18.5   Notional value of derivatives contracts outstanding held by US banks as of 1Q09 ($ trillions).
Source: Deutsche Bank, *Wall Street Journal*, Office of the Comptroller of the Currency.

from *hedging*-related trading, and, in turn, to separate all these activities from derivatives trades initiated in the banks' capacity as dealers and intermediaries. Once the Lincoln Amendment under the Dodd–Frank Act (see points 12 and 13 in Section 18.2 for details) will be enacted in practice, it will effectively create segregation between the banking subsidiary that can apply for "hedger exception" and be subject to hedge documentation of its positions, with supervision and audit by bank regulators at daily frequency (as with its other risk reports), and the market making or pure dealer subsidiary, which will be subject to higher collateral or capital requirements.

18.4.5 Proposed Reforms Will Help End Users

The end users of OTC derivatives, including some of the largest corporations on both sides of the Atlantic (such as Caterpillar and Lufthansa), have expressed concerns about the proposed reforms. Some of them have sent memoranda to their respective regulators suggesting that the proposed reforms to the OTC derivatives markets would ultimately increase their business risks, reduce investment capital and slow economic growth. To better evaluate the validity of their concerns, one should first recognize the relative importance of end users in the OTC derivatives markets and their motivation for accessing such products.

According to a 2009 ISDA survey, 94 percent of the world's 500 largest companies, located in 32 different countries, made use of derivatives. That included 92 percent of US companies, 100 percent of UK companies, 97 percent of German companies, 100 percent of French companies and 100 percent of Japanese companies. The broad use of derivatives by companies of various sizes is documented in a more detailed analysis conducted by Fitch Ratings in July 2009 based on the quarterly reports of a sample of 100 companies from a range of industries in the Standard & Poor's (S&P) 1,500 universe. The report sheds light on the trends in derivatives use within various industries. Table 18.2 details the assets and liabilities for the selected companies in each industry.

In the financial services industry, the most important user segment (the top five banks put aside), 36 companies were reviewed in the Fitch report. Of these 36, only four institutions had no exposure to derivatives.[23] In addition, Fitch reviewed 13 regional banks, and it seems that trading activity in derivatives by these banks is not as extensive as by the larger national banks. Furthermore, the study shows that interest rate derivatives make up an average 85 percent of total net exposure, while currency derivatives make up an average 7 percent of total exposure. In the insurance industry, interest rate derivatives dominate on the balance sheets of the four reviewed companies. However, and not surprisingly, AIG and MBIA Inc. show sizable total notional amounts for net credit derivatives written (AIG $256 billion; MBIA $165 billion).

Fitch also reviewed the derivatives disclosure of 14 utilities and power companies. Utilities traditionally have used derivatives to hedge pricing exposures within regulated business lines. In response to deregulation and the development of active energy trading markets, many power and gas companies also developed proprietary trading operations that allowed them to speculate on derivatives, above and beyond what was necessary to hedge their own production and purchasing. However, since the Enron bankruptcy (which was, at least in part, attributed to derivatives trading using complex special purpose vehicles), the resulting changes to accounting rules governing energy contracts require more detailed disclosure; consequently, many of these companies have either disbanded or sold their trading functions. Of the 14 utilities reviewed, only three companies (Dominion Resources Inc., Exelon Corporation and FPL Group Inc.) disclosed the use of derivatives for proprietary trading. Proprietary trading may

Table 18.2   Derivative assets and liabilities as of June 6, 2009 ($ millions).

	Company	Total Assets	Total Derivative Assets[a]	Total Derivative Liabilities[a]
Selected Insurance Companies	American International Group	819,758	10,192	5,197
	MetLife, Inc.	491,408	9,351	4,009
	Prudential Financial	427,529	7,430[b]	4,621[b]
	MBIA Inc.	27,907	1,126	5,332
Selected Utilities and Power Companies	Duke Energy Corporation	53,584	491	649
	Southern Company	49,557	20	461
	Exelon Corporation	48,863	1,437	506
	American Electric Power	45,865	710	353
	FPL Group, Inc.	45,304	1,016	1,762
	Edison Int'l	44,429	950	948
	Dominion Resources, Inc.	41,687	2,219	2,219
	PG&E Corporation	41,335	298	542
	Entergy Corporation	36,613	351	91
	AES Corporation	34,838	202	467
	Consolidated Edison, Inc.	34,224	279	464
	FirstEnergy Corporation	33,557	383	869
	Progress Energy, Inc.	30,903	5	935
	Centerpoint Energy, Inc.	19,676	142	221
Selected Energy and Oil Companies	Exxon Mobil Corporation	222,491	NA	NA
	ConocoPhillips	143,251	7,442	7,211
	Anadarko Petroleum Corporation	48,154	533	84
	XTO Energy, Inc.	37,056	2,397	66
	Chesapeake Energy Corporation	29,661	1,978	635
	El Paso Corporation	22,424	873	896
	Spectra Energy Corporation	21,417	26	22

[a]Includes the impact of netting adjustments.
[b]Presented gross without netting benefits.
Source: Fitch Ratings, quarterly filings.

be used for the purpose of price discovery or to benefit from superior market knowledge. However, for the companies reviewed it appears that the scale of trading activities is limited in relation to their overall activities.

Similar to power companies, the oil industry also has had extensive experience in the use of derivatives over the past several decades. Of the seven energy companies reviewed, six had exposures to derivatives, with a 97 percent concentration in commodity derivatives. Surprisingly, according to Fitch's review of energy companies, Exxon Mobil Corporation – the largest energy company in the United States – had no derivatives exposure at the end of the first quarter of 2009. Furthermore, two companies (ConocoPhillips and El Paso Corporation) had trading operations in addition to using derivatives for risk management of their operations. Non-trading activities typically include hedging of crude oil and natural gas production. Although oil companies actively market natural gas, crude oil and other products to customers, their knowledge of the market gained through this marketing effort is useful for trading on the prices of these basic commodities. As a result, oil companies may engage in trading activities for the purpose of generating profit from exposure to changes in the market prices of these products, rather than merely hedging.[24]

Thus, while end users of OTC derivatives do represent a significant proportion of the market in terms of the number of participants, their usage is dominated by the activities of a few large firms, in particular the large insurers. Nevertheless, these end users have expressed several concerns regarding the reform of OTC derivatives. The first concern is that an increase in the overall cost of dealer activities – due to transparency and greater margin requirements – may raise end users' own hedging costs, as dealers will, in one form or another, pass on the costs to these end users. The second concern is that reforms that force a dealer preference for standardized products cleared centrally would reduce the ability of end users to find customized hedges, thus increasing their basis risk. For example, an airline may not be able to hedge jet fuel prices, but only the price of crude oil, which may not move perfectly in line with the airline's fuel costs.

Will end users' hedging costs necessarily increase? We are unable to quantify this, as we explain in detail later. However, even if end users' costs were to go up, it may be argued that this is a fair price that society requires to balance economic growth and financial stability. The experience with the CDS market during the financial crisis highlights the systemic risks imposed by OTC contracts that did not adequately price risk to balance economic growth and financial stability. In some cases, such as FX, it may be argued that the opposite is the case and the basis risk borne by market participants swamps the systemic consequences of using customized, noncleared derivatives.

In our view, enhanced transparency and reduced counterparty risk of derivatives dealers ought to benefit end users directly in terms of the risks and costs they ultimately bear. Currently, end users manage the counterparty risk of dealers either by distributing their hedges across different dealers or by buying protection on counterparties through CDSs. Both these methods are not only inefficient but also deceptive. As the current crisis has made clear, dealers themselves are often taking similar positions. In this case, buying protection against default of the first dealer from a second dealer is not that different from bearing the default risk of the first dealer.

In contrast to current practices, up-front capital injections into central clearinghouses along with greater margin requirements on OTC positions held directly by dealers would reduce the default risk that end users face. One still cannot rule out the possibility, however remote, that a clearinghouse may itself collapse (see the next subsection). But there are mechanisms in place – such as the lender of last resort – to deal with such an extreme scenario. It would be better from a systemic perspective for the Federal Reserve to lend to a clearinghouse, effectively lending to its strongest member firms, than to the weakest ones that brought it down. Furthermore, since the risks are clearly visible from the marketwide information available within the clearinghouse, it may be possible to take preventive action earlier than under the previous regime, where the risks were largely under the regulators' radar.

Under the proposed reforms, dealer activities are intended to be efficiently margined by regulators to contain the systemic risk they pose on others. Thus, it is only fair that end users also pay at least a part of this price. The alternative scenario where these risks are not borne and paid for by the beneficiaries – dealers and end users – but are underwritten by taxpayers at large if dealers default is suboptimal. Indeed, such perverse incentives were the root cause of the credit bubble just witnessed and must be curbed before they lead to another crisis.

Another point of contention is about whether the derivatives reform should extend directly to the end users or they should be exempt. It may be reasonable to argue that end users should receive exemption from the detailed transparency reports and margin requirements that dealers will be subject to. It may also be appropriate that the margin requirements should take into account the hedged positions that the end users aim to maintain. Such exemptions, however, cannot be left entirely open-ended by regulators. It is important to recognize that once dealers are subject to higher capital requirements and transparency, and end users enjoy a hedger exception, the most likely place for buildup of excessive risks in the OTC markets would be in the space of end users. Of course, the regulations should take cognizance of the hedges that the end users maintain with their operational positions.

It is important, as proposed in the Act, that end users that choose not to be classified as dealers be brought under the same set of regulations as dealers if these end users violate certain criteria regarding their hedging status. In particular, end users should be required to provide hedge documentation of their derivatives trades detailing their underlying exposures. This hedge documentation must be subject to regular audits. End users whose audits reveal shortcomings in hedge documentation, or who are found to be maintaining substantial one-way derivatives position bets more appropriate for a dealer's warehouse or a speculative desk, should be subject to penalties and potentially have their hedger exception revoked for a sufficiently long period, effectively subjecting them to additional transparency requirements and margins.

Nevertheless, the "audit and penalize" system is not perfect and will not prevent all abuse of the hedger exception. The risk from any such abuse will be greater in case of "major swap participants," who therefore deserve greater scrutiny. Large corporations may have greater hedging needs and require larger OTC positions for hedging. However, their ability to use derivatives under the hedger exception carries the risk of ending up in a levered, too-big-to-fail position. Like dealers, they too must pay for this systemic risk.

18.4.6 Centralized Clearinghouses: Too Systemic to Fail?

Momentum is gathering – partly through industry consensus on some products such as standard credit derivatives and partly through legislation in the Dodd–Frank Act – for the establishment of a central counterparty (CCP) clearinghouse for OTC derivatives as a way to reduce counterparty credit risk. The CCP would stand between the two original counterparties, acting as the seller to the original buyer, and as the buyer to the original seller. Because its long and short positions are automatically offsetting, a CCP has no losses or gains on a derivatives contract so long as the original counterparties to the trade continue to perform. The CCP is, however, exposed to a counterparty credit risk from each of its participants. To minimize this risk, a CCP relies on a range of controls and methods, including stringent membership access, a robust margining regime, clear default management procedures and significant financial resources that back its performance.

A clearinghouse, through its opportunity to net across different asset classes and across dealers, can lead to a substantial reduction in risk and a substantial improvement in allocational efficiency. It potentially also allows market participants to reduce the amount of margin to post against their exposures if many contracts clear through the same clearinghouse. Therefore, a joint clearing of different derivative products in the same CCP would not only improve the opportunity to net counterparty exposures, but also increase the incentives for market participants to clear their derivatives trades without increasing systemic risk. At the same time, if there are too many clearinghouses, regulators run the risk of increasing the systemic risk posed by OTC derivatives due to fragmented trading (for example, if default management procedures are not coordinated in advance or if there is lack of sufficient information sharing on exposure data) and excessive use of collateral (unless there is a collateral-sharing arrangement across different clearinghouses). Nevertheless, forcing the establishment of a single clearinghouse may concentrate the risks due to the monopolistic position that it would create for clearing.

Finding the optimal number of CCPs is not the only hurdle for establishing a central clearing of OTC derivatives. One also needs to take into account the difficulties of clearing OTC trades. First, while multilateral netting can be the main advantage of a CCP in reducing counterparty risk, multilateral netting can be limited or even impossible, when the contracts traded are non-uniform and when the terms of the contract remain largely undisclosed to other participants. Moreover, if an OTC trader defaults on its promise to pay the CCP, the CCP faces a large replacement cost risk. The less standardized the contract, the larger this cost.

Even after a successful migration of derivatives trading from the OTC market to central exchanges, CCPs are not immune to the risk of failing on their obligations; if many of its trading counterparties default together or are vulnerable at once, a CCP may not have enough resources to cover all its outstanding positions. While clearinghouses have functioned well in general, a few clearinghouse failures have occurred around the world from time to time. For example, in 1974, a sharp price increase in the Paris White Sugar Market with a subsequent correction prompted the default of participants on margin calls; as a result, the Caisse de Liquidation market was closed by the French commerce ministry. Similar incidents occurred in Kuala Lumpur (Commodity Clearing House, 1983) due to defaults in palm oil contracts and in Hong Kong (Futures Guarantee Corporation, 1987) due to failures in futures trades.[25]

There are also a few instances in recent US history when exchanges were on the brink of collapse. In the 1970s, two short episodes in the commodity futures market caused serious liquidity problems with settlement delays. In 1976, as a result of a manipulation in the Maine potato futures contract on the New York Mercantile Exchange (NYMEX), the largest default in the history of commodity futures trading occurred on some 1,000 contracts that covered 50 million pounds of potatoes. A similar market disruption occurred at the end of 1979, when the price of silver jumped to an all-time record. At that time, the Hunt brothers were estimated to hold one-third of the entire world supply of silver (other than that held by governments). A change of the Commodity Exchange (COMEX) rules regarding leverage spurred a series of margin calls, causing COMEX to increase margin levels to 100 percent, which further dried up market liquidity. An SEC report on the silver crisis later stated that "for six days late in March 1980, it appeared to government officials, Wall Street, and the public at large that a default by a single family on its obligations in the fomenting silver market might seriously disrupt the US financial system."

Central counterparties in the equity arena also have experienced similar problems. In the aftermath of the 1987 stock market crash, a big counterparty of the Chicago Mercantile Exchange (CME) failed to make a large payment by the settlement date, leaving the exchange $400 million short. Its president, Leo Melamed, called its bank, Continental Illinois, to plead for the bank to guarantee the balance, which was well in excess of its credit lines. Only three minutes before the exchange was due to open, the bank authorized the backstop. Melamed has said repeatedly that if the Merc had not opened that morning, it would not have opened again. To make matters worse, the head of the New York Stock Exchange (NYSE) also noted that if the Merc had not opened that morning, the NYSE would not have, either, and the NYSE might have never reopened again.[26] Even the remote possibility of such an incident being repeated is too high a risk for the system to bear.

The collapse of Lehman Brothers in September 2008 resurfaced concerns of the likelihood, however small, of clearinghouse failures. Lehman had $4 billion in margin accounts to backstop commitments for customers and also had large proprietary bets on energy, interest rate and stock index futures on the CME. A court-appointed examiner, Anton Valukas, presented a report that reveals details about the scramble at the CME, the world's biggest futures exchange, as Lehman filed for bankruptcy. The CME ordered Lehman to liquidate bets made with Lehman's own money, but rather than selling off these positions, Lehman continued to add to them for another two days. Thereafter, the CME convened an emergency committee that conducted a forced transfer of the bank's positions, the first and only time this has been done by the exchange operator.

While the CME has dealt with a failure of clearing members before, including the 2005 unraveling of the broker Refco, the risk that the Lehman crisis posed to the CME does raise the issue that the growing pressure from regulators to shift more derivatives contracts to centralized clearing concentrates the risk of several counterparties defaulting in one place – namely, the clearinghouse. This recent episode gives some support to the concerns that the failure of a CCP could suddenly expose many major market participants to substantial losses.

As the previous examples show, oversight and intervention are often necessary to avoid the failure of a clearinghouse. Given that central clearing in some form is likely to be an important aspect of OTC derivatives, if a single party were to default, the clearinghouse would settle the outstanding trades and prevent a cascade of failures. In many cases, the centralized counterparty would be a privately owned corporation belonging to a consortium of dealers and other market participants. While this may ensure that the clearinghouse has relatively deep pockets, the risks must still be monitored the same way as any other entity with systemic risk. The risks that the centralized counterparty will naturally have to bear could be mitigated by setting margins, as discussed before, but adequacy of the initial and variation margining procedures of the CCPs must be a part of the task entrusted to the systemic risk regulator.

In this context, it is important to note that looking back at history, we find that the failure of clearinghouses due to poor risk management or excess risk taking has been relatively rare. This is in striking contrast to the case of banks and large financial institutions, where it is relatively an exception to find an example where failure is not linked to poor risk management or excessive risk taking. So, while clearinghouses are clearly systemic and perhaps too-big-to-fail members of the financial sector, their risk-taking activities have a limited scope, and on balance the moral hazard in their case is also somewhat limited. Hence, in the central clearing arena, competition among exchanges does not appear to have caused a race to the bottom in terms of risk management and control, in which clearinghouses settle for excessively low levels of contractual guarantees in an attempt to increase volume; if anything, there is a race to the top (see Santos and Scheinkman 2001).

In the unfortunate case when a centralized counterparty itself faces default, there should be little hesitation to rescue it with taxpayer resources, rather than being subject to the mercy of an individual financial institution. Such systemic risks are indeed exactly what the lender of last resort should focus on, since from a moral hazard standpoint it is far more prudent to rescue a clearinghouse than a private risk-taking institution that blows up due to its risky trades and endangers its in-house public utility function as a market maker (a case in point being Bear Stearns, which was de facto a clearer of a large number of CDS contracts). Thus, while some of the moral hazard remains, it would be much more muted than in the case of individual financial institutions, both because the clearing corporation is more transparent and because of active supervision by the systemic risk regulator. The regulatory apparatus appears well designed to reduce this risk, so that wherever there is sufficient standardization of contracts, we welcome the migration from OTC to CCPs.

18.5   CONCLUSION: HOW WILL THE DERIVATIVES REFORMS AFFECT GLOBAL FINANCE IN FUTURE?

We conjecture that there are four key areas where the proposed OTC reforms of the Dodd–Frank Act will have the greatest global impact. These concern: (1) consolidation within the United States and across countries of clearinghouses and exchanges, and potentially also of large dealer banks; (2) emergence of global transparency platforms and services related to processing of newly made available data on derivatives transactions and positions; (3) gradual transition of (some) end-user hedging demand to centralized platforms and exchanges; and (4) separation of market making and proprietary trading/asset management positions in large financial institutions.

There are two sound economic reasons why consolidation across clearinghouses and exchanges is likely to take off following the proposed OTC reforms. First, in the early years, centralized clearing will likely occur separately within the individual product spaces (e.g., credit derivatives, interest rate derivatives, etc.). We believe that centralized clearing will first occur with credit derivatives, and then with relatively standardized interest rate and FX products. Customized products will probably remain in the uncleared space, at least for some time until market innovations permit them to be moved to clearinghouses at a reasonable cost. However, absent rules across clearing platforms to share collateral in case of a dealer's default, there will most likely be a reduced portfolio margining benefit, and in the short run, an increase in collateral requirements from dealers. Yet, market infrastructure and organization will likely respond to the enhanced collateral requirement and costs. Clearinghouses and exchanges may be spurred to merge and thereby work out collateral-sharing arrangements in case of default, and in turn, offer more cost-effective collateral arrangements to dealers. Dealers may themselves find it advantageous to merge in order to ensure that they can provide as much portfolio margining to clients as possible, rather than see clients getting fragmented across dealers in different markets. Moreover, while greater transparency and trade registry at the level of individual platforms would aid regulators in the event of a large financial firm's default, such information would have to be shared across different platforms. This should also spur consolidation across platforms, especially globally, and should be partly encouraged by national regulators. Of course, such consolidation implies that systemic risk will likely get concentrated on a few platforms and in the hands of a few dealers, unless their leverage and risks are managed well. This will be a key challenge for central banks and systemic risk oversight councils in the future, particularly in order to forestall the potential failure of a large clearinghouse or exchange.

Second, related to the point on the need to coordinate transparency, a market response to such need is likely to emerge in the form of global clearing services being provided by players such as the Depository Trust & Clearing Corporation (DTCC), as well as in the form of global information gathering and dissemination provided by players such as Markit. Greater standardization of products would facilitate such global aggregation, and the consolidation proposed earlier would also necessitate such global data repositories. Furthermore, to the extent that new information would become available – even if with some delay and coarseness – third-party vendors, which mine these data and refine them into more directly useful measures of counterparty exposures and risks, may emerge. Indeed, central banks and systemic risk oversight councils may find it efficient to outsource some processing of data in this form rather than managing such risk data entirely themselves. The Office of Financial Research (OFR), proposed in the Dodd–Frank Act in the United States, will also be charged with the task of collecting transaction-level data and organizing it in forms that aid understanding of systemic risk. It would be desirable for a climate to be created for a healthy exchange – and even some competition – among the OFR, third-party vendors, policy institutions and academic research in figuring out how best to analyze the new data that are commonly available to all.

Third, it is plausible that, over time, the migration of standardized products to centralized clearinghouses and exchanges will allow entry of new dealers such as large hedge funds and specialized derivatives trading firms (the initial push for consolidation notwithstanding). This will simply be the outcome of greater pretrade and posttrade transparency offered by such platforms relative to the current veil that precludes such transparency of OTC markets. Such entry should reduce the costs of trading in these products, and end users (the hedgers) would be induced to move some of their hedging away from customized products with dealer banks to the centralized platforms, perhaps with some market innovations in combining customization with centralized clearing. There is a chance that such a movement may significantly enhance liquidity on these platforms, and in some cases, make it possible – even if not in the near future – to allow retail access to certain derivative products that are close to cash markets. For example, a CDS is best visualized as a standardized corporate bond, and ability to trade credit risk this way – with appropriate risk controls – might be valuable to retail traders and provide depth to credit markets (as we currently have with equities). Nevertheless, given the basis risk involved in hedging production schedules with standardized products, some market for customized hedging will remain in the OTC space. Overall, we believe that end users will likely face lower counterparty risk and pay for it more efficiently given the proposed reforms.

Last, but not least, there is bound to be a greater separation on the books of banks between the pure market-making function that is properly combined with traditional banking products, especially in the interest rate and FX area, and positions taken through proprietary trading and investment in asset management entities, such as hedge funds. The former cluster of businesses will be offered the traditional support under the Dodd–Frank Act through privileged access to funding and deposit insurance. The risk-taking activities, however, would be separated so that the moral hazard issues are mitigated to a large extent. It is not necessary for this separation to take place in the context of separate companies, as long as there is a separate accounting for risk, capital adequacy and regulatory oversight. One approach that we have stressed in this chapter is to organize the hedging and the dealer functions of derivatives into separate subsidiaries and adopt the "audit and penalize" strategy (explained in this chapter) to ensure that the hedging subsidiary is not a speculative arm.

While all these are interesting trends to look out for over the next decade or two, it is unlikely that the debate on derivatives will be closed anytime soon. There will always be the occasional backlash against derivatives when large defaults are imminent and some powerful firms, policy institutions or countries are at the suffering end. Perhaps such debate is useful in the sense that each time it is raised, the marketplace is reminded that while derivatives have their natural use in hedging when markets are incomplete, they also facilitate leverage, which has been found to be a key contributor to systemic risk in past financial crises. Regulating leverage thus will require certain improvements in the trading infrastructure of derivatives and possibly some restrictions on derivatives positions of large players (whose leverage contributes more to systemic risk). In the end, will we get the balance in regulating derivatives right? We will know only when the next crisis hits us, but most likely it will be where we do not anticipate it – perhaps in a new "green energy" asset class, or in the currently nascent derivatives markets in Asia, or in some other pocket that we cannot even imagine today!

APPENDIX A: ITEMS CONCERNING OTC DERIVATIVES LEFT BY THE DODD–FRANK ACT FOR FUTURE STUDY

1. Study on the Effects of Position Limits on Trading on Exchanges in the United States.
   a. The CFTC shall conduct a study of the effects (if any) of the **position limits** imposed pursuant to the other provisions of this title on excessive speculation and on the movement of transactions from exchanges in the United States to trading venues outside the country.
   b. Report to the Congress:
      - Within 12 months after the imposition of position limits pursuant to the other provisions of this title.
      - The Chairman of the CFTC shall prepare and submit to the Congress biennial reports on the growth or decline of the derivatives markets in the United States and abroad, which shall include assessments of the causes of any such growth or decline, the effectiveness of regulatory regimes in managing systemic risk, a comparison of the costs of compliance at the time of the report for market participants subject to regulation by the United States with the costs of compliance in December 2008 for the market participants, and the quality of the available data.
      - Required hearing within 30 legislative days after the submission to the Congress of the report.
2. Study on Feasibility of Requiring the Use of Standardized Algorithmic Descriptions for Financial Derivatives
   a. The SEC and the CFTC shall conduct a joint study of the feasibility of requiring the derivatives industry to adopt standardized computer-readable algorithmic descriptions which may be used to describe complex and standardized financial derivatives.
   b. Goals: The algorithmic descriptions defined in the study shall be designed to facilitate computerized analysis of individual derivative contracts and to calculate net exposures to complex derivatives.
   c. The study will also examine the extent to which the algorithmic description, together with standardized and extensible legal definitions, may serve as the binding legal definition of derivative contracts. The study will examine the logistics of possible implementations of standardized algorithmic descriptions for derivative contracts. The study shall be limited to electronic formats for exchange of derivative contract descriptions and will not contemplate disclosure of proprietary valuation models.
   d. Report to the Committees on Agriculture and on Financial Services of the House of Representatives and the Committees on Agriculture, Nutrition, and Forestry and on Banking, Housing, and Urban Affairs of the Senate within eight months after the date of the enactment of this Act.
3. International Swap Regulation and Harmonization of Margining Methods
   a. The CFTC and the SEC shall jointly conduct a study relating to:
      i. Swap regulation in the United States, Asia, and Europe.
      ii. Clearinghouse and clearing agency regulation in the United States, Asia, and Europe.
      iii. Identifying areas of regulation that are similar in the United States, Asia, and Europe and other areas of regulation that could be harmonized.
   b. The CFTC and the SEC shall submit to the Committee on Agriculture, Nutrition, and Forestry and the Committee on Banking, Housing, and Urban Affairs of the Senate and the Committee on Agriculture and the Committee on Financial Services of the House of

Representatives a report not later than 18 months after the date of enactment of this Act, including:

   i. Identification of the major exchanges and their regulator in each geographic area for the trading of swaps and security-based swaps including a listing of the major contracts and their trading volumes and notional values as well as identification of the major swap dealers participating in such markets.

   ii. Identification of the major clearinghouses and clearing agencies and their regulator in each geographic area for the clearing of swaps and security-based swaps, including a listing of the major contracts and the clearing volumes and notional values as well as identification of the major clearing members of such clearinghouses and clearing agencies in such markets.

   iii. Description of the comparative methods of clearing swaps in the United States, Asia, and Europe.

   iv. Description of the various systems used for establishing margin on individual swaps, security-based swaps, and swap portfolios.

4. Stable Value Contracts[27]

   a. Not later than 15 months after the date of the enactment of this Act, the SEC and the CFTC shall, jointly, conduct a study to determine whether stable value contracts fall within the definition of a swap. In making the determination required under this subparagraph, the Commissions jointly shall consult with the Department of Labor, the Department of the Treasury, and the State entities that regulate the issuers of stable value contracts.

   b. If the Commissions determine that stable value contracts fall within the definition of a swap, the Commissions jointly shall determine if an exemption for stable value contracts from the definition of swap is appropriate and in the public interest. The Commissions shall issue regulations implementing the determinations required under this paragraph. Until the effective date of such regulations, and notwithstanding any other provision of this title, the requirements of this title shall not apply to stable value contracts.

Table 18.3 Time line of the future studies.

Study	Deadline	Section
Study on the Effects of Position Limits on Trading on Exchanges in the US	12 months after imposition of position limits	719(a)
Study on Feasibility of Requiring the Use of Standardized Algorithmic Descriptions for Financial Derivatives	8 months after enactment of the Dodd–Frank Act	719(b)
International Swap Regulation and Harmonization of Margining Methods	18 months after enactment of the Dodd–Frank Act	719(c)
Stable Value Contracts	15 months after enactment of the Dodd–Frank Act	719(d)
Study on Impact of FOIA Exemption on Commodity Futures Trading Commission	30 months after enactment of Section 748	748
Study on Oversight of Carbon Markets	6 months after enactment of the Dodd–Frank Act	750

There are two studies that are within the bill, but are unrelated directly to our discussion:

5. Study on Impact of FOIA Exemption on Commodity Futures Trading Commission
   a. The Inspector General of the Commission shall conduct a study:
      i. Whether the exemption under section 552(b)(3) of title 5, US Code (known as the Freedom of Information Act) established in paragraph (2)(A) aids whistleblowers in disclosing information to the Commission.
      ii. On what impact the exemption has had on the public's ability to access information about the Commission's regulation of commodity futures and option markets.
      iii. To make any recommendations on whether the Commission should continue to use the exemption.
   b. Not later than 30 months after the date of enactment of this clause, the Inspector General shall submit a report on the findings to the Committee on Banking, Housing, and Urban Affairs of the Senate and the Committee on Financial Services of the House of Representatives.
6. Study on Oversight of Carbon Markets
   a. The interagency group shall conduct a study on the oversight of existing and prospective carbon markets to ensure an efficient, secure, and transparent carbon market, including oversight of spot markets and derivative markets.

APPENDIX B: CURRENT OTC DISCLOSURE PROVIDED BY DEALER BANKS

To help investors gauge the financial implications for companies that have sold CDSs, the Financial Accounting Standards Board (FASB) in the United States introduced a new standard that eliminates the inconsistency between two existing accounting standards, effective for fiscal years that end after November 2008. One of these rules covers financial guarantees, which are similar in terms of their economic risks and rewards to credit derivatives. It requires an extensive disclosure of contracts in which the buyer of the insurance owns the underlying instrument that the contract is protecting. However, if the guaranteed party does not own the asset or the instrument that is insured, then the protection is classified as a derivative and falls under another accounting standard that does not require disclosure. This is in spite of the fact that the risks of a financial guarantee and a credit derivative being undertaken by a firm under either of these kinds of instruments are the same in economic terms.

The FASB's new standard covers sellers of CDS instruments, namely the entities that act as insurers by selling protection. They have to disclose such details as the nature and term of the credit derivative, the reason it was entered into and the current status of its payment and performance risk. In addition, the seller needs to provide the amount of future payments it might be required to make, the fair value of the derivative and whether there are provisions that would allow the seller to recover money or assets from third parties to pay for the insurance coverage it has written.

We detail the collateral data, fair value, and notional value of credit exposures in OTC derivatives for Goldman Sachs (Figure 18.6) and Citigroup (Figure 18.7), two of the major

OTC Derivative Credit Exposure
($ Millions)

As of September 2009

Credit Rating Equivalent	0–12 Months	1–5 Years	5–10 Years	10 Years or Greater	Total	Netting	Exposure	Exposure Net of Collateral
AAA/Aaa	$ 1,482	$ 3,249	$ 3,809	$ 2,777	$ 11,317	$ (5,481)	$ 5,836	$ 5,349
AA/Aa2	6,647	12,741	7,695	9,332	36,415	(20,804)	15,611	11,815
A/Aa2	31,999	46,761	29,324	31,747	130,831	(111,238)	28,503	24,795
BBB/Baa2	4,825	7,780	5,609	8,190	26,404	(12,069)	14,335	8,041
BB/Ba2 or lower	3,049	13,931	2,903	1,483	21,366	(5,357)	16,009	9,472
Unrated	666	1,570	387	148	2,771	(224)	2,547	1,845
Total	$48,668	$86,032	$49,727	$53,677	$238,104	$(155,173)	$82,931	$61,317

As of June 2009

Credit Rating Equivalent	0–12 Months	1–5 Years	5–10 Years	10 Years or Greater	Total	Netting	Exposure	Exposure Net of Collateral
AAA/Aaa	$ 2,743	$ 4,524	$ 4,623	$ 3,209	$ 15,099	$ (6,221)	$ 8,878	$ 8,520
AA/Aa2	6,989	20,669	9,252	9,252	46,162	(32,641)	03,521	9,759
A/Aa2	36,715	39,178	28,307	28,760	132,960	(103,597)	29,363	25,539
BBB/Baa2	5,091	10,211	3,435	7,238	25,975	(11,908)	14,067	8,492
BB/Ba2 or lower	5,849	11,576	2,814	1,983	22,222	(5,965)	16,257	10,160
Unrated	859	1,386	623	446	3,314	(83)	3,231	2,808
Total	$58,246	$87,544	$49,054	$50,888	$245,732	$(160,415)	$85,317	$65,278

Figure 18.6 Goldman Sachs's accounting disclosures of credit default swap exposures.
Source: Goldman Sachs's annual balance sheets.

OTC Derivative Credit Exposure
($ Millions)

As of March 2009

Credit Rating Equivalent	0–12 Months	1–5 Years	5–10 Years	10 Years or Greater	Total	Netting	Exposure	Exposure Net of Collateral
AAA/Aaa	$ 4,699	$ 6,734	$ 5,994	$ 2,964	$ 20,391	$ (8,178)	$12,213	$11,509
AA/Aa2	18,619	40,015	22,228	10,095	90,957	(71,881)	19,076	16,025
A/Aa2	21,148	33,369	16,955	19,767	97,239	(66,342)	30,897	25,220
BBB/Baa2	8,185	19,413	6,833	12,571	47,002	(31,280)	15,722	10,358
BB/Ba2 or lower	8,734	9,922	3,568	1,652	23,976	(8,116)	15,760	10,339
Unrated	2,670	1,007	312	360	4,349	(371)	3,978	3,314
Total	$64,055	$116,460	$55,890	$47,409	$283,814	$(186,168)	$97,646	$76,765

As of November 2008

Credit Rating Equivalent	0–12 Months	1–5 Years	5–10 Years	10 Years or Greater	Total	Netting	Exposure	Exposure Net of Collateral
AAA/Aaa	$ 5,519	$ 3,871	$ 5,853	$ 4,250	$ 19,493	$ (6,093)	$ 13,400	$12,312
AA/Aa2	26,835	30,532	33,479	18,980	109,826	(76,119)	33,707	29,435
A/Aa2	25,416	27,263	17,009	24,427	94,115	(59,903)	34,212	28,614
BBB/Baa2	11,324	17,156	8,684	14,311	51,475	(29,229)	22,246	16,211
BB/Ba2 or lower	11,835	10,228	4,586	3,738	30,387	(12,600)	17,787	11,204
Unrated	808	803	916	215	2,832	(11)	2,821	1,550
Total	$81,737	$89,943	$70,527	$65,921	$308,128	$(183,955)	$124,173	$99,326

Figure 18.6 (*Continued*)

The following tables summarize the key characteristics of the Company's credit derivative portfolio as protection seller (guarantor) as of September 30, 2009, and December 31, 2008:

In millions of dollars as of September 30, 2009	Maximum Potential Amount of Future Payments	Fair Value Payable[1]
By industry/counterparty:		
Bank	$ 860,437	$ 46,071
Broker-dealer	301,216	17,661
Monoline	–	–
Nonfinancial	2,127	96
Insurance and other financial institutions	151,326	12,753
Total by industry/counterparty	$1,315,106	$ 76,581
By instrument:		
Credit default swaps and options	$1,314,282	$ 76,383
Total return swaps	824	198
Total by instrument	$1,315,106	$ 76,581
By rating:		
Investment grade	$ 759,845	23,362
Non–investment grade	422,865	33,231
Not rated	132,396	19,988
Total by rating	$1,315,106	$ 76,581

[1] In addition, fair value amounts receivable under credit derivatives sold were $23,324 million.

The following tables summarize the key characteristics of the Company's credit derivative portfolio as protection seller (guarantor) as of June 30, 2009, and December 31, 2008:

In millions of dollars as of June 30, 2009	Maximum Potential Amount of Future Payments	Fair Value Payable
By industry/counterparty:		
Bank	$ 899,598	$ 71,523
Broker-dealer	322,349	30,798
Monoline	123	89
Nonfinancial	4,805	231
Insurance and other financial institutions	138,813	14,756
Total by industry/counterparty	$1,365,688	$117,127
By instrument:		
Credit default swaps and options	$1,363,738	$116,600
Total return swaps and other	1,950	527
Total by instrument	$1,365,688	$117,127
By rating:		
Investment grade	$ 813,892	49,503
Non-investment grade	342,888	46,242
Not rated	208,908	21,382
Total by rating	$1,365,688	$117,127

Figure 18.7   Citigroup's accounting disclosures of credit default swap exposures.
Source: Citigroup's annual balance sheets.

In millions of dollars as of March 31, 2009	Maximum Potential Amount of Future Payments	Fair Value Payable
By industry/counterparty:		
Bank	$ 919,354	$123,437
Broker-dealer	345,582	56,181
Monoline	139	91
Nonfinancial	5,327	5,121
Insurance and other financial institutions	135,729	21,581
Total by industry/counterparty	$1,406,131	$206,411
By instrument:		
Credit default swaps and options	$1,404,928	$206,057
Total return swaps and other	1,203	354
Total by instrument	$1,406,131	$206,411
By rating:		
Investment grade	$ 808,602	88,952
Non–investment grade	362,851	79,409
Not rated	234,678	38,050
Total by rating	$1,406,131	$206,411

In millions of dollars as of December 31, 2009	Maximum Potential Amount of Future Payments	Fair Value Payable[1]
By industry/counterparty:		
Bank	$ 943,949	$118,428
Broker-dealer	365,664	55,458
Monoline	139	91
Nonfinancial	7,540	2,556
Insurance and other financial institutions	125,988	21,700
Total by industry/counterparty	$1,443,280	$198,233
By instrument:		
Credit default swaps and options	$1,441,375	$197,981
Total return swaps	1,905	252
Total by instrument	$1,443,280	$198,233
By rating:		
Investment grade	$ 851,426	$ 83,672
Non-investment grade	410,483	87,508
Not rated	181,371	27,053
Total by rating	$1,443,280	$198,233

[1] In addition, fair value amounts receivable under credit derivatives sold were $5,890 million.

Figure 18.7   *(Continued)*

players in these markets. As is clear from the disclosures, there is a fair deal of difference in reporting standards:

- Goldman Sachs reports CDS exposures by:
  - Maturity.
  - Credit rating (AAA/Aaa, AA/Aa2, etc.) of counterparty.
  - Gross, net, as well as net of collateral.

- Citigroup reports the exposures by:
  - Nature of counterparty (bank, broker-dealer, monoline, etc.).

- Type of instrument (CDSs, total return swaps, etc.).
- Fair value as well as maximum notional payable.

The new regulatory regime should require that these reports be more standardized.

APPENDIX C: SOVEREIGN CREDIT DEFAULT
SWAPS MARKETS

Since the mid-1990s, Fitch Ratings has recorded a total of eight sovereign defaults. The list of sovereign defaults includes Indonesia and the Russian Federation (both in 1998), Argentina (2001), Moldova (2002), Uruguay (2003), the Dominican Republic (2005), Ecuador (2008) and Jamaica (2010). In the wake of Greece's recent debt crisis and with the eroding credit quality of other sovereign issuers, particularly in Europe, the need for targeted regulations of the sovereign CDS market has been called into question. In May 2010, the German securities regulator, BaFin, took unilateral action by banning naked short sales of certain sovereign bonds and related CDS contracts, as well as equity securities.

From virtual non-existence only a few years back when sovereign CDSs were mostly traded on emerging market economies, the sovereign CDS market has grown rapidly to $1.76 trillion, according to data from the end of June 2009 published by the BIS (compared with $22.4 trillion for nonsovereign contracts). Given the large quantity of sovereign bonds outstanding, there is a substantial body of natural buyers of protection. Yet the lack of natural sellers of protection in the sovereign CDS market has capped its growth. The launch of SovX, the European index of 15 equally weighted sovereign entities, in July 2009 has provided an additional avenue for investors to express views on the sovereign market and has significantly improved liquidity. SovX has been seeing a steady pickup in activity relative to corporate CDS index contracts such as those of CDX and iTraxx, and is now ahead of the financial sector CDS index (see Figure 18.8). Still, the sovereign CDS market accounts for a relatively small share of the overall

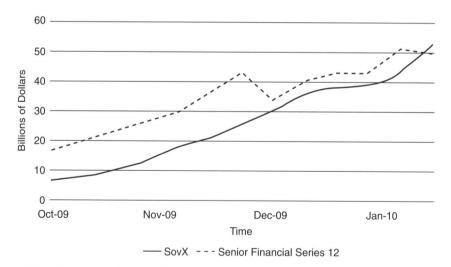

Figure 18.8   Gross notional outstanding of SovX versus financials ($ billions).
Source: Morgan Stanley Research, "Credit Derivatives Insights: Sovereign CDS Markets – A Corporate Perspective," January 29, 2010; DTCC.

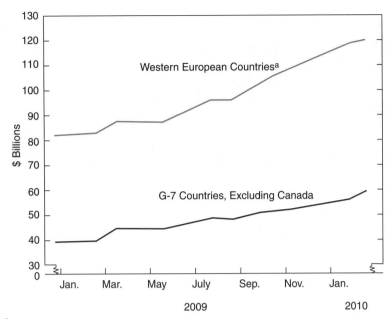

aThe Western Europe series includes the 15 members of the Markit iTraxx SovX Western Europe
Index, excluding Portugal and Norway.

Figure 18.9   Net notional dealer exposures to sovereign CDS contracts.
Source: Depository Trust & Clearing Corporation; Bank of England 1Q10 Bulletin.

CDS market, and exposures to sovereign CDSs are modest relative to the size of government
bond markets. That remains the case despite a notable growth in turnover in sovereign CDSs,
especially in terms of net dealer exposures (Figure 18.9) over the past year in which there has
been increasing attention on public finances of a number of countries. Figure 18.10 shows,
however, that wherever sovereign credit risk is more in question (e.g., recently in the cases of

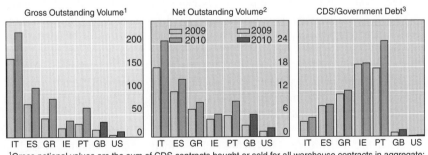

1Gross notional values are the sum of CDS contracts bought or sold for all warehouse contracts in aggregate;
in billions of US dollars.

2Net notional values are the sum of net protection bought by net buyers; in billions of US dollars.

3Net notional CDS volume as a percentage of government debt.

Figure 18.10   Gross sovereign CDSs.
Source: Organization for Economic Cooperation and Development; Depository Trust & Clearing Corporation; BIS Quarterly Review, March 2010.

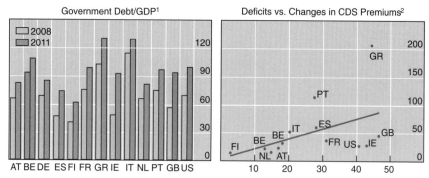

AT = Austria; BE = Belgium; DE = Germany; ES = Spain; FI = Finland; FR = France;
GR = Greece; IE = Ireland; IT = Italy; NL = Netherlands; PT = Portugal;
GB = United Kingdom; US = United States.

[1]Actual data for 2008 and projections for 2011.

[2]Horizontal axis shows the sum of government deficit as percentage of GDP for 2007–2011; vertical axis represents change in CDS premiums between October 26, 2009, and February 17, 2010. Actual data for 2007–2009 and projections for 2010–2011 for government deficit as percentage of GDP.

Figure 18.11 Government debt, deficits, and sovereign credit premiums.
Source: Organization for Economic Cooperation and Development; Depository Trust & Clearing Corporation; BIS Quarterly Review, March 2010.

Greece, Portugal, Spain, Italy and Ireland), the ratio of CDSs to government bond markets is greater, relative to safer countries (e.g., the United States and the UK). Indeed, some of the safest countries such as the UK and France have also shown signs of stress in this context.

Concerns about the market implications of large fiscal deficits came to the fore in late 2009 and early 2010. Investors' attention was first drawn to the issue of sovereign risk in the aftermath of the financial difficulties encountered by the government-owned Dubai World in late November 2009. More recently, though, the focus has shifted to the euro-zone periphery, where large budget deficits have led to the prospect of rapidly increasing government debt/gross domestic product (GDP) levels in several countries (see Figure 18.11). In October 2009, as it became evident that Greece might lose European Central Bank (ECB) funding for Greek banks and the use of its sovereign bonds as collateral at the ECB, CDS premiums and yield spreads on Greek government debt shot up, both in absolute terms and relative to the benchmark German bunds. Simultaneously, while sovereign CDS premiums shot up across the board since that period, it was primarily the European banks who suffered in terms of market valuation of their equity as well as their own corporate CDSs (more so than Asian or US counterparts), both due to reduced value of government guarantees and exposures to sovereign credit risk through their government bond holdings (Figure 18.12).

In general, sovereign CDSs are traded by a wide variety of market participants, including banks, asset management firms and hedge funds. These market participants have a multitude of reasons to trade in sovereign CDSs: trading of the basis and hedging of a specific government bond exposure, hedging of a direct exposure to sovereign credit, or simply isolating single-name corporate risk from the risk of the sovereign where the corporate is located. However, recent events in the sovereign credit markets have brought sovereign CDSs under intense market scrutiny, and have led EU politicians to call for a ban on naked sovereign CDS trades.

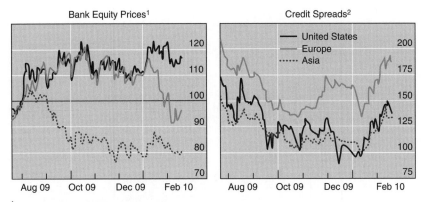

¹In local currency; July 31, 2009 = 100.

²Equally weighted average senior five-year CDS spreads for the banking sector.

Figure 18.12   Bank equity prices and CDS premiums.
Source: Datastream, Markit, Bank for International Settlements calculations; BIS Quarterly Review, March 2010.

As a knee-jerk reaction to the Greek woes, policymakers and commentators in Europe have quickly questioned the sovereign CDS market's effect on the levels at which heavily indebted countries, such as Greece, were able to refinance in the capital market. They have, in fact, given notice that they would consider banning CDS use for speculative bets in the markets. Nevertheless, as of today, there is no compelling evidence that activity in the sovereign CDS market has led to wider spreads and has limited governments' ability to borrow money, as even the German regulator, BaFin, acknowledged as it moved to restrict naked short selling. First, examination of the DTCC's reports since the beginning of 2010 shows that the net outstanding CDS position on Greece has changed little over the course of the year. The net position for Greece was $8.7 billion in the week of January 1, 2010, and has ranged between $8.5 billion and $9.2 billion since then (compared to $7.4 billion a year ago). None of the data suggests that there has been a surge of open interest in either 2009 or 2010. Second, the no-arbitrage relationship between CDSs and bonds implies that while it is relatively easy for CDSs to drive bond prices higher and yields lower, it is much harder for CDSs to force bond prices lower and yields higher, since bonds become hard to borrow and then it becomes increasingly difficult to short the bond against selling protection. The fact that basis has remained stable – that is, the government bond and CDS spreads have remained essentially in line (for most countries, including Greece) and outstanding positions have remained constant – strengthens the assertion that naked short selling activity in the CDS market has had little or no impact on the government bond market.

Another piece of evidence supporting our view that the CDS market was an effect of the euro-zone crisis, rather than its cause, is Altman's bottom-up analysis to assess sovereign risk (see Box 18.1). Using corporate financial health data of a nation's private sector to find its aggregate default risk, Altman's metric has signaled early warnings of a domestic economic slowdown in Greece and Portugal well before May 2010 (see Table 18.4).

While there is no global consensus for a ban or even restrictions on short selling of sovereign bonds or the purchase of related CDSs, it is clear that the side effects of such a ban might

Table 18.4 Financial health of the private sector of selected countries – The Z-Metrics Assessment.

Country	Number of Listed Companies	Five-Year Public Model[a]			Median PD from CDS Spreads[b]	One-Year Public Model[c]		
		Median PD	Standard Deviation PDs	Median Rating	Five-Year[b]	Median PD	Standard Deviation PDs	Median Rating
Netherlands	61	3.33%	7.52%	ZB	2.83%	0.153%	1.020%	ZB–
United Kingdom	442	3.62	11.60	ZB–	6.52	0.218	2.580	ZC+
Canada	368	3.70	12.20	ZB–	4.15	0.164	3.350	ZB–
United States	2,236	3.93	9.51	ZB–	3.28	0.139	2.320	ZB
France	297	5.51	9.72	ZC+	3.75	0.290	2.060	ZC+
Germany	289	5.54	13.10	ZC+	2.67	0.268	3.960	ZC+
Spain	82	6.44	9.63	ZC	9.39	0.363	1.360	ZC
Italy	155	7.99	10.20	ZC	8.69	0.493	1.650	ZC
Portugal	30	9.36	7.25	ZC–	10.90	0.482	0.827	ZC
Greece	79	10.56	14.40	ZC–	24.10	0.935	3.660	ZC–

[a] Based on Z-Metrics PDs from January 1, 2010, to April 1, 2010.
[b] Assuming a 40 percent recovery rate, based on CDS spreads observed from January 1, 2010, to April 2010.
[c] Probability of default (PD) is computed as $1 - e^{(-5*s/(1-R))}$.
Sources: RiskMetrics Group, 2010; Markit; Compustat.

be significant. Banks would need to use other ways to hedge country-specific risks, such as creating a short position in that country's debt or shorting a relevant stock index. Short-selling activity directly in government bonds will certainly have a greater effect on government bond prices, as it involves selling the actual instruments in the market. A ban might also remove potential demand for government debt from so-called negative basis traders (investors who buy bonds and short the associated CDSs, pocketing the difference), hindering the liquidity of the government debt market. Furthermore, the blanket restriction on naked positions would have unanticipated effects on basis hedges such as the purchase of a sovereign CDS to hedge a position in corporate bonds of the country.

Box 18.1: Sovereign Default Risk Assessment from the Bottom Up

Edward I. Altman*

Periodically, sovereign economic conditions spiral out of control and require a massive debt restructuring and/or bailout accompanied by painful austerity programs in order for the country to function again in world commercial and financial markets. Recent instances involving several Latin American countries in the 1980s, Southeast Asian nations in the late 1990s, Russia in 1998 and Argentina in 2000 are examples of situations in which a nation's severe problems not only impacted its own people and markets but created seismic financial tremors the likes of which we are now experiencing from the situation involving Greece and several of its southern European neighbors.

The dire condition of these nations usually first manifests as a surprise to most, including the agencies that rate the default risk of sovereigns and the companies that reside in these suddenly threatened nations. Similar to Greece, which was investment grade not long ago, South Korea, considered in 1996 to be one of the "Asian Tigers" with an AA– rating, one of the best credit ratings possible, was downgraded within one year to BB–, one of the so-called junk rating categories, and would have defaulted if not for a $50 billion bailout from the International Monetary Fund (IMF).

Academics and market practitioners simply have not had an impressive record of providing adequate early warnings of impending sovereign economic and financial problems using the usual macroeconomic indicators, such as GDP growth, debt levels relative to GDP, trade and financial deficits, unemployment and productivity. While there is no absolute guarantee of providing the magic formula for early warning transparency of impending doom, we believe that one can learn a great deal about sovereign risk by analyzing the health and aggregate default risk of a nation's private corporate sector – a type of bottom-up analysis. Models such as Altman's established Z-Score technique (1968), and more recently (2010) RiskMetrics' Z-Metrics system, can provide an important additional measure of sovereign vulnerability.

The Z-Metrics system combines several fundamental measures of corporate default risk – such as profitability, leverage, and liquidity – with equity market value measures and a few macroeconomic stress variables. Each factor is assigned a weighting, which when tallied up gives a measure of default probability for one- and five-year horizons. By aggregating these measures for listed companies in each country and calculating median credit scores and default probabilities, one can assess the overall health of the nation's private sector. Our Z-Score tests showed that South Korea was the riskiest country in all of Asia at the end of 1996, which was before the Asian crisis started in Thailand and spread east and north to cover most countries. Thailand and Indonesia followed South Korea closely as the next most vulnerable countries. And yet, South Korea was, as noted, considered to be an excellent credit by traditional methods.

The current situation in Europe is also instructive. In a recent test of default probabilities (see Table 18.4), using our new Z-Metrics measure, Greece clearly has the most risky and the least healthy private sector profile, with a five-year median cumulative default probability of over 1,000 basis points (10.56 percent), followed by Portugal (9.36 percent), Italy (7.99 percent), and Spain (6.44 percent). Germany and France display a moderate overall credit risk cohort (5.5 percent), with the United Kingdom (perhaps a surprise) and the Netherlands rounding out our survey as the least risky corporate sectors. The United States and Canada also display healthy metrics. With the most notable exception of Greece, our five-year median default probabilities for corporates are quite close to the median for sovereigns. Default probabilities are derived from the credit default swap (CDS) market's five-year contract over the past few months in 2010. The CDS market's default probability assessment for Greece is more than twice our median default probability for its corporate sector. Similar differences can be observed for the United Kingdom and Spain, although at lower default probability levels. Of course, 50 percent of the corporations in these countries have default probabilities greater than the median.

So, in prescribing difficult sanctions to governments in order for them to qualify for bailouts and subsidies, we should be careful to promote, not destroy, private enterprise valuations. Improving corporate health can be an early indicator of a return to health of the sovereign.

*Dr. Altman is the Max L. Heine Professor of Finance at the NYU Stern School of Business and an adviser to several financial institutions, including the RiskMetrics Group.

Regardless, the proposed reforms to the OTC derivatives markets should reassure the governments that they would have unfettered access to trading information should it be desired to rule out market manipulation motives. This is but just one of the useful roles that the much-needed transparency of OTC derivatives can serve. The transparency of the OTC derivatives market would shine a much-needed light on the market and obviate the need for desperate measures such as banning naked short selling.

NOTES

1. Even if the Treasury ultimately determines to exclude FX swaps and forwards, the bill provides that parties to such transactions are subject to certain business conduct standards and requires these transactions to be reported to a swap data repository or to the CFTC.
2. The Act divides jurisdiction over the derivatives markets between the CFTC and the SEC. The CFTC will have jurisdiction over "swaps" and certain participants in the swap market, while the SEC will have similar jurisdiction over "security-based swaps." The definition of *swap* under the Act includes interest rate, currency, equity, credit, fixed-income and commodity derivatives, with certain exceptions for physically settled commodity forwards and certain securities transactions (such as security options). Note that over-the-counter FX swaps and forwards are included in the definition of swap, but the secretary of the Treasury has the authority to exempt them from the definition of

the term swap. The term *security-based swap* is defined as a swap on a single security (or loan) or index composed of a narrow group of securities.

3. *Financial entities* includes swap dealers, major swap participants, commodity pool operators, a private fund under the Investment Advisers Act of 1940, an employee benefit plan, or an entity predominantly engaged in activities related to banking or that is financial in nature.

4. Under the Act, a *swap data repository* is "any person that collects and maintains information or records with respect to transactions or positions in, or the terms and conditions of, swaps entered into by third parties for the purpose of providing a centralized recordkeeping facility for swaps."

5. A *swap dealer* is "any person who (i) holds itself out as a dealer in swaps; (ii) makes a market in swaps; (iii) regularly enters into swaps with counterparties as an ordinary course of business for its own account; or (iv) engages in any activity causing the person to be commonly known in the trade as a dealer or market maker in swaps, provided, however, in no event shall an insured depository institution be considered to be a swap dealer to the extent it offers to enter into a swap with a customer in connection with originating a loan with that customer."

6. A *major swap participant* is "any person who is not a swap dealer, and (i) maintains a substantial position in swaps for any of the major swap categories (as determined by the Commission), excluding (I) positions held for hedging or mitigating commercial risk; and (II) positions maintained by any employee benefit plan (or any contract held by such a plan) as defined in the Employee Retirement Income Security Act of 1974 for the primary purpose of hedging or mitigating any risk directly associated with the operation of the plan; (ii) whose outstanding swaps create substantial counterparty exposure that could have serious adverse effects on the financial stability of the US banking system or financial markets; or (iii) (I) is a financial entity that is highly leveraged relative to the amount of capital it holds and that is not subject to capital requirements established by an appropriate Federal banking agency; and (II) maintains a substantial position in outstanding swaps in any major swap category as determined by the Commission."

7. The provisions of the Volcker Rule are to take effect on the earlier of 12 months after the issuance of the final rules or two years after the enactment of the Act, at which point a two year transition period begins, with the possibility of additional extensions thereafter.

8. A *systemically significant institution* is a bank holding company with total consolidated assets equal to or greater than $50 billion or a nonbank financial company supervised by the Board of Governors.

9. This prohibition on lender-of-last-resort support is commonly referred to as the "swaps push-out provision," as it effectively forces many derivatives activities to be pushed out of insured banks into separately capitalized entities.

10. The prohibition on federal assistance does not prevent an insured depository institution from acting as a swaps entity for swaps or security-based swaps involving CDSs, if those are cleared. Therefore, a beneficial consequence of this provision, which essentially allows banks to retain *cleared* CDSs in their books without losing the benefits of federal assistance, is the push toward central clearing of CDSs.

11. The Commission will have to decide on the provisions: "(i) to ensure such information does not identify the participants; (ii) to specify the criteria for determining what constitutes a large notional swap transaction (block trade) for particular markets and contracts; (iii) to specify the appropriate time delay for reporting large notional swap transactions (block trades) to the public; and (iv) that take into account whether the public disclosure will materially reduce market liquidity."

12. It is equally important for regulators to have information on derivatives' risk exposures not just in clearinghouses and exchanges in their own jurisdiction, but also in other global financial centers. The Act recognizes this and provides sufficient latitude in international information sharing across clearinghouses and data repositories. However, the implementation issues will be fairly complex and remain largely unknown.

13. Industry and regulatory sources offer varying estimates of the size of the OTC market, but they all underscore similar past and current trends. Over the past decade, the OTC derivatives market, both

in the United States and internationally, registered exponential growth (over 20 percent compound annual growth rate since 1998), with credit derivatives as a significant force behind it. Today, based on recent statistics from the Bank for International Settlements, the OTC segment accounts for 90 percent of the overall derivatives market size in terms of notional amount outstanding, and the total notional amount of all types of OTC contracts outstanding globally almost doubled to $605 trillion in the four years to June 2009.

14. In effect, our recommendation amounts to imposing a position limit, but one whose size – as it applies to each market participant – is determined by the participant, subject to the requirement that its largest position in the clearinghouse be fully collateralized. In case the clearinghouse has concerns about a particular group of firms, for example those in one industry, the definition of the single largest exposure could be broadened to include this group.

15. "Goldman Sachs Demands Collateral It Won't Dish Out," Bloomberg, March 15, 2010.

16. "The Case for Regulating Financial Derivatives," *Barron's*, March 22, 2010.

17. A total of 67 ISDA member firms responded to the 2009 Margin Survey. The Survey classifies respondents into three size groups based on the number of collateral agreements executed. The threshold for classification as a large program is 1,000 agreements; under this criterion, 20 firms are classified as large. Financial firms with 51 to 1,000 agreements are considered to be medium (25 firms fall into this classification); and the rest, financial firms that have fewer than 50 agreements, are classified as small (22 firms fall into this classification).

18. www.imf.org/external/pubs/ft/wp/ 2010/wp1099.pdf.

19. BIS Derivatives Statistics, June 2009, Table 19, memo item (www.bis.org/ statistics/derstats.htm).

20. Another, somewhat more subtle device would be to legislate that, in the event of a default, OTC counterparties are junior to any centrally cleared or exchange-traded claim. This would ensure that uncleared OTC products still exist but are subject to substantial counterparty risk or high margins; in turn, these products would be worthwhile only if customization gains are sufficiently large.

21. Aggregated reports for credit derivatives are currently being published by the Depository Trust & Clearing Corporation (DTCC), but it is clear that they fall short of the transparency standard we deem necessary to assess counterparty and systemic risks with sufficient granularity (without compromising anonymity).

22. Some economists argue that it is possible that increased transparency might destroy incentives to gather information and actually deter market makers from operating in these markets, which, in turn, might decrease liquidity. We note, however, that the illiquidity costs need to be weighed against the financial fragility costs arising when large players fail. We hold the view that suitably *aggregated* information on exposures should be disseminated to the market at large.

23. The four financial institutions without exposure to derivatives are: New York Community Bancorp Inc., Hudson City Bancorp, Vornado Realty Trust, and ProLogis.

24. Typically, an oil company's trading risk position will be net short the commodity, offset by the company's natural long position as a producer.

25. See Hills, Rule, Parkinson and Young (1999) for further details.

26. Panel on the Stock Market Crash of 1987 with Nicholas Brady and Gerald Corrigan (Brookings-Wharton Papers on Financial Services, First Annual Conference, Washington, DC, October 29, 1997).

27. The term *stable value contract* means any contract, agreement, or transaction that provides a crediting interest rate and guaranty or financial assurance of liquidity at contract or book value prior to maturity offered by a bank, insurance company, or other state or federally regulated financial institution for the benefit of any individual or commingled fund available as an investment in an employee benefit plan subject to participant direction, an eligible deferred compensation plan that is maintained by an eligible employer, an arrangement described in section 403(b) of the Internal Revenue Code of 1986 (tax-sheltered annuity), or a qualified tuition program.

REFERENCES

Acharya, V. V., Bisin, A. 2010. Counterparty Risk Externality: Centralized Versus Over-The-Counter Markets. Working Paper, NYU Stern School of Business.

Acharya, V. V., Engle, R. 2009. Derivatives trades should all be transparent. *Wall Street Journal*, May 15.

Hills, B., Rule, D., Parkinson, S., Young, C. 1999. Central counterparty clearing houses and financial stability. *Bank of England Financial Stability Review*.

Santos, T., Scheinkman, J. 2001. Competition among exchanges. Quarterly Journal of Economics 116(3): 1027–1062.

19

Governing Derivatives after the Financial Crisis: The Devil is in the Details

S.G. Badrinath and Stefano Gubellini
San Diego State University

Problems worthy of attack
Prove their worth by hitting back.

—Piet Hein

19.1 INTRODUCTION

Derivatives serve a number of functions in advanced economies. While their speculative uses appear periodically destabilizing, their benefits in hedging a range of risks are undoubtedly of value to the economic entities that utilize them. As derivative innovation has evolved, the frequency of financial setbacks has also increased. Both the stabilizing and destabilizing influences have magnified, from jump risk in credit derivatives to the globalization of risk management. Legal, accounting and regulatory bodies have attempted to balance these objectives, tilting towards one side or the other depending on the fervor with which deregulatory or regulatory motivations have dominated the prevailing social ethos. In this fashion, concerns about derivatives mimic the periodic generational discomforts with innovative ideas be they social, cultural or political.

This chapter evaluates recent financial regulation pertaining to derivatives. It describes the role of derivative products in securitizations, discusses the evolution of regulation and the challenges involved in implementing the recommendations of the Dodd–Frank Wall Street Reform and Consumer Protection Act of 2010 (hereafter the "Dodd–Frank Act") as it affects interest-rate swaps and credit default swaps. According to the ISDA, as of the first half of 2010, the notional principal underlying interest rate/currency swaps and credit default swaps is $434 trillion, and $26.23 trillion respectively. Both these instruments have been heavily used in asset securitization activities and are widely perceived to have contributed to the ongoing financial crisis.

While Dodd–Frank's primary recommendations are to create transparency in the over-the-counter derivatives markets by moving to an exchange traded environment, this chapter identifies the linkages between market participants on the trading, legal and accounting fronts that potentially obstruct the achievement of these objectives. All these linkages pose trade-offs – between hedging and speculation, disclosure and reporting burdens, and standardization versus customization of product offerings. As of this date, the agencies charged with implementation, the Securities and Exchange Commission and the Commodity Futures Trading Commission are considerably behind in terms of their implementation schedule and find their efforts further complicated by the power of the banking lobby as well as changes in the political climate. These are the details that our chapter seeks to illuminate.

Section 19.2 describes the use of these derivatives in asset securitizations. Section 19.3 places the various pieces of derivatives legislation in a historical context. Section 19.4 critically evaluates the challenges posed in implementing the recommendations of Dodd Frank as it relates to derivatives practices. Section 19.5 concludes.

19.2 SECURITIZATION AND RISK MANAGEMENT

The use of derivatives to manage interest rate risk and credit risk has been widespread in securitization activities. While detailed descriptions of securitization and its current state are available elsewhere (see for instance, Fender and Mitchell (2009) or Caprio et al. (2009)), this section provides a brief, critical review at their functioning over the years. Simply stated, securitization refers to the process of transforming illiquid individual loans into securities and distributing them to investors. We view securitization on a risk continuum with primary market loan funding at one end. Here, traditional thrift institutions originate the loan, service it, fund it with deposits and assume the associated interest rate risk as well as the credit risk of default of the individual borrower. At the other end, all interest rate and credit risk would be distributed to investors in secondary markets. In such a situation, there is no informational asymmetry as the lender does not have a stake in the quality of the loan. Securitization lies in the middle of these two extremes, where loans are bundled, risk is unbundled, some of it is retained, and the entire structure closely monitored. There is a three-step process. First, originated loans are pooled together into mortgage-backed securities enabling a diversification of borrower risk. Second, these assets are transferred in a true-sale to a special purpose vehicle (SPV) so that the cash flows from these assets cannot be attached in the event of originator bankruptcy.[1] Third, the SPV issues different tranches or slices of bonds where the cash flow is passed through from the original mortgages comprising the pool according to different rules of priority. Typically, the senior and the largest tranches are paid first and bear the least risk. The lowest or equity tranche is the first to be affected by default in the underlying collateral pool. In this manner, securitization provides access to funding sources from secondary capital markets.

As the structures are designed by the SPV, an iterative process conducted with rating agencies determines the type of credit rating that the different tranches can garner. The SPV engages an asset manager to trade the assets in the pool, a guarantor to provide credit guarantees on the performance of that pool, a servicer to process the cash flows generated from the pool and transferring them to the owners of the tranches and a trustee to oversee the activities of the SPV.

As comfort with securitization products and structures grew, numerous variations emerged over the years. In addition to the usual individual fixed-rate and adjustable-rate mortgages and mortgage-backed securities (MBS), the assets pooled into the securitization began to include loans and leveraged loans, high-yield corporate bonds as well as asset-backed securities (ABS). Thus the early collateralized mortgage-backed obligations (CMO) were augmented by collateralized loan obligations (CLO), then by collateralized bond obligations (CBO), and later their aggregated version – the collateralized debt obligation (CDO). Once the securitization infrastructure was in place at most banks, new product development even involved the re-securitization of the lower (and more risky) CDO tranches into CDO-squared structures. Demand from private investors seeking yield in an environment of low interest rates began to mean that every conceivable cash flow stream was prone to being securitized.

19.2.1   Securitization and Interest Rate Risk

On the risk continuum described above, the S&L crisis of the 1980s can be viewed as failure of the traditional banking model to concentrate risk in one set of financial institutions.[2] Indeed, after that crisis, mortgage securitization received a significant impetus, with the government sponsored enterprises (GSEs) taking on a more increased role in the mortgage market.[3] Home ownership has been a cornerstone of public policy in the US and the GSEs' mandate was to provide liquidity, stability and affordability to this market.[4]

As part of the mandate to promote home ownership, Freddie Mac purchased mortgages, packaged them into MBS and sold them to investors. In contrast, initially Fannie Mae issued its own debt and retained the interest rate risk rather than passing it through to investors. To reduce the expense of strict cash flow matching, Fannie Mae began to issue debt of a shorter duration than the mortgage itself. Declines in interest rates then triggered refinancing by borrowers holding fixed-rate mortgages. Even though the mortgage gets prepaid, the debt must still pay off at the higher original rate causing a loss to Fannie Mae. If interest rates rise, the borrower retains the mortgage and Fannie Mae still bears the loss of having to refinance its loan at the new higher rate. This feature of mortgages is referred to as negative convexity. Recall too that refinancing is essentially the exercise of a prepayment call option by the borrower. In an attempt to manage this refinance risk, Fannie Mae began to issue callable debt and later accessed the interest-rate swap market as well as employed swaptions to seek a corresponding hedge.[5] Their hedging approach largely involved maintaining full hedges against short-term likely shocks, with dynamic changes to the hedge portfolio as market conditions changed. While dynamic hedges can lower costs, they do not effectively protect against either a large shock or a series of small shocks. Indeed, derivative losses for the GSEs were large well before the current global financial crisis. In this context, the bank-like behavior of the GSE's inevitably resulted in bank-like consequences of maturity mismatch that plagued the S&Ls. Ironically, the SPVs that were structured as ABCP conduits became subject to similar maturity mis-match problems in 2009 when money market funds lost confidence in the safety of that paper.[6]

19.2.2   Securitization and Credit Risk

Credit risk was initially managed by the GSEs by strictly adhering to loan size, conformity and underwriting standards. As the mortgage market expanded and private mortgage entities entered the business, providing guarantees became a larger part of GSE operations. Loans that were bundled and sold as MBS came with a guarantee that the unpaid balances to security holders on individual mortgage defaults would be paid by the GSE. Acting on behalf of the GSE, a servicer would then attempt to recover that amount through the foreclosure process. Therefore, the security holder would not have any exposure to credit risk.

With the advent of private mortgage entities, the Collateralized Debt Obligation (CDO) became a common way in which credit risk was tranched to investors in much the same way that mortgage prepayment risk was distributed in a CMO. Although it is often described as a credit derivative, a CDO is essentially a multi-class bond with multiple tranching conventions. Simple senior/subordinate structures tranche credit risk. More complicated structures combine tranches from a number of issues. Pools of reference assets underlie synthetic CDOS. Demand for such securitized products from investors contributed to the financial meltdown of recent years.

CDO entities also managed credit risk by creating different types of credit enhancements based upon the quality of the collateral asset pool amid concerns regarding adverse selection by pool originators. Both internal and external assurances become common.[7] Internal guarantees included a cash reserve from setting aside a portion of the underwriting fee for creating the collateralized structure, or a portion of the interest received from the collateral assets, after paying interest on the tranches, or even by deliberate over-collateralization where the volume of collateral assets placed in the structure is greater than the volume of liabilities, thereby providing an additional layer of default protection. External guarantees came from the GSEs, were solicited from the sponsor, obtained by the direct purchase of credit insurance from mono-line insurance companies or offered as over-the-counter insurance through credit default swaps.[8]

19.2.3 Securitization and Credit Risk Transfer

Much has been written about the role of the credit default swap (CDS) in the trading and transfer of credit risk. A CDS is conceptually similar to a put option on credit risk.[9] Buyers of protection from a credit event pay a periodic premium. If there is a relevant credit event that affects the value of the underlying asset, then the protection buyers are made whole by the protection seller and have effectively shed the credit risk. Sellers of protection assume the credit risk in exchange for that periodic premium income. The appeal of the CDS becomes clear when it is compared with corresponding bond market transactions. Exposure to credit risk can be achieved either by owning the bond or selling the CDS. Owning the bond requires capital and also creates interest rate risk exposure while selling the CDS only requires mark-to-market adjustments and periodic collateral (since the CDS is unfunded). Likewise, being short credit risk implies being either short the bond or buying the CDS, with the latter choice widely perceived as operationally simpler.

The CDS market was essentially a loosely regulated over-the-counter market. Beginning with their use by banks to manage credit risk, the late 1990s saw increased participation by hedge funds and relatively less "insurance" or hedging activity. By offering both leverage and liquidity the CDS market easily permitted the assumption of market exposure towards credit in a manner not possible in the secondary bond market.

Several considerations complicate attempts to regulate this instrument. First, owners of the underlying credit can purchase protection against its possible default – an application similar to that of a protective put option.[10] Second, the direct purchase of a CDS without owning the underlying credit is similar to a short sale. It is important to note that with or without ownership of the underlying asset, CDS can be purchased in multiples of the outstanding loan amount.[11] Accordingly unscrupulous market participants can acquire the ability and thereby the incentive to precipitate borrower default. Only a portion of CDS purchases can be justified as legitimate hedging activity. The remainder are clearly speculative, especially when the gains from the CDS cannot directly be linked to the amount of loss actually suffered by the protection buyer. This feature is further complicated by the fact that the ability of the protection buyer to realize these profits is conditional on the creditworthiness of the CDS seller. AIG's $446 billion in CDS exposure suggests that this counterparty risk was substantial. Furthermore, a statement from its 2008 10-K report suggests that regulatory capital arbitrage was one of the less well known motives behind their selling CDS to banks.[12]

Third, from initially insuring the default risk of individual bonds, the CDS market rapidly expanded to include CDS products on loans, mortgage-backed and asset-backed securities.

Portfolio versions of these known as basket CDS and index CDS products traded in the middle of the 2000s. The now notorious ABX and TABX indexes are securities that take one or two deals from 20 different ABS programs, with 5 different rating classes: AAA, AA, AA, BBB, BBB-. The bottom two are further combined into the TABX which is the most sub-prime and experienced the most rapid declines in value at the beginning of the financial crisis.[13]

The synthetic CDO is a special purpose securitization vehicle that creatively uses the CDS instrument. The Bistro structure conceived initially by J.P. Morgan in 1997 became a template by which the cash flows to tranches of securitizations were generated from the premiums received by selling credit default swaps on a portfolio of underlying securitizable assets. In other words, instead of a pool of assets generating cash flows, the insurance premium representing their likelihood of default is itself distributed directly to the tranches. Since the rate of default in the pool of underlying assets governs the amount of the premium that will be received from credit default swaps sold on those assets, this amounts to essentially the same bet.[14]

19.2.4   Skin in the Game

In a concerted effort to revive the moribund securitization market, several proposals that require participating firms to have some "skin in the game" have been making the rounds. One proposal requires participants to retain a portion of each individual loan they originate while another suggests that a portion of the risk in securitization pool be retained. Thompson (2011) provides an excellent summary of the merits of these arguments.

19.3   THE REGULATION OF DERIVATIVE CONTRACTS

The difficulties inherent in regulating derivatives to permit "legitimate" hedging activity while limiting "undesirable" speculative activity is visible most clearly in the history of derivatives regulation. Whether to permit off-exchange activity and how to regulate on-exchange activity has been a pressing concern throughout this history.[15] Differences in regulatory orientation vary from a focus on co-regulation and principles-based regulation in the UK to the more self-regulatory and rules-based approaches of the United States. This section first provides a brief post-Depression overview of events in the latter.

19.3.1   Regulation Prior to 2000

Regulation of exchange-traded futures contracts on agricultural commodities was the purview of the Commodity Exchange Act (CEA) of 1936. Many of its central principles are worth articulating in light of the recent Dodd-Frank rules. These include transparent market-based pricing, disclosure and consumer protection rules, prohibitions against manipulation and illegal trading activity, the regulation of broker–dealer intermediaries, self regulation by exchanges and enforcement by the federal regulator. A central principle of the CEA was that a well-capitalized central clearinghouse would be interposed between the counterparties to various transactions. This clearing facility would in turn assure that derivatives traders had adequate amounts of capital by the rigorous collection of margins. Virtually all of these goals appear in some shape or form in recent legislative efforts.

In 1974, under the Commodity and Futures Trading Commission Act, the CFTC became the new regulator, whose role was expanded to include all exchange-traded futures contracts including financial futures. Subsequently, the adoption of a proposal from the US Treasury, called the Treasury Amendment, resulted in the exclusion of forward contracts such as those in foreign currency markets, mortgage, government and other debt securities from regulatory supervision by the CFTC.[16]

The subsequent rapid growth of interest rate swaps in the 1980s renewed concerns about the CFTC's ability to monitor over-the-counter activity in these instruments. Despite several soothing statutory interpretations from the CFTC, legal uncertainties still remained. Eventually, a provision in the Futures Practices Act of 1992 granted the CFTC the right to exempt off-exchange transactions between "appropriate persons" from the exchange-trading requirement of the CEA. This right was almost immediately exercised in the context of interest rate swaps. Concerns about the interest rate swap market still continued amidst turf battles in 1997–98 between the SEC and CFTC on how to regulate the broker–dealer firms in this market. A Presidential Working Group was formed comprising the Chairman of the Federal Reserve, the Chairpersons of the CFTC and the SEC and the Treasury Secretary. At this time, events pertaining to Long Term Capital Management (LTCM) and their leverage in the OTC derivatives markets came to light. After multiple hearings and a bailout of LTCM orchestrated by the Federal Reserve, the Commodity Futures Modernization Act of 2000 was signed into law.[17]

19.3.2   The Commodity Futures Modernization Act (CFMA) of 2000

Under the CFMA, over-the-counter derivative transactions between "sophisticated parties" would not be regulated as "futures" under the Commodity Exchange Act (CEA) of 1934 or as "securities" under the federal securities laws. This fragmented regulation implied instead that banks and securities firms who are the major dealers in these products would instead be supervised under the "safety and soundness" standards of banking law. A new Section 2(h) of the CEA created the so-called Enron "loophole" that excluded oil and other energy derivatives from CEA requirements of exchange trading. In addition, Title 1 of the CFMA specifically excluded financial derivatives on any index tied to a credit risk measure. The Act provided even further impetus for credit derivatives markets to engage in risk transfer activities pursuant to securitization.

In August 2009, after the financial crisis and the collapse of securitization, regulation took a 180-degree turn when the US Treasury proposed legislation that essentially repealed many of the above exemptions and argued for an exchange-traded credit derivatives market.

19.3.3   The Dodd–Frank Wall Street Reform and Consumer Protection Act of 2010

More popularly known as the Dodd–Frank Act, Section 723(a)(3) amends the Commodity Exchange Act ("CEA") to provide that "it shall be unlawful for any person to engage in a swap unless that person submits such swap for clearing to a derivatives clearing organization, or DCO, that is registered under the CEA or a DCO that is exempt from registration under the CEA if the swap is required to be cleared." It addresses swaps and security-based swaps. The Commodities Futures Trading Commission (CFTC) has authority over the former and the Securities and Exchange Commission (SEC) has authority of the latter, with joint rule making permitted in the case of derivatives with mixed characteristics. State insurance laws are explicitly prohibited from regulating swaps. All swaps must be traded through some form of centralized exchange and will have to be cleared through registered derivatives clearing organizations or clearing agencies. The Act also addresses several areas of transparency-collection of transactions data, registration of market participants, disclosure of the underlying risks and the imposition of margin and collateral requirements and position limits on counterparties. Taken together, all these recommendations pose a variety of challenges that are described below.

19.4 REGULATORY CHALLENGES AND RESPONSES

19.4.1 Fostering an Exchange-traded Credit Derivatives Market

The complexity and opacity of over-the-counter credit derivatives markets and their purported role in several scandals in the headlines makes them obvious candidates for financial reform agendas. The primary recommendation of Dodd–Frank in this regard borrows heavily from the Commodity Exchange Act of 1936 which required that futures and options trade on organized exchanges. The goal is to encourage the development of exchange-traded derivatives markets for credit.

In response, exchanges have already created templates for, and are making markets in, trading credit products. The Chicago Mercantile Exchange (CME) offers a Credit Index Event contract, which is a fixed recovery CDS product.[18] The InterContinental Exchange (ICE) has been clearing CDS, the Nasdaq OMX group and the CME have been competing for a portion of the clearing business of the nearly $3 trillion of derivatives with Fannie Mae and Freddie Mac. Since 2009, the CME offers clearing-only services for over-the-counter CDS products along with several founding members.[19] LCH ClearNet offers similar services to hedge funds and buy-side firms. The obvious motivations for the exchanges are to profit from the volume of activity in these markets. After all, currency derivatives first started trading over-the-counter and now trade in parallel on an exchange platform.

On exchanges, centralized counterparties perform novation, which is the act of interposing themselves between buyers and sellers of financial contracts. As such, counterparties both receive and disburse payments between transacting parties. Clearing relates to all activities that take place from the time such a commitment is made until settlement when the funds and securities are transferred between the buyer and seller. This contrasts with over-the-counter markets where buyers and sellers bilaterally negotiate terms and settle contracts. Governance rules for clearinghouses that are currently under consideration impose limits on the voting ability of individual clearing members as well as on the collective ability of financial firms that provide clearing facilities. Making credit derivatives exchange-traded entails several considerations.

First, by interposing itself between the buyer and the seller, the clearing-house can potentially reduce counterparty risk. As an independent entity, the clearing-house is also separate from the counterparties, unlike over-the-counter settings, where currently investment and commercial banks make a market as well as take on risk exposure.[20] Second, clearing-houses are generally well capitalized and their credit-worthiness is less likely to be called into question.

Third, exchange trading makes it possible to view market prices clearly. Exchange trading is appropriate in situations where the terms of the contract on the underlying product being traded are standardized. The need for moving toward exchange trading is less urgent if OTC markets are equally able to handle standardized derivative instruments. The objection being raised by the securities industry is that specialized complex securities do not lend themselves to an exchange-traded environment. They argue that such an environment may limit the ability of hedging end-users to correctly tailor the hedging instrument to the underlying risks and may interfere with swap accounting rules. It is also likely that the dominant motivation is the fee income generated by the provision of an over-the-counter market in such instances. Still, if the underlying securities are complex and hard to value, then market activity may be light and prices may be stale, but that may be preferable to having no prices at all.

Fourth, exchanges impose a settlement or a mark-to-market reconciliation of the exposures of the two parties on a daily basis. In contrast, mark-to-market practices in OTC derivatives are less frequent and likely to be more contaminated. For instance, hedge funds often carry leveraged positions at cost. Some OTC desks keep the books on an "accrual" basis.[21] A disposition may come into play where losses are "accrued" while gains are marked-to-market immediately.

Fifth, the contracts can be standardized along the lines of the ISDA, but incorporating default events that may be unique to the legal environment in the local market.[22] Finally, while such an exchange-traded credit derivative market is more likely to preserve the benefits of securitization, it may not be the most appropriate venue for all types of derivative transactions. Indeed, it is the last feature that appears to be the sticking point as traders are reluctant to forego past practices, pointing out that financial crises can and have happened in exchange traded markets as well.

19.4.2 Counterparty Risk

Counterparty risk refers to the inability of one of the contracting parties to make a payment as required under the contract. Transactions in securities typically terminate quickly along with the legal obligation of the contracting parties, with sellers receiving payment and purchasers retaining the risk of not receiving subsequent cash flows from the issuer of the security. In contrast, certain types of derivatives contracts such as credit and interest rate swaps have longer lives and require a series of periodic payments. Protection buyers are contractually obligated to pay the swap premium. With CDS, the exposure of protection sellers can be large following a credit event and several mechanisms involving position limits and collateral limits have developed in the OTC markets.

First, individual protection buyers limit their transactions with a specific protection seller. However, bilateral netting (also referred to as trade compression) involves the cancellation of mutually offsetting contracts. While imposing position limits on individual market participants can prevent market manipulation and reduce the potential for systemic risk, these can also limit their incentive to gather information and thereby impede price discovery (Financial Economists Roundtable, 2010).

Second, the protection seller is required to post collateral. A recent survey by the ISDA documents that roughly 60% of the positions are collateralized with about 80% of that collateral being in cash. Infrastructure delays in the return of this collateral may result in a loss of liquidity to the underlying dealer and create market disruptions.

Third, the funding of the CCP typically occurs from its members who are among the larger financial institutions that are active in these markets. Moral hazard arguments would suggest that one member may be tempted to engage in extremely risky transactions since the consequences of its failure would be borne by all members. Such issues led to the consideration of multiple CCPs as well as the types of derivatives they should clear. Duffie and Zhu (2010) carefully evaluate the recommendations of central clearing with a central clearing counter-party (CCP) as advocated in Dodd–Frank (2010). In comparison with the bilateral netting that is common practice in over-the-counter markets they show that, for credit default swaps, introducing CCP entities can reduce the efficiency of netting arrangements and that coun-terparty risk exposures can actually increase if multiple classes of derivatives are cleared by different CCPs.

Fourth, the imposition of initial margins as well as variation margin to manage mark-to-market risks in the CCP context is one more instance where fine tuning may become necessary. Indeed, Heller and Vause (2012) estimate the quantity of collateral that CCPs would require to effectively clear the interest rate swap and credit default swap positions of the major derivatives dealers. They find that while these dealers appear to have adequate assets to meet initial margin requirements, some may require additional cash to meet variation margin. These considerations underscore the complex network of credit and liquidity arrangements between derivative market participants and dealers. Several parties are involved in any given trade in addition to the client and the CCP. These clearing members and execution brokers, each have different infrastructures that will require modification. Resolving the credit side of these arrangements only remains a part of the story, albeit an important one.

19.4.3   Disclosure and Transparency

Disclosure is simply viewed as disseminating information to market participants. One impor-tant benefit of moving to an exchange-traded platform is that daily mark-to-market require-ments ensure that prices are revealed to market participants in a timely manner. Date-stamped and time-stamped price and quantity information will enable these players to accurately gauge the value of their outstanding positions and assist in their decisions to implement new ones. Furthermore, data warehouses such as the current Trade Information Warehouse of the DTCC that provide market-wide disclosure of positions would enable regulators to assess the extent of systemic risk that prevails at various times. However, Bartlett (2010) persuasively argues that simply reducing information uncertainty is not sufficient in the case of derivatives disclosure. At a minimum, both buyers of CDS should disclose adverse risks to the underlying entity and sellers of CDS should disclose their financial condition.[23] Several other arguments are offered against increasing disclosure. The first is that current disclosure already enables traders to infer the information they need. Related to this argument is the one that such sophisticated trading organizations are quite capable of regulating themselves.[24] Second, that many of the offered products are customized for individual clients and that excessive disclosure requirements may affect the client's abilities to execute their desired strategies. Third that the banking establish-ment in the US is already well regulated. Fourth, that unless there are global commonalities in terms of disclosure requirements, financial institutions in the US may find themselves at a comparative disadvantage.[25] Curiously, Arora et al. (2009) argue that, for boundedly rational investors, the computational complexity central to derivatives actually amplifies asymmetric information rather than reducing it! It is ironic that many of the same arguments were made in the late 2000s when there were concerns about option accounting. Finally, Zhong (2012) shows that dealers in non-competitive centralized markets have little incentive towards transparency as there is no potential of entry by other market makers and dealers. When centralized markets are competitive this latter threat reduces the opaqueness that is well known to be prevalent in over-the-counter markets.

19.4.4   Accounting, Valuation and Stability Issues

The intent of accounting guidelines has historically been to enable market participants to develop reasonable estimates of fair value in illiquid markets. The premise behind FAS 157: Fair Value Accounting is that orderly transactions are possible under prevalent conditions on the relevant measurement dates – conditions that can hardly be said to have existed during the depths of the financial crisis. During those years, the ability to rollover asset-backed commercial paper (ABCP) became questionable and the market valuations of lower tranches of CDOs became unreliable as subprime mortgage securities were affected by rapidly declining real estate valuations. In later stages, these valuation effects were felt in the senior and "super-senior" tranches of CDO's, often magnified by underlying CDS arrangements.

Reporting requirements for swaps mirror changes are designed to reflect their increasing use for hedging purposes. There are two types of hedges, cash flow hedges and fair value hedges. First, an ideal benchmark which exactly offsets the underlying risk is determined. Hedges are deemed to be effective if the gains (losses) from the actual derivative are less than or equal to that of this benchmark. Hedges are deemed ineffective if the gains (losses) from the actual derivative are greater than that benchmark. Ineffective gains (losses) are recorded in income. Effective gains (losses) are first recorded in other comprehensive income and then transferred to earnings when the gain (loss) impact actually occurs. Even within this broader framework, it is recognized that cash flow obligations in interest-rate swaps that exchange fixed cash flows for floating cash flows have lesser jump risk characteristics than credit default swaps, where protection sellers can be subject to large drawdowns if an adverse credit event occurs. Additionally, both swaps have speculative (trading) characteristics as well as hedging characteristics and it is impractical and inadvisable to ban one but not the other.

Bank regulators, whose overarching concern is financial stability and the early identification and management of systemic risk, view valuation from a somewhat different lens. For them, the inter-connected nature of large financial institutions and the volatility underlying fair value assessments in times of financial stress are important. This volatility can cause big changes in both earnings and capital of financial institutions from one quarter to the next and thereby adversely affect financial stability.

Shaffer (2012) optimistically points at a convergence between these two objectives. The Financial Accounting Standard Board is moving towards advocating a mixed measurement approach. Assets that are intended to be held in order to realize the underlying cash flows could be recorded at historical cost while assets that are held for the purpose of realizing profits from short-term changes in value would be recorded at fair value. Bank regulators can attempt to counter the adverse effects of the volatility in fair values by changing supervisory policies and adjusting accounting information by using prudential filters and conducting stress tests as mandated by the Dodd–Frank Act.

19.5   CONCLUSIONS

This chapter discusses the many challenges that arise in the implementation of the Wall Street Transparency and Accountability Act of 2010 as it pertains to derivatives. Beginning with the use of derivatives in securitizations, it traces the history of rule-making that culminated in this Act. It argues that some of the prescriptions of recent rules are essentially rehashed versions of ideas that have been proposed in previous regulatory efforts. It describes a balancing act between the socially desirable benefits of hedging with derivatives and the attendant discomforts of excessive speculation. As the pendulum swings to one extreme, mean reversion in regulatory efforts indubitably results while the central issues underlying societal concerns about the use (and abuse) of derivatives remains.

The inexorable growth of innovation implies that a return to a simpler regime is highly unlikely. In any event, such a regime will always find opposition from those quarters that generate wealth from opaqueness. Even much vaunted transparency arguments are in the eye of the beholder who is unlikely to understand financial complexity. Suggestions to limit complexity continue to be made without an explicit recognition that complexity will continue to be an increasing part of the fabric of finance.

Concerns about regulatory capture will also remain and indeed be strengthened by a comparison between the budgets of the enforcers and the enforced. The entire budget of the SEC is about $2 billion, while JP Morgan alone has a budget of several billion to fight lawsuits. Regulatory fragmentation as evidenced by the number of organizations that are involved in overseeing the financial system makes it even more likely that different bodies will arrive at conflicting regulation. Finally, regulatory fatigue suggests that future omnibus acts of the magnitude of Dodd–Frank are somewhat unlikely.

NOTES

1. While the special purpose entity (SPE) is a legal construct for bankruptcy remoteness, related vehicles such as structured investment vehicles (SIV) or Asset Backed Commercial Paper (ABCP) conduits use these constructs.
2. One of the primary reasons for the Savings and Loan Crisis of the 1980s was the funding mismatches caused by borrowing short (via deposits) and lending long (to 30-year fixed rate mortgages). In addition to maturity mismatches, the Regulation Q ceiling on interest payable to depositors was kept artificially low, causing them to move to alternative interest-bearing investments such as money market funds.
3. This was not, however, the starting point for securitization. Goetzmann and Newman (2009) point to a complex real estate market in the 1920s, with arrangements resembling securitization well before the GSEs were created.
4. This mission is conducted by holding mortgages and MBS as well as guaranteeing other MBS issues. Loans that meet underwriting and product standards are purchased from the lenders and then pooled and sold to investors as MBS. The GSEs received a fee for guaranteeing the performance of these securities. Second, they held some of the loans they purchase from banks for portfolio investment. Some of the holdings in the investment portfolio were themselves MBS issued by private firms (many of which have been subprime). Funding for the former is obtained from investors and funding for the latter is obtained by issuing agency debt creating moral hazard problems.
5. At of the end of 2009, the notional value of Freddie Mac's derivatives book was more than $1.2 trillion and the total notional value of Fannie Mae's derivative instruments was more than $967 billion (Business Week, April 29, 2010).
6. Kacperczyk and Schnabl (2009) document the characteristics of the asset-backed commercial paper during the financial crisis.
7. If originators have the most information about the quality of the underlying financial claims then it is reasonable to expect adverse selection on their part, only keeping the good loans and selling the bad ones. In the extreme, loan quality will decline across the board as demand for loans from securitizers weakens the incentive for originators to screen the loans. This leads to issues of information asymmetry causing rational lenders to demand a lemons-premium, Duffie (2007).

8. Understandably, the level of these credit-enhancements was critical to obtaining a favorable rating from the rating agencies.

9. Contract terms and definitions of the credit event are standardized by the International Swap Dealer's Association (ISDA). More details on the CDS are available at www.isda.org.

10. Traditional forms of insurance incorporate the notion of "insurable" interest where the primary purchasers of insurance are those owners of assets who deem it necessary to seek protection against its loss of value. Restricting CDS purchases to this class of market participants is identical to only permitting protective put options to be traded and would thus limit the flexibility of market participants.

11. In recognition of the use of the CDS as a trading tool rather than a purely hedging one, the ISDA moved towards cash settlement of single-name CDS contracts. In 2005, they created a global protocol and a credit event auction to provide more transparency.

12. Sender (2009) reports the quote as: "(selling CDS) was . . . for the purpose of providing them (banks) with regulatory capital relief rather than risk mitigation in exchange for a minimum guaranteed fee".

13. As an illustration, the ABX.HE.A-06-01 is an index of asset-backed (AB), home-equity loans (HE) assembled from ABS programs originating in the first half of 2006.

14. The charges filed by the SEC in April 2010 against Goldmans Sachs pertain to their lack of disclosure of information while such a synthetic structure was being created.

15. Dinallo (2009) reports of stock jobbing, an early version of short selling that was outlawed in New York in 1829 and then repealed in 1858 as its scope was viewed as prohibiting legitimate speculative activity. Bucket shops arose in the early 19th century as a form of off-exchange trading activity and functioned by netting out opposing trades. In extremely one-sided markets, the operators were nowhere to be found and traders held worthless tickets. The Banking Panic of 1907, J.P. Morgan's famous call to bankers to agree on a backstop for the banking system and the 1909 anti-bucket-shop law all serve to remind us that concerns about off-exchange, over-the-counter activity have long histories.

16. The thinking, summarized nicely in a speech by Federal Reserve Chairman Greenspan in 1997, was that foreign currency markets were different from agricultural markets in that they were deep and difficult to manipulate. Therefore regulating them was "unnecessary and potentially harmful."

17. A 2009 documentary on Frontline titled "The Warning" describes the 1997–98 conflicts between Brooksley Born, the Chairwoman of the CFTC and the other members of the Presidents Working Group. The former was strongly in favor of regulating OTC derivatives but the other members, who were opposed to any regulation, prevailed.

18. Since the CDX and iTraxx products described above are branded, the CME has created its own index of underlying reference entities.

19. See 'CME Group Launches Credit Default Swap Initiative; Begins Clearing Trades', Chicago-PRNewswire-First Call, Dec 15, 2009.

20. The Volcker rule, which limits such proprietary trading by financial institutions, has been one of the hot-button battleground issues of the recent regulatory debate.

21. Anecdotal evidence suggests that, at times, mark-to-market practices are postponed if the transactions will not be unwound until expiration.

22. The events of 2011 surrounding whether Greek sovereign debt restructuring constituted a "default" are a case in point, with the ISDA issuing and subsequently taking back its pronouncements.

23. In June 2012, for instance, J.P. Morgan disclosed that losses in positions created by the "London Whale" would be in the order of about $2 billion. Several weeks later, it was reported that these positions would take considerably longer to unwind and that losses in the order of $9 billion were not out of the question!

24. In testimony to the Financial Crisis Commission, Viniar (2010) argued that Goldman Sachs' exposure to AIG during the financial crisis was about $10 billion, and was backed by $7.5 billion in collateral.

25. Differences between the US and Europe are already evident in the precise nature of the "swap execution facilities" that the CFTC has recently proposed, with the latter calling for considerable less stringent rules than the former (Grant, 2011). Market historians may find echoes of these arguments in those put forth during the option accounting issues that plagued technology firms during the internet years.

REFERENCES

Arora, S., B. Barak, M. Brunnemeier, R. Ge, 2009. Computational Complexity and Information Asymmetry in Financial Products, Working Paper, Princeton University.

Gharagozlou, A. M., 2010. Unregulable: Why derivatives may never be regulated, Brooklyn Journal of Corporate Financial and Commercial Law, 4(2).

Bartlett, R. P., 2010. Inefficiencies in the Information Thicket: A Case Study of Derivative Disclosures During the Financial Crisis,

Barth, M. E., W. R. Landsman, 2010. How did Financial Reporting Contribute to the Financial Crisis? European Accounting Review,

Baxter, L. G., 2009. Capture in Financial Regulation: Can we Channel it to the Common Good, Duke Law School.

Bliss, R. R., R. S. Steigerwald, 2006. Derivatives Clearing and Settlement: A Comparison of Central Counterparties and Alternative Structures, Economic Perspectives, 4Q/2006. Federal Reserve Bank of Chicago.

Caprio, G. A. Demirguc-Kunt, E. J. Kane, 2009. The 2007 Meltdown in Structured Securitization: Searching for Lessons not Scapegoats, The Paolo Baffi Center for Central Banking and Regulation, Working Paper-2009-49.

Dinallo, E., 2010. Testimony of Eric Dinallo, Former Superintendent, New York State Insurance Department, to the Financial Crisis Inquiry Commission in the Hearing on the Role of Derivatives in the Financial Crisis, July 1.

Dodd–Frank Wall Street Reform, Consumer Protection Act, Pub. L. No. 111-203, 124 Stat. 1376 2010.

Duffie, 2007. Innovations in Credit Risk Transfer: Implications for Financial Stability. Working Paper, Stanford University.

Duffie, D., H. Zhu, 2010. Does a Central Clearing Counterparty Reduce Counterparty Risk? Working Paper, Stanford University.

Fender, I., S. Mitchell, 2009. The Future of Securitization: How to align the incentives. Bank of International Settlements, September.

Financial Accounting Standards Board, 2010. Accounting Standards Update #2010-06.

Financial Economists Roundtable, 2010. Statement on reforming the OTC Derivatives, Markets. Wharton Financial Institutions Center, University of Pennsylvania.

Gensler, G., 2010. Statement of Gary Gensler, Chairman, CFTC before the Financial Crisis Inquiry Commission.

Goetzmann, W. N., F. Newman, 2009. Securitization in the 1920s. Working Paper, Yale University, http://ssrn.com/abstract=1546102.

Grant, J., 2011. U.S and Europe Divisions emerge in derivatives. Financial Times, March 20, 2011.

Greenberger, M., 2010. The Role of Derivatives in the Financial Crisis. Testimony to the Financial Crisis Commission, June.

Gregory, J, 2009. Are we building the foundations for the next crisis already? The case of central clearing.

Heller, D., N. Vause, 2012. Collateral requirements for mandatory central clearing of over-the-counter derivatives. BIS Working Papers Number 373.

Hull, J., 2010. OTC Derivatives and Central Clearing: Can All Transactions Be Cleared? Working Paper, University of Toronto.

Kacperczyk, M., P. Schnabl, 2009. When Safe Proved Risky: Commercial Paper during the Financial Crisis of 2007–2009. Working Paper, New York University.

Kane, E., 2010. Missing elements in US Financial reform: A Kubler-Ross interpretation of the inadequacy of the Dodd-Frank Act. http://ssrn.com/abstract=1654051.

Kawaller, I., 2007. Interest Rate Swaps: Accounting vs. Economics. Financial Analysts Journal, 63 (2), 15–17.

Lowenstein, Roger, Derivatives Lobby has US Regulators on the run. April 2012. Bloomberg News.

McDonnell, B. H., 2012. Financial Regulation Reform and Too Big To Fail. Legal Studies Research Paper Series, 12-08, University of Minnesota Law School.

Murphy, D., 2012. The Possible Impact of OTC Derivatives Central Clearing on Counterparty Credit Risk. Working Paper.

Pekarek, E., C. Lufrano, 2010. The Goldman Sachs Swaps Shop: An Examination of Synthetic Short Selling through Credit Default Swaps and the Implications of SEC v. Goldman Sachs & Co., et al. Available at SSRN: http://ssrn.com/abstract=1654764.

Pirrong, C., 2009. The Economics of Clearing in Derivatives Markets: Netting, Asymmetric Information, and the Sharing of Default Risks Through a Central Counterparty. Available at SSRN: http://ssrn.com/abstract=1340660.

Roe, M., 2010. Can a Clearinghouse Really Stop the Next Financial Crisis? http://blogs.law.harvard.edu/corpgov/2010/05/06/can-a-clearinghouse-really-stop-thenext-financial-crisis/

Ryan, S., 2008. Accounting in and for the Subprime Crisis. Working Paper, Stern School of Business, New York University.

Sender, H., 2009. AIG saga shows danger of credit default swaps. Financial Times, March 6, 2009.

Shadab, H. B., 2010. Counterparty regulation and its limits: The evolution of the credit default swaps market. New York Law School Law Review 54, 57–73.

Shaffer, S., 2012. Evaluating the Impact of Fair Value Accounting on Financial Institutions. Working Paper Number QAU 12-01, Federal Reserve Bank of Boston.

Skeel, D. A., 2010. The New Financial Deal: Understanding the Dodd-Frank Act And its (Unintended) Consequences. Research Paper #10-21, The Institute for Law and Economics, University of Pennsylvania.

Thompson, E., 2011. Dodd-Frank and Basel III's Skin in the Game Divergence and why it is good for the International Banking System. http://ssrn.com/abstract=1783768

U.S. Securities and Exchange Commission, 2009. Report and Recommendations Pursuant to Section 133 of the Emergency Economic Stabilization Act of 2008: Study on Mark-To-Market Accounting.

Viniar, D. A., 2010. Statement of the CFO, Goldman Sachs before the Financial Crisis Inquiry Commission.

Wilmarth, A. E., 2011, The Dodd-Frank Act: A Flawed and inadequate response to the too-big-to-fail problem. Oregon Law Review 89 (3).

Zhong, Z., 2012. Reducing Opaqueness in Over-the-counter Markets. Working Paper, Cornell University.

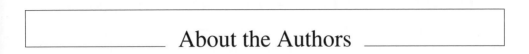

About the Authors

VIRAL V. ACHARYA, NEW YORK UNIVERSITY

Viral V. Acharya is the C.V. Starr Professor of Economics at the Department of Finance at New York University. He has research expertise in the regulation of banks and financial institutions, corporate finance, credit risk, liquidity risk, sovereign debt, crises and growth.

SWAMINATHAN G. BADRINATH, SAN DIEGO STATE UNIVERSITY

Swaminathan G. Badrinath is a Professor of Finance at SDSU. He has held faculty appointments at Rutgers University, Purdue University and the University of Arizona, prior to SDSU. His research interests are in investments and derivatives. Some of his work appears in The Journal of Finance, The Journal of Financial Economics, The Review of Financial Studies, The Journal of Business, The Journal of Banking and Finance and The Journal of Risk and Insurance.

MONICA BILLIO, CA' FOSCARI UNIVERSITY VENICE

Monica Billio is Full Professor of Econometrics at the University Ca' Foscari of Venice, where she teaches Econometrics and Financial Econometrics. She graduated in Economics from the University Ca' Foscari of Venice and holds a doctorate in Applied Mathematics obtained at the University Paris IX Dauphine in 1999. Her main research interests include financial econometrics, with applications to risk measurement and management, volatility modeling, hedge funds, financial crises and systemic risk; business cycle analysis; dynamic latent factor models and simulation-based inference techniques. She has participating in many research projects financed by the European Commission, Eurostat and the Italian Ministry of Research (MIUR). The results of these and other research projects have appeared in peer-refereed journals including Journal of Econometrics, Journal of Financial Economics, Journal of Statistical Planning and Inference, Journal of Empirical Finance, Journal of Financial Econometrics, Computational Statistics and Data Analysis, Journal of Forecasting and European Journal of Operational Research. Moreover, she is head of the School of Economics, Languages and Entrepreneurship (Treviso branch of the University Ca' Foscari of Venice), Deputy Head of the Department of Economics, President of the Teaching Committee of the Master Degree in Economics and Finance and member of the Teaching Committee of the PhD in Quantitative Economics at the same University.

TIMOTHY J. BRERETON, UNIVERSITY OF QUEENSLAND

Tim Brereton is a PhD student at the University of Queensland. He has a Bachelor of Science (Honours) in Mathematics and a Masters of International Economics and Finance, both from the University of Queensland. His research interests include simulation, computational statistics and mathematical finance.

FRANCESCA CAMPOLONGO, EUROPEAN COMMISSION

Francesca Campolongo is the Head of the "Scientific Support to Financial Analysis" Unit of the European Commission Joint Research Centre. Francesca graduated in Mathematics (Pisa University, Italy) in 1993 and completed her PhD in modeling and sensitivity analysis (Griffith University, Australia) in 1998. Since then, she has been working at the EC Joint Research Centre, where she also obtained in 2002 a prize as "best young scientist of the year." Her main research interests focus on financial modeling and financial risk analysis. Working in support of EU policy makers she has developed skills in calibration and impact assessment of financial directives, with particular attention to the banking and insurance sectors. In the last few years she has been actively involved in the work of the European Commission to improve protection for bank account holders, to create a safer and sounder financial system, and to prevent a future crisis. She has over 20 scientific publications in refereed journals and is co-author of three books on sensitivity analysis published by Wiley.

MASSIMILIANO CAPORIN, UNIVERISTY OF PADUA

Massimiliano Caporin is Associate Professor of Econometrics at the University of Padova. His research activities include portfolio allocation and portfolio risk management, financial contagion, derivative pricing, risk measurement, performance measurement, high frequency data analysis and financial time series analyses. Some of his work has appeared in the Journal of Financial Econometrics, Econometric Reviews, Computational Statistics and Data Analysis, Journal of Economic Surveys, Applied Economic Letters, European Journal of Finance, Journal of Forecasting and Energy Economics.

JOSHUA C. C. CHAN, AUSTRALIAN NATIONAL UNIVERSITY

Joshua Chan is a lecturer at the Australian National University. His research interests lie in the field of Monte Carlo simulation, especially the methodological and computational issues of adaptive importance sampling and Markov chain Monte Carlo methods, with an emphasis on economics and finance applications.

CARL CHIARELLA, UNIVERSITY OF TECHNOLOGY, SYDNEY

Carl Chiarella is currently Professor of Quantitative Finance at Finance Discipline Group in the UTS Business School at the University of Technology, Sydney. He holds doctorates in both applied mathematics and economics. He has held visiting appointments at various institutions all over the world. He is the author of over 170 research articles in international and national journals and edited volumes and the author/coauthor of 16 books. Carl is a Co-editor of the Journal of Economic Dynamics and Control and an Associate Editor of Quantitative Finance, Studies in Nonlinear Dynamics and Econometrics and the European Journal of Finance.

ASHISH DAS, MOODY'S ANALYTICS

Dr Ashish Das, Managing Director, is the Head of Research in the Structured Analytics and Valuation group at Moody's Analytics in New York. Previously he was a Vice President in the Prime Brokerage group at Morgan Stanley. Prior to this, Dr Das spent six years at Moody's KMV, where he headed the portfolio group that was responsible for the correlation research (Gcorr) and portfolio risk modeling (Portfolio Manager/Risk Frontier). He has a PhD in Finance from Kellogg, an MBA from Thunderbird School of Global Management and a Bachelor degree in Chemical Engineering from Indian Institute of Technology, Kanpur, India. Dr Das has published in prestigious journals, including Journal of Finance and Journal of Credit Risk.

FRANCESCA DI GIROLAMO, EUROPEAN COMMISSION

Francesca Di Girolamo is currently a PhD student in financial modeling at the Katholieke Universiteit of Leuven (Belgium), and she has a grant by the European Commission obtained in 2010. She is going to complete her PhD in 2013. Her research focuses on Asset Backed Securities and Contingent Capital. Since 2009, she has been working for the "Scientific Support to Financial Analysis" unit of the European Commission Joint Research Centre. She graduated in 2008 in Mathematical Engineering at "Politecnico di Milano," Italy. She developed and defended her final thesis at the "Universitat Politècnica de Catalunya" in Spain.

FRANK GEHMLICH, TECHNICAL UNIVERSITY CHEMNITZ

Frank studied from 2004 to 2009 business mathematics at Chemnitz University of Technology. He graduated in the field of financial mathematics with his diploma thesis on portfolio credit risk with shot-noise effects. Since 2009 he has been a PhD Student at the department of mathematical finance in Chemnitz. His research activities focus on credit risk modeling and filtering theory. In addition he works on statistical issues in energy markets.

ZORANA GRBAC, UNIVERSITY OF EVRY

Zorana Grbac is a postdoctoral research associate at the University of Evry Val d'Essonne, France. She obtained her PhD degree in Mathematics at the University of Freiburg, Germany, under the supervision of Prof. Dr Ernst Eberlein. Her undergraduate studies, as well as her M.Sc. degree in Mathematics, were completed at the University of Zagreb, Croatia. Her research interests are in the area of mathematical finance, especially in credit risk and interest rate modeling. She is interested in applications of semi-martingales with jumps, in particular time-inhomogeneous Levy processes, to financial modeling. Enlargements of filtrations and conditional Markov chains and their connections to credit risk models are another topic of her interest.

STEFANO GUBELLINI, SAN DIEGO STATE UNIVERSITY

S. Gubellini is an Assistant Professor of Finance at SDSU. He received his doctorate and master's degrees from the Krannert School of Management, Purdue University. His primary teaching interest is in the investments area of finance. Current research includes asset pricing, stock market predictability, trading strategies, derivatives, data-snooping issues and mutual funds. Some of his research has been published in The Journal of Empirical Finance and The Journal of Banking and Finance.

THOMAS GUHR, UNIVERSITY DUISBURG-ESSEN

Thomas Guhr, born in Giessen (Germany), studied physics at the universities of Giessen and Darmstadt where he received a Master's degree in experimental nuclear physics. He then went to the Max Planck Institute for Nuclear Physics in Heidelberg to pursue a PhD project in theoretical physics. He defended his thesis in 1989. Thomas Guhr held postdoctoral positions at the Lawrence Berkeley Laboratory (California, USA), at the Niels Bohr Institute (Copenhagen, Denmark) and in Heidelberg. In 2001, he moved to the University of Lund (Sweden) where he was first researcher and eventually full professor of physics. Since 2007, Thomas Guhr has been full professor of physics at the University of Duisburg–Essen (Germany). His field of interest is statistical physics of complex systems. For about ten years, econophysics has been a major part of his research.

ALFRED HAMERLE, UNIVERSITY OF REGENSBURG

Alfred Hamerle is a professor of statistics at the faculty of business, economics and information systems at the University of Regensburg. Prior to serving in his present position, he was professor of statistics at the University of Konstanz and professor of statistics and econometrics at the University of Tübingen. He is the founder and CEO of Risk Research Prof. Hamerle GmbH. His primary areas of research include statistical and econometric methods in finance, credit risk modeling and Basel II as well as multivariate statistics. Alfred has published 8 books and more than 80 articles in scientific journals.

STEFFI HÖSE, TECHNISCHE UNIVERSITÄT DRESDEN

Steffi Hoese is a postdoctoral fellow at the Technische Universität Dresden, Faculty of Business and Economics, and Chair of Quantitative Methods, esp. Statistics, where she works in quantitative risk analysis. Her current research interest focuses on credit risk management, in particular on the modeling of dependence structures by means of risk factor and mixture models, on the simultaneous estimation of dependence and default parameters and on the involved model risk. She has been a trainer in the SRP/IRB qualification program for supervisors of the Deutsche Bundesbank and the Federal Financial Supervisory Authority (Bundesanstalt für Finanzdienstleistungsaufsicht – BaFin) since 2004. She holds an academic degree in business management (Diplom-Kauffrau) and obtained a doctoral degree (Dr rer. pol.) from the Technische Universität Dresden.

MING XI HUANG, UNIVERSITY OF TECHNOLOGY, SYDNEY

Ming Xi completed a BSc and MPhil in Physics at the Chinese University of Hong Kong and then a PhD in Finance and Economics at the University of Technology, Sydney in 2009. She joined the University of Technology, Sydney in 2009 as a research associate working with Professor Carl Chiarella on a project about modeling and assessment of credit default risk. Her main research interests are modeling credit risk in the area of counterparty default risks, jump risks and default correlations. She has published a couple of refereed papers in international journals and edited volumes. She has also presented her research at a number of national and international conferences. Outside of academia, Ming Xi is currently working at the Commonwealth Bank of Australia in the area of credit risk under Basel II and Basel III.

STEFAN HUSCHENS, TECHNISCHE UNIVERSITÄT DRESDEN

Stefan Huschens holds the Chair of Quantitative Methods, esp. Statistics at the Technische Universität Dresden. He obtained a doctoral degree in economics and a habilitation degree in statistics and economics from the Ruprecht-Karls-Universität Heidelberg. He has been a trainer in the SRP/IRB qualification program for supervisors of the Deutsche Bundesbank and the Federal Financial Supervisory Authority (Bundesanstalt für Finanzdienstleistungsaufsicht – BaFin) since 2004. His major research interests are statistical and econometric methods of market and credit risk management.

KEN JACKSON, UNIVERSITY OF TORONTO

Ken Jackson completed his BSc, MSc and PhD degrees in Computer Science at the University of Toronto in 1973, 1974 and 1978, respectively. Following his PhD, he worked as a Gibbs Instructor and Visiting Assistant Professor in the Computer Science Department at Yale University for three years until returning to the Computer Science Department at the University of Toronto as an NSERC University Research Fellow and Assistant Professor in 1981. He was promoted to Associate Professor with tenure in 1986 and to Full Professor in 1992. He was Associate Chair of the Computer Science Department at the University of Toronto 1987–1989, 2000–2001 and Associate Chairman for Graduate Studies of the Department 2002–2005. He was President of the Canadian Applied and Industrial Mathematics Society 2003–2005.

HENRIK JÖNSSON, BNPPARIBASFORTIS

Henrik Jönsson is a researcher at the "Scientific Support to Financial Analysis" unit of the European Commission Joint Research Centre (JRC). Before joining JRC, he worked as a methodology analyst at the ABS Steering Centre, BNP Paribas Fortis, and as a research fellow in the Multivariate Risk Modellng group at Eurandom, an independent research institute. His research focused on asset-backed securities and credit derivatives pricing using jump models (Lévy models). His work on asset-backed securities modeling and rating was conducted within the research project "Quantitative analysis and analytical methods to price securitization deals" sponsored by the European Investment Bank via its University Research Sponsorship program (EIBURS). Henrik Jönsson was awarded a PhD in Applied Mathematics in Sweden 2005 and is a former Marie Curie European Research Fellow (2006–2008).

ALEXANDER F. R. KOIVUSALO, KOIVUSALO CAPITAL

Alexander is President and CEO of Koivusalo Capital LLC. He worked as a Portfolio Manager at Danske Capital in Copenhagen, Denmark. He was responsible for the market and credit risk across 15 credit portfolios, both investment grade and high-yield portfolios with a total value of EUR 4 billion. He also developed trading and risk systems for a team of seven portfolio managers (including himself). Alexander is involved in research projects at the Department of Theoretical Physics, University of Duisburg-Essen, Duisburg, Germany. These studies involve structural and reduced-form recovery models and the dependence of defaults and recoveries. He has publications in prestigious journals such as the *Journal of Credit Risk* and *Journal of Economic Modelling*. Already during his thesis he compared structural and reduced-form credit risk models at the Department of Mathematical Physics. Alexander obtained a degree of M. Sc. in Engineering, Engineering Physics from Lund Institute of Technology, Lund, Sweden.

MATTHIAS KORN, NORDLB

Matthias Korn works as Head of Product Development at Norddeutsche Landesbank Girozentrale (NORD/LB). Prior to this appointment he was in charge of valuation and risk management of structured products in a major German bank. Aside from this he developed the portfolio model and established the corresponding monitoring processes in a leading financial group in Europe.

ALEX KREININ, RISK ANALYTICS, BUSINESS ANALYTICS, IBM

Alex Kreinin has been with Algorithmics, an IBM company, since 1995, currently as the Senior Director of the Quantitative Research. Alex has PhD in Probability and Statistics from the University of Vilnius (Lithuania). He has published over 60 papers and 2 monographs. His research areas include market and credit risk modeling, numerical methods for risk management, Monte Carlo methods, calibration of stochastic models, semi-analytical methods of portfolio valuation, design of numerical algorithms and their software implementation. Current research projects are focused on operational risk modeling and backtesting problems. Dr Kreinin is an adjunct professor in the Computer Science Department of the University of Toronto and has been affiliated with the "Masters of Mathematical Finance" program.

DIRK P. KROESE, UNIVERSITY OF QUEENSLAND

Dirk Kroese is ARC Professorial Fellow at the University of Queensland. His research interests include Monte Carlo methods, adaptive importance sampling, randomized optimization, and rare-event simulation. He has over 70 peer-reviewed publications, including three monographs: Simulation and the Monte Carlo Method, 2nd Edition, 2007, John Wiley & Sons (with R.Y. Rubinstein), The Cross-Entropy Method, 2004, Springer-Verlag, (with R.Y. Rubinstein), and the Handbook of Monte Carlo Methods, 2011, John Wiley & Sons (with T. Taimre and Z.I. Botev).

FRANK LEHRBASS, RWE SUPPLY AND TRADING

Frank Lehrbass is Head of the Front Office unit Credit Risk Structuring at RWE Supply & Trading, Essen, and part-time lecturer at the University of the Bundesbank. His expertise is in the area of Banking, Financial and Corporate Risk Measurement and Management, Securities Evaluation and Structured Finance. His research work has been accepted by many publishing companies including Springer and Incisive Financial Publishing Limited. Frank started his professional career in 1994 at WestLB as Financial Engineer for exotic derivatives and intraday trading systems, followed by an appointment as Head of Analytics & Systems in the central credit risk management in 1998. In 2001 he moved on to DG HYP (DZ BANK group) in Hamburg, initially as Head of Credit Risk Controlling, since 2002 equipped with credit competence as Head of "Credit Portfolio Management and Structured Investments" in Credit Treasury. In parallel, Frank built up the special servicer "Immofori GmbH" where he was Managing Director from 2004 to 2006. In 2007 he moved to IKB Credit Asset Management GmbH and was appointed as Managing Director in March 2007. He was involved in crisis management concerning the balance sheet of IKB AG, the conduit "Rhineland" and the structured investment vehicle "Rhinebridge." Since 2009 he has worked for RWE Group in various roles and part of this work inspired his chapter.

THILO LIEBIG, DEUTSCHE BUNDESBANK

Thilo Liebig is head of the Macroprudential Analysis Division and deputy head of the Financial Stability Department at Deutsche Bundesbank. He studied Mathematics and Economics at the University of Ulm and Applied Mathematics at the University of Southern California, Los Angeles (Fulbright Scholarship). He received his PhD from the University of Ulm in 1995. Since August 2011 Thilo Liebig is honorary professor at Technische Universität Dresden. Thilo Liebig joined Deutsche Bundesbank in 1998. Until December 2009 he was head of Banking Supervision Research and deputy head of the Research Centre of the Deutsche Bundesbank.

CHI-FAI LO, THE CHINESE UNIVERSITY OF HONG KONG

Chi-Fai Lo is an associate professor in physics at The Chinese University of Hong Kong, specializing in mathematical and theoretical physics. He received his SB and PhD in physics from MIT, and he also holds a MSc. in financial management from SOAS, University of London. He is an active researcher in the field of quantitative finance, and he has been supervising the thesis research of postgraduate students in credit risk modeling and derivatives pricing for more than ten years. His papers on quantitative finance have appeared in Finance and Stochastics, International Journal of Theoretical and Applied Finance, Quantitative Finance, Asia-Pacific Financial Markets, Journal of Risk, Journal of Derivatives, Journal of Fixed Income, International Review of Financial Analysis, Journal of Economics and Business, Journal of Future Markets, International Journal of Finance and Economics and Journal of International Money and Finance. In addition, he has also written over 100 mathematical and theoretical physics papers.

SEBASTIAN LOEHR, UNIVERSITY OF HANNOVER

Sebastian Löhr is a Research Associate of Finance at the Leibniz Universität Hannover, Germany. Sebastian works in the area of Banking, Financial Risk Management and Structured Finance. In 2001 he completed his two-year apprenticeship and formal education certificate program with Commerzbank AG in banking, finance and business administration. After spending an academic year in England at the Warwick Business School, University of Warwick, he completed his studies of business administration at the Georg-August-Universität Göttingen, Germany, in 2007. Since 2008 he has participated in the PhD program of the Leibniz Universität Hannover. At the Institute of Banking & Finance he focuses his research on sustainable risk management of structured financial products like asset securitizations.

KRISTINA LUETZENKIRCHEN, UNIVERSITY OF HANNOVER

Kristina Alexandra Lützenkirchen is a Research Associate of Finance and PhD candidate at the Leibniz University of Hanover, Germany. Kristina works in the field of Banking, Financial Risk Management, Prudential Regulation and Empirical Capital Market Research. She has completed her studies of economics at the University of Hanover in 2010 (majors: Banking & Finance, Statistics and Insurance). Kristina has also worked as graduate assistant and tutor at the Institute. Currently she focuses on structured financial products and especially on regulatory capital requirements for securitizations.

KONSTANTIN MÜLLER, NORDLB

Konstantin Müller works as an analyst in the Product Development group at Norddeutsche Landesbank Girozentrale (NORD/LB). Konstantin's tasks include transaction advisory, cash flow modeling, and the pricing of credit-sensitive securities. Prior to this, Konstantin obtained a Master of Science in financial mathematics at the Technical University of Braunschweig.

LORIANA PELIZON, CA' FOSCARI UNIVERSITY VENICE

Loriana Pelizzon is Associate Professor of Economics at the University of Venice. She graduated from the London Business School with a doctorate in Finance. She was Assistant Professor in Economics at the University of Padova from 2000 till 2004 and recently Visiting Associate Professor at MIT Sloan. Her research interests are risk measurement and management, asset allocation and household portfolios, hedge funds, financial institutions, systemic risk and financial crisis. Her work includes papers published in the Journal of Financial Economics, Journal of Financial and Quantitative Analysis, Journal of Financial Intermediation, and Journal of Banking and Finance. Pelizzon has been awarded the EFA 2005 – Barclays Global Investor Award for the Best Symposium paper, FMA 2005 European Conference for the best conference paper and the Award for the Most Significant Paper published in the Journal of Financial Intermediation 2008. She teaches Financial Economics and Investments at the International Master in Economics and Finance program and Economics and Financial Economics at the undergraduate program. She has been awarded the Best Teacher in 2007 and 2008 at the Ca' Foscari University of Venice. She is one of the coordinators of the European Finance Association (EFA) Doctoral Tutorial, member of the EFA Executive Committee and member of the BSI GAMMA Foundation Board. She has been involved in NBER and FDIC projects as well as EU and Inquire Europe projects. She frequently advises banks, pension funds and government agencies on risk measurement and risk management strategies.

KILIAN PLANK, UNIVERSITY OF REGENSBURG

Kilian Plank is a research assistant and lecturer at the University of Regensburg (chair of statistics, Prof. Hamerle). His research focuses on statistical modeling and analysis of credit risks and especially securitizations. Kilian has several years of work experience in the banking industry and is still engaged in consulting projects at Risk Research Prof. Hamerle GmbH.

NATALIA PUZANOVA, DEUTSCHE BUNDESBANK

Natalia Puzanova is a researcher at the Financial Stability Department of the Deutsche Bundesbank, Frankfurt. She graduated in business administration at the Siberian State University of Technology in Krasnojarsk, Russia and obtained her doctorate degree in Economics at the Institute for Econometrics and Economic Statistics at the University of Münster, Germany. Her research interests span a variety of topics with application to credit risk and systemic risk, with special emphasis in modeling tail dependency with copulas.

MIN QI, OFFICE OF THE COMPTROLLER OF THE CURRENCY

Min Qi is the Deputy Director of the Credit Risk Analysis Division at the Office of the Comptroller of the Currency (OCC). She serves as a credit-risk modeling expert participating in exams at national banks, reviewing models used in credit risk management and in Basel II risk-based capital for wholesale and retail credit exposures. She has provided quantitative support for international and domestic policy development on Basel capital rules, and was active in the work of the Research Task Force, Accord Implementation Group and Standards Implementation Group of the Basel Committee. Prior to joining the OCC, Min was an associate professor of economics at Kent State University. Her research and publications cover a wide range of topics on quantitative modeling and analysis in economics and finance. Her recent research investigates mortgage default and loss given default, corporate default and loss given default, and exposure at default of unsecured credit cards. Min graduated from Tsinghua University in Beijing, and holds a PhD in economics from the Ohio State University.

DANIEL RÖSCH, UNIVERSITY OF HANNOVER

Daniel Rösch is professor of finance and head of the Institute of Banking and Finance at the Leibniz University of Hannover. He received a PhD from the University of Regensburg. Daniel's work covers a broad range in asset pricing and empirical finance. He has published numerous articles on risk management, credit risk, banking and quantitative finance in leading international journals. Daniel has also held numerous executive training courses and is consulting financial institutions on credit risk issues.

DOMENICO SARTORE, CA' FOSCARI UNIVERSITY VENICE

Domenico Sartore is Professor of Econometrics at the Ca' Foscari University of Venice. He held previous positions at Milan University and Padua University, and visiting appointments at London School of Economics (visiting researcher) and UCLA (visiting professor). He has published in various international journals. His main recent research interest covers Bayesian inference in dynamic models with latent factors, stochastic volatility and scenario analysis in macroeconomics.

RUDI SCHAEFER, UNIVERSITY DUISBURG-ESSEN

Rudi Schäfer, born in Lauterbach (Germany), studied physics at the University of Marburg where he received his Master's degree in experimental physics. In his PhD project he continued his research on quantum chaos in Marburg and defended his thesis in 2004. Rudi Schäfer held postdoctoral positions at the University of Palermo (Italy) and at the University of Lund (Sweden). Since 2008 Rudi Schäfer has been leading a junior research group on econophysics at the University of Duisburg-Essen (Germany).

CHRISTIAN SCHERR, UNIVERSITY OF REGENSBURG

Christian Scherr is a research assistant at the chair of statistics at the University of Regensburg, Germany. He has previously worked as a business analyst at Risk Research Prof. Hamerle GmbH & Co. KG. Christian studied physics and economics at the University of Regensburg and Bayerische Elite Akademie. His research interest focuses on continuous-time modeling of credit derivatives.

HARALD SCHEULE, UNIVERSITY OF TECHNOLOGY, SYDNEY

Harald (Harry) Scheule is Associate Professor of Finance at the University of Technology, Sydney. His expertise is in the area of banking, financial risk measurement and management, insurance, prudential regulation, securities evaluation and structured finance. He is a regional director of the Global Association of Risk Professionals. His research work has been accepted for publication in a wide range of journals including the European Financial Management, International Review of Finance, Journal of Banking and Finance, Journal of Financial Research, Journal of the Operational Research Society and The European Journal of Finance. He currently serves on the editorial board of the Journal of Risk Model Validation. He has worked with prudential regulators of financial institutions and undertaken consulting work for a wide range of financial institutions and service providers in Australia, Europe and North America.

THORSTEN SCHMIDT, TECHNICAL UNIVERSITY CHEMNITZ

Thorsten Schmidt is Professor in Mathematical Finance at Chemnitz University of Technology since 2008. Prior to this he was Associate Professor at University of Leipzig and he held a replacement professorship from Technical University Munich. Besides his interests in Mathematical Finance, in particular interest rates, credit risk and energy markets, he has a strong background in statistics and probability theory. Currently he published a book on Mathematical Statistics with Springer. His research in credit risk studies the role of incomplete information and the connection to nonlinear filtering as well as the theory of general Heath–Jarrow–Morton models, even in infinite dimensions. For the modeling of contagion effects and dependence in credit risk he proposed the use of shot-noise models, which extend the class of affine models. Applications include portfolio credit models and CDOs as well as insurance models and operational risk. His latest research contains the calibration of extended affine factor models to large time series of data.

WIM SCHOUTENS, KU LEUVEN

Wim Schoutens (Leuven, Belgium) is professor in financial engineering at the Catholic University of Leuven, Belgium. He has extensive practical experience of model implementation and is well known for his consulting work to the banking industry and other institutions. He is an independent expert advisor to the European Commission on "State aid assessment of valuation of impaired assets and of asset relief measures" and has assessed in that position about EUR 1 trillion of assets. Wim is the author of several books including Contingent Convertibles (CoCos): Structure and Pricing, the first book ever on Contingent Capital and CoCo bonds (written together with Jan De Spiegeleer). He was also (co)author of the Wiley books Lévy Processes in Finance, Lévy Processes in Credit Risk and The Handbook of Convertible Bonds. He is Managing Editor of the International Journal of Theoretical and Applied Finance and Associate Editor of Quantitative Finance, Mathematical Finance and Review of Derivatives Research and International Journal of Portfolio Analysis & Management. He is also series editor of the "Financial Engineering Explained" books for Palgrave Macmillan. Finally, he is member of the Belgium CPI commission.

MICHAEL SCHWALBA, NORDLB

Michael Schwalba works as Head of Structured Solutions & Products at Norddeutsche Landesbank Girozentrale (NORD/LB). Prior to this appointment he was Managing Director within the investment banking group of another major bank. He is a former Investment Director of Axel Springer Venture GmbH, the venture capital arm of Axel Springer AG, one of Europe's leading media groups.

OR SHACHAR, NEW YORK UNIVERSITY

Or Shachar has research interests in credit risk, regulation of financial institutions and financial economics.

ROGER M. STEIN, MOODY'S CORPORATION

Roger M. Stein is the Managing Director of Research and Academic Relations globally at Moody's Corporation. Previously, he held positions as President of Moody's Research Labs; co-head of Moody's KMV's research and product development; and head of research at Moody's Risk Management Services. He has authored dozens of professional and academic articles as well as books including Active Credit Portfolio Management in Practice (Wiley). He also serves on the editorial boards of several finance-related journals. Stein is a member of the board of PlaNet Finance, USA; a member of the Advisory Council for the Museum of Mathematics; and the President of the Consortium for Systemic Risk Analytics. He is also a Research Affiliate at the MIT Sloan School of Management. He has a PhD and Masters degree from the Stern School of Business, New York University.

MARTI G. SUBRAHMANYAM, NEW YORK UNIVERSITY

Marti G. Subrahmanyam is the Charles E. Merrill Professor of Finance, Economics and International Business in the Stern School of Business at New York University. Marti has research expertise in the valuation of corporate securities; options and futures pricing; asset pricing (especially in relation to credit, liquidity, market microstructure, securitization, the term structure of interest rates and fixed income markets); family businesses and real option pricing.

WANHE ZHANG, UNIVERSITY OF TORONTO

Wanhe Zhang has been working at Royal Bank of Canada as a quantitative analyst since 2009. Before that, he was a PhD student at the Department of Computer Science, University of Toronto. His research was on computational methods for credit derivatives. He completed his PhD in 2010. Before his PhD study, he received a Master of Science from McMaster University in 2005.

Index

Index compiled by Terry Halliday